Sustainable Development and Planning II

Volume 1

WITPRESS

WIT Press publishes leading books in Science and Technology.
Visit our website for new and current list of titles.
www.witpress.com

WITeLibrary

Home of the Transactions of the Wessex Institute.
Papers presented at Sustainable Development and Planning are archived in the
WIT eLibrary in volume 84 of WIT Transactions on
Ecology and the Environment (ISSN 1743-3541).

The WIT eLibrary provides the international scientific community with immediate and
permanent access to individual papers presented at WIT conferences.
Visit the WIT eLibrary at www.witpress.com.

E. Tiezzi
University of Siena
Italy

W. Timmermans
Alterra Green World Research
The Netherlands

R.E. Ulanowicz
UMCES
USA

J-L. Usó
Universitat Jaume I
Spain

A. Viguri
Universitat Jaume I
Spain

Y. Villacampa
Universidad de Alicante
Spain

SECOND INTERNATIONAL CONFERENCE ON
SUSTAINABLE DEVELOPMENT AND PLANNING

SUSTAINABLE DEVELOPMENT AND PLANNING II

CONFERENCE CHAIRMEN

A. Kungolos
University of Thessaly, Greece

C.A. Brebbia
Wessex Institute of Technology, UK

E. Beriatos
University of Thessaly, Greece

INTERNATIONAL SCIENTIFIC ADVISORY COMMITTEE

M. Andretta
S. Basbas
R. Brandtweiner
S.D. Brody
O.G. Christopoulou
H. Coccossis
V. Ferrara
A. Gospodini
H. Hendrickx
MD.B. Ishak
H. Itoh
B.A. Kazimee
E. Larcan
T. Oc
N.J.J. Olivier
V. Pappas
H. Schocken
M. Su
J.H.R. van Duin

Organised by
Wessex Institute of Technology, UK

Sponsored by
WIT Transactions on Ecology and the Environment

Sustainable Development and Planning II

Volume 1

Editors

A. Kungolos
University of Thessaly, Greece

C.A. Brebbia
Wessex Institute of Technology, UK

E. Beriatos
University of Thessaly, Greece

WITPRESS Southampton, Boston

A. Kungolos
University of Thessaly, Greece

C.A. Brebbia
Wessex Institute of Technology, UK

E. Beriatos
University of Thessaly, Greece

Published by

WIT Press
Ashurst Lodge, Ashurst, Southampton, SO40 7AA, UK
Tel: 44 (0) 238 029 3223; Fax: 44 (0) 238 029 2853
E-Mail: witpress@witpress.com
http://www.witpress.com

For USA, Canada and Mexico

Computational Mechanics Inc
25 Bridge Street, Billerica, MA 01821, USA
Tel: 978 667 5841; Fax: 978 667 7582
E-Mail: infousa@witpress.com
US site: http://www.witpress.com

British Library Cataloguing-in-Publication Data

A Catalogue record for this book is available
from the British Library

ISBN: 1-84564-025-X (Vol 1)
ISBN: 1-84564-050-0 (Vol 2)
ISBN: 1-84564-051-9 (set)
ISSN: 1746-448X (print)
ISSN: 1743-3541 (on-line)

The texts of the papers in this volume were set individually by the authors or under their supervision. Only minor corrections to the text may have been carried out by the publisher.

Preface

These volumes contain the contributions presented at the 2nd International
Conference on Sustainable Development and Planning, held in Bologna, Italy,
September 12 to 14, 2005. The series, which started in October 2003 in Skiathos,
Greece, is organized by Wessex Institute of Technology, UK and sponsored by
WIT Transactions on Ecology and the Environment.

The Conference addressed the subjects of planning and regional development
in an integrated way as well as in accordance with the principles of sustainability. It
has become apparent that planners, environmentalists, architects, engineers, policy
makers and economists have to work together in order to ensure that development
can meet our present needs without compromising the ability of future generations.
In recent years, there has been in many countries, an increase in spatial problems
that has lead to planning crises. Planning problems are often connected with uneven development, deterioration of the quality of urban life and destruction of the
environment. Furthermore, problems of environmental management and planning
are not restricted to urban areas. Environments such as rural areas, forests, coastal
regions and mountains face their own problems that require urgent solutions in
order to avoid irreversible damages. The use of modern technologies in planning,
such as geographical information systems and remote sensing, give us new potential to monitor and prevent environmental degradation.

Effective strategies for management should consider sustainable development
and planning, and emphasise the need to handle these matters in an integrated way.
The conference provided a common forum for all scientists, specialising in the wide
range of subjects.

The scientific topics of Sustainable Planning and Development 2005 included:

1. City planning
2. Environmental impact assessment
3. Environmental legislation and policy
4. Environmental management
5. Waste management
6. Resources management
7. Geo-informatics
8. Transportation
9. Ecosystems analysis, protection and remediation
10. Regional planning

The editors would like to thank all the authors for their presentations and in particular, the members of the International Scientific Advisory Committee who helped to review the papers.

The Editors
Bologna, 2005

Contents

(Includes complete contents and author index for volumes 1 & 2)

Volume 1

Section 1: City planning

Section 2: Environmental impact assessment

Section 3: Environmental legislation and policy

Section 4: Environmental management

Section 5: Waste management

Section 6: Resources management

Volume 2

Section 7: Geo-informatics

Section 8: Transportation

Section 9: Ecosystems analysis, protection and remediation

Section 10: Regional planning

Section 11: Rural development

Section 12: A multidisciplinary approach to territorial and environmental risk assessment and management (Special session organised by E. Larcan)

Section 13: Social and cultural issues

Section 14: Urban landscapes
(Special session organised by A. Gospodini)

Section 1
City planning

Sustainable urban freight policies in the Netherlands: a survey

J. H. R. van Duin
Transport Policy and Logistics' Organisation, Faculty of Technology, Policy and Management, Delft University of Technology, The Netherlands

Abstract

As mentioned in the white paper of the OECD the main policy objective to be tackled is the development of sustainable urban goods transport [1]. Sustainable urban goods transport should facilitate a continuing economic growth and meanwhile protecting the environment and ensuring a better quality of life for future generations.

In the Netherlands various regulations have been implemented with the aim of maintaining an urban living environment with sustainable qualities and facilitating smooth and safe traffic flows. Most of these regulations, like access restrictions based on time and/or vehicle size or weight, have been widely implemented. However, the diversity and different applications of these regulations among municipalities can cause serious (planning) difficulties for logistics operators.

For this reason it is interesting to compare and evaluate the differences of policy measures within municipalities. In this paper an inventory of policy measures have been carried out among Dutch cities. The inventory of measures has been classified according to a transportation system's view. The cities have been ranked according to the number of inhabitants. With the use of a classification of towns into large, middle and small towns a more detailed comparison can be made towards the effectiveness of policy measures.

A detailed evaluation of the measures can give us an insight into how policy measures should be implemented in order to reach a long-term sustainable urban goods transport. Also interesting to evaluate on this level is to look at the rate of harmonisation and standardisation of policies between cities. With this respect it is possible to get some idea what the impact of the OECD white paper is on municipalities in European countries.
Keywords: cost-analysis, future transport system, policy makers.

WIT Transactions on Ecology and the Environment, Vol 84, © 2005 WIT Press
www.witpress.com, ISSN 1743-3541 (on-line)

1   Introduction

The concept of "sustainability" and "sustainable development" has become increasingly influential in policy considerations in recent years. The most widely accepted definition of sustainable development is "development that meets the needs of the present without compromising the needs of future generations to meet their own needs" [2]. This was the definition used by the World Commission and then endorsed by the United Nations at the Earth Summit in Rio in 1992. This conference led to a focus on the policy action required to bring about sustainability, known as Agenda 21, which, whilst having no force in international law, has been adopted by many national governments [3].

In many European countries as a result, many local authorities have been preparing environmental strategies. A key problem to implementing an achievable sustainable strategy is determining the parameters of measurement (e.g. geographical scale, environmental and social impacts, etc.), and not surprisingly it is extremely difficult to achieve a workable, acceptable set of targets, actions and measures which will result in more sustainable cities, and a more sustainable urban freight transport system within that city.

The aim of a sustainable transport strategy is "to answer, as far as possible, how society intends to provide the means of opportunity to meet economic, environmental and social needs efficiently and equitably, while minimising avoidable or unnecessary adverse impacts and their associated costs, over relevant space and time scales" [4]. Since freight transport is part of the transport system it follows that the issue of sustainability must be addressed with regard to freight transport.

Urban freight movement can be improved so as to make it more sustainable in various ways. It is important to distinguish between two different groups who are capable of changing the urban freight system and the rationale for their doing so:

- Changes implemented by governing bodies—i.e. the introduction of policies and measures that force companies to change their actions and thereby become more environmentally or socially efficient (e.g. changing the way in which they undertake certain activities) [5].
- Company-driven change. Companies implementing measures that will reduce the impact of their freight operations because they will derive some internal benefit from this change in behaviour—i.e. companies can achieve internal economic advantages from operating in a more environmentally or socially efficient manner, either through improved economic efficiency or through being able to enhance market share as a result of their environmental stance. Company-led initiatives include increasing the vehicle load factor through the consolidation of urban freight, making deliveries before or after normal freight delivery hours, the use of routing and scheduling software, improvements in the fuel efficiency of vehicles, intelligent communications systems, and improvements in collection and delivery systems [6].

The driving forces behind these urban freight flows are factors such as the geographic location of activities, the costs of transport and related activities, land prices, customer tastes and required service levels and existing policies governing freight transport and land use. Therefore, in order to change freight transport patterns and reduce their impacts it is necessary to influence some of these factors that determine goods flows as well as simply focusing attention on goods vehicle movements. Sustainable development strategies are likely to require national policies together with measures taken at a more local level. A European and national sustainability strategy could help to ensure that urban sustainability policies do not result in some urban locations becoming less economically attractive than others. It will be necessary to find suitable measures for the town or city in question and these are likely to vary from one urban area to another.

The aim of this paper is to evaluate the rate of harmonisation and standardisation of policies between cities. With this respect it is possible to get some idea what the impact of the OECD white paper is on municipalities in European countries. A detailed evaluation of the measures (of cities in the Netherlands) can give us an insight into how policy measures should be implemented in order to reach a long-term sustainable urban goods transport. With this respect it is possible to get some idea what the impact of the OECD white paper is on municipalities in European countries.

2   Policy evaluation in the Netherlands

2.1 Facts and figures

The Netherlands is a country with relative small size but very high population density. There are around 16 million people live in this 41528 km^2 country, of which 89% lives in urban areas. It is predicted that more than 93% of the Dutch people will live in the urban areas in 2025 [8]. With the increasing population and highly concentration of economic activities in urban area, congestion becomes inevitable in downtowns as well as on highways. Like many other European countries, the freight transport experiences a substantial increase in these years due to various reasons, like economic globalization induces longer journeys and "just-in-time" delivery asks for smaller and more frequent shipments. Such tendency will last for a long time as long as the economy grows continuously. Although the country has a world famous inland water transport system, the road transport has a much high proportion which occupies 80.8% of total goods transport in 2002. The passenger cars still hold the dominant position on the road traffic which has 87% of the total vehicles. The freight vehicle takes the rest 13%. Vans, less than 3.5 tons loading capacity, represent 86% of the total freight vehicles.

2.2 Freight policy development

The attention for urban freight transport problems has already a long tradition in the Netherlands. Serious attention for urban freight problems started in the early 90's with the introductions of public distribution centres (Coopers & Lybrand, 1991). After a trial period of five years in several cities in the Netherlands the first evaluations came out (Duin, 1997) and has lead to a change of policy and policy management. Before National governmental plans had been very directive and top-down with implementing (Heijden, 1995). In 1995 the raise of the platform urban distribution caused a turn in influencing and stimulating innovative urban freight policies. The platform was a constitution of eleven parties: Union of Dutch municipalities (VNG), Ministry of Transport (V&W), Ministry of housing, spatial organisation and environmental affairs (VROM), Ministry of economic affairs (EZ), inter-province organisation (IPO) Inter-provincial debate (IPO), Association of Transport owners (EVO), Royal Association of retailers (MKB) and Dutch society of large retailers (NVG). This platform tries to stimulate and co-ordinate and support all kind of promising initiatives in the field of city logistics, namely:

- Upstream collection of goods for the same area;
- Co-operation between transportation organisations;
- Distribution outside of the opening hours of the shops;
- Ideal time windows;
  The time windows in which it is allowed to distribute goods in a particular urban area must be tuned to the specific situation in the area in order to work efficiently for the carriers;
- Central and local rules;

According to the platform the governments (central, province or local) must be one of the initiators for new policies and measures. The policies and measures themselves should not be seen as complete solutions. However it is a way to stimulate other parties to find a solution together. Therefore they have developed three kinds of process management models:

- The **Amsterdam model** (1995) – All actors decide about the best measures to be taken. Finally the municipality decides about the legislation. For specific situations exemptions are possible.
- The **Groningen model** (1999) – All actors decide about the measures to be taken, innovation is obtained by facilitating private city distribution with regional coverage. Municipality decides about the legislation of measures.
- The **Hague model** (2003) – All actors determine the rules. Innovation is obtained by searching integration with other transport modes and functions (for example garbage collection). Municipality is facilitator, less legislation of rules and responsibility for implementing is shared among the actors.

So far the effects of the platform have leaded to an increase of attention for urban freight problems and have leaded to more appropriate attention of freight issues in the political agenda of municipalities. From a survey (PSD, 2002) among 278 municipalities with more than 15000 inhabitants around 20% of the municipalities shows a growing political interest for freight transport. *However, still 38% of the municipalities has no political attention for freight!!*

2.3 Survey

280 Cities are investigated from a total of 509 municipalities and the population of sample cities ranges from 15,084 (Boskoop) to 734,594 (Amsterdam) inhabitants. The average size of the city is around 50,000 inhabitants. Therefore, middle to small-sized cities are strongly represented. To make the analysis easier to understand, we split the cities into two categories. The cities with population over 50,000 are defined as big cities and the small cities are below 50,000. The density of a city also plays a crucial role with regard to the traffic situation in general. This is particular important to the urban freight transport since the higher density means more problems will occur. From the statistics, the densities in big cities like Amsterdam ($33,574p/km^2$) and Rotterdam ($19,568 p/km^2$) are much higher than the average (for the size takes into account is only the inner city and not including the suburbs). Also like above, places with inhabitants more than $2,000p/km^2$ are defined as high-density areas.

Table 1:   The relation of size and density.

		Density		Total
		High	Low	
Size	Big city	44	20	64
	Small city	32	184	216
Total		76	204	280

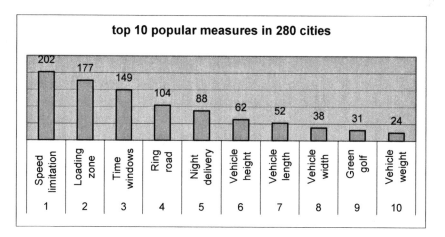

Figure 1:   Top 10 measures in the Netherlands.

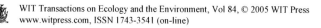

2.3.1 Frequently used policy measures
For all the measures, speed limitation, loading and unloading zones and time windows are among the top three most popular measures in the Netherlands. From these measures, the desired effects mainly to achieve are to protect people in the downtown area, regulate the goods supply flow, prevent physical damage to the inner city and create a good shopping environment.

2.3.2 Speed limitation
Speed limitation is the most popular measures in local municipalities. There are 72% of cites in favor of this measure. For these cities, more than a half restricts the speed regardless of the downtown or suburb. There is no difference of implementing the measure in terms of the size of the city. Around a quarter of the cities don't have speed regulation both in big and small cities.

Table 2:   Size and speed limitation.

Size	Yes, inside downtown	Yes, outside downtown	Yes, thinking	Yes, both inside and outside downtown	No	No, inside downtown	Total
Big city	10	11	1	25	17	0	64
Small city	39	35	0	83	58	1	216
Total	49	46	1	108	75	1	280

2.3.3 Loading and unloading zones
The use of loading and unloading zones is another important policy measure for local authorities. Sixty three percent of the cities have this policy in general. The big cities have stronger tendency to support this policy that 92% of big cities have. The difference is probably attributable to the higher frequency of social and economic activities in the big cities. The more people live there, leading to a large amount of shipments. The design of loading and unloading zone could regulate the traffic flow go in and out the downtown.

Table 3:   Load and unloading zone and size of the city.

		Loading and unloading zone		Total
		Yes	No	
Size	Big city	59	5	64
	Small city	118	98	216
Total		177	103	280

2.3.4 Time windows

Time windows are widely implemented in the Netherlands. More than 50% of the cities have this kind of measure. Five working days plus Saturday are the most frequent days. The main reason is the shops are open on Saturday. People go to the downtown to make shopping and they don't want to be disturbed by trucks. However, more than a quarter of the cities also restrict the freight traffic on Sunday. The range of the time period is widely diversified which is from one and half hours to more than 20 hours (see Figure 2). However, the time windows in the morning period from 6:00 to 12:00 count for 43.6% of the total cities. 2/3 of the cities have time range from three hours to six hours.

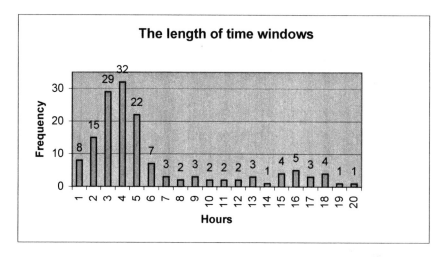

Figure 2:   Lengths of time windows.

Table 4:   The size of city and time windows.

			Time windows		Total
			No	Yes	
Size	Big city	Count	6	58	64
		% of Total	2,1%	20,7%	22,9%
	Small city	Count	124	92	216
		% of Total	44,3%	32,9%	77,1%
Total		Count	130	150	280
		% of Total	46,4%	53,6%	100,0%

2.3.5 Vehicle restrictions

The vehicle restrictions are also very popular in the Netherlands. Many aspects have regulated the movement of lorries in the downtown. 138 in 280 cities have at least one kind of vehicle restriction. As different cities may have their own unique characteristics related to historical center, transport infrastructure and economic situation, the difference of the same regulation varies considerably for each individual town. The limitation of height ranges from two meters to values of 4.5 meters. The differences observed here are also largely attributable to the local structure. Especially in the inner cities, some historical buildings limit the height of trucks. The most frequently used limitation is three or four meters high, i.e. more than 50% of the total cities. In big cities, the height limitation is higher than the small cities, ranging from three meters to 4.4 meters. The height of three meters (17%) and four meters (46%) are the top two, respectively. The width restriction ranges from two meters to four meters. Small cities use this regulation more often, i.e. 82% of the total small cities. Two or three meters limitations are used intensively, combining 76% of the total number. The length limitation is equally distributed between big and small cities. Ten and twelve meters are used more frequently, which have proportion of 23% and 31% respectively.

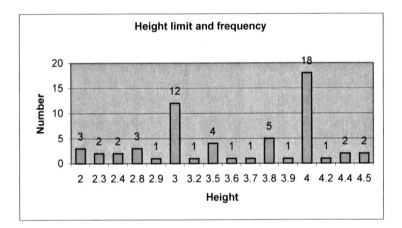

Figure 3:   Height limitation and frequency.

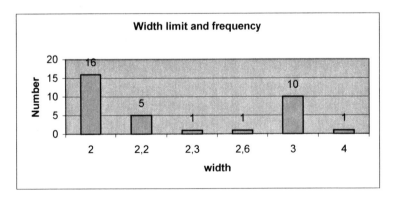

Figure 4:   Width limitation and frequency.

WIT Transactions on Ecology and the Environment, Vol 84, © 2005 WIT Press
www.witpress.com, ISSN 1743-3541 (on-line)

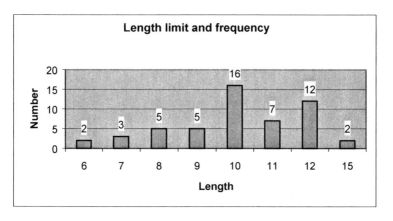

Figure 5:   Width limitation and frequency.

2.3.6 Innovative policies

With respect to innovations in the field of city logistics, the Netherlands is representative of the use of city distribution centres for freight delivery. So far it has not shown any signs of feasibility due to the low level of participation shown by carriers, who prefer direct deliveries, still possible in a low enforcement scenario. Other innovative policy to be found in Dutch cities is the designation of logistic routes, which sometimes consist of designated detours for heavy goods traffic (Amsterdam, Tilburg), and sometimes of bus lanes used for city distribution (Utrecht). Somehow innovative, but actually based on very old traditional delivery in towns, are freight carriers operating in the Dutch channels. With small vessels, in the cities of Amsterdam and Utrecht, parcel services operate to distribute in the inner centre. Underground freight transport has been studied over in the Netherlands for a couple of cities. For sustainable development of a city these systems might have the future. However, at this moment the building costs are too much expensive to be considered seriously.

3   Conclusions

In our study among the Dutch municipalities we have noticed that regulations concerning city logistics are very much the same, independent of the size and characteristics of towns. Access restrictions according to weight, occasional time windows, and load zones available until 11 a.m. represent the typical regulations, very often without a previous analysis or without having any information about deliveries in the congested areas of the city.

Along this line, city logistics policies are not very often the result of detailed analyses and evaluations. This is reflected in similar types of regulations repeated through the different cities regardless their characteristics, the same schedules for time windows and load zones, and the failure to recognise different types of urban distribution which require different types of regulations. Apart from copying regulation frameworks, however, cities do not share information, knowledge or cooperation, and the lack of national or regional bodies dealing with city logistics, as there exist for urban passenger traffic, is significant.

Time windows both for access and for the use of load zones seem to be the most widespread policies both in the Netherlands. However, the question still is: 'are these policies really the best ones for all the towns'? In the Netherlands the problem of introducing time windows has been recognised by municipalities and about 45% out of 278 municipalities shows interest in a regional coordination of the time windows.

On the other hand, it should be mentioned that in the Netherlands knowledge and experience on city logistics have been institutionalised into one platform, i.e. PSD. The commitment of the members and the information sharing among their members have led to a good common thinking for making city logistics policies. Sixty percent of the municipalities (out of 278) know what the platform stands for. Last year the platform ceased to exist and divided itself among four geographical zones in the country, in order to get more insight into the processes of supplying the inner cities with goods and the effects of measures taken by the municipalities. The platforms have more discussions in detail since not only union members will join these platforms but also the real companies operating in the city.

For the sustainable development of freight transport in Europe this ideology has been followed by the BESTUFS platform [8]. The idea is not to impose regulation frameworks on cities, but to make available for all of them a common source of data, experiences and best practices. That's why this initiative like the BESTUFS II platform represent probably the best type of institution for this knowledge exchange role and can build the bridge between academic knowledge, policy and practice. In these platforms the new roads to sustainable urban freight policies can be explored.

Acknowledgement

I thank Zhengqin Qian for his master thesis work [9].

References

[1]   OECD (2003), '*Delivering the goods: 21st Century Challenges to Urban Goods Transport*'

[2]   World Commission on Environment and Development, Our common future. , Oxford University Press, Oxford, UK (1987).

[3]   Mazza L. and Rydin, Y., 'Urban Sustainability: Discourses, Networks and Policy Tools', Progress in Planning, Volume 47, Issue 1, 1997, Pages 1-74

[4]   Himanen, V., Lee-Gosselin, M. and Perrels, A., 'Sustainability and the interactions between external effects of transport, Journal of Transport Geography, Volume 13, Issue 1, March 2005, Pages 23-28

[5]   Ogden, K.W., 'Urban goods movement; a guide to policy and planning', Ashgate, 1992

[6]   Duin, J.H.R. van, L. Yin, J. Serrano, N. A. Pecorari & V. Serrano (2003); "New Sustainable transportation solution in urban areas, S.A.T. Project: Towards a simulation modelling approach", in: E. Beriatos, C.A. Brebbia, H. Coccossis, A.G. Kungolos (eds); Sustainable Planning and Development, W.I.T. Press, Southampton, pp 681-690, ISBN: 1-85312-985-2.

[6]   Anderson, S., Allen J., and Browne, M.,'Urban logistics—how can it meet policy makers' sustainability objectives', Journal of Transport Geography, Volume 13, Issue 1, March 2005, Pages 71-81

[7]   PSD, 'Van B naar A, overzicht van maatregelen in 278 gemeenten', Den Haag (www.psd-online.nl), 2002

[8]   BCI consultants, ''CITY FREIGHT inter- and intra- city freight distribution networks, Work package 1, Deliverable D1, 2002

[9]   http:\\www.bestufs.net

[10]   Qian, Z., 'Quantification of the effect of policy measures related to urban freight transportation', Master Thesis, Delft University of Technolology, June 2005

Sustainable cities: an integrated strategy for sustainable urban design

A. Abdulgader & Y. Aina
College of Environmental Design,
King Fahd University of Petroleum and Minerals, Saudi Arabia

Abstract

It has been recognized that urban design has a vital role to play in fostering sustainable cities as urban spatial structure and form have considerable influence on the social, economic and environmental processes in the urban area. Research works have focused on the development of appropriate guidelines and frameworks for making urban design sustainable. However, the studies have not explored the development of a holistic approach to sustainable urban design. This paper seeks to develop an integrated framework, in the local context of Saudi Arabia, for promoting sustainable urban design. The paper discusses the role of urban design in promoting sustainable cities and examines the sustainable development principles that should guide urban design. The paper also discusses issues pertaining to sustainable urban design in Saudi Arabia. It concluded that sustainable urban design could only be achieved if the procedural, substantive, institutional, policy and methodological aspects of urban design are interlinked and guided by sustainability principles.
Keywords: sustainable cities, sustainable urban design, sustainability principles, urban management, land use planning, Saudi Arabia.

1   Introduction

In recent times, the major challenges to urban management and development are the spate of rapid urbanization and the subsequent impacts of increasing human activities. The myriad of factors that influence urban development have made the task of taming urban problems enormous if not unachievable. The complexity of factors to be integrated by urban planners and designers in managing urban areas is compounded by globalization. Urban development is no longer mainly directed by local forces but by global factors. Liddell and Mackie [1] noted that city form is now driven by organizations that are not local and which have imperatives that are not derived from local area. Consequent upon the influences of local and international economic forces, urban spatial structures and patterns are principally directed by economic imperatives leading to high social and environmental impacts. The negative impacts of development activities pose a great challenge to human living as close to half of the world's population lives in the city. The number of mega cities (cities with populations of over 10 million people) is expected to increase from 19 (with population of about 266.7million) in 2000 to about 27 (with population of about 374.8 million) in 2015 UNFPA [2]. That is, the environmental and social failures of the cities affect the high proportion of the world living within them.

Cities are not entirely problematic because they drive economies and it is within them that innovation occurs. Urban problems do not develop due to inherent characteristics of the cities but due to lack of effective governance and management Jenks and Burgess [3]. Land use planning and urban design have been recognized as having a major role to play in the management of urban development. Planning and urban design influence urban structure and form which eventually generate land use activities within the city. Good practice of city management requires that all the relevant dimensions (social, economic and environmental) to urban development be considered at the planning and design level. Traditionally, all these dimensions are considered in development planning during the planning process. The emergence of the concept of sustainable development has boosted the incorporation of the all the dimensions (social, economic and environmental) in the planning process. The principles of sustainable development require a balance consideration of social, economic and environmental implications of development activities. Quite a number of authors have expounded on the frameworks of integrating sustainability principles into urban design, Frey [4], Williams *et al* [5], Atkinson and Ting [6] and Carmona [7], but the frameworks have mainly explored the substantive and procedural aspects of urban design. There is the need to elaborate on the other dimensions of urban design.

In Saudi Arabia, there have been tremendous changes in urban spatial organization due to rapid urbanization and the transformation of the traditional built environment. The Kingdom has experienced a high rate of development and modernization through its petroleum-driven economy. Western urban models have been adopted to direct the development of the built environment. The western models are greatly in contrast with the traditional urban form and consequently the emerging modern urban spatial structures have generated some problems. The challenge lies in developing the built environment in a way that will be at pace with modern trend and harmonious with socio-cultural values. The integration of sustainability principles into urban design and development could open a window of opportunities for rescuing the situation. This paper seeks to develop an integrated framework, in the local context of Saudi Arabia, for promoting sustainable urban design. The paper discusses the role of urban design in promoting sustainable cities and examines the sustainable development principles that should guide urban design. The paper also discusses issues pertaining to sustainable urban design in Saudi Arabia. It concluded that sustainable urban design could only be achieved if the procedural, substantive, institutional, policy and methodological aspects of urban design are interlinked and guided by sustainability principles.

2   Urban design and sustainable development

The concept of sustainable development originated from the World Commission on the Environment and Development in 1987 and it has become the goal of every society. The broad goal of sustainable development is inter- and intra-generational equity. The principle of sustainable development advocates that social, economic and environmental issues should be given balance consideration in development activities. The objectives of sustainable development are laudable but they are seemingly elusive in practice. In order to bridge the gap between the principle and practice of sustainable development, a global action plan "Agenda 21" was formulated at the Earth Summit held in Rio de Janeiro in 1992. Agenda 21 elaborated on the need for indicators and local initiatives to promote sustainability [8]. The basis of the Local Agenda 21 initiative is that local communities need to become involved in making their neighborhoods sustainable which should, in turn, have a knock-on effect in achieving global sustainability [9]. Due to the importance of the cities, the implementation of Local Agenda 21 at the city is recognized as a vital approach to sustainability. The participation of the local authorities especially at the city level is crucial to achieving global sustainable development.

Urban design and planning offer the opportunity to guide city development towards sustainability as noted by Miller [10] that most urban areas use planning to determine present and future use of each parcel of land in the area. One of the ways in which local authorities can deliver sustainability is through making their land use planning process sustainable [11]. As planning has a vital role in achieving sustainable urban development; the planning process and the outcome of planning should be guided by the principles of sustainable development. Thus, urban design conceptualizations should include sustainable dimension in the design guidelines which hitherto make reference to morphological, functional, social and visual dimensions.

There is a tendency to weigh economic considerations more than social and environmental factors and even assume that cities are mainly shaped by economic forces. Despite the influence of market forces on the spatial organization of cities, urban design can play an important role in protecting the cities from market failures. The effects of city form and structure on sustainability cannot be disregarded because the configuration of the city influences the function and quality of the city. Frey [4] rightly observed that cities with physical structures that are strictly the products of a market economy rather than being planned become sterile, functionally suboptimal, and unsustainable. Such cities fail to maintain identity, sustainability, amenity, and diversity. Urban development should not be solely driven by market forces but by an integration of all the relevant factors. Thus, cities need to be designed and planned to foster sustainable urban development. It is the task of urban planning and design to enable and enhance the city's advantages and to minimize, if not eliminate, the city's disadvantages [4]. This poses a challenge for sustainable urban design to identify guidelines that improve environmental quality while leading to social and economic development of the city [1].

3 Towards sustainable urban design

Having recognized the crucial role that could be played by urban design in fostering livable and sustainable cities, different governments and urban administrators have tried to reestablish urban design in the arena of urban development. In Britain, urban design has started taking root in government planning guidance since 1992 and the process has culminated into the development of urban design guidance [12]. Similar initiatives have been taken by cities in the United States such as the Sustainable Seattle initiated by the city of Seattle [13]. The emerging urban initiatives make reference to good urban design based on the premise that urban design can help promote sustainability and reduce if not eliminate present urban problems. However, it has been noted especially in the United Kingdom that more drastic steps must be taken to really succeed in fostering sustainability through urban design [14]. Carmona [14] highlighted the need for design policy and guidance based on primary concern for urban design, policy mechanism based on fully conceptualized urban design framework and hierarchical approach to design policy and guidance in order to improve on the current practice in the United Kingdom.

Apart from the government institutions, urban researchers have also contributed to the debate on promoting livable cities through good design. Even different urban design and planning movements have emerged to advocate for better quality of life in the cities. The notable groups among these movements are the New Urbanism and the Smart Growth. New Urbanism is an urban design movement that is committed to the restoration of urban centers through participatory planning and design while the Smart Growth advocates for reformation of state growth management regulations to foster livable cities [15]. Most of the commentators on the issues concerning sustainable design tend to focus on the substantive and the procedural aspects (as shown by the terms of reference of the movements). It is imperative to develop a holistic approach to the issues bordering on sustainable urban design.

4 Challenges of sustainable urban design in Saudi Arabia

Prior to the 1950s, urban development in Saudi Arabia was mainly influenced by traditional Islamic urbanism. However, since the 1950s, the physical arrangement of Saudi cities has changed due to the adoption of the gridiron pattern streets and villa housing. The change has led to socio-cultural contradictions [16] including issues of privacy and security. Efforts have been directed at promoting good city design through the adoption of the New

Urbanism concepts [17]. The efforts could achieve better results if the challenges to sustainable urban design in the Kingdom are addressed in an integrated framework. The task is to highlight the challenges to sustainable urban design and then develop the framework to address these challenges. Different social, economic and environmental factors pose challenges to sustainable urban design in the Kingdom. These include:

- institutional framework – the kingdom has a centralized institutional arrangement and limited autonomy is granted to the municipalities;
- the climate factor – special design capability is needed to protect the populace from the desert climate and at the same time reduce energy consumption;
- pattern of living – the populace relies on automobile for travel and it may be socially difficult to change to public transportation;
- low level of public awareness – environmental awareness among the populace is still low;
- political will - the political will is not so strong.

The factors listed above hinder the achievement of sustainable urban design in Saudi Arabia. Some of these factors are general while some are specific to the Kingdom.

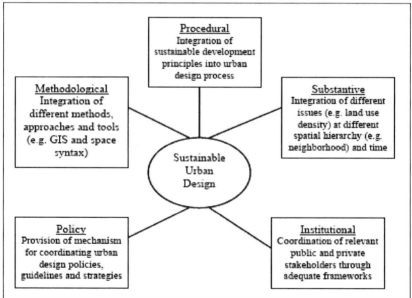

Figure 1:   The concept of integrated sustainable urban design.

5   Integrated strategy for sustainable urban design

The integrated strategy highlighted in this section is adapted from Eggenberger and Partidario [18]. The different aspects of sustainable urban design (procedural, substantive, methodological, institutional and policy), as shown in figure 1, should be integrated in a synergetic form to foster sustainable cities through urban design. The substantive aspect involves the integration of different issues relevant to sustainable design such as land use density, environmental performance, mixed-use and pedestrianization. The procedural aspect involves the urban design process. Sustainability principles should be incorporated with the urban design process. Methodological aspect involves the different tools for supporting urban design while institutional and policy aspect borders around good urban governance, integration of design policies and coordination of relevant stakeholders.

5.1 Procedural aspect

As shown in figure 2, sustainability issues and process can be integrated into the urban design process by introducing sustainability steps into the design process. The urban design process consists of about four stages: Analysis, Synthesis, Evaluation and Implementation. Each stage of the process is amenable to sustainable urban design process. Overall, the process should be proactive, flexible, allow top-down and bottom-up interactions and encourage citizen participation [19].

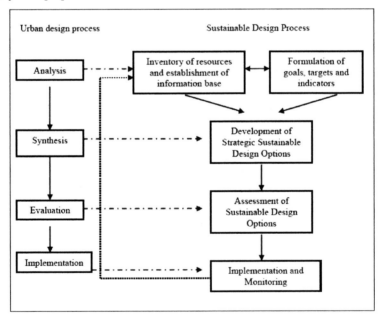

Figure 2:   Integration of sustainability into urban design process.

5.2 Substantive aspect

Carmona [7] and Selman [20] identified the key principles of sustainable development that should be integrated with urban design. These tenets include intergenerational equity, public trust doctrine (maintaining environmental diversity and carrying capacity), precautionary principle, intra-generational equity, participation and polluter pays principle. The spectrum of the spatial scale of urban design (from local to metropolitan) should be considered in applying the urban design principles. Frey [4] elaborated on the spatial scale of urban design by identifying three levels of strategic urban design interventions: individual spaces or group of spaces, city district and city/conurbation levels. For urban design intervention to achieve success and effectiveness development frameworks should be generated at these levels and in this hierarchical order. The spatial scale aspect can be managed effectively if plans are prepared at each level and the plans are coordinated with each other while maintaining their individualities [15]. Also, issues such as resource efficiency, diversity and choice, human needs, pollution reduction, intensification of land use, identity, biotic support and self-sufficiency are relevant to the substantive aspect.

5.3 Institutional aspect

The institutional aspect is very important because it involves the provision of adequate collaborative framework and the political will to promote sustainability principles. Good sustainable urban design initiatives can be frustrated by inadequate institutional framework and impeding political process. Therefore, the institutional aspect should provide frameworks that will achieve the following:

- encourage stakeholder and community collaboration and participation in development decisions,
- enhance the exchange of information and sustainability awareness
- clarify the duties and responsibilities of stakeholders

5.4 Policy aspect

The policy aspect involves the integration of principles, regulations and strategies for intervention. The integration of sustainable design policies can help in formulating design goals, indicators and targets. Integrated policy framework can also enhance the resolution of contradictory sustainability policies. For instance, the policy of encouraging high density development can contradict that of ensuring affordable housing as housing prices may shoot up as a result of high-density housing development. Differences in contexts and socio-cultural values should be considered in policy integration. A policy that works in an urban area might produce different result in another city within the same region.

5.5 Methodological aspect

The methodological aspect involves the integration of different approaches and tools to enhance the understanding of the complexity and uncertainty involved in urban development decisions. Batty *et al* [21] noted that the opportunities provided by information systems have not been fully utilized in urban design. Figure 3 shows a conceptual framework of integrating GIS and other information technology tools into the urban design process. The concept envisions the integration of all the tools relevant to urban design analysis.

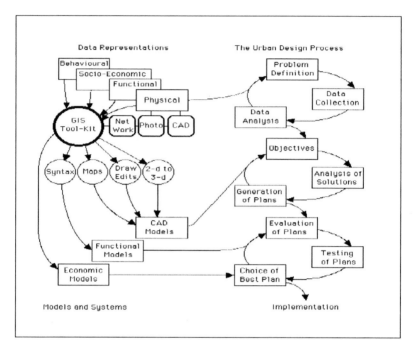

Figure 3: Integration of urban design systems (source: Batty et al [21]).

6 Concluding remarks

Urban planning and design could play a vital role in achieving sustainable development as the city structure and form influence effectiveness and quality of the city. For a balance urban development, the principles of sustainable development should be integrated with the urban design and planning process. The sustainable urban design principles could be used to rescue cities from the negative impacts of market-driven spatial organization. As there are no two communities that are the same, the context of application of sustainable design principles will vary from place to place. In this view, the challenges to sustainable urban design in Saudi Arabia are highlighted and a strategy for integrating sustainability into urban design is discussed. There is the need to further investigate into the different aspects of sustainable urban design. For instance, in the substantive aspect, the degree of compactness a city must maintain is still debatable. The application of these principles in empirical cases will go a long way to shed more light on how to use them in achieving sustainable urban development. Also, the contradictions of arising from the implementation of sustainability need to be better understood by planners and urban designers.

Acknowledgement

The authors wish to acknowledge the support of King Fahd University of Petroleum and Minerals, Dhahran, Saudi Arabia in carrying out the research and attending the conference.

References

[1]   Liddell, H. & D. Mackie., Forward to the Past. *Proceedings of International Conference on Sustainable Building*, Oslo, Norway, 2002.

[2]   United Nations Population Fund (UNFPA). *The State of World Population 2001*, United Nations: New York, 2001.

[3]   Jenks, M. & Burgess, R., (eds). *Compact Cities: Sustainable Urban Forms for Developing Countries*, E & FN Spon: London, 2000.

[4]   Frey, H., *Designing the City: Towards a More Sustainable Urban Form*, Routledge: New York, 1999.

[5]   Williams, K., Jenks, M. & Burton, E., *Achieving Sustainable Urban Form*, E & FN Spon: London, 2000.

[6]   Atkinson, R. & Ting J., Sustainable Urban Design- Saving the Status Quo or Transforming the future?, http://www.ictcsociety.org/pdf/ATKINSON,%20Rick%20&%20TING,%20Jason.pdf

[7]   Carmona, M., Sustainable Urban Design – A Possible Agenda. *Planning for Sustainable Future*, eds. A. Layard, S. Davoudi & S. Batty, E & FN SPON: London, 2001.

[8]   United Nations (UN). *Earth Summit Agenda 21: the United Nations Programme of Action from Rio*. United Nations Department of Public Information: New York, 1993.

[9]   Walsh, F. & Brand, J., Environmental Appraisal in Scotland–Local Authority Experiences. *Strathclyde Papers on Planning*, 32, 1998.

[10] Miller, T. G., *Living in the Environment: Principles, connections and solutions*, 12th edition, Thomson Learning, Inc: New York, 2002.

[11] Blowers, A., *Planning for a sustainable environment*, Earthscan: London, 1993.

[12] Biddulph, M., Urban Design Strategies in Practice: An Introduction. Built Environment, **25 (4)**, pp. 281-288, 1999.

[13] Lawrence, G., The Seattle approach. *Urban Design Quarterly*, **57**, January, pp. 23-26, 1996.

[14] Carmona, M., Implementing Urban Renaissance – problems, possibilities and plans in South East England. *Progress in Planning*, **56**, pp. 169-250, 2001.

[15] Godschalk, D. R., Land Use Planning Challenges. *Journal of American Planning Association*, **70 (1)**, pp. 5-13, 2004.

[16] Al-Hokail, A. A., Socio-cultural contradictions in the Arab/Islamic built environment: an empirical study of Arriyadh, Saudi Arabia. *Proc. of CORP 2004 & Geomultimedia04*, ed. M. Schrenk, www.corp.at, pp. 325-331, 2004.

[17] Eben Saleh, M. A., The transformation of residential neighbourhood: the emergence of new urbanism in Saudi Arabian culture. *Building and Environment*, **37**, pp. 515-529, 2002.

[18] Eggenberger, M. & Partidario, M., Development of a framework to assist the integration of environmental, social and economic issues in spatial planning. *Impact Assessment and Project Appraisal,* **18** (3), pp. 201-207, 2000.

[19] Alshuwaikhat, H. M. & Nkwenti, D. I., Developing Sustainable Cities in Arid Regions. *Cities*, **19** (**2**), pp. 85-94, 2002.

[20] Selman, P., *Local sustainability – Managing and Planning Ecologically Sound Places*, Paul Chapman: London, 1996.

[21] Batty, M., Dodge, M., Jiang, B & Smith, A., GIS and Urban Design. *CASA Working Paper*, **3**, CASA: London, 1998.

The optimum density for the sustainable city: the case of Athens

D. Milakis, N. Barbopoulos & Th. Vlastos
School of Surveying Engineering, Department of Geography and Regional Planning, National Technical University of Athens, Greece

Abstract

Over the last decade there has been a great deal of research on the definition of the sustainable city. There is also an ongoing debate on city shape and on the optimum distribution of activities. The dominant theory, often to be found in political documents, favours the compact city. Its main principles are the mix of land uses and the increase of density. It also promotes improvement of public transport and of environmentally friendly means of transport, such as cycling and walking. In this paper, we offer an estimate for a critical threshold of density for the case of Athens. This threshold reflects the density required in order for significant changes in travel behaviour to appear. It results from a statistical analysis of data concerning urban and transport characteristics. This threshold is much higher than those identified in other cities around the world. We then discuss the policy implications of such a threshold.
Keywords: residential density, socio-economic characteristics, travel behaviour.

1 The discussion on optimum density

Over the last two decades there has been a growing concern over implementing principles of sustainability in cities. The major question to be addressed is how to define the appropriate guidelines, needed to obtain to obtain urban structures that are energy efficient and do not pollute the environment excessively. There is a growing number of policy documents referring to urban planning. These documents set the following targets:

- the reduction of car use,
- the reduction of distance traveled by car, and

- the promotion of public transport and non-motorized means, namely walking and cycling.

Such documents suggest developing compact urban structures, with high residential density and mixed land uses. Two typical reports along these lines have been launched by the European Commission (CEC [1, 2]). There are also reports produced by expert advisors on the urban environment (EGUE [3]), which clearly state that land use planning must and can constitute a tool for achieving these aims.

The key notion in these new planning guidelines is density. An increase in density is considered as environmentally beneficial, causing a decrease in energy consumed in transportation. This is quite reasonable, since high density means that land uses are concentrated in less space and the ability to travel shorter distances by sustainable mean of transport is increased. This hypothesis was tested by Newman and Kennworthy [4], who elaborated data from 32 cities in four continents and found a strong negative statistical correlation (R^2=0.8594) between residential density and energy consumption per capita by car. This relationship was exponential for densities beneath 30 persons/ha and linear for higher levels.

Other studies have also come to the conclusion that residential density affects travel behavior, but have identified different critical thresholds for it. For example, Frank and Pivo [5] found for Washington DC that population density should exceed approximately 13 persons/acre (32 persons/ha), before a significant modal shift occurs from Single-Occupant Vehicles (SOV) to transit use and walking for shopping trips. In contrast, Stead [6], in his research on Britain, identified a critical range for density between 40 and 50 persons/hectare, which is associated with low travel distances.

In our paper, the influence of density on travel behavior will be investigated in the case of Athens. A comparison between density and socio-economic characteristics regarding their significance in explaining the variability of travel characteristics will be applied, too. Moreover, a density threshold will be estimated: this threshold defines the area where the increase in density will have significant impact on travel behaviour. Finally, the policy implications of the results will be addressed, given that Athens already has a very high density in comparison with other European and American cities.

2 Estimation of the range of density values corresponding to low car use and energy savings: the case of Athens

2.1 Methodology

The aim of this research is to explore the relationship between density and travel behavior and, if possible, to define a density threshold beneath which its increase will have significant effects on travel behaviour. However, in a large number of studies it is argued that socio-economic characteristics should be taken into account when exploring the relationship between urban form characteristics and travel behavior (Gomez-Ibanez [7] Stead and Marshall [8]). This is crucial, since it is possible that some of the travel characteristics may be more influenced by socio-economic characteristics, than by urban form parameters. At the second level of the analysis we investigated the significance of density in explaining travel behavior in relation to three socio-economic characteristics. To this end, five multiple regressions were applied, with density and the three socio-economic characteristics serving as independent variables and five travel characteristics as dependent.

The socio-economic characteristics (independent variables) were the following:
1. Mean household income
2. Level of car ownership
3. Household size

As dependent variables, we chose the following travel data:
1. Number of journeys/person/day by public transport
2. Number of journeys/person/day by car
3. Number of journeys/person/day on foot
4. Mean length of car journeys
5. Energy consumption per capita by car

The descriptive statistics of data are presented in table 1.

Table 1:   Descriptive statistics of data.

Parameter	Unit	Mean	SD	Min.	Max.
Independent Variables					
Net residential density	persons/hectare	218	197	6	903
Household income	euros	889	390	402	2638
Car ownership	car/1000 inhabitants	279	76	138	471
Household size	persons/household	3.13	0.32	2.50	4,13
Dependent Variables					
Journeys per person by public transport	number of journeys	0.19	0.09	0.26	0.45
Journeys per person by car	number of journeys	0.817	0.339	0.365	2.62
Journeys per person on foot	number of journeys	0.140	0.093	0.000	0.97
Mean journey length by car	meters	7108	2506	3706	13781
Energy consumption per capita by car	MJ	21.7	14.64	8.6	77.9

2.2 Data

Our study case is the Athens metropolitan area. It comprises 82 municipalities with a total population of 3833400 persons. The municipality was chosen as spatial unit of analysis, due to lack of empirical data on any lower scale. 95% of the population of the study area is concentrated in a basin of approximately 1270 km^2. This basin has physical boundaries, the sea in the south, and mountains in the north. The majority of the municipalities are located inside this basin. Their mean area is 15 km^2.

The data used is taken from the following inventories, which were compiled in 1996, by Athens Metro Development study:

- Land uses and socio-economic characteristics (AM-DPGS [9])
- Travel characteristics (AM-DPGS [10]),

A vast inventory of land uses was created, covering 74500 hectares and 66600 blocks. Travel characteristics were estimated through the analysis of data acquired through 29358 household interviews.

2.3 Travel characteristics

We define the threshold beneath which density affects significantly travel behaviour in relation to the following travel characteristics:

- Modal split
- Mean travel length by car,
- Energy consumption per capita due to car use.

To describe modal split, we employed the mean number of journeys per person per day by public transport, car and on foot. Walking journeys were defined as being longer than 500 m. The mean journey length by car (Mean Journey Length – MJL) was calculated according to the origin/destination records in the municipality level:

$$MJL_i = \frac{\sum_i t_{ij} d_{ij}}{\sum_i t_{ij}} \qquad (1)$$

t_{ij} : *number of car journeys with origin municipality i and destination municipality j.*
d_{ij}: *Euclidian distance between municipalities i,j.*

Finally, to estimate energy consumption per capita by car, we defined mean energy consumption per kilometer. For this reason we used the equations regarding fuel consumption employed in the research program CORINAIR - COPERT III (Ntziachristos and Samaras [11]), which vary according to car technology (by year of manufacturing), cubic capacity and mean travel speed in urban areas. We also drew on data concerning the composition of car fleet in the study area, provided by the National Statistical Service. The mean fuel consumption is 0.0798 liters/kilometer. This is converted to energy, given that the energy equivalent of one petrol liter being 44.7 MJ. The energy consumption per capita due to car use therefore was calculated as the product of average car journey length per capita and energy consumption per kilometer.

2.4 Results

Net residential density was found to be the most significant parameter in accounting for the variability of the four (out of the five) travel characteristics. The only exception is the parameter "journeys by car", which is explained more significantly by car ownership than by residential density (t-value: 6.572) (tables 2-6).

The same results are found in the comparison of the level of influence of the explanatory variables on travel characteristics. On the basis of standardized coefficients, net residential density exercises the strongest influence on four out of the five travel characteristics. Only in the case of journeys by car is car ownership more influential than density (0.812) (see tables 2-6).

Density was found to be positively correlated to journeys by public transport and on foot, and negatively correlated to journeys by car, mean journey length and energy consumption per capita by car. Interestingly, the relationship between residential density and all the travel characteristics is better described by a logarithmic curve. In figure 1, graphical representations of these relationships are given.

A threshold for density can be easily identified in these five diagrams. In the case of Athens, it is found to be around 200 persons/ha. Policies regarding increase in density up to this value might involve the following aspects:
1. Increase of public transport use and walking
2. Reduction of car use, mean journey length and energy consumption by car.

It is also apparent that if density increases over this threshold, public transport passengers and walkers will also increase in absolute numbers. However, the alteration of modal split will occur to a much lower degree.

For example, an increase in residential density in municipalities with 10 persons/ha to 30 persons/hectare would cause an 18.6% increase in public transport use. On the contrary, an increase in residential density in municipalities with 210 persons/ha to 230 persons/ha would cause only a 1.6% increase in public transport use. The impacts of density change between these values on travel characteristics are presented in table 7.

Table 2:   Results of multiple regressions for journeys by public transport.

	Coefficient	Standardized coefficient	t-value (sig.)
Net residential density (Logarithmic transformation)	0.054	0.626	6.271 (0.000)
Income	-3.853E-05	-0.047	-0.317 (0.752)
Car ownership	-2.051E-04	-0.143	-0.863 (0.391)
Household size	-0.036	-0.107	-1.187 (0.239)
R^2	0.594		
F-value (sig.)	28.153 (0.000)		

Table 3:   Results of multiple regressions for journeys by car.

	Coefficient	Standardized coefficient	t-value (sig.)
Net residential density (Logarithmic transformation)	-0.052	-0.191	-2.576 (0.012)
Income	-1.563E-04	-0.061	-0.554 (0.581)
Car ownership	0.004	0.812	6.572 (0.000)
Household size	0.131	0.125	1.867 (0.066)
R^2	0.775		
F-value (sig.)	66.265 (0.000)		

Table 4:   Results of multiple regressions for journeys on foot.

	Coefficient	Standardized coefficient	t-value (sig.)
Net residential density (Logarithmic transformation)	0.031	0.416	3.065 (0.003)
Income	-1.956E-04	-0.280	-1.392 (0.168)
Car ownership	7.311E-05	0.060	0.266 (0.791)
Household size	0.023	0.082	0.667 (0.507)
R^2	0.251		
F-value (sig.)	6.435 (0.000)		

Table 5:   Results of multiple regression for mean journey length by car.

	Coefficient	Standardized coefficient	t-value (sig.)
Net residential density (Logarithmic transformation)	-1987.1	-0.994	-11.744 (0.000)
Income	3.179	0.168	1.338 (0.185)
Car ownership	-12.252	-0.371	-2.638 (0.010)
Household size	-1093.265	-0.142	1.850 (0.068)
R^2	0.708		
F-value (sig.)	46.673 (0.000)		

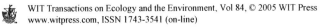

Table 6:   Results of multiple regressions for energy consumption by car.

	Coefficient	Standardized coefficient	t-value (sig.)
Net residential density (Logarithmic transformation)	-7.341	-0.629	-8.577 (0.000)
Income	0.008	0.074	0.680 (0.499)
Car ownership	0.064	0.330	2.705 (0.008)
Household size	0.951	0.021	0.318 (0.751)
R^2	0.781		
F-value (sig.)	68.641 (0.000)		

Table 7:   The effects on travel characteristics from the density increases.

	Residential density increase from 10 to 30 persons/hectare	Residential density increase from 200 to 230 persons/hectare
Journeys/person by car	+ 18.6%	+ 1.6%
Journeys/person by public transport	- 6.9 %	- 0,6%
Journeys/person on foot	+ 24.1%	+ 1.9%
Mean journey length by car	- 30.7%	- 2.5%
Energy consumption by car	- 37.2%	- 3.1%

3 Discussion: policy implications of the optimum density in the case of Athens

The central municipality of Athens accommodates about 1/3 of the total metropolitan population and occupies the area defined by the city limits as they were in the 50s. It has a very high density (750 persons/ha) in comparison to the other municipalities of the metropolitan area and is usually considered as a bad paradigm for urban development. A strong anti-density outlook exists in almost all of the municipalities. It is argued that it is environmentally correct to lower residential densities in order to increase open and green spaces. However, the implications of such a planning principle regarding transport are not taken into account. On the other hand it is apparent that any increase in densities in order to alter travel behaviour would be ineffectual, if no additional measures promoting public transport and discouraging private car use were applied.

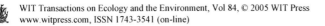
WIT Transactions on Ecology and the Environment, Vol 84, © 2005 WIT Press
www.witpress.com, ISSN 1743-3541 (on-line)

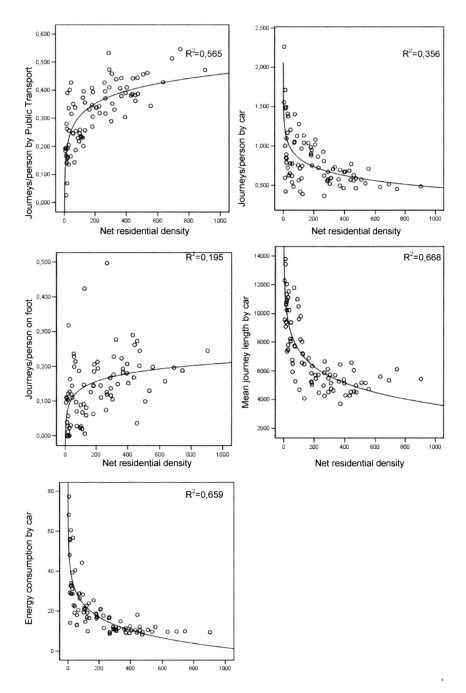

Figure 1: Graphical representation of the relationships between density and travel characteristics.

Increase in density reduces total traveling distance, which already quite beneficial. However, such increases should be accompanied by policies aimed at the reconstruction of the urban and road environment, thereby rendering making it friendlier for the pedestrian or cyclist and policies promoting public transport. Moreover, higher densities increase the number of the potential passengers of public transport.

It is a fact that the inhabitants of Athens metropolitan area immigrate to the suburbs, where they can fulfill their desire for a detached house with a garden and a less congested road network. It needs great effort in order to reverse this trend. The social acceptance of the compact city concept depends on the magnitude of the investments for appraising urban environment and public transport infrastructure. This investment will be made quickly, if it is shown that the city will consume less energy, be more attractive to the visitors and more functional.

Acknowledgements

This research is co-funded by the European Social Fund (75%) and National Resources (25%).

References

[1]   Commission of the European Communities (C.E.C.), 1990. Green Paper on the Urban Environment [COM(90)218], Office for Official Publications of the European Communities, Luxembourg.
[2]   Commission of the European Communities (C.E.C.), 2004. Towards a thematic strategy on the urban environment. Communication from the European Commission [COM(2004)60], Office for Official Publications of the European Communities, Luxembourg.
[3]   Expert Group on the Urban Environment (E.G.U.E.), 2001. Towards more Sustainable Urban Land Use. Advice to the European Commission for Policy and Action. Report of the Expert Group on the Urban Environment. European Commission, DGXI, Environment, Nuclear Safety and Civil Protection, Brussels.
[4]   Newman P. & Kenworthy J., 1989. Gasoline Consumption and Cities. A comparison of U.S. Cities with a Global Survey, Journal of the American Planning Association 55 (1): 24-37.
[5]   Frank L.D. & Pivo G., 1994. Impacts of Mixed Use and Density on Utilization of Three Modes of Travel: Single-Occupant Vehicle, Transit, and Walking. Transportation Research Record 1466: 44-52.
[6]   Stead D., 2001. Relationships between land use, socioeconomic factors, and travel patterns in Britain. Environment and Planning B: Planning and Design 28 (4): 499-528.
[7]   Gomez-Ibanez J., 1991. A Global View of Automobile Dependence, Journal of the American Planning Association 57 (3): 376-379.

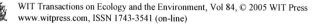

[8]   Stead D. & Marshall S., 2001. The Relationships between Urban Form and Travel Patterns. An International Review and Evaluation. European Journal of Transport and Infrastructure Research 1 (2): 113-141.

[9]   Attiko Metro S.A., Department of Planning and General Studies, 1997. Metro Development Study. Land Use and Socioeconomic Characteristics. AM-DPGS, Athens

[10]   Attiko Metro S.A., Department of Planning and General Studies, 1998. Metro Development Study. Travel Characteristics. Household surveys in Typical Period. Technical Report. AM-DPGS, Athens.

[11]   Ntziachristos, L., Samaras, Z., 2000. COPERT III. Computer programme to calculate emissions from road transport. Methodology and emission factors [Technical Report No 49]. European Environmental Agency, Copenhagen.

The transformation of residential patterns in Al-Ain City, UAE

M. Haggag & K. Hadjri
Department of Architectural Engineering, UAE University, UAE

Abstract

This paper aims at investigating some of the important features affecting the planning and transformation of urban residential patterns, focusing on availability and accessibility of serviced land on the one hand, and the characteristics of the households and the level of their wealth on the other. The study is concerned with the main factors affecting residential distribution patterns, including land value, transportation cost, and characteristics of the city structure. The study examines the current and future trends of the residential mosaic in Al-Ain city as a unique case study because of the new phenomena caused by the relationship between the post-independence urban development and modern urban planning approaches implemented in the United Arab Emirates. The paper highlights some of the key issues that are emerging as a result of the socio-economic and cultural changes of Al-Ain city. In addition, the study aims to understand the spatial configuration of key factors such as population and household structures, income distribution, social and cultural requirements, and physical and institutional constraints.
Keywords: urban transformation, residential pattern, land value, transportation cost, Al-Ain city.

1   Introduction

Urban populations utilize built space for different purposes, of which housing constitutes the largest part, and may account for over 25 percent of household expenditure [1]. Urban residential structure is not restricted to the result of the interplay between housing demand and supply, but is also shaped by other attributes, such as household characteristics. The household is assumed to find its optimal location by trading off travel cost, against housing cost; and chooses a location at a point at which total cost is minimized.

Urban planning and development can be understood to be increase and spread of values and institutions that enhance the ability of a society to generate and successfully cope with the continuing change [2]. The rate of change is a function of the level of social interaction, information exchange and communications, which in turn is a function of the physical and spatial structure of a city. The spatial quality and structure of the urban environment is one of the most examined components of urban planning. Most planners and decision makers today are mainly concerned other aspects of urban planning such as the patterns of human activities outside the home, and the mosaic patterns of residential neighborhoods.

The paper attempts to produce a clear understanding of urban patterns and changes of Al-Ain residential neighbourhoods with regards to the effects of modernization. In order to study Al Ain's growth and development, themes on power of socio-economic and cultural relationships and their effects on the urban structure are important.

To achieve the aim of the study, a better understanding of theoretical background of residential location patterns is highlighted, and the main aspects which affect the transformation of residential pattern are identified. Current and future trends of residential mosaic of Al Ain were examined. Socio-economic, cultural changes and other aspects were studied using the following variables: household structure; income distribution; ethnic groups; social and cultural requirements; land value; physical constraints; institutional limitations; transportation; and urban residential patterns. A number of neighborhoods within were selected as case studies. A field survey was carried out by the authors to identify the users' patterns of movement, socio-economic data, and housing typology in selected neighborhoods.

2   Al-Ain city and its structure development

The city of Al-Ain, is located in the eastern region of the Emirate of Abu Dhabi, within the inner desert oasis of the United Arab Emirates. It lies about 150 km east of Abu Dhabi, and 130 km south east of Dubai. The city exploded in size from a small village to a fast growing urban centre in less than 30 years. The old area of Al-Ain was located in an area of about 150 hectares with a small number of populations [3]. In 1980, the area of Al-Ain was increased to 1,800 hectares with a population of around 120,000. At the end of 1990s, with a new geographic pattern, the city has expended to about 15,000 hectares with a population number of 300,000 [4]. A unique national, regional, and local road network was developed in the city, and more than 1,800 km of road length has been built including to its hinterland. The modern development of Al-Ain came with the successful exploitation of Oil in the Emirate of Abu Dhabi and the foundation of the United Arab Emirates in 1971. During the subsequent period, a radical transformation of the area took place, which saw a modern urban development, and a new population structure with particular socio-economic characteristics. As a hometown of the ruling family of the Emirate, it has benefited from the desert. As a result, a number of standard residential types were developed for citizens and non-citizens during the last few decades, such as apartments, low cost governmental housing, small and large private villas. These types are distributed within and outside the CBD, according to many factors. The most important of which are the physical characteristics of the city, the availability of residential land, decentralization of the city cervices, the level of transportation and street network.

In 1986, a new planning process was established to accelerate the new development of the city and to create and develop new settlements outside the old area [4]. This plan was based upon new criteria in order to: encourage more residents from different tribes to live in the city; create a homogenous social structure by redistribution of the UAE citizens within the new residential districts, and create a new social system of solidarity with the new districts. During the past twenty years, a concerted effort has been made to implement the 1986 master plan with houses and roads being built and hundreds of hectares of residential land have been developed and a number of new neighbourhood units have already been built. The new physical structure pattern is highly preferred by citizens and non-citizens alike who are seeking more privacy than they had previously and large residential lots. A study of the distribution of populations by districts revealed that there is a general trend for redistribution location of residents from areas close to CBD to areas such as Hili, Zakher, and Maqam (for more details see section 4). Those who were initially living close to the CBD seem to relocate to the periphery via areas such as Mutaredh and Jimi districts. This move correlates with the changes that are seen in household incomes especially for the citizens. This raises a question of whether in the future this may lead to urban flight and urban decay to those areas close to the CBD as a result of abandoned and unoccupied buildings.

3   Urban residential pattern: theoretical background

To achieve the aim of the study, it is important to highlight the main theories of urban structure and urban land market, and how they can be fitted to Al-Ain City. Three theories of urban structure attempt to describe the different growth and functional distribution patterns of a city and show the residential location in relation to socio-economic household characteristics. These theories are: the concentric zone theory; the sector theory; and the multiple nuclei theory [5]. The concentric zone theory is based on the idea that similar activities are located at the same distance from the centre of the city. Each zone would have relatively homogeneous land use [6]. This model assumes that a city grows outward from its centre to form a pattern of concentric zones. The first zone, which is the Central Business District (CBD), is the focal point of commercial, social and civic life. It also represents the area of original settlement. The second zone is an area in transition, which is usually contain the poorest quality residence and is being invaded by business and light manufacturing. The third zone is basically an area of low-income people who desire to live within easy access of their work. Beyond this zone, the middle and high-class residential areas are distributed. This zone is followed by the commuter zone, which contains the patchy development of high-class residence associated with the fastest existing transport facilities.

The second model of city structure, the sector theory, was formulated by Hoyt after examining structure pattern of residential locations in 142 cities [5]. The idea of this model is that the pattern of residential location could be explained in terms of sectors or wedges. The wholesale and light manufactures are located at the opposite end of the city from high quality residential areas. However, low-class residential areas are located close to the manufacturing zone. The remarkable feature of this model is the way it highlights the outward migration of high-class housing districts as the city evolves. It is also clear that the sector theory may be extended to include all types of urban land use, with each of the principle functions occupying adjacent sectors of terrain.

The third model of urban structure, multiple nuclei, was developed by Harris and Ullman [5]. The basic idea of this model is that cities develop around several district nuclei rather than around one centre of origin. The nuclei, sometimes established in an earlier rapid urbanization phase, emerge as a new centre as the city expands. It should be noted that no particular significance is attached to the shapes of each zone. The emergences of separate nuclei are determined by factors such as; the interdependency of some types of activity that need to be close to each other; and the tendency for complementary activities to be near each other. It seems that the multiple nuclei model takes into account more real factors than the other two theories and it is clear that this model makes it possible to construct and elaborate a model of urban structure which is far more widely applicable than either the concentric or the sector models.

The three models are not completely opposed to each other. The first two models, which are based mainly upon conditions of developed cities, cannot fit all developing cities. In most developing cities, the residential pattern is almost the reverse of that proffered by the concentric zone model [7]. The high-income families are willing to locate near the CBD and pay the premium in cost of tenancy, while the low-income families who cannot afford to pay any extra than is necessary are pushed to the outer edge of the city. This could be attributed to the lack of high-level technology in transportation and infrastructure, and therefore the excessive amount of time spent on traveling.

The urban land market theory attempts to rationalize the location of individual activities within an urban system using components of land accessibility, trade or commerce and traveling cost as major variables to influence the household's choice. The determination of residential location is different from the location of any other activity. The household is assumed to find its optimal location by trading off its travel cost against its housing cost, and locating to a point at which total cost is minimized. The household will also consider other factors, such as social, physical, political, and availability of wealth. This relationship is known as the trade-off theory [5]. The basic assumption of this theory is that housing cost declines with increase in distance from an activity centre, but transportation costs are assumed to rise with increase in distance from that center. The model uses the bid-rent function that is a derivative of urban land market theory (see section 4). This theory is tested for Al Ain city, based on both the observed reactive empirical data and those non-reactive data collected from the field survey, and from the Municipality of Al-Ain. Contributions to residential location theory were mad by Wingo and Mills. Wingo's model focused on the way urban transportation costs affected land rent and the demand for residential land. This model assumes that the demand of residential land per household depended upon the land value and that the elasticity of demand is constant. It also emphasized the fall of population density with the distance from the CBD when land is substituted for capital in the production of housing at locations distant from the CBD [8].

The characteristics of the above residential models show that the costs in renting or purchasing land, and costs of commuting are the main factors in determining the optimal locations of residential land. It is reasonable to argue from the above analysis that the property value gradient should be affected by the land value gradient and the analysis of the empirical study of Al-Ain City shows that the rent or the property value falls with increase in distance from the CBD, but at a diminishing rate. The high income families are willing to make long commuting journeys to the outskirts of the city. However, the low-income groups are unwilling to do so because the direct cost is high as a percentage of their total income.

4   Al-Ain city and its residential distribution pattern

Al-Ain has a unique pattern of land use that is similar to most of the cities within the Gulf region. The field survey that carried out by the authors in 2001 and the structure map of Al-Ain reveal that there is a strong correlation between the residential land distribution pattern to that proffered by both the sector and nuclei models, though predominately the sector model. The high income residential areas are located radially outside the CBD on the periphery of the city boundary in areas with low residential densities. However, low-income residential areas are located close to industrial zone "Sanaiya", and this location is diametrically opposed in comparison to that of the high income residential areas. The high-rent apartment areas are located close to the CBD; however, high-rent single family houses are located a little further away from the CBD.

The study of the household characteristics, land values, and transportation system, reveal four recognizable residential types within the various sectors in the city: rented apartments, rented single family houses, popular residential lots (Shabiat), and large residential lots (villas). The first residential type is located within the CBD. It is composed of mixed-use units containing commercial and residential apartments for low-income and single-family middle-income non-citizen residents. Small urban blocks with a maximum height of 4 stories characterize this type. This area is the most densely occupied part of the city (25-30 dwellings per hectare). The second type is located just outside the CBD, and is characterized by semi-attached, two storey houses for middle-income non-citizen residents with an average density of 15 dwellings per hectare. The third residential type, the Shabiat, is occupied by the low and middle-income citizens and located a few kilometres away from the central area of the city. It is characterized by low residential density (3-5 dwellings per hectare). The high-income citizens mainly occupy the fourth residential type located on the periphery of the city. This sector is characterized by large residential lots containing large single-family residences with a very low residential density (1-2 dwelling per hectare).

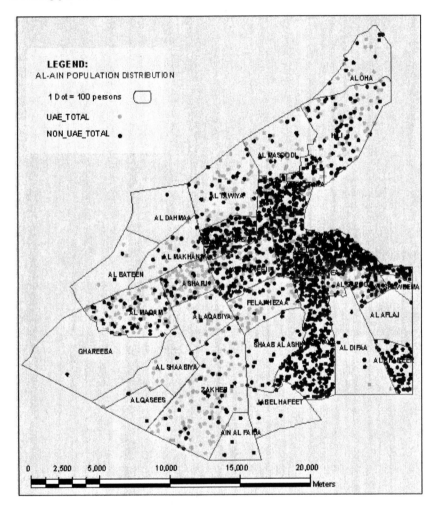

Figure 1: Population distribution pattern of Al-Ain, 2002. Source: the authors, based on the database produced by ArcView.

The analysis of the residential and household growth patterns of Al-Ain reveal that the majority of the UAE citizens live in residential areas farther from the CBD. This results in a desire to relocate farther away from the CBD, in private lot sub-divisions. This probably is a result of the government's encouragement to the citizens to develop new residential areas on the periphery of the city through provision of land and cheap financing on the opposite side of Sanaiya. The study further revealed that low-income non-citizens prefer to live in the high-density areas near the centre of activities, or other new secondary business centers. The middle-income households tend to move to just outside the CBD. The study also leads as to conclude that residential densities decrease with the distance from the CBD (see figure 1). Table (1) shows the distribution pattern of the population in selected districts. It is recognized that every district, except Sanaiya, had an increase in population with significantly very large motilities visible to areas such as Hili and Maqam. It must be noted that the majority of the redistribution is mainly by the citizens.

Table 1:   Changes in distribution of population in Al-Ain. Source: Adapted from Cox [4] and the Municipality of Abu Dhabi.

Districts	1990		1995		2000	
	Citizen	Non-citizen	Citizen % change	Non-citizen % change	Citizen % change	Non-citizen % change
Central	9,876	24,855	30.00	0.00	4.65	0.00
Jimi	7,778	10,552	5.00	1.70	5.00	0.87
Maqam	12,508	5,339	56.30	190.6	62.30	59.02
Zakher	5,745	1,518	13.10	8.60	7.76	22.2
Mutaredh	12,184	29,486	26.30	52.70	5.20	0.05
Hili	12,283	10,461	50.90	16.90	91.34	14.40
Tawaia	10,626	11,745	78.44	14.60	21.10	12.40
Sanaiya	---	20,044	---	-19.30	---	-6.90

The analysis of land tenure in UAE is somewhat different from those in other parts of the world in that the open market still has a very little role to play in pricing. The Ruler on behalf of the citizens and other non-citizens of long established residency holds all the land in Al-Ain in trust. This confers rights to plots of land for purpose of building self-residence and extra for investments without payment to all citizens. The supply and demand for the land is thus in theory determined by the needs of the citizens and family size an elements that is not very empirical since socio-political factors come into play. This creates uneasy balance between individual needs against the planning policy objectives of the region and the town as a whole.

Assumptions and modification have been made to the urban land market theory in the analysis of Al-Ain. The householders are assumed to be rational and economic persons above and beyond their other human and psychological desires. In a normal market the unit cost of land is assumed to fall with distance away from the CBD. In the case of Al Ain since land is given free of cost to the resident citizens, a measure of value of land has to be derived. We used an index based on rental rates for the various areas, unit cost of construction, which is assumed to remain constant throughout Al-Ain and analysis of maps and master plan. The theory uses the bid-rent function that is a derivative of Urban Land Market theory [9]. The bid-rent should be equated with the utility level for the lot by the householder, thus the rate of change of the bid-rent for a given household represented by the curve "b"; with distance "d" (see figures 2 and 3).

$$b = \frac{[d.Tc-Oc]}{V.A}$$

where; "Tc" represents unit value of land, which for Al Ain is related to the size and distance, the further away from CBD, the lower the unit cost of land and because of increase in size; "Oc" represents travelling costs; "V" represents actual unit value or cost of purchasing or renting of property; and "A" represents the actual area of land occupied by the householder.

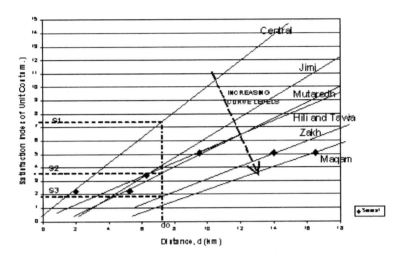

Figure 2:   Varying bid-curve levels with distance.

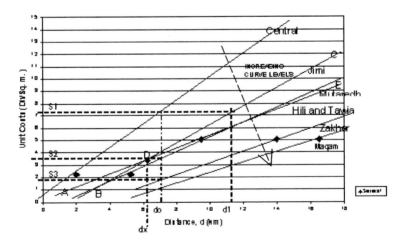

Figure 3:   Unite cost against distance from the CBD.

The household thus engages in manoeuvres aimed at lowering or reducing the unit costs levels and boosting space and levels of privacy available. It is thus typical to relate the high bid-rent curves with high land values and low bid-curves with low values. The high unit cost of land reduces the size of land or space available to the householder, thus the desire to relocate at some distance d1 to continue to enjoy the same level of amenities and utilities (see figure 3).

Respective sets of linear equations for the various districts in Al-Ain could be derived and use them as an easy differencing system for location or spatial competitiveness. The higher curves with lower bide-rents, b, will locate closer to the CBD, while the lower ones will locate further away in attempts to increase cost index and utility levels while at same time maintaining levels of satisfaction. In figure 3, there are two intersecting bid-curves for Mutaredh and Jimi districts, both have location indifference being the same distance dx from the CBD. This is the location at which both neighbourhoods have equal or matching spatial compositeness. The effective bid-rent here are A, D and DC while the failed bid-rent curve is B, D and DE respectively. The Mutaredh bid-curve results from factors such as close proximity to CBD and lower costs in transportation. As the distance d rises, the Mutaredh bid-curve fails due to new high costs in rents, congestions etc and this creates the desire in the householder to relocated further away in attempt to raise the bid-curve. The move then results in relocating to Jimi represented by the curve DC. By using these equations and empirical figure from the survey it is possible calculate the approximate location points for various household groups based on their changing characteristics.

5   Conclusion

The analysis of the residential pattern of Al-Ain City shows that, the distribution pattern of residential land is almost the same of that proffered by the Sector Model. The majority of the high-income UAE citizens are located radially outside the CBD in private large plot subdivisions. However, low-income non-citizens tend to live in the high-density areas, near the CBD. Therefore, residential density decreases with the distance from the centre of activities. The main reasons for this residential pattern can be summarized in the following points. Al-Ain has been affected by the transport revolution. The well-developed transportation network and the high technology of communication systems have encouraged high-income citizens and those with large families to own or live on a large area of land away from the CBD. The new residential districts that have been and continue to be established on the periphery create a new homogenous social structure. This structure preserves traditional and social values, and is highly preferred by the citizens; moreover, the family sizes are larger and thus necessitate the desire for a large lot of land that is not available in areas close to the city centre. The rate of car-ownership in Al-Ain is very high, which in turn encourages high-income citizens to live farther away from the CBD. Every neighborhood is well supplied with infrastructure and public utilities, and has easy access to the centre of activities.

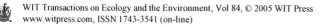

The study of Al-Ain also reveals a high vacancy rate of residential units mainly due to both oversupply of the units and lack of strong independent market forces. The encouragement of development of new residential areas at the periphery of the city creates other new problems that are associated with growth of cities. These include congested rush hour traffic, longer and pains taking travel to work and school, stratified and homogenous society that do not foster integration between various categories. There is need for further development of an efficient and reasonable public transportation since the report reveals that 80 percent of the commuter traffic is by small private vehicles.

Acknowledgement

The authors would like to express their appreciation to the Scientific Research Affairs Department at the UAE University for their financial support, and cooperation in the research project under contract number 02/11-7-24.

References

[1] Spear, A., *Residential Mobility, Migration, and Metropolitan Change*, Ballinger Pub. Co, 2000.
[2] Eisner, S. et al, *Urban Patterns*, John Wiley & Sons, New York, 1993.
[3] Abdellatif, M. *Achieving Sustainability in a Horizontally Expanding Desert City: the Case of Al-Ain City*, UAE, Proc. of the 2nd international conference on sustainability in desert region, UAE University, UAE, pp. 97-108, 2000.
[4] Cox, S., *Master Plan for the Region of Al-Ain for the year 2000*, Town Planning Department of Al-Ain, Abu Dhabi, 1986.
[5] Putman, H. S., *Urban Residential Location Models*, Martinus Nijhoff Pub., Boston, 1979.
[6] Goodman, J., *Urban Residential Mobility: Place, People and Policy*, Urban Institute Press, Washington, DC., 1978
[7] HABITAT, *The Residential Circumstances of the Urban Poor in Developing Countries*, United Nation Centre of Human Settlements, Praeger, 1981.
[8] Kivell, P., *Land and the City: Pattern and Processes of Urban Change*, Routledge, London, 1993
[9] Onyango, J. O., *The Re-constructive Master plan, Base on Traditional Model: The Case of Nairobi*, M.Arch thesis, University of Notre Dame, 1999.

Spatial conditions for the integration of combined decentralised energy generation and waste(water) management in city districts

A. van Timmeren[1,2], P. A. de Graaf[1] & G. de Vries[3]
[1]*Climate Design & Environment (CD&E), Delft University of Technology (TUD), Faculty of Architecture, The Netherlands*
[2]*Atelier 2T, Haarlem, The Netherlands*
[3]*V&L Consultants, Rotterdam, The Netherlands*

Abstract

A topic of interest in sustainable urban planning and regeneration is the lack of integration of the so-called critical streams (water, energy, waste/wastewater). Most of the times concepts and systems which are developed or realised are not evaluated, compared or combined. Combinatorial effects of different decentralised technologies are not taken into consideration or investigated. The thesis of the research is that it is more appropriate to realise the pursued replacement of existing end-of-pipe technologies with an integrated approach and healthy, sustainable solutions at the intermediate scale of an urban district. In the case of decentralising alternative systems and infrastructures, concerning energy and sanitation in city districts and/or urban ensembles, conditions concerning the environmental impact, development and maintenance processes, spatial layout of collection, generation, treatment and interconnection of the different streams are effective. This paper focuses on the spatial and social conditions for the design, integration and implementation of sustainable solutions for these essential streams at the scale of an urban district, a cluster of houses and individual houses. Emphasis will be put on sanitation and the question of scale in relation to the integration and implementation of natural technologies and the way these technologies are present to the users. An improved visibility of solutions in the living environment of users will support their consciousness, and possibly commitment. The conditions for implementation are based on projects with innovative decentralised concepts for wastewater treatment and energy generation.
Keywords: decentralisation, spatial conditions, energy and sanitation, integration.

1 Introduction

The presented research tries to demonstrate the need to include interdisciplinary approaches to the integration of strategies for raising public awareness, marketing of the different qualities of water (cascading) and energy (exergy), and establishing a service business for building and operating more decentralised installations. Within this framework integration strategies for wastewater management and sanitation, even possibly together with energy-generation, comprise direct linking with neighboring subjects like agriculture–especially urban farming–, aquaculture, horticulture, health care and food security.

The basis of this research forms an urban planning that is based on 'interconnection', as well as waste management in general and the organisation, maintenance and assurance of indispensable parts of closed cycles. The methodology of the research is based on the 'regulative cycle' of Van Strien, in which a distinction is made between theoretic parts on the one hand and practice-related parts on the other hand. The theoretical part concerns flow-analysis of existing and new sustainable technologies for the preservation of the (energy, water and waste) streams, the analysis of the different options of transportation and the belonging technical infrastructure and analysis of possible scales. The practice-related part of the research consists of case studies concerning solutions (at different scales) solving the problem of turning these essential streams into cycles. Apart from these case studies concerning only part of the main research hypothesis, in one 'integration case' the outcome will be tested in a concept and belonging device, which is called the Sustainable Implant (or S.I.) [1].

The research has been commissioned by the Delft University of Technology (TUD) as part of the DOSIS (Sustainable Development of City & Infra-Structures) project (recently continued in CD&E–Climate Design & Environment–research) to investigate and develop decentralised sanitation, energy and reuse technologies. The aim is to research the spatial, social and environment related consequences of the implementation of decentralised technologies, and to define the conditions within society, with emphasis on urban planning and building.

2 Interconnecting energy and waste(water) related systems

2.1 Circular approach of resources and waste

It is important to realise that environmental-effects not only have to be negative. There can be positive aspects too, which can possibly compensate to some extent negative effects. Well known is the 'Eco-device model', with incoming and outgoing streams and respectively linked to primary harmful aspects for the environment (in- and outgoing streams), and secondary harmful aspects (coupled to the investigated system or area). The disadvantage of the schemes like the 'Eco-device model' is its constrain to the stochastic behaviour of input and output. It is important to see the eco-device in a larger framework, as a part of what is called the 'environment-circuit' [2]. In this 'E-circuit' the chain in/out is specified to the three main units: extraction, production and consumption, which through so-called leakage-flows have a continuous relation with the ecological basis (fig. 1). An important link in the desired transformation of our society from one based on linear attitudes of resources and waste, towards a circular one, is a changed way of handling sustainable energy and (ecological) sanitation. Ecological sanitation is not merely about a new latrine design. It comes down to thinking more in nutrients and raw materials than in waste, which 'are to be disposed'.

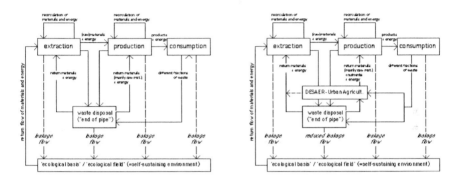

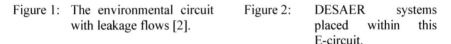

Figure 1:   The environmental circuit with leakage flows [2].

Figure 2:   DESAER systems placed within this E-circuit.

Within the figure of the Environmental circuit 'Decentralised Sanitation, Energy and Reuse' (DESAER) can be placed in between the (end-of-pipe) waste disposal and the three main units (fig. 2). It is a 'closed-loop-approach', in which excreta are returned to the soil instead of being returned to water. It comes down to a (better) formalisation of the existing 'leakage flows' between the cultural world and the natural world, or 'ecological field' as a self-sustaining environment. In this way the closed-loop approach is non-polluting, keeping fresh and marine water bodies free of pathogens and (too many) nutrients, while the environmental and human health risks are minimised or eliminated.

It is important to put this in a global perspective: unfortunately, half of humanity still does not have access to any type of sanitation [3]. On the one hand this is a threat to the ecological field. On the other hand it still might be the basis for a critical look upon existing 'conventional' approaches, which have been realised so far, and (mostly) are to be realised in these parts of the world too. The dilemma is: fast-arrangement of sanitation systems for the people who do not have access to sanitation (being a human right) and additional global environmental consequences, or ecological sanitation: on site systems with, especially in the beginning, a slower rate of implementation and therefore -in the beginning- not following the equity principle within Sustainable Development.

Apart from that, ecological sanitation is valuable for a number of other reasons, varying from better food production to secondary benefits, like improvement of soil structure and water holding capacity. The two main design features of ecological sanitation are urine-diversion and composting techniques. The first can be interconnected to nutrient recycling, the latter to nutrient and energy recycling. In both cases it is possible to manage urine, faeces or excreta with little or no water. But to ensure an ecologically secure way of managing excreta it is important to combine these systems to energy production like biogas production and/or integrated food production. Within these integrated projects concepts will have to be based on a closed-cycle flow of nutrients.

2.2 The role of technical infrastructure

One could state that the infrastructure of the essential (or critical) streams, due to its 'path-dependent', long term character and the existence of a limited number of dominant actors per network or stream [1], is determinative to what degree a project -varying in scale from a (part of a) building to a city- will or can be sustainable. In case of the energy streams for instance, conventional sources of energy are being extracted, isolated and in high concentrations brought together in central installations in which they are converted into large amounts of energy which via large distribution networks can supply large areas with energy. The loss during conversion and distribution is overshadowed by the abundance of energy that can be generated inside these centralised power plants. Most of the sustainable energy sources however are present (almost) everywhere but in relative small concentrations and most of the times less continuous available. For most of these sources it is illogical and not profitable to generate high-energy revenues and distribute it to larger areas. Especially the (waste)water infrastructure and the energy infrastructure can be characterised by transported streams which are not drawn up out of ongoing 'ecologisation' and dematerialisation but out of efficiency in central management and other economical factors. From the point of view of sustainability the technical infrastructure therefore seems to be insufficiently efficient.

Science, and increasingly the market too, bring up a rising number of solutions that imply possible smaller scales of implementation. The considered benefits are a possible reduction of infrastructure and better visibility and tuning in to the demand and therefore more flexibility. Especially in the field of small scale-, ecological sanitation systems important efforts have been made [4]. The idea behind these kind of smaller systems, often based on natural technologies, is their relative simplicity and adaptability, and therefore their possibility to create extra (real sustainable) capacities in situations where:

- centralised systems have not been built yet,
- existing systems (or surrounding environment) have reached the limits of their capacity and new buildings, districts and/or higher densities are planned; e.g. use as a (temporary) back-up,
- bio-climatical, geological or circumstantial characteristics make interventions in the subsoil difficult and/or expensive, and
- in case of desired improved environmental performances e.g. through interconnections with other 'infra' systems.

These kind of small scale alternative systems most of the times still are more expensive, due to their limitation to pilot projects, and the little 'economies of scale' in the production of components. The main cost factors are the construction and maintenance of the belonging 'small-scale networks'. This goes especially for sewage networks. Of course there are also other disadvantages. Sanitation for example is to a large extent a social phenomenon, rather than a technical. Therefore it is essential to acquire background information on cultural, social-, economic- and environmental factors influencing sanitation behaviour before actual planning can start. This is especially true when a new technology is to be introduced. In case of systems based on natural technologies one does have to take into account that these are (more) vulnerable in case of inaccurate use or sabotage. Besides they depend more on natural light and among other things this means that these renewable sources have a relative low energy density and subsequently large use of ground. Considering the use of ground of renewable, energy related technologies and the daylight dependence of the water treatment solutions which are based on natural technologies, this leads together with the ever decreasing available space to the conclusion that the optimalisation of the use of natural light and use of ground and daylight-related space(s) of surface dependent technologies should be investigated more closely. Through multiple use of ground one can prevent the rejection of small-scale sustainable alternatives on account of high costs, due to the relative large amount of needed ground surface. It can become the basis of new forms of Permaculture, because in most of the realised projects that are based on the principles of Permaculture until now, this aspect is underexposed.

3 Case studies

3.1 Examples of Decentralised SAnitation, Energy and Reuse (DESAER)

There are still few examples of living and working environments with integrated systems concerning decentralised sanitation, energy and reuse. However in several developed and developing countries examples are realised or close to completion. This research focuses on the developed countries because here the flush-and-forget technology of water closets and centralized treatment is the current status quo and alternatives have to compete with this existing standard. Seven projects in five different countries have been studied: Sustainable House Sydney (Australia) [5], Toronto Healthy House (Canada) [6], Hockerton Housing Project (Hockerton, United Kingdom) [7], Passivhaus Wohnen & Arbeiten Vauban (Freiburg, Germany) [8], Flintenbreite (Lübeck, Germany) [8], BedZED (London, United Kingdom) [9] and EVA-Lanxmeer (Culemborg, The Netherlands) [1], offering an overview of systems and scales of implementations in different circumstances.

3.2 Layout of components and scales of implementation

The applied systems are different for each project. In two cases, Flintenbreite (Lübeck) and "Wohnen und Arbeiten" (Vauban) vacuum toilet systems are used in combination with anaerobic digestion. In the other projects low flush toilets are combined with respectively a Living Machine (BedZED, London), a constructed wetland (Hockerton Housing Project), a fixed film filter (Toronto Healthy House) and a compost/fixed film tank (Sustainable House Sydney). In EVA-Lanxmeer anaerobic digestion (in combination with Living Machine) is planned but not yet installed. The anaerobic reactors in Flintenbreite –Lübeck and "Wohnen & Arbeiten" -Vauban are installed and tested, but not in operation yet.

Three scales of implementation are distinguished:

- the single-family dwelling,
- the cluster/apartment building,
- the neighbourhood/city district.

The Sustainable House Sydney (SHS) and the Toronto Healthy House (THH) are both single-family houses. The SHS is a renovated and converted terrace house in the centre of Sydney. The THH is a 3-storey house specifically designed for a competition to incorporate Healthy House criteria in a suburb of Toronto (two houses were made as semi-detached houses, both functioning autonomously). In performance the SHS and the THH are quite similar. Both are realized on (to Western standards) minimal plots (130-135 m²) and are completely self-sufficient in terms of water demand, using rainwater for drinking purposes. The wastewater is treated on site and partly reused. The surplus is infiltrated in the garden.

In these two cases however there is very little interconnection with the energy related (sustainable) solutions. Both projects concern countries with relatively high percentages of private home ownership. This might have influenced the choice for this scale of implementation. The integration of the decentralised systems on site is quite different for the SHS and the THH project. This is related to the different situation before implementation. The newly built THH has most of the components of the water and energy system incorporated in the house, except for the infiltration bed for excess treated water. In the SHS, renovated and converted to fit in the autonomous water and energy concept, the different parts of the system are placed in (and under) the garden, relatively independent of the construction.

The scale of a cluster and apartment building concerns a limited group of houses organised around a court, as terraced houses (rowhouses) or in a single building. On this scale the decentralised systems are integrated in relation to the exterior space of the cluster, which most of the times is communal space. This category concerns two of the case studies: the Hockerton Housing Project (HHP) and the "Passivhaus Wohnen und Arbeiten" (W&A). The projects differ significantly. The HHP consists of 5 terraced, earth-sheltered houses, with conservatories in front, in a rural setting. The W&A project is an apartment building in Vauban, a former French military base being converted into a new city district. The W&A project consists of 4 floors with 16 apartments and 4 offices and a basement with shared facilities and installations. In the basement and underground (outside the building) black and grey water are treated separately. The anaerobic treatment of blackwater generates methane that will be used as (supplementary) source for cooking. Greywater is treated by a membrane filter and reused for flushing toilets and for rinsing the garden. The HHP covers its entire water demand by collecting and storing rainwater. The rainwater collected from the roof of the conservatories is stored and treated with filters, resulting in drinking water. Rainwater collected from the roadside ditches and drainage in the earthwall at the back of the houses is stored in a pond and used for household purposes like washing, flushing, and showering. The black water is treated in a septic tank after which the effluent is treated in a floating constructed wetland that connects to a pond. The project can be characterised as low-tech, also as a result of the amount of space available.

An interesting reference project for concepts at this scale is 'the Biovaerk', a renovation project in Kolding, Denmark. As part of the renovation the courtyard of an existing closed building block was redesigned. The inhabitants agreed to give up part of their gardens to make room for public facilities and for a decentralised wastewater system, part of which is conducted in a large glass pyramid [10].

The scale of the neighbourhood and that of the city district show similar characteristics, although implementation characteristics and social conditions can be quite different. Due to their innovative, experimental character most projects don't exceed neighbourhood scale. Sometimes they are situated within larger districts with emphasis on sustainability or water conservation. On this scale the systems become part of collective space or common facilities building.

The BedZED development is a neighbourhood in greater London developed on a former brownfield site, while Flintenbreite is a sustainable demonstration project on the outskirts of Lübeck. The only project that could be labeled a city district is EVA-Lanxmeer. The district is situated in a water abstraction area next to the train station and near the centre of a small Dutch town. It consists of 244 houses and apartments, on either side of the most vulnerable (and therefore unbuilt) part of the area. The buildings and the water system are designed not to pollute the groundwater. Greywater is implemented at neighbourhood scale; it is led away from the centre of the district to constructed wetlands at the edge of each neighbourhood. Blackwater is collected, and led to a central facility at the edge of the district where in the future it will be anaerobically treated, similarly to the W&A and Flintenbreite projects. Here it will be combined with the EVA-Centre, an ecological information and conference centre with hotel and guesthouses. The EVA-Centre will have an integrated Living Machine (a combination of anaerobic and aerobic treatment using plants) with a Biogas plant, connected Combined Heat/Power plant and waste collecting facility (retourette). The integrated concept is called 'Sustainable Implant' [1]. It processes the wastewater and organic waste of the district. The produced warmth and power will be used in the EVA-Centre.

BedZED is a pilot project that is part of a larger strategy to develop carbon neutral one-planet-footprint housing across the United Kingdom. It combines living and working in 82 houses and incorporates all aspects of a local community. These are combined in a built-up area of 47 houses per hectare with street level access and shared facilities. The wastewater treatment is an eminent part of this approach. Therefore maximum integration and visibility of its system components have been aimed for. A Living Machine treats all wastewater and then partially reused for flushing toilets, and partially discharged to the surrounding environment or even used by others. It is situated on the first floor of a communal building, which also houses the Combined Heat and Power plant and a clubhouse. The attractive components of the Living Machine are visible, though not accessible.

The Flintenbreite plan consists of 117 houses and apartments. At this moment only part of this development is realised. It has a green setting including a slope towards a small brook. It has an anaerobic blackwater treatment system similar to that of W&A but uses the methane to generate energy. The anaerobic digester is placed in the basement of a building with collective facilities. Greywater is treated in constructed wetlands placed near the edges of the project site. From there it is led to a retention pond, working as a large swale with an overflow to the brook.

3.3 Spatial aspects of the different projects in relation to their scale and site

Local circumstances are a strong incentive for the implementation of decentralised sanitation and energy generation systems. Two of the case studies are realized in environmentally sensitive areas, where conventional building is not allowed. The HHP is situated in the countryside outside of the town Hockerton. EVA-Lanxmeer is built in a water abstraction area. By making a limited number of houses, integrating them with the natural surroundings and agreeing to very specific sustainable requirements the initiators in both cases were able to gain permission from the authorities. Of decisive importance in the HHP was the 'Land Management Plan' that was drawn up, and which has been signed by each of the inhabitants as part of the permission to live in this project. The Plan consists of detailed maintenance and management objectives for the project and its surroundings, including the obligation for the inhabitants to spend time (each household 16 hours/ week) on maintenance and educational work.

In case of the THH, the rocky soil of Toronto made it economically attractive to apply local systems. There was no connection to the sewage system for this plot and it would have been expensive to make it. The way THH is placed against a slope is used to its advantage in the collection of run off rainwater. Height differences in the terrain are also taken advantage of. E.g. in Flintenbreite and HHP, where gravity principles were used for the system configuration: both projects are situated close to brooks and use the slope in the cascade of cleaning steps and the brook as overflow for treated water and rainwater.

All case studies are situated in climate zones with annual rainfall over 500 mm. As for temperature, when space is available, low-tech outdoor systems also function in colder climates, as the HHP shows. The Living Machine in BedZED is placed indoors under a glass roof for higher (winter) temperatures and better performance, which effectively reduces the amount of space required for the system. Anaerobic systems are independent of sunlight and therefore usually kept inside and/or underground. It is uncertain if the compost/ fixed film filter used in the Sustainable House project in Sydney, with its subtropical temperatures and occasional spells of heavy rain, will function as well in humid climates (e.g. in Northern Europe).

Considering the architectonical forms, a differentiation can be made between high-tech and low-tech approaches with corresponding appearances. In general the low-tech systems take up more space and often require direct sunlight. Therefore they usually are placed in the open air or in glasshouses. The high-tech systems mostly are treated as technical installations in separate installation rooms, often in basements. Most of the times they are only indirectly (e.g. through the use of vacuum toilets) part of the everyday experience of users. The integration is technical, and innovation focuses on the integration of pipes and installations.

It is possible however to combine high-tech and low-tech approaches in one project. In that case increased visibility of the processes can be achieved more easily. Another form of integration is the spatial integration: the integration of user space and installation space. From an architectonical point of view this kind of integration offers new possibilities, as it suggests new functional combinations.

Figure 3:   Integration of 'green' wastewater treatment systems: BedZED Living Machine, laundrette in Folehaven and Biovaerk in Kolding.

Examples are 'green' wastewater treatment systems integrated in a launderette (Folehaven, Copenhagen, Denmark), in a university cafe (Folk University of Stensund, Sweden) and the Biovaerk (Kolding, Denmark) (fig.3).

The implementation of anaerobic treatment for blackwater in Flintenbreite and Vauban has a high-tech approach. In Flintenbreite blackwater sewage pipes run through an innovative conduct underneath the houses for easy access in case of maintenance or repair. The anaerobic reactor in these cases is placed in the basement of the communal building (Flintenbreite) or the apartment building itself (Vauban), and is normally not visible or accessible for inhabitants.

The BedZED Living machine is placed indoors next to a collective activities room. It is visible from the outside, but due to health regulations not accessible. Similar to THH, the SHS system only influences the private space. The design of the garden is to large extent determined by the water system: a constructed wetland/ filtration bed and a swale. In case of the SHS the terrace has a lid for disposal of organic kitchen waste, providing direct contact with the wastewater treatment.

For the blackwater treatment in EVA-Lanxmeer the choice was made to combine two innovative decentralized systems on district level (the Sustainable

Implant), while leaving them intact and visible, but not physically accessible, for educational purposes. The treatment of blackwater from the district is planned to be anaerobic, recycling energy (methane/biogas for the CHP) and nutrients that can be used in the urban farm within the district. Here the ecological information and conference centre and hotel integrates the Sustainable Implant in which some of the objectives of the EVA-organization can be shown in an appealing, educational way.

4   Conclusion: spatial and social criteria for DESAER concepts

Centralised wastewater treatment has some disadvantages that can be overcome by sustainably treating waste on a smaller scale. Apart from that there is a rise of situations in which decentralised treatment can be complementary, saving time or money with respect to necessary restructuring of the existing infrastructures (e.g. due to aging or increased, changed flow characteristics and/or capacities). With respect to the case studies it can be concluded that the location and scale of a project plays an important role in the choice for a certain technology. When a project is situated in an urban setting with little open space, possible technologies are limited to those that do not require much space, can be combined with other functions and/or can be put underground. There is no such thing as an optimal scale for implementation of DESAER-concepts. Besides, not every technology is suitable for any situation. Choosing a certain technology limits the available options further down the line. Spatial, (bio)climatical, but also social characteristics of a site have their influence on the most suitable technology.

The main spatial criteria for the implementation of decentralised alternative systems in the built environment then are: optimum fitting in (residential) areas; optimised use of (ground)surface; optimised use of materials; protection against mis-use, vandalism and sabotage; accessibility of actors; optimised collection, generation and transportation; adaptability and extensibility; and esthetical quality. The main social criteria are: maintaining / enlarging ease of use; no reduction in comfort; comparable costs (investment, maintenance and use); secure and informal; independence of specialised institutions and (complex) networks/ structures; and improvement of the visibility of solutions (raising consciousness).

Meanwhile the criteria related to the environmental quality of the alternatives are the same as those which are in force for the existing solutions: minimal pollution of soil, air and water; optimising the closing of (substance)cycles; optimising addition of raw materials, chemicals and clean water; minimal use of energy (or maximised energy production); maximum hygiene; security and consistency; flexibility (in-/decreasing streams); uniformity (economies of scale); and resilience (robustness).

In theory a larger (DESAER-)system for a larger amount of users should be cheaper per capita. However, there seems to be a social limitation to the size.

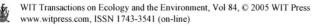

Also larger size limits the recycling of water flows because of increasing complexity. At the same time the implementation of decentralised alternatives can improve the sustainable awareness of users: The layout and design of the system components can make water treatment in the local water cycle part of people's everyday experience. However, due to health regulations and overcautious authorities, the combination with other functions is still a relatively uncovered area. Developments in related urban projects show that a symbiotic combination with public functions is possible. This would suggest that the scales of the neighbourhood or city district are appropriate scales of implementation (e.g. by integrating the DESAER-system with other facilities). Wastewater treatment as a local enterprise (e.g. reusing nutrients from the wastewater in urban agriculture) than is another possibility which, combined with a larger system, could increase the over-all feasibility.

References

[1]   Timmeren, A. van, Eble, J., Verhaagen, H., Kaptein, M., The 'park of the 21st century': agriculture in the city, *Proc. of The Sustainable City III, Urban Regeneration and Sustainability*, WITpress, Southampton, UK, 2004.

[2]   Kop, J.H., *Gezondheidstechniek, een duurzame uitdaging*, Faculteit der Civiele Techniek, Delft University of Technology (DUT), Delft. NL, 1993.

[3]   Esrey, S.A., Unicef, Closing the loop to food security, *Proc. of Ecosan in wastewater management & sanitation*, plenary. Bonn, Germany, 2000.

[4]   Otterpohl, R., New developments of EcoSan in Germany and Europe, *Proc. of the Ecosan conference 'Closing the loop in wastewater management and sanitation'*, Plenary session 2, Bonn, Germany, 2000.

[5]   Mobbs, M., *Sustainable House*, University Otago Press, New Zealand, 1998.

[6]   Townshend, A.R., *Commissioning Guide for the Toronto Healthy Houses Water Systems*, CMHC CR File No: 6740-5, Blue Heron Environmental Technology, Ontario, Canada, 1996.

[7]   White, N., *Hockerton Housing Project*, Factsheets, Hockerton Housing Project Trading Ltd, Hockerton, Southwell, UK, 1996/2004.

[8]   Panesar, A. & Lange, J., *Innovative Sanitation concept shows way towards Sustainable Urban Development*, Aturus, Freiburg, Germany, 2001.

[9]   Dunster, B., *From A to ZED, Realising Zero (fossil) Energy Developments*, Bill Dunster architects ZEDfactory Ltd., Wallington, UK, 2003.

[10] Vajnoe Jeppesen, A., *Ecological Urban Renewal in Kolding*, The Fredensgade /Hollaendervej Block Byfornyelsesselskab, Kolding, DK, 1996.

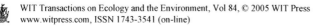

Urban model for a crowded planet – *vision42*

R. Warren
RWA Architects/vision42, New York, NY, U.S.A.

Abstract

With unremitting growth in world population, it becomes increasingly essential for humanity to devise more rational plans for compact urban development. Ecologically speaking, city dwellers impose a relatively smaller footprint on the earth and consume far fewer natural resources than suburbanites, sparing open land and its watersheds, as well as fuel in transportation. But in democratic societies, people are fairly free to choose where they live, so cities need to be made less congested and more welcoming. It is therefore vital to create more livable and workable urban models as attractive alternatives to low-density development. The sheer size of automobiles grossly inflates the scale of development, leading inexorably to urban sprawl. It follows that dense urban centers with large pedestrian populations can function more fluidly with restraints on motor vehicles, and with the simultaneous introduction of high-quality local public transportation systems. The commercial success of pedestrian streets can also be enhanced with aesthetic treatments—landscaping and other pedestrian-friendly amenities—features that are relatively affordable, and can create an inviting public realm. New York City's 42nd Street, with its high percentage of public transit riders, its confluence of a half million people every weekday, and its rich offering of cultural, civic, commercial and entertainment facilities, is in a unique position among cities in the United states for a demonstration of this principle. Results of three technical studies on the vision42 initiative for an auto-free light rail transit mall on 42nd Street support its viability and suggest that the proposal offers prospects for broad application in cities throughout the United States and beyond.
Keywords: sustainable urban development, light rail transit, pedestrian streets, urban sprawl, light rail costs, economic potential, traffic diversion.

WIT Transactions on Ecology and the Environment, Vol 84, © 2005 WIT Press
www.witpress.com, ISSN 1743-3541 (on-line)

1 Demographics and the challenge of urban sprawl

The world's current population of 6.5 billion people is projected to grow to over 9.2 billion by the year 2050 [1]. This figure could, in fact, vary between 7.7 and 10.6 billion, depending upon the actual evolving fertility rates [2]. Most of the increase is anticipated in the world's less developed regions. Yet the United States—quite unique in its relatively high fertility rates—is expected to grow to at least 400 million by that year, up from 296 million in 2005. [3].

1.1 The root causes of urban sprawl in the U.S.

It is useful to examine the case of urban sprawl in the United States, and how the trend might be effectively countered, primarily because the dominant U.S. lifestyle of auto ownership-and-dependency has set a standard that is spreading fast around the world. Since 1980, about one-half of urban sprawl in the U.S. has stemmed from population growth; the other half is the direct result of increases *per capita* in land consumption [4]. While both areas are in need of solution, it is the latter that this article addresses.

1.2 The scale of automobile-dependent development

Even if the scale of U.S. fuel consumption were cut back radically and soon, with smaller cars, the use of lightweight materials for car bodies, and utilization of more efficient engines and energy-storing flywheels, this would still not resolve the problems of traffic congestion, parking, and social dislocation wrought by the automobile. These disadvantages all stem from enormous spatial demands, since an automobile is some twenty to thirty times more massive than a human being, and its spatial requirements multiply when it is in motion.

The physical requirements for car parking and driving underlie the centrifugal dynamics of urban sprawl. According to the traditional guidelines of the lending institutions that finance new construction in the U.S., developers provide, when they build, not one, but two or three parking places per car—one at home, one at work or school, one at the shopping center, entertainment or vacation spot, etc. This is true whether the construction is in rural areas, in suburbs, or in cities, with the exception of only a few cities that are still served by regular, around-the-clock public transit systems. When access drives are included, 32.5 m^2 (350 ft^2) are typically allocated for each parking space; this, some 65 to 97.5 m^2 (70 to 1050 ft^2) are dedicated to multiple places for each private car for the purpose of its storage alone, even before streets and highways are counted.

The costs of providing this parking space are high and are a major determinant of what gets built and where. Even when it is only surface parking, and depending upon the price of land, a parking space can cost almost nothing, or more than $100,000. Parking in structures can vary enormously from city to city, and depends very much upon the type of structure—whether it is free-standing, above grade in a multi-use building, or below-grade (only built where land costs are high). Underground parking is very costly, since it requires

excavation, shoring, waterproofing, fireproofing, ramps, stairs, elevators, ventilation and lighting. So structured parking costs have varied widely—in the U.S. they have been as high as $51,000 per space in San Diego (2002) and $61,000 in Seattle.

It follows that open lots are by far the most common solution to parking needs, and their sheer size requirements are enough to draw developers and business owners toward outlying areas, where land in large tracts is more available and affordable—thereby perpetuating urban sprawl. The developer of office space, for example, typically provides one-and-one-half times as much space for cars as for employees, the cheapest scheme for commercial development being to cover 40 percent of a lot with a one-story building, and the remaining 60 percent with a parking lot. This enable the owners of businesses and shopping centers to provide "free" parking to their employees and customers (the cost of which is added to the prices of goods and services for motorists and non-motorists alike). Over 90 percent of American workers now park for free at work a fringe benefit that makes solo commuting almost irresistible [6].

Highways—which were intended to solve congestion, but as often as not have created more of the very traffic they were built to relieve—are similarly land-consuming. The space required on a highway for the safety of each moving car— some 93 m^2 (1000 ft^2) at least—exceeds by a factor of fifty the space occupied by a rider of public transit, and exceeds by more than one hundred times the space a pedestrian needs.

1.3 Consumption of land in the U.S.

More land is currently consumed in the U.S. for roadways, parking lots and garages than for housing. At the current low densities of automobile-related development, the country is urbanizing land at a *per capita* rate that is unprecedented in human history, at a scale that is five to ten times greater than that of the pre-industrial cultures [7]. In the automobile-dependent metropolitan areas of Phoenix, for example, new development is consuming land at the rate of 0.4 hectares (an acre) per hour [8].

1.4 Growth of U.S. automobile travel and petroleum consumption

Travel destinations in the U.S. have become increasingly dispersed, and the nation's inventory of cars has been growing twice as fast as the human population, as have the average lengths of trips and the popularity of large, self-protective, but fuel-inefficient vehicles. Not surprisingly, American motor vehicles now consume one-eighth of the world's total oil production [9].

With very high consumption of petroleum and other goods in the U.S., its population increases are putting major strains on available natural resources. However, this problem is hardly limited to the United States. American lifestyles and patterns of consumption—in particular, automobile ownership and suburban living—are being energetically marketed and are proliferating around the globe in countries such as China and India, where birth rates are considerably higher.

·

The results, on the one hand, are massive losses of open land and petroleum resources worldwide, and on the other hand, increasing urban traffic jams everywhere.

1.5 A resource more valuable than oil—water

One of the most compelling reasons fro curbing urban sprawl is the need to protect the quality of the planet's water supplies, many of whose persistent problems derive directly from current patterns of development. Natural landscapes are typically porous; rainwater percolates slowly through them in a filtering process on its way to underground aquifers, lakes, streams and estuaries. But when forests, wetlands and grasslands are replaced with impervious surfaces such as parking lots, roads and rooftops, stormwater becomes trapped above these surfaces, running off in large volumes, often at high velocity, picking up pollutants along the way.

There is consequently a strong correspondence between the percentage of land in a given area that is covered with impervious surfaces and the ability of our water systems to regenerate themselves. The degradation of streams begins, and fish begin to disappear, when imperious cover in a watershed exceeds 10 percent of the land area. A watershed is considered generally degraded at levels above 30 percent imperviousness. Residential subdivisions with 0.4 ha (one-acre) lots typically result in 10 to 20 percent impervious surfaces, and industrial, commercial and shopping center development in 75 to 90 percent imperviousness. Therefore, for the vital purpose of protecting regional water quality, the very best solution for new urban development is *to concentrate as much of it as possible within areas that are already developed and therefore biologically non-supporting*, allowing them to be degraded to as much as 100 percent imperiousness, in order to spare other watersheds from exceeding the 10 percent maximum threshold needed to protect the area's water quality [10]. This recommendation is *in direct synchrony with other ecological reasons for concentrating future growth within existing urban areas.*

2 Resolving dysfunctional circulation within urbanized areas

Most of the near-future increases in U.S. population will occur within already urbanized "megapolitan" areas, which are expected to gain 83 million people by the year 2040—equal to the current population of Germany [11]. However, while these areas are urbanized in terms on their high percentages of built-up, impervious surfaces, the overwhelming majority of them are insufficiently compact to be rationally served with high-quality public transportation (defined as frequent, dependable service, with transit vehicles travelling in dedicated rights-of-way, rather than having to compete with other forms of traffic). So owning and driving a car remains a requirement for convenient living within these areas—thereby perpetuating congestion. This reinforces current prejudices against urban areas altogether, and typically inspires resistance to the introduction of new high-quality transit lines, which are likely to stimulate high-density development around their stations (accompanied by increased traffic).

In densely developed countries in Europe and Asia, where the land available for development is very limited—i.e., the Netherlands, Franc, Germany, Japan, Singapore—recognition of the value of rail systems as a "down payment on a more resource-conserving urban future" [12] has been reflected in the extensive development of high-quality rail and other fixed-guideway transit networks—networks that serve to importantly support and reinforce the cities. On an international level, Europe has been famously developing its high-speed rail network, linking cities all over the continent. On an *intra*urban level, a number of European cities have retained and upgraded their streetcar systems as modern light rail lines. And in cities such as Strasbourg, Zurich, Amsterdam, Gothenburg, Bremen, Kassel and Montpellier, these have been successfully combined with pedestrian streets.

2.1 For medium-sized cities: new light rail and express bus lines

Since the early 1980s, as traffic congestion has developed to increasingly intolerable levels, 23 North American cities have followed these European examples and turned to light rail as an intermediate-capacity public transit system. Eleven additional U.S. cities are planning light rail lines. Even in Texas, new light rail networks have been inaugurated in the 1990s in Houston and Dallas, which are attracting much higher ridership than anticipated, have enormously stimulated development, and are being expanded extensively. Houston's light rail includes a pedestrian street with fountains in the middle of the city center. Other American cities that have combined pedestrianization in their downtowns with regional light rail lines are Minneapolis, San Diego, Sacramento, Portland and Buffalo. As in the case of Strasbourg, these medium-sized cities have built their light rail networks as regional systems, branching out toward the suburbs within highway medians, and serving as at-grade distributors within the cities themselves.

2.2 For larger cities: two levels of public transit needed—regional and local

Networks of high-capacity metros and commuter rail, operating on totally separated rights-of-way, provide excellent service in whisking passengers into larger cities from long distances at high speeds. However, they cannot be expected to address the problems of surface traffic or the need for fluid circulation *within* the city. In fact, if metros continue to be expanded without the challenges of surface congestion being resolved, these problems are likely to only be exacerbated with any massive new development generated by metro expansion. For space-saving local circulation, collective transport systems of intermediate capacities—distributor systems—are needed to fill this role. And for larger cities, the permanent commitment to transit infrastructure, as manifested in a light rail line, can be the most appropriate solution.

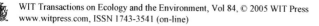

2.3 At issue: whether to remove certain streets from use by motor vehicles

How the issues of local public transit distribution are resolved depends very much upon the (basically political, rather than technical) decision as to whether street space should be taken from automobiles and given over to pedestrians.

2.3.1 No restraints on traffic, combined with automated people movers
One approach has been to assume that automotive traffic should remain uninhibited, and to propose automated people movers, traveling on elevated guideways above other forms of traffic [13]. This is an option which has certainly been extremely successful in Lille, France [14], although it is not necessarily the least expensive or most pedestrian-friendly solution.

2.3.2 Restraints on traffic, combined with manually operated light rail
Another approach—and one that is gaining increasing credibility as automotive congestion begins to cancel out the advantages of automobility, and as the value of walking in cities begins to re-gain it former popularity—is to actually close well-populated streets to traffic, making way for both pedestrians and public transit operating at street level. The advantage to this approach is that the transit system is well-integrated with the shopping street, and directly accessible without the need fro stairs, elevators or escalators.

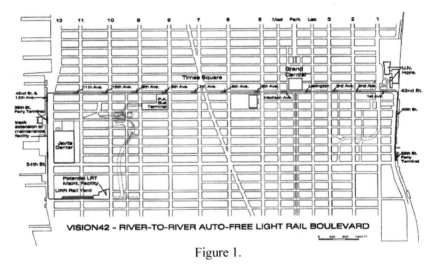

Figure 1.

3 The vision42 proposal for Manhattan's 42nd Street

This is the approach that has been proposed, as a citizens' initiative, for New York City's 42nd Street. A 4-km (2.5 mile) modern, low-floor light rail line would travel the full length of the street between the Hudson and East Rivers, within an auto-free street, furnished with landscaping, cafes, and other high-quality pedestrian amenities. Even with speeds limited to 24 km/hr. (15mph) for pedestrian safety, and stopping at every north/south avenue for traffic lights and boarding /deboarding at 16 pairs of stops, the river-to-river strip would take only 21 minutes. This is double the average speed of today's slower-than-walking buses, and would provide convenient connections with the Grand Central and Port Authority Terminals, as well as with ferries at both rivers.

Three technical studies were undertaken in 2004-05 by independent consultants, to assess the project's capital and operating costs, the plan's economic potential, and the traffic implications of closing the street to cars [15].

3.1 Estimated capital and operating costs of vision42

Halcrow, LLC, a large London and New York-based engineering firm with worldwide experience in the design of rail systems, has conservatively estimated that the light rail line and landscaped street will cost between $360 and $510 million (in 2004 U.S. dollars) to construct, depending upon the extent of utility relocations and the choice of propulsion system. The per mile cost of the light rail itself is approximately one-tenth of the cost of subway construction in New York City. The costs of utility diversions requested by the utility companies and agencies for a rail-based system are known to be major and would dominate the capital costs. However, until 1946, NYC trolleys ran right over the utilities without major problems. Modern, low-floor light rail vehicles are lighter than either the old trolleys or the many trucks that use the street today. Current restrictive policies regarding utility relocations could be modified to lessen these costs, as well as substantial temporary disruption during the construction phase.

Operating costs for the light rail will be slightly lower that operating costs for the bus services it would displace. However, the light rail will have three times the capacity of the displaced buses—important in a dense city like New York.

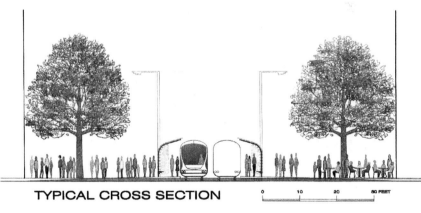

TYPICAL CROSS SECTION

Figure 2.

Self-propelled vehicles are recommended by Halcrow to avoid catenary wire and stray current issues, and will suit the operating profile of this short system. It is feasible to consider the use of fuel cell propulsion, which is scheduled to come

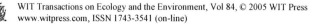

on line for rail use in the U.S. by 2009. If this direction is taken, New York may become home to the world's first fuel cell-propelled light rail line, which is appropriate for a city of its stature.

3.2 Anticipated economic potential of vision42

The firm Urbanomics, led by Regina Armstrong, former Chief Economist for the prestigious Regional Plan Association, studied the likely economic potential of vision42. Urbanomics' projections were based on an established analytic technique developed for the U.S. Federal Transit Administration, which translates improved access into increases in property value. Because of the greatly improved crosstown access provided by the light rail, major gains of $3.5 billion (in 2004 U.S. dollars) in commercial property values are forecast—a one-time increase in the asset value of real properties that represents vision42's largest single economic benefit. An increase of $13.7 million is anticipated in other properties along the corridor. Because the economic model does not include a methodology for assessing residential property increases, these were not taken into account, although, with the massive apartment towers that line the street, these could also be considerable.

The gains in commercial property values will nevertheless result in annual fiscal benefits of increased City and State tax revenues of $277.1 million, equal to more than one-half of the estimated cost of constructing the project. Thus, the gains in tax revenues alone should be enough to finance the construction in less than two years. An additional annual net gain of $250.3 million is projected in other benefits; they include benefits to individuals from travel time savings, resulting in office rent and occupancy increases, savings from a reduction in accidents, and light rail operational savings, amounting to a total of some $334.4 million—benefits that are balanced against transportation costs of $84.1 million, including the increased costs of traffic diversion and a modest increase in the cost of deliveries.

3.3 Projected traffic impacts of vision42

The traffic analysis was performed by the firm Sam Schwartz, PLLC (SSC), founded by a former NYC traffic commissioner. SSC produced an up-to-date inventory of current conditions on the 42nd Street corridor, and, using the City's projections of new development, estimated future conditions for 2010, the year that the light rail transit mall could be placed in service. It was found that, with the use of accepted standard practices fro mitigating traffic impacts, such as changes in signal timing, lane markings, and parking regulations, the relocated traffic can be accommodated on other streets with surprisingly modest impacts.

Most major office buildings along 42nd Street already provide delivery loading areas on 41st or 43rd Street, since ground floor space on 42nd Street is too valuable for this function. For ground floor retail deliveries, truck loading curb space at the intersections with avenues will need to be carefully reserved. However, there will be additional space at these intersections because vehicles will not be turning into an auto-free 42nd Street.

Options exist for reconfiguring access to the three parking garages that open directly onto 42nd Street, and alternate locations for taxi access to hotels and Grand Central Terminal can be designated. Few curb cuts and parking garage entrances have been allowed on 42nd Street in the recent past because of its high pedestrian traffic. Most taxi passengers destined for buildings on 42nd Street can be dropped off at avenue entrances or on the side streets.

The SSC traffic study used very conservative estimates of traffic "shrinkage" and projected only a very modest shift from auto and taxi travel to the light rail.

4   Re: decisions to give street space back to pedestrians

The idea of pedestrian streets is neither new nor radical. It predates the Roman Empire, but gained appreciable momentum after World War II, as the proliferation of cars inspired something of a citizens' insurrection against the effects of traffic in cities. When pedestrian zones have been initially proposed, they have often evoked reactions of wariness and even staunch opposition from local merchants because of fears that restrictions on cars would hurt their trade. Numerous experiments have nevertheless gone forward, and many of them to date, in the U.S. as elsewhere, have proven unexpectedly popular with respect to the very practical gauges of increased retail sales and real estate property values [16, 17].

Nor does the closing of a street to traffic necessarily mean that surrounding streets will become more congested. A detailed study of 47 cases of street closings in countries around the world revealed that, in most of these cases, not all of the traffic relocated to adjacent street. In fact, much of the traffic disappeared [18].

This is the very opposite of the phenomenon that, if you build more highways, more traffic will be generated. Traffic is actually quite elastic, and people are rational beings. If one driving option is closed off, and as alternate routes fill up with cars, people are likely to find other routes and/or modes of travel. Particularly if a high-quality public transit alternative is provided, people are likely to make use of it. For decision makers, this is primarily a political, rather than a technical choice, and a matter of whether the chosen priority for the center of town is for people or for automobiles.

References

[1]   U.S. Census Bureau, International Data Base, updated 26 April 2005, available at www.census.gov/ipc/www/worldpop.html.

[2]   Fornos, W., "Population to Reach 1,9 Billion", *Popline*, vol. 24, Mar-Apr 2005, The Population Institute, Washington, D.C., p. 1.

[3]   U.S. Census Bureau, Population Division, *Projected Population and Growth Rates for the U.S.*, available at www.npg.org/popfacts.htm.

[4]   Kolankiewicz, L. & Beck, R., "Weighing Sprawl Factors in Large U.S. Cities: a report on the nearly equal roles played by population growth and land use choices I the loss of farmland and natural habitat to

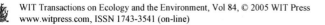

urbanization", *Analysis of the U.S. Bureau of the Census Data on the 100 Largest Urbanized Areas of the United States*, Arlington, VA, 19 March 2001, www.SprawlCity.org.

[5]   Shoup, D., *High Costs of Free Parking*, APA Planners Press, Washington, D.C., 2005, pp. 185-200.

[6]   Shoup, D. & Wilson, R., "Employer-Paid Parking: The influence of Parking Prices on Travel Demand", paper from the Proceedings of the Commuter Parking Symposium, held by the Association for Commuter Transportation and the Municipality of Metropolitan Seattle, December 1990, pp. v, 10.

[7]   Pushkarev, B.S. & Zupan, J.M., Public Transportation and Land Use Policy, Indiana University Press, Bloomington, Indiana, and Regional Plan Association, New York, 1977, pp. 4-7.

[8]   Sorensen, A.A., Green, P.P. & Russ, K., *Farming on the Edge*, American Farmland Trust, Northern Illinois University, DeKalb, IL, March 1997, pp. 2-23.

[9]   Shoup, *op. cit.*, Chapter 1.

[10] Schueler, T., *Site Planning for Urban Stream Protection*, Center for Watershed Protection and the Metropolitan Washington Council of Governments, 1995, pp. 38,43, 75-76.

[11] Lang, R.E. & Dhavale, D., "Beyond Megalopolis: Exploring America's New 'Megalopolitan' Geography", *Metropolitan Institute Census Report Series*, Census Report 15:01, Metropolitan Inst. at Virginia Tech, May 2005, pp.1-27.

[12] Pushkarev & Zupan, *op. cit.,* p. 98.

[13] Warren, R, & Kunczynski, Y., "Planning Criteria for Automated People Movers: Defining the Issues", *Journal of Urban Planning and Development*, American Society of Civil Engineers, Reston, VA, December 2000.

[14] Warren, R., "New Era for APMs: Report of 5th International Conference on Automated People Movers, Paris, June 1996", *Elevator World*, Mobile, AL, September 1996.

[15] Halcrow, LLC; Urbanomics; & Sam Schwartz, PLLC; *Technical Studies on Capital and Operating Costs, Economic Potential, and Traffic Impacts of the vision42 Proposal*, available at www.vision42.org/about/studies.php.

[16] Organisation for Economic Co-operation and Development (OECD), *Streets for People*, Paris, 1974.

[17] TEST, Quality Streets: *How Traditional Urban Centers Benefit from Traffic Calming*, TEST, 177 Arlington Road, London, NW1, 7EY, May 1988.

[18] Cairns, S., Hass-Klau, C., & Goodwin, P., *Traffic Impacts of Highway Capacity Reductions: Assessment of the Evidence*, Landor Press, London, MVA, 1998, available through Books@landor.co.uk.

Ecourbanism: designing a 'green' city

P. Viswanathan & T. Sharpe
Mackintosh Environmental Architecture Research Unit,
Mackintosh School of Architecture, Glasgow School of Art, UK

Abstract

"We should be careful to discriminate between what the notion of the City can offer and what it's offering for us for millenniums, and which we are now making the city into which is very much what you are saying an environment which is not very conducive to, what you might call, the good society. The fact remains that if we eliminate all the cities from this continent, what remains is not much. In fact, even though we Americans tend to be very sceptical about the presence of the city, we must recognize that the City is still the place where things are happening in scale and in quality which is very real otherwise."
Paolo Soleri.

This paper is an introduction to a new philosophy and outlook for eco-city design. Its analyses how to make existing cities more eco-sensitive with the help of a 'live' case study, an eco-city representing human unity in India called the "Auroville International Township", and uses this to discuss the starting point for the design of new urban sustainable settlements.

Keywords: ecopsychology, environmentally sustainable design, Auroville, green architecture, urban design of new cities.

1 Introduction

"Nature is good at conservation - of energy, water and matter. It is an exemplar of passive design and it looks after its own economy not just locally but globally."*Lovelock's [1] Gaia principle.*

Ecourbanism, a term coined by Miguel Ruano [2], "defines the development of multi-dimensional sustainable human communities within harmonious and balanced built environments". Ecourbanism is also a term now commonly associated with design of green communities and making existing cities more environmentally sensitive. Currently, over half the population of the world is living in cities and this figure is predicted to rise to 75% by 2025 [2]. Given the environmental impact of cities in the future, and the effects that climate change will have on them, it is vital that cities are designed to be ecologically sensitive and environmentally sustainable.

Although there is a great deal of research being conducted into environmentally sustainable buildings, the larger scale approach of Ecourbanism is at early stages. Such a large-scale approach is clearly required however, as last minute 'eco-touch ups' are not going to be sufficient to prevent cities becoming 'energy gluttons'. The status quo is described by Hagan [3] "The built fabric, as it presently stands in a city like London or New York is haemorrhaging energy."

The history of Ecourbanism can be traced back to traditional cities built entirely of vernacular materials and where pedestrian usage was the key to the design of circulation patterns. Such cities also made good use of natural resources and strategic planning prevented pollution by the same resources. Numerous examples can be cited for such cities and settlements like Harappa, Mohenjadaro and Roman town of Timgad (Viturvian).

This essay aims to analyse the design of the actual urban form with eco-considerations by using a case study of the Auroville International Township in India. The Auroville International Township is situated in Tamil Nadu in the Southern end of the Indian peninsula. It falls under the monsoon climatic belt, hot and humid. Auroville was founded on the 28th February 1968. It is the brainchild of two important philosophers Mira, a French spiritualist also called "The Mother" and a Bengali writer, poet and freedom fighter, Sri Aurobindo after whom the city is named.

2 Design considerations

2.1 Ecopsychology

In order to design a green city the first thing that needs to be understood is that unless its occupants understand the purpose of design logic, the city will not 'work' as planned. Hence knowledge of "ecopsychology" becomes a first step. Ecopsychology is the knowledge of ecology, which affects the brain of the user/observer. It is a term coined by T.Rozak [4] and is a branch of environmental psychology. Understanding behavioural patterns, and how these patterns are affected by changing ecology, can be used as an effective design tool while planning the urban form of the city.

Auroville was formed when 124 countries came together to form an International community and in the Inauguration ceremony, fig. 1, the Charter for the city was written by The Mother. Auroville was to be realised as a symbol of Human Unity...

Auroville began as a hot, humid climate windswept eroded land. There were no trees just canyons of red earth devoid of topsoil and ground cover.

Now, after 37 years, Auroville is a reclaimed forest, fig. 3. The community itself has regenerated all the topsoil and this gives them a sense of value over their self-built landscape. This 'ecopsychology' factor makes is a significant factor in the prevention of 'misuse' of the landscape.

Figure 1:   The Auroville Inauguration ceremony on 28th February 1968.

Figure 2:   The Early Auroville landscape.

Figure 3:   Auroville today.

2.2 Climatic, bio-regional zoning

In the days of tribal settlements, zoning depended on the boundaries and physical parameters of the bio-region rather than 'city' boundary. Such an approach to planning may solve many environmental problems as the regions are grouped on the basis of their attributes and not any other forces. For example dividing the city plan into ecological zones such as, river edge, foothills, plains, plateau and marsh, etc, facilitates planning in more sustainable terms at a micro-level. Building usage, functions, heights and densities can then be worked out in accordance to which 'bio-regional' belt they fall into thereby reducing environmental impact and producing a more precise, if not smaller, eco-footprint of the development.

In Auroville, the site has a marked elevated centre and the city itself is a 2.5km radius circle around this top point. Since it has coastal monsoon hot and humid climate, all the industrial and residential zones have been kept in the preferable North-South orientation. The cultural zone and international zones are on the East-West orientation.

Roger Anger [5], the chief architect of Auroville is from France and has a deeply spiritual outlook to the creation of the township. Recalling his own interpretation of Mother's original sketches, fig. 4, for the township he says, "Mother had given a couple of parameters: the division of the city into four areas, or zones, fig. 5, and the number of people for whom the city is envisaged (50.000). The division into those four zones (industrial, residential, international and cultural) is unique, and has no precedent in town planning".

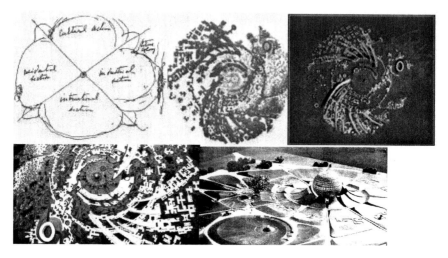

Figure 4: The Mother's sketch and development of the Galaxy Plan.

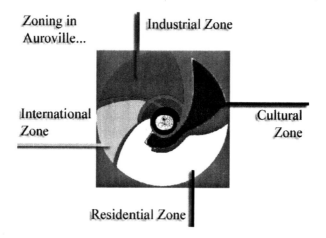

Figure 5: Galaxy Plan evolved by French architect from Mother's Sketch.

2.3 The pedestrian centre

Making city centres bio-region 'pedestrian' by reducing car use necessitates more use of public transport, more demarcation of car and non-car zones, and has the benefits of reducing parking requirements - could be used as urban parks instead – and reducing environmental problems such as noise and pollution.

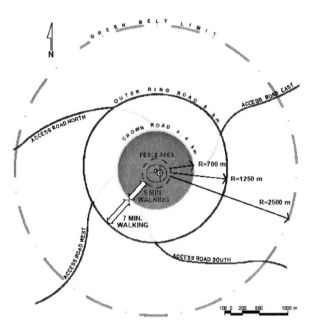

Figure 6:   The pedestrian city.

Ideally the planning strategy should incorporate walkable community living within the city itself. It should create a self-sustaining hubs and the main centre of these hubs if made pedestrian or accessible only through public transport will ensure the other centres be used efficiently. Designing picturesque cycle, jogging and walking tracks around the areas of main importance also encourages the inhabitants to cut down on the usage of the car.

In Auroville, the Galaxy plan incorporates the four zones and central genius loci called the 'Matrimandir', a meditation centre that also symbolifies human unity principle of the township. This is illustrated in fig. 6. This was planned as the centre of all focus in the urban form of the township. Around the meditation complex is the 'crown' surrounded by a fully pedestrian road (inner ring road) from which the 12 arterials roads emerge and curve around the Galaxy and finally join the second road in the periphery (outer ring road). After that the plan culminates into the final ring of a 'Green Belt' around the whole city circle much on the lines of Howard's [2] Garden city.

3   Community and design

Housing forms the very sensitive and yet crucial aspect of eco-city design. A design principle is to divide the housing needs into communities, based on work groups, which can then relate back to the 'bio-regional' plan so that the ideal locations for the work groups maybe established. A balanced mix of people catering to their own needs and sustaining their own community at a micro-scale should ideally form the work-groups themselves. The next step would be to chart out the common facilities the community requires, which is again based on a 'green' agenda such as sharing a car pool or two to three communities coming together to start a school at walking distance to all three, etc. Such a car pool idea has been successfully implemented in Malmo, Sweden, where they use IT for Internet booking facilities and follow a dependable time schedule (Hancock, C. [6]).

In Auroville, like-minded people striving towards a common 'spiritual' goal form communities. This should not be confused with religion. Mixed development is thus possible in various aspects such as age, sex, income, nationality, etc. As the community was started with a specific purpose they are also named after it... Gaia, Fertile, Courage, Surrender, Aspiration, Creativity etc. Each community has certain common goals and targets, the newcomers joining the communities have to choose which they would fit in comfortably or start a new community on their own. The aim of this kind of segregation is to make sure that the people are working for their own good as well as for the community. This approach can be compared with John Nash's [7] 'Game theory for non-co operational games', which later formed a stepping-stone for modern economics.

4 Planning and architecture

An environmentally sustainable planning model should facilitate environmentally sensitive architecture by providing answers to the 'how?' Planning standards are often aspirational, however, whilst many planning models include the word 'sustainable' in them this has not resulted in many sustainable cities. The problem is that planning requirements are undermined by minimum building standards. Building codes and regulations generally do not legislate for sustainability in a broad way.

In Auroville each community concentrates on the common township goals of low-energy eco-building. In addition, public buildings are designed as demonstration projects that enable both the communities and other groups to use as educational tools of sustainable building.

Figure 7:   The Visitors Centre- "Hassan fathy Award for Architecture" from Egypt in 1991.

5   Clean and renewable energies

A key mechanism to reduce the alarming rate of CO_2 emissions is to switch to alternative energy sources. The two major setbacks in implementing alternative energy technologies are initial investment and lack of expertise. Even if all the energy needs cannot be addressed by such measures a fraction of it certainly can be. The first few examples can then lead to further analysis and if successful more investment. Another field that is midway is 'clean' energy sources such as wooden pellet stoves, biogas digesters, etc.

In Auroville, most communities have their own solar plant of varying sizes, some have wind turbines, and biogas is extensively employed where in the domestic waste is used to produce steam. A solar concentrator has been designed for the city kitchen called "La Cuisine Solaire", fig. 8, which is capable of producing enough steam to cook for over 1000 people at one time.

Figure 8:   La cuisine Solaire and AV55-Auroville devised wind turbine.

6   Marketing ecourbanism

The crucial element of the long-term existence of even the most beautiful, successful, environmentally sustainable city is economic viability. If a city is not financially successful, then the ability to support and maintain the ecological imperative is lost. It is important however, that financial models for urban development and use account for holistic costs – non-sustainable cities may for example, not factor in costs in rubbish disposal, the effects of CO_2 emissions, health effects of pollution etc. Economic models must therefore account for the long terms costs of the present day systems and the proposed 'eco-friendly' systems. Other means of generating income for eco-friendly cities may be considered, for example to market it for tourism. Such strategies need to address changes in time, for example, seasonal shifts, and a move toward ecological norms. Governmental help at this stage becomes crucial. Educating from the grassroots helps to build the community spirit as a whole.

In Auroville during peak season, which falls in the winter months the city, is in 'credit' always, but in other times it solely depends on contributions for majority of its needs. The greatest challenge for Auroville now is to make itself a 'money free', independent and economically sustainable community.

Figure 9:   Auroville's economy!

7 Summary: ecourbanism as a wholesome approach

The Ecourbanism approach to Urban Design needs to a strong philosophy whereby the people who live in a city believe in it. Otherwise it just remains a science or an application and can never materialise into a way of life. Without active effort and co-operation from the people it is impossible to realise the environmentally sustainable city. Auroville has had a spiritual meaning ever since its conception and has grown into a close-knit yet open-minded community. Even today the Mother's Charters [8] are the backbones of its philosophy.

The Charters of Auroville:

- Auroville belongs to nobody in particular. Auroville belongs to humanity as a whole. But to live in Auroville, one must be the willing servitor of the Divine Consciousness.
- Auroville will be the place of an unending education, of constant progress, and a youth that never ages.
- Auroville wants to be the bridge between the past and the future. Taking advantage of all discoveries from without and from within, Auroville will boldly spring towards future realisations.
- Auroville will be a site of material and spiritual researches for a living embodiment of an actual Human Unity.

Ecourbanism when properly design, executed and practised would lead to physical, economical, spiritual and psychological fulfilment in the eco-city. To be able to live in a 'city' without harming the environment leaves us with only a few possibilities Auroville, a city which the Earth needs is sensitive to nature and hence is always rewarded in various levels: the Earth, the community and the individual.

"Humanity is not the last rung of the terrestrial creation. Evolution continues and man will be surpassed"...The Mother.

Figure 10:   The Matrimandir Meditation Centre: spiritual and geographical centre of Auroville.

References

[1]   Grant,N. and Liddell,H., *Eco-Minimalism - Limes versus Commonsense*: Articles from Gaia Group website [online], Scotland, Available from: http://www.gaiagroup.org/Architects/Eco-minWebsite04a.pdf.

[2]   Ruano, M., *Ecourbanism Sustainable Human Settlements: 60 Case Studies*, Editorial Gustavo Gili: Barcelona, Ed.2, pp 10-11, 2001.

[3]   Hagan, S., *Taking Shape: A New Contract between Architecture and Nature*, Architectural Press: Oxford, pp 11, 2001.

[4]   Schroll, M. A., Gaia consciousness. A review of Ralph Metzner's Green psychology: Transforming our relationship to the earth, *Resurgence*, 200, May/June, 60-61, 2000.

[5]   Anger, R., Auroville International Township Website: http://www.auroville.org/thecity/linesofforce.htm.

[6]   Hancock, C., *Malmo: towards the sustainable city*. Ecotech 4, November, pp 40-45, 2001.

[7]   Econom, J., *The work of John Nash in game theory*: Nobel Seminar, December 8, 1994, *Theory* **69** (1), 153-185, 1996.

[8]   Mira or The Mother, Auroville International Township website: http://www.auroville.org/vision.htm.

[9]   Opening quote from Ar. Paulo Soleri's Arcosanti website: www.arcosanti.org.

A land-use transition model based on building lots considering the steady state of locations and inconstancy of transition

T. Osaragi
*Department of Mechanical and Environmental Informatics,
Tokyo Institute of Technology, Japan*

Abstract

Several Markov chain models for land-use conversion have been proposed and analysed for dynamics in land-use and environmental planning. However, some problems have been encountered in the method for estimating the land-use transition probability. A new estimation method to determine the land-use transition probability is proposed in this paper. The salient features of this method are as follows: (1) In previous studies, the land-use transition probability matrix was typically estimated using time series raster data by counting the number of cells based on the land-use categories. However, the transition probability should be estimated by counting the number of building lots since building lots and not cells are the spatial unit for land-use conversion. A method to estimate the number of building lots using raster data is proposed in this paper. (2) There exist several building lots where the land-use does not vary stochastically. Therefore, building lots in the steady state should be excluded during the estimation process of the land-use transition probability. A method to estimate the number of building lots in the steady state is proposed here. The effectiveness of the proposed methods and some new findings on land-use conversion are demonstrated using numerical examples.
Keywords: land-use, Markov chain, transition probability, lot, steady state, raster data.

1 Introduction

It is important as well as necessary to analyze land-use conversion in order to evaluate the land-use policies of the past and plan for land-use in the future.

WIT Transactions on Ecology and the Environment, Vol 84, © 2005 WIT Press
www.witpress.com, ISSN 1743-3541 (on-line)

Therefore, several techniques for analyzing the structure of land-use conversion have been proposed in the discipline of city and regional planning. For instance, Kim *et al.* [1] attempted to forecast the change in land-use using a Markov chain model. Ishizaka [2], [3] proposed a method to examine the structure of land-use conversion using the eigenvalues and eigenvectors of a transition probability matrix. In addition, Aoki *et al.* [4], [5] proposed a method for evaluating the expected errors in predictions of land-use models based on the Markov chain and minimizing them by the area-dividing method. On the other hand, Osaragi and Kurisaki [6] modeled the relation between land-use transition probability and the land-use utility and measured the latter, which varies depending on the characteristics of different locations. Thus, Markov chains have been used in several urban studies to model the process of change in land-use.

First, it should be noted that the basic unit of land-use change is a building lot. However, in the models proposed earlier, the land-use transition probability matrix was typically estimated based on the area by counting the number of cells. In other words, adopting the conventional method entails the risk of overlooking the true transition structure. Second, there are some locations where land-use is in the steady state. In other words, the land-use transition at such locations should not be considered as a stochastic process. Hence, the conventional model, which assumes that the land-use transition at all locations will vary stochastically, might yield an incorrect estimate. Finally, the models proposed to date assume that the transition probability will remain stable in the future. However, it is obvious that it is necessary to consider the variations in the transition probability with time. We also need to consider the effect of various land-use regulations on the transition probability since land-use conversion depends heavily on the characteristics of the locations. Because of the limitation of pages, this article addresses the first and the second issue and improves upon previously proposed land-use models in the following manner:

(1) A method for estimating the land-use transition probability based on building lots using raster data is proposed.

(2) A method that takes into account the existence of building lots in the steady state is proposed.

2 Land-use transition probability of building lots

2.1 Concept of transition probability based on building lots

In the conventional land-use transition models, the probability P_{ij} in the change of a land-use category from j to i is estimated using the following equation:

$$P_{ij} = \frac{m_{ij}}{\sum_k m_{kj}}, \tag{1}$$

where m_{ij} is the total area of all locations where the land-use category changes from j to i during a certain time interval. In other words, the transition probability was estimated with the assumption that all the spots (cells of raster data) vary independently. However, actual spots do not change independently;

rather, all spots included within the same building lot generally change together. This implies that the spatial unit of land-use change is a building lot. A simple example of the difference between the transition probability matrices based on cells and building lots is shown in figure 1. Clearly, the transition probability matrices obtained are distinct. Therefore, in order to accurately ascertain the structure of the transition, it is necessary to estimate the transition probability by the method based on building lots. Thus, the above-mentioned conventional model (eqn (1)) should be transformed into the following enhanced equation:

$$p_{ij} = \frac{n_{ij}}{\sum_k n_{kj}}, \tag{2}$$

where n_{ij} denotes the total number of building lots where the land-use category changes from j to i. In this study, a transition matrix composed of n_{ij} is called the "transition matrix of building lots," is utilized, and its probabilistic expression is referred to as the "transition probability matrix of building lots."

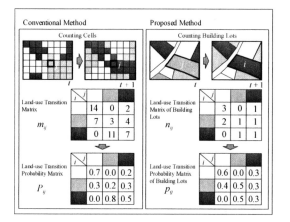

Figure 1:   Difference in transition probability estimated by conventional method and proposed method.

2.2 Estimation method of transition probability matrix of building lots

In general, a transition matrix of building lots should be estimated using vector data of building lots. However, it is relatively simple to synthesize raster data, and large amounts of such data have been gathered till date. Assuming efficient and effective use of the existing raster data, a method for estimating the transition probability of building lots using raster data is proposed. The number of building lots where the land-use category changes from j to i, denoted by n_{ij}, can be estimated using the following equation:

$$n_{ij} = \frac{m_{ij}}{a_{ij}}, \tag{3}$$

where m_{ij} denotes the total area of the building lots where the land-use category changes from j to i, and a_{ij} denotes the average area. The average area a_{ij} of building lots in the transition process can be estimated by the method shown in figure 2. If adjacent cells of the raster data display identical transition, they are considered to constitute one building lot. Therefore, the average area a_{ij} of the building lots in transition from j to i is estimated by the following equation:

$$a_{ij} = \frac{m_{ij}}{n'_{ij}}, \qquad (4)$$

where n'_{ij} is the number of building lots estimated by the method shown in figure 2. However, the number of building lots where the land-use category does not change cannot be determined by this method. Therefore, the value of the area a_{jj} is assumed to be equal to the average area of all the building lots that change from j to i ($i = 1, \dots, n$),

$$a_{jj} = \frac{\displaystyle\sum_{k \neq j} m_{kj}}{\displaystyle\sum_{k \neq j} n'_{kj}}. \qquad (5)$$

If the value of a_{ij} is calculated from the raster data using the above method, the transition matrix of building lots can be estimated by eqns (2) and (3).

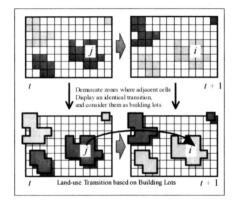

Figure 2: Estimation method of average area of building lots.

2.3 Features of the average area of building lots

The average area a_{ij} of the building lots is estimated using actual land-use data (see table 1). The study area is shown in figure 3 and the estimated values of the average area are presented in table 2. The average area is comparatively large in forests, land under development, and industrial lots. On the other hand, the average area of private residential lots is relatively small. Furthermore, in order to examine the characteristics of the average area of the building lots in detail, the average area is calculated based on the time distance from the center of Tokyo (CBD). The result is shown in figure 4. The average area based on pre-conversion is shown in figure 4(a). The average area of land under development exhibits a high value at 20 minutes from the CBD. This result indicates that large-scale development is in progress in the littoral district. The average area of forests/fields increases with distance from the CBD. On the other hand, the average area of residential and commercial lots does not depend on the distance from the CBD and remains almost constant. The average area of residential and commercial plots is much smaller than that of the other land-use categories. The average area post-conversion is shown in figure 4 (b). The average area under each category tends to increase slightly depending on the distance from the CBD. In other words, although the average area based on pre-conversion in the CBD and the suburbs is almost equal, larger building lots tend to be formed only after land-use conversion. Thus, the average area of the building lots is closely related to the pattern of land-use conversion and varies depending on the distance from the CBD.

Table 1:   Land-use data.

No.	Detailed Classification	Classification
1	Forest, Wasteland	
2	Rice field	Forest/Field
3	Field	
4	Land under development	Vacant lot
5	Vacant lot	
6	Industrial lot	Industrial lot
7	Regular residential lot	
8	Densely populated residential lot	Residential lot
9	High-rise residential lot	
10	Commercial lot	Commercial lot
11	Road	
12	Park, Green area	Public lot
13	Public facility lot	

The Detailed Digital Land Use Data (1974, 1979, 1984, 1989)
Cell Size: 10 m x 10 m

Figure 3:   Study area.

3   Land-use transition model in a steady state

3.1 Formulation of the model

According to the previously used method, the number of building lots of land-use i at time $t + 1$ is denoted by $x_i(t+1)$ and expressed as follows:

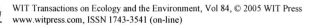

Table 2:   Average area of building lots in the process of land-use transition.

	1	2	3	4	5	6	7	8	9	10	11	12	13
1 Forest, Wasteland	9.9	9.7	9.0	26.3	4.9	6.0	2.8	1.4	1.9	3.6	1.7	4.3	5.6
2 Rice field	7.6	7.1	11.6	12.8	4.2	11.6	2.1	1.3	1.1	2.8	1.6	2.1	3.5
3 Field	8.5	9.1	5.2	16.7	5.4	4.1	2.0	1.4	1.7	2.0	1.5	3.6	1.8
4 Land under development	61.6	40.3	20.0	18.0	28.9	24.9	5.7	2.8	6.3	6.2	2.6	19.2	14.2
5 Vacant lot	9.9	8.5	5.3	37.7	4.9	6.6	2.5	1.9	2.8	3.3	1.5	4.3	3.9
6 Industrial lot	10.7	6.7	5.8	27.9	7.3	7.4	3.1	1.8	2.0	6.4	1.5	5.7	8.1
7 Regular residential lot	4.8	3.4	4.1	13.0	3.8	3.5	2.6	2.1	3.7	2.2	1.4	2.7	1.8
8 Densely populated residential lot	4.4	5.4	4.6	4.7	1.8	6.9	2.6	1.9	2.9	1.9	1.5	1.5	1.3
9 High-rise residential lot	12.3	6.1	6.3	44.8	9.3	14.2	5.6	2.6	3.0	4.5	1.7	7.4	3.9
10 Commercial lot	8.2	5.7	5.3	30.6	5.8	10.5	2.8	2.0	2.7	3.4	1.5	6.1	5.3
11 Road	2.8	2.4	2.4	4.2	2.2	2.6	1.9	1.6	2.0	2.5	1.6	3.7	2.7
12 Park, Green area	15.3	11.5	9.1	61.2	15.5	14.6	2.6	1.8	3.8	5.6	2.0	5.2	12.7
13 Public facility lot	19.5	13.4	10.3	85.0	8.5	13.6	3.3	2.0	2.9	5.7	2.2	11.9	4.4

X 100 m²

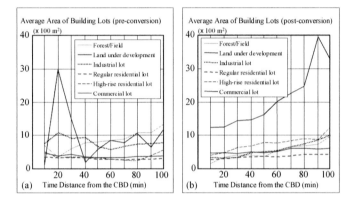

Figure 4:   Average area of building lots in the process of land-use transition based on time distance from CBD.

$$x_i(t+1) = \sum_j p_{ij} x_j(t), \tag{6}$$

where p_{ij} denotes the transition probability shown in the eqn (2). However, as described above, there may be certain locations where land-use does not vary as a stochastic process. A city or forest park with strict development restrictions is a typical example of such a location. Moreover, although forests adjacent to housing sites may be stochastically developed into residential lots, the interior mountainous regions are likely to remain in the steady state for a long time. This implies that if the building lots in the study area are also considered in this study, the above-mentioned model should be expressed as follows:

$$x_i(t+1) = s_i + \sum_j q_{ij}(t)\left(x_j(t) - s_j\right), \tag{7}$$

where s_j denotes the total number of building lots in the steady state, and $q_{ij}(t)$ is the transition probability of building lots estimated by excluding the building lots in the steady state. Moreover, since this transition probability is expected to vary with time, the description of the model should include a suffix for time t. Therefore, the estimator of $q_{ij}(t)$ is expressed by the following equations:

$$q_{ij}(t) = \frac{n_{ij}(t)}{\sum_k n_{kj}(t) - s_j} \quad (i \neq j), \tag{8}$$

$$q_{jj}(t) = \frac{n_{jj}(t) - s_j}{\sum_k n_{kj}(t) - s_j}, \tag{9}$$

where $n_{ij}(t)$ is the total number of building lots where the land-use category changes from j to i during the time interval t to $t+1$. In addition, the total number of building lots where the land-use category j did not change during the time interval t to $t+2$ is denoted by $r_j(t)$. The estimator of $r_j(t)$ can be expressed using $q_{ij}(t)$ as follows:

$$r_j(t) = s_j + \left(\sum_k n_{kj}(t) - s_j \right) q_{jj}(t) q_{jj}(t+1) \cdot \tag{10}$$

The following equation is obtained when $q_{jj}(t)$ and $q_{jj}(t+1)$ are eliminated using eqns (8) and (9),

$$s_j = \frac{r_j(t) \sum_k n_{kj}(t+1) - n_{jj}(t) n_{jj}(t+1)}{r_j(t) + \sum_k n_{kj}(t+1) - n_{jj}(t) - n_{jj}(t+1)}. \tag{11}$$

Therefore, if the values of $n_{ij}(t)$, $n_{ij}(t+1)$ and $r_j(t)$ are estimated using time series data, the number of building lots in the steady state s_j can be estimated. Furthermore, the transition probability of building lots $q_{ij}(t)$ and $q_{jj}(t)$ can be estimated using eqns (8) and (9). The framework for the estimation method is shown in figure 5.

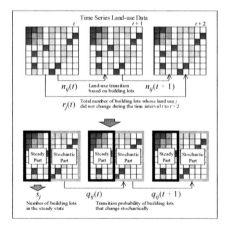

Figure 5:   Framework of estimation method for transition probability considering building lots in the steady state.

3.2 Building lots in the steady state

Actual land-use data are analyzed using the land-use transition model described above, and the number of building lots in the steady state is estimated. If areas undergoing large-scale development are considered within the study area, the estimated value of the average area becomes unstable. Therefore, the building lots that changed by 1 ha or more are excluded from the study.

To begin with, the proportion of building lots in the steady state is estimated and the results are presented in table 3. The areas of the lands under development and the vacant lots are compared with those of other land-use categories. In contrast with the other land-use categories, these building lots are unlikely to remain in the steady state. Next, in order to examine the spatial distribution of building lots in the steady state, the proportion of building lots in the steady state is estimated based on the time distance from the CBD. A part of the result obtained is shown in figure 6. The area under the vacant lot land-use category does not depend on the time distance but has a low, almost constant value. On the other hand, the proportion of residential and commercial lots is high in the CBD and low in the suburbs. Although changes in the land-use category are considered to be frequent in the CBD, the possibility of land-use conversion is actually low. In other words, residential and commercial lots are stable particularly in the CBD.

Table 3:   Proportion of building lots in the steady state.

1	Forest, Wasteland	0.811
2	Rice field	0.785
3	Field	0.668
4	Land under development	0.175
5	Vacant lot	0.381
6	Industrial lot	0.693
7	Regular residential lot	0.719
8	Densely populated residential lot	0.791
9	High-rise residential lot	0.689
10	Commercial lot	0.530
11	Road	0.694
12	Park, Green area	0.439
13	Public facility lot	-

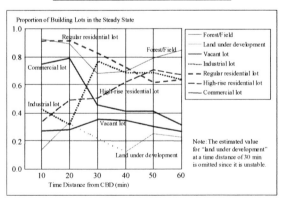

Figure 6:   Ratio of building lots in the steady state based on time distance.

3.3 Simple Markov model

In several Markov chain models, the "simple Markov" property is assumed in order to simplify the theoretical discussion. Specifically, it is assumed that "the state at time $t + 1$" is dependent only on "the state at time t." On the other hand, in a multi-Markov model, it is assumed that "the state at time $t + 1$" is dependent on "the state at time t as well as earlier states." Therefore, the following investigation is carried out to determine whether or not the actual land-use transition follows the multi-Markov process. As shown in figure 7, the study area was divided into two areas. While one of the areas did not witness land-use transition in the period from 1974 to 1979, the other did. The transition probability matrices of building lots for the periods 1979-1984 and 1984-1985 are estimated. Since the building lots that are in the steady state are likely to be located in the area that did not witness a land-use transition, the transition probability matrix for the building lots is estimated considering the building lots that are in the steady state. On the other hand, there are no building lots in the steady state located in the area that witnessed a land-use transition. The property of the Markov process is examined by comparing the transition probability matrices estimated in the two areas with different land-use transition histories. The transition probabilities of the building lots are denoted by $q_{Aij}(t)$ and $q_{Bij}(t)$, and the relationship between the values is illustrated in figure 8. No significant difference between these values was observed. We can conclude that the land-use transition process considered in this study can be adequately described by a simple Markov model.

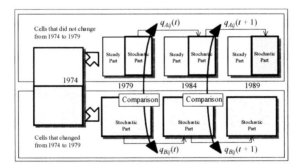

Figure 7:   Method for examining simple Markov process.

4   Summary and conclusions

In this study, certain inherent problems in the conventional method of estimating land-use transition probability were discussed and new estimation methods were proposed. The need to estimate the transition probability based on building lots was first explained. Assuming efficient use of the existing raster data, we developed a method to estimate the transition probability based on building lots from raster data. We then proved that the transition probability should be estimated by excluding the locations in the steady state in order to obtain the accurate transition structure. We proposed a method by which the number of locations in the steady state can be estimated, and then discussed the spatial distribution of these locations. To conclude, it was shown that the land-use transition process considered in this study could be described by a simple Markov mode using the proposed model.

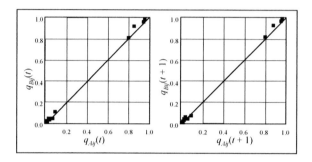

Figure 8:   Validation of simple Markov process.

Acknowledgement

The author expresses his gratitude toward Mr. Ken-ichi Masuda for the computer-based numerical calculations.

References

[1]   Kim, J.Y. et al., Analysis of Urban Land-use structure using Land-use Transition Matrix, *Transaction of Architectural Institute of Japan*, **424**, pp.69-78, 1991 (in Japanese).

[2]   Ishizaka, K., A Consideration on Analyzing Method of Land-use Transition Matrix, *Transaction of Architectural Institute of Japan*, **436**, pp.59-69, 1992a (in Japanese).

[3]   Ishizaka, K., Characteristic of Land-use Change in Relation to Distance from CBD in Tokyo Metropolitan Area, *Transaction of Architectural Institute of Japan*, **442**, pp.97-106, 1992b (in Japanese).

[4]   Aoki, Y., Nagai, A. and Osaragi, T., Area dividing method by neural network, *Third International Conference on Computers in Urban Planning and Urban Management*, Georgia Institute of Technology, **2**, pp.379-392, 1993.

[5]   Aoki, Y., Osaragi, T. and Nagai, A., Using of the Area-dividing Method to Minimize Expected Error in Land-use Forecasts, *Environment and Planning B: Planning and Design*, **23**, pp.655-666, 1996.

[6]   Osaragi, T. and Kurisaki, N., Modeling of Land-use Transition and Its Application. *Geographical and Environmental Modelling*, **4(2)**, pp.203-218, 2000.

Urban compactness and its progress towards sustainability: the Hong Kong scenario

S. B. A. Coorey & S. S. Y Lau
Faculty of Architecture, the University of Hong Kong, HKSAR, People's Republic of China

Abstract

A significant development pattern emerging in Hong Kong and many Asian cities today is the compact urban form which is an alternative to urban sprawl. It implies intensification, high density and mixed uses as opposed to low density, mono use urban sprawl. Within such a definition the compact city has caught the attention of many professionals as having a potential for achieving sustainability. But as pointed out by many researchers, the compact city has its positive and negative implications on sustainability. Positive implications are conservation of the countryside, reduced needs to travel by car, reduction in the use of fuel and pollution, the support of public transport, walking and cycling, better access to services, efficient utility and infrastructure provisions and revitalization and regeneration of urban areas. The negative implications are poor environmental quality, crowding, social acceptability, the lack of urban greenery, open spaces, and privacy, effect of urban form on ecology, wildlife, natural resources, and economic well being. Although compactness is supported as a sustainable urban form, there is limited empirical evidence to support such a contention therefore the methods for measuring such developments and the success or failure of particular initiatives are crucial in order to justify its progress towards sustainability. In this paper compactness is discussed in terms of its quantitative and qualitative attributes. The quantitative attributes are density, intensity, mix use, scale, grain and permeability. The qualitative attributes are diversity, vitality and viability. These attributes will then be discussed taking a case study in Hong Kong. As sustainability is a vast and complex area of study, this paper is limited to selected implications on sustainability as highlighted in the theoretical framework.
Keywords: compact, urban, density, intensity, mix use, scale, diversity, open space, sustainability, Hong Kong.

1 Introduction

Increase in population and emerging trends in development to meet its requirements create rapid environmental deterioration and social problems which influence the social, environmental and economic sustainability of cities. Two significant development trends as a response to increase in population and scarcity of urban land are namely high-density urban compactness and low-density urban sprawl of which, urban compactness is an emerging trend in Asia today. Compactness can be evaluated using density, intensity, mix use, scale, grain and permeability as the predominant urban variables. Such urban variables are claimed to have both positive and negative implications on the city and its progress towards achieving sustainability. A theoretical framework outlining the implications of such emerging development trends and its influence on sustainability is of urgent need in order to study the behaviour of urban compactness. For urban planners, designers and policy makers such framework can be developed as a research tool to manipulate urban compactness and its implications on sustainability.

The objective of this paper is to establish a preliminary framework outlining the concept of compactness, its theoretical measures and its claimed implications on sustainability. The paper will review the quantitative and qualitative attributes of urban compactness; the means of measuring such attributes; the claimed positive and negative implications of such attributes and its implications on sustainability. An extensive review of literature and past research findings will form the theoretical basis for analyzing a compact development. As sustainability is a vast and complex area of study, the paper focuses on selected implications of compactness that is highlighted in the theoretical framework. A compact mixed-use development in Hong Kong is selected as the case study where qualitative analysis and a questionnaire interview survey of 100 respondents is conducted.

1.1 Research questions

The following research questions are addressed in this paper in order to formulate the theoretical framework for analyzing a compact development.
1. What are the quantitative and qualitative attributes of compactness and the means of measuring such attributes?
2. What are its positive and negative implications on sustainability?

1.1.1 Hypothesis

The compact city is defined as having high density; mix uses, efficient public transport and dimensions that encourage walking and cycling (Burton [1]). Jenks [2] discuss compactness as a theory that advocates mixing of uses within concentrated environments, to prevent urban sprawl and land fragmentation. According to [3–7] compactness can be discussed in terms of its quantitative attributes such as density, intensification, mix use, scale, grain and permeability which are the critical variables for evaluating any setting of multiple uses. The quality of it according to [4, 8, 9] can be discussed in terms of its diversity, variety, vitality and viability. As established in theory and past research, such attributes have influence on city quality and thereby quality of life and sustainability.

2 Quantitative and qualitative attributes of a compact city as discussed in past research

2.1 Quantitative attributes

Density: high-density city is the most common interpretation of the compact city. Density is promoted in cities for achieving sustainability. It can be measured as density of population (gross density); density of built form (net density); Density of subcentres and density of housing (Burton [1]).

Mixed land uses: Mixing of uses takes place both horizontally and vertically and are categorized as commercial, residential, recreational, institutional and industrial uses (Coupland [7]). A refined description of mixed use is; primary and secondary uses, local and global transactions, scale and grain, public and private space relationship and spatial diffusion, linkages (Roberts et al. [4]). Primary uses are residential, employment and service functions which provide demands for secondary uses, such as commercial, restaurants etc. The activities generated by mix uses are classified as local and global transactions. Transaction means not only the exchange of commodities, but also includes the types of human exchange, in terms of conversations, and cultural and religious exchange through activities etc. (Jacobs [8]). Private space and public space in mix use is critical in influencing vitality and variety in public space (Hillier [10]).

Scale and grain: Compact developments occur within districts or neighbourhoods, streets or public spaces, building or street blocks and in individual buildings (Rowley [9] Williams et al. [6]). Scale is determined by plot ratio, and housing density. Urban Grain can be determined by size of block and the subdivisions of that block and the technique to expose urban grain is the "Figure Ground" theory. According to Jacobs [8] permeability is bound by the notion of urban scale and urban grain as fine grain and scale of buildings increase options of routes for pedestrians, and better use of functions.

Permeability: According to Jacobs [8] for a neighbourhood to support a number of small commercial outlets there is a need for multiplicity of routes – permitting pedestrians choices and variations in their journey, this idea was refined as "permeability". According to Hillier [10] permeability is more significant than distance in determining pedestrian activity and is a critical issue in shaping the allocations of mix uses across urban space. Permeability is determined by building space index (BSI) or constitutedness (the number of buildings that are both adjacent and directly accessible from the space in concern); permeability per unit area (the intensity of buildings being accessed from that space per unit area of space); degree of adjacency/impermeability (number of buildings that are adjacent but not accessible to the space); relative depth / integration (the measure of depth of the whole settlement from the space in concern) and depth of space from carrier space (the value that describes the location of the space in relation to the space surrounding the settlement also referred to as carrier space which is measured by number of axial spaces one has to pass through before reaching the space in concern) (Moirongo [11])

2.2 Qualitative attributes

Diversity, vitality and viability: All above quantitative attributes of compactness facilitates the qualitative attributes. High densities are seen to be fundamental to urban vitality and creativity (Burton [1]) but increase in development pressure and demand for uses with high value addition to land can also destroy diversity (Jacobs [8]). It is suggested that a combination of high density and mix use is important to retain diversity and vitality. According to [4, 8, 9] Mix use is a key factor that brings variety, vitality and viability to a place. There are four conditions which are indispensable in generating diversity in a city's street and district: 1. the district must serve more than one primary function. It must ensure that people go outdoors on different schedules and are in places for different purposes using many facilities in common. 2. Short blocks, streets and opportunities to turn corners must be frequent. 3. Mingle buildings that vary in age and condition and must be close grain. 4. Sufficient density or concentration of people. In combination all these four conditions must be present for effective economic pools of uses which will promote optimum diversity and variety. To maintain diversity, vitality and variety high density in combination with mix use, fine grain and permeability is essential (Jacobs [8]). Such measures can be used to evaluate the qualitative attributes of compactness.

3 Positive and negative implications of compactness

The compact city idea is identified as beneficial for quality of life by creating places that are busy, convenient, attractive, energy efficient and providing better health through less pollution (Masnavi [3]). Rowley [9] states the benefits of compactness as better social and environmental quality, vitality, urban experience and character and sustainability. Burton [5] identifies the advantages of compactness as conservation of country side, reduced needs to travel by car and thereby reduction in fuel and pollution, support public transport, walking and cycling, better access to services, more efficient utility and infrastructure provisions and revitalization and regeneration of urban areas. It is also claimed to have wider span of safe hours for walking which increases safety, security and social sustainability. Economic benefits in terms of concentrations of business and savings in infrastructure are also associated with compactness (Williams et al. [6]). In a broader sense compactness has social, environmental and economic implications. There are many debates on the validity of the above claims such as re use of urban land creates lack of urban green spaces and over crowding. According Masnavi [3] a compact city greatly favours walking with much better accessibility to facilities than a sprawling city but the quality of living environments was found to be better in low density areas, where as compact city forms suffered from perceived lack of greenery, open spaces, parks and privacy which were seen to be better in low density environment Dispersed cities suffer from inefficient transport management and long commuting trips, which leads to a high dependency on automobile in contrast to cities that are dense and fine grained that are less car dependent and having efficient public transport which is considered more efficient. But yet it is argued that low-density urban dispersal leads to less congestion, pollution, and that quality of life in this type of development is much higher. Although compact city offers benefits such as transport and land savings its benefits were not as straight forward where there are considerable costs involved which were not foreseen by advocates of the model. The challenges are mainly associated with environmental quality and acceptability (Williams et al. [6]) and although much focus has been on travel behaviour and fuel consumption the challenges associated with ecology, wildlife, natural resources, social conditions and economic well being are equally important.

4   Theoretical framework

Following the literature review a hierarchical disaggregating procedure is used to identify the measures of compactness and its implications on sustainability.

Table 1:   Quantitative and qualitative measures of compactness and its positive and negative implications on sustainability.

Quantitative Measures	Qualitative Measures	Positive Implications	Negative Implications
DENSITY/INTENSIFICATION population and building density land use density and intensity pedestrian density / plot ratio	vitality viability variety diversity	vitality/ viability/ variety / diversity in urban space alternative	Crowding perceived lack of open space lack of urban
MIX USE mix of public & private land uses mix of primary & secondary land uses / mix of local & global transactions / ratio of land use mix mix of income/social groups / mix of household rents		recreational habits to open space use better social interaction social equity better accessibility Safety	greenery/landsc ape Pollution/ poor environmental quality
FORM - scale / grain plot ratio/ housing density / size of block and vertical and horizontal subdivisions of blocks and uses average size of block		Sustainability Efficiency and Efficient use of energy reduce pollution in	
FORM -permeability (BSI) building space index/constitutedness permeability per unit area impermeability/degree of adjacency relative depth/integration depth of space from carrier space		urban space and better environmental quality **SUSTAINABILITY**	

5   Case study in Hong Kong

Hong Kong offers itself as a good specimen to study compact urban form. As discussed by [2, 12–14] its urban system with high density, high floor area ratio (plot ratio), mixed land uses, short distance between different uses and efficient public transport is a typical compact situation. HKSAR is a relatively small and high-density city, with a scarcity of buildable land. Total land area of Hong Kong is 1,103 square kilometers, with 21.8% of built up area which is concentrated in the triangular tip of kowloon and the coastal strip of northern Hong Kong Island. The built up area consists of 3.7% residential, 1.9% Government Institutional & Community (GIC), 0.3% of commercial, business and offices, and 1.8% of open space and the balance 78.2% consists of woodland, shrubs, grassland etc. (Hong Kong Planning Department, 2004). The total population is 6,882,600 with a population density of 6, 380 persons/sq.km. The Hong Kong Island, Kowloon and the New Territories hold population densities of 15, 840, 43, 510 and 3,750 persons/sq.km respectively. A plot ratio of up to 15 for commercial uses and up to 10 for residential uses have led to high rise buildings of up to 80 floors. Designers in Hong Kong have taken advantage of high density to generate prolific mixed-use designs with efficient infrastructure and higher order connectivity to urban services. The intensification of mixed use is found in a majority of city centers which are built around mass transit nodes with an efficient public transport network.

5.1   Analysis of Telford Gardens mixed use development

Telford Garden is a well facilitated and the largest private mix use development estate in Kowloon Bay district in Kowloon, with a total site area of 161,047 sq.m./16 ha, built around a mass transit node with easy access to public transport.

Mix use and density: Telford consists of a 4 storey mix use development with 100% site coverage and residential and office towers situated on the podium. The 4 levels consist of the Kowloon Bay mass transit railway station (MTR), terminal for local commuter buses, taxis, commercial and Government Institutional and Community (GIC) uses. The 41 residential blocks range from 11 to 26 floors and consists of 4992 flats with square areas ranging from 473-667 sq.ft The total resident population is 20,000 with a Net population density of 1,250 persons/ha and a Net residential density of 310.12 dwelling units/ha. The mix land uses consist of resident gross floor area (GFA) of 278,702 sq.m, commercial GFA of 83,201 sq.m, office GFA of 52,482 sq.m and GIC, GFA of 909 sq.m which include housing, offices, shopping mall, retail and departmental stores, restaurants, super market, cinema, sports and recreations, kindergarten, primary and secondary school, part of the City University, banks, post office etc.

Primary and secondary land uses: The development portrays a good mix of primary and secondary land uses with GFA of 331, 184 sq.m. and 84, 110 sq.m. respectively. Primary land uses consists of residential and office uses while the supporting secondary land uses consists of commercial, recreation and GIC uses.

Mixing has taken place both vertically and horizontally. Vertical mixing of transport, commercial, residential, and office uses is observed from below ground to podium and above podium. Horizontal mixing is observed in each of the commercial layers and podium levels, where shops, restaurants, recreation facilities, banks and schools are connected through walkways, and public spaces.

Global and local transactions: Shopping mall, retail outlets, restaurants, cinema and recreation facilities generate activity where human exchange, in terms of conversations, values, cultural and religious exchanges takes place but the office spaces generate activity and exchange at a global level and do not directly add to the vitality, variety and diversity of activity within the development.

Public and private space: mixing of public and private space has taken place vertically, where private uses are located in towers above podium while public uses are located on podium and below and the private and public is linked via open spaces and walkways. In this manner the privacy of the residents and office is secured while ensuring accessibility and integration with public functions and services. Linking of public and private space is critical in influencing the vitality of the public space in mixed-use developments (Hillier [10]).

Scale: An interdependency of primary and secondary land uses takes place not only within the development but also within two or three surrounding developments. Interdependency takes place between primary and secondary land uses of Telford and surrounding land uses such as Kowloon Bay sports ground, indoor games hall, Kowloon Bay Park and shopping and grocery markets, industry, offices and residents which are in close proximity connected by an efficient transport network. According to Lau et al. [15] scale of compactness takes place at primary, secondary and tertiary zones. When one primary node is dependent on adjoining ones for missing land uses such interdependency leads to secondary zones comprising several primary nodes and a combination of secondary zones forms a tertiary zone.

5.2 Survey on perceptions of public outdoor spaces within Telford gardens

Since focusing on all implications of compactness and its influence on sustainability is beyond the scope and limitations of this paper the questionnaire interview survey is focused on the following issues relating to public outdoor spaces within the development, such as; distribution of user groups; travel time to public space; satisfaction with the provisions of open space and use of alternatives to open space, perceptions on environmental quality, social interaction and crowding. Such issues are implications of compactness as studied in literature and important in any compact development as implying on quality of life and sustainability. A total of 100 questionnaire interviews were conducted randomly in two public open spaces within the development from 11 a.m. to 7 p.m. on two consecutive working days. Questionnaire survey focused on public open space as it is common to all user groups, and gives respondents the ease of relating to a defined spatial component within the development rather than having to relate to an entire development which would be difficult to grasp.

Distribution of user categories: A balanced mix of user categories was observed among the random sample population (fig 2). Mixing of land uses congregates a good mix of user categories for different purposes, which is essential for vitality and variety and enriches the diversity of public spaces within the development. Survey shows a relatively high ratio of visiting population which means there is a high interdependency among land uses and inhabitants in the surrounding developments. Such interdependency creates efficient use of infrastructure and services which is essential for sustainability.

Travel time to the public space: 82% of respondents spend less than 15 minutes to travel to public space for relaxing, meeting friends etc, while only 18% spend more than 20 minuets (fig 3). Accessibility to public open space is seen as an essential criterion for quality of life which is well fulfilled within the development. Reduced travel time from home to shops, to work places, recreational spaces and open space can be encouraged by space proximity, well connected walkways linking primary-secondary land sues and public-private land uses, and an efficient transport network. Reduced travel time creates neighbourhoods that people can live, work and play encouraging better social ties and sustainable communities.

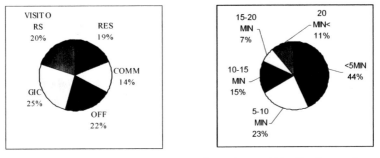

Figure 1:   Distribution   of   user   Figure 2:   Distribution   of   travel
                  groups.   time.

Provisions for open space: Although open space is claimed to be lacking in compact zones survey shows that 65% are satisfied with the provisions for open space and 52% respondents go shopping and use indoor recreation as an alternative to using open space for recreation (fig. 4). Mix uses and reduced travel time to other recreational functions have generated substitute options that are alternatives to using open space for recreation. Therefore perceptions on lack of open space in compact cities is bound by the real need for open space and changes in leisure habits where the shopping mall has become a relatively popular recreational space as a substitute to open space.

Environmental quality: 62% respondents are satisfied with environmental quality of public open spaces although situated in a district with heavy traffic and

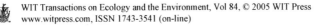

pollution. Elevated walkways and open spaces on podium buffer from noise and pollution enabling more habitable public open spaces within the development. But only 10% are highly satisfied while 52% are of average satisfaction.

Social interaction: 65% respondents are satisfied with social interaction in open space. It is mostly used to meet friends, and relax or for short breaks on the way to shopping mall, restaurants, cinema, or office. But 45% respondents are of average satisfaction while only 19% are highly satisfied. Dissatisfaction with facilities and aesthetics such as seating, tables, greenery and landscaping were also mentioned as not inducing social activity. Mix uses generate necessary and optional activity and according to Gehl [16] such activity induces social activity when a good quality public space exists. Although mix use generates active, vibrant urban spaces with more necessary and optional activity, the lack of facilities and poor aesthetic conditions discourage social activity.

Crowding: Although crowding is a negative implication on quality of life and sustainability a majority of 83% respondents perceive low to average crowding levels. Living in constrained environments could be attributed to Chinese history and culture Zang [17] and perceptions on high density are clearly culturally bounded Rapoport [18]. In this case the perceptions on crowding may be biased by the Chinese peoples' tolerance and acceptability of such a spatial attribute.

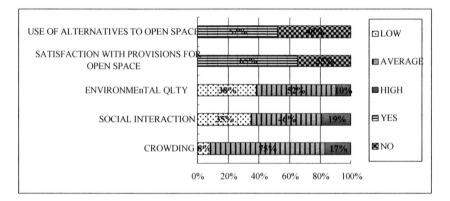

Figure 3:   Perceptions on provisions for open space the use of alternatives and the quality of open space within the development.

6   Conclusion

The case study reveals a successful intensifications and integration of mix uses that enhances activity and diversity in urban spaces. Respondents' satisfaction with open space provisions, environmental conditions, social interaction and reduced travel time are essential criteria for better quality of life. Also the interdependency of land uses within the development and neighbouring developments enables efficient use of resources, infrastructure and services. Respondents' tolerance, acceptability and adaptability to high density and crowding are bounded by culture and such behavioural attitudes are as important as urban form and land uses in the progress towards sustainability. It can be concluded that a well integrated mix use urban form has high potentials for achieving sustainability but sustainability does not depend on form alone but also on huge shifts in behaviour and attitudes which is critical when examining a development's progress towards sustainability.

References

[1]   Burton, E., The compact city: just or just compact? A preliminary analysis. *Urban studies*, **37(11)**, pp. 1969 2007, 2000.
[2]   Jenks, M., Sustainable urban form in developing countries? (Introduction). *Compact cities-sustainable urban forms for developing countries*, eds. Jenks, M. & Burgess, R., Spon press: London, pp.1 6, 2000.
[3]   Masnavi, M. R., the new millennium and the new urban paradigm: the compact city in practice (Part 1). *Achieving sustainable urban form*, eds. K. Williams, E. Burton & M. Jenks, E & FN Spon: London, pp. 64 73, 2000.
[4]   Roberts, M., Jones, L. T., Mixed uses and urban design. *Reclaiming the city: Mixed use development*, ed. A. Coupland, E & FN Spon: London, 1997.
[5]   Burton, E., Measuring urban compactness in UK towns and cities. *Environment and Planning B: Planning Design*, **29**, pp. 219 250, 2002.
[6]   Williams, K., Burton, E. & Jenks, M., (eds). *Achieving sustainable urban form*, E & FN Spon: London, 2000.
[7]   Coupland, A., *Reclaiming the city: mixed use development*, E & FN Spon: London. Ch 1, 2, 8, 9 & 11, 1997.
[8]   Jacobs, J., *The death and life of great American cities*, Random house: New York. 1961.
[9]   Rowley, A., Planning mixed use development; issues and practice. Research report founded by Royal Institute of Chartered Surveyors, UK. 1998.
[10]   Hillier, B., Space is a machine: a configurational theory of Architecture, Cambridge University Press: Cambridge, pp. 149 182, 1996.
[11]   Moirongo, B. O., Urban Public Space Patterns: Human distribution and design of sustainable city centres with reference to Nairobi CBD. *Urban Design International*, 7, pp 205 216, 2002.
[12]   Burgess, R., The compact city debate: A global perspective (Part 1). *Compact cities: sustainable urban forms for developing countries*, eds. M. Jenks, R. Burgess, Spon press: London, pp. 9 23, 2000.
[13]   Ganesan, S. & Lau, S. S. Y., Urban challenges in Hong Kong: Future directions for design. *Urban Design International*, **3**, pp. 3 12, 2000.
[14]   Zaman, Q.M. M., Lau, S. S. Y., Mei, S.O., The compact city of Hong Kong: A sustainable module for Asia (Part 3). *Compact cities-sustainable urban forms for developing countries*, eds. M. Jenks, R. Burgess, Spon press: London, pp. 255 267, 2000.

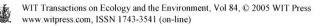

[15]   Lau, S. S. Y., Ghiridaran, R. & Ganesan, S., Personal communication, 2004, Department of Architecture, University of Hong Kong, HKSAR, China.

[16]   Gehl, J., *Life between buildings: Using public space*, Arkitektens Forlag: Copenhagen, 1996.

[17]   Zang, X. Q., High-rise and high-density urban form (Part 3). *Compact Cities: sustainable urban forms for developing countries*, eds. M. Jenks, R. Bugress, Spon press: London, pp. 245 253, 2000.

[18]   Rapoport, A., Towards a redefinition of density. *Environment and behaviour,* 7, pp.133 158, 1975.

Growth management of the cities as a function of sustainable development of the Serbia Region

M. Ralevic & A. Djukic
Department of Urban Planning and Urban Design,
Faculty of Architecture, University of Belgrade, Serbia and Montenegro

Abstract

Serbia is going through a process of transition that involves big and rapid changes, which unfortunately have some side effects in the form of a set of negative, unfavourable and uncontrolable transformations. The most obvious ones are: slow development of the cities, first of all due to the lack of funds for replacement of the old infrastructure, but also due to ruined superstructure; disturbed even and equal development of the regions within the country (districts and municipalities) – in the last two decades only the gravitational area of the biggest city in the country – Belgrade – has developed; uncontrolled changes of the cities and settlements in terms of their uncontrolled growth – the cities have expanded in such a way that they have crossed the borders of the city's constructional area, with such newly created suburbs acquiring all the characteristics of rural settlements; and illegal construction that reached its peak in the last decade of the 20th century, thus disturbing the urban order and recommendations of the city planning documents.

The basic objective of the research is to create some new approaches and methods of management aiming at the regeneration of the region and renewal of the cities. The management would mostly refer to the implementation of the city planning documents.

Expected results include an even development of the region and controlled growth of the cities – by insisting on compact cities and on prevention of further illegal construction as well as on regeneration of illegally constructed parts and cities and decrease of the differences between developed and underdeveloped regions of the country.

Keywords: region, urban planning, re-development, networks, sustainable, Belgrade.

WIT Transactions on Ecology and the Environment, Vol 84, © 2005 WIT Press
www.witpress.com, ISSN 1743-3541 (on-line)

1   Introduction

Regional level surpasses the gap between national and local. It refers to an area of special economic and social characteristics, possibilities and problems, which makes it different from other regions. Planned regions, regardless of the precision of their definition, have to be co-ordinated with administrative borders so that the plans might be successfully implemented [1]. Planning loses its point if it is not co-ordinated with the implementation programmes and with administration. In order to make a region administratively acceptable, Smith believes that it has to meet at least the following five criteria [2]:

- It has to be big enough to support a team of professional administrators
- It has to contain main migration areas in the region background
- It has to have certain gravitational areas
- It has to provide staff for its services
- It has to accept topographic factors.

Today's structure of territorial organization of Serbia is made of: autonomous provinces, municipalities, cities: Belgrade, Novi Sad, Nis and districts as special forms of organization. There are 17 districts in Serbia not counting provinces. The district has not fulfilled the role of an administrational-management unit, especially in terms of spatial-physical aspects and planning. In the Draft of the Spatial Plan of Serbia there is a scheme of functional areas totalling 37, the basis of which is a hierarchy of city centres on sub-regional level, with the idea to rationalize public services and administrative affairs even though it means rehabilitation of regionalization. The spatial plan of Serbia points out that existing districts as a form of regional or sub-regional regulation of the state's interests are not contradictory to the idea of establishing functional areas, even though they do not match territorially match.

Currently in Serbia a new Constitution is being made and a new package of laws is being defined. Frameworks of city planning will be defined with this document. It is expected, among other things, to provide institutional foundation for spatial organization of the state to suit the 21st century atmosphere. Since decentralization is enclosed in 5 priority aims, it can certainly be expected to have a regional level introduced in the level of territorial organization of the state, fully in accordance with NUTS classification.

A region is a multi-layer frame in which all processes of urbanisation globalisation, localisation, etc. take place. In majority of cases, interactions between the regions and cities are one-way and go from a city to its surrounding (during extensive growth) or in opposite direction (during intensive development) [3].

There are numerous definitions of a region and they differ both in number and in inclusion of certain criterial parameters. In order to create a problem basis of regionalization as a form of development category, initial definitions of a region can be viewed in layers [4]:

- General definition would be that a region is total space available at a given time, which with its function and its structure of accompanying systems represents a unique organization within a spatial entity.

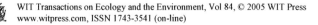

- In order to be more precise, we can say that a region represents a frame (of space, of time of contents) where different urban entities, infrastructural systems and natural resources develop.
- Generally, a region can be defined as space where urbanization processes take place, first of all settling down in order to activate the territory, and with an aim to create a unique regional complex organizational entity.

Redefinition of areas of certain cities' regions (important centres) includes the need of parallel checking through several spatial levels:

- The first level is a global level and requires that international position, location and importance of the city be determined (in the Balkans, Europe and the world)
- The second level is macro-regional and includes the dimension of the space of interest for co-ordinated development of its metropolitan area
- The third level is meso-regional and refers to a directly taken space that includes the city and surrounding settlements both close and remote.

The frist level includes the territory of urban city area that includes the area of total city agglomeration.

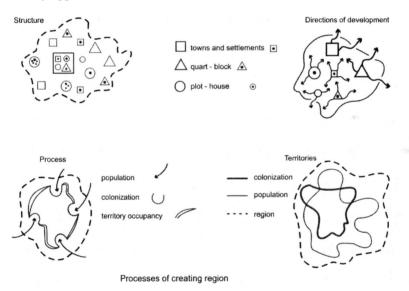

Figure 1:   Processes which create region.

In order to review all development possibilities of urban agglomerations, it is necessary to investigate the regions of those cities by taking the following model-methodic steps:

1st step   re-aggregation of development concepts by introducing polar assumptions of development of the region as a whole,

2nd step   re-balance of previous "loads" of spatial entities of close and remote surroundings of the city,

3rd step	re-structure of spatial organization by means of basic regional sub-systems,
4th step	reconfirmation of cross-linking possibilities in close and remote areas,
5th step	determination of the options of model development of urban agglomerations aiming at their co-ordinated development.

2 Possibilities of re-aggregation of Belgrade region development trajectories

Planning possibilities to improve Belgrade region are concerned with finding the options to re-aggregate the space by creating a nucleus and axes of development and by creating future settlement zones.

2.1 De-aggregation of Belgrade development nucleus

Within the proclaimed territory of Belgrade region, expansion of certain zones can be achieved through activation of development poles by changing from standard to other instruments used to establish inter-relations, such as comparative, complementary or compatible inter-relations.
In this regard, the following development circles can be distinguished:

- The first circle consists of transitional development poles – suburbs,
- The second circle of development would be the nearby settlements (of different importance),
- The third circle would include the zone of contact with other regions,
- Macro cricle is formed out of the proclaimed Belgrade region but the impacts of nearby cities, in both directions, are included.

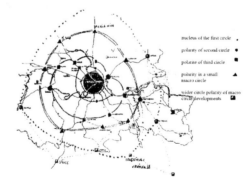

Figure 2:   Activation of potential nucleus of development in the region of Belgrade.

2.2 Re-activation of development axes of Belgrade territory

The same as with nucleus de-aggregation, this approach requires creation through spatial rings:

- The first circle of Belgrade region includes several development axes, namely: development along the Danube and the Sava banks; development towards suburban settlements, and development of roundabouts to be activated in the second phase (they connect suburban settlements like a ring)
- The second circle includes the axes out of the proclaimed region and they are: macro directions of making settlements along the river banks; development axes towards the contact zones with other cities, and axes in forms of roundabouts connecting close and remote settlments around Belgrade.

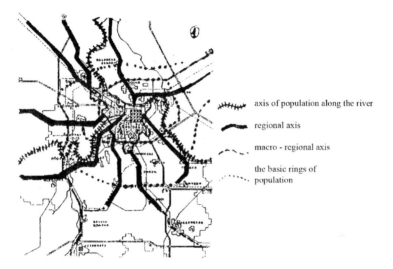

axis of population along the river

regional axis

macro - regional axis

the basic rings of population

Figure 3:   Reactivation of development axes in the area covered with spatial plan.

2.3 Re-activation of regional districts

The same as with previous two development approaches, this one also recognizes several spatial development circles:

- The first circle includes the districts inside Belgrade region, with their own available resources for settling douwn and composed of several layers: the first layer is made of edge districts created through natural expansion of a settlement within its contact zonesрних зона (Belgrade edge districts, edge districts of the development nucleuses from various circles, and edge districts of other existing settlments); the second layer is made of parallel districts representing areas close to existing axes in the forms of Belgrade connections with surrounding settlements and in the forms of the streams that connect surrounding settlements according to their spatial circles; the third layer is made of territorial districts as

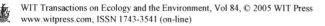

complexes that occur within a territory confined with two or more development axes.
- The second circle is made of macro-regional districts, outside Belgrade region, occupying the territory between development axes.

3   Possibilities of re-balancing the region

Re-balancing is done in order to set the actions for efficient and sustainable regional structures and connections. Development options can be viewed through discoveries of spatial assemblies that can be spatially controlled and used by means of available adequate connection systems. In this regard, it would be useful to examine all possible options of adjusting spatial loads, circulating efficiencies and to find optimal development envelopes for the region as a whole.

3.1 Load re-balance

Load re-balancing of spatial segments of a region directs us to find new balanced options of territorialization by means of several parameters, such as: population density, occupancy of the area, temporariness of changes, value of the territory, typology of inhabitants, etc [5].

Development options for above parameters could be considered through the following development options:
- Balancing of the loads between certain entities (load redistribution, load reduction on certain points, introduction of equality measure),
- Segment value determination and classification of potentials (from the centre to the periphery, along the axes or from point to point),
- Strengthening the differences among entities by the principle of contrast.

3.2 Efficiency improvement

By examining certain coding systems and setting a gradation between inhabited entities as well as by establishing new, functional grids, it is possible to improve circulation within a region.

The options of organizational improvements on regional level can be formed as:
- Co-ordination and linking of grids (natural-morphological with technological-communicational, macro-regional with local, multipolar development with multiaxial development),
- Introduction of inter-graded and multy-co-ordinated structures of territorialization through: construction of the model of multi-cyclic functioning of the region, adjustment of gradation systems between inhabited entities in the new system of cyclic flow, and establishment of different business systems as a function of speed systems.

Envelopes of territorial development offer a large number of options in the form of segmenting spatial potentials, parallel assessment of streams and trajectories of development changes [6].

For Belgrade region it is possible to form the follwoing territorialization options:

- Segmenting multi-polar and multi-axial development models, which offers two basic options:
  - o Creation of development circles, where polar cores consist of: the central Belgrade zone, Zemun and New Belgrade, then the circles from the down-town areas, peripheries, regional and macro-regional come one after the other.
  - o Creation of inter-relation networks, enabling relations among all poles and axes according to their character and importance.
- Parallel assessment of territorial impacts of different segments (the centre of the area, of middle parts, development routes), when the following can be measured:
  - ▪ Spatial belts of influence
  - ▪ Time distances of road availability
  - ▪ Impacts of attraction of certain territories.

4   Restructuring possibilities of the region

In order to restructure and re-establish regional development dimensions (especially in regions with one unique nucleus), future development plans for the region have to include   several different development options for complex spatial-urban agglomerations [7]. The region of Belgrade is currently considered a region with one development nucleus.

4.1 Planning development possibilities of loose structure

In the forthcoming period, loose structures will have a transitional role in planning development (towards matrix structures), and it will be possible to develop different types of urban agglomerations [8]:

- Dotted loosely inhabited structures cover the areas around the cities and settlements,
- Cell-like populating forms occur when a number of such areas group together as a set of individual entities,
- Areal populating forms move in two directions nowadays: as smaller inhabited entities (the size of satelite settlements) and as points of specific settlements close to cross-roads or in certain areas within a settlement.

Matrix regional structures of planned development of a region are characterised with numerous populating options:

- Linear populating matrices as a result of prefering road networks as spatial development frame, offering the following options for forming regional matrices: settling along access roads easy to get to; settling along highways not easy to get to (with cross-roads and supply points or by means of parallel access roads)

- Superficial matrices created by occupying certain zones and able to develop in several directions: as enclosed conglomerates or belts; as continuous forms developed along linear streams, or as composite groups formed close to attractive segments; and as discontinuous segments with different forms of links between each other (as leaps in time and space, in different directions from one point).

5 Possibilities of cross-linking the regions

Cross-linking of the regions within an area, in close or remote surrounding, can be various.
Establishment of cross-linking aims at establishing relations, connections or ties between different parts of regional structures. In this regard, it is possible to distinguish several forms of developing newtworks of a region.

5.1 Communicational networks

Communicational networks are products of establishing various forms of communication that increase the level of spatial cross-linkage. At this moment, new communicational systems expand daily, connecting entire regions in one global village.
  These networks are characterized with two opposing effects:
- On one side, spatial scope increases as well as the number and type of communications leading to expansion of the borders of regional entities and increase of communicational intensity,
- On the other hand, the need for direct movements through space is decreases resulting in reduced movement dynamics and revived possibilities of stable functioning of the region.

5.2 Operational business networks

Operational business networks are formed as a function of establishing different business systems, such as:
- Management-marketing streams of business network forming based on the principle of compliance with market conditions;
- Preparation of plans and designs and their distribution through hardware network, when network systems are created which are compatible with software systems;
- Educational-business internet networks.

5.3 Relation networks

These networks establish functional relations between individual entities. In this regards, depending on the mechanisms of their linking, the following forms are possible:
- Complementary networks (formed when surrounding settlements become supplements to the city they gravitate within [9]);

- Compatible networks (formed when feedback relations between the city and its surrounding occur and the region becomes a united organizational entity)
- Comparative networks (formed when all settlements become inter-competitive or encouragingly competitive through the differences of the quality they want to achieve).

6 Possibility of a planned re-agglomeration of the region

Agglomeration can be enriched on several levels by introducing spatial-morphological criteria and by applying them to basic forms of urban agglomerations [10].

6.1 Agglomeration of basic inhabited entities

This agglomeration usually starts from the inital form, from the core, with the possibility to transform further into the following types:

- Formation of stick-like forms, the multiplication of which can result in different radial forms (with one or more intersections)
- Formation of belts around existing cores or stick-like structures (of one or more layers)
- A combination of stick-like and radial with belt-stratified forms when complex ring-like or star-like forms are created.

6.2 Agglomeration of complex forms of inhabited entities

This way of agglomeration is made of the city structure with surrounding settlements, where the connecting streams play the key role [11]. It is possible to have several planning options from the basic type:

- Initial phase of "dispersed" form can grow into a phase of several "flocks" (around a single gravitaional settlement) or can form rows along existing development axes;
- Growing into more complex forms, when the grouping of "flocks" leads to "settlement clusters" and their inter-connection leads to territorial structures ("amoebas");
- A combination of previous simple forms (rows and "flocks" with "amoebas" and "clusters") results in complex forms of a "tree" or "chain".

6.3 Agglomeration of inhabiting streams in the form of complex spatial-time curves

This type of agglomeration comprises three basic typological possibilities:

- Development in the form of points (poles) and streams (axes) of development offers the possibility to have a curved wavy spiraled structure formed;
- Development of inhabited structures in the form of spatial-time waves (from one or several poles – cores or axes of development) shaped like

"rings" (from or around the pole or axis of development or by combining them);
- Development of inhabited systems in the form of galaxy by linking all previous options into a complex heterogenous system.

7 Conclusion

After considerable economic and political changes to which the space of Serbia was exposed in the laset decade of the 20th century, our cities, being the crucial knots of future integration, become the synthesis of different global trends and their local perception. Even though the problems that Serbia and Montenegro experience are big, the development of the country and its integration in regional and European networks have to be based on postulates imposed by global trends. Under the influence of technological innovations and multicultural trends, urban development assumes a multicomponent dimension, which as a time-spatial spiral starts to absorb specificities of inhabited trajectories and through their combinations reproduces new complex forms of spatial agglomerations.

The area of Belgrade region and other proclaimed regions on the territory of Serbia without provinces are treated as unique and compact, having one development nucleus. The entire system of spatial organization is formed as a function of achieving mono-centralization of the territory of the region. Decentralization and return to regionalization as a function of interregional co-operation between the countries, are basic priorities of the state and thus the first step leading back to regional development dimension of Belgrade and other regional centres is to reassess proclaimed regional borders and redefine the structure and content.

References

[1] Janjic, M.,: *Primena modela u praksi urbanistickog planiranja*, AF-PS, 1995, Beograd.
[2] Smith. B.C.: *An introduction to Regional Planning*, Hutchinson Educational, 1974, London.
[3] Alexander, C.: *The Atoms Environmental Structure*, Berkley, 1966, UK.
[4] Mirkovic,A.,: *Optimalna velicina grada*, Mladost, 1987, Beograd.
[5] Dodzidis, C.A.: *Ekumenopolis naselje buducnosti*, AF, 1970, Beograd.
[6] Wilson,A.G.: *Urban and Regional Models in geography and Planning*, JWS, 1974, New York.
[7] Manheim, M.L.,: *Hierarchical Structure, Model of Design and Planning*, MIT, 1966, Cambridge.
[8] Reif, B.: *Models Urban and Regional Planning*, IEP, 1973, London.
[9] Openheim, N.: *Applied Models and Regional Analysis*, PH, 1980, New Jersey
[10] McLokgheim, J.B.,: *Urban and Regional Planning – A System Approach*, PP, 1973, New York.
[11] Osborn, F.J.: *The New Towns – The Answer to Megalopolis*, DC, 1962, New York.

Exploring changes in land use, population, transport and economics with CAST

L. Jankovic[1], W. Hopwood[2] & Z. Alwan[2]
[1]*InteSys Ltd, U.K.*
[2]*Sustainable Cities Research Institute, University of Northumbria, U.K.*

Abstract

The paper reports on research into city modelling based on principles of Science of Complexity. It focuses on integration of major processes in cities, such as economics, land use, transport and population movement. This is achieved using an extended Cellular Automata model, which allows cells to form networks, and operate on individual financial budgets. The model uses 22 land use cell types, with detailed process definitions in each cell. The integration is achieved as an emergent consequence of complex cell interactions.

The formation of networks is based on supply and demand mechanisms for products, skills, accommodation, and services. Demand for transport is obtained as an emergent property of the system resulting from the network connectivity and relevant economic mechanisms. Population movement is another emergent property of the system, resulting from mechanisms in the housing market. Income and expenditure of individual cells are self-regulated through market mechanisms and changing patterns of land use are obtained as consequence of collective interaction of all mechanisms in the model.

Analysis of state of the art carried out by the research team has identified that the main differences between CAST and other models are in the higher integration of mechanisms of operation of the city, and in the higher level of detail of processes in cells. As CAST is being developed in collaboration with prospective end users it is believed that it addresses key issues required by decision makers.

Keywords: urban modelling, complexity, integration, land use, planning, sustainability.

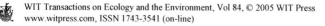

1 Introduction

Urban planning deals with phenomena of considerable complexity. Authors have long recognised the complexity of cities and that many of the features of the city emerge from the many individual and localised actions (Jacobs [1], Mumford [2]). However until recently planning and modelling tools were unable to even begin to handle this level of complexity so had to simplify analysis. In this paper we consider the complexity of cities and show how conventional urban planning tools do not have a theoretical capability to deal with this complexity. We subsequently outline the principles of complexity used in CAST – A City Analysis Simulation Tool, and demonstrate how such complexity based approach has a potential for a much more efficient planning process and thus sustainable results of planning.

City planning developed significantly at the end of the 19th century and into the 20th century. This was driven by the explosive growth of cities and population due to the industrial revolution and concerns about mass poverty, widespread disease and ill-health and in some case fear of revolution. Great plans were drawn up to re-shape cities. Some concentred on adding to the beauty and monumental nature of cities with grand boulevards, vistas and significant buildings. Others aimed to remove slums and create open spaces and parks. Underlying many was the simple idea that if the physical form of the city was changed the social conflicts would diminish, poverty and disease would be reduced, and the economic life of the city would improve. Many of these were based on simple linear models and concepts about cities. In addition the rise of the motor car added another motive (and re-enforced a linear approach) for re-designing cities – the need to speed cars traffic through the city (Hall [3]).

Beginning around the 1960s there was a growing reaction to the urban plans based on linear models. Authors such as Alexander [4], Jacobs [1] and McHarg [5] pointed to the rich multi-connections, the organic nature of cities and their complexity. This growing understanding of the complexity of cities was part of wider appreciation, in part fed by the growth of biological and evolutionary science, that reality is complex and therefore linear and reductionist science has a limited value. This trend grew to produce the ideas of Complexity Science.

Another major influence on urban modelling in the last 40 years has been the development of the computer. However until recently, most computer models, although handling large amounts of data and multiple options with outputs enhanced by fancy graphics, have based their modelling on linear approaches (Batty and Torrens [6]). In the last decade there have been various moves to use ideas from Complexity Science to explore and model cities and their changes.

Concerns with sustainabily, global economic competitiveness, regeneration, urban sprawl and social inclusion have all encouraged recent attempts to model cities. However given the complex and complicated nature of cities and the issues, this is no easy feat.

Models are often judged by their predicative powers. However this assumption is not suitable for city models. As cities have an enormously rich complexity both within themselves and in their relations with the wider world, it

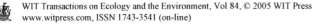

is impossible to make accurate predictions into the future. In addition as cities are contested places, there cannot be one right or wrong answer to long term urban planning. Models are, and should be viewed as, tools for exploring a range of possibilities and aids to decision making which remains a political process.

Analysis of state of the art carried out by the research team has identified that the main differences between CAST and other models are in the higher integration of mechanisms of operation of the city and in the higher level of detail of processes in cells. As CAST is being developed in collaboration with prospective end users it is believed that it addresses some of the key issues required by decision makers.

CAST, based on complexity, is a non-predictive tool which gives a range of future scenarios of possibilities in 10 or 15 years exploring different options of what urban development and change may look like. Due to its integrated nature, it is believed that the end result of this work would be a "city processor", capable of modelling cities and exploring the space of development possibilities. The paper will outline the theoretical basis for, and the approach taken in developing, the model.

2   State of the art

In this section we review the state of the art of different approaches to city modelling, and assess their usefulness for planning purposes.

Theoretical models rely on considerable knowledge of mathematics and physics and attempt to develop general theories about processes in cities (Haag [7]). Schweitzer, for example, has used the concepts of Brownian motion and the self-assembly of network-like structures, to develop theoretical models of self organisation within urban and human processes (Schweitzer, [8]). They are far removed from providing useful information to planners and decision makers.

Geometry based models are not concerned with processes, but only with application of fractal patterns to city modelling (Frankhauser [9]). As these models do not consider urban processes, they are of limited use in planning.

Process based models are developed from the ideas of Complexity Science based on Cellular Automata. The core idea is that rules operate at the cell level so that the character of the city and its processes emerge for the actions in and interactions between cells. There has been significant work exploring the potential of this approach and it has been useful to examine the broad process of urban sprawl. Examples include DUEM (Batty et al. [10]), IDEUM (Xie and Batty [11]), SLEUTH model (Silva and Clarke [12]) Simland (Wu [13]) and the work by White and Engelen [14]. While these models can be useful for decision makers, their usefulness is limited because of the simplification of the processes. Generally these models lack economic rules and in some cases the cells can only connect with their immediate neighbours as in traditional Cellular Automata models, unlike areas in real cities.

Mobile agent models, while also based on Complexity Science, rather than focus on cells, as in process models, are based on the emergent properties of the actions of mobile agents that move through the city, which represent major players in a city's development. Examples of agent based models are contained in the work of Semboloni's CityDev [15], Portugali [16], including CogCity (Cognitive City) and Benenson [17] and Torrens, including SprawlSim (Torrens [18]). These models, again have their uses, but are limited in their ability to deal with land use changes.

Rule based models are widely used to analyse specific issues, such as transport or air pollution as well as modelling of cities. They are based on largely linear rules which are generalisations of past experience, so that if a certain condition happens it has defined results. Usually the rules are applied in a top-down way at a citywide level, taking an aggregate view of the city. These models are able to handle large amounts of data and many fields of study such as population, economic activity and employment, land use and transport.

A number of these models have been developed for analysing cities, including CUF (California Urban Futures model) looking at changing land use (Landis and Zhang [19]); 'What If?' a programme that links with GIS to examine urban change scenarios, especially in cities experiencing rapid growth (Klosterman [20]) and UrbanSim looking at land use and transport use and their environmental impacts (Waddell and Evans [21]). One recent and useful example is QUEST [22], developed by the Sustainable Development Research Initiative in Vancouver to explore sustainable futures for the Georgia Basin area of British Columbia. QUEST is an interactive computer model, with highly visual and user friendly software, that allows people to develop scenarios for the future of the region. It is an aid for the public and policy makers to explore options for a sustainable future. It handles a large amount of data about the region and works through deterministic formulae based on best knowledge.

The downside of rule based models is that, as they are based on a top-down approach, they fail to represent the complexity of cities, the variations within a city and the dynamic nature of change.

In summary, rule based models have a longish history in city modelling and while providing useful support for planners, policy makers and public are limited as they are not based on the complexity of cities. The models based more on Complexity Science, include a growing area of work, but up until now have largely either been developed to explore the theoretical relationship between cities and complexity or to examine broad issue such as urban sprawl. As such they greatly simplify the processes within cities and do not integrate key processes including economics, land use, and transport (Batty and Torrens [6]). Also a number of these models have not been designed in collaboration with prospective users, and therefore it is questionable how they address the end user needs. In the next section we look into methods used by CAST, which attempts to overcome some of disadvantages of existing city models.

3 Complexity of cities

In this section we analyse the complexity of a city that consists of multiple number of components. The purpose of this analysis is to evaluate how successful conventional urban planning methods can be in demonstrating the consequences of planning decisions.

In order to evaluate the complexity, the number of possibilities, or states, in which the system can be needs to be calculated. To make the analysis clear, first start with a simple system, such as an on/off ballpoint pen, which clearly has a number of possibilities of 2. A system of two pens helps to generalise the total number of possibilities as the number of states in which each component can be, raised to the power of the number of components, shown in eqn (1):

$$D = S^N \qquad (1)$$

where D is number of possibilities, S is number of states of each system component, and N is number of system components.

To apply eqn (1) to the city, we first calculate the number of its components. A city can easily be 5 km in diameter, with an area $= \pi \times d^2/4 = 19,634,954$ m^2. If the city is divided into cells of 100 m^2, it would contain 1963 components. If it is assumed that these components interact in 5 different ways with each other, which is a significant underestimation given the interactions of transport modes and infrastructure, population numbers and profile, employment income and expenditure, skills and education, housing supply and demand, and environmental qualities, and substituting these numbers in eqn (1), the total number of possibilities in which the system can be is $D = 5^{1963}$ or 10^{1372}.

To explore this space with conventional planning tools, the total time needed could be of the order of 10^{1372} seconds, assuming that it takes one second per possibility. Comparatively, the total number of seconds since the Big Bang has been estimated as "only" 10^{17}. It is obvious that conventional tools cannot search this space, and that new tools are needed which are based on principles analogous to those operating in the city.

4 CAST method

Cities are open self-organising systems that have operated for hundreds, even thousands, of years. Cities are complex with many-layered physical networks of communication and service routes and human, economic and social relations. Many of these networks and the choices that people make are not controlled by government, economic or business power, policy or rules, but rather are based on individuals' own decisions. The visible and physical form of cities is their built environment but underlying the city, driving all its activities, are human actions.

CAST uses the ideas of Complexity and develops upon Cellular Automata (CA) approaches with the aim of capturing the key processes within cities. CA models usually confine interaction between cells only to the cells immediately adjacent to the cell which is the being considered. Clearly in a city the interactions are much more extended, as in theory any cell in the city can have an impact on any other cell. CAST recognises the extended networks of cell connections while understanding that the connections are not equal as proximity, road networks, etc create an uneven geography of connections (Fig. 1).

The structure of CAST is based upon cells that represent the built environment, the land use type, in other words the function of the cell. Unlike the natural world, structures (and non-built space) in the human environment are a product of human purposes. In addition, flowing through the cells, driving their changes, are humans and their actions, their metabolism.

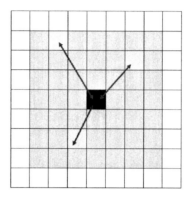

Figure 1:   A rectangular grid in which land cells form networks for interaction with other cells.

Rather than aim to capture the activity of each individual in a city, possibly millions, CAST summarises the activities of the population of a cell. This simplifies the number of calculations and recognises that it is impossible to capture the choices and actions of individual people, but statistics can reasonably accurately describe the actions of groups of people.

CAST uses a raster based grid which divides the city into cells, usually 100 metres by 100 metres. The classification of the cell type is based on the majority land use type. Fine detail is not included, such as a small corner shop, local church or minor roads, rather they are treated as the infrastructure of the cell.

The cells have been grouped into 22 broad categories which reflect their primary role within the economy (Table 1). Attached to the cell type will be a range of attributes, covering population profile, economic activity, environmental quality and building levels and standards.

Table 1:   CAST cell types.

Neutral	8. Car Park	17. Public Square
1. Water	Service	18. Urban Green Space
2. Non-Agriculture Veg.	9. Built Heritage	Production
3. Brownfield	10. Health	19. Industry & Warehouse
Residential	11. Education	20. Agriculture
4. Residential	12. Public Access Buildings	Other
Transport	13. Military & Prison	21. Other
5. Roads	14. Retail	Mixed
6. Rail & Metro Stations	15. Office	22. Mixed
7. Transport Interchange	16. Built Leisure	

CAST is a dynamic model of cities. The cells are interconnected across the city to allow for the population to seek work, gain and spend income, travel, etc. These produce a metabolism within the cell and, in summary, a city wide metabolism. These processes drive the changes within the cells and the city.

CAST recognises that cities are open systems, so there are flows in and out of the city. There can be attractors outside the city boundary such as a large retail or population centres. Additionally at a citywide level there are imposed rules and conditions, including planning policy limits on height or density of buildings or the requirement for a school for a certain number of pupils. Also there are global actions such as the state of the world economy which, while not modelled with CAST, can be imported to influence actions within the cells.

Central to the operation of CAST is the fact that in general there are not many top-down imposed rules, instead the processes within the cells are free to evolve and co-evolve based on the rules within the cells. The key concepts come from Complexity Science where the patterns of the whole are greater than the sum of the parts and emerge from the processes within the parts. The city is made up of its cells but is greater than the sum of the actions in those cells.

As the actions of the cells are not centrally controlled, but are free to evolve depending on their internal processes and the influence of other cells, this allows a change in one cell to cascade and impact on other cells across the city. Cities are made up of a rich network of connections; people live and work in certain areas but their actions spread, rippling impacts to cells which they never directly visit. A change in one area of a city impacts on other areas of the city.

CAST aims to model changes in cities, concentrating in particular on changes to the economy, land use and transport. This integration of economy, at the cell rather than city wide level, is unique to CAST. Most models of cities assume citywide economic patterns; ignoring that while one part of city's economy may be expanding, other sectors and areas can be in decline. Transport in CAST is also treated both as a land use and also as a real flow of people across the city.

Most of the processes of CAST take place in the individual cells, this is their metabolism. The formulae of change and interaction will be replicated across all cells or all cells of the same type. However, some processes take place across the city and are not primarily located within a cell or number of cells. To handle these CAST includes citywide flows and distribution boxes. Distribution boxes are used to collect and spend taxation, handle finances such as income for property (rent and mortgage) and provide loans to buy property, transport infrastructure and provision decisions, and the economic activity around construction and building maintenance.

There are several flows through the city such as transport, but the key one for CAST is the flow of money, the income of cells, gained through employment and from taxation, and expenditure on the many goods, services and taxation.

The primary outcome that CAST studies is land use, the changes, expansions and contractions. Transport has a major influence both on the operating of the economy and of the uses of land. There are a number of subsidiary systems such as pollution, education/skills, population change, and household change and movement. These are mainly of concern in so far as they affect the metabolism and land use, rather than being studied themselves, but CAST can give outputs for changes in these systems. In addition there are the process with each cell, their internal metabolism (Fig. 2).

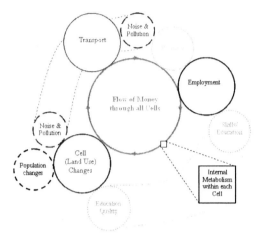

Figure 2:   Flows in CAST.

Economic modelling in CAST is achieved through differential market parameters between the city and the outside world. Thus, setting City GDP and World GDP enable the user to set economic output, and inflation and reinvestment parameters to determine how much of the output can be used to support growing population. This will influence the immigration rate into the city from the outside. Skill and property market parameters are also used to influence the city's behaviour.

5   Using CAST

When the user starts the simulation, cells start developing dynamically, based on individual rules on a cell level, and as a result, a complex model of the city land use behaviour emerges. Land use types, major roads, population, and other parameters are imported into CAST as externally generated GIS data. The user can also insert any of the 22 cell types into the grid using the CAST paint function, representing planning interventions. These new cells will then automatically be connected into networks on the basis of their rules and transition functions. Subsequently, the user will be able to observe the effects of cell insertion on city development (Fig. 3).

Using the graphical user interface, this behaviour of the city can be displayed as a number of different attributes of cells, thus showing dynamic maps of cell types, cell resources/fitness, population, and others. Interactive three-dimensional views of these attributes can also be generated.

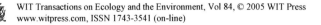

6   Conclusions and future work

We described here our research into city modelling based on principles of Science of Complexity. Unlike other models which address particular aspects of city development and ignore others, CAST attempts to integrate land use, economics, transport, and population dynamics. There are several market mechanisms in CAST, enabling the user to specify differential parameters between the city and the outside world. These market mechanisms influence population dynamics in the city which in turn gives rise to transport demand. CAST can be described as a network model of the city, where connectivity between different cell types and their individual metabolism determines the cell behaviour and the behaviour of the overall system. In CAST, connectivity, population and market parameters can be controlled by the user, to investigate different behaviours of the city under different scenarios.

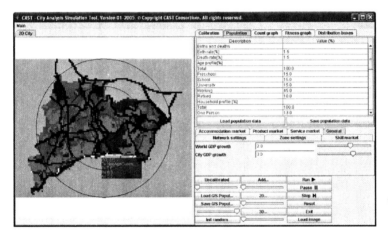

Figure 3:   CAST operating on GIS data from the Municipality of Oeiras.

CAST aims to take forward the modelling of cities by including many processes and factors previously not included in models based on Complexity. However, deciding which processes to include remains a challenge for future development of CAST, in terms of necessary data, processes and interactions.

CAST is being developed in collaboration between researchers, urban practitioners and computer scientists, and thus is a truly multidisciplinary project addressing multidisciplinary issues. Although there are some future challenges ahead in terms of streamlining the existing economic and other processes in cells and networks, CAST is already giving encouraging results and has a potential to become a versatile analysis and decision support tool for urban practitioners.

Acknowledgements

CAST project is collaboratively funded by the European Commission Contract No. EVK4-CT-2002-00079, and the CAST Consortium: InteSys Ltd, UK, (Co-

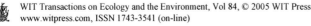

ordinator); ADENE, Portugal; Municipality of Sintra, Portugal; Municipality of Oeiras, Portugal; FIT Consulting, Italy; Municipality of Cholargos, Greece; Phaos Ltd, Greece; Sustainable Cities Research Institute, University of Northumbria, UK.

References

[1]   Jacobs J, *The Death and Life of Great American Cities*, Penguin: London, 1965
[2]   Mumford L, *The City in History*, MJF Books: New York, 1989
[3]   Hall P, *Cities of Tomorrow*, Blackwell: London, 1988
[4]   Alexander C, A City is Not a Tree, *Architectural Forum*, **122(1)**, 1965
[5]   McHarg I, *Design with Nature*, (reprinted 1993, Wiley: New York), 1969
[6]   Batty M & Torrens P, *Modeling Complexity: The Limits to Prediction*, CASA Paper 36: London, 2001
[7]   Haag G, *Dynamic Decision Theory: Application to Urban and Regional Topics*, Kluwer Academic Publishers: London, 1989
[8]   Schweitzer F, *Brownian Agents and Active Particles: Collective Dynamics in the Natural and Social Sciences*, Springer: Berlin, 2003
[9]   Frankhauser P, *La Fractalité des Structures urbaines*, Anthropos: Paris, 1994
[10]   Batty M, Xie Y & Sun Z, Modeling urban dynamics through GIS-based cellular automata, *Computers, Environment and Urban Systems*, **23(3)**, pp. 205-233, 1999
[11]   Xie Y & Batty M, *Integrated Urban Evolutionary Modeling*, CASA Paper 68: London, 2003
[12]   Silva E & Clarke K, Calibration of the SLEUTH urban growth model for Lisbon and Porto, Portugal, *Computers, Environment and Urban Systems*, **26(6)**, pp. 525-552, 2002
[13]   Wu F, A linguistic cellular automata simulation approach for sustainable land development in a fast growing region, *Computers, Environment, and Urban Systems*, **20**, pp. 367–387, 1996
[14]   White R & Engelen G, Cellular automata as the basis of integrated dynamic regional modelling, *Environment and Planning B*, **24**, pp. 235–246, 1997
[15]   Semboloni F, Assfalg J, Armeni S, Gianassi R & Marsoni F, CityDev, an interactive multi-agents urban model on the web, *Computers, Environment and Urban Systems*, **28(1-2)**, pp. 45-64, 2003
[16]   Portugali J, *Self-Organization and the City*, Springer: Berlin, 1999
[17]   Benenson I, Multi-Agent Simulation of Residential Dynamics in the City, *Computers, Environment and Urban Systems*, **22(1)**, pp. 25-42, 1998
[18]   Torrens P, SprawlSim: modeling sprawling urban growth using automata-based models. *Agent-Based Models of Land-Use and Land-Cover Change*, eds. Parker, Berger & Manson, LUCC International Project Office: Belgium, 2002
[19]   Landis J & Zhang M, The second generation of the California urban futures model Parts 1, 2 & 3, *Environment and Planning B*, **25**, pp. 657-666 & 795-824, 1998

[20] Klosterman R, 1999, The What if? Collaborative Support System, *Environment and Planning B*, **26**, pp 393-408

[21] Waddell P & Evans D, *UrbanSim: Modelling Urban Land Development for Land Use, Transportation and Environmental Planning*, U of Washington: 2002

[22] QUEST, http://www.basinfutures.net/play_gb_quest.cfm

An analysis of sustainability and urban sprawl in an Algerian oasis city

R. Meziani[1], T. Kaneda[1] & P. Rizzi[2]
[1]*Graduate School of Engineering, Nagoya Institute of Technology, Japan*
[2]*Alghero Faculty of Architecture, Italy*

Abstract

This paper examines the state of the sustainability and the urban sprawl phenomenon of an Algerian Oasis city. Our purpose is to analyse sustainability and sprawl in M'zab valley through measuring its impact on the environment by using indicators. The work consists of three parts: firstly, analysis of the urbanization process of M'zab valley and identification of sprawl impacts through a cause-effect structure from literature investigation; secondly, a brief overview of sprawl land impact indicators in order to define the analysis framework and to chose the appropriate indicators to apply to our study case; finally, calculation of the land resource consumption indicator by measuring the land use change area amounts from 1968 to 1997 in M'zab valley using GIS.
Keywords: oasis city, sustainability, second residence, loss of oasis farmland, sprawl indicators, GIS.

1   Introduction

M'zab valley has been faced with the urbanisation process and has suffered from population growth during the last 50 years. Many studies reported the problems generated from the sprawl phenomenon, especially since the 80's; the loss of oasis farmland.

Our purpose in this paper is to analyse the sprawl and sustainability of the valley through the analysis of the urbanisation process from the literature survey and to calculate the land resource consumption indicator via the land use change area amount measurement using GIS.

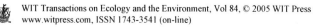
WIT Transactions on Ecology and the Environment, Vol 84, © 2005 WIT Press
www.witpress.com, ISSN 1743-3541 (on-line)

1.1 Geographical features of M'zab valley

M'zab valley is situated at the entrance of the Algerian Sahara at some 600Km south of Algiers. It is a city with one hundred twenty eight thousand people. It is known for its five old towns called Ksour with their respective oasis farmlands that were established in the 11th century and classified as a world heritage by UNESCO in 1982. M'zab valley is also known for its traditional irrigation system using the "Foggara".

From the northwest to the southeast along the valley, runs a Wadi called Oued M'zab in the local language, which floods once or twice per year. Along Oued M'zab are the Ksour, settled since 1014, characterised by their compact structure of hundreds of houses made from local material such as sand, lime and dates trees wood.

1.2 Historical features of M'zab valley

According to the literature, the history of M'zab valley is divided to three periods:

- The traditional period (1014-1850): is characterised by a construction in harmony with the nature and the environment and a land use that obey the rules designated by a local social law called "Ourf", made by a old and wise M'zab people. This period is also characterised by a local seasonal migration from the Ksour to the second residence in the oasis during the hot season (Brahim [1]). In summary, this traditional life style supported the valley's sustainability.
- The colonization period (1850-1962): this period is known by the French colonization, which opened the valley to the economical development (Commandant [2]). Thus, the modernization of the valley is the main characteristic of this period.
- The independence period (since 1962): is characterised by the industrial development of the valley, the migration flow of population attracted by the new opportunities of job and investment, the housing pressure and the sprawl phenomenon (ANAT [3]).

2 Analysis of urbanization process in M'zab valley through literature investigation

In order to analyse the urbanisation process of M'zab valley and to understand the background of the sprawl phenomenon, we did a literature investigation that allowed us to identify the following factors: historical, economical, econo-demographic, socio-cultural, geographical one and a policy factor.

- The effect of the colonization as a historical factor that brought modernization to the valley fixed the migration flow of nomad people and developed lands in some areas, which were forbidden to any construction by the Ourf during the traditional period (Raymond [4]).
- The economical development due to the industrial zone near the valley from 1962-1980 (ANAT [3]).

- The housing development pressure by migration flow through the modernization and the economical development (ANAT [3]), (Raymond [4], Helmut et al [5]). The census statistics of 1954 and 1998 show that M'zab valley faced a rapid growth of population during this period, it increased from 25,541 to 128,087 people. Especially, the population grew at a noticeable pace from 1966 to 1977 by an annual growth of 4.5% and from 1987 to 1998 by 3%.
- The decrease of the custom of seasonal migration from the Ksour to the Oasis farmlands generated the sprawl through a development of low-density neighbourhoods in the oases under the housing pressure. In fact, many second residents changed their state from temporal to permanent one (ANAT [3]). According to the census of 1998, half of the houses in Ghardaia dates farmland were always occupied. Among 2990 houses, 1345 were occupied all the time that represents the percentage of 47%, in comparison to 1540 unoccupied houses (50%). It is important to note that only 15.4% of this population work in agriculture, which threatens the preservation of the dates plantations and encourages their building-up.
- The impact of the land reserve policy that was applied in M'zab valley in 1982 to provide the land for developing housing and public facilities (Brahim [1], ANAT [3]). This policy was adopted in all of Algeria by the national government from 1974 to 1990 and consists of giving each municipality the exclusive right to use and manage the land inside the build-up area or near the boundary. The pieces of land were to be reserved and then redistributed to the national organization to promote public projects and development plans. However, the land was secured by possible expropriation were needed (Mouaouia [6]). In a case of M'zab valley, most of the provided land was located inside the oasis farmlands near the urban areas (ANAT [3]).
- The impact of the land reserve policy was from three points: 1) it provided the pieces of land in low price, which encouraged the rapid urbanization in those areas (Brahim [1]); 2) it considered the farmland of the oasis as build able land (ANAT [3]); 3) it allowed the low density, since the lots of land were designated for an individual houses or public facilities (ANAT [3]). Here we present fig.1 of the Floor Area Ratio (FAR), which is the ratio of the number of square feet of built area to land area (Oliver [7]), to show the low density in the oasis farmland that increases with the distance to the centres and to the historical cores of the cities (Ksour).
- The geography of the valley dictated the development of land along the Oued M'zab in the downhill and toward the dates farms (ANAT [3]).

As a summary, we made a cause-effect structure of sprawl in M'zab valley as Driving Forces Pressure State Impact Result (DPSIR) model, fig.2. It consists of factors that played a role of first causes of sprawl problems; we call them Driving forces, which made a pressure on the environment that generated the sprawl phenomenon. We also show aspects of sprawl as well as their consequences divided into: impacts on the urban environment and reactions of different institutions to solve the sprawl problems. Let's note that because of lack of space and time, we could not include all the impacts of the sprawl phenomenon on the society, economy and environment.

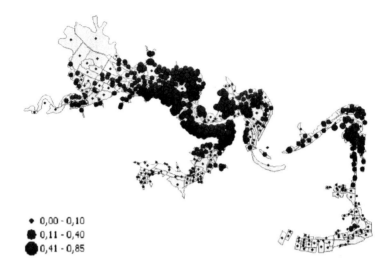

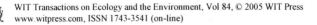

Figure 1:   The density by Floor Area Ratio (FAR) in M'zab valley.

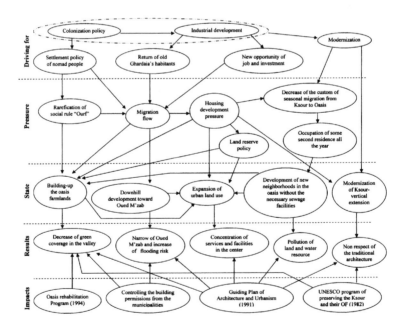

Figure 2:   The cause-effect structure of sprawl showed as a DPSIR model.

In conclusion, this diagram implies that the following impacts: the decrease of green coverage; the narrow of Oued M'zab and decrease of its flooding risk; the concentration of the services and facilities in the centres; the pollution of land and water resource; and non-respect for the traditional architecture; have been mainly caused by the econo-demographic factor (Brahim [1], ANAT [3], Helmut [5]): housing development pressure by migration flow through the modernization. Also, the sprawl problem of M'zab valley is influenced by other unique factors, such as geographical features as an oasis city and historical circumstances of the colonization, social and cultural changes according to the modernization, and moreover in the independence period, policy factor such as the land reserve policy.

M'zab valley is an oasis city, so both of its water resource and oasis farmland have functioned as the critical lifelines for sustainability. However, the results from the existing literature survey suggest that the modernization and the rapid urbanization have broken the sustainability that the traditional M'zab valley achieved.

In the next sections, we are going to do analysis-based indicators to verify what the references reported about the impacts of sprawl on the environment and measure the decrease of the green cover area in M'zab valley. But before this, an overview of the sprawl indicators is needed in order to choose those, which fit the M'zab valley problematic.

3   Sprawl land impact indicators: a brief overview

Most of the sprawl researchers linked the sprawl indicators to the density, accessibility, transportation infrastructure, and land use patterns; some of them use a fiscal and socio-economic indicator (Oliver [7]). To measure the sprawl, a calculation of indicators between two time points is usually done to evaluate the change in data. For instance, the comparison of a percent population growth over a given period of time to the percent growth of a factor such as developed area; vehicle miles travelled, number of cars, of dwellings, etc. (Kent et al [8]).

The sprawl indicators are represented by percent and by capita, such as the per household land resource consumption (PHLC), this indicator was used by the Montgomery county in USA in 1993. It is calculated by dividing the total area of land by the number of households that resides in the developed area. The increase of PHLC indicates a low density and consequently a sprawl development (US Environmental Protection Agency [9]). The difference between the per capita indicator and the percent change indicator is that the first one "provides a measure of land use efficiently of the new urban growth", however the second one "measures the impact on the selected geographic unit's remaining land resources" (John and Richard [10]). Although both representations give different kind of data, their combination is strongly recommended.

In addition to the land use pattern and transportation infrastructure, sprawl is measured through its impacts. In reference to the sustainability goals promoted by the European Union (Elena and Nancy [11]), the indicators of impacts are classified to environmental such as land resource consumption, energy consumption and atmospheric pollution; economic such as costs on housing and transportation; and social such as degree of spatial segregation between households (Oliver [7]).

Let explain more about the indicators of impact on the environment, especially the land resource consumption, which was pointed out by the references as the most noticeable impact of sprawl on M'zab valley, as an oasis city.

John and Richard [10] propose five groups of land resource consumption indicators called the Land Resource Impact indicators (LRI) as following: 1) density of new urbanisation; 2) farmland loss; 3) forest core habitat loss; 4) natural wetlands loss and 5) impervious surface increase.

In further work, John [12] used more indictors to calculate the environmental impact indices to measure new development tracts for characteristics of sprawl in Hunterdon County-New Jersey. The farmland loss indicator was used with the loss of wetlands and endangered habitat to calculate the loss of important land resources. In addition, the following indicators were used: the encroachment upon sensitive, preserved opened space indicator, the excessive per capita impervious surface coverage indicator and the explosive growth trajectory imposed on localities by new development indicator.

In fact, the increase of the impervious surface indicates less efficient land use that develops sprawl. For example, the urbanization of Kharga oasis in Egypt under a random method of land distribution by the local government decreased agricultural and date farmlands and raised both residential land use area and impervious area via streets land uses to equal surface (Arch et al. [13]).

It is clear that the application of these indicators depends on the locality's problematic, geographical scale, and the availability of data. The development of advanced technologies and the access to information encourage the wide use of GIS, aerial photos and remote sensing data, especially the land cover/land use data.

The use of such data and techniques has helped a lot in measuring the spatial and temporal change of land use and detecting the boundary change that are necessary for calculating land resource consumption indicator.

As an example, we quote the SCATTER project (Sprawling Cities and Transport; from Evaluating to Recommendations), which occurred to quantitative and qualitative analysis on six European cities in Belgium, Germany, the United Kingdom, Finland, France and Italy. The project used GIS to complete the statistical analysis of spatial change for each of the six cities (Elena and Nancy [11]).

Other example is Hyderabad project in USA, which used the remote sensing data to measure the urban sprawl of the city via land use/cover analysis. The combination remote sensing-GIS made the calculation of the density of land development (%) indicator, defined as the amount of land developed divided by the land area in each of the studies zones of the cities (Lata *et al* [14]).

Nevertheless the indicators using remote censing should not be limited to the physical attributes of sprawl; the population data should be taken in consideration. Furthermore combination with socio-economical indicators, for instance the fiscal one, is strongly recommended (Kent *et al* [8]). So, the impacts of the several factors interfering in sprawl development should be involved in the indicators calculation process.

In this section, we briefly overviewed the use of sprawl indicators in order to define the framework of our analysis. So in the next section, we are going to:

1. Use only the land resource consumption indicators to measure the sprawl impacts on the environment, because of the limitation of data;
2. Make a spatial analysis of land development of M'zab valley by using GIS in four time points from 1968 to 1997 in order to measure the land use change;
3. Use the GIS database, made by a group of Algerian and German academic researchers (Helmut *et al* [5]), and aerial photos at different scales and dates.

4 Land resource consumption indicator: measurement of land use change in M'zab valley from 1968 to 1997

In section 2, we analysed the urbanisation process of M'zab valley through the literature investigation and identified the sprawl problems. In this section we are going to measure its impacts on the environment via the land resource consumption indicators, which can be listed in reference to the literature to: density of new urbanization, loss of farmland, loss of wetland, loss of farmland core habitats or endangered habitat and increase of impervious surface.

According to the problematic of M'zab valley explained in section 2, which is focused on the decrease of green coverage, and because of the limitation of the data to population, socio-economic and history of land development, neither the wetland loss indicator, nor the loss of the farmland core habitat, nor the decrease of impervious surface are considered by our analysis.

So, in order to analyse the land resource consumption, we are going to use the density of new urbanization indicator, calculated by dividing the land development growth by the population growth for the same period, and the loss of farmland indictor, expressed by the difference of the land area amount of Oasis farmland between tow time points. For this, we are going to measure the land use change area amount of M'zab valley from 1968 to 1997.

Firstly we will make a classification of the land use into different categories, secondly will map the land use of the valley in 1968, 1982, 1991 and 1997, thirdly will measure the land use change area amount of each category in each time point, fourthly will calculate the difference in the area amount during the periods 1968-1982, 1982-1991, 1991-1997, and will calculate the percent of the land development density for each land use category.

4.1 Step 1

We classified the land use of M'zab valley to four categories based mainly on the Plant cover ratio PCR and the Building ratio BR as following: the Oasis

Farmland (OF) (1>) PCR (≥0.8) and (0.2 ≥) BR >0; the Mixed land use area (MX) (0.8 >) PCR> 0.2 and (0.4 ≥) BR≥ 0.2; the Build-Up area (BU) (0.2 ≥) PCR ≥ 0.05 and (0.7≥) BR> 0.4; and finally the historical cores of the cities, which we call Old Town (OT) (0.05 ≥) PCR> 0 and (0.85≥) BR>0.7, we also used other criteria, such as the building type, the construction age and the current land use. Let note that the dates farmlands in M'zab valley are divided to two types, those with only dates plantation that we classify with MX category and those with a cultivated vegetables, fruits and cereals under the dates palms (Djennane [15]) that we include in the OF category.

4.2 Step 2

We mapped the land development of the valley via four maps of land use change in 1968, 1982, 1991 and 1997, using GIS Arc View and based on the aerial photos of 1/25,000 scale in 1968, 1/60,000 in 1982 and 1/10,000 in 1991, we also used GIS data, which was produced from the aerial photomaps of 1/40,000 scale in 1997, the census of 1998 and the land use map scale of 1/25,000. In fig.3, we show the land use change in M'zab valley from 1968 to 1997.

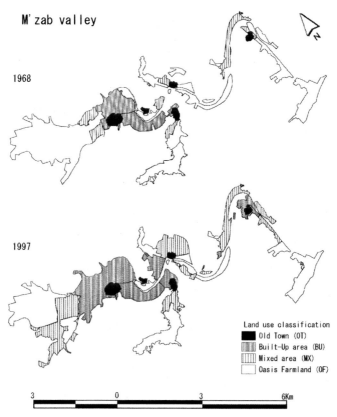

Figure 3:   The land use change in M'zab valley from 1968 to 1997.

4.3 Step 3

We calculated the land use change area amount of each category in GIS in each time point 1968, 1982, 1991 and 1997, fig.4.

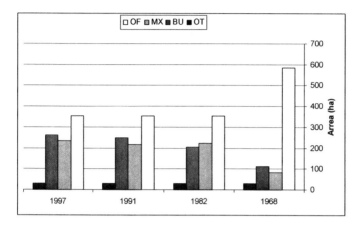

Figure 4:   Change of area amount for each land use category from 1968 to 1997.

4.4 Step 4

We made table 1, in which we show the difference in land use change area amount for each period 1968-1982, 1982-1991 and 1991-1997. Also, we represented the percent of land development density.

Table 1: The difference in the area amount and in the land development density.

	Area (Ha) 68-82	Land-Dev-DENS%	Area (Ha) 82-91	Land-Dev-DENS%	Area (Ha) 91-97	Land-Dev-DENS%
OF	-231,1	-40%	0	0%	0	0%
MX	+138,3	+165%	-4,3	-2%	+16,8	+8%
BU+ OT	+93,5	+66%	+42,7	+18%	+248,6	+89%
Total	+0,7	+0%	+38,4	+5%	+29,9	+4%

4.5 Results analysis

The results show: 1) the decrease of OF area amount from 1968 to 1982 then halted because of some countermeasures, such as the Oasis rehabilitation program (Messar [16]), the control of building permissions from the municipalities (ANAT [3]), the Guiding plan of architecture and urbanism (CNERU [17]), and the UNISCO program of preserving the Ksour and their OF

(Pietro [18]); 2) the increase of MX area amount, especially from 1968 to 1982 by building-up OF and developing a new land; 3) the expansion of BU in all periods, mainly by building up the MX through decreasing its green cover areas; 4) the area amount of OT did not change during the period of analysis.

It is important to note here that more accurate results about the change of land use and decrease of green cover area would be obtained if the use of remote sensing data could be possible.

The land development density indicated that Build up area reached the highest percent 89% during 1991-1997 and the lowest percent 18% in 1982-1991. From 1982 to 1991, the MX decreased a lot (-2%). However, it reached the percent of 165 from 1968 to 1982.At the opposite, OF decreased a lot (-40%) during 1968-1982.

These results show the decrease of the green cover area in the valley via dates farmland consumption due to the expansion of the build-up, mainly by developing the oasis farmland. So, by calculating these indicators, we verified the land resource consumption in M'zab valley during the period 1968-1997. Consequently, we confirmed one impact of the sprawl on the environment.

4.6 Considerations

Because of the availability of the socio-economic data only from the census of 1998, we could not include the land use change area amount measured from 1968 to 1997 in calculating other land resource consumption indicators, such as PHLC.

However, we consider the number of occupied and unoccupied houses in the oasis farmland, explained in section 2, as an indicator of urban density and by consequence an indicator of urban sprawl in the oasis city; in addition, we consider the percent of the population living in the oasis farmlands, that does not work in the agricultural activity, as an indicator of farmland loss.

5 Conclusion

This paper has analysed the state of sustainability and sprawl in an Algerian oasis city, M'zab valley through analysis of urbanisation process and land resource consumption. The worked consisted of literature survey and land use change area amount calculation from 1968 to 1997 using GIS, in order to measure the indicators of land development density and oasis farmland loss.

The results of our work show:
1) The sustainability that was achieved during the traditional period of M'zab valley has been interrupted mainly because of the modernization, brought by the colonization, and the rapid urbanization; nevertheless the geographical features, the historical circumstance, the traditional society and the policy factor have generated the sprawl, which has been stressed since the independence;
2) The necessity to use the oasis farmland loss indicator to measure the sprawl impact in an oasis city; so, we could verify the decrease of green coverage due to the building-up of oasis farmland in M'zab valley;

3)   The consideration of socio-economic data and socio-cultural factor such as the custom of "second residence" in analyzing the sprawl in M'zab valley;
4)   The importance of using GIS in studying the spatial and temporal patterns of sprawl phenomenon in general.

References

[1]   Brahim, B.,   L'Approche de l'espace socio-urbain, problématique, tradition et modernité, Phd. thesis in urbanisme , EPAU : Algiers, 1999.
[2]   Commandant. G., L'Oasis moderne, La Maison des Livres : Alger, 1954.
[3]   ANAT (Agence Nationale pour L'Aménagement du Territoire), Maîtrise de la Croissance Urbaine de Ghardaia ou Sauvegarde de la Vallée de M'zab, Ministère de l'Equipement et de l'Aménagement du territoire: Alger, 1996.
[4]   Raymond, J., Croissance urbaine au Sahara, Ghardaia. Les Cahier d'Outre Mer vol. XXIII (89), p.p. 46-72.
[5]   Helmut, H., Rafik, B., Brahim, B., Tahar, B., and Mohammed, B., Espace, Société et Dynamique Urbaine, Gestion des Villes- Cas des Villes de la Vallée du M'zab: EPAU, Alger, 2001.
[6]   Mouaouia, S., Eléments d'Introduction à l'Urbanisme, ed. Casbah: Alger, 2000.
[7]   Oliver, G., The Limitless City- a Primer on the Urban Sprawl Debate, Island Press: Washington, 2002.
[8]   Kent B.B., John, M.M., Martin, C.R., and Shannon, L., Sprawl Development- Its Patterns, Consequences, and Measurement, white paper, http://chesapeake.towson.edu/landscape/urbansprawl/download/Sprawl_w hite_paper.pdf
[9]   U.S. Environmental protection Agency, Green communities, Where Are We   Going?   -   Socio-Economic   Tools   –   Sprawl, http://www.epa.gov/greenkit/2sprawl.htm
[10]   John, E.H. and Richard, G.L., Land resource impact indicators of urban sprawl. *Applied Geography* (23), p.p 159-175, 2003.
[11]   Elena, B. and Nancy, C., Advanced spatial analysis-the CASA book of GIS (chapter 6). *Identifying and Measuring Urban Sprawl*, ed. A. L. Paul and B. Michael, ESRI PRESS: California, pp. 109-128, 2003.
[12]   John, H., A Geospatial approach to measuring new development tracts for characteristics of sprawl. *Landscape Journal* **23(1-04)**, p.p 52-67, 2004.
[13]   Arch, A.M.S.M., Mojmir, K. and Peter, S., Application of GIS to Describe Historical Urban Development of Kharga city, Egypt, GIS development http://www.gisdevelopment.net/application/archaeology/general/archg003 2.htm
[14]   Lata, K.M., Prasad, V. K., Badarinath, K.V.S., Raghavaswamy, V. and Rao, C. H.S., Measuring Urban Sprawl A Case Study of Hyderabad, http://www.gisdevelopment.net/magazine/gisdev/2001/dec/mus.shtml
[15]   Djennane, A., Constat de situation des zones Sud des oasis Algériennes. *Options Méditerranéenes*, **Ser. A (11)**, pp. 29-40, 1990.

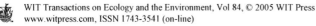

[16]   Messar, E.M., Le Secteur phoénicicole Algérien: Situation et perspectives à l'horizon 2010. *Options Méditerranéennes* **(28)**, pp. 23-44, 1996.
[17]   CNERU (Centre National d'Etude et de Réalisation en Urbaine), *Plan Directeur d'Aménagement et d'urbanisme - PDAU*, Wilaya de Ghardaia, 1993.
[18]   Richard, P., Decomposing urban sprawl, *TPR* **72 (3)**, pp 275-298, 2001.

Sustainability strategies in North American cities

L. A. Reese & G. Sands
Wayne State University, U.S.A.

Abstract

Urban areas throughout North America have traditionally evidenced little concern for sustainability in their land use and development patterns. Political fragmentation and a lack of clear policy guidelines from senior governments have combined with the consumer preferences of a largely affluent population to perpetuate discontinuous, low density sprawl as the predominant urban form. There have been few effective efforts to limit peripheral growth and ensure the sustainability of fringe developments. Inner city revitalization through property tax abatements and core area revitalizations efforts have similarly met with limited success. Business incubators, faith based organizations and other community based revitalization initiatives appear to hold somewhat more promise.
Keywords: urban sprawl, metropolitan governance, tax abatements, faith based organizations, business incubators, central business district, tax increment financing.

1 Introduction

Urban areas throughout North American have historically assigned low priority to issues of sustainability. In part, this is the result of the relative abundance of land and other natural resources. Few North American metropolitan areas are physically constrained by barriers that limit their continued outward diffusion. Even where natural resources, especially water, are limited, engineering solutions have allowed urban areas to grow. The result has been a dominant pattern of low density "sprawl" in urban areas throughout North America. This low density, discontinuous development consumes excessive amounts of land and natural resources, impacts environmentally sensitive areas, and is difficult to service. Because the marginal cost of new development is below the average cost, the long run sustainability of much of suburban development is questionable.

The predominant forms of peripheral development also have detrimental impacts on the viability of central cities. As new development occurs at the urban fringe the core areas of many cities erode. Population, employment and investment have shifted outwards, leaving behind declining neighborhoods, abandoned factories and desolate commercial strips. The central business districts of most North American cities have lost retail functions as well as much of their office employment base. As businesses and higher income residents have departed, a downward spiral has resulted in which municipal tax burdens heighten as tax bases erode and the demands for services from low-income residents increase. High taxes and poor public services create barriers to the attraction or retention of businesses and residents in central cities.

Increasingly, these problems are no longer confined to central cities but have come to extend to many older "inner ring" suburbs as well. Peripheral growth on greenfield sites continues to be the preferred model for development, leaving the built up older suburbs at a significant disadvantage (Orfield [17]). The adverse impacts of urban sprawl are many and include: redundant and declining infrastructure, environmental and resource degradation, duplication and inefficiencies in service provision, and inequities among municipal fortunes.

2 Managing peripheral growth

Although there is growing recognition that current development patterns in most North American metropolitan areas are not sustainable, efforts to control or better manage peripheral growth have had only limited success. A fragmented local government structure, strong traditions of property rights and a lack of clear policy direction from senior levels of government, make efforts to plan and manage growth for sustainability almost impossible. While Canadian metropolitan areas have fared somewhat better in terms of sustainability policies, they too are coming under increasing pressures to address peripheral growth and local sustainability.

Approaches to managing growth and preventing "urban sprawl" include coordinated planning or governance structures that emphasize regional issues, rather than the economic fortunes of single communities. Metropolitan-wide planning and governance structures may take many forms, creating a spectrum of cooperation from minimal, informal initiatives to complete structural change in the form of consolidation of local government units. The figure below illustrates the range of cooperative approaches used in the North America.

Spectrum of Cooperation						
Complete Fragmentation					Complete Integration	
Home rule	COGS	Inter-local agreements	Lakewood Plan	Tax base sharing	Two tier systems	Consolidation

The fragmented approaches on the left generally predominate. Home rule is the most common relationship between states and local governments in the US.

Municipal units are allowed under state constitutions to develop their own charters with few limitations, have wide latitude in policy and service delivery decisions, and are free to cooperate (or not) with other local units. During the 1960s the federal government encouraged local units to cooperate through entities known as Councils of Government (COGS). These are voluntary and typically lack the ability to "force" local participants into cooperative activities.

Voluntary agreements between local units of government are also widespread, albeit for limited purposes, and may provide an area of optimism for the growth of regional cooperative solutions to sprawl. The Lakewood Plan is an extreme but relatively rare formalized example of such inter-local cooperation where an individual municipality purchases all of it services from the county government lowering costs through economies of scale.

Tax base sharing in the Minneapolis/St. Paul Minnesota metropolitan area requires municipalities to contribute a portion of tax base growth to a common pool which is then reallocated among participants based on need and economic stress. This arrangement reduces unhealthy competition for economic development that often drives sprawl and the fiscal inequities among local units dependent on local property valuations.

The Greater Vancouver Regional District provides coordination of public utilities and other regional infrastructure under the direction of a board elected from municipalities throughout the Vancouver BC region. Portland OR also has an elected metropolitan-wide board that has responsibility for some public utilities, regional planning and management of growth. The Regional Board also has responsibility for establishing the urban growth boundary (UGB) for the metropolitan area. The UGB has promoted more compact, higher density development at the periphery and contributed to the revitalization of some neighborhoods.

Complete consolidation of local units is rare in the US but more common in Canada and has been touted as a way to increase coordinated planning, reduce sprawl, stimulate economic development, reduce service costs through economies of scale and reduction in redundancies, and even limit the number (and hence cost) of multiple local officials (Rosenfeld and Reese, 2004). In the US, consolidations are becoming slightly more common and have most frequently occurred in metropolitan areas of 150,000 to 800,000 (Leland and Cannon [11]) or in those under 100,000 (Durning [4]).

The experience with consolidation and other forms of regional governance has been much more extensive in Canada. Studies evaluating the outcomes of consolidation have been mixed although most agree that more coordinated, long-range metropolitan planning results and that inequities among local units are reduced (O'Brien [16]; Reese [19]). It is still unclear, however, whether this radical structural change really reduces sprawl, increases economic development, and serves to reduce costs of service provision (Carr and Feiock [3]; Wolfson and Frisken [26]).

For the most part, even where the more extreme forms of inter-governmental cooperation are in place, the results are often quite limited with respect to changing the overall pattern of development. Portland and a number of

Canadian metropolitan areas have experienced increases in density in response to limitations imposed on peripheral growth. In some instances, notably the Washington, DC metropolitan area, significant investments in rail mass transit have had visible impacts on development in older suburbs, arguably reducing peripheral growth.

3   Revitalizations strategies

Although national and state/provincial governments have provided few effective tools or incentives to curb peripheral growth and improve sustainability in urban areas, senior levels of government have provided local jurisdictions with a variety of tools that are intended to make central cities and older suburbs more competitive. While these initiatives vary considerably across jurisdictions, they typically seek to level the playing field between the redevelopment of older communities and growth at the periphery through a variety of interventions in the market. The results of these initiatives have been mixed at best.

3.1 Center city revitalization

The dominant role of the city center has continued to erode in many urban areas. For small and medium sized urban centers, with populations between 75,000 and 350,000, efforts to sustain cores have proven to be difficult (Burayidi [2]). Urban areas in this size range typically have a downtown business district (as opposed to a more limited Main Street) but are unlikely to have extensive public transit systems (Filion and Hoernig [6]).

Nevertheless, city centers are still regarded by many as important parts of the metropolitan area. Even those cores with little retail activity may continue to be major employment centers, with government, financial concerns and utilities remaining in central locations (Gad and Matthew [7]). The city center represents a substantial investment in infrastructure, both public and private. In many communities, the city core constitutes a major portion of the municipal property tax base and is the focus of transportation networks. It may also have historic character. In addition, the symbolic importance of the core area makes it the focus of revitalization efforts in many cities.

These efforts have taken a number of forms, with dominant strategies changing over time. Initial efforts to replace public mass transit with freeways and parking garages were followed by the development of suburban style shopping malls. Neither of these strategies has been particularly successful, however. More recently revitalization strategies have focused on increasing downtown population, niche market retailing and urban entertainment, including convention centers, sports venues and casinos with mixed results.

A recent survey of city planners and other urban professionals asked respondents to identify those features of North American city centers that led them to consider an area to be successful (Filion, et al. [5]). The most important were a pedestrian friendly environment, with people on the streets; active, street oriented retail; cultural events and employment. Green spaces, civic events,

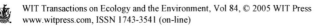

tourist activities, historic character, strong neighborhoods and architectural quality were also considered to be important. In addition, successful city centers were often found in provincial capital cities, on waterfronts and where a large university was located close to the core. Although many of these features are beyond the control of local economic development efforts, planning can contribute to the vitality of city centers by emphasizing the distinct sense of place cores areas represent and by providing infrastructure and development regulations that that support a human scale environment.

3.2 Industrial revitalization

Most states allow municipalities to offer businesses significant reductions in property taxes in exchange for commitments to invest or remain in the community and providing jobs for local residents. Although the use of tax abatements is wide-spread, it is also hotly debated, by scholars and community leaders.   Opponents argue that they are not effective, are too costly to communities that can least afford them and reward businesses for doing what they would likely have done anyway. Proponents argue that no revenue is lost because without the abatement no investment would be made, and that for older cities tax benefits are essential to remain competitive with peripheral suburban locations in retaining employment and tax base, let alone in spurring growth.

Michigan's industrial tax abatement program is representative of such programs. Michigan Public Act 198 of 1974 permits local governments to reduce by half the property tax liability on new or replacement industrial plants and equipment for up to twelve years. This has been an extremely popular program; more than 15,000 tax abatements were granted since 1974, generating investment of $53 billion. Some 37 percent of Michigan's local governments have granted tax abatements.

Most (80 percent) of the investment generated by these tax exemptions has been used to replace obsolete facilities (not for new plant construction) and retain jobs (not for new employment); jobs claimed for the program is about 210,000 while the retained jobs has been 821,000 (Sands and Zalmezak [23]).

Evaluations of the effects of tax abatement programs generally have been somewhat mixed but the preponderance of evidence has suggested that tax abatements: are only effective at the margins in business location decisions; only serve to increase the "zero sum" aspect of local development; tend to redistribute public sector revenues to private sector interests; are used primarily by healthy cities which can "afford" to forgo potential tax revenues; and, tend not to produce jobs and tax base benefits commensurate with the loss of local revenues (see for example Peters and Fisher [18]).

Concerns about the impacts of tax incentives on sustainability and inter-city equity appear well founded based on this research. Abatement use does not favor distressed areas and central cities have a higher percentage of abated jobs relative to their workforce and are spending more to create or retain each job. Investment in new plant development and jobs favors exurban areas and economic health in communities using abatements heavily has worsened over time. Overall, abatements are supporting the movement of business, people, and infrastructure investment further from central cities (Reese and Sands [20]).

That tax abatement use is widespread among communities of all types indicates that they are exacerbating extant inequities rather than ameliorating them in addition to increasing peripheral growth and reducing sustainability.

4 Community and neighborhood development

4.1 Business incubators

Small business incubators have a long history as economic development tools beginning in the United Kingdom in the early 1970s as artist cooperatives, often located in historic buildings. In the United States incubators have been driven by desires to redevelop blighted inner city neighborhoods. Beginning on a small scale – with about 40 registered business incubators in 1985 – and growing to at least 600 in 1995, the attractions of incubators as a sustainable development tool are many (NBIA [14]). The focus of these incubators is generally on small or startup businesses that are desirable because they can employ local residents and are often technologically innovative. Significant efforts must be made to ensure that businesses are not created only to fail and incubators address this reality.

Typically a small business incubator offers a common location for new firms, with lower than market rents and an array of support services designed to meet the needs of small start-up firms often owned by inexperienced entrepreneurs. Tangible benefits may include shared equipment, computing and secretarial services, assistance in business and marketing plans, legal services, joint promotion and the like. Assistance in gaining start-up capital is also a critical component of incubator projects. Intangible benefits accrue from the ability of business owners to act as support systems that can turn into tangible benefits in the form of contracting among incubator firms. The new businesses start in the incubator and then move out when they have become large or stable enough to operate without special supports. Research has suggested that incubators have been successful in stabilizing small businesses, limited job generation, and increasing sales among incubated firms for relatively small investments of public dollars (Sherman and Chappell [24]). The cost per job created for incubated jobs has been estimated at about $6,580 while the per job cost of other types of firm attraction efforts ranges from $11,000 to $50,588 (Markley and McNamara, [13]; 277).

While incubators can be a low cost way to nurture new small businesses there are some important caveats. First, it is not clear how incubated firms would have fared if they had not been incubated (Bearse [1]). It is also important to remember that, despite tangible benefits, the numbers of jobs produced is relatively small. Moreover, most incubators (about 2/3 according to some studies) are not financially self-sustaining (NBIA [15]). Thus, incubators need to be viewed as a publicly supported community development technique not as potentially revenue-generating enterprises.

4.2 Tax increment financing

Tax Increment Financing (TIF) districts provide a mechanism through which increases in property tax revenue resulting from rising property values or new development are "captured" and invested in the district to promote locally determined maintenance and improvement strategies. When an area is first designated as a TIF district, property values are established as the base. Any subsequent increases in property values, as a result of new development or increasing property values, provides the tax base for the TIF authority. The "new" tax revenue is invested in improvements in the area: infrastructure, site assembly, subsidized business financing, and so on. Capital improvements may be financed through the sale of bonds secured by future captured tax revenues.

The use of TIF is very common across the US; 49 states use or allow the use of such financing making it one of the most popular economic development tools (Johnson and Man [10]). In part, TIFs are popular because they allow for concentrated public investments in specific areas without raising taxes to do so. TIFs do divert tax revenues from other geographic areas within the municipality, and sometimes from other taxing jurisdictions (Weber [25]).

TIF districts are most effective when a significant investment occurs immediately after the creation of a new district. Small scale investment and property value inflation may not generate sufficient new tax base to make the TIF effective. Residential neighborhoods in cities where property values are rising rapidly but demands on the public sector are increasing even more rapidly may benefit from using TIFs to ensure that a "fair share" of new revenues is returned to the neighborhood. Neighborhood TIFs often have goals in addition to the common aims (job creation and business investment) of more traditional business-related TIFs, including developing housing, building social capital, and improving the general quality of life for residents of the TIF that directly contribute to sustainable communities. As a result, neighborhood TIFs may mitigate the tax diversion affects on other units by directing revenue toward the community generally rather than to individual businesses.

4.3 Faith based initiatives

Faith-based service provision (i.e. services provided by religious organizations and/or congregations) is a logical extension of both "reinvention" of government—through a focus on ends-oriented governance—and "devolution," as federal and state actors are replaced by faith based organizations Jensen [9]). Faith-based organizations (FBOs) are often seen as efficient actors, highly motivated to serve "customers" and able to impact long-term behavior in ways not possible for traditional public agencies. Some faith-based organizations have been active in community and economic development efforts traditionally focusing on housing but also included cooperative restaurants and fast food franchises, construction cooperatives, rehabilitation of former drug houses, recycling operations, auto shops, credit unions, print shops, job information centers, and day care centers (Lincoln and Mamiya [12], Reese and Shields [21]).

FBOs have a number of potential advantages as mechanisms to achieve sustainable communities. They are inherently community-based, operate from the bottom up, rest on institutions and cultures that are historically integral to the community, and the added element of faith may lead to success where secular or private sector initiatives have failed. Thus far, however, there are a number of significant limitations to this approach. The actual number of FBOs engaging in community development activities appears limited. There is, as yet, little indication that FBOs can effect city-wide transformations. Many congregations engage in collaborative efforts, primarily to limit exposure to risk. The volunteer efforts of congregants has limited sustainability over the long term, and there are often conflicts between the religious roles of FBOs and their roles as implementors for publicly funded programs (Reese and Shields [21]; Hula et al. [8]).

5 Conclusions

A long period when the abundance of land, a relative lack of barriers to the continued spread of urban development and high levels of economic prosperity has caused little concern for sustainability of North America's urban areas. The closing decades of the last century saw a growing recognition of the importance of sustainable development. However, management of development in North America's urban areas has been only occasionally and marginally successful. With notable exceptions such as Portland and Vancouver, most urban areas continue to extend themselves with little or no gain in population or employment. Moreover, the nature and form of the development occurring at the periphery is essentially unsustainable and will inhibit efforts to achieve sustainability.

Since 1990, a number of larger central cities in the US have experienced population growth, primarily due to immigration but to a lesser extent because of changing preferences among the younger generation. These trends have contributed to the relative success of downtown revitalization efforts. But core area revitalization schemes, along with industrial redevelopment, have proven to be expensive relative to gains and likely to produce few spin-off benefits that do no require high levels of public subsidy. Community-based initiatives such as business incubators, neighborhood TIFs, and faith-based efforts, may be more sustainable in the long run but their potential is not clear. While there have been occasional successes, the majority of city centers and adjacent neighborhoods remain far from sustainable.

In short, widespread sustainability for North America's urban areas remains an elusive goal. It is evident that there is little commitment to the types of structural change that will be required to produce sustainable metropolitan areas across North America. Government structures that limit regional perspectives on development, along with the continued predominance of individual (property) rights over the common good, make the continuation of low density, scattered development almost inevitable. Over the next decades, North America will develop half as much new development as currently exists. Allowing these capital investments to continue to be made under the present rules of the development game will ensure that an even larger proportion of development in North American metropolitan areas is unsustainable.

References

[1]   Bearse, P. 1998. A question of evaluation: NBIA's impact assessment of business incubators. *Economic Development Quarterly* 12: 322-333.

[2]   Burayidi, M. ed. 2001. *Downtowns: Revitalizing the Centers of Small Urban Areas.* New York: Routledge.

[3]   Carr, J.B. and Feiock, R.C. 1999. Metropolitan government and economic development. *Urban Affairs Review* 34: 476-488.

[4]   Durning, D. 1995. The effect of city-county government consolidation: The perspectives of united government employees in Athens-Clarke County, Georgia." *Public Administration Quarterly* Fall: 272-298.

[5]   Filion, P., Hoernig, H., Bunting, T. and Sands, G. 2004. The Successful Few. *Journal of the American Planning Association.* 36:328-44.

[6]   Filion, P. and Hoernig, H. 2003. Downtown past, downtown present, downtown yet to come. *Plan Canada.* Spring 3-6.

[7]   Gad, G. and Matthew, M. 2002. Central and suburban downtowns. In Bunting, T. and Filion, P. *Canadian Cities in Transition.* 2nd edition. Toronto: Oxford University Press.

[8]   Hula, R.C., Elmore-Jackson, C. and Reese, L.A. 2004. An exploration of faith-based service delivery. Paper presented at the annual meeting, Urban Affairs Association, Washington DC, April.

[9]   Jensen, L.S. 2001. Not by bureaucracy alone: Charitable choice and the reinvention of church as state. Paper presented at the annual meeting, New England Political Science Association, May.

[10]   Johnson, C. and Man, J. 2001. *Tax increment financing and economic development: Uses, structures, and impact.* Albany: State University of New York Press.

[11]   Leland, S. and Cannon, C. 1997. Metropolitan city-county consolidation: Is there a recipe for success?" Paper presented at the annual meeting, Midwest Political Science Association, Chicago, April.

[12]   Lincoln, C.E. and Mamiya, L.H. 1990. *The Black church in the African American experience.* Durham: Duke University Press.

[13]   Markley, D.M. and McNamara, K.T. 1995. Economic and fiscal impacts of a business incubator. *Economic Development Quarterly,* 9: 279-278.

[14]   National Business Incubator Association (NBIA) 1996. *10th anniversary survey of business incubators: 1985-1995.* Athens, OH: NBIA.

[15]   National Business Incubator Association (NBIA) 1992. *The state of the business incubator industry, 1991.* Athens, OH: NBIA.

[16]   O'Brien, A. 1993. *Municipal consolidation in Canada and its alternatives.* Toronto: ICURR Publications.

[17]   Orfield, Myron. 2002. *American Metropolitics.* Washington, DC: Brookings.

[18] Peters, A. and Fisher, P. 2004. The failures of economic development incentives. *Journal of the American Planning Association* 70 (Winter): 27-37.

[19] Reese, L.A. 2004. Metropolitan reorganization: Same governance, different day? *The Review of Policy Research* 21: 595-611.

[20] Reese, L.A. and Sands, G. 2005. The equity impacts of municipal tax incentives: Leveling or tilting the playing field? Paper presented at the annual meeting, Southern Political Science Association, New Orleans, January.

[21] Reese, L.A. and Shields, G. 2000. Faith-based economic development: Characteristics of active churches. *Policy Studies Review* 17: 84-103.

[22] Rosenfeld, R.A. and Reese, L.A. 2004. Local government amalgamation from the top-down, pp. 219-245, in J. Carr and R. Feiock eds. *Perspectives on city-consolidation and its alternatives*, New York.

[23] Sands, G. and Zalmezak, P. 2001. Michigan industrial property tax abatements: A summary of activity under Public Act 198 of 1974, 1985-98. Paper presented at the Urban Research Seminar, Detroit, MI.

[24] Sherman, H. and Chappell, D.S. 1998. Methodological challenges in evaluating business incubator outcomes. *Economic Development Quarterly* 12: 313-321.

[25] Weber, R. 2003. Equity and entrepreneurialism the impact of tax increment financing on school finance. *Urban Affairs Review* 38: 619-644.

[26] Wolfson, J. and Frisken, F. 2000. Local response to the global challenge: Comparing economic development policies in a regional context. *Journal of Urban Affairs* 22: 361-384.

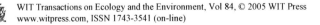

Sharpening census information in GIS to meet real-world conditions: the case for Earth Observation

J. Weichselbaum[1], F. Petrini-Monteferri[1], M. Papathoma[2],
W. Wagner[2] & N. Hackner[3]
[1]*GeoVille GmbH, Austria*
[2]*Christian Doppler Laboratory for Spatial Data from Laser Scanning and Remote Sensing, Vienna University of Technology, Austria*
[3]*Tele Atlas GmbH, Austria*

Abstract

Information about population distribution is important for planning purposes and geomarketing. Census data are often only available for large administrative units with arbitrary boundaries that convey a wrong impression of homogeneous population density leading to analytical and cartographic problems. To refine census data dasymetric methods can be used, which disaggregate them to finer scales by incorporating information on land use and land cover. In this study, census data from Vienna, Austria, are disaggregated by means of a dasymetric method, which uses as input land use/land cover data and sealing intensity information derived from very high resolution Earth Observation data as well as digital infrastructure data from Tele Atlas. This method employs a calibration procedure to assign meaningful population densities to the land use/land cover classes. The final results are 'sharpened' population density maps on the basis of regular grid cells or building blocks, the latter derived from Tele Atlas digital road network data. Such maps provide a more realistic representation of the actual population distribution than traditional coropleth maps.
Keywords: earth observation, land use, land cover, dasymetric mapping, data disaggregation, population density, census, coropleth maps.

WIT Transactions on Ecology and the Environment, Vol 84, © 2005 WIT Press
www.witpress.com, ISSN 1743-3541 (on-line)

1 Introduction

The objective of the EO-STAT service (EO derived Information for Sharpening Socio-economic STATistics) is to build an interface between information derived from Earth Observation data, census data and the road network database of Tele Atlas. EO-STAT is an EO-based service delivering spatially disaggregated ('sharpened') population data for business location analysis, geomarketing and governments.

Until recently, information about the spatial distribution of the resident population was commonly available only at administrative levels with arbitrary borders. Typical conventional map presentations of demographic data are choropleth maps, which contain aggregated population data of administrative units. The drawbacks of these maps are well known. Due to their generalized nature these maps level out variations of the local population distribution, show artificial transitions of population densities at the boundaries of the mapping units, and constitute no adequate data base to relate residential locations to other geographic units, such as river catchments or marketing areas.

Today, demographic data, socio-economic and business data are increasingly required up to the (geocoded) address level and along with them location-based services, business location analysis, geomarketing applications, and so forth. Earth Observation and derived information about urban land use, artificial and sealed surfaces combined with census data and other geospatial data can serve such user needs and offer additional application potential.

In order to model the distribution of the residential population recorded at the level of administrative units according to the actually occupied areas, areal interpolation methods are employed. Areal interpolation is the transformation of geographical data from one set of boundaries to another [1]. There are several interpolation methods but the ones that use ancillary data usually lead to the most precise results [2]. Dasymetric mapping takes into consideration ancillary data (land use and land cover) as co-variable for modelling the actual population distribution and builds upon the empirically derived correlation of EO derived building density and population density. Using a dedicated estimation procedure to link building density and population density, census data can be disaggregated into smaller geographical reference units.

The dasymetric method has been used [1,3–10] mainly with the aid of EO derived information on land use (LU) and land cover (LC). However, the approaches may vary in the LU/LC classification hierarchy, the minimum mapping unit and the assignment of representative population densities to specific land use classes. Reibel and Bufalino [6] disaggregate demographic data using a street map, whereas Sleeter [5], Yuan et al. [11] and Mennis [1] use a LU/LC map. Harvey [7] models the population density of individual image pixels by classifying them as residential or non-residential (binary method), whereas Langford [4] uses a three-class dasymetric method. A challenge for dasymetric mapping is the assignment of appropriate population densities to the land use classes. Holloway et al. [9] map population density by assigning arbitrary population percentages to the LU/LC classes. On the other hand,

Mennis [1] introduces an empirical sampling method to assign meaningful population densities to the LU/LC classes. Finally, the resulting maps can be presented on the basis of new spatial units. Some use pixels [7, 10], others block groups [1, 8, 5] or census tracts [6].

The proposed service 'sharpens' the census information by means of an improved dasymetric method which was originally presented by Mennis [1]. The sharpening comes about through the spatial and thematic detail of the input LC/LU information and a calibration procedure for assigning population densities. Final population values are provided for regular grid cells with flexible cell sizes or for homogeneous building blocks as enframed by the Tele Atlas road network. This information contributes to geocoding of population at Tele Atlas address level. By integrating EO derived information, the gap between the highly accurate Tele Atlas data on one hand (down to house number-ranges and individual house numbers) and the finest available level of the statistical data (census tract) could be closed.

2   Study area and input data

2.1 Study area

The study area is the administrative area of the city of Vienna, Austria, which covers an area of approx. 415 km², comprising 23 districts/communes and 1,364 census tracts. According to the census 2001, the total population amounts to 1,550,123. The study area can be characterized by a diverse settlement structure and population distribution. The western part of the area is dominated by the Vienna Woods, an area extensively covered by forests with low to medium density residential areas. A series of terraces descends towards the river Danube, where the historical city centre is situated, made up of mixed high density residential and commercial areas as well as green urban areas. During the last decades considerable increases of settlement area occurred mainly towards the south and the northeast. These areas show a complex and heterogeneous settlement structure from low-density single-family neighbourhoods to modern high-rise buildings and large industrial areas.

2.2 Input data

Three types of data are used in this study: Land use / land cover information derived from very high resolution Earth observation data, demographic data from the census 2001, and infrastructure and road network data from the Tele Atlas MultiNet data base.

2.2.1 EO based data
EO data from optical sources are used as they provide a good recognizability of urban features and a good separability of urban from non-urban features, as well as good discrimination of urban site density based on the presence of vegetation. The LU/LC data used in this study have been derived from very high resolution Spot-5 imagery classifying the study area into the following classes:

- Artificial surfaces, which are subdivided into
  - Urban fabric (i.e. residential)
  - Industrial, commercial and transport units
  - Mine, dump and construction sites
  - Artificial vegetated areas
- Non-artificial surfaces

The fundamental suitability of the EO data to deliver the underlying land cover information for the envisaged purpose has been proven in many practical applications [8]. The LC/LU map has been validated with aerial photographs and shows a thematic accuracy of more than 95%. The minimum mapping unit of the LU/LC map is 0.25 ha, which is necessary for population distribution modelling on a local / regional scale.

As a general assumption, the classes 'industrial, commercial and transport units', 'mine, dump and construction sites', 'artificial vegetated areas' and 'non-artificial surfaces' are considered areas with no population. Information on the building density within residential areas (i.e. 'urban fabric') is derived from calibrated vegetation index data and thresholded to derive building density classes (Figure 1).

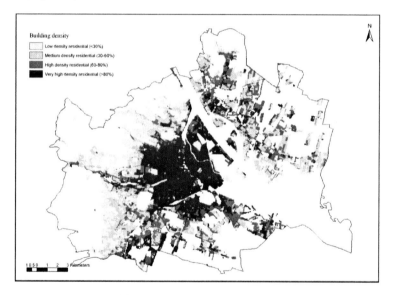

Figure 1:   Average residential building density per Tele Atlas building block.

These building density classes are taken to correspond to different population densities such as the least densely inhabited sub-urban areas, very densely occupied inner urban areas and various levels in between. In order to provide spatial reference units for the population distribution that reflect the actual settlement structures, the sealing intensity information is averaged within building blocks as enframed by the Tele Atlas road network.

2.2.2 Demographic data from the census

Publicly available demographic data (e.g. size of residential population) are usually issued at various levels of administrative enumeration units (e.g. NUTS-3 (1 unit for Vienna), district/commune (23 units), census tract (1.364 units) and grid level (1.508 units for 500m grid cells). In this study, demographic data on census tract level are used for population disaggregation. In Austria, census tracts on the average have approx. 1,000 inhabitants. Thus the spatial extent of census tracts varies significantly between urban and rural areas.

2.2.3 Tele Atlas infrastructure data (MultiNet)

Tele Atlas MultiNet is a digital geographic database carrying the complete street network and detailed traffic and address attribute information: Road geometry, geocoding attributes, routing attributes, navigation attributes and Points of Interest. As of today MultiNet covers 21 European countries and all states of the USA and is released in an updated version twice a year.

Tele Atlas road network data are used for building the geometric framework for population allocation by converting the linear road segments to polygons that make up the building blocks. Such building blocks constitute meaningful reference units for the disaggregated population as they reflect the real-world housing patterns and population distribution.

3   Spatial disaggregation of demographic data

Aggregated demographic data as visualized in choropleth maps are associated with analytical problems because they arbitrarily depict a uniform distribution of the residential population within the mapping units.

Dasymetric mapping is a technique to refine the spatial distribution of a quantitative variable (here: demographic data) by means of additional parameters (here: land cover/use, sealing intensity) that influence the character of the spatial distribution of that variable. As opposed to traditional choropleth mapping based on administrative units, the dasymetric approach applied here accomplishes a disaggregation of population data based on spatial units of homogeneous land use and site density within the enumeration units and by local/regional calibration with census data. In the end this approach results in a spatially more precise estimation of the distribution of the residential population. Population data are disaggregated from administrative entities to regular grid cells (50 / 100 m) and to building blocks as given by the Tele Atlas road network.

3.1. Estimating population densities for LC/LU classes

In the approach an empirical sampling method is employed to derive suitable population densities for each residential density class.

First, "representative census tracts" homogeneously covered by only one residential density class are identified. This step is eased by using building blocks classified into four residential building density classes, thus providing more homogenous reference units for sampling than the original pixel based data. For the representative census tracts, corresponding population densities are calculated by dividing the population by the area of the building density class. Once a reasonable number of representative census tracts are sampled for each building density class, an average population density for each building density class can be calculated at district level, which can be applied to the remaining unsampled census tracts in this district.

With the given spatial distribution of housing density in Vienna (general gradient from to centre outwards, strong local variations), it is not possible to derive representative census tracts in every district for all housing density classes. In inner-urban districts census tracts representative for low building density are missing, whereas sub-urban districts lack representative census tracts with high building density. In order to overcome this limitation, uniform population density ratios between housing density classes for the entire study area were introduced. That means all census tracts representative for a building density class (i.e. if covered to at least 90% by one density class) are used for estimating the population density of the respective housing density class for the entire study area. On this basis, the ratios between the population densities of the housing density classes are calculated. These factors are referred to as 'K-factors' (Table 1).

Table 1:   Estimated population densities and 'K-factors' for Vienna based on sampled census tracts.

Residential density	Area (ha)	Population (pop)	Estimated population density (pop/ha)	K-factors
Low density (<30%)	881. 68	23,616	26.79	1.00
Medium density (30-60%)	736.07	52,880	71.84	2.68
High density (60-80%)	153.86	18,971	123.30	4.60
Very high density (>80%)	3,331.77	651,546	195.56	7.30

3.2 Disaggregation of population data

The estimated ratios of population densities (K-factors) are subsequently applied at census tract level to calculate the number of people for each residential building density class. Since both, the total population of the census districts and the area of the building density classes are known, the population for each building density class (and its population density) can be calculated using the following equation (1):

$$Population = \sum_i Area_i * K_i \qquad (1)$$

$Area_i$ Area of building density class i
K_i K-factor for building density class i

The application of the K-factors to every building density class results in a first cumulative population estimate for the census tracts. As an essential quality requirement the estimated population of the census tract must equal the population value from the census (i.e. maintaining the so-called pycnophylactic property [10]). For this purpose a correction factor describing the relationship between the estimated population and the census population value is calculated. The correction factor is applied to the originally derived population densities resulting in final population densities. This way a variation of absolute values of population densities is achieved reflecting the differences of local population density between census tracts while keeping the original ratios as given by the K-factors.

In the last step the derived population densities are transferred to the LC/LU map and finally assigned to the final reference units for the actual derivation of the product, i.e. population figures within these units. The resulting products comprise residential population figures allocated to regular grid cells or building blocks and are provided in vector or raster format.

3.3 Results and validation

Figure 2 shows the population density map for the study area based on census tracts (A) and on building blocks (B). Map A is the aggregated census tract map with a homogeneous population distribution within each of the 1,364 census tracts (i.e. a coropleth map at census tract level). In map B the results from the dasymetric approach are shown. The total population of Vienna is allocated to 7,850 building blocks within the residential area.

The validation of the disaggregated population data quantifies the degree to which the spatially refined distribution of the population meets the truth. This is done using population grid data from the census. These population grid data are provided as a new product by Statistik Austria but still lack 2-3% of all Austrian address coordinates. In Vienna a total number of 25,382 inhabitants (i.e. 1.6% of the total population of Vienna) is missing and has to be accounted for in the validation. For all 500m grid cells the sum of the modeled population is calculated and subsequently compared with the census population counts. The average relative error of the disaggregated population amounts to 12.44%. If disaggregating commune level population, what for most countries is the most detailed data available, without using ancillary LC/LU data, the average relative error is 102.08 % compared to the original grid population data.

4 Conclusions

The focus of the EO-STAT service is on providing a scalable EO-based service delivering spatially disaggregated population data. This shall serve as an intermediate product between the detailed, address resolved geodata database of Tele Atlas and publicly available census data. The offered service is expected to address information needs of the private and public sector in fields such as geomarketing, business location analysis, risk assessment, urban, regional and spatial planning.

The results presented in this paper use EO derived LC/LU information in order to assign census population data to smaller reference units. Transferability of the method to other regions is given by the flexible method to estimate population densities for the different building density classes. The estimation procedure is eased by both, the use of Tele Atlas building blocks as more homogeneous reference units (than pixels of remote sensing data), and the summation of sampled population densities to produce region-specific K-factor-matrices. Furthermore, the local correction of the assigned population densities based on the census district population refines the generalized assumptions and allows accounting for local patterns of population distribution. The disaggregated population values can be provided for all types of spatial units (e.g. regular grid cells of flexible cell sizes or building blocks) resulting in a more realistic representation of real-world conditions than arbitrarily delineated administrative units.

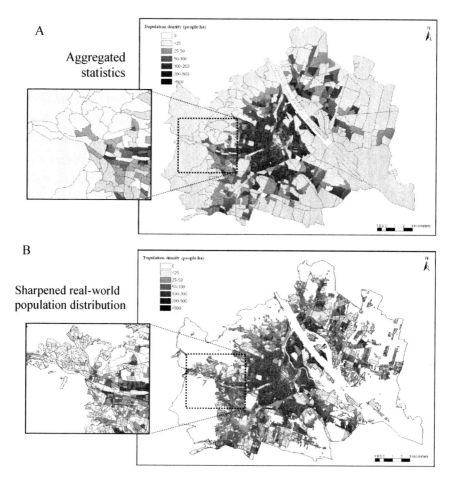

Figure 2:   A: Population density based on census tracts. B: Population density based on building blocks.

Future developments relate to the refinement of the product using more detailed or additional input information (e.g. address point information distributed by Tele Atlas) and the augmentation of the products by using third-party information layers to derive for example population exposure maps and economic location analysis.

The information on 'real-world population' distribution will soon be available for all of Austria. Extensions to Germany and eastern European countries are planned for the near future.

Acknowledgement

EO-STAT service development is funded by ESA/ESRIN Contract No. 18713/05/I-LG.

References

[1]   Mennis J., Generating Surface Models of Population Using Dasymetric Mapping. *The Professional Geographer*, 55 (1), 31-42, 2003.

[2]   Hawley K. A Comparative Analysis of Areal Interpolation Methods. A Thesis. Ohio State University, 2005.

[3]   Liu X.H. Dasymetric mapping with image texture. ASPRS Annual Conference Proceedings Denver Colorado, USA, 2004

[4]   Langford M. Obtaining population estimates in non-census reporting zones: An evaluation of the 3-class dasymetric method. *Computers, Environment and Urban Systems*, in Press.

[5]   Sleeter R. Dasymetric mapping techniques for the San Francisco Bay region, California. *Urban and Regional Information Systems Association, Annual Conference Proceedings*, Reno, Nevada, November 7-10, 2004.

[6]   Reibel M., and Bufalino M.E. Local Housing Unit Counts and Changing Enumeration Districts: Street Weighted Areal Interpolation Using Geographic Information Systems. Proceedings of the *International Conference on Methodologies in Housing Research, Stockholm Sweden, 22-24 September 2003.*

[7]   Harvey J., 2000. Small area population estimation using Satellite Imagery. *Statistics in Transition*, 4 (4), pp. 611-633, 2000.

[8]   Hoffmann, C.; Steinnocher, K.; Kasanko, M.; Grubisic, R. (2002): The Role of GIS and very high Resolution Image Data as Planning Support Tools-Case Study of Belgrade. In: Manfred Schrenk (Hg./Ed.), MULTIMEDIAPLAN.AT & IEMAR, CORP2002 Proceedings, Band 2, Vol. 2, S. 375-378, TU Vienna.

[9]   Holloway S.R., Schumacher J., Redmond R.L. People & Place: Dasymetric Mapping Using Arc/Info. *Cartographic Design Using Arcview and Arc/info*, Missoula: University of Montana, Wildlife Spatial Analysis Lab, 1997.

[10] Tobler, W. (1979): Smooth pycnophylactic interpolation for geographical regions (with discussion). Journal of the American Statistical Association, 74, 519–536.

[11] Yuan Y., Smith R.M., Limp W.F. Remodeling census populations with spatial information from Landsat TM Imagery. Computers, Environment and Urban Systems, 21(3/4), pp. 245-258, 1997.

[12] Bumi P., Lewis M., Blake M. Estimating the population distribution using remotely sensed data, 10th Australasian Remote Sensing and Photogrammetry Conference Proceedings. (Abstract), 2000.

Survey on the transition in urban retailing space from the evolution of location choice by applying information technologies

H. C. Chang[1] & K. W. Tsou[2]
[1]*Department of Asset Science, Leader University, Taiwan*
[2]*Department of Urban Planning,*
National Cheng-Kung University, Taiwan

Abstract

The demand for traditional urban commercial space is mainly influenced by location choice theory which is dominated by the agglomerate economy. Recently, the popularity of information and communication technologies has formed a new operating pattern of e-commerce and has impacted the character of conventional location choice. This paper attempts to explore the relationship of the effect between the agglomerate economy and information technologies on retailing location choice. This study examines the extent of the application of e-commerce by conducting a questionnaire survey for various types of retail stores, constructing and analyzing the relationship between them from managers' cognitive viewpoints, and further clarifying possible transitions of urban commercial spaces in the information age.
Keywords: agglomerate economy, e-commerce, information technologies.

1   Introduction

To plan spatial use patterns and modes by combining the development and application of information and communication technology is one of the critical issues facing the sustainable management of cities. The means of information and communication technology have eventually made the city boundaries unintelligible, therefore a new space of flows has been formulated. Theoretically speaking, it is possible to associate with the world through a real-time system, and new economic and social activities which are not restricted by distance or time have emerged.

The conventional concept of urban spatial patterns is being challenged by these developing trends. Many economic, social, and cultural activities entering the network space have produced the living behavioral model of residents and the demand for urban space to create structural changes (Graham [1]; Garrison and Deakin [2]; Hall [3]).

Because e-commerce is becoming increasingly popular, conventional urban commercial space utilizes instantaneous information to lower inventory costs and save storage space, and it can contact each place's consumers without opening branches everywhere to save fixed costs for operating space. Therefore, we can predict that a new commercial space concept which differs from the tradition one will eventually be substituted for the conventional regional spatial structure.

Although some studies have argued that the demand for downtown business areas is declining (Wong [4]), there is no direct evidence to support this idea, and there is also a lack of comparative analyses for different businesses. Thus, the major concern of this article focuses on whether or not the decline in the agglomerate economy factor of retailing location choice has been affected by information technologies. We examined the informational suitability of various retail business patterns as the study object and constructed and analyzed the influential relationship of the agglomerate economy factor on location choice by the application of e-commerce to further clarify possible transitions of urban commercial space in the information age.

2 Retailing location choice vs. the agglomerate economy

The location choice of the retailing industry has long been mainly impacted by major factors of the agglomerate economy. Patterns of the agglomerate economy include the interior economy and external economy. The interior economy, also called the scale economy, means that long-term production and management costs will decline when the operation scale of the manufactory itself is expanding. The external economy can be classified into a localization economy and an urbanization economy.

The agglomerate economy of retail industry location mainly emphasizes the scale of sales marketing, which differs from the production-oriented efficacy of conventional industries. Therefore, the capability of the agglomerate economy primarily relies on the size of the market. The range of the size of the market depends on the scale and density of the population. At the same time, the population scale also reflects the degree of specialization for reducing transaction costs of hiring a labor force. Thus, the major factor influencing retail industry location is the degree of urbanization of the economy.

3 Information application vs. spatial location

The introduction of information technology has directly influenced the transition of urban land spatial location. Urban spaces have become more energetic, and some of the core business areas have gradually expanded to the surrounding suburbs, where small business districts have been built up (Wong [4]).

Hepworth [5] thought that the ability of telecommunications to substitute for transportation greatly depended on the conditions of time and space limitations which were changed by the urban activity system. The original locality advantage of a core business area which is closer to the market has been exterminated by the popularity of communication networks. Non-core business areas have greater competitiveness due to lower rental costs.

Miller [6] considered that network shopping will cause conventional mega-supermarkets to lose their superiority. Roulac [7] pointed out that technological innovations have created large-scale retail markets on a global scale, and this means that consumers must pay more attention to service and spatially oriented exhibitive sales functions. The monopolization of spatial locations is no longer important.

On the demand side of retailing space, Burt [8] thought that the impact of e-commerce on spatial dimensions can be observed from two directions: one is the linear decrease in substantial space demand, while the other one is the reduction in the operating function of some assets which further indirectly reduce the demand for those assets. As to retail real estate, the shopping mall has experienced the greatest impacts caused by e-commerce. It is anticipated that the substantial retailing floor area of GAFO in 2005 (which includes the industries of general, apparel, furniture, and others) will be diminished by 15% to 17%. Baen [9] considered that when network shopping becomes even more popular, commuting trips by consumers to substantial stores will decrease, and impulsive consumption will drop. The lower the profit of a merchant is, the greater the competition will be, which may cause a decrease in the demand for retail real estate and increase the vacancy rate. Researches pointed out that the current percentage of network shopping only occupies a small portion of the entire retailing industry. Even if network shopping grows rapidly, the present retailing space will become part of the network sales channel to enable the handling of goods received and after-sales service. Furthermore, when the profit of network shopping increases, the rental affordability also enlarges, which will cause an increase in the demand for sales space. Bakos [10] optimistically thought that network shopping unexpectedly has the possibility of increasing the demand for retailing space. One reason for this is that the existing brand recognition from a substantial store will make distribution channels more diversified and mutually reinforcing; and second is that competition from the network will enable the merchant employing more-efficient and cheaper services to attract consumers to increase consumption, thus continually investing in the store.

To summarize the aforementioned literature, the dramatic development in information technology has changed human being's commercial activity models. The retail merchant can utilize real-time information to seek lower costs and more-efficient operation patterns. Simulated stores of the network break through the restrictions of timing, space, and location essential to past operations, and under the boundless expansion of the variety and volume of merchandise, information technology has been substituted for face-to-face interactions between human beings. The agglomerate economic efficacy brought about by conventional urbanization may change any time. Information has reduced the significance of transportation costs, and workers are no longer greatly concentrated in the city, thus the phenomenon of center removal has obviously impacted the effect of the agglomerate economy.

4 Methodology for estimating relationships

This study uses a questionnaire survey based on managers' subjective cognition. The pattern of information application is separated into transition and influences of the agglomerate economic effect on traditional retailing location choice.

4.1 Establishment of information application and the agglomerate economy model

This paper employs static cross-sectional data to analyze and compare information technologies of various industries and different comparative benefits which are formed by the agglomerate economy on location choice. The model is presented here:

$$Y = \alpha + \beta f(x_i) + r D_{t-1} + \varepsilon_i;$$

where Y is the variable of agglomerate economy,
$f(x_i)$ is the production function of the information application variable for number i,
D_{t-1} is a dummy variable of the t type of urban pattern,
α, β, and γ are regression coefficients, and
ε_i is a residual item.

X_i represents the variable of applied information technology which includes information search technology (information flow), transition technology (monetary flow), goods receiving technology (material flow), etc. $f(X_i)$ represents the production function of each aforementioned information application technology. Due to the patterns of production function differing according to various industries and areas, this article initially selects the Cobb-Douglas production function to conduct the analysis and discussion.

4.2 Analysis of the relationship model for information application and the agglomerate economy

In the analysis of the retailing industry, patterns based on former investigations of the degree to which e-commerce is employed are classified into the following patterns. First, there is the deeper specified merchandise pattern such as traveling, ticket affairs, and commodities of 3C; its application popularity for e-commerce is the highest. Second, the currently developing degree of general specified merchandise, such as computer software, books, films, and music, for e-commerce is common; while for lesser specified merchandise such as drinks, foods, flowers, etc., the development extent of e-commerce is lower.

In the process of analysis, parameter correction was first conducted according to the overall investigation sample of the retailing industry; then three kinds of retailing industries were targeted to separately carry out parameter modification and determine the sign of each coefficient by an empirical method to probe its theoretical meaning as well as to explore comparisons of influential effects by various patterns of different merchandise.

5 Empirical analysis

The study object was the Taiwan area, and a sample survey was undertaken at a standard of confidence level of 95% and a sampling error of 5%. The results are analyzed here.

To the retail industry as a whole, the relationship of information application input to the agglomerate economy showed significance ($p < 0.05$), meaning that information application has already truly impacted the factor of location choice of the agglomerate economy. The sign of the coefficient (b < 0) indicates that the relationship of information application and the agglomerate economic factor is negative. The higher the degree of information application, the lower the influence of location will be in the agglomerate economy. This implies that the factor of location choice in the information age has actually already changed.

Table 1: Model of the agglomerate economy of various merchandise patterns and information applications.

	Transverse distance (α)	Information flow technology (β)	Monetary flow technology (β)	Material flow technology (β)
Total retailing industry	-5.7689 (-40.507)*	-0.3698 (2.337)*	-0.1068 (2.043)*	-0.4001 (4.588)*
Traveling ticket affairs (higher specification)	-1.6908 (-8.063)*	-0.4468 (3.387)*	-0.1856 (2.473)*	-0.3201 (2.443)*
Computer software (common specification)	-3.9852 (-14.263)*	-0.4633 (3.996)	-0.0557 (0.603)	-0.0038 (0.127)
General merchandise (lower specification)	-5.6089 (-19.593)*	-0.0983 (2.752)*	-0.0198 (0.927)	-0.0026 (-0.189)

* $p < 0.05$; ** $p < 0.01$.
Values in parentheses ( ) are t-values.

Next, the development degrees of e-commerce for different retail industries were compared and analyzed, and the model showed that the relationship of the first retailing industry pattern with the agglomerate economy was significant, while the relationships of the factors of the second and third retailing industries were unremarkable. This discloses that the retail industries with higher degrees of e-commerce will easily overcome the impact of the factor of location choice of the agglomerate economy, and also implies that they possess greater flexibility in the spatial dimension for the location model.

As to the information technology orientation, a discussion is conducted on three parts of shopping behavior of information search, transaction processing, and goods receiving to substitute for the traditional retail industry. Preliminary research discovered that the three kinds of industry all express significance on the function of submitting information search technology, while regarding the technologies of transaction (monetary flow) and receiving (material flow), neither shows a notable status. This implies that general merchants have confirmed that the information flow technology is apparently reducing the factor of location agglomeration, possibly because current network search technologies are being popularly employed; therefore, the results are quite clear. Some doubts still exist as to the proportion of the on-line payment transaction technology or network merchandise delivery technology being employed, but they are considered to currently be having little impact on the effect of location in the agglomerate economy.

6 Summary and conclusions

6.1 Conclusions

According to the built-in model and a preliminary investigative analysis, the conclusions of this paper are summarized here.

1. The popularity of information technology application has impacted the location and spatial arrangement of retail industries. The study shows that a more-flexible phenomenon exists which is created by location. In the past, the demand side of the urbanization economy emphasized restrictions of location choice, but changes in space demand have occurred with input from utilization of information technologies. It is possible that new structural characters for spatial patterns of retail industries will be created in the age of information in the future.

2. The degrees of development of e-commerce for various retail industries present varied effects on location agglomerate economic factors which are accompanied by whether or not the product is suitable for network sales with higher specifications. Our preliminary study found that retail industries are enjoying greater popularity with the application of e-commerce, and the influence of technological applications on the agglomerate economy is more noticeable. This reveals that the various retail industries have endured the discrepancies of structural characters of merchandising and differences of fitness exist for e-commerce, which also enable the variations caused by the flexibility of location choice.

3. This study found that only the function of information search technology has

exhibited a notable influence on location agglomeration in a discussion of impacts on patterns of information technology applications to retail industries. Because it is possibly being affected by the technology recognition of the merchant and whether or not there is doubt about its function, this part has to wait until utilization of information technology becomes more popular, then we can further analyze its ability to influence these factors.

6.2 Suggestions

1. This article is a preliminary study which only attempts to examine a portion of the retail industry as its research target, and the suitability of information technology varies according to discrepancies in business patterns. Therefore, the character of commercial space in the age of information still needs to be explored and observed.
2. In this article, the measured model of the production coefficient for information technology employed the frequently used Cobb-Douglas production coefficient as the exercise base, and it is not further discussed. We suggest that a successive study be further conducted to discuss patterns of production coefficients.

References

[1]   Graham, S., Telecommunications and the Future of Cities: Debunking the Myths. Cities, 1 (14), pp.21-29, 1997.
[2]   Garrison, W. L. & Deakin E., Travel, Work, and Telecommunications: A View of the Electronics Revolution and ITS Potential Impacts. Transportation Research A, 4(22), pp.239-245, 1988.
[3]   Hall, P., The Future of Cities. Computers, Environment and Urban Systems, 23, pp.173-185, 1999.
[4]   Wong, T. C., The Changing Role of the Central Business District in the Digital Era: The Future of Singapore's New Financial District. Land Use Policy, 21, pp.33-44, 2004.
[5]   Hepworth, M. E., Planning for the Information City: the Challenge and Response. Urban Studies, 4(27), pp.537-558, 1990.
[6]   Miller, N. G., Telecommunications Technology and Real Estate. Real Estate Finance, 13(2), pp.18-24, 1996.
[7]   Roulac, S. E., Retail Real Estate in the 21st Century: Information Technology + Time Consciousness + Unintelligent Stores = Intelligent Shopping Not!. The Journal of Real Estate Research, 9(1), pp.125-150, 1998.
[8]   Burt S., Sparks L., E-commerce and the Retail Process: A Review. Journal of Retailing and Consumer Services, 10, pp.275-286, 2003.
[9]   Baen, J. S., The Effects of Technology on Retail Sales, Commercial Property Values and Percentage Rents. Journal of Real Estate Portfolio Management, 6(2), pp.185-201, 2000.
[10]   Bakos Y., The Emerging Landscape for Retail E-Commerce. The Journal of Economic Perspectives, 15(1), pp.69-80, 2001.

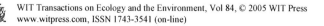

Homes for the future – accommodating one-person households the sustainable way

J. Williams
Bartlett School of Planning, University College London, U.K.

Abstract

Recent growth in one-person households in the UK has led the government to seek more sustainable housing models for accommodating them. Cohousing could provide one option. However, cohousing has been relatively unsuccessful in the UK so far. This paper sets out to prove that cohousing is sustainable and that it also has the potential to be a popular housing form amongst one-person households. It goes on to explore how development of cohousing communities could be encouraged in the future through a more proactive planning system.
Keywords: sustainable housing, one-person households, pro-active planning, cohousing.

1 Introduction

Ever since the release of the 1996-based UK household projections, the question of how best to accommodate the growth in small households and one-person households in particular has been a key planning issue. The issue is not simply one of accommodation, but of sustainability. UK Government guidance now calls for new residential developments to be environmentally and socially sustainable, for domestic resource consumption and waste to be reduced, and for local communities to be re-invigorated. Thus accommodation for one-person households would ideally encourage lower levels of resource consumption and waste production and greater local social capital. Resource consumption in particular appears to be an issue for smaller households. According to a growing body of research, increases in domestic consumption of space (land), energy, materials, packaging, and goods and the production of waste are linked with an increase in small households (Table 1). Thus an increase in one-person households is likely to result in a significant increase in domestic resource consumption and waste production.

Table 1:   Comparison of consumption of energy, materials and production of waste annually per capita in households of different sizes (one-person household =100).

	1 person	2 persons	4 persons	Data Source
Products per capita	100	75	62.5	INCEPEN
Packaging per capita	100	75	58	INCEPEN
Indirect energy per capita	100	63	42	INCEPEN
Electricity per capita	100	68.5	45	Noorman and Uiterkamp
Gas per capita	100	64.5	39	Noorman and Uiterkamp
Solid waste per capita	100	88.5	75.5	Noorman and Uiterkamp

Source: compiled using data from ICPEN [1], Noorman and Uiterkamp [2].

Research completed in the UK, Williams [3] showed that an increase in one-person households would result in a significant increase in both domestic energy and land consumption. The research showed that one-person households consumed 23-77 per cent more electricity, 38-54 per cent more gas, and 45-65 per cent more space than individuals in two- or four-person (all-adult) households, respectively. These estimates are likely to be conservative as they are based on current consumption patterns. The research also found that resource consumption was likely to increase in the future among one-person households especially as the group became more affluent; as married people began to live separately from their spouses (since they tended to double-up on all of their resources in two homes); and as the consumption culture penetrated further across the generations.

Research (Putnam [4]; Williams [5]) does not suggest that there is likely to be a decline in local social capital with an increase in one-person households living in residential areas. Marital status, employment status, social status, location, and age appear to be more likely to influence local social capital than household size. However, according to research undertaken by the OECD [6] local social capital in the UK does appear to declining, in terms of trust and informal socialising among all household types. The main driver for re-building local social capital has been the various social benefits it brings, such as increased safety and security, increased mutual support networks, and so on; but there are also benefits to be gained in terms of domestic resource consumption, waste reduction, and pro-environmental behaviour (Williams [5 and 7]; Meltzer [8]; Pretty and Ward [9]). Thus in both social and environmental terms it is important that higher levels of local social capital are achieved in residential development for one-person households if they are to be sustainable.

2   Cohousing – one novel solution?

In recent years the UK Government has been searching for more sustainable housing options. One rather novel option has so far been over looked – cohousing. Cohousing is a model that offers high levels of local social capital and pro-environmental behaviour (Williams [7]). It also offers considerable domestic resource savings and appears to be popular amongst one-person households (Williams [5] and [10]). Cohousing is a form of collaborative housing. It has both private units and indoor and outdoor common space. It combines the autonomy of private dwellings with the advantages of community living. It can be built at low, medium and high densities and in a variety of layouts, with a variety of tenure types. Communities can be new build or retrofit.

Social contact design (SCD) principles are used to encourage more casual social encounters and increased opportunities for informal socialising cohousing communities (Williams [11]). The principles include:

– provision of indoor and outdoor communal facilities;
– good visibility into all communal spaces;
– car parking outside the community or car-free communities;
– gradual transitions between public and private space;
– provision of semi-private outdoor spaces close to private units for socialising; and
– positioning of key facilities and access points on walkways.

Generally the private dwellings tend to be smaller than average unit size (with limited facilities provided). However, the loss of space in the private unit is offset by the provision of communal facilities – for example communal kitchen/dining areas, a laundries, gyms, workshops/hobby rooms, guest bedrooms, entertainment rooms, gardens, and storage space, which are available for all residents and their guests to use. This enables space and facilities that are normally under utilised in private units (e.g. storage space, gym, work space) to be more efficiently used by the community as a whole.

The role of residents is more participative, and they can be involved in the recruiting, development, and design of the community, depending on which development model is adopted (Table 2). In the standard model (adopted in the UK) all the activities are resident led. In the streamline model (adopted in the USA) the development and design processes are developer led. In the speculative model all activities are developer led. Resident involvement in these activities helps to develop local social networks and build capacity in the community. However, it also slows down the development process and increases the cost of the units. In addition, without a developer all the financial risk of the development will be borne by the residents.

In all models, residents are involved in managing and maintaining communities. They are involved in the maintenance and management of indoor and outdoor communal spaces; the preparation of communal meals (one to three times per week); the organisation of social events within the community; and liaising with the wider community. Residents are also involved in ongoing design and recruitment decisions made within the community. All decisions are made using the consensus decision-making process.

Table 2: The development models.

Model	Standard cohousing - self development model	Core-group Cohousing	Streamlined Cohousing	Speculative Cohousing
Description of model	Resident led	Two phase Model – resident led.	Group and developer partnership.	Developer led
Community Visioning	All residents involved	Core group of residents involved	All residents involved	Developer
Recruitment	All residents involved	Core group of residents involved	All residents involved with professional help	Developer
Legal structures and financing	Resident led with professional help	Resident led (core group) with professional help	Developer led	Developer
Design Process	Resident led with professional help	Resident led (design committee) with professional help	Developer led with resident input.	Developer
Community development	Resident led with professional help prior to living in community and throughout life of community	Resident led with professional help prior to living in community and throughout life of community	Resident led with professional help prior to living in community and throughout life of community	Resident led once living in community

Source: Davis [12].

Although still very restricted in its coverage the cohousing model (in all it's forms) is becoming more widespread. Various forms of cohousing can be found in Europe, USA and the Pacific Rim. This has partly been facilitated by the diversity of the cohousing models developed globally. Supportive governments that believe cohousing to be a more sustainable form of accommodation have also encouraged the spread. For example in Denmark, Sweden and Holland cohousing principles are introduced into all new housing developments, encouraged through design guidance, a pro-active planning process and financial assistance from the governments.

Cohousing exhibits many of the characteristics of new urbanism both in terms of objectives and design strategies (Torres-Antonini [13]). Its ability to deliver the objectives of new urbanism suggest that although cohousing is currently a restricted housing form (playing a limited role in housing provision) it could well become a more common in the future. Finally the social, environmental and economic benefits of cohousing make it a more sustainable housing model and attractive to governments.

Table 3:   Sustainability benefits of cohousing.

Sustainability objective	Detailed empirical research - testing the theories	Research to support this
Strong social networks and cohesion	Cohousing design (social contact design) positively impacts on social behaviour. In cohousing communities informal and formal social factors and personal characteristics influence use of communal facilities and level of social interaction that in turn increases social capital. Cohousing helps people to organise themselves as a residential group to overcome the alienation of modern neighbourhoods by building mutual support and sociable relations between households.	Torres-Antonini [13]; Williams [5]; Brenton [14].
Social Inclusion	Cohousing communities tend to be diverse in terms of household size but not in terms of education, income, religion, ethnicity. However there were positive attempts to be inclusive in selection procedures. Communities also made efforts to integrate into the wider community. Various approaches were adopted: canvassing local people about the development proposal; recruiting residents form the local community to live in the development; supporting local services / facilities (e.g. shops, schools, etc); opening the community facilities and events to visitors from the locality; becoming involved in local social networks (e.g. local religious groups, parents associations in schools, clubs and societies).	Williams [5]; Brenton [14].
Pro-environmental behaviour	High levels of social capital in cohousing has encouraged pro-environmental behaviours in cohousing:	Meltzer [8]; Williams [5]
Reduce resource consumption	Significant space, energy and good savings can be made by those living in cohousing. On average 31% space savings; 57% electricity savings and 8% good savings. Residents tend to share second cars and thus ownership of second cars is lower. Resident ownership of washing machines, tumble driers and freezers was reduced by 25% by living in cohousing communities because people tended to use communal laundry facilities. Ownership of DIY and gardening tools was also low, again because the tools were shared communally. Ownership of privately owned lawn mowers reduced by 75% when residents moved into cohousing.	Williams [5]; Meltzer [8]
Well-being	The benefits of living in cohousing include an increase in well-being resulting from increased opportunities for socializing, support, security, sharing chores, sharing expertise, living with people with similar interests, inter-dependent living. These benefits are built through a combination of social contact design and process (resident involvement in decision-making and community formation. Well-being is generated through empowerment – empowerment model.	Williams [5]; Meltzer [8]
Affordable lifestyle	Cohousers highlighted significant savings in daily expenditure as a result of sharing facilities, vehicles and goods.	Williams [5]
Affordable accommodation	Higher capital costs borne by resident or developer. However, there are opportunities to reduce costs through restricting customisation and altering the development model. Also higher re-sale values.	Williams [5]

3   Sustainability benefits

A review of theory, cohousing literature and empirical research suggests that cohousing is potentially a more sustainable form of housing (Williams [7]). With stronger more cohesive communities, more affordable lifestyles, higher levels of resident well-being and pro-environmental behaviour cohousing has a lot to offer in terms of fulfilling sustainability objectives (Table 3).

Strong social networks are built in cohousing communities through SCD, capacity building and high levels of participation among residents in all processes. These networks are further developed through the adoption of a non-hierarchical social structure and the formal organisation of communal activities. This in turn creates more cohesive communities, a greater sense of well-being amongst residents (associated with affordable lifestyles greater opportunities to socialise, stronger support networks and greater security) and encourages more pro-environmental behaviour.

Pro-environmental behaviour is encouraged in cohousing in a number of ways, including:
– Strong social networks facilitate reciprocal learning within the community - raises residents' awareness of environmental problems and practices.
– Strong social networks effectively generate pressure on residents' to adopt more pro-environmental behaviour, i.e. peer group pressure.
– Acting as a community enables environmental technology / schemes to operate more effectively.
– Visible environmental benefits can be seen at a local level that sustains pro-environmental behaviour.

In the case of one-person households cohousing has a significant advantage in enabling a reduction in individual resource consumption. Domestic resource consumption is significantly lower among one-person households living in cohousing compared with those living in self-contained accommodation, particularly in terms of electricity and space consumption. This is because one-person households living in cohousing have small private units and share communal facilities (for example laundry, kitchen, and dining facilities) and thus space, energy (for heating, lighting, appliance use), and appliances (especially kitchen and laundry appliances). In addition, activity spaces that would generally be under-utilised by one-person households if provided in their private unit (for example guest bedrooms) are provided in communal facilities. Under-utilised goods (gardening equipment, DIY tools, seasonal goods, etc.) are also shared between households.

4   Market potential

Currently demand for cohousing in the UK is very limited, and so it is difficult to predict future demand for it among one-person households based on UK evidence. However, evidence from California (Williams [5]) suggests that there is potential demand for a number of reasons. One-person households living in cohousing communities in California were surveyed to determine the factors that had attracted them to live in cohousing. California was chosen for the study because of the high percentage of one-person households living in cohousing. The research found that cohousing offers one-person households the opportunity to live independently in a community. Those who live alone tend to rely more on their local community than larger households for social interaction and support. Cohousing offers both. One-person households are a diverse group, and so their needs vary greatly. According to the results of the California study, cohousing appeals to a wide range of one-person households for a variety of reasons.

For the elderly it offers a safe and secure living environment, with support networks that enable them to live independently and healthily. For the young it offers the opportunity to socialise in their locality with others with similar interests, and gives them access to various leisure and entertainment facilities. For the more affluent it offers the opportunity to be involved in designing their homes and neighbourhood. It also offers safe and secure living environments, with greater social caché that enhances resale values for properties. For the less affluent it provides access to facilities that would otherwise be unavailable, reduces living expenses (which are shared within the community), and provides some financial security.

For single women in particular it provides attractions in that it gives them access to kids, pets, and families. For those who are working and single men, cohousing provides "convenience living". It helps busy people to meet others in their locality "convenience socialising". It also enables residents to share time-consuming chores (maintenance, cooking, gardening, etc), "convenience meals" cooked on a rota by others in the community are particular popular amongst single males. Thus cohousing has the potential to be a popular accommodation option among one-person households.

5   Pro-active planning to facilitate cohousing

The social and environmental benefits of cohousing should make it very attractive to planners. Using four UK case studies that included communities at all stages in the planning process (both new-build and retrofit), research was undertaken to determine the extent to which the planning system has prevented, slowed, or facilitated cohousing development (Williams [5]). It found that although the UK planning system itself doesn't create barriers to the development of cohousing, it doesn't positively promote it. A more pro-active planning system could be used to facilitate the development of cohousing communities or the inclusion of cohousing principles (more specifically SCD, capacity building exercises and resident participation in the creation and management of their community) into residential development. This could be achieved in the following manner.

5.1 Material considerations

Policy, design guidance, development plans, building regulations, and land use classifications could be used to support cohousing, SCD principles or encouragement of greater resident participation in the planning and management of their local areas by making them material considerations (i.e. a matter which should be taken into account in deciding on a planning application). As a material consideration planning authorities can require the development of cohousing communities or application of the principles through section 106 agreements (i.e. planning gain – where the developer agrees to provide additional benefits, usually in the form of related development supplied at their expense) in new developments.

Design guidance could be used to specify the use of SCD in mainstream housing developments. To an extent it already is in the UK, for example residential design guidance specifies higher densities, reduced parking spaces, and parking on the periphery of housing projects. However guidance does not cover other cohousing principles including the provision of communal facilities or the division of public and private space. These additional features could be specified in guidance.

Preference for residential development based on cohousing principles (SCD, capacity building and resident participation in all processes) could also be expressed in development plans (site specific or general statement), making it a material consideration. Sites particularly for cohousing projects could also be identified. The cohousing principles could be reinforced through the sequential test for housing (a set of national criteria used to reinforce sustainable housing development in the UK).

In addition, community strategies (an action plan for the economic, environmental and social well-being of local areas in the UK) could be used to promote greater resident involvement in local areas. The provision of communal facilities in residential developments could be specifically addressed by setting minimum unit sizes in building regulations and significantly lowering those limits (to increase densities) if communal facilities are provided in a development (as the major barrier to the provision of communal facilities in new-build development is the profit loss to the developer resulting from building at lower densities).

One further problem that has been encountered in the UK is the classification of cohousing. In some instances planning authorities have separately classified communal facilities in cohousing (especially office space and leisure facilities) from the residential element. This has had implications for obtaining sites, for parking and infrastructural requirements, which in some cases have actually prevented development. Communal facilities should be classified as ancillary uses in order to overcome this problem.

5.2 The planning process

Fast-tracking applications that adopt cohousing principles would also help to promote development. This would reduce the development times and thus reduce the risks and costs to the investors (developers or residents). Certainly the length of the planning process was identified as a problem in the UK by cohousing groups and developers. Greater resident involvement in the design and management of their locality could be encouraged through a more inclusive and facilitative planning system. Residents could be encouraged to take a greater responsibility for their local environment, while planners could adopt a more facilitative role.

Educational programmes and capacity-building exercises for residents and professionals will be needed to provide them with the skills for their new roles. In the UK there is a long history of top-down decision-making processes, thus fairly radical cultural and institutional changes would be needed to encourage a truly bottom-up approach. Resident groups will also need to be given greater autonomy in decision-making and encouraged to be more proactive.

5.3 Allocating sites

In addition to sites for cohousing development being identified in development plans, planners could allocate sites (owned by the local authority) through the Best Value programme, as one of the objectives of Best Value programme in local government is to ensure sustainable development (if they regarded cohousing as a more sustainable housing form). Allocating sites for cohousing development through the Best Value Programme would reduce land costs to a developer thus releasing funds for SCD features and resident capacity-building exercises.

5.4 Identifying funding streams

Planners could also usefully identify suitable funding streams for demonstration projects, retrofitting SCD features in existing residential developments and resident capacity-building. However, these funds will need to be made more widely available and not just targeted at deprived areas as they are currently. Tax breaks could also be given to developers adopting SCD features, including resident involvement in the development process and capacity-building in new-build projects.

6 A sustainable way

Is cohousing one solution to accommodating one-person households in a sustainable way? This research certainly suggests that it is a more socially and environmentally sustainable housing form, which has proved popular amongst one-person households. Thus it could provide a sustainable and potentially popular accommodation option for one-person households in the UK. Adoption of some of the cohousing principles in residential areas and in new-build housing developments would also help to build environmentally and socially sustainable communities. This paper suggests that the development of such communities could be encouraged by a more proactive and facilitative approach by planners in the UK.

References

[1]   International Consumer Protection and Enforcement Network (2001) *Towards Greener Households Producers, Packaging and Energy.* London: ICPEN.

[2]   Noorman, K and Uiterkamp, T (1998) *Green Households: Domestic Consumers, Environment and Sustainability.* London: Earthscan Publications

[3]   Williams, J (2005) *One-person households – a resource time bomb?* in Ecosystems and Sustainable Development, Advances in Ecological Sciences, Vol 22. ISBN: 1-84564-013-6.

[4]   Putnam, R (2000) *Bowling Alone: The Collapse and Revival of American Community.* Simon & Schuster, New York.

[5]   Williams, J (2003) *Homes for the Future – A Means for Managing the Singletons Consumption Crisis.* Unpublished PhD Thesis, Bartlett School of Planning, University College London.

[6]   Organisation for Economic Co-operation and Development *(2001) The Well-being of Nations: The Role of Human and Social Capital,* OECD: Paris.

[7]   Williams, J (2005) Sun, Surf and Sustainability – Comparison of the Cohousing Experience in California and the UK, *International Planning Studies Journal,* 10/2.

[8]   Meltzer, G (2000) *Cohousing: Towards Social and Environmental Sustainability.* Unpublished PhD Thesis, Department of Architecture, University of Queensland, Brisbane, Australia.

[9]   Pretty, J and Ward, H (2001) Social capital and the environment. *World Development,* 29 (2), pp.209-227

[10]   Williams, J (2005) Homes for the Future – Accommodating One-Person Households the Sustainable Way! *Town and Country Planning Journal* April 2005.

[11]   Williams, J (2005) Designing Neighbourhoods for Social Interaction – The Case of Cohousing, *Journal of Urban Design,* vol 10/3.

[12]   Davis, Andrea Paloma (2001) *Creating Community: Development and Design Alternatives in Cohousing.* Unpublished Masters Thesis, University of Washington.

[13]   Torres-Antonini, M (2001) *Our common house: using the built environment to develop supportive communities,* unpublished PhD Thesis, Graduate School University of Florida.

[14]   Brenton, M (1998) *We're in Charge: Cohousing Communities of Older People in The Netherlands – Lessons for Britain?* The Policy Press, Bristol.

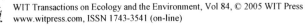

Towards a sustainable and tourism-led urban regeneration objective: Eminonu historical city core

P. Özden[1] & S. Turgut[2]
[1]Department of Public Administration, Istanbul University, Turkey
[2]Department of Urban and Regional Planning,
Yıldız Technical University, Turkey

Abstract

As one of the oldest settlement areas of Istanbul located within the Historical Peninsula, Eminonu District encompasses a highly distinctive and privileged structure with its historical assets, the considerably different functions undertaken, and the cultural and social diversity it shelters as also accompanied by the rich cultural and natural entities reflected on physical space. However, despite all these assets which Eminonu possesses, the district could not escape from becoming a "deprived" area where serious levels of urban decay are experienced especially in social terms.   In this paper, following the brief information and examination of the existing structure and organizational system, the incrementally-given planning decisions for specific parts of the area in question will be considered. In light of these decisions that will be analyzed and the evaluations made accordingly, the "tourism-led" regeneration objective in a socially "deprived" area under "decay" will be scrutinized in the context of sustainability and related proposals will be revealed.
Keywords: tourism-led regeneration, urban decline and deprivation, housing development policy.

1 Introduction

The Eminonu Region is one of the oldest settlement areas of Istanbul. It is located in the "Historical Peninsula" accepted as a cultural heritage with the intercultural civilizations and values it has embraced for many centuries, has a unique and distinguished structure with its historical values, many different functions it has assumed, the cultural and social diversity it contains, and many cultural and natural assets that have also been reflected in the physical space as well. "The Historical Peninsula" and the Eminonu District in paeticular attracts more attention with its trade centers and trade functions. The general outlines of the trade sector in the "Historical Peninsula" is determined when informal trade caused by tourism, which has a unique structure and the entertainment sector that is directed mainly by the tourism sector are added to these functions (Kaptan [1]).

Historically, the Eminonu region has always been the core of the city in terms of trade as well as production and trading of traditional handcrafts. It is the most important center of Istanbul for retail and wholesale of textile and leather products, furnishings, food, jewellery, wickerwork and woodwork, carpets and rugs. Resulting from the commercial identity of the region, banks, offices, insurance companies, the Chamber of Commerce, hotels and restaurants have chosen to settle in this area. As a traditional center, it displays quite a strong structure against the new centers (CBD) of the city which develop in an organized manner. However, because of its proprietorship structure and the announcement of the Historical Peninsula as a registered area as a whole, it has not become attractive for global investments which prefer to shape urban space as they wish and Eminonu has gradually become an urban deprivation area.

2 Potentials, opportunities and threats

As mentioned above in the previous section, both the Historical Peninsula and the Eminonu region have a very lively identity. It is one of the most significant opportunities for Istanbul with the values and potentials that it possesses. The region, with its regional characteristics, is a very special area incorporating many opportunities, threats and significant potentials that are in contradiction with each other. The region incorporating different functions such as housing, tourism – entertainment, wholesale and retail, commerce, manufacturing, education – culture, services, press-broadcast, administration etc. is also a significant meeting and distribution point with its characteristics of being a "destination" and "transfer". The diversity in physical texture possesses a dimension incorporating sub-groups in socioeconomic structure as well, such as social differences, religious differences, differences in the level of economic income, those having settled after migration from rural areas, minorities, singles, "others".

3 The analysis of the planning process and policies directed at the region

3.1 The Historical Peninsula and the Eminonu Region within plans with higher scales

To date, two plans with higher scales covering the Istanbul Metropolitan Area have been prepared. There are no special provisions and decisions with regard to the Historical Peninsula in the Regulatory Plan dated 1980 for the Istanbul

Metropolitan Area. However, the provision reading "Adjustments shall be made in the urban areas constituting the historical core and the construction plans shall be implemented accordingly in accordance with the decisions of the Civil Heritage and Monuments Supreme Committee" is included in a general sense with regard to the historical urban areas.

The plan dated 1995 has foreseen the development of the Historical Peninsula as a historical, tourism and retail trade center. It emphasizes topics such as shift of historical residential areas in the Eminonu region and Central Business District functions outside the city walls, their protection from the constraints of CBD and prevention of their destruction and vanishing, restoration of dilapidated areas, decentralization of unfavorable functions causing dilapidation, decentralization of small industries, warehouses and manufacturing as they destruct historical texture. Also, the boundaries of tourism centers within the Historical Peninsula were determined according to the decree of the Council of Ministers and they have a determining role in the plan decisions to be adopted.

3.2 The planning process of the Historical Peninsula

The Regulatory Construction Plan aimed at preserving the Historical Peninsula was prepared in 1990. The purpose of the plan was indicated as saving the Historical Peninsula from being a "Central Business District (CBD)" and an urban crowd area and to transform it into a living historical, cultural, tourism and recreation area that is integrated with its settled population". However, the plan was abolished on grounds that there was no public benefit in the implementation of the plan as a consequence of a lawsuit filed by the Chamber of Architects.

While this process was carrying on, all of the Historical Peninsula was announced as a registered area. Then, the Planning and Construction Management of the Istanbul Metropolitan Municipality started planning activities. After a long process, the plan has just been approved at the beginning of May in 2005.

3.3 The policies foreseen for Eminonu by the plans of the Historical Peninsula

The Regulatory Construction Plan dated 1964 with a scale of 1/5000 for the Region within the city walls: The Historical Peninsula is divided into parts according to its different functions and features. The plan does not include decisions directed for the Eminonu region as a whole.

Istanbul Metropolitan Area Regulatory Plans dated 1980 with a scale of 1/50000: In the Plan, the following provision is included with reference to the Historical Urban Areas "For the urban areas constituting the historical core, adaptations shall be made in accordance with the decisions of the Civil Heritage and Monuments Supreme Committee when needed and the approved construction plans will be implemented". Since there are no special provisions and decisions about the Historical Peninsula in the Regulatory Plan dated 1980, there are also no specific plans for Eminonu as well.

The Implementation and Construction Plans dated 1993 for Eminonu for Preservation Purposes with a scale of 1/500: Areas to be protected and different functions and structuring conditions for other areas were determined in these plans.

The Construction Plan dated 2005 for the preservation of the Historical Peninsula: The plan that was approved at the beginning of May 2005 was prepared with a more participatory comprehension when compared with previous planning works. The tools and planning principles directed towards the aim of the plan within the framework of general principles were determined with the effective participation of the actors concerned.

The plan puts forward basic decisions for the Eminonu region such as the decentralization of all functions (small manufacturing facilities and industries) that are not compatible with the cultural and historical identity of Eminonu, bringing functions that are identical with the identity of the region, removal of the reasons causing physical and social decline and dilapidation in Eminonu, transforming it from being an area of decline and dilapidation, preservation and development of socio-cultural functions, provision of their sustainability, etc.

It emphasizes that the determining factor for the development and sustainability of the Historical Peninsula is tourism and that this should definitely be take into consideration in the plan. Eminonu on the other hand is an important area that can undertake this mission. When the distribution of tourism areas are analyzed in the Regulatory Construction Plan for the Preservation of the Historical Peninsula, Eminonu catches attention with a share of 53.87% and 1.70% of the district area in tourism areas that covers only 1.03% in the whole Historical Peninsula. In Eminonu, prestige residence and housing functions are recommended for certain regions in order to attract the elite class for housing purposes. Newman [2] indicates that investments to prestige projects prefer city centers, hence areas within or close to cultural values and existing attraction points. In his opinion, the unfavorable parts of large projects are accepted widely and continue to be attractive and are significant for competing cities.

It is indicated in the plan that the commencement of trade and tourism in housing areas lead to the disappearance of the residents and to the transformation of housing areas to trade and tourism areas that provide higher returns. The plan dated 2005 foresees the development of Eminonu with a tourism identity but has also taken into consideration the point that the housing function should also be increased and that it should not be damaged from the tourism function.

4 Estimations about tourism-led regeneration and housing development strategies in the Eminonu region

Besides assuming the function of being the most fundamental center, Eminonu has a very strong potential both for housing and tourism functions due to the intensity of civil and monumental architectural examples and its special status within the city. However, balancing the functions of housing and tourism are among the basic problems in the region as also indicated in the Historical Peninsula Plan 2005.

4.1 Scenarios

The Plan of the Historical Peninsula was constituted on different scenarios. Each one of these scenarios foresees a different mission for the area. It seems useful to take a brief overview at the scenarios at this point:

Scenario 1: A trade identity is foreseen for the Historical Peninsula. The identity that the Historical Peninsula will gain when the existing situation continues will be based on a development based on housing and trade. It was assumed that there will be a development with emphasis on housing, trade and services as a consequence of the decentralization of functions such as manufacturing and warehousing that are harmful for the texture, environment and the identity of the area that are prerequisites.

Scenario 2: It aims to increase physical and social quality by establishing a tourism-based identity in the Historical Peninsula where the inventory of historical works of art is intensive. Furthermore, it was also aimed at encouraging high quality and culture-led tourism by planning large public buildings and large public areas on an urban scale as tourism oriented facilities. Also, it was aimed to provide contributions to trade by encouraging the development and diversification of tourism based trade. Housing areas were preserved, trade areas were decreased, and housing + boarding and trade + boarding functions were introduced with the tourism areas. Since the second scenario places more emphasis on tourism, there is a decrease in pure housing areas. Housing areas are decreased by 10% in the second scenario. The areas of existing boarding areas were increased by 21 times and it was made possible to increase the diversity of tourism and to construct boarding areas that can address all kinds of tourist profiles.

Scenario 3: The third scenario aims to evaluate the housing, cultural, tourism and trade functions in the Historical Peninsula, their distribution in a balanced manner, to liven up and provide the sustainability of areas with emphasis on old historical works. It was aimed to emphasize the historical and cultural identity that the Historical Peninsula bears for many centuries, to develop housing areas along with this identity.

Scenario 4: The fourth scenario ranks first in terms of cultural areas as it supports the revitalization of all historical art works and their use for cultural purposes. It foresees the combination of utopia, earthquake scenario or the ancient – modern synthesis, aims to emphasize the traces of the past 3 cultures (Roman, Byzantine and Ottoman) in the Historical Peninsula and to form a synthesis by also adding modern comprehension as well.

4.2 Tourism-led regeneration in Eminonu and development of housing areas

The plan dated 2005 emphasizes that the determining factor in the development and sustainability of the Historical Peninsula should be tourism and that this should absolutely be taken into consideration for all decisions related with the plan. Hence, while the plan comes up with different scenarios of its own, it indirectly accepts the 2nd scenario. Therefore, within the scope of this section, it would be useful to focus on the contributions of a tourism-oriented development in Eminonu and their effects on the development of housing areas.

One of the most important points that should not be forgotten within this framework is the changing situation of the tourist profile beside the internal dynamics of the region. "The findings of the tourism researches conducted lately have much more to say about the supply dimension of the matter rather than the demand dimension. However, there are also certain studies conducted, which focus on the growing cultural tourism sector. It is known that the profile of visitors coming to the cities is changing. Urban tourists are typically independent and experienced travelers that generally repeat their visits. They may prefer new locations that are outside the center and may also be attracted to prestigious spaces with architecture and ambience as well as certain points of attraction. What the urban tourists are in search of are the spaces necessary for consumption (Newman [2]). Comprehension of the characteristics of certain places needs to query how a number of certain factors are combined. At this point, history, environmental quality, opinions of the local population and consumption areas is important. The most important class that will contribute the support of locations is the "middle" class. Their interpretative qualities will provide an opportunity for the revaluation of all the potentials of the area (Newman [2]).

The sustainability of the Eminonu region within the framework of its core values is directly related with provision of sustainability of culture in societies, taking into consideration and development of all values that were present in the past in a conscious and multidimensional manner for this purpose and coming up with rooted policies for this purpose as indicated by Ergun [3] as well.

Within this framework, all decisions and strategies to be developed in this context should be interpreted in accordance with these data. The matter is a very serious and comprehensive process that should be dealt with within the framework of logic of planning. The existence of such an extensive plan based on comprehensive analysis is an advantage for the region. However, there is need to concentrate on the nuances here. When the 2nd scenario emphasized by the system, central government and departments concerned is analyzed by keeping these points in mind, it is observed that no special emphasis is placed on the housing function and the weight is placed on the tourism function. However, searching for a balance that will provide an opportunity for the coexistence of tourism and residences is indispensable. It is natural that the tourism values and tourism function of the region is emphasized. However, the use of large buildings for tourism purposes and the settlement of prospective 5 star hotels with a large volume, which most probably belong to a chain and displaying a dominant character will not only damage the identity of the area but will also harm the unique identity of becoming a mystical synthesis of the east and west.

Strengths: The tourism function will provide economic returns to the region, strengthen its domestic economy and help its development, intensification of tourism in such a sub-region and attracting investments in different scales and profiles will provide action for the region and transform it into a center of prestige and attraction as the most important historical center of the city. This tendency will be able to attract large scale projects and prestige projects into the region. The profile with respect to proprietorship of houses will also change in the region, the status of which will improve and a movement of socialization will be observed where the higher income and culture groups will also be attracted.

Urban regeneration movements will be observed in the areas that especially have a very intensive potential culturally. The areas that are desolate in the evenings and the criminal regions in the existing structure will be able to get rid of these negative points. The region will be able to get rid of the social sub-groups that impose a problem within the existing structure. It will be possible to preserve, renew and enliven the historical values and architectural inventory of the region. It will be possible to enliven certain unique areas of activity that are starting to be lost within the region. The historical, cultural and geographical data of the area are very strong for prestige projects and large-scale investments.

Weaknesses: The social context of the area is being neglected. Since the boundaries of tourism are not determined, the socioeconomic level and quality of the area may be under threat against the danger of a negative growth in tourism. The area may be treated and perceived as an "object" in time with the pressure of tourism, which may damage the identity of the areas as well as the existing potentials. One of the most important features of the area is the fact that it incorporates housing areas belonging to different periods and different cultures. Weakening this function will automatically cause the loss of certain values that have existed within the historical process.

Opportunities: The traditional identity of the area and the potentials that it has are strong. The potentials concerned are supported not only by national but also by international institutions and organizations. The stock of buildings in the area is very diverse and strong in terms of cultural and historical aspects. The existence of large buildings provides an advantage for the fulfillment of certain functions.

Threats: Some problems may be encountered with respect to making the region attractive. In the event that the existing large structures are used for tourism purposes, there will be a profile for a tourism facility that is not compatible with the identity of the area. This structure will lead to an outcome that is not compatible with the existing identity of the region and the tourist profile. The prospective extreme and uncontrolled growth that may take place in the tourism sector will lead to the exclusion of housing functions as a whole. The area that has adopted a tendency of nobility against tourism will lose its existing structure for the social profile. The users of houses belonging to the upper income group, which will replace the middle class, will lead to a social transformation in the region and the process that will start will directly affect the dynamics of the region. Along with tourism, social erosion will be inevitable, the tourism texture will pose a threat for the area and damage historical texture with the pressure of reaching a spatial structure. An economic activity such as tourism, which has high economic returns will increase speculative actions. It will be necessary to plan the social and technical fitting areas that the high number of visitors who will come to the area shall need and to organize the technical service areas to meet all needs.

5 Conclusion and assessment

In conclusion, the Eminonu region possesses the potential to set up its future absolutely with tourism. However, there is a need for a tourism scenario that will not be in contradiction with the scale and general identity of the region within a profile that is compatible with the region. When we evaluate the matter by taking into consideration the givens and scenarios of the Historical Peninsula, the conclusions and recommendations given below are reached:

Within the strategic tourism planning studies to be conducted for the whole city in general, the Eminonu region should be handled in a manner that is different from other regions with its special and unique location. When the question of "Should Eminonu be an area of transformation in a tourism oriented manner in the future" is asked and the existing potential in the region is reviewed, it is possible to conclude that a transformation in a tourism oriented manner is inevitable. Notwithstanding the foregoing, Eminonu, just like the whole Historical Peninsula, has to adopt a means of development incorporating the housing identity as well in order to provide its sustainability. It has to develop and emphasize this identity with the measures that it will take in the medium and long run. When a correct balance in terms of use and functioning is established between tourism-housing in the region, the use of tourism and housing shall provide contributions to the traditional identity of the Eminonu region and will assume an effective role for the provision of sustainability. The first thing that should be done for the establishment of such a balance is to query the type of tourism targeted. The tourism aimed for the region is the kind that does not need large stocks of buildings, will not be transformed into chain hotels, will display civil architectural examples compatible with its function, tourism oriented, far from show off, emphasizing the identity of the Eminonu region (boarding houses provided by inhabitants, boutique hotels etc), that do not damage the housing function, does not lead to a decrease in owner occupation and does not encourage private rented housing. The transformation in the pattern of change of proprietorship in the area and consequently of tenure pattern will speed up (Aaen [4]). The local governments should play a significant role for guiding this process in a correct manner and prevent speculations and they should provide structures and fittings that will be able to follow up the process in an effective manner. It is necessary to supply houses that are accessible for the potential users in order to provide an incentive for the uses of houses and the basis to provide legality should be prepared. A contemporary, rehabilitated housing function will nourish and develop this target. Because good housing helps to improve health, reduce crime and enhance quality of life (Edgar and Taylor [5]). Hence, the tourism capacity in the region will increase. The tourism development strategy can assume a fundamental function for the economic transformation in a city as Shutt [6] suggested. Therefore, it is necessary to take into consideration that any tourism oriented transformation strategy in the region might have a trigger effect both for the area specifically and for the cit as a whole in general. Business opportunities supporting the tourism function on one side and providing business opportunities for the inhabitants of the region should be created, local governments should be effective for developing the tourism oriented business capacity in the region. Within this framework, the strategies developed for the regions in the area for tourism and housing, will contribute the sustainable development of the region in interaction with each other and create a strong social structure, a unique tourism profile and a trade function supporting this structure.

Relying only on a single factor for the preservation and development of an area is considered to be a weak attempt for the provision of the sustainability of the area when the prospect of extinction of that single factor is considered to take place in the long run. For this region, although tourism may seem as a basic function providing income and returns for today and for the medium run in the Eminonu Region, the axes may change as a consequence of planning decisions or a strategic movement that comes from top. In this case, it seems beneficial to also hold on tightly to the housing function. Because, the most fundamental component that makes an area live until the very end is the house; hence the human factor. Developing the social structure with educational projects, health projects, social goals such as sports and recreation will contribute to the transformation of the region in a tourism-oriented manner in the long run. It is deemed useful to remind that the investments made in the areas within the city for this purpose Report on the DoE Inner City Programs [7] always reach their goal. Similarly, decentralization of office buildings located in the traditional centers (Walton and Milner [8]) that damage the identity of the area and intensification of prestigious office buildings in the area should be taken into consideration as another factor that will contribute the sustainability of the region.

References

[1] Kaptan H., Economic, Social, Geographical Space Definition in the Historical Peninsula,, YTÜ – DPT Research Project Report , Istanbul, pp. 5, 2000

[2] Newman P., Cultural Transformation, Tourism and Urban Management, Symposium of Transformation into International Cities: Kucukcekmece Workshop, Istanbul, 2004.

[3] Ergun N., Provision of Cultural Identity within the Process of Renewal, Yapı 199/ Haziran 1998, Istanbul, pp. 91-96

[4] Aaen S., National Strategies for Urban Renewal and Housing Rehabilitation in Norway, Housing Renewal In Europe, Policy Press, UK, 2000, pp.203-240

[5] Edgar B and Taylor J., 2000. Housing, Urban Regeneration: A Handbook, ed. by Peter Roberts, Hugh Sykes SAGE Pub., London, pp153-175

[6] Shutt J., 2000. Lessons from America in the 1990's, Urban Regeneration: A Handbook, ed. By Peter Roberts, Hugh Sykes SAGE Pub., London, 257-280

[7] Renewing the Cities: A Report on the DoE Inner City Programs in 1988-1989, 1990. England

[8] Walton B., Milner S., 1990. People, Places and Production, Great Britain

The operative process in sustainable urban planning

M. P. Amado
Departamento de Engenharia, Faculdade de Ciências e Tecnologia da Universidade Nova de Lisboa, Portugal

Abstract

This document is intended to present a contribution to the development of urban planning actions through the establishment of an operative process that allows a sustainable development either for existing or for new urban areas.

This operative process is theoretical, supported and adapted to the environmental and territorial planning. This process was previously checked in an application to establish the main factors and critical aspects in the achievement of the goals of the sustainable development.

The checking list of objectives and sustainable strategies was carried out in the beginning through criteria based on the feasibility of the process. It is clear that the determinate factors of the process promoted the participation and conduct of the population in the planning phase. Nonetheless, the operability of the process was checked one could realize that a critical aspect related to the enormous amount of data to collect was mislead in the implementation of stage 2. This situation may lead to an eventual loss of objectivity in case it is not verified an efficient and simultaneous coordination.

In conclusion, the document shows the base of a new operative process that promotes the inclusion at any level of urban intervention of the concept of sustainable development. This inclusion is established as the main strategy in the transformation of the use of the land.

Keywords: sustainable development, urban planning, process, goal, reference situation, conception, implementation phases.

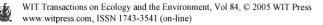
WIT Transactions on Ecology and the Environment, Vol 84, © 2005 WIT Press
www.witpress.com, ISSN 1743-3541 (on-line)

1 Introduction

The enlarged use of the concept of sustainable development had as starting point two conferences of the United Nations on environmental and development (WCED, 1987), where the need to adopt new development strategies at local and global level was recognized.

That need had already been felt in 1969 by a study developed by UNESCO, which admitted that, in the year of 2000, the urban population would be equivalent to the rural population in just 15% of the area.

In 1993 another study by the World Bank pointed the 2010 year as the one when the population will inhabit in cities which represents a very problematic situation for the urban systems with related consequences and for the rural areas in what desertification and shortage of resources concerns.

However, until recently the use of the concept, even of the expression "sustainable development" was only used by the political class who always intended to mean that any development proposal should be framed in the spirit and orientation of the concept. Being not significant, this fact was however enough for the dissemination and implementation of the concept.

2 The sustainability in planning process

Through the Green Book of the Urban Environmental (UE, 1990), the reinforcement appears in the sense of the city as one of the main step of action in the process of sustainable development. The same book relates the matter of the expected expansion of the urban areas in an exponential degree the same as the issues that one will create to the urban planning.

The necessary approach to the process of action and the concept of sustainable development will be guaranteed through the process of territorial planning "... the regional and urban planning is directed to the communities, its population and for the use of land and economics' structures, through processes of goals definition, planning actions and rules..." (Slocombe, 1993).

To Nogueira and Pinho (1996), it is possible to consider three different perspectives for the territorial planning process towards the actions of the sustainable development – the conceptual perspective, the operative and methodological perspective and the politics and institutional perspective.

The first – conceptual perspective – is dedicated to the rule of the planning with environmental politics and sustainable development, process and methodological.

The second embraces the integration of new objectives in the phases of planning process.

The third and last – politics and institutional - is related to the management of interests among the several social and economics agents involved in the process.

On the other hand, Winters (1994) refers that territorial planning has always integrated sustainability concepts through the objectives definition in programs of long term, and the interaction of social dimensions, economics and environmental protection. However, although we cannot check this position, it is possible to verify that the practical results don't show this contribution for the performance of the development process.

Another contribution to this issue is given by Redclift (1989), who refers that territorial planning is limited to seek better locations for the human activity admitting more growth. This situation is hardly accepted by social consent when faced to the economic, environmental and social justness goals.

For Marshal (1992) the main role of territorial planning to reach the sustainable development takes place when avoiding or reducing negative impacts and in having a leader role through solutions adapted to the environmental changes.

Owens (1993) facing the expectable demographic and urban growth of the cities refers that although limits may exist to prevent the growth and that development may become unsustainable the territorial planning can be a valuable assessment to turn those limits more elastic when associated to the components of the sustainability.

In addition to these different contributions to the process of planning to reach to the sustainable development is the Thomas (1994) position. He refers that the growing of politics positions of the society and the consequent involvement of the population in the process of social education will contribute to the creation of a new type of political redistribution of costs and benefits associated to an appropriate implementation of the sustainable development.

Blowers [4] refers that the sustainable development will never be effective if an articulation between environmental and development promoted by the integration in the traditional planning of the social concerns does not exist.

The planning as preponderant vehicle for the actions of transformation of the use of the land and the promotion of life's quality of the population's lead, according to Jacobs (1991), to integrate sustainability measures, of intensities differentiated in agreement with the objectives. The same author still refers that according to the defined goals these can be ponder and changed for other, in elapsing of the process, or then to facilitate that the environmental subjects are treated as determinate for the warranty of effectiveness of the process. On the other hand, and taking into consideration the resultant plan of the action of territorial planning, as a head office of support approaches the taking of decisions, we have the process of transformation of the use of the soil.

In this activity the subjects of economic social and environmental ambit are articulated on the space dimensions of the administration of the territory, and its contribution for the sustainable development will depend on the existence of a conceptual structure that facilitates to assist to the interactions between use of the land and environmental alterations and simultaneously make possible the definition of a methodological theory that identifies the "critical" natural capital (Healey and Shaw - 1993) and the "thresholds of the sustainability" (Blowers [4]; Jacobs 1991).

Another important aspect for the territorial planning is to contain in its process the specific analysis of the environmental and social components, in the sense of valuing its importance in the actions, integrated in the debate on the objectives and development strategies, promoting the discussion and inducing to the obtaining of consents among all the intervening agents.

Other aspect in the planning, which compete in the promotion of the sustainable development, is that it has to take into consideration the obtaining of consents in the goals and strategies, through the different political, social agents' responsibility and economics with view to a larger procedure celerity from where it will result evident gains for the communities embraced by the planning actions.

Such notorious responsibility is due to a larger animation and transparency of the process and to the promotion of a new posture for the citizenship, avoiding that the process promotes conditions for the occurrence of situations of social exclusion or economic discrimination.

In conclusion, one can say that sustainable development is possible to reach at an operable level by the use of a new process of territorial planning, which should guarantee the promotion of the integration and inter-relationship in equal ways to the three sustainability components – economic, social and environmental.

2.1 The process to sustainable urban planning

For process it is understood that it is "the way of doing a thing" (Porto Editora, 5 Ed°), understanding this as corresponding to the intended objective of promoting the sustainable development through the urban planning.

The necessary relationship that exists between the objectives of the sustainable development and the operative process of the sustainable planning corresponds to the decisive factor for the success of the development.

That role fits to the operative process with a view to its interpretation and forward action in the field. This action, as developed, shows us the disjointed expectations between the real capacities of the natural resource and the effective satisfaction of the expectations of the population, coming to attend a preference for the accomplishment of the promoters' economics expectations. Nonetheless the legal board of framing process doesn't guarantee the results of the elaborated plans, in its totality, to be considered framed in the sustainability concept.

The social subjects are not always treated and when it happens they don't have the same depth level that is used for the treatment of the economics subjects in special the related with financial profits of the operation. On the other hand, the actual process of urban development, to be continued, will bring disastrous consequences for the future generations, face to the overload that is done on the natural resource and to the excessive consumption of natural resources as well as to the absence of actions in the social field. Conditions are not created so that the future generations can continue to use certain natural resources and to live with safety with the same or superior level of quality life comparing to the actual one.

Another negative aspect of the present development process is the absence of solutions that promote the social and cultural integration among differentiated groups, as well as measures that foresee the resulting swinging movements of the options of centralization of functions and activities side by side with actions of promotion of conviviality places in natural spaces and which conservation should be promoted.

It is the time for the urban development to stop being dictated almost exclusively by the economic component that since the sixties has led the process, by using a new and actual operative process of urban planning, to promote framed actions in the concept of sustainable development in according to the possible warranties of obtaining through its application.

Just as in the beginning of the industrial revolution, the mechanization of the productive system intended the improvement of the work conditions and productivity, the process of urban planning also wants to guarantee the improvement of the quality of life of the populations in an effective manner. This situation needs to be promoted by the public institutions, in its role of guaranty of a social justness and of operation of the public systems, through the production of new legal diplomas.

It is also understood that the "new" process of urban planning will need to guide strategies that seek the effective promotion of the improvement of the quality of life of the populations, of the largest and more efficiency enlargement of the systems of infrastructures, larger and better relationships of urbanity, more safety in the public spaces and a larger effectiveness in the relationship with the natural field. It is considered to be possible the guarantee of the treatment and observance of these aspects in the ambit of the operability in the "new process" of urban planning to develop. This way the need of the existence of a "new" process elapses of the adaptability lack that today is recognized in the existing process and of its framing in the concept of sustainable development, that it intends implemented in a more widespread way. This situation is tied to the need that the growth of the urban agglomerates was to be processed in a harmonious way, guaranteeing the maintenance of a high level of life quality.

The great urban centres in its majority, present a preponderance of the economics relationships face to the social ones and they are one of the origin of the swinging movements of the populations and of the urban expansion. However, the continuity of the development of the economics actions only has viability in case they increase, in number and in rhythm and the social relationships set as way of balance in global development board. This new way to face the global system of social relationships requires innovative solutions to be adopted, one of which can be the work through a new process of the actions of the urban planning. That process should allow giving a driven answer and adapted to the challenge that the sustainable development places to the transformation of the use of the land and of the social relationships and those that the urban centre promote.

Considering that it has been the environmental component whose treatment is more careless in the actual system of development of society, the new process should guarantee that it should be this component to assume the decisive role in the future actions not only for the implications that certain type of solutions can provoke but also as that determination it will constitute a factor in the promotion of the treatment justness, in a process that the economic component is far too much influential in the determination of the level of quality of life of the populations. This new process will have to handle and to relate the countless variables that specific situations recommend they be treated in an expedite way for the team of the plan, and accompanied by the public entities and population.

The accompaniment by the part of the population in its civic role can be promoted through inquiries regular information and direct intervention with base in opinions and petitions.

According to Sanoff [10], these procedures increase the transparency of the process and its efficiency, because the continuous accompaniment allows a reduction of periods so much of approvals as of implementation and a better future appropriation of the site where take place the transformation.

3 Proposal of process to sustainable urban planning

By the analysis of several theoretical aspects related to the methodological process of the urban planning, and to the need of the introduction in a clear way of the environmental component in it, becomes evident the existing disconnection of the processes used until now in the practice of the urban planning. The need that the interventions on the territory don't commit the expectations of the presents and futures generations and in parallel they guarantee the sustained administration of the natural resources is one of the various factors that conditioned the process of the urban planning. Such is related, until today, to the fact that the environmental component has not been integrated in the process of urban planning in a continuous and large form.

The possibility of the process to develop to endow and to guide the intervention in the sense of preservation and rehabilitation, so much on the natural space as in the built, it turns the challenge of conception of the process more incentive for the result that it can drive, face to the sustainable development.

To guarantee the execution of the goals of sustainable development it is necessary that the new process of sustainable urban planning possesses a simple structure with clear goals and is easy to use. It will owe that process to facilitate the obtaining of gains possible to quantify in the several action areas, in way to assure the satisfaction of the largest number of sustainability strategies.

As strategic beginnings of sustainability, important evidencing in the ambit of this way are the constant ones in the following table for they be including and they cover the environmental, social and economics areas and still of the participation of the population:

Table 1:   Strategic beginnings of sustainability.

Use sustainable of the natural resources;   Reduction of consumptions and wastes;   Preservation of the natural diversity, economic and cultural in a relationship of justness;   Promotion of the economy and employment places;   Promotion of the use of energy renewed;   Involvement of the local population in the process;   Promotion of the popularization and information on the foreseen development and verified along the process.

These strategic beginnings present an adaptation to the picture of the territorial planning, tends as reference the Aalborg Chart.

Together with these sustainability beginnings of having enlarged action ambit, it is necessary for articulation in the process, that goals must be enumerated and beginnings of action taken into consideration for the interdisciplinary equips of the plan, in the elaboration of its work and conception of the urban drawing.

To the level of the measures and essential beginnings that the process of sustainable urban planning should contain and guarantee they are considered the constant of the following table:

Table 2:   Measures and essential beginnings.

Definition of the strategic goals of the intervention;
Definition of the reference situations in the environmental aspects, economic, social and urbanistic;
Motivation to the participation of the population and local players;
To assure the balance between different sectors and social groups;
Promotion of new mobility types;
Motivation for the modernization in the activities sectors;
Motivation to the saving of energy and the use of solutions of energy renewed;
Promotion of quality in the urban space.

The presented list has the characteristic of being open and, for the goals conditions of application; it should be enlarged and adapted according the case being the referred elements the ones that it can consider as anchors of the process of sustainable urban planning.

3.1 The process

The process of sustainable urban planning comes with a structure of conception composed for 4 stages, stages that are developed with base in the process of logical reasoning and are sequential of the development of an urban intervention supported in the practical sense of the empiric knowledge, that until today it has been characterizing in an enlarged way in every action of the urban planning process.

The process comes with different stages and complemented actions to each one of these owing actions to be combined in the way more adapted to the problem's approach, in function of the environmental landings, economics and social, intended or wanted. Another aspect of the process is the consolidation in the same of the weight action in the participation of the population foreseen in the stages 2 and 3, informed of the evaluation. This action can even drive to the need of an objective reformulate.

The existence of an evaluation action in the process increase the capacity of decision and it reduces the risk of the arbitrary act when allowing the evaluation of the solutions in face to the alternatives, situation that would not be possible to appear with so much efficiency in face to the well-known methods.

In pointing out the process presented it possesses the characteristic that it could embrace all the expansion projects and urban renewal, independently of its dimension or location.

Table 3:   Concept structure.

STAGES			ACTIONS
	1 – Intervention objectives	Defined of strategic goals	
	2 – Reference situation	Environmental Analyse Economic Analyse Social and urban analyse Commitments and potentialities Definition of criteria's	
	3 – Conception	List of Land proprieties Commitments Strategies and sustainability factors Location of equipments and open spaces Plan of roads Creation of lots Proposal	
	4 – Implementation	Check list of implementation	

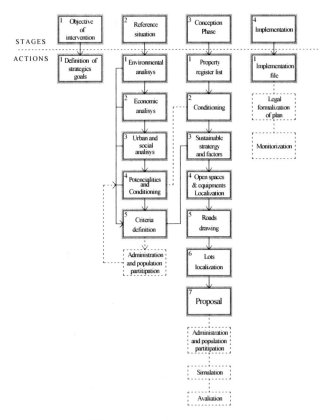

Figure 1:   Process structure.

Those stages of development inter-relational behave in itself acutance action and its sequence is developed in each one of the stages of the process. The structure of the process is synthesized in Fig. 1, which presents actions whose development doesn't only depend on the project team, but also on the activities congregation of everybody interested and involved in the intervention.

3.2 Determinant factors of process

The objective of the developed process is the creation of an operative instrument to support the promotion of the sustainable development, through the urban planning. The elaboration of the proposed process tends to give execution to the objectives and sustainability strategies that are materialized through the urban planning.

In a second point, the process still intends to facilitate an effective marking of the works and a coordination of the teams of the project in its several tasks and specific studies tends in view the obtaining of efficiency gains and to minimize losses.

The inclusion of the three components of sustainability in an equal weight in the process, in a way to facilitate the satisfaction of the conditions to implementation of the human activities, is the other of the aspects of the viability of the process.

The possibility of effective participation and the accompaniment of the developing of the works by the population are in the sense of obtaining, with its participation, more knowledge, preventing the occurrence of possible problems and conflicts of interest, guaranteeing simultaneously a faster acceptance of the new spaces in the urban city. These results are a decisive factor of the new process. Another decisive factor of the process is the implementation stage and its efficiency warranty. The phase of implementation of the plan, foreseen to develop in an alone action it is controlled through records that have the objective of providing gain of efficiency in the three components.

The possibility separation by functional areas of the actions to implement with the plan would facilitate that for each one of the sustainability components, specific steps are given in the correct way and still the information of new sustainability practices with rigidity and warranty of results. Those results could be comparable to face the sustainability indicators used during the development of the elaboration of the plan.

The result of the application of this process of sustainable urban planning would constitute a reference for future expansion actions and urban renewal supported in a base of data of the relationships: action ↔ relationship. That base of develop for public entities and its diffusion and availability to all urban planners would not allow the occurrence of less efficient actions with negative effects.

4   Conclusions

The diversity and environmental sensibility should always create differentiated urban solutions. Therefore the mere application of parameters and urban indexes are not possible to continue to be observed.

The need of a way to implement the actions of urban planning according to a new operative process has to be obligatorily structured in "another way". In the inevitability of the development of the human activities and the continuous demographic growth and economic, forces all taking new attitudes face the necessary expansion and urban renewal. On the other hand, the process of urban planning has become to rise as a privileged way of leaving in "inheritance", for the future generations, a way to reach how to use the available common resources on the planet. Therefore, facing the innovation proposal through a new process of sustainable urban planning, it was foreseen that this is one of the possible roads for the integration of the development concept sustained in the mentioned process.

It was verified although, for its structure, that the proposed process can be applied to interventions of quite differentiated dimensions due to the open structure that supports it. In addition this process allows to determine which are the potentialities, weaknesses and opportunities of the intervention place possesses, facilitating the same ones as soon as is benefited, for the resulting orientation of the planning process.

Lastly, it is possible to verify that it is not through the simplification of the planning process that the integration of the concept of the sustainable development is gotten, but on the contraire, by the compatibility and reinforcement of the content of information and selection of data for support of the conception stage, with a view to a large responsibility of all the intervenient on the process which tends to clear what is the cause of its improvement of the quality of life of the populations and its preservation through the coming generations.

References

[1] Amado, M. (2005), *O Processo do Planeamento Urbano Sustentável*, Edições Caleidóscópio, Lisboa

[2] Beatley, T. (2000), *Green Urbanism, Learning from European Cities*, Island Press, Washington.

[3] Becker, E.; Jahn, T. (1999), *Sustainability and the Social Sciences*, Zed Books, New York.

[4] Blowers, A. (ed) (1993), *Planning for a Sustainable Environment*, a Report by the Town and Country Planning Association, Earthscan Publications, London.

[5] Cartwright, L. (2000), Selecting Local Sustainable Development Indicators: does consensus exist in their choice and propose?, in *Planning Practice and Research*, 15

[6] Doak, J. (2000), Consensus-building for environmental sustainability, in *Integrating Environment + Economy*, Routledge, New York.

[7] Eichler, M. (1999), Sustainability from a Feminist Sociological Perspective: A Framework for Disciplinary Reorientation, in *Sustainability and the Social Sciences*, Zed Books, New York.

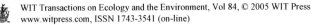

[8]   Gouldson, A.; Roberts, P. (2000), *Integrating Environment + Economy*, Routledge, New York.
[9]   Redclift, M. (1999), *Sustainability and Sociology: Northern Preoccupations, in Sustainability and the Social Sciences*, Zed Books, New York.
[10]   Sanoff, H. (2000), *Community Participation Methods in Design and Planning*, John Wiley & Sons, Inc. New York.

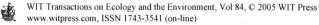

Building regulations based on sustainable principles in Italy: state of the art and trends

C. Carletti, P. Gallo, C. Gargari & F. Sciurpi
University of Florence, Dept. TAeD Tecnologie dell'Architettura e Design "P. L. Spadolini", Italy

Abstract

The future of Europe regarding environmental conservation is based on the success of the energy consumption reduction policies and of the renewable energy sources development. As regarding energy and resources consumption, the building field is particularly important and economic incentives play a fundamental role to promote environment pollution reduction.

All these incentives concern different technologies and strategies, such as: photovoltaic, thermal solar, biological and sustainable architecture. Recently institutions such as Government, Districts, Municipalities, issued economical incentives and money contributions in favour of those projects oriented towards environment conservation and respect. These contributions mainly regard energy saving and renewable energy use, as well as waste recycling, low emitting vehicles, biological agriculture, water saving, local fauna preservation and so on. Local actions support regional ones in different ways: co-financing, capital account, urbanization and building concession charges; while some Municipalities stress the importance of thermal solar, others point out the importance of ecological materials or energy saving policies.

The aim of this work is to critically present a comprehensive survey of the Italian actions based on sustainable principles which will play an important role in the aspect of our cities.

Keywords: building regulation, sustainability, incentives.

1 Introduction

In 1987, the World Commission on Environment and Development (Brundtland Commission) asked for the development of new ways to measure and assess progress towards sustainable development. This call has been subsequently echoed in Agenda 21 of the 1992 Earth Summit and through activities that range from local to global in scale. The Sustainable Construction concept aims at the creation and responsible management of a healthily built environment based on resource cy and ecological principles. It takes care of environmental and life quality issues, social equity, cultural issues, and economic constraints. Buildings have to integrate environmental quality in each stage of their life: planning, design, construction, use and possible redevelopment, re-use, demolition or deconstruction.

2 The sustainable development strategies in Italy

Pursuing a sustainable development means to try to improve quality of life, encouraging economic assets and consistent behaviours with the resources for next generation. For this reason a lot of efforts have been done as a strategy for national sustainable development.

Starting from the approval in 1993 of the National Plan for Sustainable Development, in Implementation of Agenda 21, by the Interministerial Committee for Economic Planning (CIPE), an Interministerial Committee was set up to monitor progress in the Plan-s implementation, to co-ordinate the collection of data on operational projects and to prepare an annual report on Agenda 21 targets related to the 12 priority "Themes" of intervention; Water, Urban Environment, Biodiversity, Biotechnology, Decontamination site, Climatic changes, Electromagnetic fields, Indoor Pollution, Sea and Coasts, Quality of the air, Waste and Territory.

The solution to these urgent problems lies in focussing actions on the more traditional economic sectors (manufacturing, agriculture, tourism), on basic infrastructure (energy, transportation), and on the need to radically alter the attitudes of public and private entities towards waste.

In the building sector, as a reply to the increasing demand of eco-compatible quality, significant efforts to assess performance have been made by corporations, non-government agencies, academics, communities, national organizations.

Crucial, in this sense, the operational contribution of different private organizations (NGO): these are developing indicators to get quantitative measures of the progress towards an environmentally sustainable development, or participate in experimental campaigns and benchmark for the validation of the lists agreed upon international level.

For example, the Annual reports prepared by Legambiente, the "Urban Ecosystem report", the Italian Forum ICITE/CIB, the Working Group for Eco/sustainable construction GL13 activated by UNI (National Standardization Body), the code of self-government for public Authorities on the environmental quality of energy in buildings and open spaces produced by ENEA, the CasaKlima certificate showed by province of Bolzano and every other Quality an Sustainability Marks like CasaQualita, Natureplus, Ecolabel. Not to forget, moreover, that Italy is first in the list of Countries involved in the European project SHE (Sustainable Housing Europe) to realize 714 "green" lodgings in 4 different Nations.

Nevertheless in Italy, sustainable architecture remains marginalized in the building market and it is still missing a complete picture about the major sources of resistance to sustainable building and about useful methods to lower those resistances. The lack of appropriate incentives or policies and supporting legislation has been identified as major impediments to the implementation of sustainable architecture. In Italy, a national integrated implementation framework is missing and there is a lack of consensus on preferred implementation methods for sustainable architecture. There has also been no agreement on who should be responsible for orchestrating initiatives, and whether measures should be applied on a voluntary or mandatory basis. Actually recent bills for a sustainable building have been proposed by individual town councils or local government but latest experience developed in a regional context, and legislative local adjournment confirm right in the middle the essential processing for national regulation fit to take in the demand-pull for a more and more sustainable building.

3   The body of laws

In Italy, law providing energy certification of buildings (article 30 of Law n. 10/91) isn't enforced yet since enabling legislation has not been passed.

The article 30 of the Law 10/91 really introduced some innovation even in the European legislative survey; it provides some operative aspects summarized as follows:

- during renting or conveyance on sale the buyer must take notes of the energy certification of the building;
- the owner or the letter can ask for these certifications to the Municipality.

In order to affect the real market energy, saving strategies should aim at introducing a tax relief system meanwhile reducing urbanization burdens for those buildings whose efficiency will be proved by the certificate. The latter should also report synthetically the main performances of the building, first of all, its energy consumption expressed in an easily understandable unit such as kWh/m^2year.

In the meantime, a new EU Directive (2002/91/CE) governing energy efficiency in building sector will have to be incorporated into Member State Legislation by February 2006.

The EU Directive while improving standards concerning energy efficiency at the same time urges the consumer to evaluate energy features of the building itself.

The EU Directive aims at improving the building energetic performances assuring that only energetically efficient and economically conscious enterprises will be undertaken.

In short, the building's energy certification should be mainly:

- a simple way to describe both energy features (such as thermal insulation) and efficiency of the building;
- suggest some action to be undertaken in order to improve the above-mentioned energetic performances;
- to see the building-plant system as a whole from the planning and the design phase of the project as well as the building management.

The energy efficiency of the building should be assessed by some indicators evaluated as a function of the following parameters: thermal insulation, technical features of the HVAC systems, climatic characteristics of the building site, building form and orientation. Probably it will be worthwhile to include even a CO_2 emission indicator.

Even active energy strategies will be included in this evaluation as a lot of European States have been investing in solar technologies and renewable energy (district heating and cogeneration) for some time.

The energy building certification will be adopted by every EU Member State and revised no more than every five years.

4 Incentives for sustainability in buildings

In the last few years, in order to promote environment and human health protection and respect, a lot of Italian Public Institutions (Municipalities, Regions, Ministry) have issued incentives and economic contributions regarding principally energy saving and use of renewable energies in buildings, waste recycling, use of less polluting vehicles, biological agriculture, water consumption reduction and so on.

To all the actions and contributions from central government (Ministry and Regions), like as the Programs "Tetti Fotovoltaici" (D.M. 12/11/2002), Thermal Solar (D.M. 13/12/2002), "Fotovoltaico ad alta valenza architettonica" and "Comune Solarizzato", have been added different actions which distribute in different way (co-financing, capital account founds, urbanisation tax reduction, ecc.) public contributions in order to promote sustainability in buildings by local government (principally town councils).

Some municipalities provide incentives for the use of thermal solar in buildings (Modena, Naples, Caserta, Salerno, Lecce, Cosenza, Catania, Agrigento, etc.), others for the use of non polluting material in buildings (Trent, Calenzano, Nonantola, Vezzano Ligure, Schio, Poggibonsi, Carpi, Faenza, Forlì, etc.), others for the use of energy saving technologies in buildings (Bolzano, Udine, etc.). In Tables 1 and 2 some incentives provided by different Italian Public bodies in order to promote sustainability in buildings are reported.

Table 1:   Incentives provided by different Italian municipalities.

Municipality	Kind of instrument	Incentives and contributions
Municipality of FAENZA (Ravenna)	P.R.G. - 1996	Incentives of the volume or the useable surface for those projects which use energy saving strategies (building orientation, structures insulation, etc.); glasshouses without heating systems used for solar gain are not charged on the building volume.
Municipality of Nonantola (Modena)	D.C.C. 45/2001	Tax reduction of the urbanisation charge for bioclimatic buildings and for those projects which use energy saving strategies.
Municipality of Cavalese	P.R.G.	Tax remission for those projects which use energy saving strategies or solar energy in buildings.
Municipality of Calenzano	D.C.C. 115/2002	Tax reduction of the urbanisation charge for bio-ecological buildings.
Municipality of Florence	R.E. – D.C.C. 346/2000	Urban parameters concessions and tax reduction of the urbanisation charge for those projects which use energy saving strategies or renewable energies in buildings (glasshouses, etc.).
Municipality of Rignano sull'Arno	D.C.C. 70/2000	Urban parameters concessions and tax reduction of the urbanisation charge for sustainable buildings (extra-thickness of the wall and the floor, thermal inertia, ventilated roofs, etc.).
Municipality of Pesaro	P.R.G. 2003	Clear surface and additional surface increment as far as full 5% of permitted one and full 30% of clear feasible surface, for all new Building and Demolition/ Rebuilding housing projects which use bio-architectural techniques.
Province autonomous of Trent	L. P. 1998	Incentives for those projects which use energy saving strategies (thermal insulation of walls, roofs, windows, etc.), or renewable energies in buildings, or for low energy consumption buildings (passive buildings, etc.).
Province autonomous of Trent (Municipality of Trent)	L.P. 22/1991	Tax reduction of the urbanisation charge for sustainable buildings.
Province autonomous of Trent	L. P. 1998	Incentives for those projects which use energy saving strategies (thermal insulation of walls, roofs, windows, etc.), or renewable energies in buildings, or for low energy consumption buildings (passive buildings, etc.).
Province autonomous of Bolzano	L.P. 04/1993	Tax contributions for those projects which use energy saving strategies or renewable energies in buildings.

Notes: D.C.C. = Deliberation of the Municipal Council; R.E. = building regulations; L.P. = Provincial Law; P.R.G. = town-planning scheme

Table 2:   Incentives provided from different Italian regions.

Regions	Kind of instrument	Incentives and contributions
Emilia Romagna Region	D.G.R. 849/1998 D.G.R. 21/2001	Tax reduction of the urbanisation charge for bioclimatic or bio-ecological buildings.
Veneto Region	L.R. 21/96	Urban parameters concessions for those projects which improve the indoor human comfort and the energy saving (extra-thickness of the wall and the floor, thermal inertia, etc.).
Friuli Venetia Julia Region	L.R. 04/1999	Tax contributions for the use of energy saving strategies or renewable energies in buildings.
Tuscany Region	L.R. 45/97	Tax contributions and promotion for the use of energy saving strategies and renewable energies in buildings and the development of new energy saving technologies.
Tuscany Region	D.G.R. 03/03/2003	Tax contributions for thermal solar in buildings.
Latium Region	D.G.R. 1329/2002	Tax contributions for the construction of low emission buildings.
Umbria Region	Law 61/1998 D.G.R. 5180/1999	Increase of the contributions for the reconstruction of the buildings damaged by the earthquake of the 1997, for those projects using bio-ecological or bioclimatic strategies, energy saving techniques and materials recycling.
Umbria Region	L.R. 38/2000	Urban parameters concessions for those projects which improve the indoor human comfort and the energy saving (extra-thickness of the wall and the floor, glasshouses, etc.).
Umbria Region	D.P.G.R. 374/1998	Tax reduction of the urbanisation charge for those projects which use energy saving technologies (solar panels, electrical energy production using renewable sources, thermal insulation, etc.).
Marches Region	D.G.R. 579/2003	Increase of the transfer price of those houses (subsidised building) built according to sustainable principles

Notes:
L.R. = Regional Law
D.G.R. = Deliberation of the Regional Council
D.P.G.R. = Deliberation of the President of the Regional Council

5 Conclusions

The present government structure and division of responsibilities is a primary obstacle; implementation is inhibited by the lack of leadership and coordination between various levels of government, agencies and industry groups.

This may be the result of different priorities and the lack of clarity or consistency of initiatives for all levels of government, so conflicting objectives and strategies need to be solved.

Actually fragmented actions exist at different level of government, but it is necessary an 'harmonization', through a global action plan for sustainable building or a shaping of packages related to the sustainable building at national level.

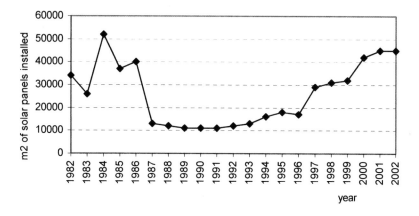

Figure 1:   Italian market of thermal solar in the last twenty years.

One of the actions in this direction should be, for instance, to prepare a 'set of measures for Sustainable Building' in order to harmonize different sets of local authorities requirements used until now. The set would be a collection of criteria, indicators, measures and recommendations that can be taken in the field of sustainable building. It could work as an instrument on sustainable building for local authorities because they could select appropriate measures for their policy on sustainable building.

Broad consensus in construction industry, product manufacturers, developers and government should be achieved on the definition of these sustainable measures. The sets of indicators are now used to define criteria for ambitions in new project developments, to create agreements in project consortiums and to define eligibility for green financing schemes.

References

[1] Carletti C, Cellai GF., Sciurpi F., "Certificazione energetica ed incentivi ai fini del risparmio energetico negli edifici", Abitare il Futuro SAIE 2003
[2] AA.VV   "Le Regioni italiane e la bioedilizia", EdicomEdizioni, Monfalcone, 2002
[3] ENEA "Verso un libro verde per l'edilizia sostenibile"- La qualità energetico ambientale dell'edificio, Conferenze Nazionale Energia e Ambiente, Roma 1998

[4] M. Colagrossi, R.A. Mascolo "Sviluppo sostenibile e indicatori", ANPA, 1998
[5] G. Guenno, S.Tiezzi: The Index of Sustainable Economic Welfare (ISEW) for Italy. FEEM 1998 nota di lavoro 5.98
[6] M. Wackernagel, W.E.Rees: L'impronta Ecologica, Edizioni Ambiente Milano, 1996
[7] www.she.coop!¬"NM

Criteria for choosing tunnels as a possible corridor for urban public installations

R. Spaic & M. Terzic
Faculty of Building Management,
The European University of Belgrade, Serbia and Montenegro

Abstract

This work defines the criteria for choosing corridors in planning and constructing urban public installations.

On the basis of general urban solutions for public technical infrastructure corridors in the pre-investment analysis it is possible to develop in detail three corridor variants: the first is in the trunk of a planned road (beneath the road), the second is a public tunnel, and the third one is a combination of the previous two.

For the given investment task are defined appropriate criteria: investment expenses, expenses of using and managing the object, stimulus in developing urban public system, and ecological effects. These criteria are adapted for application of the multi-criteria optimization method for the purpose of achieving an optimal solution.

This all-inclusive and real procedure brings to the front the public tunnel as a long-time solution for the urban installations corridor.

Keywords: public corridor, urban installations, optimization, criteria, public tunnel.

1 Introduction

The process of programming public corridor is a hierarchy series of activities of erudite investigation for planning and constructing urban public tubes. The essence is in a creative role of the planner and the programmer in a team coordinated work. In practice, these are real problems with a very compound structure, and optimal solutions are very difficult to find.

Since it is necessary to make decisions during the process of realizations of urban plans and in the programs of public development, this process should be developed through the form of several possible solutions, using when and whenever it is possible mathematical methods of optimization.

The first step is in finding urbanistic solutions by checking technically and operatively possible variants with at least two variants presented: one as a corridor in a planned street on the surface of the terrain (fig. 1 – put all installations [3]) and the other as a tunnel gallery (fig. 2 – put possible pipes [7]). Sometimes all necessary installations cannot be found in a tunnel corridor but even though gallery type is used for most of them, therefore other pipes (sewerage system, for example – due to the limitation concerning the slope of the pipe) take their own route (by pressing or similar) and this would be the third real variant. Depending on the configuration of the terrain, geodesy conditions, the character of the corridors, the position and the number of connections to pipes, geotechnical and hydro-geological conditions, etc, the fourth variant can be made. Most often only two exist and they are enough for analysis and research.

In any case, variants should be precisely defined – they are general engineering solutions with enough data for optimization, so that these general projects enable further analysis of variants and the application of the methods for valuing them.

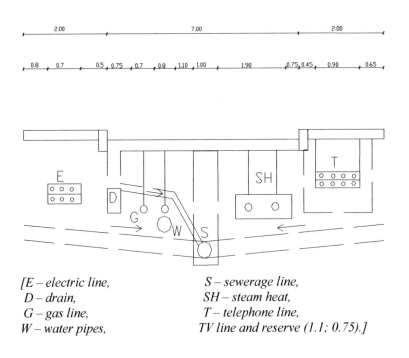

[E – electric line,   S – sewerage line,
D – drain,   SH – steam heat,
G – gas line,   T – telephone line,
W – water pipes,   TV line and reserve (1.1; 0.75).]

Figure 1.

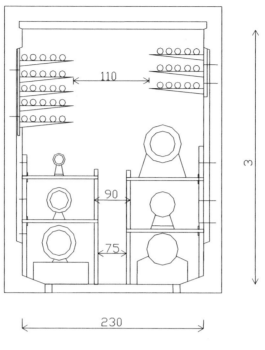

Figure 2.

2 Defining of the criteria for choosing the variant

Any variant solution for the corridor - streets, tunnel galleries or combined, is checked from the standpoint of acceptability concerning:

-   functionality and usage
-   total economy
-   socially developing stimulus
-   ecological conditions. In order to optimize the final solution – the general aim of construction of a corridor installation – such a compound system is presented by the general form of the criteria function *(Fi)*, which is simply adjusted to methods of multi-criteria analysis:

$$F_i = \Sigma_j P_{ij} \, \alpha_{ij} \; ; \; (i=1,2,...,20); \; j=1,2,...n) \tag{1}$$

where: P_{ij}- real values of indicators and

α_{ij} – weight coefficients by which the influence of each indicator is shown. Since the indicators are of a different structure, the general aim must be selected into several separate aims with suitable criteria like:

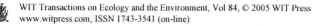

2.1 The investment aim

The investment aim is to achieve the full technical and technological functionality with the minimum of investment in construction, that is:

$$\min f_{1i} = \Sigma_j \ Q_{ij} \ c_{ij} = \Sigma_j \ P_{1ij} \tag{2}$$

$$(j=1,2,...,n; \ i=1,2,...,5)$$

where: Q_{ij} – indicators of quantities according to types of work,

c_{ij} – prices of separate types of positions,

P_{1ij} – the value of expenses of construction according to specified indicators.

The indicators of investment expenses are:

K_{11} - expenses of planning and programming of the project,

K_{12} - expenses for the preparation of the construction,

K_{13} - expenses of constructing

K_{14} - expenses of supervision and control of constructing

K_{15} - expenses of managing the project.

All expenses are given in monetary units.

2.2 Minimal expenses

The minimal expenses of using and managing the object, present the second aim of the project which is expressed through monetary units as:

$$min f_{2i} = \Sigma_j A_{ij} \ a_{ij} = \Sigma_j P_{2ij} \ ; \ (j=1,2,...,n; \ i=1,2,...4) \tag{3}$$

where: A_{ij} – quantities of i – indicators of criteria,

a_{ij} – suitable unit prices

P_{2ij} – total value of expenses for maintaining and using.

The indicators of these criteria of expenses are:

K_{21} – the expenses of investment maintaining

K_{22} – the expenses of current maintenance

K_{23} – the expenses of unexpected maintenance

K_{24} – the expenses of managing by using it.

2.3 Third group

The third group of criteria concerns the stimulus of the development of public standard of the city and consequently it concerns the stimulus of the development of the city on the whole.

These criteria are defined on the basis of the economically – developed analysis and the plans which enable the more exact data for expressing these criteria. The indicators would be:

K_{31} – the increasing of public standard of space area,

K_{32} – the stimulus of social development
K_{33} – the stimulus of industry development
K_{34} – the stimulus of urban planning

Since these indicators are of different dimensions, of quantitative and qualitative nature, their coordination is achieved by introduction of weight coefficients (α_{ij}). Then the analytic form of criteria function will be:

$$maxf_{3i} = \Sigma_j \alpha_{3ij} P_{3ij} = \Sigma_j P'_{3ij} \; ; \; (j=1,2,...,n; \; i=4) \tag{4}$$

where: P_{3ij} – suitable real indicators,
P'_{3ijj} – reduced values of indicators which define space entities,
α_{3ij} – weight coefficients by which the importance of each indicator is expressed in the way that they are reduced to uniform estimating in the function of maximization of effects.

2.4 Fourth group

The fourth group of criteria has the aim to reduce the negative stimuli on space and living surroundings (ecological criteria).

This sub function is minimized because the aim is to have the minimum of bad effects on existing and planned state of living and space surroundings when constructing and making functional new limitation which are regulated by the low, professions and science, made by research and study.

The indicators are:

K_{41} – noise,
K_{42} – vibrations and the danger of gas explosions, impact, etc,
K_{43} – electromagnetic radiation of energetic pipes and plants,
K_{44} – air pollution
K_{45} – water pollution
K_{46} – earth pollution
K_{47} – worsening of the healthy surface (greenery).

These indicators are of quantitative nature and are expressed by m2 but of different purpose, so the criteria function is minimized:

$$min f_{4i} = \Sigma_j P_{4ij} \alpha_{4ij} = \Sigma_j P'_{4ij} \; ; \; (j=1,2,...,n; \; i=7) \tag{5}$$

Analogous to the previous indicators and holding to mathematical realization of operators, here are:

P_{4ij} and P'_{4ij} – real and reduced values of indicators and
α_{4ij} – suitable weight coefficients

3   Conclusion

By all this the basic approaches of valuing criteria and matrices of aims are defined, which is enough for the development of a specified model of programming of investments into public pipes as a basic element of planning (economic, urban and technical). Only by such general recognition of criteria for the selection, the tunnel as a public corridor will get much wider application than before.

This project should be followed by a more detailed work (proposal) of a practical application of this methodology (variation of solutions, numerical expression of the value of all indicators and multi-criteria optimization).

References

[1] Acic, M. Lakicevic, M.: *"Construction of objects of public facilities"*, Collection of works, "Civil engineer calendar" Yugoslav Engineers Union, Belgrade, 1996.

[2] Ivkovic, B.: *"Carrying out projects in civil engineering"* Science, Belgrade, 1994.

[3] Maletin, M.: *"Urban lines of communications"*, Faculty of Civil Engineering, Belgrade, 1996.

[4] Petric, J.: *"Operational Research I and II"*, Modern administration, Belgrade, 1979.

[5] Spaic, R. Djindjic, M.: *" Running construction of urban public facilities"*, University for Management " Braca Karic" and a review of Serbian Civil Engineering's Union, "Construction", Belgrade,1999.

[6] Zegarac, Z.: *"Facilities"*, Faculty of Geography, Belgrade, 1998.

[7] Spaic, R: *Standardizing underground buildings for city public facilities purposes"*, Collection of works of Technical school in Nis, Nis, 1996.

[8] Spaic, R.: *"Rationalization in planning of construction of public objects in towns"*, M.A. dissertation, Faculty of Civil Engineering in Nis, Nis, 1989.

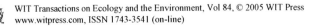

Ningbo – a new sustainable city for China

R. Edmond
HASSELL Pty Ltd, Melbourne, Australia
RMIT University, Melbourne, Australia

Abstract

This paper describes the winning entry in the international competition for planning of the expansion of the city of Ningbo, China, for 350,000 people on a 4000ha site; and the design of its new Centre by HASSELL, with engineering consultant Hyder in late 2002.   Shortlisted competition entrants included Obermayer from Germany, Kurokawa from Japan and the Beijing Planning Bureau. The winning scheme blends traditional Chinese practices in sustainable farming, aquaculture and soil and water management evolved over four millennia, with 21st Century technologies, to create a city which is sustainable to a degree greater than most contemporary cities. At the same time, the new city design embodies urban design qualities rarely found in contemporary Chinese cities, and compliments a fine city building tradition which spans 4000 years.

ESD components are woven throughout the fabric of the new city. The largest parks and waterbodies accommodate storm and wastewater treatment and storage for recycling, and sustainable energy generation from wind and wastes; the smaller urban canals and waterways provide drainage and water distribution into wetlands for cleaning. The ESD agenda for the new Ningbo will reduce externally supplied water and energy requirements by half that of a conventional city, while providing a physical environment equivalent to the most advanced contemporary cities. The concept includes a comprehensive public transport system, which minimises incentives for growth of private vehicles and energy use, by providing an excellent standard of service.

HASSELL is continuing its involvement with detail design of the project through the Shanghai and Hong Kong offices of the firm.

1   Introduction

The Ningbo Urban Planning Bureau briefed competition entrants, to provide clear strategies to guide the future expansion of Ningbo beyond the boundaries of the old city, to encompass the New District of East Ningbo (NDEN). The Brief included a more detailed urban design of a new business and commercial centre on 7km2 and urban expansion by 350,000 population over the total 39km2 site, and a requirement for a 'Model Environmental City'.

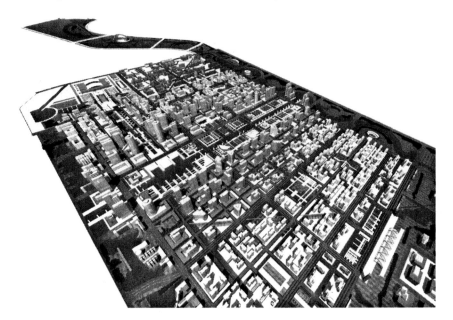

Figure 1:   The New City Centre.

2   The legacy and the future

Ningbo is growing and evolving into what will be one of the great cities in China in the 21st century. Ningbo is already the No.2 port in China, has a major export trade in textiles, clothing and other manufactures, and is a major centre for high-tech research and education, banking and finance.

The old city centre of Ningbo dates back to 700AD. It has a unique character epitomised by the scale and design of its older areas, the river system; new parks and plazas within the city and on the riverfront accompanied by well-designed new building complexes.

This leads to a city mixing a thriving business and commercial sector, with an active street life, reminiscent of much larger Chinese cities.

2.1   Urban design concept

The concept for the new center is based on traditional Chinese town planning principles of "the magic square" and the "field of nine divisions" leading to a grid of boulevards aligned to existing and proposed new canals. The grid is centred on the existing grand canal which links to the old city and provides a visual connection to the mountains beyond.

Figure 2:   City Centre Grand Canal Axis.

The vision for the NDEN is to reinforce the unique qualities of the old city centre and create a second centre for the metropolitan area. This will allow for central functions to be expanded within the new centre without destroying the unique qualities of the Old City. The express rapid underground transit system is proposed to link the two centres via a 5-10 minute journey, thus allowing shared central functions to be practically realised between the two centres.

The rich intellectual tradition of Ningbo is reinforced through the creation of the Knowledge Axis in the New City, while cultural facilities are located in the Urban Axis, which forms the major transport and green space link between the new and the old city centres.

The concept aims to achieve harmony and balance between the old city centre and the NDEN and to create a unified world city with two complimentary centres.

WIT Transactions on Ecology and the Environment, Vol 84, © 2005 WIT Press
www.witpress.com, ISSN 1743-3541 (on-line)

3   City size and density

By 2020, the Ningbo Urban Planning Bureau estimates that the Three River Division of Ningbo (including the NDEN and the old town) will have 1.5 – 2.6 million people, on 146km^2 of land. The NDEN portion will have approximately the same density of population as Berlin.

4   Creating a sustainable environment

The project brief called for the new Ningbo to be a model environmental city. The HASSELL approach was to blend traditional Chinese sustainable practices in agriculture, with modern ESD practices and technologies specifically developed for large cities. These are described in more detail in section 10.

5   Making better use of the NDEN site

The site allocated for the eastern expansion of Ningbo, is 39km^2 of former agricultural land running from the Yong Jiang River in the north, to the agricultural land intersecting the hills to the southeast. The main characteristics of the site which have influenced the concept development are listed below.

Site Element	Planning and Design Response
Existing canals	■ Adapt, re use and change to an urban role –performing a wider range of ESD functions ■ Re-use the best where appropriate ■ Replace the worst where heavy metal or nutrient build-up is excessive ■ Add complimentary soft edged wetlands, which will provide storage for flood control, drainage, and treatment for re-use.
Existing development	■ New areas and buildings to be retained where possible ■ Gradual replacement of poor quality environments ■ Retention of areas of the best traditional development, such as the town of Quiga. These include canals, streets, and buildings of cultural significance ■ Retention of new roads and canals, bridges and parks ■ Ensure incubator buildings have a prominent location in the new plan, as symbols of a high-tech city
Hospitals, Schools and Convention Centre	■ Retain wherever possible ■ Integrate within urban design ■ Incorporate in core area, allow for new hotels and business park adjacent as complimentary uses ■ Locate main public transport routes and tourist water transport to service these facilities

Soils and terrain	▪ Incorporate soil conservation and reuse program from development sites in allotments; open spaces; urban forestry opportunities, and wetlands ▪ Utilise flat terrain for minimal energy use in transport and efficient storage and distribution of stormwater for the recycling program
Existing Roads	▪ Connect new grid of roads to existing grid to the west and proposed new roads surrounding the site. Incorporate bicycle and public transport routes for staged development, from bus to light rail
Yong Jiang River	▪ Create a new park system and open up views to the river ▪ Recognise the significance of the river by the diagonal axis within the core ▪ Locate a boat harbour and neighbourhood centre on the river front ▪ Conversion of one existing tidal gate to water transport adding locks to allow river connection to old city centre
Hills surrounding to east	▪ Celebrate the hills to the south-east of the site by creation of a diagonal axis within the core area ▪ Allow views down the main canal to frame the hills, as a backdrop to the urban area
Vegetation	▪ Wherever possible conserve the few trees which remain ▪ Schedule major planting programs in boulevards and parks; and the macrophyte establishment programme, for urban waterways
Existing Rail System	▪ Allow for planned expansion at urban and regional level, and incorporate into regional and local public transport system within the Ningbo metropolitan area

6   Water transport

City development from 700AD onwards was always closely reliant on trade goods brought by water transport from the region and other parts of China, and then transferred for shipment by sea to other Chinese ports and beyond.

As with many port cities based on rivers, the Yong Jiang River is no longer able to provide the port function for the scale of shipping now generated by Ningbo. Nonetheless, the layout of the old port city has survived 1200 years almost unchanged. Although the main port has moved down river to the open sea due to size of vessels and cargo handling requirements, the legacy of water orientation of the city is a major area of potential interest to visitors to Ningbo. The HASSELL / Hyder concept for NDEN seeks to extend and enhance the experience of water for transport in and around the city.

The main potential water transport routes utilises two east west canals connecting the NDEN site to the old city. With the addition of some locks, the Yong Jiang River becomes a potential for routes between the NDEN and the Old Ningbo centre. The new centre plans show the routes between two urban centres and docking facilities next to major new cultural attractions on the Urban Axis. As much of the navigable canal routes are in newly constructed waterways, there is an opportunity to ensure depths are sufficient for navigation, and new bridges are designed with sufficient clearance for river craft. Existing canals to be developed, as navigable waterways will require dredging to allow appropriate boat clearances at maximum storage levels required for the water recycling system. Dredging will also remove nutrient rich silts from existing canal floors, minimising risk of algal blooms in the new water system.

7   Waterway function

The existing canal system which is retained for drainage and flood control, has been redesigned to perform the following additional functions:
- Drainage and flood control for an urban, rather than rural runoff
- A transportation network capable of being used by watercraft to connect the new and old centres
- Improved water quality by installing litter and oil traps, to remove pollutants associated with stormwater runoff, prior to entering water ways
- Provision for storage of stormwater for:
    a)   cleansing by removal of nutrients and bacteria in wetlands
    b)   re-use as a substitute for reticulated town water (non potable)

Addition of aquatic vegetation to waterbodies will improve the aesthetics of the canals, as well as removing suspended solids and nutrients, which will result in water quality improvement throughout the entire water system.

Smaller canals will distribute urban stormwater to the new wetland treatment areas, which are distributed around the system to provide an even level of treatment.

8   Sewerage treatment

- A reticulated sewerage system to the New District of East Ningbo will be provided to collect waste effluent from all forms of development.
- Waste will be treated to a tertiary level, suitable for recycling back into the NDEN for use on local garden and landscape watering, non-potable domestic use; and industrial water cooling; or for discharge into the Yong Jiang River.
- Provide for recycling of solid waste (sludge) from the treatment plants, for urban forestry, parks, agricultural uses, and other purposes both on and off site.

9   Landscape and open space

Planning of the landscape and open space system responds to the site in a manner that assists in the achievement of the overall goals. Key components are:-

9.1   The axes

The creation of the axes are both symbolic and functional. They trace the relationship of the site to the river and the mountains. They provide for a system of complex and diverse water bodies. These in turn provide an even distribution of water based ESD initiatives throughout the whole site; and create landscapes of functionality and delight, ranging from broad-scale water bodies, lakes and canals, to formal plazas and the public realm of the urban areas. They also provide the setting for major public facilities and the location of waste and wind power generators.

9.2   The linear parks

The park system performs a number of functions, including a buffer and screen to freeways and roads, opportunities to facilitate aquaculture, urban forestry, garden allotments; and an extension to water treatment methods.

The riverside parkland marks the importance of the river in the history of Ningbo, and the site. It aims to redress practices of the recent past, in which the river had become visually and physically inaccessible, so great has been the pressure of commerce and industry in the last decade of development of Ningbo.

9.3   The canal system

Smaller linear parks are proposed along the canals, which distribute water from development into the main water bodies for treatment and storage. These will be augmented by a still smaller system of canals and water bodies, developed within each development super lot. Smaller canals will be incorporated in the neighbourhood open space of each housing development, and be the responsibility of the building developer, rather than part of public infrastructure provision in the first instance. The penetration of the waterways into every part of the city will encourage their stewardship by the whole population.

9.4   Recreation facilities

Main sporting facilities will be provided as part of the major facilities programme. Other facilities such as walking and cycle tracks, playgrounds, pavilions and picnic areas, will be incorporated into smaller parks, and small sporting venues within neighbourhood centres and nodal points.

10   ESD strategy - preliminary performance assessment

10.1   An ESD agenda for Ningbo

Our objective has been to challenge the conventional wisdom traditionally adopted when planning large urban developments, by using ESD as a key driver in the design process. This approach will help deliver the model environmental city required in the brief.

The following project initiatives were suggested with performance indications:

10.2   ESD initiatives

10.2.1 Green power

50% of all electrical energy used in the new city is proposed to be green power harvested on site. Wind, solar and tidal energy sources, are considered and located on the ESD plan.

For wind power, up to 500 cylindrical wind turbines are proposed, located in:
A. The Knowledge axis
B. Within the eastern freeway buffer zone

Each wind turbines is rated at 800kw. The power produced will be approximately 1,750,000 megawatt hours/year. New technologies in compact, cylindrical wind turbines have demonstrated high efficiencies with the lower wind speeds prevailing in Ningbo, as well as reduced noise and visual intrusion.

10.2.2 Energy recovery from municipal wastewater

Two anaerobic egg digestors are to be installed as part of each existing wastewater treatment facility in order to produce power from biogas (predominantly methane).

Energy generated will provide power requirements for the wastewater treatment facility, with excess power being fed into Ningbo's electricity grid. A total of four Eggs are proposed as noted on the ESD plan.

10.2.3 Brown power: cogeneration

50% of the power is to be generated through a number of high efficiency gas fired cogeneration plants. Waste heat will be recycled for industrial heating and the heating of residential buildings.

10.2.4 Urban stormwater management

When all initiatives are complete, water usage from external sources in NDEN, will fall by 50% of existing levels in other urban areas of Ningbo.
ESD initiatives have been proposed for every part of the water cycle: -

The volume of stormwater that can be stored within the canal system is 2.5 million m^3. This is 3.8% of the total volume available from rainfall. More water can be stored during the dry season when flood protection requirements are reduced.

Approximately 50% of the total rainfall volume can then be recycled, depending on the future detailed design and operation of the system.

The existing 373ha of canals are to be reformed, with a proposed water area of 367ha that will include canals, waterways and wetlands.

Approximately half of the new water area will be in the form of soft edged water bodies, with peripheral emergent macrophyte plants: submerged macrophytes in deeper areas.

The catchment of the urban development area will produce approximately 40,000,000 m^3 of water per year.

Gross pollutants and petrol/oil traps will minimize entry of oil, litter and nutrient laden sites to waterways.

The improved water area will provide:

1. Storage for urban stormwater for cleansing, using natural ultra violet light and absorption of nutrients by macrophytes
2. Supply of treated stormwater for irrigation of nearby parklands and other non potable uses in urban development
3. Navigable water bodies which will connect the Old City Centre to the NDEN Centre and environs
4. Use of parts of the water bodies for aquaculture in adaptation from traditional Chinese practices, for the production of ducks, fish and water plants, and to encourage a fish population to predate mosquitoes

A third pipe system will be added to urban infrastructure to supply recycled water to all water consumers separate from potable water, with on-site ancillary treatment of recycled stormwater using UV and high rate filtration, after withdrawal from the wetland system.

Additional uses of recycled stormwater and cooling water will include: Fire fighting; wash down; industrial use and toilet flushing.

Figure 3:   New urban waterways.

10.2.5 Topsoil conservation

Topsoil has been gradually improved over several thousand years of traditional Chinese agriculture in the Ningbo area. The aim is to minimise waste and misuse of topsoil.

Proposed conservation measures:

1. Strip and store for reuse prior to construction or landfills
2. Avoid mixing topsoil with subsoil or other contaminants

3. Reuse on site in parks, wetlands, urban forestry, and productive allotments, as well as development of open spaces in residential areas, and outside site for agriculture

10.2.6 Land allotments
Land allotments will maximise the opportunities for residents to produce food in the city and will be provided in some residential areas. Reuse of topsoil and recycled water will be practiced in these areas.

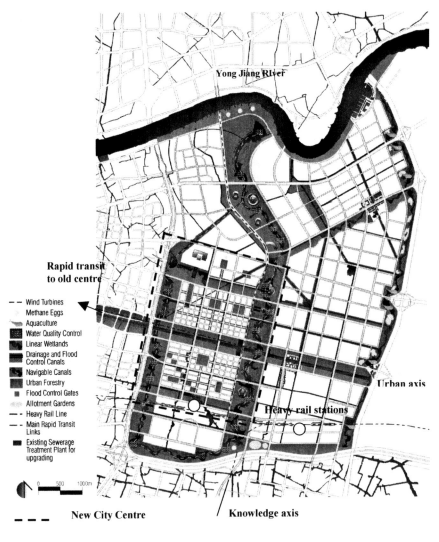

Figure 4:   New District of East Ningbo- ESD Framework.

10.2.7 Urban forestry

Urban forestry will be incorporated to provide the following benefits:
1. Buffer zones along freeways
2. Disposal of composted sewage and other wastes
3. Reuse of topsoil and recycled water, and other composted wastes
4. Noise absorption, air purification and visual screening. Harvesting of forests may be considered on a periodic basis.

10.2.8 Transport modes

Ningbo presently uses high levels of cycling (60%) and walking (20%) for journeys to work, by comparison with most major cities outside China.

Western cities utilise higher non-renewable energy levels on transport. New systems for Ningbo will minimize the increase in private car use, as community living standards improve.

As more mechanical transport is demanded, utilisation of public transport will be maximized by bus and lightrail routes in main road reservations; and the underground rail line along the Urban axis, the Rapid Transit Line linking the two urban centres, and the heavy rail centre and regional connection.

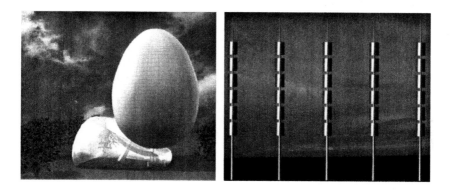

Figure 5:   Methane eggs and wind turbines.

10.2.9 ESD building design

A detailed schedule of ESD initiatives to be incorporated in individual developments was developed to compliment citywide ESD planning and infrastructure set out above.

11   Conclusion

The speed and quantum of China's urbanisation is unparalleled with 500 million additional population planned for cities by 2020. Modern sustainable systems for cities relate strongly to Chinese tradition and culture. The pattern of future growth of China's new cities, and the degree to which they can be made sustainable will affect all our futures.

References

[1] Ningbo Competition Brief – Ningbo Urban Planning Bureau – 2002
[2] The Magic Square – Alfred Schinz, Axel Mengez, Stuttgart, London, 1996
[3] Farmers of forty centuries: organic farming in China, Korea, and Japan / F H King, Dover Publications, Mineola, N Y (originally published 1911)
[4] Ningbo – New Urban District Concept Plan and Centre Design- HASSELL Hyder Competition Report, Melbourne, 2002

Underground development:
a path towards sustainable cities

D. C. Kaliampakos & A. A. Mavrikos
National Technical University of Athens,
School of Mining and Metallurgical Engineering, Greece

Abstract

The utilization of underground space has provided viable solutions with regards to many serious problems that modern cities are faced with. Underground development releases valuable space on the surface, improves the environmental quality and preserves the city-scape and the landscape. Lately, interest in underground space utilization in Greece is more intense than ever. This paper presents two characteristic cases from Greece's experience. Furthermore, important issues such as the public's considerations and land ownership are discussed.
Keywords: underground development, urban planning.

1   Introduction

Nowadays, the majority of the population of a given country lives in large urban areas, where the centre of today's life revolves. This situation begun to take shape during the beginning of the previous century and the trend continues to our days. The concentration of many people and human activities in relatively small surface area created the need to expand in order to fulfil the demands for better living conditions. Cities begun to expand "horizontally" or "two dimensionally" and the urban sprawl consumed neighbouring "green areas", while free surface space was evidently diminishing. We all experience the repercussions of this model of urban expansion as we bear witness to the degradation of the environmental quality, the deterioration of the living conditions, the scarcity of free space, the high land prices and other urban-related problems. At the same time, infrastructure and the industry demand all the more surface areas and as a result land prices continue to rise.

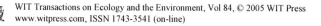

It is only lately that urban planners are beginning to realize that there is a resource practically unexploited so far, a resource with potential to alleviate the above-mentioned problems, as it has been proven in several cases, that resource is the underground space. Today underground development encompasses both the relocation of several surface land uses or activities, which are difficult, impractical, less profitable, or even environmentally undesirable to be installed on ground level, into subsurface built environments and the development of a strategic, multi-disciplinary vision about the use of space as integral part of the future physical planning and zoning [1]. Among the main advantages of the utilization of underground space are the release of space on the surface, the preservation of "sensitive" areas, such as historical city centres, archaeological sites and considerable energy savings. At the same time the installation of hazardous processes (industrial uses, hazardous waste treatment and disposal, etc.) below ground level ensures minimum risk and disturbances (visual impact, noise pollution, odours, etc.) generated by these activities [2].

One of the main interests of the Laboratory of Mining and Environmental Technology (LMET) of the National Technical University of Athens (NTUA) has been to raise public awareness regarding issues of underground development. Among the research activities of the LMET, two characteristic cases are presented and several issues related with underground development are discussed.

2 Underground development in Greece

2.1 General

The historical background of the utilization of underground space in Greece displays several contradictions. On the one hand there are records that prove that the Ancient Greeks had achieved a remarkably high level in the field of underground engineering. Their ability to construct complex mining underground works, such as shafts and adits, in difficult geological conditions such as in the case of the ancient Lavrio mines or important infrastructure works, such as the Eupalinus aqueduct on the island of Samos, gains more respect and admiration if one takes into consideration the primitive tools and limited resources available [3]. On the other hand during the following centuries underground works were considered to be a very difficult task and with only a few exceptions, underground solutions were disregarded. Therefore, apart from the Athens' first metro line, which included an underground tunnel and was inaugurated in 1895, fact that makes it one of the oldest in Europe and the underground works undertaken by the Greek Public Power Corporation (PPC), only limited underground construction actually took place. In contrast, Greece is experiencing, today, a significant increase in the number of underground infrastructure projects. The majority of them concern transportation tunnels. Approximately 16 new tunnels with a total length of 36 km will be constructed until 2010, while more than 20 tunnels having length between 500 m and 1000 m will have been commissioned by that year [4].

However, it was only a decade ago when the underground construction for sections of the Ymittos Western Peripheral Motorway (YWPM) was regarded as an almost impossible and non-feasible prospect. The technical feasibility of the tunnels was put into question both by construction companies and governmental authorities. What is more, they argued that the construction of underground sections would result in an overwhelming cost. Subsequently, a surface alignment was chosen for the motorway that would follow the foothill of Mt. Ymittos, hence destroying a large part of one of the few remaining forests in Athens. Inevitably, the proposal was met with strong opposition from the public and a research project for the preliminary investigation of the underground solution was assigned to the LMET. The findings supported that the underground construction was a realistic, environmentally friendly solution and the construction cost would be slightly over twice the respective cost for the surface road [5]. The research project's findings combined with the environmental benefits of an underground alternative and the intense public protests resulted in the project's redesign, which finally included almost 6.5 km of tunnels.

The above-mentioned case marked a gradual shift among the technical world of Greece regarding the development of underground projects. Nevertheless, there still remains a challenge. The technical community has not yet realised that underground development is more than the establishment of transportation infrastructure. Thus, the part of underground development that involves the integration of several underground facilities in the modern city's life, which perhaps is the most beneficial, has not been fully developed yet.

In support of this perception, LMET has undertaken research efforts focusing on the design of underground plans that will promote sustainable solutions compatible to the Greek conditions. The studies thoroughly cover all aspects of the underground endeavour, such as the excavation and support design, safety measures, mechanical installations, market research, living environment and finally the financial appraisal of the project as a whole. The concept behind each project is to study the specifications and requirements of specific activities on the surface and then try to transform the underground space in an ideal working environment, in compliance with all necessary standards.

With a view to displaying the true potential of underground development in Greece two selected cases of underground development in urban areas are presented hereinafter. Apart from these cases, there is a number of other ongoing promising projects, such as the underground car parks in the internal hills of Athens using the room-and-pillar method, the development of underground repositories for hazardous waste disposal, etc.

2.2 Underground logistics warehouses

According to a recent market research, the demand for modern storage facilities in the wider area of Athens is high. However, the construction of new logistic facilities is a very difficult issue, as it has to overcome serious obstacles concerning the scarcity of unified free land and its high cost.

On the other hand, the development of underground storage facilities can provide feasible solutions. Underground space that would have all the necessary features to host such activities can be created using the "room-and-pillar" mining method, as it has been thoroughly investigated [6, 7]. Furthermore, the evaluation concerning the establishment of underground logistic centres in Attica has demonstrated very promising results [8].   The site selected for the development of the underground storage facility is located in the south-eastern parts of Mt. Ymittos, near the Mesogeia region. The underground space will be converted into a state-of-the-art underground warehousing-logistics centre that would be as ergonomic, efficient and functional as a relevant surface facility.

The necessary modifications include the installation of utility networks (electricity, water supply, ventilation, lighting, communication network, safety arrangements, etc.) and the creation of the cross-docks. Taking into account the specifications set for the storage area, a square-patterned room-and-pillar layout was used, having a height of 11 m. The width of both the rooms and the pillars are 11 m, yielding about 62.000 m^2 of free space to be utilized and approximately 1.8 million tn of very good quality limestone that can be sold as aggregates. Calculations estimate the total construction cost for this underground storage facility at 94 €/m^2, which is significantly less than the respective cost for a typical surface facility in the same area, taking into consideration the average land price.

2.3 Underground oil storage facility

The tank farm in the Perama district near Piraeus is vital for the supply of refined oil products to the greater area of Athens. In these facilities, covering an area of about 30 ha, 175.000 m^3 of various oil products are stored in 102 steel tanks. The placement of the facilities within the urban fabric, just a few meters from the houses, has resulted not only in harmful environmental impacts but also in serious threats to public safety.

In search for a feasible solution to the growing problems and disputes the relocation of the tanks to another surface area has been investigated. This solution confronts two serious obstacles, the protests of the neighbouring communities and the land cost. Approximately 500 ha are required for the establishment of the tank farm, costing, with moderate assumptions, around € 12.5 million.

Table 1:   Comparative cost analysis between the surface and underground relocation of the Perama tank farm.

Cost categories	Underground (10^3 €)	Surface (10^3 €)
Land Cost	1,000	12,630
Civil Works	26,840	17,400
Mechanical Installations	18,300	21,480
Piping	2,000	16,140
Contingencies	7,140	10,150
Total	55,280	77,800

A possible alternative can be the relocation of the tank farm to an underground oil storage complex constructed in the same region [9, 10]. The project suggests the construction of 5 storage caverns with a total capacity of 200.000 m^3. The limestone bedrock is of good quality and can sustain such type of excavations without encountering significant difficulties. Without overlooking the financial benefits of the project, the main advantages lie in the environmental superiority compared to any surface alternative. The initial estimations of the cost of the project [11], including all surface installations (e.g. truck loading stations), piping and coastal facilities range at about € 55 million, almost 30% lower than the initial surface relocation alternative (Table 1).

3 Some important issues

3.1 Underground development and the environmental benefits

As a general rule the economic feasibility of underground works is judged on the grounds of the comparison between underground construction cost and surface construction cost plus the land cost. However, this comparison reflects only a part of the truth. It has been already mentioned that underground development offers certain environmental and social advantages. Therefore, in order to provide an answer regarding the social benefits of underground solutions, it is necessary to evaluate all the benefits and costs, including the so-called externalities. In other words, underground solutions should be assessed on the grounds of social cost-benefit analysis, using bottom-up approaches and environmental valuation methods. Although there are difficulties in environmental valuation, internationally the use of environmental economics in project appraisal has significantly increased, since it results in better decisions [12, 13].

Towards this direction, both primary research, based on revealed (e.g. Travel Cost and Hedonic Pricing) and preference methods (Contingent Valuation), as well as Benefit Transfer studies have been conducted. Empirical evidences show that the scarcity of free space, the need to protect existing green areas from further degradation and the will to enhance living conditions in modern urban centres tend to increase the cost-effectiveness of underground development and, consequently, the net social benefits.

To illustrate the above with an example let us consider the case of an underground parking facility. This plan allows for a corresponding increase of free space in the surface, which could be reforested. According to a recent research [13], it was estimated that an urban park of 20.000 m^2 in a densely populated region of Athens affects the dwelling prices at a range between 1 – 4 blocks. Within this zone, a dwelling attracts, on average, a premium of 14% up to 31%. More specific, given that the average unit price of an apartment, in the case examined, was about 1.320 €/m^2, the value of the green space capitalized in property prices of the surrounding dwellings ranged between 185 up to 409 €/m^2. It is apparent that one should compare the construction cost of an underground facility with the cost of building it aboveground, plus the cost of purchasing the land, plus the benefits created by the green area. If the value of non-market goods and services of the environment are taken into account, the result would be that in many cases an underground solution would be justified not only on the basis of environmental and social criteria but also on strict financial grounds.

3.2 Underground development and land ownership

Among the principal issues that hinder the promotion of underground development in many countries including Greece are the legal matters and in particular land ownership. Since the roman times, it has been accepted by most western laws that the "the owner of the surface also owns to the sky and to the depths" [14]. However, laws that control land ownership vary among countries, resulting in a state of uncertainty regarding the ownership of subsurface.

According to a survey carried out by ITA three main systems have been adopted [15]:

- Unlimited ownership to the centre of the earth
- As far as reasonable interest exists
- Only to a limited depth.

Some countries, having recognised the need to revise their legislation in terms of land ownership, have already started investigating three-dimensional delimited real estate. For example Oslo (Norway), has already adopted the three-dimensional real estate model [14]. In Japan the State owns the subsurface below 50m, the so-called "deep underground". In the case of the city of Montreal [16] it is widely accepted that the development of the underground city of Montreal would have not been accomplished, unless urban planners had decided to stratify the property rights both vertical and horizontal, etc. On the contrary, in Finland the landowner's right to the underground space is unlimited [1].

The latter condition stands for Greece. With the exception of the exploitation of certain mineral resources, the owner of the land is also the owner of the subsurface. Hence, the issue of who owns the underground space with respect to non-mining activities, especially in urban areas, where several conflicts exist between private and public interests, remains so far unsolved and the need to revise the Greek legislation, regarding land ownership, is more pressing than ever.

3.3 Public's common misconceptions

Currently, the public's perception of underground space is far from modern reality. Common prejudices and misconceptions usually prevail and more often than not an underground space is described as a dark, humid and claustrophobic environment. However, modern underground workplaces have nothing in common with this picture. They are supported with good lighting, sufficient fresh air, controlled climate and well-designed, safe and high-quality interior environment.

Undoubtedly public perception towards underground places plays a critical role and it should be taken into consideration. Accordingly, in order to

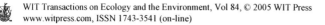

familiarize the public and the end-users with the modern underground solutions, state-of-the-art 3D visualization and virtual reality techniques have been employed. The results so far underline the fact that visual scene simulation is essential in persuading non-experts. Furthermore, 3D visual representation of underground spaces could alleviate, to a certain extent, the psychological reservations regarding going underground.

4   Conclusions

Undoubtedly the underground space will be intensively exploited in the future. The growing environmental concern and the principles of sustainable development force urban planners towards the utilization of underground space. Accordingly, unwanted or polluting activities and facilities should be placed underground, releasing, in that way, valuable surface space and improving environmental conditions and the quality of life.

Underground development can change the scenery regarding major problems of modern urban centres. Nevertheless, in order to achieve this goal, certain issues affecting the underground's ease of use, such as the ownership rights and the public's hesitations, as well as to some critical issues that affect the final decision, e.g. externalities should be addressed.

References

[1]   Ronka, K., Ritola J. and Rauhala, K., Underground Space in Land Use Planning, *Tunnelling and Underground Space Technology*, vol. 13, no. 1, pp. 39-49, 1998.

[2]   ITA, Underground Works and the Environment, Report of the Working Group on Underground Works and the Environment, *International Tunnelling Association*, 1998.

[3]   Kaliampakos, D.C., Mavrikos, A.A., Underground development in Greece: History, current situation and trends, *Proc. of the international conference, Sustainable Development and Management of the Subsurface*, 5-7 November, Utrecht, The Netherlands, 2003.

[4]   European Commission, Proposal for a Directive of the European Parliament and of the Council on Minimum Safety Requirements for Tunnels in the Trans-European Road Network, COM 2002/769, 2002.

[5]   Kaliampakos, D., Panagopoulos, K., Koumantakis, J., and Sofianos, A., The Environmental Importance of Using Underground Structures: The Case of Ymittos Western Peripheral Motorway, *KEDE Journal*, vol. 125 – 132, Jan. 1995 – Dec. 1996.

[6]   Benardos, A.G., Kaliampakos, D.C., Prousiotis, J.G., Mavrikos, A.A. and Skoparantzos, K.A., Underground Aggregate Mining in Athens: a Promising Investment Plan, *Tunnelling and Underground Space Technology*, vol. 16, no. 4, pp. 323–329, 2001.

[7]   Kaliampakos, D., Benardos, A. and Mavrikos, A., Underground Storage Warehouses in Attica, Greece: A Feasible Long – Term Solution, *Proc. 9th*

Int. Conf., Urban Underground Space: a Resource for Cities, 14-16 November, Turin, Italy, 2002.

[8]   Zevgolis, I.E., Mavrikos, A.A. and Kaliampakos, D.C., Construction, Storage Capacity and Economics of an Underground Warehousing – Logistics Centre in Athens, Greece, *Tunnelling and Underground Space Technology*, vol. 19, no. 2, pp. 165-173, 2004.

[9]   Kaliampakos, D. Benardos, A. and Mavrikos, A., Underground Oil Storage Perspectives in Greece, *Proc. of the Int. Symp., Geotechnological Issues of Underground Space Use for Environmentally Protected World*, pp. 333-338, June 26-29, Dnipropetrovsk, Ukraine, 2001.

[10] Benardos, A.G. and Kaliampakos, D.C., Moving Tank Farms Underground. A case study in Greece, *Tunnelling and Underground Space Technology* (under publication), 2004.

[11] LMET – Lab. of Mining & Environmental Technology, Pre-feasibility Investigation for the Construction of Underground Oil Storage Complex in Perama – Underground excavations. (in Greek), 2003.

[12] Damigos D. and Kaliampakos D., Economic valuation of mined land reclamation: An application of Individual Travel Cost Method in Greece, *Proc. of the International Conference, SGEM 2001: Modern Management of Mine producing, Geology and Environment Protection*, Bulgaria, 2001.

[13] Damigos, D. and Kaliampakos, D., Environmental Economics and the Mining Industry: Monetary Benefits of an Abandoned Quarry Rehabilitation in Greece, *Environmental Geology*, Vol. 44, Number 3, pp. 356-362, 2003.

[14] Landahl, G.M., Planning of Underground Space, eds Franzèn T., Bergdahl, S. and Nordmark, A., *Proc. of the Int. Conf. on Underground Construction in Modern Infrastructure*, pp. 95-100, Stockholm, Sweden, June 7-9, 1998.

[15] Sterling, R., Legal and Administrative Issues in Underground Space Use, *a Preliminary Survey of Member Nations of the International Tunnelling Association*, ITA, 1990.

[16] Escobar, M., The Next Urban Frontier - The Inner City and the Role of the Evolution of Real-Property Law in the 21st Century - A Montreal Perspective, *Proc. of the 9th International Conference, Urban Underground Space: a Resource for Cities*, 14-16 November, Turin, Italy, 2002.

Residential palimpsest: a novel dimension to city sustainability

G. Holden
School of Architecture, Victoria University of Wellington, New Zealand

Abstract

Wellington's city centre residential population has increased nearly threefold in the past twelve years to over seven thousand people. About two-thirds of city dwellers live in new apartments on the top of or within converted buildings. Apartments on top of buildings may be considered as a form of palimpsest in the conceptual sense of introducing a new layer. The new city residents make a significant contribution to the increased social vitality and economic activity of the centre. Restaurants, convenience stores and retail business have opened to service the population and give new life at the pedestrian level of buildings. By comparison with demolishing existing buildings to make way for new construction, 'residential palimpsest' literally builds on and uses the existing infrastructure. It generates relatively low-cost residential densification with little disruption. Architectural heritage and sense of urban place is largely sustained with this typology, though theoretical questions about architecture as object are raised when the design 'integrity' of the existing building is challenged by the addition, especially when visual compatibility is low. City centre residents mostly walk to their place of employment. They have the lowest car ownership in Wellington, thereby reducing motor vehicle impact on the city and studies elsewhere would suggest that with regular exercise as pedestrians their health is better than the general population. Residential palimpsest is enhancing the liveability of Wellington in a sustainable way improving environmental, quality of life and economic outcomes. The model could transfer to other cities.
Keywords: apartments on top of existing buildings, palimpsest, typology, layering, city sustainability, liveability.

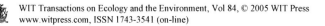
WIT Transactions on Ecology and the Environment, Vol 84, © 2005 WIT Press
www.witpress.com, ISSN 1743-3541 (on-line)

1 Introduction and context

Wellington is gaining a new building layer, adding to its already distinctive urban character, fig. 1. Previously a city with few inner-city residences, new apartments are being constructed on the top of existing buildings at such a rate that they indicate the emergence of a new typology. By extending the life of existing buildings and accommodating a significant proportion of the centre's population this phenomenon is contributing to the city's greater liveability, vibrancy and sustainability.

Figure 1:   Overview of Wellington city centre.

The population growth for greater Wellington, at 8.64% from the census years of 1991 to 2001, is less than for the whole of New Zealand (10.75%). However the city centre area at 250% increase has experienced a very much higher growth. Of this the South low-city area of TeAro, at 695% increase, generated outstanding growth and it is here that the majority of building-top apartments occur. Te Aro will be the focus of this paper [1].

TeAro has a history of layers of European settlement on earlier Maori use of the area. From the first European building activity in 1841 until the 1950's it has largely been a working-class mixed residential and service-warehouse-light

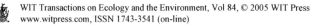

manufacturing area. Following two decades of decreasing residential population, in the 1970's and 80's TeAro was affected by strategic traffic movement changes together with a city centre building boom and national and regional economic restructuring during the period. The social and functional mix of the area remained diverse but with fewer permanent residents. Demolitions prevailed because of artificially high land values that undermined economic viability of the old buildings in favour of new development potential. Many buildings were un-occupied and their fabric was deteriorating [2].

In the favourable economic climate of the early 1990's TeAro started rejuvenating, influenced by several factors. A greater Wellington plan was established that contained the city's growth by re-zoning land on the perimeter from future urban to rural. Within the city centre many buildings were given an extended life through subsidised earthquake reinforcement and a new district plan created the potential for development in the air space above roof level to a maximum datum height. At the same time a new national performance-based building code was launched permitting light-weight (timber-frame) construction for apartment buildings. Together these circumstances contributed to a climate within which new construction on top of existing buildings became profitable for many small developers. All that was needed was market demand.

Inner city living in Wellington has become increasingly attractive for many people, seen as a more fulfilling alternative to suburban lifestyle. This appears to be influenced by sub-urban frustrations of travel time and property maintenance with the converse of easy access to work and facilities and easy maintenance of apartments. It is also influenced by increasing numbers of urbanites experienced through travel and through increasing numbers of immigrants from city-living cultures. Studies confirm that the strongest motivation for inner-city living is the centre's stimulation appeal, amenities and creative opportunities [3, 4].

2 Palimpsest

Palimpsest literally means "a piece of written material or manuscript on which later writing has been written over the effaced original writing" (Oxford Dictionary). If used outside of this definition palimpsest is metaphorical.

It has been suggested [5] that the use of 'palimpsest' in architecture, urban design and planning potentially may apply to a number of concepts. These include collage, erasure, tracing, scribing and what seems to be the most appropriate in this discussion, those of 'layering' which is understood as successive layers that make up the whole at any given moment and of 'transparency' which is understood in spatial terms as the overlap between separate elements that is claimed by both.

3 Typology

While building-top apartments do not yet appear as a model category in typical texts about residential typologies, which normally include terraces, town-houses, multi-story, duplexes etc. apartments-on-top can be discussed at the level of performance comparatively with other models. Horizontal and vertical access, building depth, site orientation, number and size of units, floor plan, the idea behind the design and its visual express are all relevant typological sub-topics for building-top-apartments together with other residential buildings.

Adopting the common sub-topic agenda mentioned, Holden [6] has proposed elsewhere that building-top apartments may be considered as an emerging independent typological model because of the distinctive characteristic of being built on top of existing buildings. The argument for this is that apartments-on-top must address several design matters of a constraining kind that do not apply to buildings that are built from the ground up. Key matters derive from the size, construction, strength and visual significance of the host building as well as opportunities to access the top through the base building.

Figure 2:   Building-top apartments in Te Aro.

Two thirds of Wellington's city apartment complexes atop existing buildings have been classified. Most contain between four and six apartments though there are several large complexes with up to thirty apartments. Sizes of independent apartments range from forty square metres up to two hundred square metres. Accommodation mostly falls within the range from single to three bedrooms.

Design of the new tops varies considerably influenced by responses to the sub-topic factors mentioned previously but especially by the relationship with the base-building design, materials and style. Generally the new apartments are of light-mass construction (commonly timber framed walls), constrained by the carrying capacity of the foundations of the host building and the intrinsic or reinforced structure of the host. About half of the classified cases are designed in a contemporary-modern style that contrasts with the host building while the others adopt a style that attempts to be compatible with the host.

The quality and performance of the type varies from excellent to poor. In some examples greatest concern lies with inadequate construction standards leading to waterproofing problems and failure of the structure and cladding. In others there is sub-standard internal planning providing inadequate natural light and sunlight or inferior ventilation. These deficiencies are capable of being addressed through more stringent application of the building act, including performance inspections. Other problems derive from the district plan's lack of treatment of design guidance for the type, including that 100% site cover is permitted without regard to implications for blocking access to light and air.

4   Sustainability

Residential palimpsest is recent in Wellington. While of itself constructing additions on top of existing buildings is not unusual, there being many examples across cities and across time, what is especially significant about Wellington is the extent of building-top apartments built in the past ten years and the consequential impact of the new residential population on the character and liveability performance of the built-environment and on economic outcomes.

Te Aro is one square kilometre. Over two thirds of its apartment complexes are independent building-top developments or building-top developments combined with conversion of at least part of the host building into apartments. Ground floor spaces of many of the developments accommodate retail outlets.

By comparison with demolishing buildings to make way for new construction residential palimpsest literally builds on and uses the existing infrastructure, constrained as mentioned earlier by the carrying capacity of the host building. Existing water supply and sewerage pipes are usually upgraded and new power cabling is installed. In most cases the building remains occupied to some degree during construction work on top, causing less disruption to users within the building and to nearby sites and passing traffic than new building construction.

The urban fabric and sense of place of the immediate area is largely sustained at street level because of the retained building, though the presence of new construction on top is obvious and potentially engaging if clearly visible from street level. In the Cuba Street heritage sensitive area within Te Aro, a precinct plan requires new additions on top to be set back from parapets thereby interrupting sight lines from the street [7]. Most examples of hidden building-top additions are so successful as to leave the casual pedestrian completely un-aware of the extent of residential palimpsest in their immediacy, fig 3.

Figure 3:   Out-of-sight building-top apartments set back from the heritage building's parapet.

In architectural terms the more aesthetically successful and intellectually valid additions that are visible are those which are un-ashamedly contemporary. These clearly contrast with the heritage host, fig 4. Contrasting is a philosophical approach that acknowledges the importance of each era to express architecture in the materials and forms of its time and to not engage in false heritage nostalgia. In this both parts of the assemblage retain full architectural respect as the eye is drawn to the qualities of the new and the old separately, rather than to the interconnecting zone of 'transparency' that tempts compatibility.

The residential population of Te Aro is approaching thirty five people per hectare, which while well below many European cities (eg. Copenhagen 59/ha, Vienna 67/ha) in new-world city terms it is relatively high. The population is predominately made up of the two distinct categories of young adults (20-40 years) at 53%, a high proportion of whom are university students, and middle-age and older people (50+) at 32%. There are slightly more males than females, the reverse of the national profile, and household size at 2.4 people compares with 2.6 for Wellington City and 2.7 for the whole of New Zealand. Only 32.6% of dwellings are owned compared with 61.7% for Wellington and 67.8% nationally, reflecting the relatively high university student population as well as investor driven ownership. More than half of the population have post-school qualifications, compared with 32% nationally. 66% of households have access to a motor vehicle compared with 90% nationally. European ethnicity prevails in the area at 86% compared with 80% nationally, with the next largest group being Asian at approximately 9% slightly ahead of Maori people. The median income of people in Te Aro is the highest in New Zealand, equal with other nearby areas in Wellington. There are very few families in Te Aro [1].

Figure 4:   Design integrity of new apartments contrasting on top of offices with shops at ground floor.

The demographics of Te Aro raise more questions than can be addressed here, but what appears to be significant in this discussion is that the area is undergoing rejuvenation attracting mobile people with high incomes. However this is not a process of gentrification in that it does not fit the normal conditions for gentrification wherein there is displacement of previous residents. In this case there were relatively few earlier residents and indications are that a high proportion of them remain.

Research by McMurray [4] into city centre apartment demand concluded that family status is a key location determinant in New Zealand cities, with apartments generally not being considered suitable for families. He proposes that as most discretionary spending goes to lifestyle choice categories, and that choosing apartment living is mainly a lifestyle decision, then greater attention than at present should be given to the quality and scope of urban elements and services that contribute to this. He also forecasts that with increasing numbers of young people delaying having children and with the nation's growing number of divorcees and elderly people there is a growing proportion of the population that will be attracted to apartment living. Increasing employment opportunities in the city centre has also contributed to the demand for apartments.

With relatively high disposable incomes and attracted by lifestyle, dwellers in the city centre spend more on food, housing, socialising and entertainment than the average for New Zealand. This expenditure has fuelled the growth in numbers of restaurants, bars, food outlets, convenience shops, art galleries, theatres and places of entertainment as well as the provision of services. It has been said anecdotally that Wellington now has more restaurants per capita than New York. Higher numbers and diversity of facilities is giving greater vitality in the centre and more people from the outer suburbs and more out of town visitors are also attracted to engage with the lifestyle opportunities that this offers. Recognising the link between quality of urban space and urban liveability, Wellington City Council has progressively been giving greater attention to the up-grading of public spaces including streets, sidewalks, squares, parks and the integration of artworks. Plans are under development with the assistance of international public space design expert Jan Gehl of Copenhagen.

At approximately 13%, Wellington has the highest Australasian rate of city workers who walk to work. While this compares reasonably favourably with many European cities it is considered that more can be done to achieve even greater pedestrian participation in the city. A project conceived to guide pedestrian engagement is that of 'Active Journeys', a research proposal to evaluate the relationships between: quality of the urban environment (experience of the journey including obstacles & barriers to the journey such as vehicle crossings); distance travelled (convenience and comparison with conventional thinking taking account of terrain and weather); legibility and permeability (clarity of way-finding and scope of choices of journey); health of the walkers compared with general population and implications on national cost of public health. Although this research has not yet commenced it promises to generate information to guide future policy and actions for greater city sustainability.

'Active Journeys' seeks to explore links between motor vehicles and pedestrian participation in the city, as identified by Woodward's [8] comments on relevant studies in Australia and New Zealand. He suggests that *"disease attributable to traffic pollution may be at least as great as that caused by road accidents"* and that *"perhaps the most serious public health implication of car-dependent societies is the unprecedented level of sedentariness that this lifestyle encourages"*. Woodward discusses the implications of declining physical activity including increased bodyweight leading to higher risks of cardiovascular disease and diabetes and also links between inadequate physical activity and certain cancers.

Woodward's sustainable city health message echoes true for several achievements in Wellington including: limiting urban sprawl, locating facilities closer to where people live and reducing the occurrence of low-density housing. However more needs to be done to increase 'active journeys' including improving public transport, footpaths and cycle ways and improving the quality of public space.

Wellington's economic performance is healthy because of its overall 'creative class' profile (after Florida [9]). Based on Florida's methodology studies undertaken by Zolner [10] indicate that Wellington is the only New Zealand city that is in the same league as the top centres of creativity in the United States, rating comparatively at about sixth. It is significant that the central city area represents 67% of the 'high-flying' creative class.

Florida (p290) writes that *"creative cities want to attract more creative people and are running out of suitable space to accommodate them unless existing well-serviced areas are rejuvenated and intensified for residential living"*. He points to the importance of proximity of research universities in the creative economy of cities, which he sees as *"a basic infrastructure component more important than railroads and freeways systems"*. Wellington is blessed with two universities located within walking distance of the Te Aro area. As well adding considerably to the city's economy through infrastructure and staff and student spending, the institutions provide technology, talent and a culture of tolerance. These are seen as key elements of a city's sustainable creative culture which helps develop social capital and capacity to respond to change.

5 Conclusion

Residential palimpsest in Wellington was not explicitly planned, it being more of a private developer led opportunistic outcome of the policy, regulatory and economic conditions that prevailed. However there is growing awareness of the importance of this typology to the city's sustainable development and it is likely that guidelines will be forthcoming to improve the minimum standard of construction and quality of habitable space. Cognisance has been taken by the local authority of the interest that residential palimpsest gives to urban character.

The urban spaces of the city are planned to be upgraded further to enhance city living and visitor experience. The improving liveability of the city is attracting new citizens, more investment and more jobs in the creative industries that are seen as major economic drivers of contemporary cities. There are obvious sustainable benefits of residential palimpsest in conserving and giving new life to old building stock and apartment occupants are contributing to sustained cultural, social and economic activity in the city centre.

Many of Wellington's existing buildings have adapted and grow for new residential use, and thereby contribute to a more sustainable future for the city. Residential palimpsest is a novel phenomenon that could transfer to other cities that have conducive property economic circumstances and a willing local government.

References

[1] Statistics New Zealand, *2001 Census: Population and Dwellings Statistics: Territorial Authority and Area Unit by Census Usually Resident Population Count, 1991, 1996 and 2001; Territorial Authority and Area*

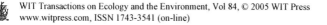

Unit by Private Occupied Dwellings, 1991, 1996, 200, Statistics New Zealand, Wellington

[2] Wellington City Council, *Cuba Precinct Plan,* Wellington City Council, 1990.

[3] Criscillo, v., Tong, H. *Wellington City Apartments: The Survey,* Moore Warburton, Wellington, 1999.

[4] Murray, S.A., *The Demand for Inner City Apartments: A Case Study of Wellington,* New Zealand. Master of Arts, Victoria University of Wellington, 1996.

[5] Palimpsest: writing material (as a parchment or tablet) used one or more times after earlier writing has been erased. Palimpsestic architecture: a working bibliography. http://www.xostudio.com/xostudio/palimpsest.htm

[6] Holden, G., Building-Top Apartments: an Emerging Typology. *The Planned City,* Petruccioli, A. et al (eds), Uniongrafica Corcelli Editrice, Bari, pp135-140, 2003.

[7] Wellington City Council, *Wellington City District Plan: Central Area Design Guide; Courtney Character Area Design Guide; Cuba Character Area, Wellington City Council,* 1994.

[8] Woodward, A.J., The motorcar and public health : are we exhausting the environment? *The Medical Journal of Australia,* Vol 177, No 11/12, pp592-593, 2002.

[9] Florida, R., *The Rise of the Creative Class,* Basic Books, 2002.

[10] Zolner, E., *The significance of employment in the Creative Class in New Zealand's eight largest urban areas,* Wellington City Council, 2002

Section 2
Environmental impact assessment

Quantitative approaches to landscape spatial planning: clues from landscape ecology

R. Lafortezza[1], R. C. Corry[2], G. Sanesi[1] & R. D. Brown[2]
[1]Department of Plant Production Science, University of Bari, Italy
[2]School of Environmental Design and Rural Development,
University of Guelph, Ontario, Canada

Abstract

Quantitative approaches to analyse and interpret landscape spatial patterns have developed rapidly during the last decade. The landscape ecological paradigm, based on a foundation of island bio-geography and meta-population dynamic theories, has emerged as a conceptual basis for incorporating such approaches to sustainable landscape planning and development. In this paper we describe two approaches to landscape pattern analysis that originate in landscape ecology: landscape pattern indices (i.e. landscape metrics) and cost-surface modelling. Landscape pattern indices quantify the composition and configuration of ecosystems across a landscape (e.g., patch size, shape, nearest-neighbor distance; proximity index; etc.) thus allowing quantitative comparison between different landscapes or within the same landscape at different times. Cost-surface modelling evaluates potential pathways between landscape elements (e.g., habitat patches) thus allowing quantitative estimation of landscape connectivity and/or fragmentation. The two approaches are described in terms of data requirements, GIS-based algorithms, and results interpretation. The approaches are then compared for applicability to landscape planning and we discuss the validity of approaches for different planning objectives. The two approaches are illustrated with examples on rural landscapes from Canada and Italy and the resulting quantities compared for implications to landscape planning. We conclude with practical advice for professionals seeking to incorporate quantitative approaches to sustainable landscape planning and development.
Keywords: spatial planning, landscape ecology, sustainable development, GIS.

WIT Transactions on Ecology and the Environment, Vol 84, © 2005 WIT Press
www.witpress.com, ISSN 1743-3541 (on-line)

1 Introduction

As a basic foundation of the landscape ecological theory, the study of landscape pattern has acquired relevance in the process of planning and developing sustainable landscapes. Quantifying the spatial distribution of landscape elements (i.e., patches and corridors) is a way to determine the degree of fragmentation and spatial heterogeneity of landscape mosaics, Gustafson [1]. Landscapes are heterogeneous systems composed of clusters of interacting ecosystems that vary in size, shape and spatial distribution, Forman [2]. Interactions among landscape elements are commonly described in terms of energy flows, nutrient cycling, and flora/fauna dispersal, which in turn determine the survival of species population and the persistence of the landscape in a "steady state" over time, Turner *et al* [3]. The ability to quantify landscape spatial patterns is therefore a prerequisite to predict landscape functions and changes, McGarigal and Marks [4], and to achieve sustainability in landscape spatial planning and development. Through pattern analysis, planners may gain additional information and knowledge on the: (1) composition and spatial configuration of the landscape as it currently appears; (2) transformation of landscape elements in response to ecological and social factors; and (3) evolution of the landscape under different planning and development strategies (i.e., alternative landscapes or landscape scenarios). For example, spatial attributes such as habitat area and structure, land uses, vegetation pattern, and distance between habitat patches may help planners to develop more ecologically sound plans and decisions. Starting from these considerations, in this paper we describe two basic approaches to landscape pattern analysis as part of a unique framework that originates in landscape ecology: landscape pattern indices (i.e. landscape metrics) and cost-surface modelling. Landscape pattern indices quantify the composition and configuration of ecosystems across a landscape (e.g., patch size, shape, nearest-neighbor distance; proximity of patches; etc.), thus allowing quantitative comparison between different landscapes or within the same landscape at different times. Cost-surface modelling evaluates the spatial configuration of landscape elements (e.g., habitat patches) allowing a quantitative estimation of landscape connectivity and fragmentation. The two approaches are described in terms of data requirements, GIS-based algorithms, and results interpretation. The approaches are then compared for applicability to landscape planning and we discuss the validity of approaches for different planning objectives. The two approaches are illustrated with examples on rural landscapes from Canada and Italy and the resulting quantities compared for implications to landscape planning. We conclude with practical advice for professionals seeking to incorporate quantitative approaches to sustainable landscape planning and development.

2 Landscape pattern analysis

The analysis of the landscape pattern generally involves the adoption of quantitative approaches and methods along with dedicated tools based on geographical information systems (GIS) and remote sensing (RS) technologies. Once spatial information on landscapes have been made available and/or derived from remotely sensed data, pattern analysis can take place considering each landscape unit (e.g., land-cover type) as part of a discrete patch mosaic: each patch is intended as a structural element of the landscape bounded by other patches that may be more or less similar. Landscape units are then subject to further analysis and computation aimed at determining quantitative measures of landscape composition and spatial configuration. In general, landscape composition refers to the relative amount of landscape units within the landscape mosaic, whereas landscape configuration refers to the spatial arrangement, location, and functional connectivity of landscape units. A basic scheme of the procedure for analysing landscape patterns is illustrated in fig. 1.

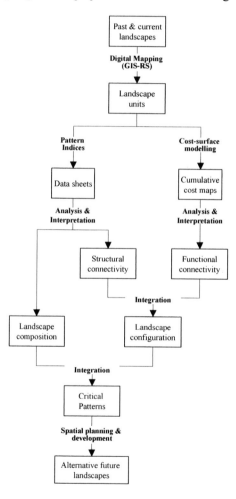

Figure 1:   Basic scheme of the procedure for the analysis of landscape patterns.

WIT Transactions on Ecology and the Environment, Vol 84, © 2005 WIT Press
www.witpress.com, ISSN 1743-3541 (on-line)

The analysis of landscape pattern is therefore a complex process of understanding the critical patterns of the landscape and their reciprocal interrelationship and interdependency. As a consequence, performing pattern analysis requires a full integration between the expanding technology (GIS-RS) and the theory in landscape ecology that lies behind numbers and algorithms. This integration could be achieved combining two basic approaches that originate in landscape ecology: landscape pattern indices and cost-surface modelling. These approaches to landscape pattern analysis have to be integrated in a unique-holistic framework, figure 1, while defining the "future" of the landscape through the acts of planning, designing and alteration of patch patterns.

2.1 Landscape pattern indices

In the pattern:process relationship, landscape pattern has been commonly described by the use of indices that quantify the elements of a landscape (composition) and how the elements are spatially arranged (configuration), [1]. Landscape pattern indices are calculated on digital map data. Spatial data, most often in a GIS, is classified for an ecological property of interest and measured with selected landscape pattern indices. Two immediate issues arise: the landscape classification system used, and the landscape pattern indices applied. Landscape classification for design and planning purposes usually yields land cover types with descriptive labels for human purposes: "road", "park", "orchard", "field", "forest", "lake", etc. While these labels may be entirely adequate for communicating a spatial design concept to stakeholders, they are not very useful for quantifying ecological consequences of plans or designs, Corry and Nassauer [5]. Landscape classification for ecological purposes requires that broadly-described land cover types be re-classified as, for example, habitat quality or units of landscape for some target guild or species. Even small changes in management, such as changes in farm tillage from conventional to minimum tillage, have implications for ecological outcomes such as carbon sequestration, runoff, soil loss, and habitat, Nassauer [6]. Indices commonly applied in landscape pattern analysis are myriad. In current versions of FRAGSTATS (a very popular index-calculating software), there are hundreds of indices available that can apply to a single patch, to all patches of a particular type, or to every patch in the landscape, [4]. It is imperative that indices be carefully selected because of a hypothesized relationship with an ecological property, Wu [7]. Applying dozens of indices and sifting through results to find an index which confirms the investigators' suspicion is not a valid use of landscape pattern analysis, [1]. Landscape pattern indices range from very simple measures (such as number of patches, or area of a class of land covers) to complex (such as edge contrast, or interspersion and juxtaposition of patch types). These metrics are applicable to either raster or vector spatial data. Some indices are applicable only to one data type (e.g., contagion cannot be calculated on vector data), and values can differ for an index calculated for the same landscape represented as either vector or raster data. If raster data are used (more indices apply to raster data than vector data) individual polygon identities should be preserved such that neighbouring, contiguous patches remain distinct, [5]. That is, if patches begin to blend together, index values become difficult to interpret because of how patches are connected through the landscape and measured as a single large patch with a net-like shape. Table 1 lists a small number of landscape pattern indices and how they are calculated. For a fuller description of how landscape pattern indices are computed on spatial data, including formulae and interpretation, see [4].

Table 1: Sample landscape metrics, algorithms and meaning. Modified from [4].

Index	Algorithm	Description	Implications in landscape planning and development
Percentage of landscape	$P_i = \dfrac{\sum\limits_{j=i}^{n} a_{ij}}{A}$	Percentage of landscape equals the sum of the area of a particular class (a_{ij}), as a proportion of the landscape area (A)	For ecologically-functional land cover classes, higher percentages are better; for disturbed or hostile land cover classes, lower percentages are better
Mean patch size	$MPS_i = \dfrac{\sum\limits_{j=i}^{n} a_{ij}}{n_i}$	Mean patch size is the sum of all patch areas of a particular class (a_{ij}), divided by the number of patches in that class (n_i)	For ecologically-functional land cover classes, larger mean patch size values are better; for disturbed or hostile land cover classes, lower mean patch size values are better
Aggregation index	$AI = \left[\dfrac{g_{ii}}{g_{ii}(\max)}\right] \cdot 100$	Aggregation index calculates the number of like adjacencies (joins) between pixels of patch type (g_{ii}) as a portion of the maximum number of like adjacencies for a particular class	For functional classes, increased aggregation is better; for disturbed or hostile land cover classes, less aggregation is better
Modified Simpson's evenness index	$MSIEI = \dfrac{-\ln \sum\limits_{i=1}^{m} P_i^2}{\ln m} \cdot 100$	The modified Simpson's evenness index is the proportional abundance of each patch type (P_i) relative to the maximum possible diversity for that number of patch types (m)	For highly fragmented landscapes, greater evenness is better than less evenness (implying that the landscape is more heterogeneous)

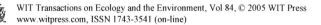

Landscape pattern index values are reported by FRAGSTATS in separate text files or data sheets for the individual patch, land cover class, or landscape level indices. Indices differ in their range (some are range-limited, while others are not) and units (some are unit-less, while others may be reported as percentages or in map units). Interpreting indices with different units or ranges can be difficult, and as mentioned, determining an ecologically-significant change in index values is challenging. Landscape pattern indices may be best interpreted by relating the change in pattern to some beginning or "baseline" condition. This condition may be the current or *status quo* landscape, and index values for alternative plans or designs can be relative to that baseline condition. Interpreting values relative to the baseline eliminates the difficulty of units and ranges, but does not resolve the issue of ecological significance. The landscape pattern index values can be useful to quantify how alternative landscapes compare to a baseline, and possibly rank alternatives for changes in landscape pattern that are desirable – if not ecologically significant. The missing connection for landscape pattern indices, as with many quantities, is determining if in fact a change in pattern will have a positive ecological outcome. The structural aspects of pattern are much more easily quantified than the functional aspects of pattern. However, landscape pattern indices are useful tools for comparing alternative patterns, though their value for inferring ecological function is questionable, [3, 5]. Landscape pattern index values are easily tested for statistical significance, which is part of their appeal. A statistically-significant change in index values, however, does not necessarily equate to an ecologically-significant difference in landscape patterns, [1, 3]. More empirical research is needed to identify the relevance of changes in landscape pattern and the difference in measures of landscape composition and configuration, Wu and Hobbs [8]. Of particular interest for planning and design applications is, finally, the issue of "scale". In terms of spatial analysis, "scale" refers to the extent and resolution of a study area. Changes in either, or comparisons among different extents or resolutions, affects landscape pattern index values, [3], Li and Wu [9]. Planning and design decisions often apply at resolutions from several to a few metres – towns, farms, highways, to walkways, roadsides, hedgerows. This challenges landscape pattern indices to be able to discriminate large, often poor-quality habitat patches, from very fine-scale bits of relatively-high biodiversity, Corry and Nassauer [10].

2.2 Cost-surface modelling

One of the basic principles in landscape ecology is that large and heterogeneous habitat patches and networks of habitat connections support higher level of species diversity by increasing the probability of interbreeding among species populations, Peck [11]. Under a planning perspective, habitat connections are essential elements to be investigated in order to ensure a balance between human and animal/plant needs. Dealing with organisms in the landscape (i.e., functional connectivity) implies broadening the common approach of planners to landscape assessment: from a mere site approach (object of planning) to more spatially explicit models and methods: landscape planners must be able to determine potential pathways among habitat patches and compare alternative patterns as consequence of alternative plans and decisions. As part of the landscape pattern analysis, the cost-surface modelling approach can be used to derive quantitative information on the spatial configuration (isolation *vs.* connectivity) of landscape elements, in absence of direct species movement observations. In applicative terms, this approach involves the adoption of a simple algorithm called: 'least-cost', Adriaensen *et al* [12] or 'least-resistance path algorithm' (*lrp-alg*), Lafortezza *et al* [13]. The algorithm requires 'gridded' landscapes in which patches are identified by a contiguous group of cells of the same mapped category, [3]. Specifically, two grid-layers are needed to run the algorithm: (1) a *source grid* that defines the source and destination patches (e.g., habitat patches from which species are expected to emigrate) and a *cost grid* (or friction layer) that assigns an impedance in some uniform unit measurement system that depicts the 'cost' involved in moving through any particular cell (as part of the intervening landscape matrix grid cells). In the *cost grid*, the numerical value assigned to each cell is assumed to represent the 'cost' *per* unit-distance of passing through the cell, where a unit-distance corresponds to the cell width, ESRI [14]. In landscape planning applications, the 'cost' may represent the degree to which landscape elements facilitate or impede movement of species across the landscape, considering the behavioural aspects of a focal species and/or a group of species, Taylor *et al* [15]. These values are preferably based on empirical data, or else on expert appreciation and assessment, Chardon *et al* [16]. Over the two input data, the 'least-resistance path algorithm' calculates, for each cell, the minimal cost (i.e., least cost) to reach a given patch from a source cell or set of source cells, Verbeylen *et al* [17]. The outcome of the cost-surface modelling is a *cumulative cost grid*: for any vertical or horizontal movement from cell A_i to cell A_{i+1} the cumulative cost, $CC(A_{i+1})$, is computed as the cost to reach cell A_i, $C(A_i)$, plus the average cost to move from cell A_i to cell A_{i+1} multiplied by the cell size (*d*), fig.2:

$$CC(A_{i+1}) = C(A_i) + d \cdot \left[\frac{C(A_i) + C(A_{i+1})}{2} \right] \qquad (1)$$

$$CC(A_{i+1}) = C(A_i) + d \cdot \frac{\sqrt{2} \cdot [C(A_i) + C(A_{i+1})]}{2} \qquad (2)$$

In the case of diagonal directions, eqn (2), the cost is multiplied by the square root of two to compensate the longer distance, [12]. The cumulative cost is thought to be the 'effective geographical distance' between landscape elements, [17]. The use of the cost-surface modelling approach in landscape planning and development is therefore a way to quantify the functional connectivity between habitat patches (landscape metrics are indeed indicators of structural connectivity) and to predict species dispersal in the landscape. In addiction, this methodological approach can be used to develop several alternative future developments (landscape scenarios) for a given landscape, each one corresponding to a different planning strategy and/or decision.

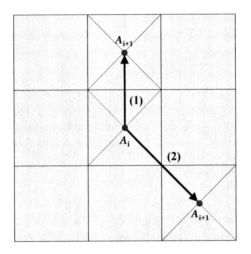

Figure 2:   Exemplificative scheme of the cost-surface modelling: (1) vertical and horizontal directions; (2) diagonal directions (see text for corresponding equations).

2.3 Pattern analysis in landscape spatial planning and development

As above mentioned, the co-use of pattern indices and cost-surface modelling may augment the understanding of landscape patterns and processes. The two approaches must be seen as complementary processes within the same unique framework, fig.1, which considers the clues from landscape ecology as foundational. Pattern indices provide information on the structural features of the landscape mosaic (physical composition and configuration) without explicit reference to ecological functions: landscape elements are thought of as independent elements in a landscape matrix, primarily with relationships only within a single land cover type. Cost-surface modelling considers the matrix in between habitat patches as an important factor affecting species movement and therefore the functional connectivity of the landscape. The integration of these quantitative approaches in the process of planning and development sustainable landscapes represents a key challenge for landscape ecologists. Especially in the case of highly fragmented landscapes, this integration may help planners in determining the amount of habitat remnants (e.g., forest fragments) and their reciprocal arrangement from a species perspective. A common task in landscape planning is indeed the allocation of new elements (introduced patches) in patchy mosaics: planners identify optimal positions for new housing developments, industrial sites, recreational areas, forest plantations, etc. Besides the consideration of economic and social factors (e.g., distance from main roads, water and soil availability, etc.), the plan must contain solutions that strengthen ecological processes inside and/or outside new patches. New patches have to be planned, designed and developed using quantitative information coming from the analysis of landscape pattern. The general composition of the landscape context indicates the variety and abundance of patch types along with the average size, shape and proximity distance among patches (as a measure of the structural connectivity). The configuration of the landscape describes the spatial character of patches based upon species-specific resistance values of the intervening matrix (as a measure of the functional connectivity). As a consequence, planners can acquire a better knowledge on "what has to be planned" and "how to plan" in order to meet the target of sustainability. Another recurrent objective in landscape planning is the creation of alternative future landscapes in response to land-reorganization projects, like brownfield sites rehabilitation, [13]. Planners have to build alternative options for their plans and decisions, thus recommending the one that best fits specified criteria and/or constraints. The analysis of landscape pattern may provide, in quantitative way, useful insights for predicting the effect of each option on the surrounding landscape elements: enhancement of landscape connectivity/fragmentation; modification of the general pattern of existing patches and corridors, etc. An example of the complementary use of pattern indices and cost-surface modelling as been recently proposed by Lafortezza and Brown [18] for the development of a new golf course in the rural Mediterranean landscape of Apulia, Southern Italy. New patches of Mediterranean vegetation have been planned and designed within the recreational area, considering: (1) the *pattern* of the neighbouring fragments of natural vegetation, expressed in terms of number of patches, average size, shape, and core area; (2) the *spatial arrangement* and *functional connectivity* of Mediterranean scrublands and pine/oak plantations with undergrowth in relation to the behavioural aspects of species like the Hermann's tortoise (*Testudo hermanni*). Another application of the pattern analysis in landscape planning and development has been described by Corry and Nassauer [10]. Indices were applied to ecological landscape planning alternatives for highly-fragmented Corn Belt agriculture watersheds (Iowa, USA). Corry and Nassauer [5], tested the applicability of landscape pattern indices for judging alterative landscape design and management across small watersheds (56-87 km^2). Using a small set of landscape pattern indices, results showed that not all indices ranked alternatives similarly for amount of habitat, heterogeneity, landscape connectivity, and landscape grain size. That is, while an index might imply that an alternative landscape may be better connected, another index might imply reduced landscape heterogeneity. When compared to spatially-explicit population models (small mammals) applied to the same alternative landscapes, indices did not validly imply ecological consequences. However, indices were reported to be adequate measures of changes in landscape pattern, and useful for judging alternatives for their pattern consequences, [5].

3   Conclusion

Planning for sustainable landscapes is a complex task that necessarily requires the adoption of quantitative approaches and methods that originate in landscape ecology. In this paper, we described two emerging procedures to investigate landscape patterns as part of a unique and holistic landscape ecological framework. Landscape pattern indices and cost-surface modelling represent 'two facets of the same medal': from one side, there is a need to determine the physical or *structural* characteristics of patches considered as discrete entities in themselves (e.g., woodlands, wetlands, prairies, grasslands, etc.); from the other side, it is critical to analyse the *functional* joinings or connections between target patches (e.g., habitat patches) in relation to one or more species of interest. Combining structure and function of landscape elements, landscape planners may strength their plans and decisions with new insights and ecological considerations. In practice, professionals seeking to incorporate such principles in their works can find in the proposed quantitative approaches two valid methods to: (1) appreciate the inherent heterogeneity of patches that surround the object of planning and development (patches typified by a fine-grain texture are likely to concentrate relatively high diversity in small areas); (2) estimate whether the shape of surrounding patches is regular or not (for a given size, a rounded shape ensures less points of interaction with the adjacent patches than an elongated or convoluted shape); (3) identify the appropriate size and shape of new green patches (larger and irregular patches of vegetation tend to support more suitable habitats for a wide range of species, and are more likely to be intercepted and colonized by dispersing species); and (4) determine the optimal location of the patch/patches being introduced through the analysis of the high-permeability pathways assessed in the *cumulative cost grid* (patches located along potential pathways are likely to facilitate or impede movement of species, acting as conduits or barriers). Despite the prominent value added by pattern measurement to landscape planning and development, it is important to note that quantitative measures must be tested in the field before extensively used. For example, monitoring protocol and indicators could be established to analyse long-term data collected in the study area and to weigh comparative applications at multiple scale of resolution (from coarse-to-fine scale). The definition of validation procedures of pattern indices and cost-surface modelling might be a productive topic to focus further study. Having a clear indication of the meaning of each quantity will certainly help to bridge the gap existing between fundamental theories (conveyed by academics and researchers) and final applications of principles (exerted by professional planners) in the field of sustainable planning and development. Planners and designers should continue to seek suitable quantitative tools for objectively judging the outcomes of planning. Landscape pattern indices and cost-surface models have revealed to be suitable, applicable tools that can be capably applied by planners and designers. Quantities that describe the structural pattern (composition and configuration) and functional connectivity of alternative plans or designs can be useful to infer ecological consequences. While it is questionable to use landscape pattern indices to imply an ecological consequence, index values can quantify the differences in landscape pattern. Alternatively cost-surface modelling can yield better information about ecological consequences, but usually for a single or few species, [16, 17]. Both quantitative tools seem to be useful within a set of limitations. The limitations do not fatally diminish the value of either tool for landscape ecological planning. In fact these tools have been legitimately promoted for improving applications of planning and design, Botequilha Leitão and Ahern [19]. In order to achieve more ecologically functional future landscapes, tools that quantify the structural complexity and functional implications of alternative plans are needed. Landscape pattern indices and cost-surface models are promising tools that have only begun to be developed and tested for landscape planning. Used wisely, and with full knowledge of the usefulness of each, these tools can lead landscape planning to more desirable outcomes.

References

[1]   Gustafson, E.J., Quantifying landscape spatial pattern: what is the state of the art? *Ecosystems*, 1, pp. 143-156, 1998.
[2]   Forman, R.T.T., Land mosaic: the ecology of landscapes and regions. Cambridge University Press, 632 pp, 1995.
[3]   Turner, M.G., Gardner, R.H. & O'Neill R.V., Landscape ecology in theory and practice. Pattern and process. Springer-Verlag, New York, 401pp., 2001.
[4]   McGarigal, K. & Marks, B.J., FRAGSTATS: spatial pattern analysis program for quantifying landscape structure. Gen. Tech. Rep. PNW-GTR-351. Portland, OR: U.S. Department of Agriculture, Forest Service, Pacific Northwest Research Station. 122 pp., 1995.
[5]   Corry, R.C. & Nassauer, J.I.., Limitations of using landscape pattern indices to evaluate the ecological consequences of alternative plans and designs. *Landscape and Urban Planning*, in Press.
[6]   Nassauer, J.I., Agricultural Landscapes in Harmony with Nature. *Visions of American agriculture*, ed. W. Lockeretz, Iowa State University, Ames, Iowa, pp. 60-73, 1997.
[7]   Wu, J.G,. Effects of changing scale on landscape pattern analysis: Scaling relations. *Landscape Ecology*, 19, pp.125-138, 2004.
[8]   Wu, J.G. & Hobbs, R., Key issues and research priorities in landscape ecology: An idiosyncratic synthesis. *Landscape Ecology*, 17, pp. 355-365, 2002.
[9]   Li, H.B. & Wu, J.G., Use and misuse of landscape indices. *Landscape Ecology*, 19, pp. 389-399, 2004.
[10]   Corry, R.C. & Nassauer, J.I., Managing for Small Patch Patterns in Human-dominated Landscapes: Cultural Factors and Corn Belt Agriculture. *Integrating Landscape Ecology into Natural Resource Management*, eds. J., Liu & W., Taylor, Cambridge University Press, Cambridge, Massachusetts, pp. 92-113, 2002.
[11]   Peck, S., Planning for biodiversity. Issues and examples. Island Press, Washington. 256 pp., 1998.
[12]   Adriaensen, F., Chardon, J.P., De Blust, G., Swinnen, E., Villalba, S., Gulinck, H. & Matthysen, E., The application of 'least-cost' modelling as

a functional landscape model. *Landscape and Urban Planning* 64, pp.233-47, 2003.

[13] Lafortezza, R., Sanesi, G., Pace, B., Corry, R.C & Brown R.D., Planning for the rehabilitation of brownfield sites: a landscape ecological perspective. *Brownfield Sites II. Assessment, Rehabilitation & Development*, eds. A. Donati A., C. Rossi & C.A. Brebbia, WIT Press, Southampton, UK, pp. 21-30, 2004.

[14] ESRI, Using ArcView GIS. Environmental Science Research Institute, Inc., Redlands, California, 1996.

[15] Taylor, P.D., Fahrig, L., Henein, K. & Merriam, G., Connectivity is a vital element of landscape structure. *Oikos* 68, pp. 571-573, 1993.

[16] Chardon, J.P., Adriaensen, F. & Matthysen, E., Incorporating landscape elements into a connectivity measure: a case study for the Speckled wood butterfly (*Pararge aegeria* L.). *Landscape Ecology* 18, pp.561-573, 2003.

[17] Verbeylen, G., De Bruyn, L., Adriaensen F. & Matthysen E., Does matrix resistance influence Red squirrel (*Sciurus vulgaris* L. 1758) distribution in an urban landscape? *Landscape Ecology*, 18, pp. 791-805, 2003.

[18] Lafortezza, R. & Brown, R.D., A framework for landscape ecological design of new patches in the rural landscape. *Environmental Management*, 34(4), pp. 461-473, 2004.

[19] Botequilha Leitão, A. & Ahern, J. Applying landscape ecological concepts and metrics in sustainable landscape planning. *Landscape and Urban Planning*, 59, pp. 65-93, 2002.

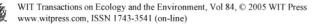

Estimating the environmental risk of construction activities on the ecological receptors along the Egyptian Red Sea coast

A. H. Sherif[1], A. H. El Sherbiny[2] & A. N. Hassan[3]
[1]Construction Engineering Department,
The American University in Cairo, Egypt
[2]Komex "Environment and Water Resources", Cairo, Egypt
[3]Institute of Environmental Studies & Research, Ain Shams University,
Cairo, Egypt

Abstract

Tourism is one of the main contributors to the Egyptian economy. The Red Sea coastal area represents one of the major tourist attractions. It has witnessed a large increase in tourism developments. Uncontrolled tourism developments, with their associated construction activities, have led to deterioration in the ecological resource base of the region. The paper investigates the construction activities and associated stressors that could result in deterioration of the valuable ecological components existing along the Egyptian Red Sea coast. Fulfilling that aim required estimating the ecological risks associated with the construction of an already established development, and tracking backward the stressors that were responsible for high-risk levels. An Environmental Risk Assessment (ERA) Model was used. It estimates the risk of causing environmental harm to existing ecological receptors, while considering the cumulative effect of different stressors and impacts resulting from various construction activities. As a result, changes in the master plan, construction methods and/or mitigation measures were suggested to decrease the magnitude of these stressors and minimize the ultimate impacts and final risk over existing significant ecological receptors.

Keywords: tourism coastal development, construction activities, environmental risk assessment, ecological risks, El-Gouna tourism center, Red Sea, Egypt.

 WIT Transactions on Ecology and the Environment, Vol 84, © 2005 WIT Press
www.witpress.com, ISSN 1743-3541 (on-line)

1   Introduction

Tourism is one of the main contributors to the economy of Egypt. It is among the three main sources of foreign exchange after oil and Suez Canal [1]. It contributes about 11.2 % of the Gross Domestic Product (GDP) [2]. In 2002, the number of tourist nights they bought was 2.3 million [3]. It is expected that the number of tourists in Egypt would reach 14 Million by year 2017 [3]. The Red Sea is planned to accommodate about 14 % of the tourist nights coming to Egypt in 2017 [4]. Besides its sunny climate, sandy beaches and tranquil sea, the Red Sea area is characterized by unique marine and terrestrial environment. The area contains more than 1,500 km of coral reefs and associated ecosystems such as Mangroves [5]. The marine ecosystem is home to over 300 species of coral, 500 species of aquatic plants and numerous fish and marine animals [6]. In addition, the magnificent valleys of the coastal Wadis support the highest diversity of terrestrial plants in Egypt [5].

The Egyptian Government has been encouraging investment in tourism development in the Red Sea area. Uncontrolled tourism developments have led to deterioration in the resource base of part of the Red Sea. The northern part of the Red Sea, for example, has witnessed a great deal of development that was responsible for the deterioration of some unique natural resources [7–13]. El-Gouna region, located north of Hurghada, has witnessed a great deterioration in the existing Sabkha, Sea grasses and Mangroves due to their direct removal [14]. It became apparent that unless there are management tools to regulate the relationship between development and natural conservation, the natural resources would deteriorate placing economic growth at jeopardy.

Construction along the Egyptian Red Sea coast could be very damaging due to the presence of highly sensitive ecosystems that could be easily affected by direct impacts, such as dredging in the reef flat, as well as indirect impacts, such as sediments transport to nearby corals.

2   Aim and methodology

This paper aims at investigating construction activities and associated stressors that could result in deteriorating the valuable ecological components existing along the Egyptian Red Sea coast.

This entailed: 1) Selecting an already established development; 2) Utilizing an ERA model to estimate the ecological risks associated with its construction; 3) Comparing the model results with previous research work that identified the adverse ecological changes associated with its construction; and, 4) Tracking backward stressors, and thus construction activities that were responsible for high-risk levels.

The ERA model, proposed by El-Sherbiny, Sherif and Hassan [15], was utilized to estimate the risk over each receptor from various impacts. After comparing the model results with previous research that considered adverse impacts associated with the construction of the case study project, a backward tracking analysis was performed for the impacts responsible for high-risk levels.

Thus, different alternatives regarding proposed master plan, mitigation measures and/or construction methods were analyzed and the risk was reevaluated according to the new conditions.

3   Description of the ERA model

An ERA model is utilized to estimate the risk of causing an environmental harm to the ecological receptors existing along the Red Sea coast as a result of proposed developments. It describes the various links between construction activities and the ecological receptors existing along the Red Sea coast (Fig. 1). In addition, it depicts and tracks secondary order impacts, which represent possible deterioration to the ecological receptors, and its relation to lower-order impacts and related stressors.

As presented by El-Sherbiny et al. [15], the ERA model incorporates four parts: area investigation, project analysis, risk characterization and risk evaluation. Area investigation is concerned with identifying the ecological receptors that exist within the study area, as well as evaluating their status significance and sensitivity. Project analysis involves specifying the project components and activities conducted during the construction phase as well as identifying the volume of work of each activity to evaluate the stressors magnitude. As for the risk characterization, it entails identifying the probability of stressors' transport through different pathways, impacts' duration (short term versus long term) and any direct removal that could be encountered during construction for existing ecological receptors. Finally, the risk estimation involves integrating the outputs of the previous three parts.

4   Description of the case study project

A case study was selected for this purpose. El-Gouna tourism center was selected based on its size, and accomplishment level, as well as the availability of data on construction activities and environmental conditions before and after development.

El-Gouna is located in the northern part of the red sea coast, 20 km north of Hurghada. It lies on the northern part of the alluvial fan of Wadi Abou Shaar and Wadi Umm Diheis, and the southern part of the alluvial fan Wadi Bali [14]. It is concentrated along the coastal strip with a length of about 10 km. It is built through in-land dredging to create a number of man-made islands that are separated by a number of artificial lagoons and channels, and connected by a complex system of roads and bridges. It includes 14 hotels, real estate villas and apartments, complete infrastructure and extensive support facilities and services, such as marinas, restaurants and cafes, sports and health clubs, nursery and school, hospital and pharmacy, aquarium, museum, airport, etc. (Fig. 2). Most of El-Gouna tourism center has been developed completely. However, according to El Gamily [14], modifications are continuously in process.

Prior to the area development, the existing location of El-Gouna resort was characterized by the presence of significant natural resources and unique habitat.

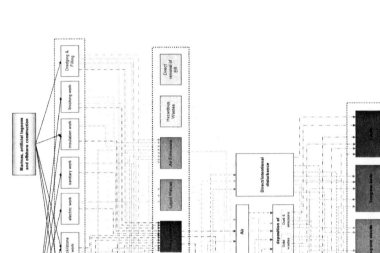
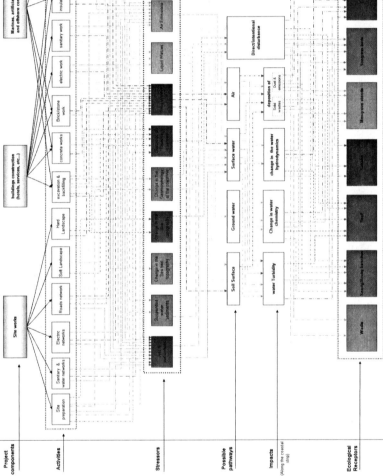

Figure 1: Model network diagram.

The coastal plain of El-Gouna region consisted of Sabkha, Mangrove Stands, Seagrass beds, reef and Corals [14]. The area was dominant with Sabkha deposits that used to cover about 6.3 km2. In addition, there was a Reef flatparallel to the coastline. Sea grass beds were also found along the coastline and next to the offshore reef. Coral communities only existed in the northern and southern part of El Gouna, and along the edge of the offshore reef. Mangrove stands were also scattered along the coastline.

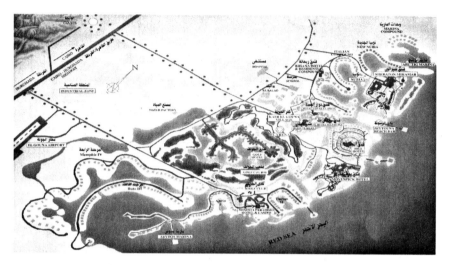

Figure 2:   El-Gouna Master plan (Tourism development Authority).

Previous research studies have been performed to assess the adverse impacts of El-Gouna development on existing ecological receptors. El Gamily [14] indicated that Sabkha is the most deteriorated ecological receptor. He estimated that 51% of the existing Sabkha was directly removed and substituted by other soil, 45% changed to man-made canals, 2.03% changed to various anthropogenic activities such as buildings and 1.26% deteriorated from construction related activities. The study also indicated that Mangrove stands followed by Sea grass beds are impacted mostly by the direct disturbance associated with the direct removal and changes in the geomorphology of coastline.

In another research [9], it was clear that the land-cover along the coastline was completely substituted with man-made canals and buildings. He indicated that the deterioration of corals is limited to the southern part of the development where two small marinas are located. He also added that the reef flat was distressed from the excavation and construction of near shore pathways.

5   Risk evaluation

Fig. 3 presents the maximum risk over each receptor. Sabkha is subjected to the highest risk level (1.00). It is then, followed by Mangrove stands (0.70), and sea grass beds (0.50). As for the corals and reef, they are exposed to risk levels below the mean (0.35 and 0.1, respectively). This output is consistent with the results of previous research work [9, 14] through which adverse changes associated with El-Gouna development were identified. Running the ERA model on El Gouna tourism center yielded the expected risks over each ecological receptor from related impacts (table 1).

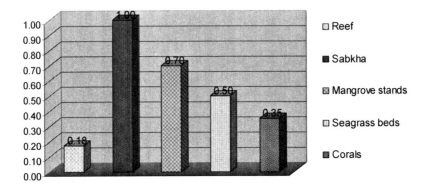

Figure 3: Maximum risk over each receptor.

Table 1: Individual risk, risk from related impacts.

Impacts	Ecological Receptors						
	Wadis	Sabkha	Mang. Stands	Seagrass beds	Reef	Corals	Beaches
Water turbidity	x	x	x	0.13	0.12	0.18	x
Change in water chemistry	x	x	0.00	0.00	0.00	0.00	x
Change in water hydrodynamics	x	0.35	0.50	x	0.09	0.35	x
Direct deposition of:							
- *Solid wastes*	x	0.00	0.00	0.06	0.00	0.04	x
- *Dust and particulates*	x	x	x	0.18	x	0.18	x
Direct disturbance by:							
- *Change in the site topography*	x	1.00	x	x	x	x	x
- *Change in coastline Geomorphology*	x	1.00	0.70	x	x	x	x
- *Direct removal of the ecological receptor*	x	1.00	0.50	0.50	0.18	0.00	x

(x) No relation

According to table 1, Sabkha is exposed to three sources of high risk attributed to direct/intentional disturbance: direct removal (1.00), changes in coastline geomorphology (1.00) and changes in site topography (1.00). Mangrove stands are also exposed to a high-risk level from three sources. The first source is the direct/intentional disturbance by changes in the geomorphology of coastline (0.7) and the direct removal (0.5). The other source is the changes in water hydrodynamics (0.5). As for the Sea grass beds, the highest risk emerges from the direct removal (0.50). However, the dust deposition and water turbidity posses risk levels of 0.18 and 0.13 respectively. For the Corals, the highest risk sources include the changes in water hydrodynamics (0.35), dust deposition (0.18) and water turbidity (0.18). As for the reef, it is exposed to a risk level of 0.18 due to its direct removal.

5.1 Backward tracking

According to the presented results, impacts that endanger the existing ecological receptors include:
1. Direct/intentional disturbance through direct removal
2. Changes in the geomorphology of the coastline
3. Changes in the site topography
4. Changes in water hydrodynamics
5. Dust deposition and water turbidity.

Tracking each impact backward through the network diagrams presented in Fig. 1 provided related stressors responsible for the high-risk levels (table 2). There are four stressors, generated from almost all the development related activities, responsible for the identified impacts. These stressors include the direct removal of the specified receptors; changes in the geomorphology of the coastline, dust and particulates generated and air emissions as well as changes in the seabed topography.

Table 2:   Receptors at risk and related impacts/stressors.

Ecological Receptors	Impacts	Stressors
Sabkha	- Direct/intentional disturbance	- Direct removal - Changes in coastline geomorphology - Change in the site topography
Sea grass beds	- Direct/intentional disturbance - Dust deposition - Water turbidity	- Direct removal - Dust & particulates - Air emissions - Dust & particulates - Water suspended sediments
Mangrove stands	- Direct/intentional disturbance - Changes in water hydrodynamics	- Changes in coastline geomorphology - Direct removal - Change in the Sea bed topography
Corals	- Changes in water hydrodynamics - Dust deposition - Water turbidity	- Change in the Sea bed topography - Dust & particulates - Air emissions - Dust & particulates - Water suspended sediments
Reef	- Direct/intentional disturbance	- Direct removal

5.2 Alternative construction activities and mitigation measures

After identifying ecological receptors at risk, and tracking backward responsible stressors and activities, required changes in the master plan, construction methods and/or the mitigation measures could be identified. Thus, the input data could be modified, and the risk could be estimated according to the new conditions, if the model was to be applied before the construction phase.

Since Sabkha, Mangrove and Seagrass beds are subjected to the highest risk levels, they were considered the receptors at risk. Some of the mitigation measures that could help in decreasing High-risk levels could include [16]: Avoiding disturbing high quality areas; using siltation control: silt curtains, settling ponds and/or appropriate dredging techniques; productive use of dredge spoils; proper disposal of contaminated spoil; working with natural topography as mush as possible; timing of construction to avoid migratory and spawning seasons; applying grading controls and require rapid re-landscaping of disturbed areas; fencing the construction site to contain litter and secure construction materials; daily pick up and proper disposal of construction wastes; applying emission limits; and control use of dangerous and hazardous material.

Within that respect, the ERA model was employed over four hypothetical consecutive cases to reevaluate the risk associated with each case. Consequently, the most suitable alternatives could be selected as early as possible before commencement of construction activities. Fig. 4 presents the obtained risk levels in each case in comparison to that of the original one.

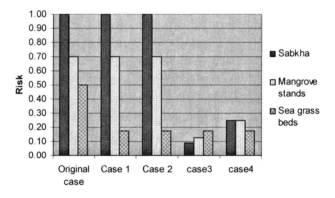

Figure 4: Comparison between the results of the effects of the mitigation measures and that of the original case.

In the first case, it is assumed that there is no direct removal, while keeping the magnitudes of other stressors in their original values. Eliminating the direct removal practices effectively reduced the risk over Sea grass beds. However, other receptors were still under stress. This consequential effect was expected. As mentioned earlier in the results analysis section, the maximum risk over the sea grass is associated mainly with the direct removal. However, other receptors, Sabkha and Mangrove stands, are subjected to other sources that posse high risk levels.

In the second case, it is assumed that the mitigation measures were revised so that the magnitudes of concerned stressors regarding related activities were taken to be either mild or negligible (i.e. stressors having negligible magnitude were kept the same, while others with severe, high or mild were considered to have mild magnitude). Suggested mitigation measures were not enough to decrease the risk levels. Sabkha and Mangrove stands are still under stress mainly from the direct disturbance. Sabkha suffers from the performed changes in coastline geomorphology and site topography. Mangroves are under stress from the changes in the coastline geomorphology and the changes in water hydrodynamics.

In the third case, it is assumed that direct/intentional disturbance due to changes in the coastline geomorphology and the site topography were eliminated, while keeping the status reached from the previous case. As shown in Fig. 4, this action has significantly decreased the risk over Sabkha and Mangroves.

In the fourth case, instead of eliminating the direct disturbance, it is assumed that the mitigation measures were revised so that all concerned stressors, shown in table 4, have negligible magnitudes. Such modifications also effectively decreased the risk levels.

6 Conclusion

As coastal zones are considered distinctive areas with sensitive ecosystems, rapid and unregulated development can lead to a great deterioration in coastal and marine environment. Adverse changes in the land-use/land-cover have been already witnessed along the coastline of developed zones. Investigating the ecological deterioration in El-Gouna region showed that Sabkha is the most deteriorated receptor, followed by Mangrove stands, Sea grass beds and finally the corals and reef flat.

Impacts that endanger existing ecological receptors included direct/intentional disturbance, changes in water hydrodynamics, dust deposition and water turbidity. Four stressors were found to be responsible for the generated impacts; they are direct removal of the specified receptors, changes in the geomorphology of the coastline, dust and particulates generated and air emissions as well as changes in the sea bed topography. Finally, activities generating previously identified stressors and related impacts were specified through backward tracking to include most of the construction related activities. Accordingly, different alternatives regarding the master plan, construction methods and/or the mitigation measures were examined, such that appropriate changes and precautions would be applied to significantly decrease the risk over existing ecological receptors.

References

[1] Euromonitor International. *Travel and Tourism in Egypt,* September 2000. www.euromonitor.com/travel_and_tourism_in_egypt.htm

[2]   Egyptian State Information Service. *Tourism industry contributes by 11.2% of GDP,* 24 July 2003, www.sis.gov.eg/online/html9/o240723j.htm

[3]   Egyptian State Information Service. *Egypt's tourism reports good harvest in 2002,* 27 Jan. 2003. www.sis.gov.eg/online/html8/o270123q.htm

[4]   General Authority for Urban Planning. *Urban development plan for Red Sea governorate: Year 2017,* General Authority for Urban Planning: Cairo, 2000.

[5]   Tourism Development Authority *Environmental management guidelines for coastal hotels and resorts: volume I,* Egypt: Tourism Development Authority: Cairo, 2000.

[6]   Egyptian Environmental Affairs Agency, Tourism Development Authority and Red Sea Governorate, *Red Sea coastal and marine protected area strategy,* Egypt, 1999.

[7]   Fanos, A. M, Khefagy A. A., Abu Aesha K. A. and Frihy O. E., Human impacts on the coastal zone of Hurghada, northern Red Sea, Egypt. *Geo-Marine Letters,* 16, pp. 324-329, 1996.

[8]   Hawkins, J. P. and Roberts C. M., The growth of coastal tourism in the Red Sea: present and possible future effects on the coral reefs. *Biological Conservation,* 76 (2), pp. 216-216, 1996.

[9]   Moufaddal, W. M. Remote sensing approach for assessment impacts of some human activities on the sensitive habitats of the NW Egyptian Red Sea coast. *Proc. of the International Conference on Tourism Development in Environmentally Sensitive Areas,* Cairo, Egypt, 2003.

[10]   El Gamily, H. I., Naser S. and Raey M. E., An assessment of natural and human induced changes along Hurghada and Ras Abu Soma coastal area, Red Sea, Egypt. *Int. J. Remote Sensing,* 22 (15), pp. 2999-3014, 2001.

[11]   Abozaid, M., *Impact of various human activities on the natural resources of the Red sea.* Egypt: Report, 2003.

[12]   Tourism Development Authority, *Land use management plan, south Marsa Alam, Red Sea coast.* Egypt: report, 2003.

[13]   United Nation Environment Program, Assessment of land-based sources and activities affecting the marine environment in the Red Sea and Gulf of Aden. *UNEP Regional Seas Reports and Studies,* No. 166, UNEP: Nairobi, 1997.

[14]   El Gamily, H. I. Assessment of environmental deterioration due to the land use/land cover changes using multi-dates LANDSAT, case study: El Gona region, Red Sea, Egypt. *Proceedings of the International Conference on Tourism Development in Environmentally Sensitive Areas.* Cairo, Egypt, 2003.

[15]   El Sherbiny, A., Sherif A. and Hassan A., A model for Environmental Risk Assessment of Tourism Projects' Construction on Egypt's Red Sea Coast. *Journal of Environmental Engineering,* under review, 2005.

[16]   Tourism Development Authority, *Best practices for tourism center development along the Red Sea Coast,* Tourism Development Authority, Cairo, 1998.

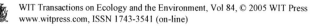

Dealing with uncertainty – integrated sustainability assessment based on Fuzzy Logic

R. J. Baumgartner
University of Leoben, Austria

Abstract

Assessing environmental and social impacts is associated with uncertainties caused by applied assessment tools, the definition of the object of assessment, system boundaries of assessment and data quality. In order to deal with these uncertainties the concept of Integrated Sustainability Assessment on the basis of Fuzzy Logic is presented. Integrated Sustainability Assessment combines ecological, social and economic assessments in one tool and consists of the steps definition of goal and scope, ecological assessment, economic assessment and general assessment. In the first step system boundaries and the object of assessment have to be defined. The ecological assessment evaluates the ecological impacts caused by the assessment object. For the social assessment, specific criteria have to be defined. For the economic assessment common economic concepts can be used. The crucial step of Integrated Sustainability Assessment is the general assessment, where the ecological, social and economic assessments are combined through Fuzzy Logic in order to consider the specific conditions of the decision situation. Preferences of decision makers are modelled with case-specific fuzzy sets. The result of Integrated Sustainability Assessment can be used as a basis for strategic decisions.
Keywords: integrated assessment, Fuzzy Logic, sustainable development.

1 Introduction

Integration of sustainability questions in corporate decision processes has been discussed for many years. Nevertheless, studies and analyses show that for instance ecological effects of products, services or technologies are barely or not regarded in business decisions (Dreyer [1], Hibbit and Kamp Roelands [2], Summers Raines [3]). Beside a higher environmental load as necessary, economic advantages through increasing competitiveness and innovation potentials due to a sufficient and adequate consideration of ecological questions can't be recognized.

In this paper the concept of Integrated Sustainability Assessment is presented, which is a step-by-step approach to integrate ecological, social and economic aspects of products, services or technologies into one assessment tool. It has been developed at the Department of Economics and Business Management, University of Leoben (Baumgartner [4, 5, 6]) and allows the integration of ecological and social aspects into corporate decision processes. It is strongly based on the concept of Sustainable Development, but flexible for specific corporate decision situations.

2 Sustainable development

The concept of Sustainable Development has been developed in forestry and came in mind by the so-called "Brundtland report" (World Commission on Environment and Development [7]); it consists of ecological, social and economic sustainability (Baumgartner [8]).

The objective of Sustainable Development is sustainability, which can be characterized by four principles. First, contribution to systematic increase in concentrations of substances from the earth's crust has to be eliminated. Second, contribution to systematic increases in concentrations of substances produced by society has to be eliminated. Third, contribution to the systematic physical degradation of nature through over-harvesting, introductions and other forms of modification has to be eliminated. Fourth, contribute as much as possible to the meeting of human needs in our society and worldwide, over and above all measures taken in meeting the first three objectives (Robert et al [9]).

3 Uncertainty in sustainability assessments

Assessing objects in the light of Sustainable Development is linked with several requirements, challenges and uncertainties. The requirements are that the ecological, economic and social dimension of Sustainable Development has to be assessed and that the decision situation has to be regarded. The first challenge is that each dimension of Sustainable Development is assessed with different measurements and scales, which have to be combined to the final result. And second, any sustainability assessment has to measure absolute and relative contributions of the assessment object to Sustainable Development.

Uncertainties of an assessment occur by the definition of the assessment object, the definition of the system boundaries for the assessment, the selection of assessment methodologies and tools, the quality of the data for the assessment and the integration of assessments based on different scales. To deal with these sources of uncertainty, the assessment object and the goal of the assessment has to be defined and described carefully. Based on this definition, the system boundaries can be determined. The selection of assessment tools has to be based on the requirements of the decision situation; the data quality has to be regarded with sensitivity analysis and simulation, whereas for the integration a suitable approach, which can integrate different scales, has to be chosen. These challenges and uncertainties are regarded in the Integrated Sustainability Assessment, which is described in the next section.

4   Integrated sustainability assessment

The concept of Integrated Sustainability Assessment assesses step-by-step ecological, social and economic aspects of products, services or technologies. It supports both strategic and operative decisions and follows main requirements of Sustainable Development. The concept is subdivided into the modules definition of goal and scope of the assessment, ecological assessment, social assessment, economic assessment and general assessment (Baumgartner [10]). In order to illustrate the concept, an example for the application is integrated in the next sub-sections. An innovative process technology is assessed regarding social, ecological and economic aspects in comparison to an established one (Baumgartner [11]).

4.1   Goal and scope of assessment

First module specifies the object of assessment and describes the decision situation and objectives of assessment. On the basis of these specifications, criteria for the following modules are derived. The object can be a product, a service or a technology. A detailed description and definition of the object is the basis for data ascertainment as well as for description of the decision situation (Baumgartner [12]). The assessment object is a new process technology; it is assessed relative to an established process technology. The assessment result is the basis for the purchase decision of the new technology.

4.2   Ecological assessment

In this module ecological effects are evaluated. First, system boundaries of the observed system have to be specified in order to build up a balance sheet of material and energy flows, which is the basis for the ecological assessment. This material and energy balance of the assessed object has to be evaluated with an ecological assessment tool. The tools Sustainable Process Index (SPI) (Narodoslawsky and Krotschek [13]), Eco-Indicator 99 (Goedkoop et al [14]), Eco-Points (Ahbe et al [15]) and CML (Hofstetter [16]) can be used. On the basis of the objectives a corresponding ecological assessment tool has to be selected which can be done with a specific rule set (see Table 1).

First of all, it has to be examined if the assessment is carried out for a strategic or an operational decision: a strategic decision is characterized through a long-term effect, a huge investment or a radical innovation. In case of unavailability of data for a material and energy balance sheet, qualitative criteria have to be used, as ecological assessment tools cannot be applied.

Regarding our example, the system boundaries have to be defined first. Due to lack of data concerning the life cycle and lack of resources to survey them, in this example the production process with inputs, outputs and emissions is regarded. Regarding to Table 1 a quantitative assessment tool is suitable. Due to the application of a new technology is a strategic decision, rule 1 is valid and the method SPI was chosen. The result of the ecological assessment shows that the environmental performance, measured with SPI, of the production could be improved by 75 percent with the new process technology.

Table 1:   Selection of ecological assessment tool (Baumgartner [17]).

	Rule 1	Rule 2	Rule 3	Rule 4
Strategic decision	Yes	No	Yes	No
Operational decision	No	Yes	No	Yes
Material and energy balance available	Yes	Yes	No	No
Applicable tool	SPI Eco-Indicator 99 CML	SPI Eco-Indicator 99 Eco-Points		
Using qualitative criteria			X	X

4.3 Social assessment

For social assessment, no integrated assessment method is applicable. Therefore qualitative and quantitative criteria have to be used. Examples are job satisfaction, working conditions, gender equality or wage level (Steven [18]). These criteria have to be defined for the assessment individually. In case of two or more selected criteria, the results have to be summarized for the social assessment. This can be done by value benefit analysis (Zangemeister [19]), which has several disadvantages (Bechmann [20]) or can be done with Fuzzy Logic.

For the social assessment of our example, the criteria working conditions and job enrichment have been defined. The first describes the physical working conditions regarding dust, heat, noise and malodor. It is assessed relative to the established technology on a scale of 0 to 100 and transformed to a linguistic variable. The variable consists of the terms "better", "identical" and "worse". The second variable job enrichment describes the mental working conditions and is also measured on a scale of 0 to 100 and transformed to a linguistic variable with the terms "better", "identical" and "worse". The two variables have to be combined with fuzzy logic to the social assessment. The criterion working conditions is assessed with 80, the criteria job enrichment is assessed with 40. The working conditions can be improved significantly with the new technology, due to a higher automation the job enrichment declines.

4.4 Economic assessment

This module assesses economic aspects of the assessment object. If data regarding costs and benefits caused by the assessment object are available, the quantitative instruments cost comparison method (Lechner et al [21]), benefit comparison method (Lechner et al [22]), return on investment (Schmalen [23]), net present value method (Horvárth and Reichmann [25]) and internal rate of return (Lechner et al [24]) can be used. Additional to these methods, or in case of lack of data instead, qualitative criteria can be used for the economics assessment. Examples are logistic performance, market situation or customers benefit (Hahn et al [26], Hering [27]).

For the economic assessment of our example, the cost comparison method is used. With the new technology, 20% of the production costs can be saved.

4.5 General assessment

In the last step single results of sub-assessments are integrated to a global result in order to generate realizable directives for business decision. The challenge of this global integration lies in the fact that sub-assessments are using different scales and that circumstances of decision and temporary changing determinants strongly affect final result.

A suitable approach to handle this complexity is based on Fuzzy Logic (Zadeh [28]). This method enables specific weighting of social, economic and ecological aspects and translates blurred input signals into stable global results. The structure of a fuzzy-based scoring model consists of the steps defining logical composition rules, fuzzification, inference and defuzzification (Mechler et al [29]).

4.5.1 Defining logical composition rules

The logical composition rules are defined as If-then-conclusions. The rules consist of a condition and a consequence part. An example of a rule could be as follows: "If the improvement of the environmental performance is small and the creation of value is strongly worsened then the total evaluation is unacceptable."

In the condition section several premises (here "environmental performance" and "creation of value") can be combined with the help of logical relations. Premises and consequences are linguistic variables, the values of the variables are words or sentences, the concept is illustrated in following example: consider the word "age" in natural language, it is the summary of the experience of enormously large number of individuals and cannot be characterized precisely. Employing fuzzy sets, age can be described in a mathematically process able form. "Age" is the linguistic variable whose values are words like "very young", "young", "middle age", "old" and "very old". They are called terms or labels of the linguistic variable "age" and are expressed by fuzzy sets on a universal set U $\subset R_+$ called "operating domain" measured in years. It represents the base variable age; each term is defined by an appropriate membership function μ, which can have triangular, trapezoidal or bell-type shapes (Bojadziev and Bojadziev [30]). In our case, triangular membership functions are suitable.

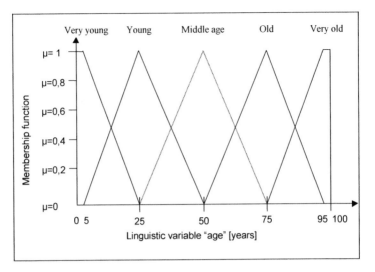

Figure 1: Linguistic variable age, based on Bojadziev [31].

The variable "age" on the universal set U = [0, 100] (operating domain of x (basis variable)) represents age in years by triangular and part of trapezoidal numbers which specify the terms "very young", "young", "middle age", "old" and "very old". The membership function can be derived through the gradient of the numbers; it shows the membership of an input to the terms of the linguistic variable, for instance a person with age of 15 is with $\mu = 0.5$ member of "very young" and $\mu = 0.5$ member of "young" (see Figure 1).

In case of Integrated Sustainability Assessment, the results of the ecological, social and economic assessment are transformed in linguistic variables. Therefore the specific circumstances of the assessment can be regarded through the definition of the terms and the operation domain.

4.5.2 Fuzzification

The membership functions of the terms of the linguistic variable have to be determined, which is called fuzzification. For instance, for a person of 15 years they membership functions are $\mu = 0.5$ member of "very young" and $\mu = 0.5$ member of "young", for a person of 50 years, $\mu = 1$ member of "middle age". This means, that a person of 50 years is exact part of the term "middle age". This fuzzification has to be done for all linguistic variable of the condition part of the defined rules (Kahlert [32]).

4.5.3 Inference

In the next step, the inference, conclusions from the premises to the consequences have to be made. For instance a rule is defined as followed: "If the improvement of the *environmental performance* is small and the *creation of value* is strongly worsened then the *total evaluation* is unacceptable". The membership function for environmental performance (small) is $\mu = 0.3$ and for value creation (strongly worsened) is $\mu = 0.7$, the inference defines the membership function for total evaluation (unacceptable). Consists the condition part of the rule of one variable the conclusion has the same value for μ. For two or more variables, it depends on the logical operator used in the condition part. Basis operators are "and", which represents a minimum operator, and "or", which is a maximum operator. In our example, "and" is used, therefore the conclusion is defined with $\mu = 0.3$ (Figge [33]).

4.5.4 Defuzzification

Here a sharp value of the membership functions of the conclusions is calculated. Therefore different methods exist - a simple, but sufficient represents the so-called Singleton procedure (Figge [34]).

For the general assessment the results of the ecological, social and economic assessment have to be transferred into a linguistic term. These results are united by logical rules for general assessment. With logical rules inputs (premises, conditions) are transformed to outputs (conclusions). The conclusion is represented again as linguistic term and be reflected the preferences of the users. The result of the conclusion can finally be defuzzificated, a single value for the general assessment is obtained. The application of this integrated assessment method is presented in the next session.

4.5.5 Example

The general assessment combines the results of the ecological, social an economic assessment. The results of these assessments have to be transferred in linguistic variables, the composition rules have to be defined, followed be fuzzification, inference and defuzzification. To support this process, the software "Fuzzy Control Manager" (Fuzzy Control Manager (Version 1.5), TransferTech GmbH, D-38118 Braunschweig) is used.

The linguistic variable for the ecological assessment is defined as "Ecological Assessment" with the terms "better", "identical" and "worse". The social assessment is the result of combining the variables "working conditions" and "job enrichment", represented in the variable "social assessment" with the terms "better", "identical" and "worse". The economic assessment is represented by the variable "economic assessment" with the terms "better", "identical" and "worse". The result of the general assessment is represented in the variable "general assessment" with the terms "applicable", "conditional applicable" and "not applicable" on a scale of 0 to 100 points. All linguistic variables are represented as triangular fuzzy sets.

The next step, the composition rules for the social assessment and the general assessment have to be defined. The rules reflect the preferences of the decision maker in this specific assessment and can differ in different assessments. Besides the sub-assessments, this is the central step of the Integrated Sustainability Assessment, as company-specific circumstances can be regarded in defining these rules. As the social assessment consists of two variables (working condition and job enrichment), they have to be combined with composition rules. For the general assessment, the social, ecological and economic assessments are combined. For instance one rule is defined as "If the ecological assessment is worse and the social assessment is identical and the economic assessment is better then the general assessment is not applicable". In total, 27 rules have to be defined. The general assessment represents the applicability of the new technology. In case one of the condition variables is worse, the general assessment is also worse. This means in this case, that advantages in one dimension cannot be balanced with disadvantages in other dimension. This would represent the preferences of a decision maker who refers to the concept of Sustainable Development. Of course, not every decision maker in every decision situation will decide in this way. But this assessment concept makes the necessary trade-offs between the ecological, social and economic dimension of Sustainable Development transparent.

The next step is the fuzzification. As the improvement of environmental performance is 75%, this value represents the membership function $\mu = 0.75$ for the term "better" and $\mu = 0.25$ for the term "identical" of the variable "ecological assessment". For the variable "job enrichment" the result is for the value 40 $\mu = 0.8$ for the term "identical" and $\mu = 0.2$ for the term "worse". For the variable "working conditions" the values $\mu = 0.6$ for the term "better" and $\mu = 0.4$ for the term "identical" is obtained. The improvement of production costs of 20 % represents $\mu = 0.2$ for the term "better" and $\mu = 0.8$ for the term "identical".

The inference and defuzzification according to the composition rules for this example was done by fuzzy control manager and shows following result: the new technology is represented through the value of 66. Remember that the value for the term "conditional applicable" is 50 and for "applicable" is 100. Therefore the application in this case can be seen positive, but maybe in depth analysis to the points "job enrichment" and "cost saving" should be made. An improvement in these criteria would improve the assessment results significantly.

5 Conclusion and outlook

In this paper the concept of Integrated Sustainability Assessment has been presented. This tool allows the integration of social, ecological and economic aspects into decision processes regarding assessment of technologies, products or services. Using Fuzzy Logic, individual preferences of decision maker and circumstances if decision situation can be regarded and makes them transparent in the decision process. An example for the assessment of a new process technology shows the practical applicability of this instrument.

References

[1]   Dreyer, P. Ökologisches Life Cycle Assessment (LCA) als Instrument des Umweltmanagements: Integration in betriebliche Abläufe und Strukturen, Transfer Verlag: Regensburg, ISBN 3-86016-062-1, 1997.

[2]   Hibbit, C., Kamp-Roelands, N. Europe's (Mild) Greening of Corporate Environmental Management. Corporate Environmental Strategy, 9(2), pp. 172 - 182. 2002.

[3]   Summers Raines, S. Implementing ISO 14001 - An International Survey Assessing the Benefits of Certification. Corporate Environmental Strategy, 9(1), pp. 1 - 10. 2002.

[4]   Baumgartner, R. Integrierte Bewertung für betriebliche Entscheidungsunterstützung. Umweltwirtschaftsforum, 11(1), pp. 54-58. 2003.

[5]   Baumgartner, R. Integrierte Bewertung für betriebliche Entscheidungsunterstützung - Teil II. Umweltwirtschaftsforum, 11(2), pp. 63-68. 2003.

[6]   Baumgartner, R.J. Sustainability Assessment - Einsatz der Fuzzy Logic zur intergrierten ökologischen und ökonomischen Bewertung von Dienstleistungen, Produkten und Technologien, Techno-ökonomische Forschung und Praxis, DUV: Wiesbaden, 2004.

[7]   World Commission on Environment and Development, W. Our Common Future, Oxford University Press: Oxford, 1987.

[8]   Baumgartner, R. Tools for Sustainable Business Management, Ecosystems and Sustainable Development - Volume I, ed. Tiezzi, E./Brebbia, C./Úso, J., WIT Press: Ashurst Lodge, Southampton, pp. 187-197, 2003.

[9]   Robert, K.-H. et al Strategic sustainable development - selection, design and synergies of applied tools. Journal of Cleaner Production, 10(3), pp. 197-214. 2002.

[10]   Baumgartner, R.J. Integrated Sustainability Assessment in the Mineral Industry - Framework and Example, Sustainable Development Indicators in the Minerals Industry, Vol. 1, ed. Martens, P.N., Glückauf: Essen, 2005, p. 405

[11]   Baumgartner, R.J. Integrated Sustainability Assessment in the Mineral Industry - Framework and Example, Sustainable Development Indicators in the Minerals Industry, Vol. 1, ed. Martens, P.N., Glückauf: Essen, 2005, pp. 410

[12]   Baumgartner, R.J. Sustainability Assessment - Einsatz der Fuzzy Logic zur intergrierten ökologischen und ökonomischen Bewertung von Dienstleistungen, Produkten und Technologien, Techno-ökonomische Forschung und Praxis, DUV: Wiesbaden, 2004, p. 131

[13]   Narodoslawsky, M., Krotschek, C. The Sustainable Process Index - A new dimension in ecological evaluation. Ecological Engineering, 6(4), pp. 241 - 258. 1996.

[14]   Goedkoop, M., Effting, S., Collignon, M. The Eco-Indicator 99: A damage oriented method for Life Cycle Impact Assessment (Manual for Designers), Pre Consultants B.V.: Amersfoort, 2000.

[15]   Ahbe, S., Braunschweig, A., Müller-Wenk, R. Methodik für Ökobilanzen auf der Basis ökologischer Optimierung, Schriftenreihe Umwelt Nr. 133, Bundesamt für Wald, Umwelt und Landschaft (BUWAL): Bern, 1990.

[16] Hofstetter, P. (eds). Bewertungsmethoden in Ökobilanzen-ein Überblick, GAIA, 1994.

[17] Baumgartner, R.J. Sustainability Assessment - Einsatz der Fuzzy Logic zur intergrierten ökologischen und ökonomischen Bewertung von Dienstleistungen, Produkten und Technologien, Techno-ökonomische Forschung und Praxis, DUV: Wiesbaden, 2004, p. 88

[18] Steven, M. Integration der sozialen Dimension des Sustainable Development in Rechenwerke. Umweltwirtschaftsforum, 9(4/2001), pp. 29-33. 2001.

[19] Zangemeister, C. Nutzwertanalyse in der Systemtechnik - eine Methodik zur multidimensionalen Bewertung und Auswahl von Projektalternativen, Wittemann: München, 1971.

[20] Bechmann, A. Nutzwertanalyse, Handwörterbuch der Wirtschaftswissenschaften, ed. Albers, W., G. Fischer: Stuttgart, 1982, p. 39

[21] Lechner, K., Egger, A., Schauer, R. Einführung in die allgemeine Betriebswirtschaftslehre. Vol. 19, Linde: Wien, 2001, pp.301

[22] Lechner, K., Egger, A., Schauer, R. Einführung in die allgemeine Betriebswirtschaftslehre. Vol. 19, Linde: Wien, 2001, p. 303

[23] Schmalen, H. Grundlagen und Probleme der Betriebswirtschaft: Studienausgabe. Vol. 11, Wirtschaftsverlag Bachem: Köln, 1999, p.587

[24] Lechner, K., Egger, A., Schauer, R. Einführung in die allgemeine Betriebswirtschaftslehre. Vol. 19, Linde: Wien, 2001, p. 311

[25] Horvárth, P., Reichmann, T. (eds). Vahlens großes Controllinglexikon, Vahlen: München, 1993, p. 341

[26] Hahn, D., Hungenberg, H. PuK: Planung und Kontrolle: Wertorientierte Controllingkonzepte. Vol. 6, Gabler: Wiesbaden, 2001, p. 372

[27] Hering, E. Prozessorientiertes Controlling-Management, Carl Hanser: München, Wien, 2001, p. 65

[28] Zadeh, L.A. Fuzzy Sets. Information and Control(8), pp. 338-353. 1965.

[29] Mechler, B., Mayer, A., Schlindwein, A., Wolke, R. Fuzzy Logic: Einführung und Leitfaden zur praktischen Anwendung. Vol. 1, Addisn-Wesley: Bonn; Paris; Reading, Massachusetts, 1993, p. 69

[30] Bojadziev, G., Bojadziev, M. Fuzzy Logic for Business, Finance, and Management, Advances in Fuzzy Systems - Applications and Theory, World Scientific: Singapore, London, New Jersey, 1997, pp. 44

[31] Bojadziev, G., Bojadziev, M. Fuzzy Logic for Business, Finance, and Management, Advances in Fuzzy Systems - Applications and Theory, World Scientific: Singapore, London, New Jersey, 1997, p. 45

[32] Kahlert, J., Frank, H. Fuzzy-Logik und Fuzzy-Control: eine anwendungsorientierte Einführung, Vieweg: Wiesbaden, pp. 339, 1993, pp. 54

[33] Figge, F. Öko-Rating: ökologieorientierte Bewertung von Unternehmen, Springer: Berlin, 2000, p.123

[34] Figge, F. Öko-Rating: ökologieorientierte Bewertung von Unternehmen, Springer: Berlin, 2000, p.124

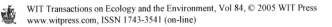

Environmental and hazard perception: a case study of a periurban area of Central Portugal

J. Gaspar[1], A. Tavares[2] & J. Azevedo[1,2]
[1]Geophysical Centre, FCT Coimbra University, Portugal
[2]Earth Sciences Department, FCT Coimbra University, Portugal

Abstract

This paper describes an attempt to understand environmental and risk perception in a periurban area. Based on physical characteristics, an analysis of surface processes and the identification of the development of land use, certain environmental vulnerabilities were isolated. The study area corresponds to a small-scale hydrological basin which enabled an inventory of local affinities and common interests to be produced. A survey was undertaken of a sample of 220 local residents in order to assess concerns about natural resources, hydrological, soil and atmospheric contamination, natural and technological hazards, the general quality of life and community needs. The results show that the major concerns focussed on natural resources, especially ground waters, noise and light pollution. Natural hazards do not appear to be relevant concerns, in spite of a long history of flooding. Conservation laws are identified as being important for the development of the local community, as opposed to planning and remediation measures.
Keywords: periurban area, water demands, environmental vulnerabilities, local survey data, local concerns, sustainable management.

1   Introduction

Studying the public's perception of quality of life and the general welfare of the community has become an important issue (Marris et al. [1]; Lima and Castro [2]). Vulnerability analysis, consisting of the identification and evaluation of natural and technological hazards, is nowadays both a concern for planners, politicians and residents and an area of interest for the media (Slovic [3]).

Human activities produce land disturbances which reflect both advanced technology and social concerns. The consequences of these disturbances present varying levels of areal extent, intensity and duration that require trigger impact recognition and mitigation development. The public and decision-makers' perception of environmental parameters and hazardous activities make it easier to adopt and provide institutional support for restrain and reclamation practices (Weston [4]).

These aspects are of particular relevance in periurban areas where changes in land use, different developments in particular areas and alterations and deterioration in the environmental parameters are evident (Tavares and Soares [5]).

The aims of this paper are to characterise the public's perception of environmental parameters and hazard vulnerability and their relevance in a residential community located in Central Portugal in a periurban area of Coimbra (Figure 1).

Figure 1:   Location of the study area in Central Portugal.

2   General description of the area

The area studied corresponds to a small-scale hydrological basin of about 21.4Km^2, with a SE-NW orientation that has two inflections (Figures 2 and 3).

The thread physical characteristic is the Ribeira de Frades water shed which flows into the large River Mondego floodplain. The flow regime is perennial in the mainstream and intermittent or ephemeral in the remaining stream network. The water stream has influenced land use and human occupation and is the most relevant environmental parameter in terms of local perceptions.

The hypsometry expresses values ranging from 259 m to 11 m in a sharply widening valley. The upstream slope angles of the basin have values ranging from 10-15%, and the downstream valley has less than 5%, with a 10-20% side slope.

The upstream valleys are cut into dolomitic and marl limestones Jurassic units, in contrast with the wide downstream valleys which rest on Cretaceous and Tertiary conglomerate, sandstone and mudstone units (Figure 2).

The main water input in the area studied comes from atmospheric precipitation. The annual precipitation (P) is close to 900 mm and about 50% is consumed by evapotranspiration. The remainder goes into infiltration (about 30% of P) and surface runoff.

Within the specific hydrological basin there are several aquifer units, organized into two aquifer systems. The upper and unconfined system lies on the Tertiary and alluvial deposits and has an important hydrodynamic relationship with the perennial stream-flows and discharge into several small springs; the depth of the water table changes from 0.5 m to about 16 m. The lower and confined aquifer system rests on the Cretaceous and Jurassic formations.

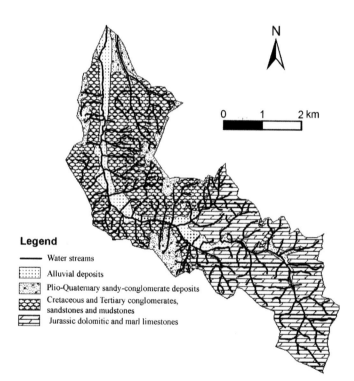

Legend

—— Water streams

Alluvial deposits

Plio-Quaternary sandy-conglomerate deposits

Cretaceous and Tertiary conglomerates, sandstones and mudstones

Jurassic dolomitic and marl limestones

Figure 2:   Geological and hydrological characteristics of the study area.

Figure 3 shows five main areas of land use: (1) agricultural areas with a significant share of natural vegetation; (2) forest and semi-open areas; (3) three important road networks and associated areas; (4) urban, with general discontinuous built-up areas (Assafarge, Palheira-Antanhol, Ribeira de Frades; (5) industrial and commercial units close to an airport structure.

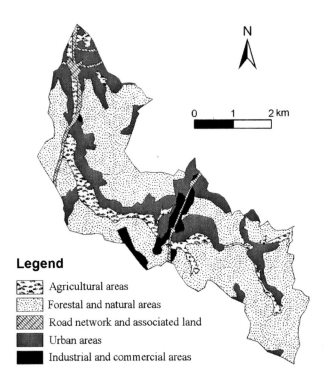

Legend

- Agricultural areas
- Forestal and natural areas
- Road network and associated land
- Urban areas
- Industrial and commercial areas

Figure 3:   Land use of the study area.

The area has about 10,000 residents with a very asymmetrical distribution. In the upper regions, the population density is close to 123 p/Km^2 and human activities are concentrated on agglomerations mainly involved in forestry and some agricultural activity. In the middle and lower areas the density is close to 300 p/Km^2 and the main human activities are in the service sector, with some industry.

Two highways and a national road cross the area and have had environmental impacts that have involved separating local communities and increasing urban pressure.

3   Methods and techniques

Geomorphological, geological, structural and soil occupation approaches were mainly supported by the available bibliography, thematic maps (Tavares [6]), and aerial photography, as well as fieldwork. Detailed physical cartography, including the surface instability processes, was undertaken on a 1/25000 scale. The hydrological setting was based on the meteorological and hydrographical data for the surrounding region and the geological and hydrological classifications were mainly supported by field observations and measurements.

The inventory of environmental problems and vulnerabilities was based on data from fieldwork collected during the year 2004.

The local survey questionnaire was planned and tested between February and April 2004 and administered in May and July 2004. The sample was divided according to physical and environmental characteristics and the number of residents in the periurban areas. The data was analysed with descriptive statistics, ANOVAs performance and the Statistical Package for the Social Sciences software in October, November and December 2004.

4 Environmental vulnerabilities

On the basis of physical characteristics an assessment of the changes in land use in recent decades, certain environmental vulnerabilities and hazardous activities can be identified:

- The rural features of the area have diminished, particularly due to forestry, the semi-natural reduction and deterioration of areas and a poor understanding of local water resources.

- The growth of continuous built-up areas for residential, industrial or commercial use has created large impermeable areas involving serious changes to the drainage network and infiltration rates.

- There has been a significant increase in water demand over the last two decades. The surface and ground water, as well as the soil, reveal considerable contamination. There are a few localised points that have serious pollution problems related to the excessive use of fertilisers in agriculture or to car repair activities and the packing industry.

- The downstream floodplain area traditionally used for agriculture has been abandoned and replaced by a built-up area, which has increased the future risk of damage and loss.

- The deforestation associated with slope cuts and anthropogenic fill due to road-building and construction activities has produced new evidence of mass movement and an increase in activity and surface erodibility.

- Road and urban land occupation and the growth of agricultural activities and forestry have increased the risk of fire in forests and areas covered with shrubs and herbaceous vegetation.

- The road network and associated areas have divided organised communities, leading to worsening public and social amenities, air pollution, noise and vibration impacts, light pollution, and soil loss.

- There has been a reduction in the quality of building work, involving changes in the types of buildings constructed and the materials used and also new demands on local access to services and community facilities. All of these factors have lead to conflicts in planning projects.

5 Local survey

5.1 Questionnaire organisation and interviews distribution

A structured questionnaire which incorporated elements relating to environmental and risk perception and also to the balance between public needs and planning policies was administered to 220 residents. The methodology involved direct and confidential interviews. Seven per cent of the sample was dropped out because of unreliable answers.

The questionnaire included 49 questions organised into six main sections: (1) definition of the natural resources, (2) forestry and agricultural needs, (3) hydrological and atmospheric contamination problems and their management, (4) perceptions of natural and technological hazards, (5) personal satisfaction with physical infrastructures, namely public sanitation, sports and recreational facilities, access to services, refuse collection, the water supply, proximity to work and public safety, (6) the general quality of life in relation to land use and overall planning.

The questionnaire included mainly closed questions with dominant scaled responses on a Likert or rating scale.

5.2 Survey data

The results show that a large majority of the interviewees (84%) considered that the area had a mixture of urban and rural characteristics, but assumed that local residential areas were rural. The younger groups in the panel generally tended to undervalue these rural characteristics.

Questions about the importance of forest land and related activities showed that about 70% considered this important or very important, as it was connected with commercial clear-cutting or was valued as an energy resource. There was a general understanding that the forest and open areas were well organized and clean.

The agricultural soil and agricultural activities were important or very important for 82% of the population interviewed because of their effect on the family budget, as an essential or supplementary resource. The agricultural roads were good but the fields were only fairly well tended.

The water courses were important to 48% and very important to 26% of the respondents, as they constituted a water supply (for irrigation and domestic use) and for ecological and aesthetic reasons. 47% classified the local water as being of poor quality, 37% stated that the quality was good and 16% did not know what to answer.

Only 10% of the sample considered the groundwater was not important, otherwise 48% of the residents thought it was very important, based on its importance as a supply of water and for environmental reasons. 71% of the sample considered the groundwater to be of good quality.

Figure 4 shows the importance of the specific environmental parameters for the respondents.

When questioned about atmospheric quality in their local area, 24% + 37% of responses stated that it was bad or poor and 39% indicated that the quality was fair. The most relevant factors affecting atmospheric problems were proximity to industrial and commercial areas and the presence of intensive lighting from the road network and associated infrastructures.

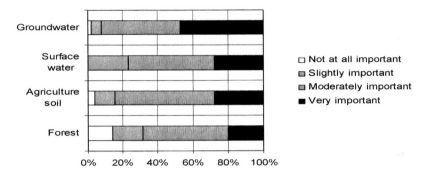

Figure 4:   Importance of the specific environmental parameters.

As far as proximity to, and knowledge of, the Ribeira de Frades watershed was concerned, it was clear that there was a better understanding of this in the downstream valley area, although over two thirds of the sample did not recognise the species of flora and fauna.

The welfare factors indicated by the residents are shown in Figure 5. Basic social concerns about the water supply, waste collection and sanitary sewing were indicated by more than 15% of all groups. Good access to health care services and good public order policies were factors selected by 13% of the sample. As observed in Figure 5, land planning and the issue of urban amenities and building projects were not important to local residents, especially the younger group in the sample (15 to 25 years old), who did not cite these in their answers.

Concerning the recycling of waste, only a few residents said that they never separated their waste. Paper and glass were the materials that were usually separated and half of the sample also separated plastic products and batteries from their household waste. Nevertheless the answers show a local lack of concern for recycling (38% rarely; 39% sometimes). Only 25% indicated problems with the refuse collection; the main reasons are related to a lack of information or a lack of effort.

When asked about risk perception, multiple answers were allowed and more then one hundred of the interviewees focussed on forest fires and water and air contamination. The results are shown in Figure 6. Natural (climatic and geological) hazards do not appear to be relevant concerns, despite a long history of flooding. No one reported seismic risk as a local issue and only a quarter of the respondents were concerned about traffic accidents. The sample also reveals a local concern for public safety.

WIT Transactions on Ecology and the Environment, Vol 84, © 2005 WIT Press
www.witpress.com, ISSN 1743-3541 (on-line)

When asked about public concerns that should be discussed or should be the subject of new management policies, several areas were mentioned, as shown in Figure 7. Conservation legislation relating to water, air and forest land was indicated, as were strategies for reducing the risk of floods. Urban planning and ecological conservation were not important for a large number of the population.

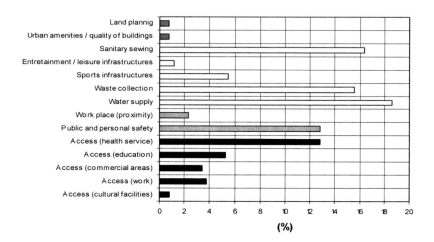

Figure 5: Importance of the welfare factors.

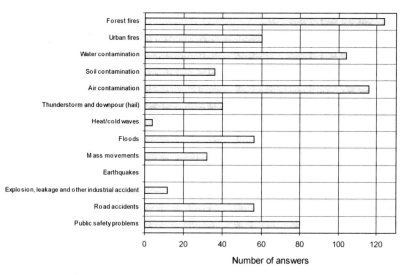

Figure 6: Local evaluation of the hazard targets.

When questioned about the interests of local politicians, access and land planning were mentioned, which suggests a difference of opinions.

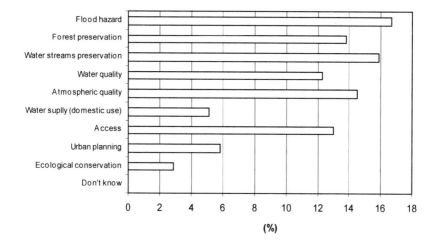

Figure 7:   Local environmental and hazardous concerns issues.

6 Conclusions

Recent developments in the study area have led to a significant increase in urban characteristics and new demands for employment, together with a lowered perception of natural parameters. However, a large majority of the residents stated that they liked living in the area and appreciated the rural lifestyle.

The results show a high level of local concern for water quality (streams, aquifers and the domestic supply), according to the environmental vulnerability detected. Atmospheric pollution also worries residents. The agricultural use of land is considered to be more important socially and for economic reasons than forestry. On the other hand, the aesthetic and environmental role of the forest area was also emphasised.

Social and community facilities and infrastructures are considered inadequate. The basic social concerns still focus on the main welfare factors, associated with access to healthcare and public or personal safety.

The recycling of waste has not yet become a habit.

There were marked differences between the major community issues and concerns and the interests of the local politicians and institutions.

General knowledge and perceptions of risk and of the environment allow for sustainable management of the natural parameters and for improvements to be made to the local potential for dealing with vulnerabilities.

References

[1]   Marris, C., Langford, I.H. & O'Riordan, T., A quantitative test of the cultural theory of risk perceptions: comparison with the psychometric paradigm. *Risk Analysis*, **18(5)**, pp. 635-647, 1998.

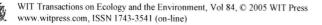

[2]   Lima, M.L. & Castro, P., Cultural Theory meets the community: Worldviews and local issues. *Journal of Environmental Psychology*, **25(1)**, pp. 23-35, 2005.

[3]   Slovic, P., Perception of risk. *Science*, **236(4799)**, pp. 280-285, 1997.

[4]   Weston J., EIA and public inquiries (Chapter 6). *Planning and environmental impact assessment in practice*, ed. Joe Weston, Longman, Essex, pp.120-140, 1997.

[5]   Tavares, A.O. & Soares, A.F., Instability relevance on land use planning in Coimbra municipality. *Proc. Int. Conf. Instability, planning and management*, eds. R. McInnes & J. Jakeways, Thomas Telford, London, pp. 177-184, 2002.

[6]   Tavares, A.O., Condicionantes físicas ao planeamento. Análise da susceptibilidade no espaço do concelho de Coimbra. Ph.D. Thesis Coimbra University, Portugal, 346 p.+ 26 maps, 1999.

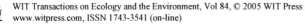

Tailoring the precautionary principle to pharmaceuticals in the environment: accounting for experts' concerns

N. A. Doerr-MacEwen & M. E. Haight
School of Planning, University of Waterloo, Canada

Abstract

Over the past decade, scientists have detected an increasing number of pharmaceuticals in surface water and groundwater in urban areas. The effects of these pharmaceuticals on aquatic ecosystems are uncertain, although in some cases pharmaceuticals have been linked with effects such as the feminization of fish. As concern exists that pharmaceuticals in natural waters could have subtle, long-term effects on the reproduction, development, and/or behaviour of aquatic species, the precautionary principle could arguably be applied to induce management action to reduce the release of pharmaceuticals to aquatic environments. As part of a larger study on the management of pharmaceuticals in the environment, we interviewed 27 experts on pharmaceuticals in the environment from the academic, government, and industrial sectors, to ascertain their views on the precautionary principle, and its implications for pharmaceuticals in the environment. Most had a favourable opinion of the precautionary principle, but many also cautioned that it must be applied in a proportional and carefully balanced manner, and that it should include continued research. Based on the results of our interviews, we discuss how the precautionary principle can be tailored to the problem of pharmaceuticals in the environment, addressing the concerns of scientific and management experts, and reducing the levels of pharmaceuticals being discharge to aquatic environments.
Keywords: precautionary principle, pharmaceuticals, risk management, scientific experts, proportionality, adaptive planning, aquatic environment, uncertainty, surface water, interviews.

WIT Transactions on Ecology and the Environment, Vol 84, © 2005 WIT Press
www.witpress.com, ISSN 1743-3541 (on-line)

1 Introduction

The precautionary principle (PP) is a decision making tool meant to guide society towards a sustainable future, by protecting human and environmental health. The best known definition is likely the one adopted from the Rio Declaration on Environment and Development: "Where there are threats of serious or irreversible damage, lack of full scientific certainty shall not be used as a reason for postponing cost-effective measures to prevent environmental degradation." [1, Principle 15]. The precautionary principle is founded on several premises, including: 1) prevention of harm is preferable to attempting to undo damage once it has occurred, 2) lack of scientific certainty 3) reasonable scientific basis suggesting a potential for serious harm, 4) duty to act [2, 3]. Inherent in the precautionary principle is the concept that deciding to do nothing – to maintain the status quo – *is* a policy decision, and that a decision to do nothing should be considered and reviewed as carefully and as skeptically as a decision to mitigate risk [4].

The precautionary principle can arguably be applied to the problem of pharmaceuticals in the environment, a problem concerning which scientific understanding continues to emerge. Pharmaceuticals, or medications used to maintain human and animal health, have been detected at low (μg/L-ng/L) concentrations in surface water and groundwater in a number of countries, throughout the past decade [5-7]. This paper focuses particularly on human pharmaceuticals, which are often detected near urban areas, especially in developed countries, where relatively large quantities of pharmaceuticals are consumed. The main route through which human pharmaceuticals enter the environment is consumption, followed by excretion, sewage collection, and then treatment at a wastewater treatment plant. Improper disposal of unused pharmaceuticals can also lead to their entry into wastewater. Unfortunately, wastewater treatment plants are not designed for the removal of pharmaceuticals, and removal rates are therefore low, often near 60%, depending on the compound [7]. As a result, residual quantities of pharmaceuticals are discharged to surface water as part of treated wastewater effluent.

While it is becoming clear that pharmaceuticals are ubiquitous in aquatic environments, their effects on aquatic species and ecosystems remain uncertain. Many researchers believe that pharmaceuticals could have long-term, subtle, detrimental effects on aquatic organisms, due to their bioactive nature [8, 9]. 17α-ethinylestradiol, the active ingredient in the birth control pill, is believed to have contributed to fish feminization [10], and the anti-depressant fluoxetine has been found in laboratory studies to induce spawning in mussels [11]. However, most pharmaceuticals have not been tested on aquatic species, and for those which have demonstrated effects in laboratory tests, the question of whether or not similar effects would be seen at lower, natural concentrations, remains. Assessment of effects on organisms and ecosystems is further complicated by the possibility of additive or less than additive effects of mixtures of pharmaceuticals and other compounds [12, 13]. Traditional environmental risk assessments are generally ill-suited to pharmaceuticals, as they rely predominantly on acute tests, whereas pharmaceuticals in the environment are only expected to have subtle, chronic effects [9].

In order to successfully integrate science into management, scientific experts are increasingly expected to work together with managers and to play a role in environmental decision making [14]. The purpose of our study was to assess the views and concerns of experts regarding the precautionary principle and its application to pharmaceuticals in the environment. Based on these, we discuss how the precautionary principle can be tailored to pharmaceuticals in the environment while meeting the needs of experts.

2   Research methods

As part of a larger study on the management of pharmaceuticals in the environment, 27 scientific experts from universities, governments of all levels, and industry, from Canada, the U.S., and Europe, were interviewed. The interviewees were mainly selected based on their contribution to the literature on pharmaceuticals in the environment and their participation in meetings and conferences on pharmaceuticals in the environment, although some were also chosen based on personal referral from other interviewees or contacts. Interviews were conducted in person whenever possible, with telephone interviews and e-mail questionnaires/interviews being used otherwise. Interviewees were asked two questions related directly to the precautionary principle, on which we report here: 1) Do you support the use of the precautionary principle in environmental decision making? Why or why not?, and 2) What do you think the precautionary principle means for pharmaceuticals in the environment?

3   Results

3.1 Concerns about the precautionary principle (Table 1)

In general, there was support for the precautionary principle among the experts interviewed, with 63% expressing a positive view of the principle, including 90% of European interviewees, 50% of Canadian interviewees, and 40% of interviewees from the U.S. However, several experts, including those who were in favor of the precautionary principle, expressed concerns about it. Their concerns mainly fell into 4 categories (Table 1):

1) Proportionality. The experts emphasized that precautionary action should be of a reasonable scale, proportional to the risk presented by pharmaceuticals in the environment (or other substances). Several experts stated that they felt the banning of pharmaceuticals because of environmental impacts was neither reasonable nor appropriate. The concern was raised that the precautionary principle had the potential to impede the development of technologies, such as pharmaceuticals, which might be beneficial to human health and well-being. A U.S. expert from the government sector believed the precautionary principle

Table 1: Examples of experts' concerns about the precautionary principle.

Proportionality of precautionary action	Definition	Socioeconomic balance	How much evidence is enough?	Other
"It doesn't mean you ban chemicals; it means you take an action, an appropriate action. Some people interpret the precautionary principle as in if there's any uncertainty, you ban it. And that's a very inappropriate response." – University, Canada	"The Rio Declaration, paragraph 15, is unintelligible and you cannot use it in public policy making." – University, Canada	"With limited resources, you have to reallocate some of them to these issues, and you take away from issues that are maybe more of an issue." – Government, Canada	"The question is, it's still a grey area around how much information is enough…what's appropriate time to jump in?" – University, Canada	Adaptivity: "If such concerns can be reasonably ruled out, then restrictions should be loosened." – Industry, Europe
"What can you possibly do to somebody who needs to take a medicine?...Let's assume it does something to the environment, let's say if you think of a million people taking Advil all across the country, what possibly could Health Canada do that would solve the problem?" – Industry, Canada	"I think that the appropriate application of the precautionary principle with the intention of the preamble of CEPA (Canadian Environmental Protection Act) and Rio is very appropriate." – University, Canada	"No I do not [support the use of the precautionary principle]. Again, that's based on the use of public dollars." – Government, U.S.	"All the examples I read are times where with hindsight you should have used the precautionary principle. So I don't know at this stage, how serious it has to get, that you use it up front." – Government, Europe	Stakeholder participation: "All stakeholders have to be informed properly so that they can act properly." – University, Europe
"There's some people who say, you must not do anything because you don't know what the future holds...If the guy who invented immunization was around today, the precautionary principle wouldn't allow it to be developed. You don't know what immunization might do to people. But how many people's lives have been saved, and the quality of that?" – Industry, Europe	"The thing about the precautionary principle is that there are already diverging opinions about what it really means, how to use it." – Government, Europe	"My feeling is that all risks need to be balanced versus economic costs and other risks." – University, U.S.	"The real question is how robust is the scientific evidence on which to base judgement as to environmental risks/threats for various types of drug molecules." – Industry, Canada	Dialogue/Debate: "You need a dialogue, where people can actually have a debate, raise the questions." – Industry, Europe

would require a goal of zero concentration to be set for pharmaceuticals in aquatic environments; the expert felt this was an unreasonable goal.

2) Definition. Several experts expressed concern about the lack of a clear definition for the precautionary principle. Perhaps not surprisingly, however, those who did discuss defining the precautionary principle did not agree on how it should be defined .The main concern regarding the definition was that a lack of definition would open the principle up to inappropriate use.

3) Socioeconomic Balance. The proper distribution of resources was of concern to several experts; financial concerns were the main reason cited by those who did not support the precautionary principle. Several interviewees emphasized that the risks of pharmaceuticals in the environment had to be balanced against other risks, including the risks incurred by taking precautionary action. There needed to be a prioritization of risks, as allocating funds to address the problem of pharmaceuticals in the environment would mean that the funds would not be available to address other problems. Several experts were concerned that the precautionary principle would not allow for such prioritization, and would lead to improper allocation of funds and unnecessary expenditures.

4) Sufficient scientific evidence to invoke the precautionary principle. A number of experts wondered about the level of scientific evidence required to invoke the precautionary principle. A European government expert pointed out that it is often only in hindsight that it becomes clear that management action should have been taken at a certain point; it is difficult to ascertain, as evidence of an environmental concern emerges, when the appropriate time is to engage in mitigative action

In addition to these four theme areas, individual interviewees raised several other concerns. A European industry expert who supported the precautionary principle made the case that it should be applied adaptively, with regulations and management strategies being adjusted to newly acquired information. A European university expert made the case that precautionary management needed to include disclosure of information to stakeholders, including the public, so that they could decide for themselves what sort of action to take. A second European industry expert emphasized the importance of societal debate concerning environmental problems, and expressed his concern that the precautionary principle did not allow for such debate.

3.2 Implications of the precautionary principle for the management of pharmaceuticals in the environment

Sixteen of the twenty-seven experts believed that applying the precautionary principle to pharmaceuticals in the environment required the implementation of management actions beyond research or risk assessment; however not all of them indicated which management strategies might be considered. Seven of the experts believed that the principle meant increased research into the problem of pharmaceuticals in the environment. Many researchers also felt that the precautionary principle meant pharmaceuticals should undergo environmental assessments, despite the current difficulties in applying traditional environmental assessment methods to pharmaceuticals. Environmental assessment regulations for human pharmaceuticals exist in the US [15] and are under development in the EU and Canada [16, 17]. Those experts who did suggest specific management strategies as a result of applying the precautionary principle to human pharmaceuticals in the environment, favored, in particular, enhancement of sewage treatment technology; reduction of pharmaceutical over-use; development of 'green' (i.e. biodegradable, less toxic) pharmaceuticals; and environmental labeling of pharmaceuticals, although other management strategies were also suggested. Two experts listed negative implications, related to their concerns in Section 3.1: increased costs and difficulties in developing and marketing pharmaceuticals, and an artificial goal of zero concentration being set for pharmaceuticals in water.

4 Discussion

4.1 Defined or flexible precautionary principle?

While some experts were concerned that the lack of universal definition of the precautionary principle would lead to its being used inappropriately, we suggest that the flexible nature of the precautionary principle holds great potential, as it allows the Principle to be tailored to specific problems [18], such as the problem of human pharmaceuticals in the environment. Rather than resulting in its inappropriate use, the 'fuzzy' nature of the precautionary principle makes capable of being shaped by stakeholders, including scientific experts, so as to become most appropriate to a particular environmental problem. Thus the precautionary principle can be thought of as a source of both guidance and dialogue for environmental problems, rather than an artificially restrictive dictum.

4.2 Point of invocation of the precautionary principle

Among the main concerns of the expert interviewees was the question of the level of scientific evidence of harm required for the precautionary principle to be invoked. This question has also been the subject of discussion in the academic literature on the precautionary principle [19-21]. For example, Müller-Herold et al. [21] propose a scientific screening system for chemicals, through which the more persistent, bioaccumulative and toxic substances would be selected for precautionary management action, including banning. This approach is not well suited to pharmaceuticals in the environment, however, because pharmaceuticals are 'pseudo-persistent', being ubiquitous in aquatic environments due to constant release, rather than inherent persistence. Also, many of the subtle effects which pharmaceuticals may have on aquatic organisms are not linked to traditional toxicity or bioaccumulation [13, 22]. Furthermore, requiring a scientifically measurable and quantifiable basis for invoking the precautionary principle is somewhat paradoxical, as the precautionary principle is meant to address situations in which scientific measurements and quantification are lacking [18].

Perhaps these difficulties in defining a point at which the precautionary principle is invoked should suggest that a clear 'point of precautionary action' is illusory, and furthermore, unnecessary.   As Rogers [19] points out , an as the comments of our experts imply, it is mainly the nature of the action resulting from application of the precautionary principle that leads to controversy.   We suggest, therefore, that the discussion should focus on the nature of the *precautionary action* called for as the understanding of the problem of pharmaceuticals in the environment emerges, rather than on trying to identify a point at which the precautionary principle should be invoked.

4.3 Precautionary action: proportionality and balance

Proportionality of precautionary action to the risk presented by pharmaceuticals in the environment, and the balancing of the various costs of management action against benefits, were among the main concerns of the experts in our study. Proportionality is also one of the criteria emphasized by governments advocating the use of the precautionary principle; discussion papers on the precautionary principle produced by the European Commission and the Canadian Government both stress the need for proportionality of risk management based on the precautionary principle [23, 24].   What might proportionality mean for pharmaceuticals in the environment?

The concept of proportionality recognizes, as many of our experts underlined, that management action carries with it a cost, whether social, economic, or in the form of an increase in a different risk (or a combination of these).   Therefore, precautionary actions with minimal costs – social, economic, and risk related – which at the same time meet the risk management goals, should be chosen. Risk management goals include a level of protection of the environment, but they may also incorporate elements which lead society broadly towards sustainability: for example, environmental stewardship, and environmental awareness. For human pharmaceuticals contaminating the environment, banning is not a proportional response. The costs in terms of human quality of life are too high, as there may be patients for whom only the medication in question can alleviate their symptoms. Instead, a more proportional and reasonable management strategy would be the labeling of the pharmaceutical as harmful to the environment, so that doctors can choose other medications when possible; or the listing of the medication as a last option drug. Pharmaceutical returns programs for unused medications could reduce the release of pharmaceuticals to the environment, while increasing consumers' awareness of the impacts they, as individuals, have on the environment. Having a goal of zero concentration for pharmaceuticals in the environment is neither proportional, nor is it achievable.   In fact, the European Commission's discussion paper on the precautionary principle specifically states that zero concentration for environmental contaminants should not be a precautionary management goal [23].   Instead, an attempt should be made to reduce pharmaceutical concentrations in aquatic environments to being as low as *reasonably practical*.

Proportionality may also mean that upgrading *all* wastewater treatment plants to include enhanced treatment methods, such as ozonation or membrane filtration, is not a good management option at this time. Firstly, this option would be extremely expensive [25], and would divert resources from other areas. Secondly, a European industry expert raised the point that upgrading wastewater treatment facilities would lead to greater energy use. Although water quality would be enhanced, the release of carbon dioxide to the atmosphere would be increased; both environmental compartments must be considered. Therefore, it may be more reasonable to target urban areas which release the greatest loads of pharmaceuticals to the environment, and areas where there is little dilution of wastewater, for enhanced wastewater treatment technology. Areas with other water quality problems resulting from the discharge of wastewater, which could be partly remediated by implementing enhanced treatment methods, should also be targeted. Monitoring of the quality of surface waters and wastewater treatment plant influents and effluents can be used to determine which areas are best suited for investments in enhanced wastewater treatment technology.

4.4 Precautionary action: adaptivity and research

Adaptive planning theory suggests that environmental management strategies should be flexible, account for uncertainty, and that the results of research and monitoring should be the basis for modification of management strategies [26, 27]. Ensuring that precautionary action adheres to the theory of adaptive planning may help to address the concerns of experts who emphasize the need for management action to be driven by continuing research. For pharmaceuticals in the environment, adaptivity may mean implementing management options such as pharmaceutical returns programs, pharmaceutical labeling, and education programs in the immediate future, while the effects of pharmaceuticals in the environment are still highly uncertain. These management strategies are easy to modify, if research indicates that environmental contamination by pharmaceuticals is either of greater or lesser concern than our current understanding suggests. If further evidence emerges that pharmaceuticals have detrimental effects on aquatic ecosystems, more permanent and more effective management options, such as advanced wastewater treatment technology, should be implemented in addition to existing strategies. Continuing research is essential to ensure that optimal precautionary management action is implemented.

4.5 Informing stakeholders and communicating risk

Several interviewees alluded to the importance of informing stakeholders such as the public about pharmaceuticals in the environment, and of having broad discussions of the issue. Informing and listening to stakeholders is an important component of the precautionary principle [28, 29], and the public should certainly be made aware of this environmental concern. Suggestions that the public need not be informed about the issue of pharmaceuticals in the environment due to the high degree of scientific uncertainty surrounding it [30] are misguided. Such secrecy will only increase mistrust of scientists and governments by the public [31, 32].

5   Conclusions

The experts we interviewed regarding the application of the precautionary principle to pharmaceuticals in the environment were generally supportive of the precautionary principle.   Their main concerns were the degree of evidence required to invoke the precautionary principle; the need for precautionary action to be proportional to the risk presented by pharmaceuticals in the environment; accounting for all costs, financial and otherwise, of precautionary action; and the lack of a universal definition of the precautionary principle.   The need for adaptive management, and for communication with stakeholders, was also highlighted. We suggest that the lack of definition of the precautionary principle is an advantage, allowing it to be tailored to specific situations like pharmaceuticals in the environment, and that rather than defining a specific point at which the precautionary principle is invoked, the discussion should focus on the types of precautionary action which suite the needs of scientific experts and managers.

References

[1]   United Nations General Assembly, Report of the United Nations conference on environment and development. Rio de Janeiro. pp. 5, 1992.
[2]   Quijano, R.F., Elements of the precautionary principle. Precaution, environmental science, and preventive public policy, ed. J.A. Tickner. Island Press: Washington. pp. 21-27, 2003.
[3]   deFur, P.L. & Kaszuba, M., Implementing the precautionary principle. The Science of the Total Environment, **288**, pp.155-165, 2002.
[4]   Santillo, D., Stringer, R. L., Johnston, P. A., & Tickner, J,. The precautionary principle: protecting against failures of scientific method and risk assessment. Marine Pollution Bulletin, **36(12)**, pp. 939-950, 1998.
[5]   Heberer, T., Occurrence, fate, and removal of pharmaceutical residues in the aquatic environment: a review of recent research data. Toxicology Letters, **131**, pp. 5-17, 2002.
[6]   Kolpin, D.W., Furlong, E. T., Meyer, M. T., Thurman, M. E., Zaugg, S. D., Barber, L. B., et al., Pharmaceuticals, hormones, and other organic wastewater contaminants in U.S. streams, 1999-2000: A national reconnaissance. Environmental Science and Technology, **36**, pp. 1202-1211, 2002.
[7]   Ternes, T.A., Occurrence of drugs in German sewage treatment plants and rivers. Water Research, **32(11)**, pp. 3245-3260, 1998.
[8]   Daughton, C.G. & Ternes, T.A., Pharmaceuticals and personal care products in the environment: Agents of subtle change? Environmental Health Perspectives, **107**, pp. 907-938, 1999.
[9]   Sanderson, H., Johnson, D. J., Wilson, C. J., Brain, R. A., & Solomon, K, Probabilistic hazards assessment of environmentally occurring

pharmaceuticals toxicity to fish, daphnids and algae by ECOSARS screening. Toxicology Letters, **144(3)**, pp. 383-395, 2003.

[10] Jobling, S., Nolan, M., Tyler, C. R., Brightly, G., & Sumpter, J. P., Widespread sexual disruption in wild fish. Environmental Science and Technology, **32**, pp. 2498-2506, 1998.

[11] Fong, P.P., Zebra mussel spawning is induced in low concentrations of putative serotonin reuptake inhibitors. Biology Bulletin, **194**, pp. 143-149, 1998.

[12] Chen, C.-Y. & Lu, C.-L., An analysis of the combined effects of organic toxicants. The Science of the Total Environment, **289**, pp. 123-132, 2002.

[13] Daughton, C.G., Non-regulated water contaminants: emerging research. Environmental Impact Assessment Review, **24(7-8)**, pp. 711-732, 2004.

[14] Steel, B., List, P., Lach, D., & Shindler, B., The role of scientists in the environmental policy process: a case study from the American west. Environmental Science & Policy, **7**, pp. 1-13, 2004.

[15] FDA, Guidance for industry: Environmental Assessment of human drug and biologics applications. Government of the United States of America. 1998. Online, http://www.fda.gov/cder/guidance/index.htm

[16] CPMP, Discussion paper on environmental risk assessment of non-genetically modified organisms (non-GMO) containing medicinal products for human use. Committee for Proprietary Medicinal Products: London, UK., 2001.

[17] Health Canada, Health Canada to require environmental assessments of products regulated under the Food and Drug Act, 2002. Online, http://www.hc-sc.gc.ca/english/media/releases/2001.2001_98e.htm.

[18] Adams, M., The precautionary principle and the rhetoric behind it. Journal of Risk Research, **5(4)**, pp. 301-316, 2002.

[19] Rogers, M.D., Scientific and technological uncertainty, the precautionary principle, scenarios and risk management. Journal of Risk Research, **4(1)**, pp. 1-15, 2001.

[20] Sandin, P., Peterson, M., Hansson, S. O., Rudén, C., & Juthe, A., Five charges against the precautionary principle. Journal of Risk Research, **5(4)**, pp. 287-299, 2002.

[21] Müller-Herold, U., Morosini, M. & Schucht, O., Choosing chemicals for precautionary regulation: a filter series approach. Environmental Science & Technology, **39**, pp. 683-691, 2005.

[22] Sanderson, H., Johnson, D. J., Reitsma, T., Brain, R. A., Wilson, C. J., & Solomon, K. R., Ranking and prioritization of environmental risks of pharmaceuticals in surface waters. Regulatory Toxicology and Pharmacology, **39**, pp. 158-183, 2004.

[23] Commission of the European Communities, Communication from the Commission on the precautionary principle. Brussels, 2000. Online, http://europa.eu.int/comm/environment/docum/20001_en.htm.

[24] Government of Canada, A Canadian perspective on the precautionary approach/principle: discussion document, 2001. Online, http://www.ec.gc.ca/econom/discussion_e.htm

[25] Ternes, T.A., et al., Ozonation: a tool for removal of pharmaceuticals, contrast media and musk fragrances from wastewater? Water Research, **37,** pp. 1976-1982, 2003.

[26] Holling, C.S. (ed). Adaptive environmental assessment and management. International series on applied systems analysis. John Wiley & Sons, Chichester, 1978.

[27] Lessard, G., An adaptive approach to planning and decision-making. Landscape and Urban Planning, **40,** pp. 81-87, 1998.

[28] Jordan, A. & O' Riordan, T., The precautionary principle in contemporary environmental policy and politics, Protecting public health & the environment: implementing the precautionary principle, eds. C. Raffensperger and J.A. Tickner, Island Press: Washington, D.C. pp. 15-35, 1999.

[29] Gustavson, K.R., Applying the precautionary principle in environmental assessment: the case of reviews in British Columbia. Journal of Environmental Planning and Management, **46(3)**, pp. 365-379, 2003.

[30] Aumonier, J.R. Risk management of pharmaceuticals in the environment: the human pharmaceutical industry viewpoint, EnvirPharma, Lyon, France, 2003.

[31] Slovic, P., Perceived risk, trust, and democracy. Risk Analysis, **13(6)**, pp. 675-682, 1993.

[32] Hance, B.J., Chess, C. & Sandman, P.M., Setting a context for explaining risk. Risk Analysis, **9(1)**, pp. 113-117, 1989.

Applying a CBA model to assess the Three Gorges Project in China

R. Morimoto & C. Hope
Toulouse Business School, France and Judge Institute of Management, University of Cambridge, U.K.

Abstract

The world's largest hydro project in China is currently under construction. The project is controversial as large environmental and social impacts are anticipated despite the fact that the project is supposed to control the region's severe floods, to generate 18.2 GW of hydropower, and to improve river navigation. This study employs a quantitative approach to bring the major economic, environmental and social impacts of this massive project together. This comprehensive probabilistic cost benefit analysis model takes into account the project uncertainty and its empirical application tries to deliver more robust and justifiable results than those produced by the more usual deterministic cost benefit analyses or multi criteria analyses. The mean and the 95th percentile of the cumulative net present value at a 5% discount rate estimated by the model are to be positive, whereas the 5th percentile is to be negative. Sensitivity analysis shows that the variables with the largest contribution towards the uncertainty in the cumulative net present value are the benefits of power generation, the associated economic growth, the benefits of clean hydropower, and the costs of construction, resettlement and archaeological loss. However, these results obtained by the model need to be treated carefully, as they are sensitive to the valuation methods, the choice of discount rates, and the large project uncertainty.
Keywords: CBA, China, dam, energy, sustainable development.

1   Introduction

The most environmentally controversial project in China today is the construction of the world largest dam, the Three Gorges project (TGP) on the Yangtze River in western Hubei province. It is currently under construction and would be completed in 2009. The dam site is surrounded by scenic landscape with beautiful gorges and many important cultural heritage sites. The area to be submerged is fertile and densely populated.

There are numerous studies on economic, environmental and social impacts of this gigantic project [1, 2, 3, 4, 5, 6, 7, 8, 9]. This research assesses the project again using a different approach from the previous studies. It employs a quantitative approach to bring the major economic, environmental and social impacts of this massive project together. This comprehensive probabilistic cost benefit analysis (CBA) model takes into account the project uncertainty and its empirical application trying to give more robust and justifiable results than the ones that a more usual deterministic CBA or multi criteria analysis (MCA) produces.

The next section discusses the main issues of the TGP followed by a detailed explanation on methodology in Section 3 and the presentation of the results including a full sensitivity analysis in Section 4. The probabilistic analysis allows the distribution of the net present value (NPV) to be calculated, and the most influential impacts to be identified. The final section concludes the study by considering the significance of the results.

2 Three Gorges Project

Construction of the TGP is divided into three stages. The river was blocked at the end of the Stage I (1993-1997), then the hydro power station started operating at the end of the Stage II (1998-2003), and the project will be completed at the end of the Stage III (2004-2009).

The TGP is intended to provide one tenth of China's existing energy needs, to raise flood control capacity from the present 10-year frequency to 100-year frequency, and to improve navigation along the river [2]. In order to generate the same amount of electricity, 50 million tons per year of coal, 25 million tons per year of crude oil or 18 nuclear-power plants would be required [10]. China's high dominance of coal use creates serious environmental problems such as air, land and water pollution. According to Chinese officials, electricity supply would have to increase by 20-30% to eliminate present power shortages; the economic cost of these power shortages is very high [11]. Growth in electricity consumption in China is projected at 5.5% per year until 2020 [12]. More electricity is required in order to boost the economy, including still underdeveloped regions, to meet expected future economic growth, and to meet future increases in household electricity consumption as a result of increased use of electric appliances due to improvements in the standard of living. Currently, the electricity transmission capacity is limited. However, once this distribution problem is solved, a huge increase in electricity consumption in remote areas will be expected.

The Yangtze River has produced some of China's worst natural flood disasters. For example, in 1954, the Yangtze floods killed 30,000 people [13]. In Hubei province alone, the 1998 flood resulted in total economic losses of

$3.6 billion. Agricultural production in this region accounts for about 22% of GDP and the flood inundated about 1.7 million hectares of crops [14]. Thus, these losses saved must also be taken into consideration in the creation of a realistic model of the project.

Opposition around the world continues to argue that the project will be a social and environmental disaster, having seen the tragedies of large dams elsewhere in the world (e.g., Aswan High dam in Egypt). One of the major concerns is that the dam would affect a massive area of this densely populated region. The world's third largest river, the Yangtze heads North East to surge through a spectacular 200km stretch of deep, narrow canyons known collectively as the Three Gorges. The Yangtze River valley is China's agricultural and industrial heartland. It presently supports one third of the country's population, produces 40% of the nation's grain, 70% of its rice, and 40% of China's total industrial output [15]. The project would displace about 1.98 million people, submerge 100,000 hectares of this fertile farmland, 13 cities, 160 towns, 1,352 villages, 1,500 factories. There is also a possibility of dam failures and earthquake [14]. Large dams can be a prime military target; as seen in the case of Kajaki dam in southern Afghanistan being bombed by the American air force on the 1st November 2001.

Biodiversity is also a great concern. The river possesses 300 species of fish (of which one third are endemic) and its annual aquatic production output accounts for 50% of the whole nation's gross output [2]. However, there is a fear of depriving downstream fisheries due to a decline in water quality after constructing the dam [14], [16]. The change in habitat may benefit some species but most likely adversely affect others given that different fish species have often quite specific ecological niches [2]. According to [17], over 3000 factories and mines are in the reservoir area; they currently produce 10 billion tons of waste annually containing 50 different toxins. [17] argues that if we assume the waste water level remains unchanged, the waste content will increase 11 times in some areas due to the dam.

The reservoir area is a great tourist attraction, with its scenic natural landscapes as well as cultural relics and heritage, all carrying a high aesthetic value. The cultural value of the area is also significant. About 12,000 cultural antiquities and 16 archaeological sites will be submerged due to the project [5]. Construction of the dam will result in not only the loss of a large number of cultural relics from this area, but also the destruction of an important link in understanding the birth and early development of China's ancient civilization. Only a limited number of archaeological remains can be removed or replicated for posterity due to lack of time and funds [2].

Finally, there is a risk associated with the generation capability of the dam. The water of the Yangtze River carries the fifth largest sediment discharge in the world, most of which is conveyed during floods. The Three Gorges area has been intensively cultivated so that soil erosion has become a very serious problem due to a loss of a forest cover [2]. Sedimentation problems are likely to reduce power generation capacity.

 WIT Transactions on Ecology and the Environment, Vol 84, © 2005 WIT Press
www.witpress.com, ISSN 1743-3541 (on-line)

3   CBA model

CBA is a project-based approach focusing on net benefits. The most fundamental task of analysis is to define alternative options and quantify their impacts on the objectives established for national energy planning [18]. MCA evaluates multiple objectives simultaneously, which can provide decision-makers additional information to NPV. Least Cost Analysis focuses on the entire power system and seeks to minimize total system costs. Hydropower projects generally involve streams of costs and benefits that span many years. Calculating NPV is a relatively easy way to examine the profitability of the project, and it provides policy makers with useful information for their decision-making process. However, in reality, often only certain engineering or economic costs and benefits are included in the analysis. Hence, this paper focuses on the widely used CBA analysis in a broader context, trying to incorporate environmental and social issues into the economic analysis. The model is aimed to lie somewhere in between the highly practical MCA (see for example, [19]) and the highly theoretical CBA (for example, those described in text books on CBA, such as [20, 21, 22, 23], with the aim of giving robust and highly justifiable results.

The TGP is selected in the paper, as this is currently the dominant option, which is supposed to produce the highest benefit, and indeed it is already under construction. The second dominant alternative scheme is to build a thermal power station. This is justifiable, as about 80% of electricity in China is currently generated by thermal [24]. Other possible alternative schemes to the construction of the TGP are building a series of dams that generate equivalent amounts of the electricity in the less populated upper reach area that has more active water volume whose construction is technically less challenging than the TGP, simply not building a dam, building nuclear power plants [25]. The costs and benefits are calculated by determining what might have happened in the absence of the project under construction.

The specification of the model is given in [26]. Some key variables in the model, PG is non-environmental cost savings on incremental power, EG is a willingness-to-pay for incremental power, and CP is the cost of environmental damage saved as a result of building TGP instead of thermal plants. They are externality costs for SO_2 emissions based on a number of domestic studies and the marginal costs of CO_2 mitigation. The variables EG and CP are multiplied by the factor P and (1-P) respectively, where P is the proportion of time that alternative power generation is not available. This is because the clean power benefit CP is obtained only when the alternative power generation is available, and EG is only obtained when the alternative generation is not available. This process avoids double counting. Other variables in the model are NI (navigation improvement), FC (flood control benefit), FI (negative impact on downstream fishery), DE (mitigation cost of downstream water pollution) and AS (archaeological loss). The size of the dam is massive, therefore an expression of the possibility of dam collapse due to special circumstances (earthquake, technical failures and being a military target) is also added to the evaluation of the variable AC (accident cost). Descriptions of the main parameters in the model and their details are presented in Table 1. The rest of the parameters are found in [26].

Table 1:   Main parameter values and descriptions.

Parameter	Minimum	Most likely	Maximum
Initial proportion of time during which an alternative power generation technology is not available	0.17[a]	0.2[b]	1[c]
Parameter which describes the rate of decrease in P over time	0[d]	0.018[e]	0.085[f]
Initial expected increase in economic output due to increased power supply (Yuan/MWh)	3200[g]	7800[g]	12500[g]

Notes: PERT distribution (a special form of Beta distribution) is used for all the parameters except EO which is described by a triangular distribution. [a] About 40 million rural households out of 232 million have no access to electricity. 40/232=0.17 (*China's Energy: a forecast to 2015*); [b] The State development and planning Commission estimated that about 20% of China's area suffered power shortages in 1998 (*South China Morning Post 10 December 1998* 'Obstacles block path to reform of industry' China Business Review: Power and Infrastructure). See also [27]; [c] The projected rate of China's total energy requirement is increasing continuously in the next 20 years [28; [d] According to [29], coal cannot be considered as an alternative to hydropower as a source of peaking power due to its inefficiency. Gas turbines could be an alternative, but would offer fewer benefits. Hence, assume that alternative techniques would not be available in a feasible period; [e] Electricity generated by coal and gas fired thermal power plants increased by 1.8% in 1998 (China Energy Efficiency Information Bulletin March 1999); [f] Electricity generated by coal and gas fired thermal power plants increased by 8.5% in 1995 (China Energy Efficiency Information Bulletin March 1997); [g] In China, each kWh of power shortage results in a loss of economic output of $0.38-1.5 [30]

Some of the data used in the analysis may not be very accurate or precise. However, this is inevitable, as many variables are not readily quantifiable and some data have a limited availability because of the project complexity. Hence, the data are given as ranges representing our best attempts to extract as much up-to-date information as possible from various sources. All the parameters in the model are assumed to follow either triangular or Beta distributions, and assigned a minimum, most likely and maximum value. Then, 10,000 Monte Carlo simulations are run to generate an expected NPV. Repeated runs of the model obtain a probability distribution of possible outcomes, which is a more defensible procedure than just using single values for inputs that are in reality not well known.

4   Findings

4.1 Net present value

There are three large positive impacts, EG (economic growth), PG (power generation), and CP (clean power), and three large negative impacts, CC (construction cost), AS (archaeological loss), and RE (resettlement cost) as shown in Table 2. The scale of resettlement for the TGP is extremely large compared to most dams since the area is densely populated.

Table 2: Cumulative mean NPV for the fourteen variables at t=100 in $ billion.

Benefits		$ billion	Costs		$ billion
PVEG	Economic growth	82	PVCC	Construction cost	50
PVPG	Power generation	31	PVAS	Archaeological loss	15
PVCP	Clean power	17	PVRE	Resettlement	12
PVFC	Flood control	5	PVOM	O&M cost	5
PVNI	Navigation improvement	3	PVAC	Accident cost	3
			PVDE	Downstream effect	3
			PVFI	Fishery loss	0.7
			PVLT	Tourism loss	0.4
			PVIN	Land inundation loss	0.2

Source: CBA model runs.

The finding also shows that the variable PG (power generation) seems to have a long-lasting positive impact. The magnitude of the impact of EG (economic growth) is much higher than the other variables, though it ceases more rapidly, mainly because alternative power generation techniques would gradually become more readily available, and also the country's energy scarcity is likely to reduce as time passes. The variable CP (clean power) gradually moves downward as the level of electricity generation is reduced due to sedimentation. The variable AS (archaeological loss) initially shows a downward trend and then stabilised. Although both capital costs and resettlement costs are huge, they are required only during the construction period.

The evolution of the 5th percentile, mean, and the 95th percentile of the cumulative NPV with a 5% discount rate are shown in Figure 2. The final values are $US −14, 51, 159 billion respectively. The cumulative NPV is initially negative due to the large construction and resettlement costs. However, a rapid upward movement follows as a result of increased clean electricity sale and stimulated economic growth. The benefit never outweighs the cost for the 5th percentile of the cumulative NPV, due to the reduction in electricity generation because of sedimentation problems, low prices for electricity, ongoing costly operation & maintenance cost, and the loss of important archaeological sites. The likelihood of a negative NPV for the project is 11%. This low level of risk appears to be due to relatively low environmental and social costs compared to the proposed benefits of the project. However, the sensitivity of the results to the huge uncertainty of the project should be noted. The model includes a premature closure option, where if the ongoing costs outweigh the benefits, the dam is closed down rather than keep making an increasing loss. In practice for the TGP, the possibility of premature closure does not affect the result, even at the 5th percentile since the possibly recoverable costs of OM (O&M cost), AC (accident cost), DE (downstream effect), and FI (fishery loss) are not very significant. Therefore, premature decommissioning would be highly unlikely to take place.

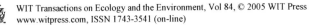

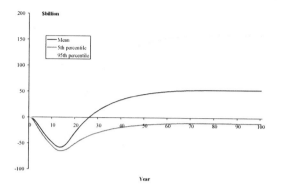

Figure 1: Range of cumulative NPV with a 5% discount rate by year. Source: CBA model runs.

4.2 Sensitivity analysis

Table 3 shows that the following input parameters have the most significant impact on the cumulative NPV: P0 (Initial proportion of time during which an alternative power generation is not available.), φ (Parameter which describes the annual rate of decrease in P (proportion of time during which an alternative power generation is not available)), EO (Initial expected increase in economic output due to increased power supply). The sensitivity of each parameter has the correct sign and is therefore consistent with the model. Although this massive project demands a huge construction cost, it seems not to have one of the largest impacts on the NPV. This may be due to the fact that a fairy small range of data, 470-660 billion Yuan ($US 57-80) is used, as it is thought that this parameter is fairy well known.

Table 3:   Statistically significant parameters.

Parameter	Description	Student b coefficient
P0	Initial proportion of time during which an alternative power generation is not available.	+ 0.58
φ	Parameter which describes the annual rate of decrease in P (proportion of time during which an alternative power generation is not available)	- 0.54
EO	Initial expected increase in economic output due to increased power supply	+ 0.39

Note: The input parameter values are regressed against the output (NPV). The student b coefficient is a coefficient calculated for each input parameter in the regression equation. Source: Sensitivity analysis runs

Note that several variable discount rates were used to see the effect of different rates of pure time preference. The finding shows that the choice of pure time preference rate has a strong effect on the value of the cumulative NPV. The fixed discount rate of 5% used for the basic analysis lies in between a pure time preference rate of 1% and 2%. The mean value of the cumulative NPV becomes negative when the pure rate of time preference is approximately above 5%. Therefore, this analysis clearly indicates that the cumulative NPV is sensitive to the choice of discount rates.

5 Conclusion

This paper has illustrated the use of a CBA model of hydropower projects using China's massive Three Gorges Project as a case study. The application of the comprehensive probabilistic CBA to this controversial project is challenging and novel, as it assesses whether the project involving such complex environmental and social problems would contribute to China's sustainable development. Quantification of the project outcome gives a clear picture of this complicated project and helps policy makers in their decision-making process. The variables with the largest contribution towards the cumulative net present value were PG (power generation), EG (economic growth), CC (construction cost), CP (clean power), RE (resettlement cost), and AS (archaeological loss). The sensitivity analysis has shown that the parameters P0 (Initial proportion of time during which an alternative power generation is not available) and φ (Parameter which describes the annual rate of decrease in P (proportion of time during which an alternative power generation is not available)) have particularly significant impacts on NPV. The inclusion of the premature decommissioning possibility did not give a noticeable change to the outcome for the TGP. The improvements of the results could be seen only if sedimentation problems of the TGP were assumed to be even larger than expected, when premature decommissioning would take place.

The mean and the 95th percentile of the cumulative NPV at the 5% discount rate at year 100 were positive, whereas the 5th percentile was negative. It is difficult to compare these findings with those from the past studies on the TGP, as the most of the previous studies have focused only on each impact of the dam and have employed mainly a qualitative approach. However, the finding in this paper supports the view that the social and environmental implications of the project are not negligible despite the fact that the benefit of power generation is expected to be large. Furthermore, these results obtained by the model need to be treated carefully, as they are sensitive to the valuation methods, the choice of discount rates, and the large project uncertainty. Theoretically, positive NPV implies that gainers should compensate losers, as some people obtain more benefit than the others. However, such distributive effects have not been investigated in this study. Given the large size and geographic scale of the project, investing those effects would be useful in the future research.

Finally, we have tried to use the most representative data which are also readily available, in order to obtain the best possible results. However, it is admitted that data collection was one of the most difficult part for this research, as there are so many parameters included in the model, and the project is not easy to scrutinize. Wider ranges are used for the particularly uncertain figures.

The strength of the model is its simplicity - if the figures used are considered not to be so accurate or representative, they can easily be replaced and the model run again to obtain better results. For example, the paper shows that the variable AL (archaeological loss) has a significant impact on NPV according to the sensitivity analysis. Therefore, further efforts to search out better estimates for this parameter would be worthwhile in order to improve the accuracy of the result.

Acknowledgements

We would like to thank Mr Tang Jie (World Bank) and the staff from China Three Gorges Project Corporation (CTGPC) who provided us with some useful data and information as well as arranging the tour of the dam site and the visit to the research institute of Yangtze sturgeon. Apart from this, all data and information have been obtained from our own independent study.

References

[1]   Canadian Yangtze Joint Venture, *Three Gorges Water Control Project Feasibility Study*, CYJV; Canada, 1998.

[2]   CTGPC, China Three Gorges Project Corporation, *Environmental Impact Statement for the Yangtze Three Gorges Project*, CTGPC; China, 1995.

[3]   Qigang, D, What are the Three Gorges resettlers thinking?, in Qing (1998), chapter 6, pp. 70-89, 1998.

[4]   Guojie, C, The environmental impacts of resettlement in the Three Gorges Project, Qing (1998), chapter 5, pp. 63-69, 1998.

[5]   Ren, Q, Discussing population resettlement with Li Pong, Qing (1998), chapter 4, pp. 39-62, 1998.

[6]   Qing, D, ed, *The River Dragon Has Come!*, IRN; Barkeley, 1998.

[7]   Hui, H, Water pollution in the Three Gorges reservoirs, Qing (1998), chapter 11, pp. 160-170, 1993.

[8]   Leopold, L, Sediment problems at the TGD, Qing (1998), Appendix B, pp. 194-199, 1996.

[9]   Bing, D, Military perspectives on the TGP, Qing (1998a), Chapter 12, pp. 171-176, 1998.

[10]   Thurston, K, Rebuilding China, *The Newsletter of Environmental Geology: Environmental Focus* (Miami University) 5/1/96, pp.1-3, 1996.

[11]   Wu, K, and B Li, Energy development in China: national policies and regional strategies, *Energy Policy*, **23**(2), pp. 167–178, 1995.

[12]   EIA (Energy information administration), *China Country Analysis Brief* EIA; Washington, 2001.

[13]   Fung, S, That dam project!, *Across the Board*, May, pp. 46-49, 1999.

[14]   Saywell, T, A river run wild, *Far Eastern Economic Review*, April, pp. 38-40, 1998.

[15]   Morrish, M, The living geography of China, *Geography*, **83**(354), January, pages 3–16, 1997.

[16]   ASCE, American Society of Civil Engineers, *Journal of the Boston Society of Civil Engineering Section*, **12**(1), Spring/Summer, 1997.

[17]   Topping, A B, Dai Qing, voice of the Yangtze River Gorges, *The Earth Times*, available at <http://weber.cusd.edu/-dmccubbi /chinadaiqingjan11_97.htm>, last accessed on 26/04/04, 1996.

[18]   Munasinghe, M and Meier, P, Incorporating Environmental Concerns into Power Sector Planning, World Bank; Washington, 1993.

[19]   Hope, C, and R Palmer, Assessing water quality improvement schemes: the multi attribute techniques of the UK's environmental agency, *Integrated Assessment*, 2, pp. 219–224, 2001

[20]   Zeerbe, R O Jr, and D D Dively, *Benefit–Cost Analysis–– in theory and practices*, Harper Collins; New York, 1994.

[21]   Layard, P, and S Glaister, 2nd ed, *Cost Benefit Analysis* Cambridge University Press; Cambridge, 1994.

[22]   Brent, R J, *Applied Cost–Benefit Analysis*, Edwards Elgar; Cheltenham, 1996.

[23]   Boardman, A E, D H Greenberg, A R Vining and D L Weimer, *Cost–Benefit Analysis*, Prentice Hall; New Jersey, 2001.

[24]   Zeng, Q. Y, Song, Y.H, Electricity market develops in China', Transmission & Distribution – An Itertec/Primedia Publication; USA, **50** (5), pp.36-41, 1998.

[25]   Fang, Tian, Fa-Tang, Lin, and Cun-xi, Ling, *On the Macro-Level Decision Making on TGP* Hunan Press of Science and Technology, 1988.

[26]   Morimoto, R and Hope, C, The CBA model for the Three Gorges Project in China, *Impact Assessment and Project Appraisal Journal*, **22**(3), pp.205-220, 2004.

[27]   Sinton, J E, and D G Fridley, What goes up: recent trends in China's energy consumption, *Energy Policy*, **28** (10), pp.671-687, 2000.

[28]   US Department of Energy, *China's Energy: a forecast to 2015* USDE; Washington, 1996.

[29]   WCD (World Commission on Dams), *Dams and Development: a new framework for decision- making* Earthscan; London, 2000.

[30]   MOF (Ministry of Finance), *Energy in China* The Ministry of Energy Press; Beijing, 1990.

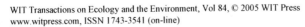

Environmental impact assessment as a step to sustainable tourism development

N. Raschke
Environmental Resources Management ERM GmbH, Germany

Abstract

ERM GmbH conducted an Environmental Impact Assessment (EIA) for the Urban and Tourism Development of Ulcinj, Montenegro on behalf of Deutsche Investitions- und Entwicklungsgesellschaft (DEG). The Project was designed to support the Municipality of Ulcinj in the preparation and implementation of an Urban Development Plan prepared by the architects Albert Speer & Partner. Ulcinj is located at the Montenegrin Mediterranean coast west of the border to Albania. Along the coastal stretch "Velika Plaza", south–east of Ulcinj town, the staged establishment of accommodation (hotels, resorts) and leisure facilities as well as related infrastructure is envisaged. Main ecological features of the area to be protected are endemic oaks, halophyte (salt-tolerant) vegetation and Important Bird Areas in the vicinity.

Phase 1 EIA consisted of a strategic oriented Environmental Assessment plan aimed to evaluate the principal suitability of tourism development of Velika Plaza from an environmental perspective. As a result, the western part of Velika Plaza was identified as being suitable for development. The eastern part however with extended marshland area, natural forest vegetation and halophyte vegetation was found to be of high conservation value in particular due the different habitats for bird life. The determination of these areas in the first phase was a very important step for sound and sustainable tourism development. Phase 2 provided a detailed analysis of the environmental impacts likely to occur when implementing the architects' concept. Mitigation measures were outlined, design recommendations, construction and operation patterns were provided and an Environmental Management Plan was organised to provide guidance to the developers of the Tourism project.

Keywords: Environmental Impact Assessment EIA, sustainable tourism, tourism development, Montenegro, Adriatic Coast.

 WIT Transactions on Ecology and the Environment, Vol 84, © 2005 WIT Press
www.witpress.com, ISSN 1743-3541 (on-line)

1   Introduction

An Environmental Assessment of the proposed Urban and Tourism Development of Ulcinj, Montenegro was prepared. The Tourism Development project at Ulcinj is one of the model projects identified by the Tourism Master Plan for Croatia and Montenegro, which was prepared on behalf of DEG (Deutsche Investitions- und Entwicklungsgesellschaft) in 2000/01. ERM GmbH, Germany who closely worked with the Montenegrin Company MonteCEP was commissioned by DEG to conduct the Project, which was designed to support the Municipality of Ulcinj in the preparation and implementation of an Urban Development Plan prepared by Albert Speer & Partner in Germany.

The study was divided into two phases. The purpose of the first phase was an "Environmental Screening and Initial Assessment", to identify ecological sensitive areas to enable the project developer to consider environmental constraints and enhancement opportunities from the start of the development. In the later Project Phase 2, a detailed EIA was conducted for a selected sub-area.

2   Description of the environment

2.1 Project area

Ulcinj is located at the southeastern part of the Montenegrin Mediterranean coast west of the border to Albania. The study area is located east of Ulcinj town and the Porta Milena channel. It covers the coastal stretch to the border, and has a length of approx. 13 kilometres and a width of approx. 2 kilometres (area approx. 2,600 hectares).

The regional road R 17 Ulcinj - Port Milena - Ada Bojana passes along the northern edge of the study area, by which the region is connected to Ulcinj. The main road M 2.4 (E752) connects the region of Velika Plaža with other settlements on the coast and the capital of Montenegro, Podgorica.

Along the coastal stretch south–east of Ulcinj town, the stepwise establishment of accommodation (hotels, resorts) and leisure facilities as well as related infrastructure is envisaged with a final capacity of up to 35.000 beds as a maximum option. Presently, the project is in a conception stage, i.e. planning is preliminary and only key features are defined. These include tourism infrastructure including hotel buildings, internal access roads, other auxiliary and ancillary facilities (roads, paths, water/energy supply and distribution, wastewater/waste collection and disposal), parks and green spaces. The possibility of the establishment of a golf course and the construction of a marina is also an option.

The investigation area is limited by the sea, port Milena, the road R-17 and the eastern branch of Bojana River, and by this also including Ada Island. The project area is characterized by decreasing human utilization from West to East. From Port Milena towards the East some residential areas exist as well as a larger hotel complex.

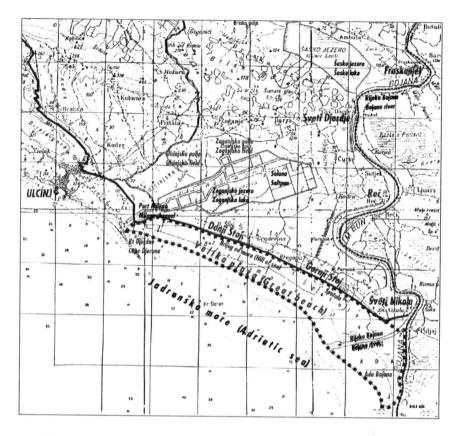

Figure 1: Investigation area in Montenegro at the Albanian border.

Close to the regional road little settlements and scattered single houses with garden and orchards together with agricultural use (mostly meadows) are dominating. In the stretch, which is closer to the sea wetlands, swamps and other less intensively used land prevail. In the coastal stretch, dunes (only low in height) and a broad sandy beach are typical features of the landscape. In some parts smaller forests resp. groves are occurring. In the Eastern section the two river arms of Bojana River surround Ada Island. The island itself is mainly covered by wetlands. Nearby the beaches hotel and old resort facilities are situated. The island of Ada is a famous region for nudist vacation. The eastern branch of Bojana River forms the border to Albania.

2.2 Physical environment

Velika Plaža with the fluvial plane in the hinterland is made of small grain sand that originates from Skadar Lake catchment area. The material is transported by Bojana River towards the littoral part of the sea and then transported by the long shore currents and deposited along the Velika Plaža beach. Wind also has some influence on erosion and transportation of sand. In the coastal stretch, dunes (only low in height) and a broad sandy beach are typical features of the landscape. The river transports and deposits large amounts of sediment at the delta. Currents deposit the sediments on the Great Beach.

Figure 2:   Bojana River mouth with reed vegetation.

Montenegro's coasts enjoy a Mediterranean climate, having dry summers and mild, rainy winters. The average monthly air temperature for Ulcinj is 15.8°C with an average maximum of 27°C in July/August and an average minimum of about 5°C in January. The average yearly rainfall amounts to 1,109 l/m². There are 108 days/year of summer days in Ulcinj.

Bojana River is partly navigable and forms the natural border between Albania and Montenegro. The river enters the Adriatic Sea via a delta with sandy Ada Island that divides the mouth of the river into two branches. The flow is slow and with small gradient.

Due to the large water volumes in the southern Adriatic Sea the water temperature does not decrease below 12°C during wintertime. At the end of summer surface layers reaches temperatures of up to 27°C or more.

2.3 Ecological resources

In the Ulcinj area a particular autochthonous flora is developed due to the special ecological conditions such as maritime impacts of the Adriatic Sea, Mediterranean climate and regular seasonal flooding. Different types of habitats are present in the investigation area (salted and brackish inland and wetland habitats, dry pastures, natural and semi-natural forests, arable land and orchards). The biotope types with the highest ecological sensitivity and the highest conservation value are the salt-tolerant halophyte vegetation and the natural forest vegetation. Important plant species are the endemic Skadar Oak (*Quercus robur ssp. scutariensis*) and the highly endangered Sand Lily (*Pancratium maritimum.*).

Figure 3:   Sand Lily (*Pancratium maritimum*).

In Velika Plaža area important aquatic ecosystems such as marshes and permanent water-bearing ponds are located. Important areas for amphibians and reptiles are e.g. both sides of Bojana River (important reproduction areas of several endemic species). West of Bojana River are important nesting areas for protected bird species. The Bojana River is an important habitat for fish and has a specific importance as migration route to the sea for several fish species. The marine part in front of Bojana River mouth is an important feeding area for migratory birds (important fish spawning area). Ada Island is important nesting and feeding area for Pygmy Cormorant and other protected bird species. The Bojana River delta (its right stream) is very important for the feeding and resting of birds during winter and migration. Sasko Lake and Ulcinjska solana are important areas in the vicinity.

The area east of the investigated area with a very high ecological value and a high conservation value is proposed as a potential conservation area.

3   Evaluation of environmental suitability and restrictions

3.1 Sensitive areas

In order to provide guidance recommendations about areas, which should be excluded from development, and which areas are regarded suitable for development from environmental view, the ecologically sensitive areas with high conservation value have been identified and are depicted in Table 1. It can be summarised that most of the ecological sensitive areas are located east of the investigation area. Whereas less sensitive areas, with the exception of single locations and the Skadar Oaks are situated in the West.

Table 1:   Ecological sensitive areas.

Important areas for birds
West of Bojana River - important nesting area for protected bird species
Marine part in front of Bojana River mouth is important feeding area for migratory birds (important fish spawning area)
Ada Island is important nesting and feeding area for Pygmy Cormorant and other protected bird species
The undeveloped open beach, dunes and landscapes and temporary wetlands/marshlands behind the dunes are bird habitats
Important areas for Amphibia/ Reptiles
Both sides of Bojana River are important reproduction areas of several endemic species
Area East of existing hotel complex is important reproduction area for lizards and newts
Dunes with halophyte vegetation are habitat for lizards
Important floristic areas
Coastal stretch with protected halophyte vegetation
In the Eastern part and on Ada Island occurs natural forest with Skadar Oak, Alder etc.
Small grove in the western part with Skadar Oak
Natural forests in the western part with Skadar Oak, Ash, Poplar, affected by human activities

3.2 Recommendations for area development

It is recommended to restrict future development in the western part. The area in the eastern part of the investigation area with a very high ecological value and a high conservation value is recommended to be protected as a Conservation Area. Development should be clearly restricted, the area should be strictly protected and impacts and damages should be avoided.

A golf course which is also a planning option could be integrated into the existing landscape and could act as a buffer zone between more intensively used recreational areas and areas with high ecological value in the East of the investigation area.

Single locations in the western part with a high conservation value, such as the Skadar Oak grove should be protected and integrated into the planning as far as feasible, e.g. they could be developed as visiting points for nature interested tourists; cutting of single Skadar Oaks should be avoided as this species is endemic and total abundance in this region is limited. In particular, large and old specimen of Skadar Oak should be conserved.

The planned green spaces between the development fields should be designed to protect the natural vegetation of the wetlands, pastures and woodland to preserve the present habitat functions for birds, amphibia and reptiles.

The natural forest with Skadar Oak, Field Ash and White Poplar also has a high conservation value, but at its present state is already affected by human activities. If cutting of this natural forest vegetation cannot be avoided, compensation is regarded feasible. Other smaller single areas with ecological value should be preserved, but if this is not feasible, appropriate compensation measures will be possible.

Any measures for conservation compensation, protection or supervision/ management require to be made conditional for the future developers.

3.3 Options for protection, mitigation and enhancement

The further planning in environmental context should be based on the general understanding of a planning policy, which aims at:

- Maintaining and enhancing biodiversity and natural landscapes of the area
- Minimising pollution of soil, air and water and the sea
- Minimising the consumption of resources, particularly water and non-renewable resources
- Increasing tourist's awareness of the importance of these objectives for sustainable use of the area for recreation.

The general concept should be to protect the eastern part of the investigation area and to allow an environmental sound development in the western part of Velika Plaža. The former requires adequate regulatory and institutional setup and monitoring, the latter requires careful planning integrating the existing ecological sensitive areas and protecting habitats of important species. Any habitat damage by visitor pressure should be avoided and kept to a minimum by establishing respective buffer zones around sensitive areas and by guidance of tourists. The effectiveness of the proposed mitigation measures should be monitored and an appropriate institutional setup established.

Following main considerations are recommended for protection, avoidance, mitigation and enhancement.

Forest vegetation

Cutting of Skadar Oak should be avoided to the maximum extent possible. Compensation planting of Skadar Oak should be established if any would be cut on locations designated for future construction. A compensation factor of 1 on 3 is proposed. The area of Spatula (in the East) is an appropriate area for compensation planting. It can be additionally improved if a conservation area would be created in the area of Spatula as mentioned above. It is recommended that important habitats are connected in order to prevent habitat fragmentation.

Halophyte vegetation

For the access areas to the beach it is recommended to construct boardwalks to bridge the halophyte vegetation. Wooden footpaths are appropriate for that construction. Boardwalks are protection measures at sandy beaches to protect vegetation against destruction by trampling. Examples of these protection measures can be found at many European beaches. If properly maintained they are well accepted, as boardwalks also facilitate walking in the sandy area. The boardwalks in the access areas should be interconnected to provide a footwalk communication system. Cleaning and maintenance of the beach should be carefully undertaken in order not to damage halophyte vegetation. Use of bulldozers and similar heavy equipment should be limited to the beach area without vegetation at Velika Plaža.

Birds
The parts of the Velika Plaža near the Bojana River, as well as greater part of Ada Island are a valuable ornithological reserve and should be protected. In these areas the vehicle traffic should be restricted, and tourists, visitors and other pedestrians should only have limited access through guided paths. This area is suitable for controlled bird watching activities. The erection of bird watching towers and appropriate information panels and other information material should be provided.

Herpetofauna
It is recommended to maintain and protect the wetland areas in the Velika Plaža - Ada Bojana region, especially small ponds and sand-excavation holes. In the forests and groves, overgrazing by domestic animals should be reduced. Some of the existing ponds are polluted by waste. Cleaning of these sites is recommended.

In cases where it will not be possible to exclude important ponds and wetlands from the development of tourist complexes, important species (e.g. newt) should be transferred to nearby existing habitats under expert control. The creation of new habitats for loss should be considered (e.g. sand excavation). Furthermore habitat improvement by cleaning (i.e. removing of solid waste) should be considered where appropriate.

Landscape
In order to minimize impacts on landscape and visual environment due to the erection of buildings and facilities it is recommended to restrict the number of storeys. Planting of green screens and roadside trees are appropriate mitigation measures.

Transport and traffic
The construction phase will require attention regarding nuisances for the residential areas along main access roads. For operation it is expected that increase in road traffic will lead to additional air pollution and increased ambient noise levels near road sections, which serve as access to the tourist development area. Also traffic communication from the development area to Ulcinj town may increase and result in traffic congestion. The development should include attractive public transport to minimise adverse impacts.

Waste and water

Presently it is not clear whether the new tourist resort development will be connected to a possible future municipal wastewater treatment plant. It is recommended to construct appropriate wastewater treatment facilities for Ulcinj, which can also effectively treat the effluents from the tourism complex. Any additional discharge of untreated sewage water is environmentally unacceptable and will be no sound perspective for tourism development. In this context the existing high transparency of the seawater should be highlighted as a valuable asset (also attractive for scuba-diving).

It is recommended to develop a waste management concept which can be an effective tool to reduce waste amounts resp. enhancing the use of more environmental friendly products and encourage recycling of residues in the tourist as well as in Ulcinj municipality.

Use of resources

In general, drinking water resources should be responsibly managed. Presently, the pipe distribution system network in the Uljincj service area has losses due to leakage up to 60%, this should clearly be improved.

Tourist development will increase water demand in summer peak months. The project should implement modern water saving techniques to reduce consumption, e.g. rainwater collection from roofs and underground storage, separate grey water pipes for e.g. toilet flushing etc.

The new development should demonstrate saving on non-renewable energy by implementing solar heating (hot water etc.), photovoltaic etc.

Golf course

In case the planning pursues to establish a golf course, excessive use of ground water for irrigation should be avoided by respective techniques. It is recommended that a separate detailed environmental assessment including green space concept with the intention to make the golf course function as an ecological buffer zone between the intensively used western area and the areas proposed for protection in the east should be undertaken.

Marina

The establishment of a marina is part of the development planning discussion at the present project stage. It is recommended that in case of building of a marina, clear priority should be given to a location within the Port Milena. A construction at the river mouth of Bojana should be avoided for ecological as well as hydraulic reasons. It is important to understand that any construction within this site would significantly disturb or stop further feeding of the beach and cause erosion of the beach at Velika Plaža.

4 Results

Phase 1 EIA consisted of a strategic oriented plan Environmental Assessment aiming at evaluating the principal suitability of tourism development of Velika

Plaza from an environmental perspective. As a result, the western part of Velika Plaza was identified as being suitable for development, with infrastructure already installed and significantly influenced by present land use. The eastern part however, with extended marshland area, natural forest vegetation and halophyte vegetation was found to be of high conservation value, in particular due the function of the different habitats for bird life. In general, it was found that the ecological value and sensitivity of Velika Plaza increases from West to East. These findings were adopted by the development concept of the Masterplan. As a consequence only the western half of the Velika Plaza was envisaged for development, which is intended to be realised stepwise from west to east with a total of six development modules alternating with green corridors. To account for habitat sensitivities, the eastern development modules were set back further away from the beach in order not to adversely impact habitats in particular the halophytic vegetation and the marshlands behind the dunes, which constitute important bird habitats. A major recommendation of the Phase 1 EIA study is that a nature conservation area should be established in the eastern part of Velika Plaza.

The Phase 2 EIA Study, on the example of the development module No. 2 was selected as the prototype for the urban design planning in the Masterplan, demonstrated how environmental impact assessment and environmental planning should be integrated into the planning layout of the single development modules.

The area envisaged is located in the western part of the investigation area and by this complies with the general recommendations given above. The study focused on the actual area selected for development and investigated also impacts during the construction phase. The location of single Skadar Oak trees, esp. tall and old trees worth to be preserved, was surveyed. The actual status of the halophyte vegetation including existing impairments was investigated. Both results provided planning guide for placements of buildings and structures, roads etc. Appropriate measures have been developed to mitigate adverse impacts. An Environmental Management Plan was developed to ascertain compliance with agreed environmental protection standards and environmental good practices for construction and operation of the planned hotel facilities including mitigation measures and monitoring.

References

[1] Busković, V. and Ražnatović, V.; Environmental Management in Montenegro. Public Document. Ministry of Environmental Protection. Podgorica, 1997.
[2] ERM Lahmeyer International; Environmental Assessment of Urban and Tourism Development Plan Ulcinj, Montenegro. Phase 1, Environmental Screening and Initial Assessment. 2002.
[3] ERM Lahmeyer International; Environmental Assessment of Urban and Tourism Development Plan Ulcinj, Montenegro. Phase 2, Environmental Study of Urban Design Plan for Development of Module No. 2 - Environmental Impact Assessment. 2002.

[4] Karajovic, S. (eds); Stvorene vrijednosti (Manmade resources). Basic study for the Coastal Area Spatial Plan. RZUP, Podgorica and MonteCEP, Kotor, 1999.

[5] Pulevic, V.; Bibliografija o flori i vegetaciji Crne Gore. CANU, Bibliografija 1, 1-235, Titograd, 1980.

[6] Puzovic, S., Grubac, B.; Federal Republic of Yugoslavia. pp. 725-745 in M.F. Heath and M.I. Evans, eds. Important Bird Areas in Europe: Priority sites for conservation.2: Southern Europe. Cambridge, UK: BirdLife.

[7] Schneider-Jacoby, M.; Euronatur, Short international assessment of the ecological importance of the Ulcinj area including the Bojana estuary and the Velipoja Lagoon/AL (internal paper). 2002.

[8] Shoqata, M.; Buna Bojana; Tirana, 2000.

[9] SR Montenegro; Act on Protection of Rare, Endangered and Threatened Animal and Plant Species (Rjesenje o stavljanju pod zastitu rijetkih, prorijedjenih, endemicnih i ugrozenih biljnih i zivotinjskih vrsta). Official Gazette of SR Montenegro, Nr.36/82, Podgorica, 1982.

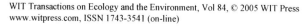

Section 3
Environmental legislation and policy

Planning for safety: a sustainable interface between chemical sites and urban development, European experiences and perspectives

C. Basta[1] & R. B. Jongejan[2]
[1]*Interfaculty Research Centre Sustainable Urban Areas (SUA)*
[2]*Risk Centre, Delft University of Technology, The Netherlands*

Abstract

With the Seveso II Directive of 1996, the European Union brought together two traditionally independent disciplines: technological risk assessment and land-use planning. Article 12 of the Directive requires Member States to adopt regulations for land-use planning in the vicinity of major industrial hazards. To minimize the risk to both humans and the environment, opportune safety distances should be observed. Though the requirement came into force almost ten years ago, regulations are still evolving: while the UK and The Netherlands have been developing a systematic method for land-use planning in risky areas since the early 1980's, regulations in France and Italy are from recent date and, in new Member States, mostly in development. As Member States have considerable freedom in implementing the Directive, developed methods and procedures are often remarkably different. The paper presents an overview of the various ways in which Article 12 has been implemented in national legislations, outlining methodological and procedural differences. In doing so, the paper wants to stimulate the reflection among planners and policy makers on the theme of risk in land-use planning.
Keywords: risk assessment, land-use planning, risk acceptability, Seveso II Directive.

1 Introduction

Twenty years after the accident at Seveso in Northern Italy, in which a large rural area was polluted by a dioxin release, the Seveso II Directive [1] formalized the need of "bridging the gap" [2] between two traditionally independent disciplines: risk assessment and land-use planning. The "gap" consisted of both a disciplinary one – a focus on technology vs. a focus on social factors – and a professional one: safety authorities and plant operators *vs.* planning authorities and project developers. In the light of their common objectives (safety, economically sustainable choices) but different approaches and backgrounds, bridging the gap involved finding a common language.

As shown by the major industrial accident at Toulouse [3], the risk of major accidents is ever-present. Risk in fact is commonly defined as a combination of adverse events and associated probabilities. Therefore, a society without risk is impossible since all activities that are intended to produce some benefit are accompanied by a probability of adverse effects, no matter how small. Major accident risks can however be reduced, either by reducing the probability of failure or by reducing the consequences associated with failure. As demonstrated by the tragic disaster at Bhopal in 1984 in which thousands of residents near the plant were killed or severely injured, safety is strongly related to land-used planning. An important way to limit adverse effects is after all the adoption of a land-use policy that restricts spatial developments in the vicinity of major industrial hazards. Thus, in response to catastrophic risks that cannot be reduced to zero, a planning policy should be adopted that is sustainable, where "sustainability", in this context, assumes the meaning of "safety".

Considering the risk as a central element in the decision-making process regarding land-use planning is a main contribution of the Seveso II Directive. Article 12 requires the adoption of land-use regulation guarantying *opportune safety distances*, minimizing the risks to both humans and the environment. In spite of this common objective, Member States have had considerable freedom in implementing Art 12 in national legislation; consequently, it has been implemented in various ways, and methods and procedures are often remarkably different [4, 11]. Moreover, Member States have been considering the matter of risk in land-use planning since considerably different times: while the UK and The Netherlands have been working on a systematic method for land-use planning in risky areas since the early 80's, new regulation came into force in France and Italy only recently. In new Member States, policies and regulations are mostly under development.

The paper analyzes the policy-making challenge arising from the implementation of Article 12 of the Seveso II Directive presenting an overview of its implementation in MS regulations, with a focus on the Italian case. In doing so, the paper wants to stimulate the debate among planners and policy makers around the theme of risk in land-use planning. Is there a future for a European policy guarantying a sustainable interface between chemical sites and urban development?

2 Risk in land-use planning: a policy-making challenge for Member States

Risk is commonly defined as being composed of two variables: effects (what is the severity of potential damages?) and probabilities (how likely are the adverse events?). The risk the Seveso Directive is concerned with is the probability of events such as explosions, fires or toxic releases causing major consequences. Generally low, frequencies are estimated between 10^{-3} and $10^{-12}/10^{-16}$ events per installation per year. The English Health and Safety Executive assigns the following qualitative attributes to these low probabilities [5]:

1.   unlikely to occur: $10^{-3} > F > 10^{-5}$;
2.   highly unlikely, but may exceptionally occur: $10^{-5} > F > 10^{-7}$;
3.   incredible (extremely unlikely that the event will ever occur): $F < 10^{-7}$.

Consequently, a major accident is a rare and unlikely event. On the other hand, the potentially great magnitude of losses means that the risk cannot be ignored. An efficient internal safety policy, focusing on plant safety, is necessary and it is required by European laws since two decades, when the first version on the Seveso Directive came into force (1982) [6].

The more recent regulations focus on external safety and include a set of preventive en proactive policies aimed at minimizing the consequences of accidents outside the plant. Among them, the external emergency plan (EEP) concerns logistic support in response to risk incidents (prompt evacuation, disaster abatement), while restrictions to land-use planning (LUP) limits the number of persons at risk. The connection between the prevention of industrial disasters and proactive land-use planning in the vicinity of major industrial hazards is evident; the outcome of the decision-making process about the acceptability of a certain level of risk is less obvious. Decision makers have to consider the risk to third parties as determined by three variables [7]:

1.   the possible accident scenarios;
2.   the estimated probabilities of these scenarios;
3.   the vulnerability and number of exposed objects.

From a decisional point of view, striking a balance between these variables is essentially the resolution of a conflict: due to the scarcity of land, a balance must be found between the level of residual risk and the loss of urban area. The name of this balance is acceptable residual risk: the higher the level of acceptable residual risk, the lower the loss of urban area and vice versa. Clearly, it is not a purely technical nor a purely subjective issue, but a multi-faceted policy-making problem for Member States.

This integrated view on the necessary political management of risk is confirmed by the increasing literature dedicated to risk studies [8-10, 12]. In recent years, the "formal" concept of risk as only a set of frequencies and consequences has been replaced with that of a "social" concept of risk as a construct that is influenced by social, cultural and psychological factors [2, 8]. According to this perspective, risk acceptability is strongly influenced by risk perception as well as safety culture. These factors can be used to explain the different implementations of Article 12 in the various Member States. Moreover, country-specific variables such as population density and affluence directly influence the balance between the safety need and the loss of land [9, 12]. A classification of approaches and methods is presented in the following paragraph.

3 Overview of Member States approaches: deciding on risk or deciding on effects?

As mentioned before, the relation between consequences, probabilities and vulnerabilities determines the level of risk from a methodological point of view. Because probabilities cannot be reduced to zero unless the hazardous activity is banned or all vulnerable objects removed, risks cannot be completely reduced to zero.

When assessing risk to humans, it becomes necessary to derive consequences (e.g. lethality, serious injuries) from accident scenarios (e.g. an explosion). Risk analysts use specific indicators (over-pressure, IDLH, thermal radiation) and probit-functions (the relation between exposure and harm) to determine the level of harm associated with the accident scenarios. These estimated effects on humans are the effects most regulations are primarily concerned with: the number of fatalities.

Two main approaches to land-use planning in the vicinity of major industrial hazards can be discerned [11]. The first, explicitly based on both effects and probabilities, is the risk-based approach. The second, based only on possible adverse consequences, is the effect-based approach. Note that the boundary between the two approaches is rather fuzzy: implicitly, the deterministic effects-based approach also accounts for frequencies. After all, the reference scenario selected for planning purposes (e.g. "worst case scenario", "most credible scenario") involves a frequency judgment. However, in probabilistic risk-based regulations, probabilities are explicit decisional elements for land-use planning that can be legally binding, such as the criterion for individual risk in The Netherlands.

From the early beginning of their policy developments, the UK and The Netherlands have both opted for a risk-based approach. In the UK, the Health and Safety Executive has developed a systematic risk assessment procedure with a strong quantitative component: probabilities and consequences are expressed in quantitative terms. The character of UK's decision making process is that of a case-by-case assessment, based on the mandatory consultation of HSE when vulnerable objects are present within the "consultation zones" the agency determines around each plant. The HSE interacts directly with the LPA (Local Planning Agency) when the latter has to decide on a risk situation. The advice is presented in matrix form, in which effects and frequencies as well as limits to the number of exposed, vulnerable objects are laid down. Though not legally binding, the advice by the HSE is accepted and implemented in the majority of cases (source: HSE, 2005).

In The Netherlands, a risk-based policy has been adopted. Because of the high population density, with 475 persons/km^2 the highest in Europe, land is relatively scarce. A policy focused on effects only would result in too costly spatial claims. A risk-based approach had been used for the optimization of the flood defences of the low-lying Netherlands prior to its application in land-use planning with respect to industrial safety [9, 14]. Industrial risk is considered from two distinct perspectives: that of the individual and that of society. Individual risk criteria are

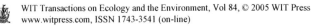

to ensure that no person is disproportionally exposed to industrial risks. Individual risk is limited by law to 10^{-6} per year for new establishments and developments. Because individual risk is defined as the probability of death of an average, unprotected person that is constantly present at a certain location, it is a property of location rather than an actual person. As such, iso-risk contours can be plotted on a map and these form a practical tool for spatial planners. Within the 10^{-6} contour, so-called "vulnerable objects" like houses, hospitals and schools are not allowed. Societal risk criteria limit the too frequent occurrence of large accidents to limit societal concerns. It is defined as "...*the probability that a group of more N persons would get killed due to an accident connected with a dangerous activity*" (see Bottelberghs 2000 [14]). The societal risk criterion is an FN-limit curve of $10^{-3}/N^2$ per year per installation, where N is the number of fatalities per accident. As in the UK, the municipalities in The Netherlands are the final decision-makers on the acceptability of risk. When doing so, they have to adhere to the individual and societal risk criteria that have been set by the Ministry of Housing, Spatial Planning, and the Environment.

In contrast to the UK and The Netherlands, effect-based approaches have been adopted by Germany and France, where risk regulation is currently in a transitional phase. Germany combines a deterministic, effect-based risk assessment with a planning tradition based on a zoning system, requiring a strict separation of industrial and residential areas. The Seveso II Directive is integrated in the EIA (Environmental Impact Assessment) procedure. Therefore, most ordinary German industries are also not allowed in the vicinity of residential zones and vice versa [15].

This brief overview of the ways in which Article 12 of the Seveso II Directive has been implemented in various European countries illustrates the considerable national differences that currently exist. Present research aims at clarifying the relation between each country's adopted safety policy and it's social, economic and political profile. A conclusion stemming from this preliminary analysis is that the early implementation of risk-based approaches can be found in countries dealing with greater scarcity of land. For illustrative purposes, a more in-depth analysis of the way in which risk control and land-use planning have been integrated in Italy is presented in the following paragraph.

4   The Italian implementation of Art 12: the RIR

In Italy, article 12 of the Seveso II Directive has been implemented in the DM 9 Maggio 2001, which extended title can be translated as "*Minimum safety requirements for urban and land-use planning in the areas exposed to the risk of major accidents*". The Decree applies Article 14 of Legislative Decree 334/99, implementing the Seveso II Directive in national legislation [16-17].

In order to describe the general decisional process leading to the urban and land-use policies in Italy, a brief background regarding the country's institutional structure is presented first. With the adoption of Decree n 112 of 31 March 1998 and the successive amendment of Article 117 of the Constitution, a strong devolution process from National to Local Authorities has been instituted [18].

Motivated by the excessive centralization of the former administrative system, roles and competences involved in the territorial governance are shifting towards greater local autonomy. In a country with considerable cultural and socio-economic differences across the regions, this process is responding to practical as well as political needs.

Currently, the 20 Regions and 103 Provinces have the right to define their own statutes. Regions can define their own regulations with respect to crucial themes such as regional planning, urban-planning, social security, industrial safety and civil protection. The Republic is concerned with national legislation and it can promote ordinary laws only. Hence, the analysis of the implementation of an EU environmental/planning Directive involves the national transposition of its text and its implementation in each of the regional statutes. Though this multi-level implementation often leads to a slow enforcement of national laws within local procedures, the increased autonomy of the Regions allows them to consider their own specific needs and sustainable strategies.

In DM 09 Maggio 2001, the general assignment of competences is defined as follows:

- Regional Authorities: they adopt the Decree, define roles, actors and competences to be involved in the procedure and the areas subject to the regulation on the basis of the Regional Plan;
- Provincial Authorities: they consider the individual areas subject to land-use regulation falling under the requirements of the Decree, under the Regional regulation and the Territorial (provincial) Plan;
- Municipalities: they produce a Technical Paper (whose original acronym is *RIR – Rischio di Incidenti Rilevanti*) in which each establishment is presented with its associated land-use planning restrictions. The RIR is attached to the Urban Plan, has the status of a public document and is subject to public consultation.

Clearly, the municipal Technical Paper is the planning instrument that "bridges the gap" between risk assessment and land-use planning. The report is based on the advice of a technical committee (generally representatives of the regional division of the Environmental Protection Agency plus experts from the Fire Brigades and the Safety at Work Authority) and it has to contain updated information on:

- The identification of hazardous establishments and, for each of them, the (selected) accident scenarios with effect distances and frequency estimates;
- The identification of urban and environmental vulnerable objects;
- The overlap between effect areas and vulnerable objects, including frequency estimates.

A graphic representation of the data on a map is the final stage of the municipal risk report. The decision making process is based on this document. The risks have to meet the threshold values of the matrix reported in DM Maggio 2001, shown in Table 1. The matrix sets limits based on effects, frequencies and vulnerabilities. Explicitly referring to UK-legislation, the Italian legislator opted for a decision-making procedure in which frequency estimates are explicitly taken into account [19]. The matrix of DM 9 Maggio 2001 applies to chemical accidents only (flammable LPG is not included). Accident frequencies are ordered in the left column and effects are listed in the top row. Depending on the frequency and estimated damage, limits are set to the acceptability of certain developments.

Table 1:   DM 09/05/2001, the compatibility matrix (applicable without urban variant).

Frequency of the event	Estimated damage (categories)			
	Elevated mortality	Mortality	Irreversible damage	Reversible damage
$F < 10^{-6}$	DEF	CDEF	BCDEF	ABCDEF
$10^{-4} < F < 10^{-6}$	EF	DEF	CDEF	BCDEF
$10^{-3} < F < 10^{-4}$	F	EF	DEF	CDEF
$> 10^{-3}$	F	F	EF	DEF

Planners verifying the acceptability of vulnerable objects in a risky area have to compare the information collected in the RIR with the threshold values listed in the matrix. With respect to the vulnerability of persons, the general criterion of "evacuation capacity" is used to assess the vulnerability category of houses (floors/units that have to be evacuated), hospitals (number of beds), schools (number of persons) etc. With respect to the environmental vulnerability, the criterion is the time necessary for the restoration of a specific environmental degradation caused by an accident (longer or shorter than 2 years; in the first case, the vicinity of the environmental object has to be considered incompatible with the plant). At the state-of-the-art of the environmental risk assessment discipline, the reliability of this criterion is however insufficient and further studies are being performed (source: Italian Ministry of Environment, 2005).

The Italian legislation is quite recent and only few municipalities have already implemented the RIR. The few experiences are not enough to draw strong conclusions about its functioning. Nevertheless, some feedback about local experiences is already available in literature [19-22]. General agreed points are:

- In an evaluation characterized by a high level of uncertainty, the quality, reliability and availability of territorial as well as risk information play a crucial role;
- An efficient and prompt exchange of information among all actors is necessary; a shared database to be used as common reference is advisable;
- Bridging the gap between risk and land-use planning also requires attention for perception, expectations and specific values of involved communities. Therefore, a proper risk communication strategy must accompany the decision-making process.

Though the nation-wide introduction of the RIR will undoubtedly present several specific problems, it already offers an opportunity for the creation of new synergies among the actors involved. Moreover, its status as a public document responds to a fundamental principle of sustainability: the transparency of territorial governance. Transparency is also one of the key features of the Seveso II Directive.

5   Conclusions: which horizon for a European policy in the field of risk in land-use planning?

Article 12 of the Seveso II Directive has obliged EU-member states to explicitly consider industrial risk in land-use planning. In this paper, a brief overview is presented of the several ways in which this is done by various Member States. Two distinct regulatory approaches can be discerned: risk-based and effect-based approaches. In risk-based regulations, both probabilities and adverse effects are considered, as is the case in e.g. the UK and The Netherlands. In effect-based regulations only effects are considered explicitly, as is the case in e.g. Germany.

For illustrative purposes, the way in which the Seveso II Directive is implemented in Italy is analyzed more extensively, with a focus on methods, roles and competences involved in the decision-making process. The Italian planning instrument RIR, reporting in an accessible and easy-reading form potential incidents, probabilities and urban/environmental vulnerabilities, has been positively evaluated as a bridge between risk analysts and spatial planners. Though the RIR-document is susceptible to improvements - particularly regarding the reliability of the information and the environmental vulnerability analysis- it is a promising tool for the inclusion of the matter of industrial risk within ordinary planning decisions.

The Italian case shows that the integration of risk control in land-use planning policies is strongly dependent on contextual, institutional and social factors. A strive for a uniform land-use planning methodology in the European Member States thus appears to be difficult as well as undesirable. The diversity of the ways in which the Seveso II Directive has been implemented in the various Member States should clearly not be considered as a flaw. Rather than on a harmonization of methods, the joint European effort should focus on the exchange of information and best practices for risk control in its territory, where "territory" assumes the supra-national meaning indicated by the European Spatial Planning programme funded by the European Commission [23].

This address has been confirmed by the first amendment of the Seveso II Directive in the end of 2003 [24], requiring to the Commission to establish a common accident database to be used by all Member States. The amendment requires also the definition of Guidelines for the implementation of Article 12, promoting "principles of best practice" for LUP in risky areas [25]. Both these requirements illustrate the possibilities to improve external safety regulations throughout the EU territory by a constant learning process of all Member States.

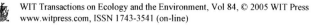

References

[1]   Council Directive 96/82/EC of 9 December 1996 on the control of major-accident hazards involving dangerous substances. Official Journal of the European Communities, L 10/13, Brussels, 14.1.97

[2]   Horlick-Jones T., Meaning and contextualization in risk assessment. *Reliability Engineering and System Safety* 59, pp.79-89, 1998

[3]   Risoluzione del Parlamento Europeo sull'esplosione di una fabbrica a Tolosa (Francia), B5-0611, 0612, 0614 and 0615/2001, 3/10/2001

[4]   Jones, A. V (eds.). *The regulation of major hazards in France, Germany, Finland and the Netherlands*, Health and Safety Executive, UK, 1997

[5]   HID Safety Report Assessment Guide: Explosive, Health and Safety Executive, UK, Online. http://www.hse.gov.uk/comah/sragexp/crit34.htm

[6]   Council Directive 82/501/EEC of 24 June 1982 on the major-accident hazards of certain industrial activities. Official Journal of the European Communities, L 230, Brussels, 5.8.82

[7]   Giove S., Basta C., Environmental risk and territorial compatibility: a soft computing approach. *Proc. Of the 14th Italian Workshop on Neural Nets*, eds. Apolloni B., Marinaro M., Tagliaferri R., Springer Verlag: Berlin, pp. 195-201, 2003

[8]   Slovic P., Emotion, sex, politics and science: surveying the risk assessment battlefield, *Risk Analysis* 19(4), pp.689-701, 1999

[9]   Ale B.J.M, Living with risk: a management question, *Reliability Engineering and System Safety,* article in press, 2005

[10]   Amendola A. *Integrated Risk Management – Recent paradigms and selected topics, IMDR Research Booklet* 2, June, DPRI, Kyoto University, 2000

[11]   Smeder M, Christou M.D and Besi S., Land Use Planning in the context of major accident hazards – An analysis of procedures and criteria in selected EU member states. Report EUR 16452 EN, Institute for Systems, Informatics and Safety, JRC Ispra, Ispra (I), 1996

[12]   Amendola A., *Gestione dei rischi: dai rischi locali a quelli globali.* Quaderni CRASL (Centro di Ricerche per l'Ambiente e lo Sviluppo sostenibile della Lombardia) 2, pp.37, 2000, Online. http://www.crasl.unicatt.it/

[13]   Health and Safety Executive, *Risk Criteria for land use planning in the vicinity of major industrial hazards*, HMSO, UK, 1989, Online. http://hse.gov.uk

[14]   Bottelberghs P.H., Risk analysis and safety policy in The Netherlands. *Journal of Hazardous Materials* 71, pp59-84, 2000

[15]   Deuster B., Ministry of the Environment (FRG), Regional Planning and Agriculture: Land Use Planning and Plant Safety, *Proc. Of the Health and Safety Executive Conference on the Major Hazards Aspect of Land-Use Planning*, Chester, UK, 26-29 October 1992

[16]   Ministerial Decree of 9 May 2001, Requisiti minimi di sicurezza in materia di pianificazione urbanistica e territoriale per le zone interessate

da stabilimenti a rischio di incidente rilevante, Gazzetta Ufficiale della Repubblica Italiana, No.138, Rome (I), 16.6.2001

[17]   Decreto Legislativo 334/99 in attuazione della Direttiva 96/82/CE relativa al controllo dei pericoli di incidenti rilevanti connessi con determinate sostanze pericolose, Gazzetta Ufficiale della Repubblica Italiana No. 228, Supplemento Ordinario n. 177, 28 settembre 1999

[18]   Decentralization of European decision-making, European Commission, Committee   of   the   Regio   (COR),   2003,   Online. http://www.cor.eu.int/en/documents/progress_democracy.htm

[19]   Colletta P., Manzo R., Spaziante A. (eds.), *Pianificazione del territorio e rischio tecnologico – il D.M. 9 maggio 2001*, Celid, Italia, Torino, 2000

[20]   Provincia di Venezia, La sicurezza del territorio: valutazione e pianificazione concertata del rischio industriale. *Urbanistica* Dossier 62, INU Edizioni, pp.32, 2003

[21]   De Marchi B., Learning from citizens: a Venetian experience. *Journal of Hazardous Materials* 78, Elsevier, The Netherlands, pp.247-259, 2000

[22]   Pellizzoni L., Ungaro D., Technological risk, participation and deliberation. Some results from three Italian case studies. *Journal of Hazardous Materials* 78, Elsevier, The Netherlands, pp. 261-280, 2000

[23]   European Spatial Planning Observatory Network (ESPON), European Commission, 2004, Online. http://www.espon.lu.

[24]   Directive 2003/105/EC of the European Parliament and of the Council of 16 December 2003 amending Council Directive 96/82/EC on the control of major-accident hazards involving dangerous substances, Official Journal of the European Union, L 345/97, Brussels 31.12.2003

[25]   European Working Group on Land-use Planning (EWGLUP), Joint Research Centre of the European Commission, Major Accident Hazard Bureau, Ispra, Varese, Italy, 2003, Online. http://landuseplanning.jrc.it

To control or not to control? The role of sustainable planning in order to accommodate informal brickyards in the integrated development plan of the Mangaung Municipality

G. M. Steenkamp & J. J. Steÿn
Department of Urban and Regional Planning,
University of the Free State, Bloemfontein, South Africa

Abstract

During 1994 and 1999, the Bloemfontein Municipality amalgamated with five other municipalities to form the Mangaung Municipality. The Mangaung Municipality now has a population of ± 740 000 and covers an area of 6 363 km². Some areas are totally urban, while in others, people are living in informal settlements. The unemployment rate is 35%, but in some areas, it has risen to as high as 48%.

Poor people in the city cannot afford to buy burnt bricks from the major suppliers of bricks. Informal brickyards were established all over the given areas where clay and/or water were available. These brickyards are now producing good home-made burnt bricks and are creating jobs in a sea of unemployment.

The problem however is that from a planning and sustainability viewpoint, all is not well. Although the location of the brickyards brings about a saving in costs for the transportation of bricks from the formal brickyards, of which the nearest is 300 km away, the coal-burning activities of the informal brickyards are creating air pollution. Furthermore, no prior environmental impact studies were carried out for the location of the brickyards. Most of them have simply been established haphazardly, in any available spot.

This paper will show how these problems could be handled within the context of sustainable planning. The environmental issues will need to be evaluated from a socio-economic perspective. A proposed policy to guide future development will have to be part of the integrated development plan; and this paper will show how this could be effectuated in practice.
Keywords: poverty, brickyards, earth bricks, sustainable planning, housing, unemployment, rammed earth.

WIT Transactions on Ecology and the Environment, Vol 84, © 2005 WIT Press
www.witpress.com, ISSN 1743-3541 (on-line)

1   Introduction

One of the problems of planning in developing countries is "to control or not to control" meaning that you are pressed to create jobs for the large number of unemployed people.

The Mangaung Municipality consists of the city of Bloemfontein (365 000 persons), Thaba 'Nchu (110 000), Botshabelo (225 000) and three other (rural) areas (40 000). The latter two are approximately 60 and 45 kilometres east of Bloemfontein on the N8 road. Population densities are very low with 70 000 informal houses. There are 150 000 erven and 100 000 formal houses in Mangaung. The population growth rate in Bloemfontein was 2.3% between 1991 and 1996, Thaba 'Nchu was 1.2% and Botshabelo has a negative growth rate of 3.5% showing that people are moving to Bloemfontein. With no industrial development to speak of the unemployment rate is 35 to 48% (MLM [1]).

This part of the Free State is in the grassveld biome, which is a flat area, dotted intermittently with small hills. The soil is clayey with numerous drainage courses. The average annual temperature has a relatively wide range of 15.2°C, while the annual rainfall is 564mm and occurs in the summer months in the form of thunder-showers (Department of Constitutional Development and Planning [2]). Because the Free State is in a relative dry area the environment is more sensitive to damage.

2   Background of the settlements of Mangaung

The first inhabited place in the present day Mangaung was Thaba Nchu. Thaba Nchu, which means "Dark Mountain", was first inhabited by a Barolong tribe under Chief Moroka, with two Wesleyan missionaries, in approximately 1833. The missionaries were Jac Archbell and J. Edwards, who lived there with their families. Chief Moroka was the heir of Siffonello who came from the north near Makwassie, on the run from Moselekatse. Chief Moroka entered into a transaction with Moshesh, the chief of the Basotho, in terms of which nine head of cattle and seventeen sheep or goats were paid to Moshesh in exchange for the land (Van der Wath [3]).

In 1836 the Voortrekkers arrived in Thaba Nchu and they constituted their own government before trekking to Kwa-Zulu Natal after two years. Some settled in the area of the present day Mangaung (Van der Wath [3]). The relationship between the Barolong and the Afrikaners was a good one. During the Anglo Boer War, one of the chieftains looked after the cattle of a neighbouring farmer when the English were killing all the Afrikaners' livestock, and he returned the cattle to the farmer after the war (Steÿn [4]).

Major Warden bought the farm Bloemfontein from Johannes N. Brits in 1846 to establish the town Bloemfontein. It became the capital of the former Free State Republic and today is the seat of the Provincial Government of the Free State and is also the seat of the Court of Appeal. Bloemfontein has an educational, commercial and service sector. The city is divided according to

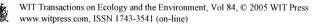

racial lines. Industrial areas form buffer zones between the separate townships (MLM [1]).

After 1948 the new government implemented the policy of separate development, better known as apartheid. Thaba Nchu became part of the Bophuthatswana homeland in December 1977. In February 1979, the South Sotho-speaking people were driven out of Thaba Nchu after an ethnic clash. About 60 000 Basothos were relocated to Botshabelo situated to the south-west of Thaba Nchu (Steÿn [5]). "Thaba Nchu has a more scattered development pattern with 37 traditional villages surrounding the urban centre as far as 35 km from the urban core (MLM [1])". Thaba Nchu has a rich cultural history. The indigenous people have their own distinctive style of earth construction. The building of earthen houses and the decoration of the buildings are linked to their culture and form part of an annual event. The urbanization of the local people has alienated the people from their culture to a large extent.

Figure 1:   Locality map of the area.

Botshabelo means "sanctuary" (Coetzee [6]). In 1988 Botshabelo housed about 207 000 people who had moved from farms and homelands where they had been restricted by law. The population subsequently grew to 225 000, according to the Integrated Development Plan for Mangaung of 2003. Botshabelo was developed according to a modern plan, with large arteries connecting the neighbourhoods. The layout of the town is not compact, but the town stretches over a vast area with big open spaces, (mostly flood plains) and the Klein Modder River runs through it (MLM [1]). This layout did not suit the inhabitants, who had to walk far distances, since very few of them owned vehicles.

In the townships around Bloemfontein, many people still live in houses built of raw earth, but today only the very poor build houses of raw earth.

3 Poverty

"There is also a growing realization that poverty is both a cause and effect of environmental degradation. In many developing countries poverty and environmental degradation combine in a vicious circle" (Whitman [7]). The Millennium Development Goals of the United Nations and Agenda 21 of the Rio Earth summit place emphasis on poverty alleviation and sustainable resource management. Poverty is viewed as being interrelated with environmental degradation and stress (United Nations [8]).

Thaba Nchu, Bloemfontein and Botshabelo was demarcated as a growth pole and an industrial development point in 1982, which offered a wide range of incentives to attract industries (Department of Constitutional Development and Planning [2]). These incentives were withdrawn after 1994. The industries declined and the number of workers dropped from 16 000 in the nineties to 9 000 in 2004. Many of the inhabitants of Botshabelo came from the mines. In the Free State gold-mining industry, 120 000 jobs were lost during the last decade. The gold-mine crisis is the result of the low gold price and the strong rand in relation to the dollar. The situation has worsened in the last decade: for example, a million jobs were lost in the agricultural sector. The unemployment figure is 35%, and has risen to 48% in Thaba Nchu (MLM [1]).

In Thaba Nchu, Bloemfontein and Botshabelo, there are many poor people who live in informal housing. People who wish to improve their housing conditions have to order bricks from Bloemfontein but no bricks are presently manufactured in Bloemfontein. Bricks are transported from Gauteng and Odendaalsrus. Gauteng is about 400km away and Odendaalsrus, 200km. The bricks are expensive and as a result of the high transportation costs, the option of buying these bricks is out of reach for most people. If material has to be transported to the site, the costs and environmental impact increase (Twinshare [9]).

Hall sees the strengths of the informal sector as a means of enabling developing countries to create better conditions for economic growth and employment-generation (Hall [10]). This is in accordance with the policy of the South African government to create jobs at local level. The Integrated Development Plan theoretically empowers municipalities to link development to their budget, and to implement it locally. Stapelberg shows that the municipalities can be agents for Local Economic Development (LED) by acting as coordinators, facilitators, stimulators or entrepreneurial developers (Stapelberg [11]).

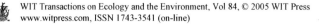

4   Types of bricks using earth

There are (a) different types of earth construction, such as mud bricks, rammed earth as well as wattle and daub.

- Mud bricks are dried in the sun and consist of clay, straw and water (Twinshare [9]). They are made by pouring a puddled mixture of clay, straw and sand into a mould and leaving the mixture in the sun to dry (Moor and Heathcote [12]). The walls made from these bricks have to be plastered.
- Rammed earth is a dryish sand mixture rammed into wall moulds. The usual thickness is 600mm, but in cases where cement is added, a thickness of 300mm is common (Moor and Heathcote [12]).
- A third technique involving the use of wattle and daub, is well known The roof is supported by a wooden structure. A lattice of wooden sticks is planted in between, and the structure is packed with clay (Moor and Heathcote [12]). Sometimes cow-dung is used instead of clay, for example in the Kalahari, owing to the scarcity of clay (the author grew up in such a house).

And (b) transformed earth bricks in the form of stabilized earth bricks, cement blocks and burnt bricks

- Another kind of brick can be produced by stabilizing the earth with 7% cement. This mixture dries more quickly and houses built of these bricks do not need plastering.
- Cement bricks and blocks are crushed stone mixed with sand and cement; sometimes they used coal ash or clinker.
- The people prefer burnt bricks if they can afford a choice of material. Water, clay and coal are needed to produce burnt bricks. The burnt bricks are made from a mixture of clay and are then sun-dried before being packed into a ziggurat-like (staggered tower) shape with pieces of coal in between, sealed off with clay. This home-made kiln is set alight.

Selection and testing of soil is important in order to determine the desired qualities such as strength, low moisture absorption, high resistance to erosion and to chemical spills. Top-soil is not suitable for making earth bricks, as it contains organic material such as humus. The top-soil has to be removed and returned after the extraction, as part of the rehabilitation of the area. If earth brick houses are not built with wide eaves, they require a great deal of maintenance (Twinshare [9]).

One way of alleviating poverty by the local entrepreneurs is to make earth bricks and burn it in kilns. In this way they supply the market with building material and create jobs. The problem is the environmental consequences.

5   Production and location of brickyards

Most of the brick industries are situated around a suitable clay pit, or near to a source of water. In Thaba Nchu the brickyards are near to markets while in Bloemfontein and Botshabelo they are mostly located near water.

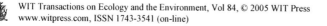

Some of the benefits of informal brickyards are as follows:
- Informal brickyards can create jobs.
- They are suitable for operation by small production units such as families.
- They use local resources, and the work can be done by unskilled labourers.
- They are labour intensive.
- A low level of capital investment is required.
- The product is tailor-made for clients, and production occurs close to the client base.

In Australia, earth bricks are most suitable for the needs of owner-builders with little money and a lot of free labour (unemployed people have the time to build their own houses) (Dobson [13]).

A survey was done in March 2004 on brickyards in Thaba Nchu and Botshabelo. The following was found namely:
- The brickyards can be classified into two groups. "Semi-formal" means that the brickyard is located on a formal lot, allocated by the former municipal authority. However, no levy of any kind has been imposed. "Informal" means that there is no formal site and the brickyards are scattered all over the settlement, mostly in public open spaces.
- This activity has created 133 jobs in settlements with high unemployment rates.
- The burnt bricks (±400 000) and cement blocks (24 000) per month contribute to the building of a large number of houses. The burnt bricks are not environment-friendly but they represent great savings in terms of transportation costs.

At that stage no brickyards were found in Bloemfontein but due to the economic success in Thaba'Nchu and Botshabelo several had been established in Bloemfontein in the last year.

6 The following factors are relevant in respect of the impact of the brickyards on the environment:

Brickyards have a negative influence on the environment because:
- Clay is extracted from informal clay pits without any impact studies having been conducted.
- The brickyards are located in open-space areas or near water-courses.
- Kiln-fired bricks require high temperatures, using large amounts of energy and producing high volumes of greenhouse gases and pollutants.
- If the kiln is not watched closely, the bricks could overheat. When this happens the bricks melt and cannot be used. On these brickyard sites, stacks of these melted bricks have accumulated. In most cases, when the manufacturers abandon the site, they tend to leave without rehabilitating the area. These melted bricks cannot be recycled.

7   Benefits of unfired earth bricks as building material

The following benefits are associated with unfired earth bricks namely:

- The greatest advantage of an earth constructed wall is the thermal mass. A wall of this type is usually thicker than walls constructed of burnt bricks. In areas with extensive fluctuations between day-time and night-time temperatures the thermal qualities of earth bricks are considerable. Thermal properties refer to the balance between thermal transfer insulation and thermal storage insulation. More research on earth flooring is necessary in this regard.
- Earth-building techniques are the most cost-effective in comparison with other construction methods.
- Construction with these materials generates less pollution.
- Earth-building materials are the most recyclable of all masonry products.
- Other benefits include good acoustic properties. In earth buildings there is no problem with reflected sound; and the thick walls prevent the transmission of sound.
- Mud brick walls are fire resistant.
- The levels of energy consumed during the building of the earth-brick house are very low. Moreover, the low energy use during the life-span of the building represents a considerable saving. At the production level mud bricks require only $1/700^{th}$ of the energy used by fired bricks.
- Some people love the colour and texture of earth buildings.
- Earth buildings have low toxicity levels and are allergen-free.
- Well-designed earth buildings require low maintenance.

By combining the traditional techniques of earth building with waterproofing and durability, the beneficial properties of earth building can be increased (Dobson [13]). Unfired earth is the ideal material for a sustainable future.

8   Sustainability in housing

Sustainability in housing means the use of less energy in building the house and in producing the material. It also entails reducing the need for cooling and heating throughout the life of the building. Another important aspect is the recyclability of the material of the house. In Australia buildings must have an adequate level of thermal performance to ensure efficient use of energy for heating and cooling, before building plans are approved (Dobson [13]).

Habitat for Humanity International resolved to make maximal use of locally-available materials. This has an empowering effect on the people of the community, and is better for the environment. Good housing becomes available to more people in this way, money is kept within the local economy, rather than being spent on importing materials, fuel and replacement parts (Nelson [14]).

According to some estimations, 30% of the world's population still live in houses of raw earth, while in Africa; the percentage may be as high as 50%

(Moor and Heathcote [12]). The problem is that soil tends to be regarded as the building material of the poor. Recently, people who are concerned about the environment have begun to use raw earth as building material, and regard it as a source of job creation. Many countries use raw earth as a sustainable solution to minimize energy use for example in Australia (Moor and Heathcote [12]).

The University of the Free State and the Technical University of Eindhoven in the Netherlands, funded by SANPAD (the South African Netherlands Research Programme on Alternatives in Development) are engaged in a three-year research project on earth bricks. One of the foci of the project concerns the attitude of the local population and the brick makers, and how to change this attitude.

When a single house is built with soil from the earth, a hole of about 2 x 3 metres in diameter, and 300mm deep, is formed. This hole soon disappears. The earth used is usually subsoil; and the hole can be filled with topsoil, which can be used for gardening or agriculture.

The main problem occurs when there is a need to make a large number of bricks. In such cases the soil must be obtained from elsewhere, such as a quarry, to prevent environmental damage. Reducing the distance that a product travels brings ecological and economic benefits.

All over the world there are examples of communities using earth- building materials to construct houses and other buildings, creating wealth in the process.

9 How to control these brickyards and make them sustainable

In a sea of unemployment, the brickyards are rendering a service; there is a demand for the bricks and jobs are thereby created. The clay pits could be controlled by local government and made available to the people at a minimal price, as part of Local Economic Development projects. The Integrated Development Plan should be amended so as to allow for this new land use in demarcated areas. Long-term funds should be allocated to develop these brickyards, in order to supply local bricks for the government housing projects.

The local government should rezone the erven for the kilns or give consent for the use of the current erven for a period of time. The occupants of the adjacent erven should be consulted as well. The site could be rented or granted rent free privileges. In terms of environmental impact, a rehabilitation plan should be put into place for all the brickyards and the clay pits. A partnership between the local government and the entrepreneurs could be entered into for the rehabilitation of the sites.

The local government should change their building standards so as to accommodate houses built from earth bricks.

In the meantime, with the aid of the project funded by SANPAD, attitudes may change. A modern earth brick could then be produced, resulting in environmental benefits.

Management skills could help to increase the number of bricks produced per person per day.

10 Conclusion

Local government should see the informal brickyards as an opportunity to create jobs and to render a service to the very poor. If the attitudes of some people could be changed, the environment would benefit from building with earth bricks. Local government, the local population and the brick-makers could build a sustainable future for all concerned.

References

[1]   Mangaung Local Municipality (MLM) Integrated Development Plan 2003/2004
[2]   Department of Constitutional Development and Planning, Bloemfontein and Environs Guide plan Government printer, Pretoria 1986
[3]   Van der Wath, I Notes on the history of Thaba'Nchu by an inhabitant born in 1902.
[4]   Steÿn, J.J. A narrative of a white Afrikaner and his family: their experience of colonialism and the so-called post-colonialism in the South African history and planning. The South African Planning History Study Group Conference University of Free State, Bloemfontein 2003
[5]   Steÿn, J.J. The role of small local brickyards in economic development: a case study of Botshabelo, South Africa Regional Studies Association's annual conference in London 2004
[6]   Coetzee, J.K. Botshabelo: the face of "orderly urbanization". Development Southern Africa Vol 5(3):336-347.
[7]   Whitman, J The sustainability challenge for Southern Africa Macmillan Press Ltd London 2000.
[8]   United Nations. The road from Johannesburg.2002
[9]   Twinshare,   Earth,   stone   and   bricks http://www.twinshare.crctourism.com.au/earth,   stone   brick   visited 29/4/2005.
[10]   Hall in Glasson, J Introduction to Regional Planning Hochinson Linder 1985
[11]   Stapelberg, H. A critical analysis of legislative planning and development instruments in the Free State. Unpublished Masters dissertation of the Department of Urban and Regional Planning. Bloemfontein 2003.
[12]   Moor, G & Heathcote, K Earth building in Australia - Durability Research http://www.dab.uts.edu.au visited 29/4/2005.
[13]   Dobcon, S Terra 2000 Continuity of tradition: New earth building http://.hahaha.com.au visited 29/4/2005
[14]   Nelson,   W   Compressed   earth   blocks http://www.networkearth.org/naturalbuilding/ceb.html visited 29/4/2005.

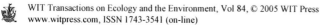

Integrating environmental issues into the Portuguese planning system – 10 years of emerging challenges and persistent problems

T. Fidelis
Department of Environment and Planning, University of Aveiro, Portugal

Abstract

It is frequently stated that land-use planning in Portugal has not only been unable to prevent environmental problems but that it has, itself, contributed to other ones. These include urban sprawl and the destruction of natural areas. Environmental problems related to land-use planning constitute an emerging concern in Portuguese society and explain part of the relevance attributed to planning by the Constitution and by an important body of legislation. This article analyses two main sides of such evolution. Firstly, the recent legislation establishing the Portuguese planning system and its weaknesses regarding the integration of environmental concerns. Secondly, the main features of current planning practice and development control as well as the way environmental problems have been dealt with. The article argues that, despite consolidation of the planning system, land-use plans still remain, practically, a series of regulations dominated by geometric and volumetric issues, legitimising a mechanized decision-making process, and leaving aside issues weakly dealt with in plans such as environmental matters. The analysis showed that the evolution of the planning system has not resulted from an internal process of critical assessment about the experience gathered. On the contrary, it has resulted from external pressures, which have led, mainly, to the mere addition of new types of plans to the system. In spite of approaches and tutelage, they do not necessarily represent a real modernization of the planning system and practice able to promote full and systematic integration of land-use, development control and environmental concerns.
Keywords: planning system, legislation, environment, sustainable development, Portugal.

 WIT Transactions on Ecology and the Environment, Vol 84, © 2005 WIT Press
www.witpress.com, ISSN 1743-3541 (on-line)

1 Introduction

It is widely, and for long, recognized that many changes in land use patterns encompass a potential source of environmental impact. Land-use planning should, therefore, control those alterations and prevent the consequent ecological imbalance they may cause. The most influential contributor to the articulation between environment and new development was perhaps McHarg through his revolutionary book 'Designing with Nature', advocating the design of land use plans according to natural features. However, an overemphasis on social and economic perspectives and urban design principles has hindered the widespread enforcement of such land use planning and related development control methods (O'Riordan and Turner [1]). The academic and political debate around the concept of sustainable development following the Bruntland's Report [2], however, brought a new incentive to review how planning integrates environmental concerns. Selman [3] recalled three main arguments for the theoretic potential of planning:

(i) A significant portion of land use planning's inspiration is based on an ecological perspective on the relationship between country and city;

(ii) In spite of the limitations of environmental legislation, land use planning has the potential to safeguard scarce natural resources and regenerate degraded places, and,

(iii) Planning can provide the integrated vision, the mediation and the negotiation that has been lacking in environmental protection and restoration.

Following the impact of the debate on sustainable development and the major challenges put forward regarding planning contribution, many countries were impelled to review their own planning systems. The revisions aimed, among other issues, the adoption of some principles associated with sustainable development. Among the various ways followed by national jurisdictions, was the integration of sustainable development principles and guiding objectives into national constitutions and planning legislation. Although these measures do not immediately transform current practices, they strengthen the arguments advocating new practices and procedures.

In Portugal, it is frequently stated that land-use planning has not been unable to prevent environmental problems but that it has, itself, contributed to several other ones in the Portuguese territory. These problems include the urbanization in flooding and environmentally sensitive areas, and the permission of high urban densities associated to a high dependence on private transport, running, therefore, against many of the sustainable development principles. This article analyses two factors of the recent evolution of the Portuguese planning system. Firstly, the main features of the Portuguese planning system and its features regarding the integration of environmental concerns, as established by recent legislation. Secondly, the main characteristics of the current planning practice and development control, as well as, the way environmental problems have been dealt with.

2   Environment and sustainable development in planning – *attitude* and *process*

Planning is conceptually related to sustainable development. It includes approaches to deal with development and economic options, to prevent environmental damage and to involve public and stakeholders in decision-making processes. The success of land-use planning' contribution to sustainable development largely depends upon the definition of integrated political strategies and on the design of land-use plans where the environmental component structures the development options. The growing interdependence between environmental and economic factors, however, requires that a strategically integrated approach to natural resource conservation and pollution control becomes incorporated in planning practice. Planning for environment and development requires adequate attention to goals, to public interest, to actors, as well as to politics and processes which have been a distinguishable characteristic of mainstream planning. Simultaneously, spatial development planning requires the substantive, ecological and environmental contributions that have been at the core of environmental planning (Slocombe [4]).

Four main phases of the planning process, namely policy design, plan-making, implementation and evaluation, as shown in table 1, integrate the planning process. It is a decision-making cycle that must be fully understood and undertaken (Tonn *et al* [5]). Its full compliance is a key factor to improve planning contribution for sustainable development. Planning policy design through integrated and participated processes to foresee new development options is a major issue referred to in the literature. Boucher and Whatmore [6] defend that planning contribution is improved with a strong participation process, particularly during policy design. Increasing politicization and public involvement in decision-making processes valorise the role of planning, by educating the general public and contributing to the creation of new re-distributive policies on costs and benefits associated to the implementation of sustainable development (Meadowcroft [7]). While some groups advocate the need for consensus-building across all stakeholders groups in the planning process, Naess [8] argues for an alliance-building, as it appears to be a more viable strategy in the, often, conflicting aims of sustainable development.

Other contributions focus on the plan-making phase and on the need to adopt methodologies that facilitate the survey and treatment of environmental information in order to frame economic development. Included in this group are environmental planning and management models, which are based on the concept of bio-areas (Rees [9]) and consider different multi-sector approaches to alternative development strategies (Yin and Pierce [10]). These integrated approaches to environmental planning have been subject to some criticism. Correcting measures require investment in gathering appropriate information base and in additional efforts to involve public opinion. Critical viewers also call for additional investments for devising appropriate theoretical (Briassoulis [11]) and institutional support to allow the integration and management of different development scenarios in the decision-making processes. Consistent implementation is also a key factor for planning success.

Table 1: Planning for sustainable development.

Planning phases	Aims
Policy design	Promoting the identification of a vision for the future through an integrated view of environmental, social and economic dimensions of development, involving as many actors as possible. Defining clear development objectives and goals.
Plan-making	Designing plans as a decision-making set of criteria where environmental features guide development location and intensity and where "critical natural capital" is safeguarded. Publishing the planning documents which must be understandable by the public.
Implementation	Using technical and political analysis through various stakeholders in decision-making instead of intuitive scrutiny. Promoting accountability in the various actors and stakeholders.
Evaluation	Verifying the implementation of development objectives and goals and updating options and methods.

Evaluation is a fundamental issue when considering the planning process and sustainable development issues. Promoting monitoring has a special role in seeking sustainable development. It may enable the assessment of planning and development control and, consequently, the improvement of accountability and effectiveness of planning and governance (Voogd [12]). The process followed for monitoring and evaluation can be viewed as an adaptive management process. The promotion of a valuable monitoring depends upon a strong conceptual framework that enables the structuring and organization of ideas underlying its development and interpretation. Implementation of monitoring, however, requires a clear definition of objectives, suitable data and evaluation methodologies, as well as, the appropriate spatial and temporal scales. The institutionalization of monitoring is also a key issue, assuring that it becomes mandatory and is undertaken systematically. Hoering and Seasons [13] point out as obstacles to monitoring (i) unwillingness of local managers to risk, admit or report failure, (ii) differing interpretations of monitoring and (iii) conflicting perspectives on what action to take.

Planning for sustainable development requires the improvement of ‘*attitude*’ and ‘*process*’. ‘*Attitude*’ relates to the ecosystem approach, essential to deal with the undeniable interdependence between human activities and nature. It implies

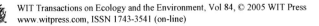

ethical, political and social responsibility. '*Process*' relates to full accomplishment of the planning decision-making cycle as a requirement to promote sustainable development, as pointed out in table 1.

3 The Portuguese planning system

3.1 A descriptive view

Environmental problems related to land-use planning constitute an emerging concern in the Portuguese society and are at the basis of the relevance attributed to planning both by the Constitution and by an important body of legislation. These documents state the special role planning must play for the implementation of a coherent planning policy, adequately aware of environmental spatial specificities. Until the end of the eighties, only a draft of a planning system existed in Portugal. Today, fifteen years later, a lot has changed.

The Portuguese Constitution (4th revision, Constitutional Law no. 1/97 of 20/9) integrates several principles directly related to environment, planning and sustainable development. These principles are included in article 9, related to the main duties of the state, and in articles 65 and 66, which are related to housing and planning, and to environment and quality of life, respectively. Their contents reflect the recognition of the need to promote sustainable development by articulating development, environment and social issues, and the contribution national planning system must give for its implementation.

The main objectives, structure and processes of the Portuguese planning system, are stated in the Framework Law 48/98 on Spatial Planning and Urbanism, and complementary legislation. The Framework Law 11/87 on Environment, although particularly focused on environmental issues, is also a relevant document as it states the role planning instruments should play for the protection of environmental values and for the promotion of sustainable development (art.27). According to Law 48/98, the planning system aims to achieve integrated sustainable development in an economic, social, cultural and environmental way throughout different regions and urban centres. It includes the main objectives of planning policy, the structure and hierarchy of spatial plans and the process for their preparation and approval. This law also introduced an innovative perspective in the planning process by establishing the need to promote evaluation of planning policies and decisions. A year later, the Decree-Law 380/99 of 22 of September was enacted in order to specify the implementation of many principles stated by the previous law. It defines the articulation between the national, regional and local levels of planning, the broad land-use regime, and the process of plan elaboration, approval and evaluation.

The planning system is now organized according to three levels of approach – national, regional and local (see Figure 1). The national level is related to the National Land Use Plan, defining the main strategic guidelines for spatial development, and to the Sector Plans with spatial incidence. From the responsibility of central government are also the Special Environmental Plans, including the Protected Areas Plans, Public Water Catchments Areas' Plans and

Coastal Plans. The regional level is related to the Regional Land Use Plans. These aim to establish the regional spatial development strategies. The local level is implemented through the Municipal Land Use Plans, including the Local Master Plans, the Urbanization Plans and the Detailed Plans. The Law 48/98 ended up to allocate significant planning powers to local level with respect to land-use and construction, while providing the regional and national levels with instrumental roles for more strategic planning related to economic development and protection of natural resources.

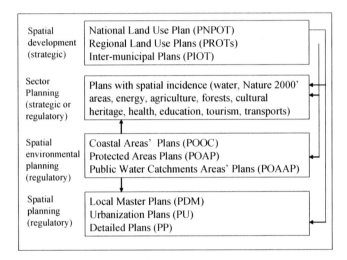

Figure 1:   Planning framework in Portugal.

Until the end of the eighties land use planning was mostly established by Local Master Plans, which are general regulatory zoning instruments covering the territory of municipalities. They also include environmental concerns but these are limited to the definition of areas where development should not take place. Local Plans have to be consistent with the strategies defined in plans prepared at central level of the administration. Local Master Plans, when approved by the central government, give the municipality the right to approve Urbanization and Detailed Land Use Plans. Furthermore, the adoption of Master Plans is a condition for municipalities to have access to specific funding from central government. These plans are considered to be the most important planning instruments in Portugal.

The adoption of Spatial Environmental Plans, as described in Figure 1 is relatively recent. They aim to preserve special natural and protected areas and natural resources. Their rules have to be translated into Local Master Plans, seeking to achieve the sustainable use of space, particularly in areas with specific natural features.

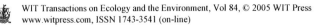

3.2 A critical view

In the last decade, the Portuguese legal background related to planning has revealed strong dynamics. Nowadays, a planning system has been institutionalized with a clear and coherent set of land-use plans, special plans and other instruments aiming to promote a balanced use and development of the land. Shortly, Portugal country will also have a national plan to implement the recently elaborated national strategy for sustainable development.

In spite of this positive background and of the increasing recognition of the importance of sustainable development, as testified in the guiding principles and objectives of spatial planning policy, practice has not yet fully absorbed the new challenges it implies. Several problems associated to land use and consequent environmental impacts still persist in the Portuguese territory and in the planning system itself (Fidelis [14]). Some of them are closely related to the requirements pointed out in table 1. This section outlines a few of them.

3.2.1 Policy design

In general, the policy-design phase under the Portuguese spatial planning system reveals a strong lack of clarity, where the exercise of visioning and formulating goals does not receive due attention. Objectives are basically defined in a very broad and superficial way, being difficult to criticize later on in the process. This weakness has, then, a negative influence on all the planning process. Without a clear set of objectives and goals, plan making is more likely to be influenced by private interests, and plan evaluation becomes unviable. In addition, policy-design tends to focus on where development may, or may not, be located rather then on a more proactive contribution in the promotion of sustainable development and natural resources management. When environmental concerns are considered, there is often a strong hiatus between policy objectives and related practice, due to, among other things, the lack of stricter environmental rules, control mechanisms, environmental responsibility and political will.

In addition, public involvement in this phase is almost inexistent. Legislation foresees mechanisms for public participation. This, however, is mainly undertaken at a later phase of the planning process, after a preliminary version of the plan has been concluded. The weak encouragement for pubic involvement in development decision-making processes, together with the weak tradition of planning and public participation in Portugal, hinders the contribution of planning to the promotion of sustainable development.

3.2.2 Plan-making

There are still serious environmental problems that the planning system has not been able to prevent or deal with, like urban growth in agricultural or natural areas, high urban density areas and excessive use of motor vehicles. In the majority of the Portuguese territory, the zoning process has not been framed by a comprehensive environmental analysis that would allow new alternative land-use development scenarios and related environmental impacts. The recent evolution of environmental legislation concerning air, noise, water or biodiversity, has brought new provisions with relevant technical requirements for planning. They are, however, still far away of becoming fully integrated into planning practice. Spatial environmental plans do establish strict measures for protected and special natural areas but hardly propose measures for their surroundings and inform Local Master Plans how to protect natural values.

Land-use regulations which define where new development can or cannot take place result from an almost intuitive process, dominated by the concern of managing urban growth and consolidating existing settlements. Plan documents are of significant complexity, thereby, deterring public interpretation and consequent discussion before approval. In spite of the consolidation of the planning system, land-use plans still remain, in practice, a series of regulations dominated by geometric and volumetric issues, legitimising a mechanized decision-making process, and leaving aside issues poorly dealt with in plans such as environmental matters. In addition, traditionally, the establishment of land-use parameters has been a task of architects and civil engineers, and has focused on the control of land use and urban development. The lack of a clear framework defining the terms of professional activity in planning and the dominance of a particular corporative view, explain, partially, the weak synergies with other professions hindering, consequently, the transformation of existing divergences into complementarities.

3.2.3 Implementation

In comparison with other European countries, the Portuguese planning system is considered rigid, as spatial development is controlled by plans of a regulatory nature. If, on the one side, the development control becomes more predictable with such a framework, on the other side it becomes less flexible, preventing the adoption of solutions different from those considered in plans. In addition, the system reveals low levels of implementation and related control.

The complex articulation between the political and private sectors in the planning system is at the basis of major criticism. Plans, which are responsibility of public authorities that aim to safeguard public interest, too often result from the views of a limited group of actors. Projects proposed in the plans are often resulting from private sector, whose interest do not always agree with the general aim of public good, environmental quality and sustainable development of communities.

3.2.4 Evaluation

The Law 48/98 and related regulations brought an innovative perspective for the planning process by establishing the need to promote the evaluation of planning policies and decisions. Although the main objectives of plan evaluation have been defined in legal documents, no methodologies or procedures have been established to undertake it. The construction of a national data base and planning observatory are also still to be implemented. Some scattered examples of tentative evaluation of plans exist. As established by the new legislation, however, comprehensive plan evaluation is yet to be put into practice in Portugal. With a lacking of evaluation phase, the planning decision-making cycle is not concluded and the system is persistently incomplete. A learning process, where successes and failures are identified, analyzed and disseminated is neither implemented nor used to improve planning performance in Portugal.

The recent evolution of the Portuguese planning system has resulted more from pressures external to the system, translated into the adoption of new types of plans (the spatial environmental plans) than from an evaluation process about the experience gathered so far. The adoption of these new plans, although necessary, reveals, in a certain way, the incapacity of the system to deal with spatial specificities and their articulation between environment and development.

4 Conclusions

In spite the consolidation of the planning system, land-use plans still remain, in practice, a series of regulations dominated by geometric and volumetric issues, legitimising a mechanized decision-making process, and leaving aside issues poorly dealt with in these plans such as environmental matters. The present analysis showed that the evolution of the planning system has not resulted from an internal process of a critical assessment of the experience gathered. On the contrary, it has resulted from external pressures, and lead, mainly, to the mere addition of new types of plans to the system. In spite their approaches and tutelage, and the recognition they give to the poor treatment of environmental concerns in conventional planning, they do not necessarily represent a real modernization of the planning system and practice, seeking full and systematic integration of land-use, development control and environmental concerns. Improvements should urgently focus on three aspects. Promoting the exercise of visioning and goal formulation phase, involving as much stakeholders and public as possible. There is an urgent need for reviewing the plan-making phase, (seeking adequate treatment of environmental and sustainable development concerns), simplifying planning documents to allow their understanding by public, and controlling plan implementation. Finally, the planning decision-making cycle should be concluded by an evaluation phase, where successes and problems are identified, analysed and communicated.

References

[1] O'Riordan, T. & Turner, R., *An Annotated Reader, in Environmental Planning*, Pergamon Press, UK, pp 139-143, 1983.
[2] WCED, *Our Common Future*, World Commission for the Environment and Development, Oxford University Press, UK, 1987.
[3] Selman, P., *Environmental Planning*, Chapman, London, pp. 2-10, 1992.
[4] Slocombe, D., Environmental Planning, Ecosystem Science, and Ecosystem Approaches for Integrating Environment and Development, in *Environmental Management*, **17(3)**, pp. 289-303, 1993.
[5] Tonn, B., English, M., Travis, C., A Framework for understanding and improving environmental decision making, *Journal of Environmental Planning and Management*, **43(2)**, pp.163-183, 2000.

[6]   Boucher, S. & Whatmore, S., Green Gains? Planning by Agreement and Nature Conservation, in *Journal of Environmental Planning and Management*, **36(1)**, pp. 33-49, 1993.

[7]   Meadowcroft, J., Democratic Planning and the Challenge of Sustainable Development, ProSus Report 1/97, 1997.

[8]   Naess, P., Urban Planning and Sustainable Development, *European Planning Studies*, **9(4)**, pp503-524, 2001.

[9]   Rees, W., Carrying Capacity and Ecological Footprints – A New Imperative for Urban-Rural Sustainability, paper prepared for the Second International Training Session, Leadership for Environment and Development, Okinawa, Japan, pp. 1-10, 1996.

[10]   Yin, Y.; Pierce, J., Integrated Resource Assessment and Sustainable Land Use, in *Environmental Management*, **17(3)**, pp. 319-33, 1993.

[11]   Briassoulis, H., Theoretical Orientations in Environmental Planning: An Inquiry into Alternative Approaches, in *Environmental Management*, **13(4)**, pp. 381-392, 1989.

[12]   Voogd, H., The Changing Role of Evaluation Methods in a Changing Planning Environment: Some Dutch Experiences, *European Planning Studies*, **5(2)**, pp. 255-265, 1997.

[13]   Hoering, H. & Seasons, M., Monitoring of Indicators in Local Regional Planning Practice: concepts and issues, in *Planning Practice and Research*, **19(1)**, pp. 81-99, 2004.

[14]   Fidelis, T., *Planeamento Territorial e Ambiente*, Principia, Estoril, pp.258-261, 2001.

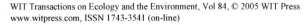

A conceptual device for framing sustainability in project development and evaluation

C. Bogliotti[1] & J. H. Spangenberg[2]
[1]*International Center for Advanced Agronomic Studies in the Mediterranean, Bari, Italy*
[2]*Sustainable Europe Research Institute, Bad Oeynhausen, Germany*

Abstract

The exclusive use of sustainability criteria does not seem sufficient to orient sustainable development towards the complexity of the societal requirements and to cope with them. The paper provides a heuristic device to determine sustainable development with a more comprehensive vision. The device represents an explicit and transferable back-to-basis approach based on 3 functions: -) sustainability (S), a field of macro-variables underlying normative criteria; -) governance (G), a field of macro-variables pertinent to the organisation of the society in which sustainability is plunged; -) Ethics (Є), a field of principles used to explicitly orient sustainability towards a higher level of individual values. The interlinkages among S, G and Є are explored to enable comprehensive planning and evaluation of sustainability accounting the fair balance among sustainability criteria, governance variables and explicit ethical principles.
Keywords: sustainability, governance, Ethics, orientation of sustainability.

1 Introduction

Criteria of sustainability alone do not seem able to comprehensively frame sustainable development in project development. The term project is used here to cover a large range of human actions, from programmes, master plans, strategies to decision making and policies. Neither traditional impact assessment approaches nor applied sustainability seem able to cope adequately with the dynamic character of our modern society, which seeks balancing between material and non-material values [1, 2]. The purpose of the paper is to present a holistic model which can support planning and evaluation of sustainability by exploring the interlinkage of sustainability, governance and Ethics, and in the same time systematise sustainability, governance and Ethics in separate fields of explicit criteria or variables. In general, the interlinkages of these variables are not explicitly and analytically considered when planning and assessing sustainable development. Very often the same or very similar variables are used simultaneously to characterise sustainability, governance and Ethics in the social, economic and environmental dimensions. The following questions are posed. Is governance an implicit sub-function of sustainability? Do we have to treat the notions of governance, although complementary to sustainability, in a separate and more explicit field? The general paradigms framing relationships of sustainability vs. governance are mainly centred on the fact that sustainability must be adequately plunged in a system of good governance [3]. Also Ethics is essential to determine the quality of choices for sustainable development [4, 5]. But what are the ethical principles inspiring sustainability? How do we establish useful interlinkages between sustainability and Ethics? They should rather be explicitly expressed and systematised and used as reference for orienting projects since their early-stage phase of design and during their assessment. The proposed model is an underlying criterion for the integration of ethics and governance in sustainability as inspired by the existing literature [2, 4, 5] but not yet analytically explored with satisfactory results. The proposed approach is also inspired by the EU values prevailing in the Treaty of Amsterdam (art. 2), further developed in the published European Commission Communication "Guidelines for Programmes in the period 2000-2006 (OJ 1999/C 267/02) and in the acts of the Process of Lisbon [6]. But perhaps the most relevant EU document for the contextualization of ethics and governance in designing and assessing sustainable development is the Framework Programme-FP for research, technology and development [7]. The final text of the 6th FP makes explicit reference to the EU aim of integrating notions of governance and ethics into sustainable development, without giving an analytical model for integration.

2 Conceptualising a new framework

The model enhances a back-to-basis heuristic approach based on the separate use of three fields of macro-variables: -) Sustainability (S), a field of macro-variables defining normative criteria for sustainable social, environmental and economic development; -) Governance (G), a field of macro-variables pertinent to the organisation of the society, ensuring the realisation of Sustainability; -) Ethics (€), a field of macro-variables inspired by values residing in individual's motivation to determine orientation of choices and paths of sustainable development.

A macro-variable is defined here as the result of the combination of sub-sector (e.g.: economic or socio-economic) measurable variables (e.g.: income, economic growth, production, productivity, etc.). The multi-dimensional interlinkages of S, G and € inscribe the space in which early-stage design or evaluation of projects should be conceptually inscribed (Fig. 1,a). The triangle of Fig. 1.a is the way to simply represent the conceptualisation lying at the base of the model, where the space delimited by the simultaneous interaction of multi-level variables S, G and Є is explored. The first step of the work consists in the systematisation of the arena of variables gloomed in current concepts and methods used in project design and assessment, trying to differentiate them in discrete groups of macro-variables for each S, G and Є field. It is important to underline that the presented methodological outline intends to stimulate the discussion about the reliability of a conceptual model based on separate, pseudo-orthogonal, S, G and Є fields, the potential and the limits to this regard and the need of more analytical forms to frame sustainability in project scheme development. A conceptual heuristic device based on a 3-D matrix, encompassing the macro-variables of the separate fields, is a useful tool for the graphical representation and analytical exploration (the second step) of the complex nature of the SGЄ field and internal interlinkages (Fig. 1.b).

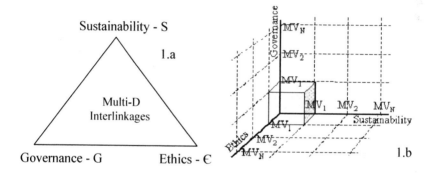

Figure 1:   a) The SGЄ triangle inscribing multi-dimensional interlinkages
            b) The multi-dimensional interlinkage of S, G and Є illustrated by a
            3-D matrix (MV = macro-variable).

3   Systematisation of the main elements

3.1 Sustainability - S

We consider the field of sustainability as a vector resulting from the combination of normative macro-variables pertinent to the societal, environmental, economic dimensions and their interlinkages. The discreteness proposed for the S field is given by a set of macro-variables generalised from the imperatives of sustainability proposed by Valentin and Spangenberg [8] for the social, economic and environmental dimensions and interlinkages established between the above dimensions. The S-field is expressed by 6 macro-variables (Table 1). An extensive description of these macro-variables is given in the recent literature [8,9,10,11]. In order to avoid the fuzzy coexistence and combination of sustainability and governance variables under the same non-linear function, and with the aim of systematising them in separate fields, we have assumed the institutional dimension to be an element of the sphere of governance and not of the domain of sustainability.

Table 1: MV_1–MV_6 are the six macro-variables of the Sustainability field.

Dimensions and interlinkages	Macro-variable (MV)
Economic	Improve competitiveness (MV_1)
Social	Safeguard cohesion (MV_2)
Environment	Limit throughput (MV_3)
Environment-Economics	Eco-efficiency (MV_4)
Environment-Social	Access (MV_5)
Social-Economic	Burden sharing (MV_6)

3.2 Governance - G

Governance is that state of minimum regime based on established rules, collective capabilities and knowledge, integration of all social parties, roles, participation, interdependences shared by individuals, households, groups and institutions. Such a type of regime is at the base of governance to enhance sustainability through the tool of policy. The institutional dimension, although important, does not constitute a main variable of governance, as the concept of governance is centred on the collective capacity to govern without government [12]. Governance as such should rather be characterised by the combination of macro-variables describing the dynamics of societal participation, knowledge society and societal capability, as these elements are at the base for building the system of societal interdependences.

3.2.1 The triangle of governance
Although we recognise the high complexity, we assume that in a simplified but justifiable fashion governance can be described as the vector resulting from the interactions of three main macro-variables: i) knowledge, KN; ii) critical mass, CM and iii) capacity – CA.

Knowledge-KN
A good governance system depends on the development of factual knowledge shared by all the components of the society from individuals to groups and institutions. The knowledge is an important element influencing the orientation and mode of governance. Building shared factual knowledge is at the base of the knowledge society, necessary – although not necessarily sufficient - for bridging the positions and interests of different stakeholders, institutions, citizens and societal groups enabling self-organisation for effective governance.

The knowledge based on trans-disciplinarity helps to build comprehensive knowledge, conveying the diversity of expertises, from technical to economic, social and humanistic sciences to support problem resolution with a holistic approach.

Critical mass-CM
Critical mass includes two concepts: i) the integration of the diversity of notions, established by the overall volume of integrated disciplines and knowledge and ii) the integration of people, established by the cooperation of an high diversity of institutions, stakeholders and citizens [3,12]. If critical mass is low there is no strong condition for sustainability. Reaching a high diversity of participation is the main target for designing and assessing the critical mass.

Capacity-CA
Capacity is related to concepts like ability and readiness of the system to ensure sustainable development. Capacity is a "dominium" in which the entities involved can act in certain ways and have the assets and-or power to accomplish objectives for progress [13]. Capacity is a key element to improve governance. Its design and evaluation is difficult, as progress varies greatly depending on the specific reference values of the evaluator. However, there is a general acceptance that the greater the collective capacity in the society, the higher the opportunity of governance. Effective capacity depends on the quality of collaboration, communication, reciprocal understanding and participation of people and institutions in the process of governance.

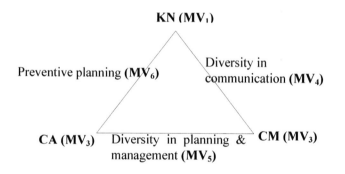

Figure 2:   The triangle of governance (KN=Knowledge, CM=Critical Mass, CA=Capacity, MV=macro-variable).

KN-CM-CA interlinkages
KN, CM and CA variables express the necessary conditions of governance at different scales and levels, without giving information on the character of their interlinkages. The connections among KN, CM and CA are encompassed in the triangle of Fig. 2. The interlinkages of Fig. 2 establish the operability criteria for a balanced integration of KN, CM and CA. The triangle of governance illustrates the following interlinkages: 1) the *expression of diversity in communication society*, 2) the *collective preventive planning* and 3) the *diversity of planning and management*. Balancing KN and CM establishes the interlinkage based on the involvement of high diversity and equity of access to knowledge through the

enforcement of diversity in networks of stakeholders, citizens and institutions, including genders and minorities. The second interlinkage between KN and CA establishes the collective capacity to make the best use of societal shared factual knowledge to develop preventive planning to mitigate effects of system perturbations. The third interlinkage trades CM and CA for strengthening the bulk of societal participation in planning and management. Unfolding the triangle of governance and interlinking the KN, CM, CA variables with the macro-variables of the S and C fields enable the exploration of the interlinkages among S, G and C. As we will see later in the paper, only KN, CM and CA will be used for the exploration of the S,G,C interlinkages. The choice of accounting only the three main variables of the G-field is enforced by the need of prioritising and reducing the number of interlinkages to be explored, while in the same time leaving the choice to extend in the future the exploration of interlinkages involving all the variables of the triangle of governance (Fig. 2).

Table 2:   List of ethical principles proposed as macro-variables (MV) of ethics.

Macro-variables	Characterization	Pertinent links
Prosperity (MV$_1$)	Development of co-existing material and spiritual benefit	Economic
Fraternity and love (MV$_2$)	Pursue the "me and you"	Social, Economic
Peace (MV$_3$)	Non-conflicting co-existence of different desires and stakes	Social, Economic
Wisdom (MV$_4$)	Enhancement of conflicts, crisis and degradation	Environmental
Truth (MV$_5$)	Trustfulness in relationships	Environnent
Ecological responsibility (MV$_6$)	Collective responsibility to respect and restore biodiversities	Environmental, Economic
Ecological enrichment (MV$_7$)	Minimal use of resources	Social, Environmental
Individual life (MV$_8$)	Rights of individuals to spiritual and material happiness	Social
Living in community (MV$_9$)	Union of Solidarity	Social, Economic

3.3 Ethics - C

Ethics is conceptually incorporated in the framework by principles that can support sustainability. The sphere of Ethics is constellated by different types of ethical values. We excluded the ones based on ego satisfaction, consumerism or "me or you" business as usual, as these kind of ethical principles do not support sustainable development as such. Ethical principles should be sought to support societal orientation towards sustainable development, accounting for more reflexive and modern economic, social and ecological models [13]. The kind of Ethics referred to in the paper should encompass the main motivations for sustainability that reside as non-expressed values in the individuals. The use of Ethics helps to express more explicitly those values which are attracted by sustainability but remain often hidden. If Ethics is an important device to plan and assess sustainable development, it must be explicitly and analytically linked to notions, models or variables of sustainability [14, 15, 16]. To give a practical example, nine ethical principles are proposed as macro-variables of the $\mathfrak{C}$ field, to support the orientation of Sustainability (Table 2). Although the ethical principles of Table 2 could pervade the whole sphere of sustainability, we have considered that some principles are more pertinent than others when considering the interlinkage with one or the other dimension of sustainability.

4   Exploring the S-G-$\mathfrak{C}$ interlinkages

The systematisation in of S, G and $\mathfrak{C}$ in different groups of variables, although it remains a subjective exercise, it opens further the discussion on the type of variables to be arranged in each field. However, it gives the opportunity to develop early-project design and assessment accounting for a more comprehensive concept of sustainable development, extended along the multi-dimensional system of governance and ethical variables. Separate S, G and $\mathfrak{C}$ fields only express some partial, although necessary, conditions to frame sustainable development in early-stage project design, keeping alive the separate three functions, without giving any explicit information on the overall volume of the SG$\mathfrak{C}$ field delimited by the interlinkages. It is very important to pay the attention to the interlinkages as they constitute the tool for establishing the balanced integration of S, G and $\mathfrak{C}$ in project development. Exploring the meaning of the interlinkages should be also a target of future research, in order to further the knowledge regarding the nature of the SG$\mathfrak{C}$ field. The model offers also an interesting matter for future mathematical modelling development. However, the operability of the model is centred on the translation of the simultaneous interaction of macro-variables of the SG$\mathfrak{C}$ framework into a scheme of interlinkages' headings usable as a preliminary guide for planners and evaluators. The simultaneous interaction of S, G and $\mathfrak{C}$ variables is framed by the theoretical 3-D matrix of Fig. 1.b, where the SG $\mathfrak{C}$ interlinkages (ITKG) are inscribed.

4.1 An outline of the new interlinkages

Exploring the interlinkages at each of the 6 macro-variables of Table 1 for given ethical principles and governance variables has lead to the abstraction of 18 main headings (Table 3). Some general remarks on the S-G-$\mathfrak{C}$ interlinkages and possible framing in design and evaluation process are given.

Improving competitiveness vs. Governance vs. Ethics - The economic dimension of sustainability is mainly expressed today through the concept of competitiveness [8]. One main limitation of the concept of competitiveness as such, is the scarce level of ethical notion embedded in the concept self. The operability of competitiveness is often interpreted to support economic benefit or power of small groups or individuals against others. Does this kind of interpretation align with the perspectives of sustainability? The new interlinkage establishes a different concept of competitiveness, seeking both material and non-material profit, involving a high level of diversities and affirming value of justice (Table 3). The interlinkage orients the concept of competitiveness to production and consumption mechanisms based on systemic logic and reflexivity, material and non-material prosperity, repositioning citizens as manipulator of production and consumptions needs.

Safeguard cohesion vs. Governance vs. Ethics - The opportunity of exploring the concept of cohesion in the new interlinkage enables a more explicit characterisation of paths and targets of the social dimension. Interlinking the social dimension with KN and CA variables and Ethics put the emphasis on a concept of cohesion built on the societal access to knowledge, to enhance the collective determination of the decision-process (democratic process) oriented towards the relevant ethical principles. The involvement of CM orients the formulation of cohesion based on diversities of people and knowledge in decision-rights, prioritising the democratic process on the ethical values. The new interlinkage gives the opportunity to further orient the concept of democracy, already established by Valentin and Spangenberg [8] as the interlinkage between social (cohesion) and institutional dimensions. The new interlinkage orients the evaluation of democracy not only on the base of the co-decision process (participation) but also on the collective determination of democracy based on higher level of values like fraternity, peace, ecological enrichment and individual life (Table 3).

Limit throughput vs. Governance vs. Ethics - The imperative of "limit throughput" [17] resembles the environmental imperative of sustainability, although it is not referenced by explicit governance and ethical variables. The regulation of material and spiritual conciliation of human being in ecosystem science-technology and the building of relevant knowledge channelled in the principle of dynamic ecosystem equilibrium and integrity are established by the new interlinkage. In Valentin and Spangenberg [8] the interlinkage between environmental and institutional dimensions is established under the heading of "care". The new interlinkage orients the concept of "care" towards the minimization of resources use (particularly in regions with scarce resources), shared on the base of trans-disciplinary and trans-sector diversities of stakes and minorities, and tutoring minimal use of resources with creative policy to regulate ecosystem perturbation (Table 3).

Eco-efficiency vs. Governance vs. Ethics - The variable "eco-efficiency", established by the connection between the economic and environmental dimensions of sustainability conceptually addresses accountability between the protection of natural resources (based on the "limit throughput") and the economic development [8]. The main limitation in conceptualising the interlinkage of eco-efficiency is the scarce level of ethical knowledge attached to the traditional concept of eco-efficiency. The main question is: how eco-efficiency should be ethically pursued and on what ethical perspectives? Eco-efficiency must leave the inspiration of traditional production-consumption models and valorise the intrinsic values of resources. Knowledge and capacity to develop ecosystem resources in terms of natural intrinsic value and minimal use lies at the base of the interlinkage between eco-efficiency, governance and ethical values like ecological enrichment and ecological responsibility (Table 3).

Table 3: Representation of the 3D interlinkages in a bi-dimensional matrix S vs. G, at selected ethical principles (Є-MVn).

	Knowledge (G-MV$_1$)	Critical mass (G-MV$_2$)	Capacity (G-MV$_3$)
Improve competitiveness (S-MV$_1$)	**Є-MV$_{1,2}$** Material - non material benefit and reflexive production-consumption mechanisms to enhance cooperative competitiveness and equity (based on the principle of equivalence).	**Є-MV$_{1,2}$** Collective cooperation to repositioning the individual as manipulator of production-consumption. Equity extended beyond cultural boundaries.	**Є-MV$_{1,2}$** Improve diversity in collective innovative choices beyond the short time horizon.
Safeguard cohesion (S-MV$_2$)	**Є-MV$_{2,3,7,9}$** Shared knowledge to improve determination of collective decision-process.	**Є-MV$_{2,3,7,9}$** Diversity of players, individuals and minorities in steering ethics in co-decision process.	**Є-MV$_{2,3,7,9}$** Strengthen democracy based on collective determination of the future.
Limit throughput (S-MV$_3$)	**Є-MV$_{4,5,6}$** Knowledge to regulate conciliation of human being in ecosystem science-technology.	**Є-MV$_{4,5,6}$** Care mechanisms oriented towards the minimization of resources use based on trans-disciplinary and trans-sector diversities stakes involved.	**Є-MV$_{4,5,6}$** Tutoring minimal use of resources and creative policy to enhance policies to support adaptation to ecosystem perturbation.
Eco-efficiency (S-MV$_4$)	**Є-MV$_{6,7}$** Shared knowledge of natural resources intrinsic value and minimal use.	**Є-MV$_{6,7}$** Collective involvement of diverse economic stakes in enhancing minimal use of resources.	**Є-MV$_{6,7}$** Capacity to improve policy enhancing intrinsic non-material value and minimal use of resources.
Access (S-MV$_5$)	**Є-MV$_{7,9}$** Knowledge of the balanced individual-societal-ecosystem sanitation and happiness.	**Є-MV$_{7,9}$** Develop access for all levels of economic and social strata of society, gender and minorities.	**Є-MV$_{7,9}$** Regulation of balanced collective material and spiritual values in using resources.
Burden sharing (S-MV$_6$)	**Є-MV$_9$** Models of solidarity to enhance real union.	**Є-MV$_9$** Union of diversities.	**Є-MV$_9$** Forms of regulation ensuring continuous solidarity.

Access vs. Governance vs. Ethics – The new interlinkage enhances individual and societal sanitation and happiness, conciliation with the criteria of no-perturbation of environment, collective/multi-stakeholder involvement and the regulation of the conflict between collective material and spiritual satisfaction from using resources (Table 3). The access to resources must more explicitly prioritise the non-material aspects, in order to enforce the intrinsic value of the resource, enforcing the orientation towards ecological enrichment.

Burden sharing vs. Governance vs. Ethics - The concept of solidarity is established by the interlinkage (Table 3). Description of burden sharing is given in Valentin and Spangenberg [8]. The interlinkage establishes the concept of solidarity and union based on the high diversity of societal and economic interests, building forms of regulation to ensure continuous union.

The set of new interlinkages can be used in multi-stakeholder meetings to design or evaluate the orientation of project goals. The interlinkages are the datum points in the process of sustainability goal prioritisation, while covering the balance of a broad sphere of elements. Tools like the Logical Framework [18] can be connected to the SG€ meta-framework for the purpose of expressing SG€ interlinkages in a hierarchical sequence of project goals.

5 Conclusions

The representation of separate fields of explicit macro-variables of S, G and € and their integration operated by multi-dimensional SG€ interlinkages helps to illustrate in a holistic, systematized and explicit way some main conceptual criteria usable to embed sustainable development in projects. The new interlinkages enhance a more comprehensive determination and framing of sustainable development, improving the transferability of interpretation of the main imperatives (macro-variables) of sustainability. The introduction of Ethics, as a separate domain, although complementary to sustainability and governance, emerges as a need to avoid fragmentation of visions of sustainability and consequent risk of shifting away from the genuine common objectives of sustainability-self. The attention must be given to the kind of approach and not to the type and number of variables or ethical principles used. What matters is the option provided by the heuristic framework of leaving traditional designing and evaluation of sustainability based on reductive and implicit approaches. The paper intends to stimulate the scientific community as well as project proposal makers, evaluators and practitioners to consider a different way of framing sustainability when developing or evaluating projects, programmes, strategy plans or policies.

Acknowledgements

Many thanks to Dr. M. Aglietti-Zanon and Prof. U. Stefani for the inspiring discussions and fruitful exchange of ideas.

References

[1]   Pope J., Annandale D., Morrison-Saunders A. Conceptualising sustainability assessment. Environmental Impact Assessment Review, 24, 595-616, 2004.

[2]   Jickling, B., A future for sustainability?. Water, Air and Soil Pollution, 123, 467-476, 2000.

[3]   Sampford, C., Environmental governance for biodiversity. Environmental Science & Policy, 5, pp. 79-90, 2002.

[4]   De Paula, G.O., & Cavalcanti, R.N. (2000) Ethics: essence for sustainability.   Journal of Cleaner Production, 8, pp. 109-117, 2000.

[5]   Robinson, J., Squaring the circle ? Some thoughts on the idea of sustainable development. Ecological Economics. 48, pp. 239-384, 2004.

[6]   Commission of the European Communities (2005). Working together for growth and jobs – A new start of the Lisbon Process – SEC, 192/193, 2005

[7]   European Commission. The 6th RTD Framework Programme, www.cordis.lu N-1-2, pp.107-121, 1995

[8]   Valentin, A., & Spangenberg J.H., A guide to community sustainability indicators. Environmental Impact Assessment Review, 20, pp. 381-392, 2000.

[9]   Spangenberg, J.H., Omann, I, & Hinterberger, F., Minimum benchmarks and scenarios for employment and the environment. Ecological Economics, 42, pp.429-443, 2002

[10]   Spangenberg, J.H., Pfahl, & S., Deller, K., Towards indicators for institutional sustainability: lessons from an analysis of Agenda 21. Ecological Indicators, 2, pp. 61-77, 2002

[11]   Funtowicz S., Ravets J., O'Connors M. (1998) Challenges in the use of science for sustainable development. Int. J. Sustain. Dev. 1

[12]   Rodhes, R.A.W., The New Governance: Governing without Government. Political Studies, XLIV, pp.652-667, 1996.

[13]   Chaskin, R.J., Building Community Capacity. New York: Aldine De Gruyter, 2001.

[14]   Balakrishnan, U., Duvall, T. & Primeaux, P., Rewriting the Bases of Capitalism: Reflexive Modernity and Ecological Sustainability as the Foundations of a New Normative Framework. Journal of Business Ethics, 47, pp. 299-314, 2003.

[15]   Collins, D., Virtuous Individuals, Organisations and Political Economy: A New Age Theological Alternative to Capitalism. Journal of Business Ethics, 26, pp. 319-340, 2000.

[16]   Weil, P., The new ethics. Editora Rosa dos Tempos, 1998.

[17]   Spangenberg J.H.. Environmental space and the prism of sustainability: frameworks for indicators measuring sustainable development. Ecological Indicators, 2, 295-309, 2002.

[18]   Eggers, W. H., Project cycle management revisited. The Courier. 169, pp. 69-72, 1998.

WIT Transactions on Ecology and the Environment, Vol 84, © 2005 WIT Press
www.witpress.com, ISSN 1743-3541 (on-line)

Economic analysis of an environmental policy instrument for basins protection in Colombia

J. A. Vásquez P.
Business Management School, EAFIT University, Colombia

Abstract

This paper accomplishes an economic analysis of a governmental policy instrument for basins protection in Colombia. According to the Colombian environmental regulation, every project that uses the hydric resource from a natural source, shall perform a mandatory investment in protection of the involved basin of 1% of the total economic cost of the operation project. (Act 99, 1993. Republic of Colombia). This paper is based on a case study of an hydroelectric power project on the Chico River's basin, located in the municipality of Belmira, Department of Antioquia (Colombia, South America). The analysis is based on the economic value that the Community of Belmira assigns to the environmental services, product of water resource, within the influence area of the Chico River's Basin. This economic value is obtained using the Conjoint Analysis Method. Finally, it is concluded that this governmental policy instrument (the mandatory investment of 1% of operation project total economic cost) is not apt or recommended to preserve the water resources of the Chico River's basin, since the investments that accomplishes the hydroelectric power project in protection of the basin does not compensate the economic value that the Belmira's Community assigns to their water resources. In that sense community does not have incentives to protect the hydric resources of the basin and the policy is not effective since it does not complies with the objective it was designed for.
Keywords: environmental economy, conjoint analysis, environmental services, environmental legislation, environmental policy, natural resources.

1 Introduction

Environmental policy instruments: technological environmental, standard of emission, taxes to the contamination, and subsidies, among others, seek in general terms the achievement of goals of the environmental quality. The subsidies act as an incentive so that the agents (companies or people) they adopt a less aggressive behavior toward the environment and therefore don't generate negative externalities. The taxes to the contamination act as a mechanism of pressure to revert the behavior of the polluting agents (companies), for that which use of the principle is made "who contaminates pay". In the design of a tax to the contamination, it is assumed that the State estimates the economic value of the externalities that the companies generate with the contamination to the community, this is, deterioration of the health, deterioration of the quality and quantity of natural resources, among others. The economic value of such externalities will be paid by the companies to the society with that which is considered that it has been compensated the damage or deterioration to the environment, that is to say the responsibility of the externality is assumed. The appropriate design of policy instruments will should therefore, to compensate to the community for the environmental deterioration and to incentivate to the companies to not contaminating. In this investigation it was carried out the economic analysis of policy instruments (tax) as mechanism for the basins protection in Colombia. This instrument is expected that it acts as a payment for environmental services, with that which would be incentivated to the community to protect the natural resources. The investigation is based on a case study of a hydroelectric power project in the basin of the Chico River, located in the municipality of Belmira, Department of Antioquia (Colombia, South America). For it is considered it the economic value of the externalities (deterioration of natural resources) and the economic value of the tax decreed by the State. To estimate the economic value of the natural resources of the basin affected by the project, use of the methodology of combined analysis is made averagely used in the environmental economy, as well as of the concept of environmental services. The economic analysis of the instrument consists basically on the comparison of both values, to determine that so appropriate it is as mechanism for the protection of the basin in the case study.

2 Instruments of environmental policy

In accordance with the Colombian environmental regulation, all project that during the construction stage and / or operation makes use of the resource it dilutes coming from a natural, superficial or underground source, it will carry out a mandatory investment of 1% of the total cost of the project in the protection of the natural source's basin (Act 99, 1993).

3   Environmental services:

The environmental services are those that toast fundamentally, the wild areas, this is: forests, swamps and, reefs, swamps, plains, savannas). The areas that conform ecosystems, and the basins in their group. For the case study the following environmental services were identified:

Environmental services associated to the Forest:
Cleaning of the Air
Regulation Climate
Retention of Waters
Control of lost grounds
Strong floors
Matter production prevails and foods
Landscape Recreation
Animal refuge

Environmental services associated to the Water:
water to consume
Input for Production
Input for the Generation of Energy
Recreation and landscape
Animal refuge

Environmental services associated to the Grasses (vegetable coverings) :
Animal food
Decrease superficial water
Landscape
Recreation

4   Economic valuation of environmental services

By means of the application of the method of combined analysis, the economic value of the derived social benefits of the environmental services was obtained that provide the natural resources in the basin of the Chico River.

The method of Conjoint Analysis is used averagely for the estimate of the value of public goods or that they don't have market price. The method allows to study the effects of the combined action of two or but qualitative attributes on the preferences of people, providing a quantitative measure of an attribute in front of others. To apply the methodology it is required to carry out four phases: identification and election of attributes, gathering of data, estimate of the utilities and interpretation of results. In the case study, the method allowed to estimate use values and no use value of the natural resources, starting from the environmental services that they lend to society.

5   Materials and methods

In the investigation an economic and environmental characterization of the Chico River's basin was necessary. Three resources natural forest were identified, it dilutes, grasslands whose environmental services are of appreciable importance for the environmental quality of the basin. Next was carried out an economic valuation of the environmental services that identifies the community in the resources waters, grasses, forests, of the study area, using the Conjoint Analysis method. Finally the economic value of the investments was compared in protection of the basin, carried out by the hydroelectric Power Project Rio Grande II that it makes use of the water services of the basin, with the commercial value of these services in the Conjoint Analysis.

6 Results and discussion

The economic value of the environmental services of the basin that was obtained applying the Conjoint Analysis methodology was the following one:

Table 1: Economic valuation of the environmental services associated with the forest.

Environmental services	Value of the service
Cleaning of the Air	1'452.630.874
Regulation Climate	1'380.400.609
Retention of Waters	1'404.477.364
Control of lost grounds	1'380.400.609
Strong floors	1'356.323.855
Matter production prevails and foods	1'316.195.930
Landscape Recreation	1'372.375.024
Animal refuge	1'420.528.534
Total	11'083.332.800

Table 2: Economic valuation of the environmental services associated with the water.

Environmental services	Value of the service
Water to consume	16'040.240.267
Input for Production	15'951.127.821
Input for the Energy Generation	15'505.565.591
Recreation and landscape	15'683.790.483
Animal refuge	15'505.565.591
Total	78'686.289.752

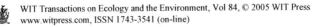

Table 3:   Economic valuation of the environmental services associated to the grasses (vegetable coverings).

Environmental services	Value of the service
Animal food	1'346.010.752
Decrease superficial water	1'064.641.273
Landscape	1'269.964.947
Recreation	1'224.337.464
Total	4'904.9544,37

7   Comparative analysis

The value of market of each natural resource, was used to find the monetary value of the environmental services lent by the Chico River's basin. The total value of the services threw an annual value of $94.674.576.989.

In accordance with the environmental legislation, it was considered that the value of the annual investment carried out by the hydroelectric power project Río Grande II for basin protection was of $833.000.000 (it is equal to 1% of the total economic cost of the project)

The difference between the economic value of the environmental services and the investment of 1% of the total cost of the hydroelectric power project in protection of the basin, shows that the environmental services lent by the basin of the Chico river, are very undervalued, since the benefits are not recognized that these they contribute to the society and the productive system of the basin.

In the case study, the community values in a very homogeneous way the environmental services associated to each one of the natural resources, although the environmental services of the resource dilute they are those but appreciated. What could imply a bigger cultural level regarding the resource dilutes that to the other resources.

8   Conclusions

The Conjoint Analysis method allows to determine valuing economic that the community assigns to the natural resources starting from the environmental services.

The Conjoint Analysis method allows to estimate the economic value of the derived externalities of the deterioration of the environmental quality.

With regard to policy instrument the investment of 1% of the total cost of the project in the basins protection, is possible to affirm the following thing:

When perishing problems of design of the instrument they exist, since it doesn't compensate the economic value that the community assigns to the environmental services of the resource it dilutes and therefore the economic investments don't incentives to the communities to protect the natural resources of the Chico River's basin in the municipality of Belmira.

Policy instruments or measures of protection of the basin of the Chico River that it determines the Colombian state, should be centered in the resource it dilutes, to achieve a bigger positive impact in the community.

The investments dedicated to the conservation and preservation of ecosystems should consider the preferences of the community, with regard to the environmental services with the purpose of that it provide a bigger environmental benefits.

References

[1]   Aguilar, Hernán D y Álvarez, J. Rafael. *Valoración Económica de Bienes Ambientales*. En Semestre Económico, No 09. Enero-Junio. pp 95-106. 2001.

[2]   Bishop, Joshua. *Valuing Forests: A Review of Methods and Applications in Developing Countries*. International Institute for Environment and Development. London. pp. 13 –95. 1999.

[3]   Contraloría General de la República de Colombia. Evaluación de las Transferencias del Sector Eléctrico a las Corporaciones Autónomas Regionales. Contraloría delegada para el medio ambiente. Bogotá, Colombia. pp. 46-65. 2002

[4]   Chomitz, K.M., and Kumari, K. *Los Beneficios Locales de los Bosques Tropicales*: Revisión critica." Traducción de "The Domestic Benefits of Tropical Forest Preservation: A Critical Review Emphasizing Hydrological functions." World Bank Research Observer, pp 13-35. 1998.

[5]   Empresas Públicas de Medellín. *Aprovechamiento múltiple del Río Grande*: Estudio de factibilidad informe final. Julio de 1982.

[6]   Espinoza N. GATICA J y SMYLE J. El Pago de Servicios Ambientales y el Desarrollo Sostenible en el Medio Rural. En ruta IICA. Junio. 1999

[7]   Estrada Rd, Quintero M. Conferencia *Propuesta Metodológica para el Análisis de Cuenca: Una alternativa para corregir las deficiencias detectadas en la implementación del pago por servicios ambientales*. III Congreso Latinoamericano de Protección de Cuencas Arequipa, 9-13 de junio de 2003

[8]   Herrador, D, and Dimas L. *Payment for Environmental Services in El Salvador*. Mountain Research and Development, El Salvador, pp 306-309, 2000

[9]   Ina, T Porras. Conferencia *Valorando los Servicios Ambientales de Protección de Cuencas: consideraciones metodológicas*. International Institute for Environment and Development [1] (IIED) Presentado en el III Congreso Latinoamericano de Protección de Cuencas Arequipa, junio de 2003

[10]   Johnson, N, A. White, and D. Perrot. *Developing Markets for Water Services from Forests: Issues and Lessons for Innovators*. En: Conservation Finance Alliance CFA. New York, pp. 125 – 170, 2001.

[11] Kaimowitz, D. *Useful Myths and Intractable Truths: The Politics of the Link Between Forests and Water in Central America.* San Jose: CIFOR pp. 85 –112, 2000

[12] Ministerio del Medio Ambiente, Republica de Colombia. Ley 99 de 1993, Editorial Legis. Bogotá, 1994

[13] Rosa, Herman. Herrador, Doribel, y Gonzalez, Martha. 1999. *Valoración y Pago por Servicios Ambientales: La experiencia de Costa Rica y el San Salvador*: PRISMA No 35. pp 1-19.

[14] Varela, Jesús y Braña Teresa. *Análisis Conjunto: Aplicación de la investigación comercial.* Madrid: Edición pirámide Madrid, 1996

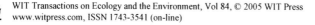

Economic instruments for environmental control: perspectives

S. M. V. G. de Araújo & I. da A. G. M. Juras
Legislative Consulting Department, Environment Unit,
House of Representatives, Brazil

Abstract

Brazil has been facing a series of difficulties in order to introduce and to put into practice its environmental public policies. The country has rigorous and complex environmental rules. Nevertheless, the deforestation rates are still alarming. The Brazilian system of environmental agencies is comprehensive and involves the Union, states and municipalities. Nevertheless, the problems related to the air, water and soil pollution are very serious.

Many environmental technicians believe that a significant part of Brazilian problems in this area are related to the governmental priority to use command-and-control instruments. They defend the stress on the economic instruments as an important strategy for achieving sustainable development and effectiveness in environmental policies. Brazil has some pioneering experiences using economic instruments for the environmental control. The country has been applying a water use payment system and other kinds of financial compensation for the use of natural resources, and it has been adopting some innovative fiscal incentives for biodiversity conservation. These experiences, however, are still at the beginning. There is a process in the Brazilian National Congress to change some relevant rules related to our taxation system. The "Tributary Reform" is analysing, among other aspects, the green taxation.

In this paper, we intend to analyse the Brazilian experiences related to the use of economic instruments for the environmental control, comparing them with similar international experiences. We intend, also, to propose some guidelines to the changes in the Brazilian taxation system.

Keywords: environmental policy; economic instruments; green taxation; green fiscal reform; environmental taxes; environmental fiscal reform; Brazilian environmental policy.

WIT Transactions on Ecology and the Environment, Vol 84, © 2005 WIT Press
www.witpress.com, ISSN 1743-3541 (on-line)

1 Introduction

The concerns related to the environmental crisis have led many countries to improve their environmental management systems in order to make them more efficient and effective. In this context, traditional command-and-control regulations are too costly and low effective in some circumstances, or incapable to achieve the desired objectives in others. Thus, policies based on market-based economic incentives have increasingly been used. They are considered by economists and other policymakers as the most cost-effective method for addressing a wide variety of environmental problems.

In this paper, we intend to analyse the Brazilian experiences related to the use of economic instruments for the environmental control, comparing them with similar international experiences, specifically those of OECD countries.

In some approaches, payments like fees (non-compliance fees, waste fees, license fees), fines (fines for air and water pollution), civil compensation for damage to victims or administrative penalties are considered as economic instruments. These instruments are very used in Brazil. Since many authors [1, 2] consider them as directly linked to command-and-control regulations, we have decided not to include them in this paper. Here, we deal essentially with the market-based instruments. We also include the analysis of governmental subsidies.

2 The use of economic instruments in Brazil

2.1 Brazilian National Alcohol Program (*Proalcool*)

Established in 1975 within a struggle against the petroleum crises, the *Proalcool* program, using public subsidies to encourage the production and consumption of fuel ethanol, had a big impact on the size and structure of the sugarcane industry. A large-scale production of alcohol cars was launched. The Brazilian gasoline consumption was reduced a lot and this situation lasted for years. The petroleum self-sufficiency, however, was not obtained by this way: the refining level was not really altered since diesel oil consumption in Brazil was (and still is) high. The self-sufficiency is being achieved with the increase in the exploitation of large oil deposits in the Brazilian sea.

Proalcool problems of reaching economic viability led to a cut in the governmental subsidies and control associated to the program. In 1991, the presidential decree establishing *Proalcool* was revoked. It must be said that one successful national rule derived from this program, the use of gasoline blended with 20% anhydrous ethanol, is still in force.

In the recent years, many voices began to claim *Proalcool* reactivation, mostly because of its environmental benefits regarding low emission vehicles. The private sector believes on the reactivation. "In July 2003, Volkswagen announced plans to have its entire Brazilian fleet's engine converted from conventional to bi-fuel version by 2006" [3].

Talking about clean burning alternative fuels, it must be also said that Brazil has recently approved, on January, a law regulating the insertion of biodiesel in the Brazilian Energetic Matrix. The Ministry of Science and Technology is developing an important initiative in this field, the Brazilian Program of Technological Development of Alternative Fuels.

2.2 The *CIDE* tax on fuels

Brazilian Federal Constitution gives power to federal government to establish economic domain intervention contributions, a special kind of tribute (*Sonderabgaben* in German doctrine), very close to a tax.

In 2001, the government created an economic domain intervention contribution that is based on the import and marketing of fuels, the *CIDE tax*. Consistent with the "polluter-pays" principle, the *CIDE tax* levied on gasoline imports and commercialisation is higher than those levied on the imports and commercialisation of other oil and alcohol derivatives. Serodio [4] explains that "this difference does not aim to encourage alcohol consumption, but: (a) to provide competitiveness conditions between the national and the imported gasoline; and (b) to collect funds to finance environmental projects related to the oil and gas industry, as well as transport infrastructure programs".

The reality has been showing neither "green" governmental purposes, nor the intention to solve the big problems of the transport sector. The *CIDE tax* on fuels has collected almost U\$ 5 billion in the first two years, but this money has been mostly used to maintain the primary *superavit* demanded by IMF. Several economic sectors and the society in general are pressuring federal government in order to apply the *CIDE tax* resources in the projects legally linked to this specific tribute.

2.3 National Fund for Environmental Protection

The National Fund for Environmental Protection (*FNMA*) was created by law in 1989 to allocate funds for environmental protection activities and scientific research, as well as for projects related to sustainable development, developed by the public sector and NGOs. Nowadays, the *FNMA* more important sources are: (scarce) resources from the federal budget; 10% of the environmental fines charged by *IBAMA* (Brazilian Institute for Environment and Renewable Natural Resources - the federal environmental executive agency); a small part of special royalties eventually received by the Union when the concessionaires of petroleum exploitation have a high production volume; and money received under the Project 1013/SF-BR financed by the Inter-American Development Bank.

Until now, the fund has applied almost U\$ 35 million, divided in more than 100 thousand projects [5]. This amount is extremely low compared with the public money invested in other sectors. Even inside the Environmental Ministry, the *FNMA* has not been properly taken into account in the most important decisions regarding environmental policies. The fund has not really been used as an instrument to fit together federal money destined to the environmental sector.

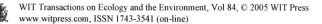

Maybe the reason for this is associated to the participatory manner that *FNMA* adopts to decide about the application of its resources, by means of a managing committee that has the participation of the public sector and NGOs.

2.4 The public banks and the environment

In 1995, the federal government decided to redirect its efforts to introduce the environmental dimension in governmental economic policies. Signing the Green Protocol, all the important public banks undertook not to finance environmentally damaging projects, and also to increase the financial support to environmental sustainable initiatives. The environmental analysis was officially introduced in the public credit system.

The Green Protocol has already generated relevant progresses towards sustainable development patterns, but there is still a lot of work to do. The rules do not involve private banks and the financial world is in some degree always impervious to the environmentalist perspective. Governmental efforts towards the consolidation of the Green Protocol, including the private funding agents, are nowadays not as strong as they could be.

The Brazilian Development Bank (*BNDES*), a federal public company that is associated to the Ministry of Development, Industry and Foreign Trade, can somehow be considered a pioneer in this area. The bank created in 1986 a financial support program with more favourable conditions for the environmental adaptation of companies, and has an environmental unit since 1989. The *BNDES* environmental responsible behaviours have potentially very big effects since its total disbursements on many different kinds of projects in 2003 reached U$ 11 billion.

One relevant example of *BNDES*' actions related directly to environment is the Program for the Treatment of Pollution at the Hydrographic Basin of the *Paraiba do Sul* River - *PRODESPAR*. This program finances city halls, public and private sanitation companies and private companies in the productive sector, in actions such as implementation of collection nets and sanitary sewage treatment systems, treatment of industrial residues and others. *Paraiba do Sul* basin is located in the most populous and industrialised region of the country and was the first one to implement charges for water use and disposal.

PRODESPAR works to join efforts to the Water Basin Cleaning Program (*PRODES*), co-ordinated by the National Water Agency (*ANA*). *PRODES* deals with a purchase-like system applied to treated sewage. State and local sanitation companies are reimbursed for a relevant part of the costs incurred in the construction of sewage treatment stations.

2.5 Ecological *ICMS*

The *ICMS* (tax on sale of goods and services), tribute which operates at state level in Brazil, constitutes an important source of revenue for local governments. The Brazilian Constitution of 1988 stipulates that 25% of the revenue raised by the *ICMS* should be allocated by the state government to the counties. A further requirement of the Constitution is that 75% of the total passed on to local governments should be allocated according to the value added generated by each county. The state governments have the authority to determine distribution criteria for the remaining 25%. Typically, the state governments have utilised criteria based on population, geographical area and primary production. But certain local authorities of counties with environmentally protected areas, or watershed protection areas, have began to argue that these land use restrictions were preventing them from developing productive activities and generating value added. Thus they were losing out in the allocation of the *ICMS* revenue as so much of it depended on value added. They stressed that without some form of compensation it would be difficult for them to maintain compliance with such land use restrictions. In response to their concerns, in *Paraná* State, a new *ICMS* distribution system included an ecological criterion for 5% of the total distributed. Of this 5%, half would be for counties with watershed protection areas and half for those with protected areas. Other states have observed *Paraná*'s experience with the ecological *ICMS* and decided to introduce similar systems.

2.6 The rural land tax

For many years, the rural land tax (*ITR*) has not encouraged the rural owners to keep important areas from the environmental point of view. To calculate the *ITR*, the environmentally preserved areas were included among the usable areas.

In 1996 this rule has been changed by the Law 9.393, so that permanent preservation areas (areas along rivers and others water bodies and sloped areas, for example) and other important ecological areas are now considered as non-taxable and non-usable.

Areas of forest on farms, that were formerly classified as "under-utilised" and subject to higher tax rates, now pay the lowest rates, but only if the farmer publicly registers these areas as the farm's forest reserve. Unused areas not registered as forest reserve are charged through the highest rates.

Unfortunately the *ITR* value is very low to have strong positive impact in environmental conditions.

2.7 The water extraction charge

Due to scarcity in quantity and quality the water hasn't been considered as free resource anymore. In the contrary, water now has an economic value legally recognised in Brazil. The Law of National Hydric Resources Policy (1997) established a water extraction charge to be paid by everyone who extracts or diverts water from surface waters or ground waters, dumps substances into surface or ground waters, or uses water for energy generation. Insignificant uses aren't charged.

The water extraction charge has two main objectives: to recognise that water has an economic value and give the user an indication of its real value; and to encourage people to rationalise water use.

The value to be paid is defined by the watershed committee and the collected money is applied in the same watershed.

2.8 Forestry taxes

Brazilian Forestry Code (1965) states that those exploiting or utilising forestry raw materials are obliged to undertake forestry reposition of appropriate species equivalent to the exploiter's consumption level. This requirement covers logging as well as consumption of charcoal and firewood with unknown origin. Since 1978, however, a federal norm allows for those consuming less than 12,000 m^3 of forest raw material per year the option of paying a deforestation contribution, instead of investing in reforestation. According to Seroa da Motta [6], this contribution, which may be regarded as a type of tax, was not primarily conceived as an economic incentive to curb deforestation and, in fact, did not work out as such. Funds from the contribution have mostly been used for budgetary purposes of *IBAMA* rather than for reforestation activities. Only recently has the government allowed part of this revenue to be diverted to the states and NGOs willing to invest in forest activities in municipalities where reforestation may either create economic opportunities or recover deforested areas.

2.9 Royalties

Brazilian Constitution establishes the payment of royalties for oil and gas exploration and water draw for electric energy generation. Companies pay proportionally to the economic value of the exploited resources. The collected amount is divided among the states, the municipalities and some governmental agencies such as those of environment and science and technology.

The money generated by this way is significant, especially in a country with financial problems as Brazil. In 2004, the oil royalties amounted U\$ 1.6 billion and the hydropower royalties amounted U\$ 430 million. There is growing criticism against the absence of rules regulating the application of these financial resources.

3 Towards an environmental fiscal reform

Brazilian Constitution previewed in 1988 that five years later there would be set a general revisional process of its own precepts. This process took place during 1993 and 1994 and ended without significant results: six punctual amendments were approved, none of them related to really important national issues. This process, however, has generated debates about some relevant themes. One of them was the polluter-pays principle. The representative requested to report the amendment proposals related to environment has suggested inserting the polluter-pays principle in the Constitutional Text. This suggestion, unfortunately, was not submitted for vote.

In the middle of the 90's, within broader initiatives concerning modernisation of the State, the federal government began to discuss some sectorial legal reforms. The fiscal reform has been elected as an important political challenge. The discussions over this theme have opened various fields of work. One of

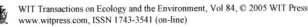

these fields is the environmental fiscal reform. In 1999 the special committee created to analyse the fiscal reform suggested, among many other proposals, two constitutional amendments: i) the insertion of the directive that the taxation system should be used as a tool to protect the environment; and ii) the prevision that the Union could establish by law an environmental intervention contribution.(*Sonderabgaben*). These proposals were not submitted for vote either.

In 2002 a new president was elected, linked to the leftist Workers Party. The fiscal reform agenda of President *Lula* was presented to National Congress without any explicit political concern regarding environmental issues. As in the previous government, the main focus has been set to the rules related to the tax on sale of goods and services, the *ICMS*. The existing rules about this tax were providing favourable conditions for fiscal war among states and therefore creating conflicts in the federation.

It must be said that the proposals related to the *ICMS* being discussed in the scope of the fiscal reform can have environmental implications. The more direct potential impact is related to the proposals that interfere in the way part of the revenues raised by the *ICMS* are transferred to the municipalities. The fruitful experiences with the ecological *ICMS* shall not put at risk.

Although the initial text prepared by *Lula* government did not contain any initiative regarding an environmental fiscal reform, during the discussion process in the National Congress the representatives have presented relevant proposals in this sense, e.g.: i) inserting of the polluter-pays principle in the Constitutional Text; ii) applying green selectivity on the state tax on sale of goods and services, as well as on the federal tax on industrial products; iii) authorising the Union to establish by law environmental intervention contributions; iv) establishing grant for renewable and clean energy; and v) creating tax exemption for forestry owners.

4 A quick overview of the use of economic instruments in OECD countries

OECD countries have a large experience in the application of economic or market based instruments for environmental control. Green taxes, emission charges, user charges, product charges, marketable emission permits, deposit-refund systems, environmentally motivated subsidies and other instruments have been more and more adopted for environmental protection.

The OECD Working Party on Economic and Environmental Policy Integration conducted a survey on the use of economic instruments for pollution control and natural resource management in OECD countries [7]. In that survey, it was considered separately the use of economic instruments for pollution control and for natural resource management.

Concerning to pollution control, the majority of the countries reported the use of some kind of economic instruments. Almost all countries use charges, basically of two types: emission charges, including user charges, and product charges. Emission charges are applied in several environmental fields on the basis of pollutant emissions or waste. The main ones are: charges on air pollution; user charges on municipal waste collection and treatment; charges on hazardous waste; water effluent charges; wastewater user charges; and charges on aircraft noise. Product charges can be classified in the following product categories: motor vehicles; ozone depleting chemicals; batteries; lubricant oils; packaging; charges on agricultural inputs; and other product charges.

Many countries use deposit-refund systems, traditionally concerning glass drink containers. However, in recent decades, other products have also been brought under such systems. These include other food packaging (cans, PET bottles), batteries, lamp bulbs, pesticide containers, home appliances, and lubricant oil.

Subsidies are very used for pollution control and they include a very broad series of schemes financially supporting activities in the fields of air pollution control, wastewater treatment, waste management and noise reduction measures. These general environmental funds are fed by revenues arising from charges imposed on air and water pollution and waste generation.

Non-compliance fees and liability payments are also used in a number of countries for pollution control. Tradable permit systems and performance bonds are less common. Tradable permits are used especially in US and they are mainly related to the emission of air pollutants. The use of tradable permits for water management and land management is quite limited.

Economic instruments for natural resource management are almost as widely applied as economic instruments for pollution control. Only a few OECD countries did not report any use of economic instruments for natural resource management.

According to that survey, "many countries apply economic instruments (primarily abstraction charges or taxes) for water quantity management, and two report the use of transferable water quota schemes. In the field of fisheries, the use of some taxes or fees was reported, but transferable fishing quotas were found to be the most frequently used economic instrument. Many countries use economic instruments in forestry management, primarily in the form of charges or subsidies. The use of economic instruments for wetland management is less common, but where it does exist it appears to be primarily in the form of financial assistance to wetland owners or users. Wetland compensation fees and wetland mitigation banking are also found in the United States."

"Economic instruments aimed at preserving the quality of land and soil are more widespread. Some of these instruments are related to restructuring the agricultural sector and may have a predominantly economic character. Many of the instruments reported in the category of natural species and wildlife relate to hunting and sport fishing permits and fees. Entrance fees for national parks and subsidy programmes for conservation purposes are also found, with almost all countries reporting their use".

An increasing number of OECD countries are implementing green tax reforms. The revenue from (pollution oriented) environmentally related taxes averages roughly 2% of GDP in OECD countries. In these countries, there are several successful examples of the introduction of green taxes, but also some cases in which the role of such taxes in achieving environmental goals remained limited (France, Ireland and Spain) [8].

In OECD countries, "the fear of loss of sectoral competitiveness and the fear of negative income distribution impacts have been singled out as the most important political obstacles for governments contemplating undertaking an Environmental Fiscal Reform"[9]. This situation is very similar in Brazil. Many Brazilian politicians and other policymakers share worries with the industrial entrepreneurs that environmental related taxes and charges may impact negatively the competitiveness of certain sectors. Their concerns about income distribution are also clear and must be taken into consideration.

The recent discussions about OECD experiences brought some lessons to address these specific issues. Regarding competitiveness, the integration of environmental fiscal reform with broader fiscal reforms is a recommendation that should be certainly followed. Regarding income distribution, the equilibrium must be sought using mitigation and compensation measures. The experts believe that "compensation measures are to be preferred over mitigation measures, because the incentives are maintained" [10].

5   Final considerations

The government and the society in general should have long-term strategies to tackle the key environmental issues (climate change, air quality, protecting natural resources and the biodiversity, etc.). Among these long-term strategies, the marked-based instruments of environmental policy certainly play an important role.

Brazil has a long path ahead regarding the adequate use of economic instruments. We have largely based our environmental policy on administrative regulations and mandatory reporting systems. The command-and-control perspective is deeply inserted in the policymakers' soul, in a way that makes things difficult to the acceptance of changes. But the environmental experts and even the politicians seem to realised the significant potential of the economic instruments. The experiences with the ecological *ICMS* are being progressively spread. The water extraction charge is being applied in our most polluted watershed, *Paraiba do Sul*. The National Congress is beginning to discuss the green taxation within a broader fiscal reform perspective.

Brazilian scenery in this field does not seem to be so different from those of the more developed countries. OECD countries are years in advance in the adoption of market-based instruments of environmental policy, but they also have problems in achieving their environmental goals.

Based on the previous experiences of other countries, our opinion is that the more important advance that we should assure in the discussions about the green fiscal reform are: i) the insertion of the polluter-pays principle in the Constitutional Text as a principle to be followed in all the tributary system; and ii) to establish the application of the green selectivity on the state tax on sale of goods and services, as well as on the federal tax on industrial products.

References

[1]   Clausen, H. & Rothgang, M. Innovations and Sustainability in the Water Services Sectors – Institutional Framework, Actors, and Policy Instruments. Paper prepared for the Workshop *"Recent Advances in Applied Infrastructure Research"*, Berlin, 12 October 2002, captured in http://wip.tu-berlin.de/workshop/2002/

[2]   Seroa da Motta, R. & Young, C.E.F. (Coord.) *Instrumentos Econômicos para a gestão ambiental no Brasil*. Rio de Janeiro, 1997, captured. in http://www.mma.gov.br

[3]   US Government. *Brazil: Environmental issues*, 2003, captured in http://www.eia.doe.gov.

[4]   Serodio, E. *Review of Sugar Policies in Major Sugar Industries – Transparent and Non-Transparent or Indirect Policies*. Paper prepared for American Sugar Alliance, January 2003.

[5]   FNMA/MMA captured in http://www.mma.gov.br/port/fnma/, May 2005.

[6]   Seroa da Motta, R. *The Economics of Biodiversity in Brazil: the case of forest conversion*. Texto para Discussão n° 433. IPEA, Rio de Janeiro, 1996.

[7]   OECD. Economic instruments for pollution control and natural resources management in OECD countries: a survey, 1999, captured in http://www.olis.oecd.org

[8]   OECD. Implementing Environmental Fiscal Reform: Income Distribution and Sectoral Competitiveness Issues. *Proceedings of a conference held in Berlin, German, June 2002*, captured in http://www.olis.oecd.org

[9]   *idem*

[10] *ibidem*

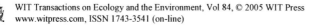

Management of noise in the case of infrastructure works

M. Clerico & G. Pizzo
Dipartimento di Ingegneria del Territorio,
dell'Ambiente e delle Geotecnologie, Politecnico di Torino, Italy

Abstract

The Italian noise legislation is based on the principle of protection of the population exposed to several types of noise sources. The noise exposure, beyond the direct effects on the auditive apparatus, could cause sleep disturbance, speech intelligibility, psycho physiological effects, that generate important states of annoyance. The real goal of the noise legislation is to reduce annoyance. Such legislation, however, is not sufficient for particular types of noise sources, like those generated by infrastructure works. In these cases the law gives authorisation notwithstanding the provisions in force, exceeding the limit values, but without creating damage conditions. The local authorities should then manage these derogations by characterizing the parameters that could be used to take control of the noise, and then to avoid several states of annoyance. The purpose of this study is to take into account the parameters that have been identified and to set up guidelines aimed at establishing limit values for derogation for the infrastructure works. The first step will be to distinguish between the different noise produced by different types of infrastructure works. The limit values will then be different for a building or street yard and for great infrastructure works such as a tunnel or high-speed way construction. The main differences are the plants and the machinery used for the works, but in particular the duration of the work. The limits will then be more rigid for long term infrastructure works, which are often also active in the night, because of a longer population exposure. These guidelines will be finally discussed with the local authorities in order to manage the noise produced by the temporary infrastructure works and to avoid the worsening of the quality of life.
Keywords: noise, annoyance, infrastructure works, building yards, derogation.

WIT Transactions on Ecology and the Environment, Vol 84, © 2005 WIT Press
www.witpress.com, ISSN 1743-3541 (on-line)

1   Introduction

The environmental legislation in Italy has ruled many aspects concerning several types of sources of impact, in order to safeguard the population and the environment itself. However there are some particular cases which should be analysed and managed, since the law is still not able to guarantee the protection of the population.

This study belongs to the Communitarian issues of health and environmental protection, as expressed by DIR 2002/49/EC on the assessment and management of environmental noise [1].

In the Green Paper on the future noise policy (1996) the European Commission defines noise as one of the most environmental problems in Europe, with the necessity to take measurements and specific actions to contain it.

Noise exposure of the population to the different sources is calculated taking into account the medium equivalent exposure of the sound pressure level without taking into account other dynamics of annoyance nor the significant temporary sources.

The entity of the problem, in urban habitats, has reached and exceeded the values fixed for the annoyance, and is expanding towards rural and protected areas, not involved in this problem up to now. This last aspect is the most impacted on by the noise of infrastructure works, since it presents, before the event, a more delicate acoustic situation.

In Italy standard conditions are controlled by noise mapping, that represents the instrument put in charge for territorial acoustical management, and it is very important for containing noise pollution and for limiting future emissions, which could be generated by new sources. This instrument however is not able to guarantee the absence of the annoyance, for the temporary activities, normally managed with derogation.

Noise produced by infrastructure works is one example that should be better studied by the local authorities, since it could represent a critical situation, in particular depending on where the infrastructure work is placed.

The Italian legislation permits one to overcome the noise limit values, giving authorization notwithstanding the provisions in force if the noise does not exceed the damage conditions. This principle could be respected if all the sources of noise, belonging to a specific work, are temporary. In this way the exposure criteria is respected.

In an infrastructure work, if the effective time of work construction is longer than few months or the intensity of emissions provokes immediate damages, or if the polluting factor is "non dose dependent", then the criteria of human health and different ecosystems protection are not respected and the derogation is not justified, since it wouldn't be a derogation to the law parameters but to the safety conditions. This is true for many parameters such as dust, visual impact, induced transport, but for the noise, this is very significant, since noise has an immediate perception, generating annoyance to the exposed people.

The absence of people does not justify that in some areas the problem of protection does not exist.

In northern Italy there are several examples of great infrastructure works in urban areas, such as tunnels, public facilities and transportation systems, but there are also other examples in rural areas, characterised by high environmental quality. These areas are often crossed by infrastructure works and need to be protected, in order to pursue the principle of sustainability, instead of only the principle of compatibility.

This study is based on the principle of sustainability, then on the respect of the quality values, not only to safeguard the human receiver, but also for the protection of the environmental components.

The presence of an infrastructure work for a long period in a specific area, could generate a worsening of the environmental quality for that time, and then an irreversible damage.

It is necessary to carry out rules which show in advance and manage these particular events, not permitting derogation tout court but characterizing guidelines that would show, also qualitatively, the parameters on which the derogation can be granted.

Such parameters have already been identified (Clerico and Pizzo) [2] for the risk factor of noise and will be used to set up a regulation that would be presented to the city Councils, in order to show possible criteria to manage the noise in the infrastructure works.

The meaning of this regulation is not to show new limit values, but to express in an official document the parameters that, although exceeding the limit values imposed by law, allow one to respect the same, or greater, safety conditions.

The limit values of the law has been calculated by taking into account standard exposure time, with standard reference time and with sources of noise belonging to permanent installations.

According to the available data (Franchini et al.) [3], the environmental noise with Leq < 50 dB(A) are not able to cause annoyance to the population. The day level, continuous and stationary, should be <55 dB(A) to protect the majority of the population from being highly annoyed and <50 dB(A) to protect the population from being moderately annoyed, as expressed in the "Guidelines for Community Noise" (WHO) [4].

The annoyance conditions for non continuous and non stationary noise, for example the traffic noise or the infrastructure works, are estimated at 62 dB(A) (day) and 55 dB(A) (night).

At night the noise level should be 10 dB under the correspondent values for the day (Berglund et al.)[5].

If the infrastructure work is similar to a permanent installation, because of the dimension of the infrastructure or of the long time work, then there is no possibility to give an authorization notwithstanding the provisions in force and the parameters presented in the following regulation can not be applied.

If an infrastructure work is placed on the same area for a very long time (this is the typical case of a great infrastructure work) it is no longer considered temporary, but it becomes a stationary and continuative source for the damage and the annoyance to the population.

In these cases the protection of the population is possible by imposing the respect of the noise mapping Leq with no derogation.

2 Guidelines for a regulation on the management of the environmental noise produced by the temporary works

The following guidelines want to represent a reference scheme for the application of law requirements about temporary activities. Such a law prescribes that temporary activities, like building yards and open space manifestations, using noisy machinery and plants, must be authorised, even notwithstanding the provisions in force, if necessary.

Each city council must establish the necessary prescription to limit acoustic pollution.

The aim of these guidelines is to present to the city councils a possible regulation to manage the noise produced in the outside environment by the temporary activities, when they exceed the limit values established in the Noise Mapping.

The following guideline wants also to define the modality to give authorisation to the temporary activities.

The meaning of temporary refers to the activities being undertaken for a variable period, such as buildings and street yards, public works that involve wide or restricted areas, that can be authorised notwithstanding the provisions in force.

In this guideline, temporary activities such as musical and popular manifestations, public shows, Luna Park, and every kind of permanent activity, that are already regulated by law, will be excluded.

Temporary activities are automatically authorised if they respect the limit values of law, like emission and immission values of Noise Mapping, and differential limit values.

The following regulation refers to annoyance for a period defined by the city council, using the 2002/49/EC range periods of DENL (h.7-19; 19-23; 23-7).

2.1 Building and street yards

Building and street yards are typical temporary works characterised by period of time not that extended and dimension restricted to a limited number of years. Whether time and extension exceed the limits expressed in the regulation for buildings and street yards and if the city council decides that the noise produced by these works should be managed with particular criteria, it will be necessary to refer to the regulation of great infrastructure works and great building yards.

Plants and machinery used in the infrastructure works must be in accordance with the homologation and certification norms and must be placed in so as to limit the noise in the environment and the annoyance to the exposed population.

For machinery that is not considered in the norms, such as manual tools, it is necessary to reduce their noise or the annoyance in some way.

Sound signals should be used when it is not possible to use signal lights, always respecting safety norms.

The activation of noisy machinery and the execution of noisy works in the building yards exceeding the limit values established by law is permitted during the week in the following periods:
- from h.8 to h.13 and from h. 15 to h. 19 during the summer;
- from h.8 to h.12.30 and from h. 14 to h. 18 during the winter.

The activation of noisy machinery and the execution of noisy works in the street yards exceeding the limit values established by law is permitted in the week, from h. 8 to h. 20.

The activation of building and street yards exceeding the limit values of the law is not permitted near sensitive receivers (hospital, schools) or in the protected areas established by the Noise Mapping.

However, it is possible to activate building and street yards exceeding the limit value near the schools after the normal school time.

The bibliography [6] indicates for street yards a maximum length in time of 20 working days. For longer time periods it is necessary to refer to the regulation for great infrastructure works and building yards.

For building yards the length of the works is not the administrative length, that could be several years, but the summary of the working days per year. Depending on the territory, the city council has to decide the number of working days to give an authorisation notwithstanding the provisions in force.

For lengths more than 30 days per year the city Council can decide to manage the building yard noise authorisation as a great building yard.

The maximum emission limit during the day is 65 dB Leq (A).

During the day the differential limit value is not important.

Further permissive limits can be permitted by the city council, depending on the characteristics of the territory, for limited periods of time (i.e. emission of 80 dB(A) for 1 hour per day [7]).

The companies that lead the works for maintenance of the streets and sub services have to ask the local authorities for an authorisation notwithstanding the provisions in force, if necessary, that will be valid for the entire length of the work and containing:
1. the limit values to reach towards the annoyed receivers;
2. a declaration that the machinery used for the works will respect the noise emission limit values established by the national and international legislation.

When for the programmed works it is seen to exceed the limit values established in the general derogation, the companies have to present the same documentation for the authorisation of the great infrastructure works and building yards.

2.1.1 Authorisation notwithstanding the provisions in force

Temporary derogation on noise authorised by the city council must contain the necessary indications for reducing the annoyance and the temporal and spatial limits of the authorisation.

The city Council saves a schedule of the derogation authorised on each area.

The emergency works are always authorised: the city Council can indicate particular disposals for the companies that work for public emergencies.

The demand to obtain the authorisation notwithstanding the provisions in force must be made 45 days before the beginning of the works to the local authorities, that can require specific noise monitoring plans.

For building and street yards in urban areas not in proximity to schools and hospitals, it is possible to ask for a simplified authorisation notwithstanding the provisions in force.

The demand for this simplified authorisation and the relevant documentation, must be presented to the local authorities 15 days before the beginning of the work.

To obtain the derogation for exceeding particular limit values in a restricted period of time, established by the city council, the company must add a programme underlining in which periods the noisy machinery would work. The eventual variation of the programme must be immediately communicated to the local authority.

The activities that do not have the characteristics for the simplified authorisation notwithstanding the provisions in force, or that cannot respect the conditions, will refer to the derogation for great building yards.

Buildings and street works with lengths between 5 and 30 working days must present the following documentation to obtain the authorisation notwithstanding the provisions in force:

1. a report to show the conformity to the national and international law of noise;
2. a list of the noise emission levels of the machinery that will be used and that need acoustical certification;
3. a list of the technical devices and procedures that will be used to reduce the annoyance;
4. a detailed plan of the area with the indication of the civil buildings.

Such documentation must be produced by an acoustical competent technician.

Building and street yards shorter than 5 days must present just a communication to the local authorities instead of the demand for authorisation notwithstanding the provisions in force.

During holidays and night periods the possibility to ask for an authorisation notwithstanding the provisions in force is excluded.

The emergency works for restoration of public services (electric plants, drain ducts, potable water, gas, transport system), for dangerous situations for the population or the environment, can be done without any noise authorisation.

2.2 Great infrastructure works and great building yards

The great infrastructure works are represented by the infrastructure, building and city planning intervention, of public interest that require particular authorisation notwithstanding the provisions in force.

The directory of the great infrastructure works and great building yards that must be subjected to this regulation will be discussed and approved by the city Council, during the public works planning.

Infrastructure works that exceed the noise limit values established for the area in which the works take place are not permitted in proximity to hospitals, schools and sensitive receivers in general, or in the protected areas established by the Noise Mapping, without an authorisation notwithstanding the provisions in force.

Great infrastructure works must respect the limit values established by the Noise Mapping and the differential limit values established by law.

The city council can identify further acoustical indicators (i.e. number of events, Sound Exposure Level (SEL)) to manage the noise produced by the infrastructure works and building yards.

It is moreover necessary to define day and night SEL value. Since UE did not establish such reference values nor defined further indicators other than the Leq to manage the annoyance, it will be up to the scientific community to propose future values and indicators aimed to manage particular events.

Great infrastructure works and great building yards generally endure for long periods, so this regulation can then be applied to all the works that have indefinite lengths of time, or in general endure for more than 30 working days.

The whole length of time of the noisy work, and the relevant timetables, must be communicated to the population by public warnings in the area of the works.

2.2.1 Authorisation notwithstanding the provisions in force

When the person responsible for the infrastructure work thinks that, for important motivation, it is necessary to exceed the limit values of this regulation, he has to ask for authorisation notwithstanding the provisions in force, 45 days before the beginning of the work. The local authorities examine the documentation and give authorisation notwithstanding the provisions in force, that could contain prescriptions, as the prohibition to use at the same time noisy machinery, or the compulsory use of sound absorbents and/or an insulating shell on the border of the site or as protection from the noisiest machinery.

In the contest for contracts for great infrastructure works and great building yards the obligation for the companies to obtain authorisation notwithstanding the provisions in force, according to the legislation and to this regulation must be included.

The authorisation is divided into two different steps:

a) a general part that can be obtained by presenting a form containing:

    1. a general report describing the activity, written by a competent acoustical technician with an indication of the limit values to reach towards the annoyed receivers;

    2. a procedure of acceptance written by the director of the infrastructure work containing:

        - the characteristics of the machinery that can be accepted on the site,

- the name of the responsible person for such decisions,
- the procedure of testing the suitability of the machinery,
- the procedure of registration of the accepted machinery and its identification;

3. the individuation of the access path to the site.

b) a detailed part for each phase of the work, where the company must present:

1. a list of the procedure that will be adopted to limit the annoyance and its description

2. a detailed layout of the area with the identification of the annoyed buildings;

3. a report to show the conformity to the national and international law of noise, and a list of the noise emission levels of the machinery that will be used and that need acoustical certification. The report must define:

- the length of time of the work ,
- the timetable of the several activities,
- the limit values that the company want to be authorised and the relevant motivation, for each of the activities.

The period in which the infrastructure works can operate is defined by the city council, using the 2002/49/EC range periods of DENL (h.7-19; 19-23; 23-7). The choice could be to exclude every noisy activity, not permitting derogation, during the holiday and the evening/night periods (from h.19 to h.7), but the city Council, depending on the specific territory, can decide to use more restrictive periods (i.e. from h.19 to h.8).

Another choice could be to exclude every activity in these periods.

Those not respecting this regulation are subjected to the administrative sanction established by law and to the suspension of the activities by local authorities.

The population can communicate annoyance to the local authorities by using appropriate procedures of request.

3 Conclusions

According to the principles of health and environmental protection expressed by DIR 2002/49/EC on the assessment and management of environmental noise, it is necessary to take into account the different noise sources with important annoyance effects on the population.

The noise source due to temporary works is an issue that, in urban habitats, has reached and exceeded the values fixed for the annoyance, and is expanding towards rural and protected areas, not involved in this problem up to now.

The Italian legislation is nowadays not sufficient to manage these particular types of noise sources, since the law gives authorisation notwithstanding the provisions in force, exceeding the limit values, generating possible annoyance conditions with a general worsening of the existing environmental quality.

The guidelines that have been set up are aimed to help the city councils to manage the noise produced by temporary works.

Such temporary works should be managed by distinguishing between the noise produced by building and street yards and great infrastructure works and great building yards.

The main difference is the duration of the work. The limit values and the relevant authorisation should then be more rigid for works of longer duration, because of a longer population exposure. According to this, the great infrastructure works and the great building yards should respect the limit values established by the Noise Mapping and the differential limit values established by law, while for the building and street yards the maximun limit during the day is represented by the maximum limit values established by the Noise Mapping and the differential limit value is not considered. The city council can decide to adopt different parameters to manage the noise produced in particular by great infrastructure works and great building yards.

In holiday and night periods great infrastructure works can be activated if they respect the limit values given by the Noise Mapping, but the city council can decide to adopt more restrictive periods of time, using the DENL periods.

The authorisation given notwithstanding the provisions in force will be more rigid for the great infrastructure yards and for the great building yards than for the building and street yards, including detailed information on the procedure used to reduce the noise.

These guidelines represent a technical instrument to manage the noise produced by temporary infrastructure works and will be finally discussed with the local authorities in order to maintaining the standard of environmental quality reducing the annoyance on the population.

References

[1] DIR. 2002/49/EC, *"Assessment and management of environmental noise"*, European Parliament and Council, Luxembourg, 25 June 2002.

[2] Clerico, M., Pizzo, G., *Environmental limit values for habitat infrastructure works: the problem of the identification of parameters based on the exceptions to the law*, IABSE Symposium 'Metropolitan Habitats and Infrastructure', Shangai 22-24 September 2004 ; p. 134-137 ; CD p. 1-6.

[3] Franchini, A., Callegari, A., Barchi, A., *"Impatto del rumore da traffico stradale sulla popolazione: effetti e reazioni"*, Atti Convegno Nazionale "Traffico e Ambiente", Trento, Febbraio 2000.

[4] World Health Organisation (WHO) *"Guidelines for Community Noise"*, 2000.

[5] Berglund, B., Lindvall, T., (eds.), *"Community Noise"*, Document prepared for the World Health Organization, Archives of the Center for Sensory Research, Stockholm University and Karolinska Insitute, Vol. 2, N.1, 1995.

[6] Comune di Prato, Regolamento delle attività rumorose, approved with D.C.C. 24.01.2002, n. 11; modified with D.C.C. del 27.01.2005, n. 10.

[7] Comune di Pisa, Regolamento comunale per la limitazione delle immissioni sonore nell'ambiente prodotte da attività temporanee, DCM 29.04.1994, n.88.

Section 4
Environmental management

Planning and management of protected areas in Greece

El. Beriatos
*Department of Planning and Regional Development,
School of Engineering, University of Thessaly, Greece*

Abstract

In Greece, nature protection as an integrated and cohesive policy has a relatively recent history. The last five years, many efforts have been made to formulate such a policy in order to achieve a better management and planning for the natural environment in all its aspects. In this respect the role of protected areas, as a planning tool, becomes very important not only for nature protection and conservation but also for local sustainable development. This paper refers to the current situation of the network of protected areas in Greece giving special emphasis on the main problems and causes of malfunction and inefficiency characterizing this network. At first, there is a critical examination of the recent developments regarding the completion of the institutional framework and especially the scientific, technical and administrative procedures required for the establishment of the appropriate managing authorities of the most important protected natural areas. Secondly, the paper investigates the role of the main institutional and organizational components as well as the socio-political parameters, which have influenced these developments. Finally, there is an attempt to elaborate the strategic guidelines (guiding principles) and priorities not only for the establishment but also for the assurance of a continuous and appropriate operation of these areas, as well as the respective managing authorities, in the framework of the national environmental policy and the policy for spatial planning and development.
Keywords: nature protection, protected areas, managing authorities.

1 Introduction

The protected areas as institutional and functional means for the protection of nature have, at the international level, a history of roughly one and a half-century. Indeed, at the end of the 19th century a generalised tendency emerged for the creation not only of archaeological but also of natural history collections and museums. The idea of preservation of nature's forms and shapes as well as of the 'monuments of nature' leads to the creation of the first 'natural parks'.The first applications based on this tendency are realised in France at the time of Napoleon 3rd (forest Fontainebleau) and in USA in 1872 (national park Yellowstone), which were the precursors of contemporary protected areas.

A general opinion in agreement with current perceptions, which also constitutes a blending of various definitions that have been attempted at times, is that protected areas (PAs) are designated the spatial units and the localities where it exists, (in relation to the surrounding space) high concentration of ecological (and caltural) values that deserve to receive special protection and 'treatment' or they are actually protected. In relation to other countries, in Greece the institution of protected areas does not have a long tradition. The entire system of the protection of nature, in which that institution is included, faces various problems (big and small) that render it only slightly effective.In fact, and in spite of all these problems, the PAs constitute today the spearhead of official policy for the national planning of the natural environment in the context of the 3rd CSF (Community Support Framework) and specifically of the Operational Programme for the Environment [9] within which action for the PAs is also dictated by international and Community obligations of a country; something that renders yet more imperative the care for their protection and, consequently, any debate and examination for that purpose.

The paper's aim is to give a concise quantitative picture of the PAs as well as to show the lack of satisfactory protection and management of nature in those regions (but also outside of them), based on real data, and to attempt to investigate the reasons and the causes that are still accountable for the observed insufficiency and the inefficiency of the environmental policy in that particular field. An additional objective of this paper is to try to identify future prospects and developments and, on the basis of lessons learnt, to discribe certain fundamental directions of strategy, always from the spatial and environmental planning point of view.

2   The existing situation in Greece

The protected areas of all categories in Greece constitute roughly 20% of the country's land surface, a large enough percentage compared to other European countries, which is justified partly by the large density in space of sensitive ecosystems and ecological values (species of flora and fauna, habitats, landscapes, etc). In Tables 1 and 2 are presented the overall classifications of Greece's protected areas, ordered by main categories, as given by the Ministry of the Environment, Physical Planning and Public Works [9] and the Organisation for Economic Cooperation and Development (OECD) [7] In these categories are included the controlled hunting areas (Game Farms) and the wild life shelters (refuges) whose purpose of establishment is not directly related to the protection of the natural environment. Other regions are also included - such as archaeological sites and 'landscapes of natural beauty'(there are no precise data).

It should be marked that concerning the quantitative information and sizes (the number of PAs and their territory) there are often differences of estimates and disagreements originating from different criteria that are taken into consideration in the calculations. That is to say, the need to define each time what should be considered as a PA. A basic aspect of this matter, creating divergence of views, is the existence of institutional protection of PAs through national legislation. If one accepts this criterion, as does OECD in its Report of Environmental Performance - Greece, p. 103-104, [7] then the total area of PAs (that corresponds to the specifications of protection of the IUCN's categories I to IV) [5] amounts to 2.6% of the country's land cover.

Table 1:   Categories of protected areas in Greece (land cover).

No.	Category of PA	No. of PAs	PA Territory (in hectares)
1	RAMSAR Convention	11	1,65,000
2	National Parks	10	70,000
3	Aesthetic Forests	19	33,000
4	Preservable Monuments of Nature	51	16,500
5	Special Protection Zones	15	14,500
6	Mountain ranges, height > 900m. (The National Parks and Aesthetic Forests are excluded).	87	1,488,500
7	Wild Bird Protection Areas. (The Mountain Ranges, RAMSAR and National Parks are excluded).	14	40,000
8	Wild Life Shelters (refuges)	615	9,450,000
9	Controlled Hunting Areas(Game Farms)	7	100,000
Total		829	2,872,500
10	Archeological Sites	No accurate data exist	
11	Areas of Special Natural Beauty (TIFK)	No accurate data exist	

Source: Ministry of Environment and Spatial Planning (2000) Greece: Europe's Ecological Reserve [9].

Similarly, the WCMC's (World Conservation Monitoring Center) estimates give the corresponding percentage to 1.68%, placing Greece in the last places of the list [8]. On the contrary, if Greece's international agreements and 'obligation'(European Union, International Conventions, etc.) are accepted as a base, then the figure gets to around 16%. Of course it is one thing reporting on a list of protections and it is another enacting particular legal measures for the protection and management of those areas. In the first case it could be claimed that it is a pre-institutional situation that constitutes a first stage in the process of establishing a PA. And of course this is of a major importance for the practical side of this issue (i.e. determining the type of effective regulations in such 'semi-

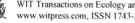

enacted' areas) that immediately concerns both the protection of the environment and other social benefits and/or citizen's individual rights.

Table 2: Protected areas in Greece according to OECD (2000).

Source: OECD (2000): Reports of Environmental Performance-Greece [7].

	Year started	Ministry (a)	No. of Areas	Land Cover	
				(in hectares)	(%) (b)
National Parks (hinterland)	1938	MIN.AGR.	10	68,090 (c)	0.6
Aesthetic Forests	1973	MIN.AGR.	19	32,050	0.2
Monuments of Nature	1975	MIN.AGR.	51 (d)	16,070	0.1
Landscapes o Special Natural Beauty	1950	MIN.AGR.	264	....	....
Controlled Hunting Areas	1975	MIN.AGR.	7	1,007,090	8.2
Wild Life Shelters (refuges)	1979	MIN.AGR.	584	964,400	7.4
Wild Life Breeding areas	1976	MIN.AGR.	20	31,600	0.2
Built-up Control Areas (ZOE)	1987	MIN.ENV.	10	14,700	0.1
Natural Reserves	1990	MIN.ENV.	2	....	....
National Parks (marine)	1992	MIN.ENV.	2	254,100 (e)	0.1

(α) MIN.AGR. = Ministry of Agriculture (forestry department), MIN.ENV.= Ministry of the Environment, Physical Planning and Public Works, YPPO = Ministry of Culture. (b) % of total land cover (hinterland), some protected areas overlap. (c) It includes 34,300 hectares belonging to regional zones. (d) 1,5 hectares and 36 monuments of nature (trees or bushes). (e) 18.300 hectares of hinterland and 2,358,000 acres of marine cover, only the hinterland is %.

Another point that should be stressed is the content and the type of protection in relation to the various categories of PAs. For example, there is the question whether the aforementioned Controlled Hunting Areas (CHA), included in the OECD's tables above, could be considered as PAs. Taking into consideration the wide meaning of a PA, the answer is positive [7]. It is simply the degree of protection that differs. Precisely at this point enters the critical issue of the definitions and categories of the PAs, as well as their coding on international level so that comparable and reliable estimates can exist between different countries. Moreover, it is necessary to have a compatibility between international and national systems of categorization and classification. It could be considered that, from a spatial planning perspective, exist mainly two levels of study/examination: the level of the real 'objects of protection' (e.g. habitats, wetlands, monuments, of nature) and the level of functional areas, which constitute management units (ie PAs). Consequently, there is a difference (in scale and content), for example, between the spatial units of type 'sites' (ecologically sensitive areas) or the special conservation zones of Natura 2000, or zones of special protection (directive 79/409/EU) on the one hand, and on the other hand, the protected areas as wider regional planning units.

Table 3:   Existing and new areas of the 10 National Parks.

National Parks	Core		Peripheral Zone		Total
	Old Territory (in hectares)	New Territory (in hectares)	Old Territory (in hectares)	New Territory (in hectares)	New Territory (Core and Peripheral Zone) in hectares
Olympus	3,993	7,150	0	16,690	23,840
Parnassos	3,513	3,629	0	44,660	48,290
Parnitha	3,812	8,535	0	9,140	17,676
Ainou	2,862	2,893	0	4,723	7,616
Samarias (White Mounts)	4,850	6,315	0	18,279	24,594
Oitis	3,010	3,010	4,200	16,348	19,358
Valia Kalda (Pindos)	3,393	4,170	3,534	4,922	9,093
Vikou - Aou	3,400	3,407	9,200	9,538	12,945
Prespes	4,900	4,900	14,570	24,970	29,870
Sounion	750	750	2,750	2,750	3,500
Total	34,483	44,760	34,254	152,022	196,782

Notes: 1).Even though at the introduction of the National Parks it was forecasted that all of them were going to have peripheral zones, these zones were defined in only 5 of them. 2).The extensions are bases on the proposals of administrative studies of GGDFP of Ministry of Agriculture. Source: Ministry of Agriculture. .Managing plans and Ministerial Decisions for the designation of National Parks / information processed by us [6].

Specifically, for the 'sites' of the national list of the Natura 2000 network - which amount roughly to 270 (the scientific catalogue lists roughly 300) - it should be stressed that almost all of them (roughly 85-90%) constitute existing 'commitments' for the protection of the natural environment [4]. These commitments come either from national legislation or from international agreements ratified by Greece or from Community obligations (EU directives), most important of which is the directive of Natura 2000. However, the program's advantage lies in the new meaning given to the term 'network' incorporated in the protection of nature.

Both the simple zones of protection and preservation and the more complex PAs should not constitute isolated 'islands', without a relation between them, but they should constitute the nodes of an integrated hub that thus will be viable due to the scale and interdependences (ecological and administrative).

As for the quantitative dimension of nature protection (area covered by PAs), the example of national parks (which are considered by international organisms to better cover the specifications and the requirements of legal protection), is characteristic from a point of view of distortion between declarations and acts: An overdoubling of their total territory (core and regional area) is envisaged, from 68,737 to 196,782 hectares, i.e. an increase of 35% (Table 3). The new territory of national parks will represent the 1.5% of national territory (from 0.5% that it is today). Of course the increase of the core area (102,774 acres) is relatively smaller to that of the peripheral area (117,767 hectares)

3 The current institutional framework of protection and management and related problems

The institution of PAs was 'imported' in Greece with the law 856/37 that led to the establishment of the (first) national park, Olympus, in 1938. Of course care for nature and, generally, for the natural environment existed since the constitution of the Greek state (a century ago) through the forestry legislation and the powers given to the Ministry of Agriculture's forestry services. Afterr the 2nd world war, with law 1469/50 certain areas could be defined as 'Landscapes of Particular Natural Beauty'.

Much later, during the period of the postwar years and specifically in 1980, with the introduction of the Ministry of Regional Planning of Settlements and the Environment as well as the passing (five years later) of law 1650/86 on the protection of the environment, a modern legislative 'arsenal' is created that constitutes an important turning-point in the history of environmental policy in Greece on the whole, but also specifically regarding the protection of nature and the landscape (the first systematic categorisation of the PA). After 13 years of 'elliptical' application (or even of no application) of law 1650/86, the law 2742/99 is passed for the 'Regional Planning and the Sustainable Development' that explicitly advances of the institutionalisation of the PA's managing authorities

Here, should be mentioned, the institutional context at the European Union level which is based on two statutes (directives): Directive 79/409 on the conservation of wild birds and the known directive 92/43 on the conservation of natural habitats and species of flora and fauna . As it has already been reported, on the occasion of the classification of habitats the planning and management of PAs in Greece in a systematic way was openly raised as a question.

Today at a national level the basic legislation on the protection of nature and the protected areas more specifically, is generally reported mainly in three different sectors of the public policy forestal policy (L.D. 86/69 and L.996/79), environmental policy (L.1650/86) and the spatial planning policy (L.2742/99) that are in effect and function in parallel not so much in a complementary but in a competitive way, as it also appears also from the findings that follow.

a) A first element of disfunction, on a regional planning level, constitutes the relative ambiguity that exists in the categorisation of those areas. This situation has also practical consequences in the determination and in the characterization of the PAs because there is no common language of communication and agreement between the co-responsible bodies but also the special scientists that are asked to implement the national strategic planning for nature in this field. As it was reported already, according to international institutions Greece is considered as being one of the countries with the smaller rate of PAs territory. Thus, in the public dialogue for the protection of nature in Greece, there is a contradictory discussion: on the one side are the protests (by ecologists and environmentalists) for the small percentage of substantially enacted and protected areas and, on the other side, are the problematics and countercharges (by the advocates of development) for the large percentage of territory attempted to be protected, which is considered as being over 16% despite the fact that there is still no national legal protection and the content of the measures to be taken is still unknown.

b) A second and also basic element of the system's disfunction constitutes the subordination of protection of natural environment to two different governmental institutions, initially to the Ministry of Agriculture and later on (after 1980) to the Ministry of Regional Planning, Settlement and the Environment that produce incoherent and many times conflicting legislative regulations and actions. Moreover,   because of the 'parallel' juristictions there are often embroilments in the incorporation of Community regulations (directives) in the national legal framework as it happened some years ago with directive 92/43 on the preservation of natural habitats and species (Natura 2000 network).

c) A third element of disfunction that plays decisive role – beyond the weaknesses and the problems on a legislative level – is the social acceptance or reaction to the meausers proposed by the studies. Those measures (when they are not unrealistic) usually clash with the interests of local social groups, mainly of small land-owners, whose attitude depends on the role that each time they play in the consultation and negotiation processes (as land-owners or as residents – 'consumers' of that particular region's environment) [1].

d) A fourth important element (reason) that intensifies the aforementioned difficulties is the factor of 'time' (with respect to delay) due to bureaucratic ankyloses, conflict of interests but also lack of organisation in the public administration that are accountable for large temporal divergences during the process of planning. The most serious consequence of that is the disappearance of any confidence in the relation between state and citizen that in Greece is particularly traumaticc in all policy areas. According to information from timetables of the Ministry of Environment and Spatial Planning these delays for the cases of the Special Environmental Studies (SES) as well as of the special spatial plans often reach up to 500% of the normally required time interval (i.e. 8-10 or even more years instead of the 2 years respectively).

e) A fifth, final and very important, element of inefficiency is the lack of a more general administrative organisation (suitable structures and institutions) that would contribute towards a stronger cohesion of the environmental protection system. A more specific weakness constitutes the lack of relative know-how in the public administration on central level, accentuated on the level of regional services and local self-government [3], a weakness that mainly comes from the lack of specialised and experienced personnel in the sector of management of nature and more specifically of the PAs.

Inferred from the above, but also as an evidence of the inefficiency of the system of protection, which it is related to the institutional framework and to sociopolitical parameters, we report the absence of new designations of PAs based exclusively on the law 1650/86. Indeed, the only designations of recently protected areas done in the 18-year period of the standing law 1650/86 are that for the two marine parks "Northern Sporades" in 1992 and "Zante" in 1999. It should be stressed here that these designations were announced following powerful pressure by the European Union.

4 The managing authorities as a key element for the operation and enhancement of the PAs

As it was said in the beginning, there is still no complete or evolved system of protected areas in Greece. Consequently, the special managing authoritiescould play a fundamental role in this situation. These institutions, without being panacea, constitute a catalyst for the achievement of economic, sociopolitical and tehnological know-how parameters of an effective policy for the protection of nature in the PAs.

During the last years there have been enough efforts towards that direction both on the legislative level and on the level of planning and financing. Indeed, in the context of training of the 3rd CFS (Operational Programs for the Environment on central and regional level) a study was carried out on the National Planning for the natural environment (Master Plan), in which it was attempted for first time a comprehensive consideration and facing of the issue, in which the management authorities of PAs have been called to play the leading role [9].

In this study the protected objects of nature of protection (mainly the Natura 2000 network sites) have been grouped in 162 PAs that constitute organic geographic units with spatial continuity and functional cohesion and which should be under some type of managing authority (cf. Fig 1). It could be noticed that the geographic distribution of PAs - at least, the most important that are presented on the map - is balanced and it covers the entire land and marine Greek territory.

More specifically, concerning the managing authorities (MAs) of the PAs it should be stressed that law 1650/86 (article 21, paragraph 2) did not provide definitely their constitution, but it mentioned only the possibility of 'special services'.

The introduction of law 2742/99 covers the void, in an explicit and categorical way, with regard to the managing authorities of the PAs. The relative provisions can be found in chapter E under the title 'Administration and management of protected areas'. The Managing Authorities (MAs)are henceforth legal persons of private legal status but supervised by the Ministry of Environment and Spatial Planning (MIN.ENV.).

NATIONAL SYSTEM OF PROTECTED AREAS IN GREECE

Figure 1: Master plan of protected areas in Greece, Source: Ministry of Environment and Spatial Planning [9].

It is expected for one to wonder why the regulations of article 15 remained inactive for three years. The more likely reason is that the formation of the institution of management of a PA cannot be realised unless the protected area is delimited first, the limits of which will constitute the corresponding territorial authority. Therefore, a managing 'authority' cannot exist in a legally and administratively 'non-existent'area. However, the designation and the spatial delimitation of a PA often faces essential difficulties mainly because of the restrictions and prohibitions that are imposed for the protection of the environment (unfavourable building regulations etc.). Almost always, these regulations create reactions in the local societies that through applied political pressure achieve to cancel or at best to postpone 'in perpetuity' the proposed measures [1].

Given the above, it is not by accident the fact that a special provision was incorporated (article 13) in the new law 3044/2002 on the Transfer of Development Rights with which are founded (directly from the law) 25 MAs of the most important PAs of the national territory.

However the first mass application of the MA's institution, it could be distinguished a certain reserve on behalf of the governmental body (MIN.ENV.) responsible in the attribution of administrative powers (in the sector of the environment) to the self-government institutions and to society, as the spirit of the law 2742/99 would have required. Of course, the aforementioned do not cancel or decrease the great importance of the fact of the first attendance of self-government and NGOs in decision-making bodies that practise environmental policy.

5 Conclusions and suggestions: towards an "undertaking" for environmental 'reconstruction'

According to what was shown previously and attempting a synopsis, our position on this subject is to stress that is very important and necessary to persevere a constant course of improvement of the system for the protection of nature and the PAs in the context of more general environmental policy. Regional planning is called upon to play a decisive role and it should be based on certain modern principles with regard to the protection of nature and the PAs already mentioned

- Achievement of protection through rational use and management of nature
- Networking of protected natural areas of all categories and levels
- Incorporating local populations and societies in the process of protection.
- Interdisciplinary and intersectoral approach.

Specifically for the MAs, it has already been said that they constitute a basic and essential organisational tool for the application of modern principles of planning and management of the PAs. Their major advantages are their ability to facilitate the (self)financing of those regions as well as the participation of the local society according to the principles mentioned previously (the MAs constitute an institutional instrument precisely because they bring into the 'game'of nature protection all those 'players' that were institutionally excluded from it up to now). Regarding the first issue of economic resources, this should also be seen through a new perspective. Thus if the state undertakes the investment expenses, the operational and maintainance expenses of protected areas should be ensured by those who 'benefit' from those particular goods.

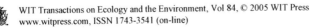

Regarding the support (from the centre) for the cohesion and co-ordination of the whole system of the Pas and MAs that was mentioned in the problems of the functional context (chapter 3), the following are given as necessary actions:

a) The enactment of a Special Planning Framework (national guidlines of strategic character) according to article 7 of L.2742/99 which is reported in the natural and the cultural heritage and will simultaneously constitute the framework or context for basic choices of policy in that sector and provide the essential input for plans and programs on lower levels.

b) The activation of existing and the introduction of new institutions of land policy (utilizing every effective constitutional regulation) that is essential for the control of the property regime of the various zones of PAs.

c) The replacement of rules and legal acts with 'contractual' tools, that is to say negociations between the interested groups where dominates a process of 'give' and 'take'for the interest of both. Indeed between a pointless or useless expropriation excessively costly (hence prohibitory) and a lawful regulation that does not cost anything but has little or no effect, the contractual process appears to bring together most advantages and to have the less disadvantages.

Adoption of the above proposals depends on many factors and it is not easy to forecast obstacles of political, organisational or technical character. However, experience gained up to now from the environmental action of the 2nd and 3rd CFS is precious. In any case, the future course will show if the experiment of MAs in Greece will be achieved and if the new tools will be utilized in the most suitable and effective way, that is to say, with political and social responsibility by all those that will be called to undertake responsibilities. Undoubtedly, without been considered a panacea, the MAs could be an important institution and an effective means of policy for the protection of nature in Greece.

References

[1] Beriatos, E. "New approaches to planning and protection of the natural and cultural heritage' "Topos": *A Review on Spatial Development, Planning and the Environment*, issue 18, 2002, Athens, 2002.

[2] Conseil de l'Europe *'Reseaux ecologiques en Europe'*, 'Naturopa', No.87, Strasbourg, 1998.

[3] Daoussi Ch. (1992) La tradition hellenique d' auto-administration locale et son institutionalization dans l' etat neo-hellenique a partir du XIX siecle. These de doctorat d' etat en droit, Universite Paris I – Sorbonne. Paris

[4] Goulandris Museum of Natural History-EKBY, *The work of the habitats in Greece: Natura 2000 Network* (Guidance 92/43 EU), Thessaloniki, 1998.

[5] IUCN Guidelines for Protected Area Management Categories, Cambridge, IUCN, 1998.

[6] Ministry of Agriculture - General Secretariat of Forests and the Natural Environment *Protected Areas*, Team Work Coordinator's Report, Athens, 1998.

[7] OECD - Organisation for Economic Cooperation and Development, *Environmental Performance Reviews – Greece*, Paris, 2000.

[8] Phillips, A. 'The Challenge of Restoring Europe's Nature and Landscapes', *International Planning Studies*, Volume 1. No.1, pp.73-93, 1996

[9] Min.Env. (Ministry of the Environment and Spatial Planning) *National Planning for the Natural Environment,* Athens. (a study in the context of the 3rd CFS 2000-2006), 1999.

Land use planning around high-risk industrial sites: the factors that affect decision-making

I. Pappas, S. Polyzos & A. Kungolos
Department of Planning and Regional Development,
University of Thessaly, Volos, Greece

Abstract

The new Council Directive 96/82/EC, among other requirements, included provisions for Land Use Planning. The Directive itself does not include any detailed guideline or suggestion on the length of the safety distances around high-risk industrial sites. On the contrary, it allows the Member States and the competent authorities to quantify them and to evaluate their adequacy. The political, cultural, structural, technical and other differences of the Member States are thus acknowledged as a parameter of distinction. The main target of this study is, under certain assumptions, to present a framework for the support of decisions concerning land use planning around high-risk industrial sites. The main purpose of this article is to present all factors which are involved in risk assessment. A general framework for risk management is also suggested as well as the configuration of land uses.
Keywords: land use, planning, industrial safety.

1 Introduction

The importance of Land Use Planning role in the prevention and the restriction of consequences of major hazard accidents were shown, after seriously extent material damage accidents, such as those of Bhopal (India) and in Mexico City. With reference to these accidents, the Land Use Planning close to installations or areas where the storage or treatment of dangerous substances takes place constituted a new requirement of Directive Seveso II with special report to the article of 12 Directive [1]. In the Directive the requirement from the States - Members is formulated in order to the applied policies for the land planning use to include the objectives for the prevention of major hazard accidents as well as the restriction of their consequences [2]. In addition, the field of application is determined and it concerns the planning of new enterprises and the operation of existing industrial ones. Specifically, while the restrictions for the arrangement and the operation of new industrial units are described, they fix the land uses in the areas that surround the existing units, considering the fact that their transport is difficult or economically disadvantageous. It is worth mentioning that in both cases specific measures were not determined in the Directive, but the responsible authorities received the general framework [3]. The article is characterized by the lack of explicit definition of safety distances imposing deliberations where the policy of participation appeared and subsidised in the decision-making.

However, during the period after the Directive Seveso II we had the recording of important major hazard accidents such as the Toulouse (France), the Baia Mare (Romania) and the Enschede ones (Netherlands). Each one of the above added a different datum and caused reflection about the level of application of Directive and in the number and the acceptable limits of dangerous substances. [4]. As a result the field of Directive was decided to be extended with the publication of Directive 2003/105/EC that results to constitutes modification of Directive Seveso II.

In the field of application of the new Directive the areas of waste management of the mining industry are included. At the same time in the level of planning the growth is included and the socio-economic criteria that are indicated for the first time create a suitable frame for the determination of the optimal point in the relation of safety and growth.

In this frame, a general evaluation report of the significance of endangerment and a concise description of factors is included. Additionally, is described the process of risk management in the direction of minimisation of consequences, that can be caused from an accident.

2 Factors of risk configuration

2.1 Generally

It is important to realise that decision-making regarding risks is a very complicated process not only from the technical aspects, but from the political, psychological and social aspects which are of great importance. For the general management of a planning model, the following are essential: a suitable goal, the determination of all essential indicators and criteria that are involved in the question and finally a rational planning. The basic objective in the management of all subjects is the selection of suitable conditions, with the tension to ensure a secure labour and exterior environment, the promotion of competitiveness and growth while satisfying the expectations of employers - workers - public - state. The successful harmonisation of the involved and their balanced attendance presuppose the inclusion of many parameters that influence each interested in a different way and at a different degree.

The rejection or acceptance can be categorized in the following groups: (a) Human safety, (b) Environmental protection, (c) Economic cost and (d) Social acceptance.

In each category, many indicators are included that determine it. The objective of exercising a public policy such as that of accidents management in installations that manage hazardous substances, many times includes contradictory objectives regarding the fact that it is nature constitutes compromising process of refuted social objectives.

2.2 Determination of risk sources

From a technical point of view, the extent of risks and the effects of risk reduction measures can be quantified in a quantitative risk assessment (QRA). Thus, the QRA can provide a basis for rational decision-making, regarding risks. In literature, 4 phases on quantitative risk assessment are referred [5]:

- *Qualitative analysis*, which includes definition of the system and the scope, identification and description of the hazards, failure modes and scenarios.
- *Quantitative analysis*, which includes determination of the probabilities and consequences of the defined events.
- *Risk evaluation*, which includes the evaluation of the risk on grounds of the results of the former analysis.
- *Risk control and risk reduction measures*, which may have to be taken to reduce the risk.

The first phase of the process of estimating risk, studies the pointing out all the sources of danger, which is the determination of this work for which the experience, the existing statistical elements and the more general perception of specialists (scientists, researchers) in the particular areas show that bring dangers for the safety of workers.

According to the above, a concise classification of possible dangers, which characterizes the industrial enterprises, is the following:

1. Dangers related to mechanical and technological equipment of the installation.
2. Dangers related to the natural risk of the recommended materials and the ability for creating explosive mixtures in contact with other substances.
3. Dangers from the use of explosives, liquids or gases of fuels.
4. Dangers from the exposure of workers in radiation, noises, dangerous biological or chemical agents, etc
5. Dangers related to the operation phases of production units of installation.
6. Dangers that result from the existing arrangement of various units in the installation (i.e. reservoir of flammable material placed near the areas of offices, etc.).
7. Dangers related to the rules of fire fighting that have been received.
8. Dangers emanated from the level of noise in the installation especially in internal spaces (i.e. disorientation of workers with the continuous noise of visible danger due to error of handling, not valid notice of workers in case of accident for evacuation of the area, etc.).

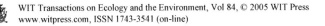 WIT Transactions on Ecology and the Environment, Vol 84, © 2005 WIT Press
www.witpress.com, ISSN 1743-3541 (on-line)

Apart from the above dangers of technological origin, other dangers also exist. These dangers emanate from natural reasons and many times constitute the initial cause of challenge of accident or other times play important role in the spread of consequences of accident. These are: (A) The earthquake risk of the region, (V) Topography of the region and the morphology of territorial area, (C) Existence of areas that include dangers in case of intense natural weather phenomena (i.e. in cases of floods - mainly filled with rubble, or forests which can be exposed to fire risk etc.)

The role of human activity in total management and support in the phase of operation at an installation is identified at the level of prevention, as well as at the level of management of crisis. Certain anthropocentric parameters that influence the degree of risk are reported below:

1. The briefing and know-how of workers regarding subjects related to the correct operation of phases of production but also substances and mechanic parts that they manage.
2. The specialisation of workers in the particular work they carry out in their unit that renders so capable on issues relating to prevention to rational management to unexpected events.
3. The suitable arrangement of workers in the unit ensures comfort in work, created flexibility of escape in case of accident.
4. The time fluctuation of work. The alternation of work time not only weekly but also on daily base reduces the workers' sychological advantage of complete repetition and it decreases the stability that lends "usual".
5. The stability of labour relation. The uncertain labour situation and the seasonal work usually affect the psychology via the economic insecurity that lends to the practice of work.
6. The hygiene of working place. The cleanliness of working places, the environment surrounding and protection from the diffusion of other annoying tobacco particles, and dangerous substances for man affect considerably the effectiveness and the secure implementation of his work.
7. The measures of labour place protection that inspires the worker a sentiment of safety.

Except for the above process of localisation of dangers, it is possible to use solid methods and techniques. The most important of them are:

- Analysis of human error: The method is used for the localisation of equipment operations, which are probably responsible for the human error.
- Safety inspection: It is used in order to estimate installation dangers and it aims in the localisation of conditions, which are functional parameters of productive process and possible to lead in accident. It includes interviews with all workers participating in each productive process.
- Preliminary analysis of danger: It seeks for the localisation of dangers in the initial stage of planning of an installation or a productive process and records the dangers and the dangerous situations.
- Lists of control: They seek the determination of known types of danger, errors of planning, reduction of dangers based on previous experience,

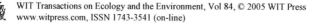

guarantee of equipment operation according to the applied practices and the present models.

- Consequences Analysis: It includes the analysis of undesirable facts consequences by experienced technicians with the system of questionnaires.
- Failure and Result Analysis: The mechanic equipment failure categorized, the results and their repercussions are determined and a list of equipment is drawn up, including the possible ways of failure and their repercussions.

The above techniques that analyze the various parameters of danger should include the uncertainty of conditions in which it is possible for an accident to take place as well as the way and the importance of the event. It is known that the risk constitutes a composition of significances, the undesirable consequence and the uncertainty that characterizes realisation [5-6]. At the process of risk assessment, uncertainty can indicatively result:

1. By the lack of knowledge with regard to the future situation of system (uncertainty of script).
2. By the rarity of data, as the phenomena of accident are not usual and the experimentation is propitiatory.
3. By the false estimation of probability in each case.
4. By the imperfections in the software and mathematic models of description.
5. By the faults of coding and numerical approaches
6. By the territorial and time fluctuation of meteorological cases that can influence the duration of phenomenon.
7. By the uncertainty in the population's behaviour.
8. By the statistical nature of consequences size.

The existence of many sources of uncertainty imposes the need of quantitative determination of risk as a condition for the existence of a reliable model of forecast and confrontation [7]. The presence of such models renders also feasible the possibility of definition of distances safety delegates, which are the decisive element for the rational planning of land uses around installations and areas that where dangerous substances management takes place.

2.3 Calculation of accident probability and the consequences

This action refers to the calculation of probability of accident challenge, after the undesirable development in the space of installation that manages dangerous substances and activates danger in the source. The collection of essential data and information, as well as the calculation of frequency which is expected for the realisation of a damage or an undesirable fact is required. Consequently, the use of statistical elements and secure proof of experience is necessary for the quantification and the essential calculations. Considering the given frequencies of damage or appearance of undesirable facts, a selection of participants (technicians, workers), all frequencies exceed a given and an acceptable value (e.g. for frequency $\geq 10^{-10}$ / year). For the calculation with the use of models, the determination of their parameters is essential. These parameters include the frequencies of appearance for undesirable facts, the probabilities of various human energies, etc. In case sufficient elements do not exist, it is possible to be used empiric values from the implementation of similar work. The calculation of consequences of accidents in the health of workers follows. The process of this calculation requires particular attention due to the likely depreciation of work danger. The possibility to follow the reverse course exists. That is to say, the calculation of consequences cost precedes and follows the calculation of probability of undesirable facts appearance.

2.4 Risk estimation

Risk measures play an important role in communicating the whole risk assessment process. A risk measure is defined as a mathematical function of the probability of an event and the consequences of that event. The risk measure constitutes the basis for the evaluation of risks by the decision-makers. Limits and standards, set an acceptable risk level, and the risk measure can be used as an instrument to show the effect of risk reducing actions.

The risk quantitative analysis follows the above mentioned phases. With the risk quantification, we put the bases to get over problems that are focused in the absence of common acceptable limits of risk for many parameters. Similar problems are also located in the case of critical limits quantities determination. The limits of report that have been established up to now by various organisations (IDLH, ERPG etc) are checked for their effectiveness with regard to the protection of special categories of population [8]. In addition, disagreements have been formulated with regard to the degree of reliability of intensity of natural phenomenon (stocking of toxic substance, intensity of thermic radiation, overpressure etc) as a criterion for the characterization of the repercussion of an accident in health, electing the need for calculation of the relation between doses - response. According to this proposal, the effect in health is interrelation of exposure time in the phenomenon of dose (eg toxic substance). The relation between doses - response reduces a concrete dose in probability of specific damage in human health. A different formulation constitutes individual risk, which makes the same reduction but determines the probability of death. The individual risk of an accident is fixed by the frequency (probability per unit of time) of an accident challenge in a worker, who works in a place (x,y). A mathematic expression of individual risk is given by the relation:

$$R = \sum_{i}^{n} f_i E_i S_i \qquad (1)$$

where:

R   = Indicator of individual risk.
i   = Indicator that takes values from the field of definition events that can cause an accident.
f_i = Indicator of frequency of appearance for event i.
E_i = Indicator of time duration of workers' exposure in danger.
S_i = Indicator of danger consequences.

The relation one allows the comparison of accidental risk of different causes and different intensities. Besides the individual risk, as mentioned above, four other expressions are described [5,9]. A different definition is used by the UK's health and safety executive board [5]. According to this body, the individual risk is a risk that a typical user of a development is exposed to a dangerous dose of toxic substance, heat or blast overpressure. To limit the risks usually the next constraint is set $r \leq 10^{-6}$ (per year) [10]. The measure of individual risk is used to determine the risks of hazardous sources and it is possible locations with equal individual risk levels to be shown on maps that facilitate land use planning applications. Figure 1 shows a typical risk contours for a hazard source.

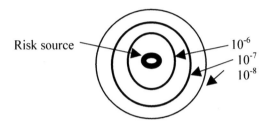

Figure 1:   Characteristics individual risk contours.

Then the relation of collective risk allows the comparison of accidents involving different individual risks but in a region with different demographic density and distribution. The collective risk is depicted in the form of the relation of the curves between   frequency and number of accidents (F, N) and is estimated by the following equation:

$$N= \sum_{i}^{n} p_i w_i \tag{2}$$

where:

N   =   The number of accidents that can be caused in an entrepreneurship by the event i.

p_i =   The probability for the event i to take place.

w_i =   The number of workers who work in the entrepreneurship or in a part of it which is affected by the event i.

The values f_i and E_i is possible to oscillate between 1 and 4, when the probability $P_i = f_i E_i$ will get values between 1 and 16, as between 1 and 16 it is possible the values of indicator S_i to be oscillated.

A different equation of risk estimation which is possible to be used for the planning is the following [5]:

$$N= \iint_A R(x,y)H(x,y)dxdy \tag{3}$$

where R is the individual risk on location (x, y), H(x,y) number of houses on location (x, y) and A is area for which N is determined. By integrating the individual risk and the population density the expected values of the number of fatalities or injuries can be determined:

$$E(N)= \iint_A R(x,y)m(x,y)dxdy \qquad (4)$$

where E(N) is the expected value of the number of fatalities or injuries per year and m(x,y) is the population density on location (x, y).

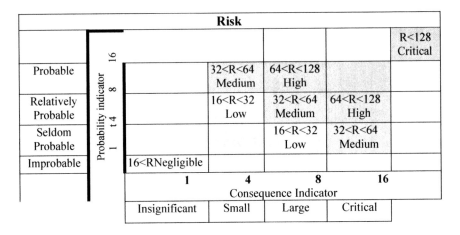

Risk						
						R<128 Critical
Probable	16		32<R<64 Medium	64<R<128 High		
Relatively Probable	8		16<R<32 Low	32<R<64 Medium	64<R<128 High	
Seldom Probable	4			16<R<32 Low	32<R<64 Medium	
Improbable	1	16<RNegligible				
		1	4	8	16	
		Consequence Indicator				
		Insignificant	Small	Large	Critical	

(Probability indicator on vertical axis: 16, 8, 4, 1)

Figure 2: Risk estimation.

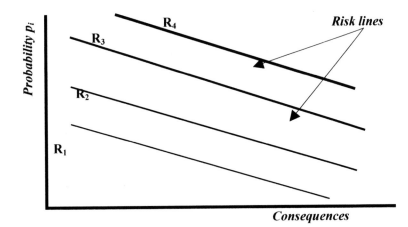

Figure 3: Interrelation between Probability and Consequences for different risk degrees.

A different form of the cross-correlation of probability for challenge of industrial accident and the consequences that will be caused for different risk areas is presented in Figure 3. It is obvious that the lines of high danger concern regions in small distance from the risk source, while the removal from the risk source decreases intensity of consequences.

3 Risk management

The quantitative analysis of previous phases creates an important background for the extraction of essential restriction rules of dangers for the workers and the minimisation of working accidents. The beforehand taken actions aim to the alleviation of the probability of an accident to happen and the alleviation of the consequences of the accident, if this happens.

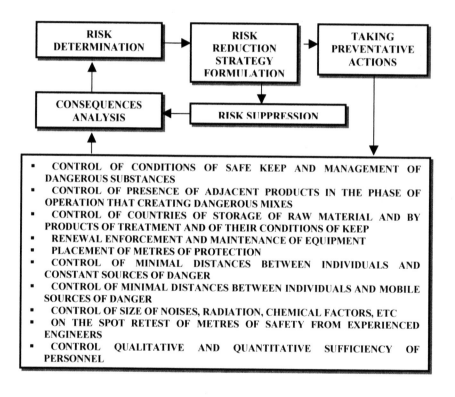

Figure 4: Risk management in plants and units that handle hazardous substances.

The process of action taken is displayed in Figure 4 and it is related with the values of R in Figures 2 and 3. If the risk is negligible, it is not required to take actions. In small or medium risk it is required to take actions in a short time. In high risk it is required to take actions immediately, while in critical risk it is necessary to interrupt work, the immediate action taken, the modification of the productive process provided the actions do not limit effectively the danger. As it was mentioned before, the endangerment constitutes the resultant of an accident's probability to happen and the consequences of accident. The risk management aims to the reduction of probability to happen an accident and for this reason prevented actions have to be taken, as well as the restriction of consequences with the taken actions of repression. The taken actions firstly require the acceptance of "bearable level of risk", since the effort for entire risk obliteration is still considered unfeasible or even the cost for the reduction of accidents is disproportionate to the profit that will result.

The actions of prevention in the process of risk management are of particular importance. The effective prevention action taken presupposes the attendance of experienced and capable engineers, especially for dangers related with the natural environment, for which the uncertainty is considerable and the risk quantification requires knowledge and experience.

4 Conclusions

A general report of the factors that influence the creation of industrial accidents and the way of estimating the individual and social risk has been presented in this study. A description of stages that include the risk of management is shown. Equations and Diagrams of calculating the consequences were given in a general frame.

It was shown that the effective management of risk in the industrial enterprises requires precise quantitative determination of risk sources, the probability of accident and the diffusion of consequences in the area. This will lead to the determination of risk areas from risk sources and will shape proportionally the land uses. The attendance of the involved ones is necessary as in that way it is ensured the better determination the risk sources and probabilities of accident facilitating the management of its consequences.

References

[1]   Council Directive of 9 December 1996, On the control of major-accident hazards involving dangerous substances (96/82/EC). Official Journal of the European Communities No L 10, 14.1. (1997) 13–33.

[2]   Christou M. "Land Use Planning and the location of Industrial units which handle hazardous substances", Technika Chronika *1/2000, p. 20* [in Greek]

[3]   Christou M. and Porter S. (Eds), "Guidance on Land Use Planning as required by Council Directive 96/82/EC (Seveso II)", European Commission, 1999.

[4]   Council Directive 2003/105/EC of the European Parliament and of the Council amending Council Directive 96/82/EC on the control of major-accident hazards involving dangerous substances (Seveso II) Official Journal of the European Communities No L 345, 31.12.2003, 97-105

[5]   Jonkman S. N., Van Gelder P., Vrijling J. K. (2003), "An overview of quantitative risk measures of loss of life and economic damage", Journal of Hazardous Materials, pp. 1-30.

[6]   Papazoglou J. "Quantitative risk determination and rational management of industrial installations safety", Technika Chronika *1/2000, p. 47*[in Greek]

[7]   Georgiadou H., "Major Hazard Industrial Accidents: Metholodical and Informative Guindance", *EL.IN.Y.A.E.*, Athens, 2001. [in Greek]

[8]   Georgiadou H. "Methodological and organisational problems for the combined application of directive SEVESO and legislation on the health and safety of workers", Conference TEE, Risk Management. Application of Directive SEVESO I & II in Greece, 2003. [in Greek]

[9]   Saloniemi A. (1998), "Accidents and fatal accidents – some paradoxes", SAFETY SCIENCE, 29, pp. 59-66.

[10]   Botelberbs P. H. (2000), "Risk analysis and safety policy developments in the Netherlands)", Journal of Hazardous Materials, 7, pp. 59-84.

State of the art of environmental management

R. Brandtweiner & A. Hoeltl
Department of Economics and Management Science,
Danube University Krems, Austria

Abstract

Enterprises are confronted more and more with environmental issues of increasing complexity, environmental regulation and public pressure which they have to manage in a new way. An environmental management system is an appropriate instrument which may be certified and accepted internationally and offers answers to the new challenges in a cost efficient manner.

Environmental management systems are assigned to the "third" way of environmental policy instruments. The main feature is the voluntary participation of enterprises to such measures. There are many advantages in participating in an international systematic certified system like EMAS in Europe. Participation is voluntary, but the organisation must meet minimum standards to be EMAS registered.

Due to the fact that environmental management systems can make an important contribution to a sustainable economic development as well as to reach the Kyoto targets, the European Union should enforce the promotion of EMAS registration especially concerning small and medium-sized enterprises.

Keywords: environmental management system, state of the art, EMAS, environmental policy instruments, voluntary measures, environmental performance, SMEs.

1   Introduction

Environmental regulation measures and the public sensitivity concerning environmental issues constitute growing challenges for the business world. An important tool for taking on these challenges is the implementation of an environmental management system (EMS) in the organisation.

Thereby the organisation is on the one hand able to demonstrate its willingness for an improved environmental performance to the public and to the authorities and on the other hand able to manage the environmental challenges in a cost efficient way.

The paper shows the motivations for and the benefits of an EMS from the government's point of view as well as from the point of view of the organisation which implements the system.

It makes sense to decide for an international systematic certified approach of an EMS, because of its international acceptance and because of the controls carried out by the authority. So we bring a synopsis of the EMS in the European Union, called EMAS.

EMSs make an important contribution to the improvement of the environmental performance of an organisation, a country and the world. By the voluntary approach of these systems it corresponds to public policies on cooperation and consensus with reaching the environmental goals in an economic efficient way. International systematic certified approaches like EMAS should be promoted by the authorities in an intensified way.

2 Environmental management systems

2.1 Economic background

Almost all good productions, activities and services by organisations effect negative externalities - effects of production and activities not directly reflected in the market. Because externalities are an important reason of market failure and produce economic inefficiencies, policy measures are required. Systematic EMS which are certified by an authority are assigned to voluntary agreements as the "new" way in environmental policies.

2.2 Benefits for organisations

Due to asymmetric information between authorities, consumer and organisation about its environmental performance, a participation in an international systematic certified environmental management system can help to reduce problems concerning this asymmetry. With such participation an organisation signals to the public its importance of improvement of the environmental performance.

The implementation of an EMS is a suitable method to recognize financial inefficiencies representing inefficient use of resources. So an international systematic certified EMS is able to bring out, in addition to indirect cost effects with an improved environmental performance on the market, a direct cost reduction due to elimination of economic inefficiencies.

2.3 Advantages for policy-makers

EMSs are assigned to voluntary agreements as a "third" way in environmental policies in addition to the classical policy intruments command-and-control and market-based measures.

2.3.1 Command-and-control

This legislative policy mainly consists of enforcements and restrictions. Harmful environmental impacts are controlled through environmental permits, limits on emissions, prohibitions of the use of certain substances, the limitation of certain activities in special areas or the enforcement of certain technical standards. Command-and-control measures still play an important role in environmental policies, however they should be limited as much as possible because of their low economic efficiency.

2.3.2 Market-based measures

Such environmental economic instruments can provide positive financial incentives to promote a more sustainable business world. Market-based measures include taxes and user charges for products with negative environmental impacts, insurance/liability schemes and tradable permits, as well as various kinds of subsidies for improved environmental performances.

The advantage of this approach in comparison to the command-and-control policy is that the organisation has, according to its cost structure, the choice, for example, of either paying the fee or reducing the emissions, which is what it should do if it is marginal costs of abatement are less than the emission fee.

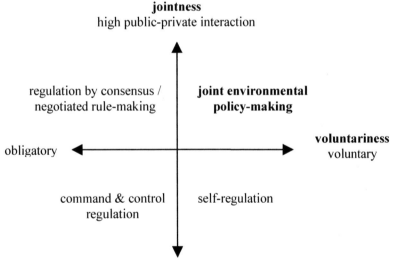

Figure 1:   Placing joint approaches. Source Ingram (1999).

2.3.3 Voluntary measures

In addition to regulations and market-based measures, companies and other organisations may voluntarily improve their environmental performance by

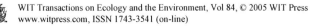

participating in public programs which are usually negotiated between economy and authorities. Voluntary agreements should strengthen the commitment of organisations to environmental goals.

Due to the limits of regulation and a tendency towards environmental policy making on consensus and cooperation, instead of confrontation, between the authorities and the economy, voluntary measures are increasingly replacing or complementing other environmental policy instruments.

Voluntary agreements can be characterised as joint environmental policy-making. Figure 1 shows the placing of voluntary agreements in the area of environmental policies.

The political tendency to deregulation promotes the increasing application of voluntary approaches. They enable organisations to develop their own solutions in the most cost effective way. Corporate relations between the authorities and the economy often facilitate better results than traditional regulations.

The European Commission has a clear interest in developing and implementing voluntary approaches in its environmental policy. It takes an important step with the regulation for the environmental management system Eco-Management and Audit Scheme, called EMAS.

3 EMAS

In our opinion organisations should choose an international systematic certified EMS rather than any other EMS. EMAS is the unique certified EMS in Europe, where the organisations commit themselves to improving their environmental performance, which is the main difference to other EMSs, especially to the international standard EN/ISO 14001. Therefore we show a synopsis of EMAS and its development.

3.1 What is EMAS

According to the regulation (EC) No 761/2001 of the European Parliament and of the Council, the environmental management system Eco-Management and Audit Scheme (EMAS) is a voluntary scheme designed for companies and other organisations that are willing to commit themselves to evaluate, manage and improve their environmental performance. EMAS is applied in all Member States of the European Union and the European Economic Area (Norway, Iceland and Liechtenstein).

EMAS was launched in 1993 and revised in 2001 by adding several new features such as the access for organisations in all public and private sectors, the integration of EN/ISO 14001 and the involvement of employees.

An environmental management system includes all economic targets, decisions and activities appropriate to minimize negative environmental impacts of an organisation as an independent goal and for supporting other organisation's goals. An EMS is an integrated part of a generic management system, where negative effects from activities of the organisation should be recognized, if possible be avoided and environmental impacts as low as possible should be guaranteed. The employees of the organisation should be involved in the continual improvement of the organisation's environmental performance.

EMAS provides organisations, regulators and the public with an instrument to evaluate and manage the environmental impact of an organisation and is designed to benefit the environment. Because of the systematic approach it is possible to evaluate and compare different companies and organizations, which provides a basis for feasible promotion of environmental protection by the government.

It is important to recognize that an EMAS certification does not mean that all services and products of the organisation are ecologically produced or ecologically convenient, however the organisation commits itself to improving its environmental performance.

3.2 Stages for implementation

In order to get the EMAS registration an organisation has to go through the following steps:

3.2.1 Environmental review
An environmental review means an initial analysis of all environmental issues, impacts concerning the products, services and activities of an organisation. Above this the legal and regulatory framework of the activities and the existing environmental management practices and procedures has to be considered.

3.2.2 Environmental policy
The environmental policy should provide the framework for all activities of the organisation concerning environmental objectives and targets. It has to become a part of the entire organisation's policy, which means that the overall aims and principles of action take into consideration and promote an improved environmental performance.

3.2.3 Environmental management system
On the basis of the results of the environmental review, the organisation has to implement an environmental management system. To do this the top management must define the environmental policy of the organisation, lay down environmental goals, responsibilities, means, communication systems, training needs etc.

3.2.4 Environmental audit
The organisation has to carry out an internal environmental audit to assess the implemented environmental management system and its conformity with the environmental goals of the organisation and with relevant environmental regulations.

3.2.5 Environmental statement
An organisation whose aim is the EMAS registration, has to provide an environmental statement to the public, to show the current environmental impact

and performance and the planned future steps to be undertaken in order to improve the organisation's environmental performance.

3.2.6 Environmental verification

An accredited EMAS verifier has to approve the environmental review, environmental management system, the internal environmental audit and the environmental statement. After this procedure the validated statement must be provided to the EMAS Competent Body for registration and has to be made publicly available. Then an organisation is allowed to use the EMAS logo. In Europe there are currently 311 EMAS registered verifiers' organisations.

Table 1: Number of EMAS accredited verifiers in the EU Member States (last update of the list 13/01/2005). Source European Union.

Member State	Austria	Belgium	Czech Republic	Denmark	Finland	France	Germany	Greece	Italy	Luxembourg	The Netherlands	Norway	Portugal	Slovenia	Spain	Sweden	The UK
#	11	6	4	3	2	7	219	4	12	1	6	5	4	1	9	6	11

3.3 EMAS logo

EMAS registered organisations are allowed to use the EMAS logo to demonstrate their participation in this certified EMS and their commitment to improve the environmental performance.

Figure 2: EMAS logo Version 1 and Version 2. Source European Union.

Version 1 of the EMAS logo demonstrates the EMAS registration of the organisation, which means the implementation of an environmental management system conforming to the requirements of EMAS. This version of the logo can be used for example on letterheads, invitations, websites, posters, door signs, buildings and flags.

Version 2 of the EMAS logo can be used for example in combination with a particular piece of information the organisation wants to communicate to the public. By this the organisation can show its environmental performance in combination with their products, services or activities. Such information has to be especially validated by an EMAS verifier.

3.4 Costs and benefits of EMAS for an organisation

For each organisation contemplating registration for EMAS, the costs and benefits concerning the implementation of this environmental management system are an important issue.

3.4.1 Costs of EMAS

On the one hand there will be external costs for the environmental verifier, the registration fees and possible additional external support, and on the other hand internal costs particularly for required internal resources to implement the EMS.

Environmental verifiers are independent private consultants who charge the normal market prices for consultancy. Registration fees can vary from zero to 1500 Euros in the case of large companies. The EMAS Regulation recommends reduced registration fees for small and medium-sized enterprises (SMEs) to encourage higher participation. Further external costs will arise by the publication of the environmental statement.

Internal costs are more difficult to quantify. They depend on the size of the organisation, the experience with environmental management systems and the complexity of environmental issues of the specific organisation. After the implementation and first registration of EMAS, the maintenance of the system won't require as many resources.

3.4.2 Benefits of EMAS

Most environmental impacts also have financial implications because they represent inefficient use of substances. An environmental management system like EMAS could help to show such inefficiencies and by doing this contribute to cost reductions.

The most common benefits of EMAS implementation are, for example, a quality environmental management due to the use of a highly developed scheme, resource savings and lower costs, reduction of financial burdens due to reactive management strategies, benefits through better control of the entire operations of the organisation, compliance checks with environmental legislation by EMAS verifier, improved quality of workplaces, marketplace advantages and improved stakeholder relations.

3.5 EMAS registered organisations

Figure 3 shows the absolute numbers of registered sites and organisations in different European countries. Considering the relative numbers of registration, per one million inhabitants, Austria is first with 31.60 organisations, followed by Denmark with 23.35, Germany with 19.65, Spain with 11.24, Sweden with 11.13, Finland with 7.71 and Norway with 6.20.

The number of EMAS registered organisations has increased in recent years and this trend is expected to continue. Many registered organisations are also interested in the environmental management practices of their suppliers. It is usually more cost effective for an organisation to anticipate such expectations and work with foresight towards EMAS registration in a planned way.

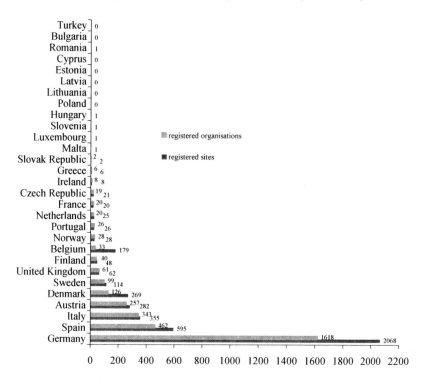

Figure 3: EMAS organisations and sites (as of 11/04/2005). Source European Union.

4 Future and conclusions

European Member States should promote increasing participation in EMAS, because by the implementation of an EMS, organisations often fully recognize for the first time their environmental impacts and economic inefficiencies. Another important point is that registered organisations commit themselves to an improvement of their environmental performance.

Especially small and medium-sized enterprises (SMEs), enterprises with fewer than 250 employees, are often not fully aware of their environmental impacts, and they are not always well informed about their legal environmental obligations. Currently the participation of SMEs in EMAS is very low. However

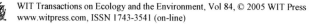

SMEs are, with 99 per cent of all private enterprises, a very important part of the economy in the European Union.

Figure 4 shows the main driving forces, barriers and results especially for SMEs concerning the implementation of an EMS according to Nutek (2003).

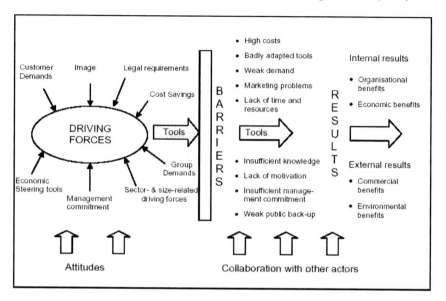

Figure 4:   Driving forces, barriers and results for SMEs. Source Nutek (2003).

In future more innovative EMAS related subsidy schemes should be implemented, for example for promoting SME networks. Such schemes have already produced positive results for SMEs in different arrangements and countries and may be more successful than conventional schemes for small organisations. The funding for EMAS implementation could be linked more intensively to financial support for traditional investments. The future revision of EMAS should enforce an easier implementation for SMEs, possibly by the introduction of a staged approach. More information about the potential benefits and practical experiences should be provided to interested organisations and the public.

A crucial point for the further development of EMAS will be to take into consideration the adoption of environmental management accounting (EMA) by EMAS registered organisations. EMA provides a scheme to fully measure and identify the environmental costs of the organisation's activities, to evaluate the benefits of cleaner processes and to integrate environmental costs and benefits in the conventional accounting systems and thereby in the decision-making of an organisation.

Additionally to the traditional environmental policy instruments the enforced promotion of EMAS registration can make an important contribution to a development of the European Union to a more sustainable economy and environment.

References

[1] Clausen, J., The State of EMAS in the EU. European Conference: "The EU Eco-Management and Audit Scheme – Benefits and Challenges of EMAS II", Brussels, 2002.
[2] EMAS; European Union. http://europa.eu.int/comm/environment/emas
[3] European Commission, Public policy initiatives to promote the uptake of Environmental Management Systems in small and medium-sized enterprises, Brussels, 2004.
[4] European Parliament and Council of the European Union, Regulation (EC) No 761/2001 of the European Parliament and of the Council allowing voluntary participation by organisations in a Community eco-management and audit scheme (EMAS). http://europa.eu.int/eur-lex/pri/en/oj/dat/2001/l_114/l_11420010424en00010029.pdf
[5] Fischer, T.C.G. & Waschik, R.G., Managerial Economics. A Game Theoretic Approach, Routledge: London and New York, 2002.
[6] Ingram, V.J., An environment for consensus?, CAVA Working Paper, **98/11/2**, 1999.
[7] Jasch, Ch., The use of Environmental Management Accounting (EMA) for identifying environmental costs, Journal of Cleaner Production, **11/6**, 2003.
[8] Liefferink, D., The voluntary approach: European experiences in joint environmental policy-making. http://www.psa.ac.uk/cps/1999/liefferink.pdf
[9] Nutek, Environmental work in small enterprises – a pure gain?, R 2003:7, 2003.

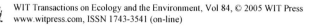

The effects of urbanization on the natural drainage patterns and the increase of urban floods: case study Metropolis of Mashhad-Iran

S. R. Hosseinzadeh
Department of Geography, Ferdowsi University of Mashhad

Abstract

Alluvial fans create a special type of flash flood threat, especially in arid and semi-arid areas where the fans support urban development. Most of the cities in Iran have developed in such environments, and are facing flash and urban floods because of the rapid growth of the cities, and the deficiency of urban planning in the last four decades. The present study aims at analyzing the urbanization effect on natural drainage patterns and their immediate result, namely the increase of vulnerability of the metropolitan city of Mashhad. Mashhad, as the second religious metropolis of the world, and second metropolis of Iran has an annual 12 million pilgrims, and 3 million population. The results of this study indicate that the rapid growth of the city from 1966 to 2002 has had excessive destructive effects on the catchments area, and has caused the decrease of impervious surfaces, and the increase peak discharge of the urban floods.
Keywords: urbanization, flash flood, urban flood, drainage pattern.

1   Introduction

The effects of urbanization on the hydrology and morphology of watersheds have been studied by Leopold [16, 17], Hammer [8], Hollis [9], Dunne and Leopold [5], Klein [15], Arnold [2], Gordon et al. [7], Arnold and Gibbons [3], Christopher [4], Paul and Meyer [21] and White and Greer [23]. According to previous studies, development of cities in the watershed increases the area of impervious surfaces which decreases infiltration of precipitation and in creases runoff. Runoff increases in proportion to the cover impervious surface in a watershed and the increased storm runoff increases peak discharge and flood

Magnitudes. Reduced infiltration of precipitation to groundwater aquifers may reduce groundwater recharge, and stream base flow [13].

Although the increases of flood and runoff have been mentioned in the previous studies, their effects have not been noticed in relation with the city itself, and urban population. The present study analyzes the effects of urban development on flash and urban floods and the deficiency of urban planning in its increase and seeks a way to decrease the environmental effects of these floods on metropolitan cities in Iran as most of these cities are located on alluvial fans where many small watersheds join them from the mountain sides. Urbanization disrupts the hill slope profiles, ruptures of vegetation, compacts soils and disrupts the stream long profiles. It also changes the natural drainage patterns and increases the urban flood hazard [5].

2 The study area and methods

The Metropolis of Mashhad in the Khorasan province is located in the North-eastern part of Iran and in the Kashaf Rood basin. To study the effects of the development of this city in urban floods, an area of 576 sq. kilometers between 36^0 13' to 36^0 25'N and 56^0 28' to 56^0 44'E were chosen. This area includes three geomorphologic features: mountain, pediment, and flood plain. The expansion of Mashhad starts from the flood plain toward the mountain and covers the whole Alluvial fans. To study the role of the city in inundation, the analysis was mainly carried out based on the historical geomorphologic method along with and its combination with the experimental methods as follows:

- The mountain landscape was subdivided into 19 stream catchments and the basic studies and the effects of urbanization were carried out through topographical maps, Air photographs, field observations and peak of the flood in each watershed have been calculated according to the recurrence of 2 to 100 years. The aim of this calculation was to determine the maximum discharge of flood entrance to the urban area from the catchments.

- On the pediment, alluvial fans and flood plain landscapes, the boundary of the city were determined by the air photographs of 1966, and the geomorphologic terrains, and the natural drainage networks were extracted and drawn on the basis map. Thereafter, the effects of the expansion of the urban area on the previous geomorphologic terrains were indicated, using satellite images.

- The changes that were caused by the expansion of the city in the natural drainage network, especially in the main channels, were measured and analyzed through air photographs and field observations.

- By the zonation of area into 8 impermeable regions according to the coverage area of each main urban canal, the maximum of flash flood in each level and the flood peak of each watershed in the mountain area were calculated and the discharge surplus in each canal was estimated.

- Finally, after a careful consideration of the original conditions of the canals, especially their width before the expansion of the city, corrective solutions for each component area were presented.

3 The discussion and the result

3.1 Catchments and the indirect effects of urbanization

The watersheds leading to Mashhad are named with abbreviations: A1 to A19 and their physical parameters are presented (table 1). All of the catchments contain high slope and have short concentration time. Nearly all of the watersheds are formed in the metamorphic and ultrabasic Permian rocks with extensive stone outcrops, little infiltration and dispersed thin soils. Due to low precipitation (an annual of 280mm) the vegetation in these areas is disperse and poor.

Table 1:   Physiographic characteristics of catchments.

Catchments	Area (km^2)	Circus (km)	Gravels coefficient	Elevation (m)			Stream length (km)	Time of cons (hour)
				Min.	Max.	Mean.		
A1	1.22	4.94	1.25	1067	1473	1192	1.98	0.25
A2	0.92	4.67	1.36	1080	1479	1215	2.01	0.23
A3	2.21	7.08	1.33	1092	1509	1261	2.62	0.31
A4	1.48	5.92	1.36	1090	1367	1194	2.99	0.40
A5	0.40	2.98	1.32	1039	1240	1111	0.99	0.15
A6	0.91	4	1.17	1050	1260	1133	1.36	0.18
A7	1.93	6.81	1.37	1100	1430	1235	2.75	0.35
A8	2.47	6.99	1.24	1120	1423	1253	2.58	0.33
A9	1.30	5.84	1.43	1140	1443	1269	2.39	0.30
A10	0.64	3.82	1.33	1100	1256	1147	1.59	0.23
A11	3.46	13.31	1.55	1090	1510	1277	5.33	0.65
A12	3.46	8.33	1.25	1120	1534	1289	3.38	0.40
A13	1.59	6.17	1.37	1119	1521	1220	2.65	0.30
A14	1.59	6.98	1.27	1160	1526	1280	2	0.21
A15	0.42	2.69	1.15	1159	1310	1124	1.01	0.15
A16	3.23	8.57	1.33	1170	1500	1312	2.67	0.33
A17	0.89	4.2	1.26	1160	1350	1220	1.66	0.21
A18	0.42	3	1.3	1120	1265	1160	1.02	0.13
A19	0.35	2.6	1.23	1120	1230	1112	0.92	0.13

The development of the city of Mashhad in the last four decades, in addition to the change in Microclimatic conditions [7] has also caused extreme changes in the morphology of the watersheds. These changes have increased the flood velocity and the volume of Flash flood sediments. The changes include the following:

• *The disruption of the slope stability:* The urban need for stone resources has caused the disruption of the stability extraction from the 100 mines in the watersheds and has developed the escarpments. It has also formed holes with a diameter of 50 to 100 meters in the location of each mine and has left a high volume of loose rubbles on the sides and the bottom of valleys.

• *The disruption of the stream long profiles:* the need for sand and gravel resources for the construction of highways and streets of the city has caused a great volume of sand and gravel to be taken away from the main river-beds. This withdrawal has changed the river beds greatly and has made them unstable. Furthermore, the disposal of building wastage in the valleys has completely blocked some stream channels and formed anthropogenic landforms. As these instances are very varied concerning their forms and material, they are very sensitive to eroding hence capable of making sheet floods during heavy rains.

• *Soil compaction and the destruction of Natural vegetation:* More than 60 kilometers of the roads are constructed in the catchments which in addition to destroying the vegetation also disrupt the steep slopes, reduce of penetrability and the produce of unconsolidated materials or loose rubble layer.

3.2 Flash flood frequencies and discharge

Concerning the physical conditions of the basins and the destructive effects of urbanization and based on the magnitude and the frequency of rainfall curves of Mashhad synoptic station, the flood crest in the watersheds has been calculated for recur 2 - 100 years and the result has been presented in table 2.

Table 2:   Estimation of highest flood discharge (Peak Flood).

Catchments	recur 2 years m^3/s	recur 5 years m^3/s	recur 10 years m^3/s	recur 25 years m^3/s	recur 50 years m^3/s	recur 100 years m^3/s
A1	3.82	6.10	7.62	9.96	11.29	13.74
A2	2.88	4.60	5.74	7.51	8.51	10.35
A3	7.51	11.13	14.10	18.86	21.24	25.84
A4	3.69	5.44	6.92	9.43	10.63	12.94
A5	1.83	2.74	3.35	4.27	4.88	6.09
A6	3.73	5.96	7.44	9.73	11.03	13.42
A7	6.56	9.72	12.31	16.47	18.55	22.57
A8	8.42	12.47	15.80	21.13	23.80	28.96
A9	4.41	6.54	8.28	11.08	12.48	15.19
A10	1.72	2.76	3.44	4.50	5.10	6.20
A11	12.62	18.25	23.48	32.56	37.31	45.43
A12	8.63	12.74	16.20	22.05	24.86	30.27
A13	4.54	6.73	8.52	11.40	12.84	15.63
A14	7.33	11.73	14.64	19.14	21.70	26.40
A15	1.28	1.92	2.34	2.98	3.41	4.26
A16	11.00	16.30	20.64	27.61	31.10	37.84
A17	2.17	3.88	4.92	6.23	7.32	8.2
A18	1.07	1.96	2.45	3.08	3.62	4.05
A19	0.9	1.63	2.04	2.57	3.02	3.39

3.3 Urban development pattern and its direct effects

The expansion of the city of Mashhad during the last four decades has been shown on the geomorphologic map from 1966 to 2002 respectively. (Figures 1 and 2) Based on figure 1, the area of the city in 1960s has been 29.1 sqkm. And has mainly been located on the flood plain. This area has increased to 228.1 sqkm in 2002 and has covered more varied geomorphologic features. (Table 3) The resulting changes from this process can be studied as follows:

- *The increase in the impenetrable surfaces:* Through field observations, it was evident that except of the flood plain, the other geomorphologic features had a very high rate of penetrability before the expansion of the city. After the expansion, 118.4 sq. kilometers of the plains had high penetrability in the Alluvial fans and 80.6 sq kilometers had low penetrability in the flood plains as more than 80% of urban areas were turned into asphalt areas. As the steepness of the Alluvial fans was more than the flood plains steepness (2 to 3%) the urban watersheds were capable of more runoff and floods.

Table 3:   Geomorphologic features and urban development.

Landscape type	Landscape area		Average slope (%)	City area on 1966 (Km^2)	City area on 2002 (Km^2)
	Km^2	%			
Mountain, Incelberg, Buttes	42.63	7.4	20	0	0.6
Pediments	137.1	23.8	2	0.05	14
Alluvial Fans	137.4	23.6	2	0.975	104.4
Flood Plain	251.68	43.6	> 1	28.075	109.7
Total	576.6	100	--	29.1	228.7

Table 4:   Changes in drainage systems associated with urbanization.

Watershed	Area (Km^2)			Eliminated or obstructed main channels		Eliminated secondary channels		Section of new canal
	Urban	Natural	Total	Number	Length (km)	Number	Length (km)	
Nu 1	9.2	5	14.2	5	12	32	17.6	2-9
Nu 2	7.62	0.42	8.04	4	11.13	69	29.2	5
Nu 3	4.87	7.39	12.26	7	16.11	21	15.6	6
Nu 4	6.8	--	6.8	5	8	50	31.6	3
Nu 5	3.02	6.38	9.4	6	11	35	13.5	6
Nu 6	6.5	5.7	12.2	7	10.6	47	22.4	4
Nu 7	2.21	1.31	3.52	3	2.4	13	6	4
Nu 8	2.71	5.83	8.54	6	11.7	10	4.8	6
Total	42.93	32.03	74.96	277	140.7	43	82.9	--

Based on the urban land cover maps, an average 25% of the land uses have been appropriated to streets and green areas, 50% to houses, and 25% to the commercial and public units. The runoff of all streets; and the runoff of 25% of the roofs enter the urban drainage systems. In the field measurements, it became clear that the time of concentration of urban floods has doubled, and the flood frequencies have increased to 100%.

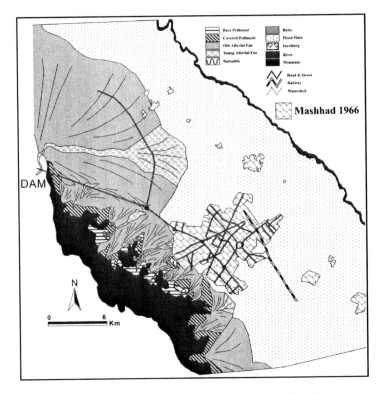

Figure 1:   Map of geomorphologic features of study area.

- *The change in the natural drainage pattern:* on the Alluvial fans, and in the flood plain, the expansion of the city has destroyed 277 natural secondary channels, about 140 kilometers long and 43 main channels measuring 82.9 kilometers long have been blocked or changed extremely. (Figure 4) The main natural channels including drained channels from the mountain and wide channels (wider than 10 m) were located on the Alluvial fans. The main channels, due to the urbanization limitations were blocked or their courses had been changed merged into one another. These 19 channels were finally connected to 9 main urban canals. The secondary channels had the same destiny as the main channels and vanished altogether.

Urban drainage system includes streets, canals and water passages of the sidewalks which are eventually concentrated in the main urban canals. According to the coverage area of each canal we can divide the Alluvial fan area of the city that faces the serious problem of flood into 8 new urban watersheds and study the resulting changes according to table 4 in each one of them.

3.4 The weakness of urban drainage system

Urban texture and its drainage system does not correspond very much to the natural drainage patterns, because in the urban development planning, rivers, as one of the most important landscapes, have been omitted and canals with low capacity have replaced them. Measure weakness of urban drainage system, the maximum probable peak in each natural urban watershed is calculated. The results of the calculations have been presented in table 5.

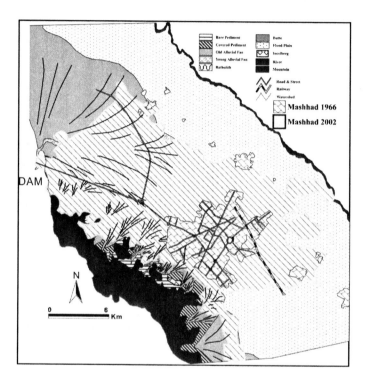

Figure 2:   Map of landforms and urban development.

Table 5:   Peak flood in natural and urban drainage basins.

Water shed	Urban area (ha)	Runoff coefficient	Peak flood of urban main canal (m³/s)						Total of peak flood	
			2	5	10	25	50	100	50	100
Nu 1	920	0.55	19.26	31.6	40.76	51.44	59.4	67.46	73	83
Nu 2	762	0.47	16.6	28.1	34.8	44.8	53.7	59.7	57.1	101.8
Nu 3	487	0.5	12.8	21	28.4	35.8	40.6	47.3	100	119.6
Nu 4	680	0.47	14.8	25.1	31.1	39.9	47.9	53.3	47.9	53.3
Nu 5	302	0.47	8.7	15.8	19.7	24.8	29.2	32.7	71.6	99.4
Nu 6	650	0.3	9.04	15.7	18.9	24.4	29.2	32.5	45.16	52.01
Nu 7	221	0.4	5.4	9.8	12.3	15.5	18.2	20.4	34.1	39.91
Nu 8	271	0.43	7.1	12.9	16.2	20.4	23.9	26.9	75.6	89.77

The comparison probable floods with recur 50 years, indicates that the existing urban canals are not capable of carrying the flash floods. The flood hazard will increase by the year 2015 when the asphalt covering will include all the urban areas. Table 6 shows the features of the main urban canals and the surplus peak during the 50-year recurrence floods, while according to the field measurements and through air photographs, the width of none of the main natural canals before this development was more than 20 m, and the change in these conditions brings about the peak surplus.

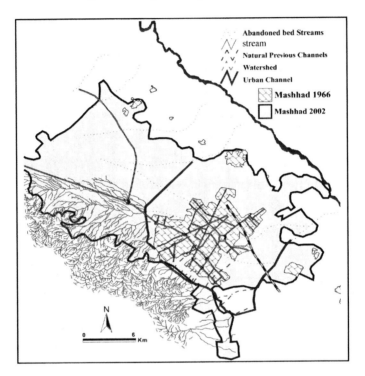

Figure 3: Map of urban development and change of the Natural drainage patterns.

Table 6: The characteristics of urban canals and non capacity for flash floods.

Water shed	Number of canal		Main canal section (m²)	Length of canal (km)	Slope of canal (%)	Surplus discharge for 50 yearly floods (m³/s)
	Secondary	Main				
Nu 1	1	1	2-9	8.25	1-2	60
Nu 2	--	1	5	2.87	3	69.9
Nu 3	2	1	6	3.75	3	78.5
Nu 4	1	1	3	3.7	2	45.5
Nu 5	1	1	6	2.43	3	48
Nu 6	--	1	4	3.92	2	33.2
Nu 7	With Nu 6		4	0.625	2	39.9
Nu 8	1	1	6	0.4	4	60.3

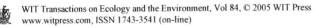

4   Conclusion

The following results can be obtained from the sum of this study:

- The residential areas on the banks of the main channels of 8 watersheds are exposed to flash floods which will probably entail the destruction of houses and deaths of residents. The main exit water passage from the mountain in these areas enters to narrow streets and the water level rise to more than 2 meters in them.
- The neighboring areas around the main urban canals in Nu1, nu2, nu3, nu5, nu6 and nu8 measuring 6/1 sq. kilometers are exposed to urban floods and the damages are mainly done on residential units, and public land uses. As these areas have been built on unstable soils, they face a high risk.
- Nearly 80 sq. kilometers of the urban area in the flood plain which now is exposed to surface water covering leads to slow movement of traffic during the annual rainfall.
- The main reason for the increase of flood potential of the city is the defect in urban design and urban drainage system which have been done with no consideration to natural environmental conditions and applies a high density of land use in these areas.
- To reduce the danger of flood, a master plan for the reduction of this danger should be taken under consideration. This plan is an interdisciplinary investigation including the following items:
- The extraction of sand and gravel resources catchments should be forbidden and all the disposed waste material in the streambeds should be evacuated. The flood control plans within the watersheds should be put into effect.
- The main canal passages inside the urban area should be reconstructed, and the channels should be led to their original natural path.
- The urban drainage system and the original natural pattern should be matched with each other.
- The density of land use, in urban texture, should be reduced and permeable surfaces increased.

References

[1]   Alizadeh. A. Applied Hydrology. Astaneghods Publisher 1989. Mashhad – Iran. P 292.
[2]   Arnold.C. L. P. J. Boston and P.C. Patton. 1982. Sawmill Brook. An example of rapid geomorphic change related to urbanization. Journal of geology 90.pp155-166.
[3]   Arnold. C. L. and C. J. Gibbons. 1996.Impervious surface coverage, the emergence of key environmental indicator Journal of the American planning Association .62(2) pp243-258
[4]   Christopher. Cumulative effects of urbanization on small stream in the Puget sound London Excoriation. Applied physics laboratory, collage of ocean and fishery sciences. University of Washington. pp 51-70.

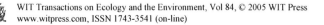

[5]   Dunne.T., Leopold. L. B. 1978. Water in environmental planning. W. H. Freeman co San Francisco, CA. USA.

[6]   Geological survey and mineral exploration of Iran. "Geological Map of Mashhad" scales 1:250000.

[7]   Gordon. N. D., Mcmahon. T. A, Finlayson. B. L.1992. Stream Hydrology, An Introduction for ecologists. John Wiley & Sons Ltd England.

[8]   Hammer. T. R. 1972. Stream channel enlargement due to urbanization. Water recurrence interval. Water Resources Research.66.pp.84-88

[9]   Hollis. G.E. 1975. The effects of urbanization on floods of different recurrence intervals. Water Resources Research. 66. pp.84-88

[10]   Hossienzade. S. R. "Environmental crises in Iranian metropolitan cities" sustainable city book 2004. Wit Press England 2004, p 183.

[11]   Hosseinzadeh. S. R. "The effects of Mashhad development on the natural drainage patterns and increase urban floods" a plan for flood control. Ferdowsi university of Mashhad. 2003.

[12]   Jahadi Toroghy Mahnaz. "Expansion of metropolises and changes in the fluvial systems in arid regions. Joint International Geomorphology conference. Abstract volume 2004 England. P 77.

[13]   Jahadi Toroghy Mahnaz. "Specifying the process of changes in precipitation and temperature of Mashhad during the 1951-94 Geographical reserch volume 54-55, 2000 Mashhad – Iran. P 154.

[14]   Keith Smith. "Environmental hazards" by Rutledge 2001 England. pp 261-265.

[15]   Klein. R. D. 1979.Urbanization and stream quality impairment. Water Resources Bulletin.15.pp 948-963

[16]   Leopold. L. B. 1968. The Hydrologic Effects of Urban land use. A Guide book of the Hydrologic effects of urban land use.USGS.554

[17]   Leopold. L. B. 1994.A view of the river. Harvard university press. Cambridge. MA.USA

[18]   Mahdavi, M. "Applied Hydrology volume 2" University of Tehran publisher. 1992. Tehran-Iran. P 108.

[19]   National cartographic center of Iran. "Air photos of Mashhad region for 1966". And topography maps of the city in 1:20000 scale for 1999.

[20]   National Geographical organization of Iran. Topographical Map of the study area in 1:5000 scales.

[21]   Paul. M.J, Meyer J.L. 2001. Streams in the urban landscape. Ann. Rev. Ecological Systems.32. pp 333-365

[22]   Remote Sensing survey of Iran "T.M land sat Images" for 2002 year.

[23]   White and Greer. "The effects of watershed urbanization on the stream hydrology and riparian vegetation of lospenasquitos, Greek, California. Landscape and Planning Journal Article in press England 2005. PP 1-2.

The role of environment in sustainable development and its relation with development management

K. Loloei
Faculty Member of Islamic Azad University, Mahallat Branch, Iran

Abstract

The desired object of national development and environment protection is nothing but improvement of the homeland in order to prepare appropriate environmental conditions for the flourishing of the intellectual and material potentials of the society. It is obvious that there is a possibility for the appearance of environmental problems in the course of the developmental process. Therefore, it has become necessary to employ engineering sciences for environment protection and to decrease the reverse effects of the civil and developmental projects on the environment to the minimum possible levels. When the development plan aims at preparation of an appropriate basis for the boom of the potential talent and capability of the society, and the increase of the life quality on a national level, the process of making an environment plan can be defined as the design of a suitable strategy for promotion of living standards on a national level, relying on the national intellectual and capital resources, with little reliance on non-native facilities. Through this paper the factor "Environment" and its role in Sustainable Development and its relation with Development Management and Planning has been studied, with due consideration of the aspects concerned.
Keywords: sustainable development, development management, environment management.

1 Preamble

For a long time, civil residences as residential complexes have been affected by factors all originating from human societies. It is not irrelevant if we say that human beings have had some plans for their residences, but these plans were different in different times and places from many years ago. What we are going to study through this paper is the plans made in recent centuries. From the beginning of the twentieth century, the changes in human ecology have had effects on the traditional civil geography, and drawn the attention of this branch of geography from the fatalistic school of geography to the local differences [1].

Of course, the changes in the trends and plans are not limited to this era and this case. Parallel to fast social and economic changes, started from several centuries ago, the changes in the trends and plans have occurred with considerable speed in recent centuries. The plans originating from the changes in trends have numerous and specific varieties. Through this paper we do not deal with all the changes in geography, urban planning and environment domains, but we study some specific subjects. For instance, after 1950, Amos Howly, in his writings under the title Human Ecology, emphasized on human life generality and defined, in his book, the shape and structural development of the society as a general harmony of a group of people with their own environment. In fact the theories of Amos Howly moot the ecological theories of our time in Sociology [1, p 8].

2   Factors of stability or instability inside the ecological social systems

The development (and sometimes growth) of homeland and residences has always been one of the most usual and lasting models of human beings. In order to achieve such goals, individuals and society have had plans and activities. As to stability or instability inside the present ecological social systems, four factors are emphasized in general, i.e.:
- Population;
- Technology;
- Structure of the System (Organization); and
- Environment.

These four variable factors have some interrelationships as well [1, p 9].

In order to present a perfect definition for these four factors we have no alternative but to return to the said reference and to define the same from the viewpoint of the writer:
- Population: Human Ecology studies the common interrelationships among human groups and environment. Increase or decrease of the number of human groups determines the degree of competition for occupying the residence space [1, p 11]. Movement and motion are among the specifications of population that are investigated in urban ecology in different ways like Study of permanent population, transitory population, movements inside cities, between city and suburbs, quality of urban population, etc [1, p 11].
- Technology: Harmony between human and environment is achieved by technology. Technology gives power to human beings to make their environment in compliance with their own desires. This power is limited to the capabilities of the technology employed [1, p 11].

- Organization or System Structure: Organization or system structure is a decisive factor in ecological complexes. Organization or system structure covers all social – economic relationships of human groups [1, p 12].
- Environment: Population lives in a natural environment. Natural environment means climate, natural resources, plant and animal life, topography and natural phenomena.

Human groups need harmony with their natural environment for survival [1, p 13].

As per the above description, human environment as one of the very important and vital factors of social ecological systems is defined in form of social systems only, and it is understood that such complexes that are separated from the pertinent natural factors will be abstract, subjective and unreal.

As to the development of human residences we must pay special attention to environmental factors. As a rule none of the said four factors has more priority than others. They are strongly related to each other. These interrelations are sometimes weak or strong. The subject that is known as Sustainable Development is based on an economic system, and this economic system was modified in its content, methodology, and main objective during different eras [2, p 10].

By sustainable development it is necessary to meet today's needs without making any limitation for future generations in meeting their needs. In fact, sustainable development emphasizes a balanced relationship between social and economic growth on the one hand and environmental needs on the other [3, p 237].

3   Environmental problems in the route of growth and development

As per the traditional theory, growth means industrialization and industrialization is a synonym for growth of urban areas. Arthur Lois, according to his theory, believes that growth is a result of the transfer of extra labor power from rural sectors to the urban industrial sector. In compliance with such a definition it is clearly observable that environment and natural resources will be sacrificed as a result of industrialization. The situation in underdeveloped countries and developing countries has become worse since the second half of the twentieth century. After World War II, some of the capital cities gained the title of the most polluted regions in the world, for example Mexico City for air pollution, Bombay (India) for solid garbage and Manila (The Philippines) for water pollution achieved the first rank in the world [2, p 73]. Urban garbage and untreated wastewater are specifications of most of cities. During the last twenty-five years, in developed/industrial countries the demand for clean water, soil and air has been increased. But the endeavors unfortunately have not been very effective and considerable [2, pp 73–74].

4 Solutions

The complexity of the problems on the route of development and useless planning in different countries has made these countries become hopeless in planning for some domains and to submit themselves to destiny, interim and short-term plans. On the other hand, lack of a clear definition from the function and duties of each operating unit and unspecific role and legal stand of the said (governmental or private) units have led to severe damages to the organization or system of these countries. Therefore, according to the present circumstances, it seems that the only solution for development problems is the creation of harmony among all legal sectors. As to Environment Management in particular, close cooperation between government and industrial sectors (private sectors) makes the performance of environmental laws and regulations easier in developing countries [2, p 75]. Many of these countries have hot jungles, marginal lands, mountains and large deserts with areas of thousands of sq. miles in their territories and they can protect these natural capitals under the title of Protected Zones from the destructive business operations of the residents of such zones [2, p 94].

Indeed, cooperation between government and industrial sector and other economic sectors shall not mean the direct interference of government and execution of projects by government, but a large number of the advocators of Sustainable Development support less governmental comprehensive business planning, ownership and supervision on industrial and agricultural sectors [2, p 140].

In fact, governments must make the general policy of development in different economic sectors such as industry and natural resources. By forming the governmental policies for achievement of such a goal we will need natural resources accounting and resource management and planning. In other words, natural resources and environment planning shall be on the basis of an accounting system, by which the governmental authorities will be able to calculate and scrutinize the environmental effects and reverse effects of economic operations such as energy consumption and the like on natural resources [2, p 141].

As one of the profits arising from planning for national or global natural resources in the form of regional plans, a plan for national resources must include and cover the various effects of economic operation on environment and natural resources and the counter effects among environmental assets [2, p 142].

On the other hand, Sustainable Development can be defined as a return to nature after one century ruling of industrialization, trade and urbanism, as the indices of national development [2, p 27].

The protection of environment and natural resources is a very important point in any economic development plan [2, p 27]. We can define the counter effect of basic natural resources and the economic system as a flow of the existing natural resources toward the process of production, consumption and return of waste products to basic natural resources [2, p 30].

Although it is impossible to increase the natural resources of the globe, it is possible to increase and optimize their productivity:

a)   Growth of natural resources and increase of utilization in comparison with each reserved unit of natural resources.

b)   Increase of goods and services produced and supplied by one unit of natural resources.

c)   Increase of efficiency of goods produced by natural resources for final consumption [2, p 30].

Most of the advocates of environment emphasize the subject of sustainability on the basis of the capacity of the basic natural resources in order to protect and increase the level of human welfare according to the amount of the marketable and unmarketable goods and services [2, p 32]. First of all it must be mentioned that "Sustainability as an economic concept shall not be defined as a physical concept such as reinstatement and protection of all natural resources [2, pp 33-35]. For definition and in operative stage, we must study the detailed items carefully and to express an operative definition for each item. Therefore, in order to analyze Sustainable Development, we must study the following three types of resources independently:

1-   Global Resources

2-   Recyclable Natural Resources

3-   Non-recyclable Natural Resources.

Although all development plans on a universal level have similar objectives, there is no detailed plan that guarantees regional sustainable development in all countries. Short-term reforms such as the supply of credits, promotion of agricultural exports, supply of capital in the form of infrastructure installations, wide irritation projects, and the performance of developmental projects in marginal districts and lands have not been very successful in promoting sustainable development. Therefore, every single area and district requires its research, experiences and experiments in order to determine successful operations in the course of time [2, p 94].

5   The community's culture: the way of energy consumption and environment protection

It is obvious that pollution is a result of population increase, but the increase of population is not the sole cause of pollution. Pollution appears when people start using energy sources and materials. Under such circumstances, the degree of pollution will depend on the way people use different resources and the type of technology employed. The recent factor shows the amount of pollution resulting from the utilization of each unit of resources by each individual [4]

To estimate pollution or environmental changes, as a result of the consumption of resources by human beings, a pattern is offered. As per this pattern pollution is related to the following three factors:

-   Number of people (population)

- Amount of the concerned resource utilized by each person
- Pollution resulting from utilization of each unit of resources.

Pollution (environmental changes) = Number of people (x) amount of resource utilized by each person (x) pollution resulted from utilization of each unit of resources [4, p 18].

But the number of people is not the sole factor in the appearance of pollution. The way the population is distributed has a key and effective role in pollution. The worst form of air and water pollution appears when a large number of people are living in a city. On the other hand, population will have a bad effect on land. Economic, political and moral factors must be added to the above pattern. It is possible to control pollution through economic methods by including the pollution control expenses in cost price of products. In this way, pollution will be controlled by making effective regulations tactfully. In any event, all efforts for pollution control through amending economic and political patterns will be null and void until the time an active political group reaches this point; that the unbalanced utilization of our living system is irrational and immoral [4, p 25].

6 Conclusion

Analysis of the natural resources and environmental problems and subjects, together with the original classification of plans and programs, expresses the necessity for evaluation of plans, from an environmental point of view, by governments and international supporting organizations. These evaluations must be conducted before approving the plans and programs and are more comprehensive than a usual project evaluation.

In any case, Sustainable Development deals with the subject beyond (minor) private plans and projects. Certainly we need Comprehensive Development Policies for section of governmentally supported plans and projects and in order to encourage the private sector to observe the requirements of Sustainable Development [2, p 115].

It will be a sign of inexperience, if we accept that technology is the first cause of pollution. Modern technology is not always harmful. Many techniques have been employed to protect and preserve the environment and natural resources since World War II. Their benefits are as follows:

- Substitution of rare resources
- Optimization of the ways of utilization of resources
- Removing a large amount of pollution
- Presenting products with less contaminating danger instead of previously used products [4, p 20].

To globalize the idea of employing Appropriate Technology is a logical way for employing technology. Advanced and modern technology is great, complex, concentrated and expensive and intends to use machines instead of humans. But Appropriate Technology is small, simple, not concentrated and inexpensive. It emphasizes the following subjects:

- Application of small and interfacial machinery which are useable and easily repairable.

- Application of producing methods that aim at the protection of materials and energy and making little pollution.
- To assist human societies to reach self-sufficiency by getting benefit from the local materials and capabilities in order to make their required products [4, p 23].

References

[1] Shakoui, Hossein – *Social Geography of Cities*, Tehran, Jihad Daneshgahi Publication, Page 7

[2] Raymond F. Mixcel – *Economic Growth & Environment*, Translated by Hamid Reza Arbab, Tehran, Plan & Budget Organization Publications

[3] Badkoubi, Ahmad, "Environment Education for Achievement of Sustainable Development", *Lectures and Essays presented to Environment, Religion and Culture_International Congress*, Environment Protection Organization, Tehran, 2001

[4] G. T. Miller, *Living in Environment*, translated by Majid Makhdoum, Tehran, Tehran University Publications, Page 17

Environmental management and planning in urban regions – are there differences between growth and shrinkage?

U. Weiland, M. Richter & H. D. Kasperidus
UFZ Environmental Research Centre Leipzig-Halle, Germany

Abstract

The question is whether the different processes in the development of growing and shrinking urban regions implicate the necessity to adjust and to differentiate between traditional environmental management and planning concepts. It is argued that urban planning in growing and shrinking urban regions does not require completely different planning procedures but locally adjusted solutions with better integration of sustainability issues. This paper briefly presents a conceptual approach that proposes a better integration of sustainability principles in planning processes by the categories *space management*, *resource management*, *spatio-temporal management* and *process management*. These categories will allow for complementing existing formal planning instruments with strategic, economic, and participatory approaches.
Keywords: urban shrinkage, urban growth, environmental management, environmental planning.

1   Introduction

At the beginning of the 21st century more than half of the global population is living in cities and urban regions, many of them in agglomerations. This major trend of global urbanisation is expected to continue during the next decades [1]. Urbanisation is related with multiple other issues of global change like changes in economic structures as well as in social and political structures and of cause with changes in environmental conditions. Facing the structural change from industrialized to service-oriented and information-based society, current urban functions are in continuous process of decline and reorganisation and/or revitalisation. International finance transfers and modified price building procedures produce modified conditions and expectations in the regional division of labour. From this point of view growth and shrinkage are two sides of one coin. They represent different facets of the dynamic processes in urban development. Therefore, in many cities growth and shrinkage processes appear simultaneously.

Many cities and urban regions spread out due to business cycle expansion and the increase of jobs, commercial zones, inhabitants, and the resulting additional needs for space. Metropolitan areas grow more and faster than small and medium-sized cities and towns outside of metropolitan areas. The new urban structures of growing cities have been described as "inter-cities" [2], "regional cities" [3] or "network-cities" [4] connected with the request to acknowledge the chances they imply. In economic less favoured urban regions, cities loose jobs and inhabitants, gain derelict areas and fallow fields; the result has been discussed as "perforated cities" [5].

Obviously, the management of land use is insufficient – despite sometimes polished urban and landscape planning systems, and thus not only in Europe [6]. Government structures of agglomerations are often dissipated, and especially in fast growing agglomerations often not existent on the regional level. Thus, environmental problems cannot be solved in a regional context [7].

The formal planning forms are loosing importance given the "withdrawal of the state". As economic processes speed up, the authorities have to act and react faster in planning processes. As more people participate in planning processes with the aim of safeguarding their interests, both the planning processes and the planning culture are changing. The importance of formal plans is being relegating by negotiations and bargaining between the administrations and investors as well as other private actors. Because growth and shrinkage processes occur simultaneously in most of the European urban regions – despite differences in the economic status and priorities in urban development strategies – locally adjusted approaches to urban development are required, that contribute to the guideline of "sustainable urban development".

2 Environmental consequences of urban growth and shrinkage

Due to changes in production, household-structures and life styles, *suburbanisation* occurs in most urban regions, whether they are economically prospering or not. Suburbanisation is combined with an increase of individual transport and tangential traffic movements; between the growth of urban regions and the increase of traffic and resulting environmental problems exist a vicious circle. Although the average environmental pollution partly decreases in shrinking (parts of) urban regions due to the decline of economic activities and the loss of inhabitants, and although valuable wildlife areas can arise from wastelands [8], environmental loads remain substantial.

From an environmental point of view, suburbanisation, i.e. the *networking* of cities, causes a *fragmentation* of nature and landscapes, the transformation of habitats into different forms of land use and the loss of natural areas. Urban

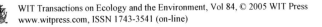

sprawl and new traffic lines raise surface sealing, the dissection and loss of wildlife habitats as well as air and water pollution, and additional noise. Furthermore, suburbanisation impedes a considerate use of resources as well as resource sparing supply and disposal technologies.

Urban regions are "importers" and "intermediate stores" [9] of large masses and a large variety of resources [10]. The quantitatively most important fluxes are those of energy, water, food, and building materials. Because recycling processes exist barely, warmth, waste water, garbage, and waste air are deposit, pass through the urban environmental systems and cause local, regional, and partly global environmental problems. Urban regions contribute to the increase of greenhouse gases and thus to climatic change at a considerable amount [11].

Recent societal changes are connected with an acceleration of economic and societal processes. Between spatial and temporal structures exist dense but to date hardly recognized linkages; the changes with regard to time (speeding-up, just-in-time-production etc.) have a major influence on spatial structures

3 Environmentally sustainable development as basic principle of environmental urban management and planning

Despite environmental loads and structural problems, the urban style of dwelling with a high density of buildings is more environmentally sound than rural settlements or suburbs with respect to the average land and resource use per person. As there is no alternative to cities and urban regions, conceptual frameworks and approaches are required to make their *environmentally sustainable development* possible.

Environmentally sustainable development is a subset of sustainable development [12] that concentrates on the environmental issues with their related procedures and institutional structures. Environmentally sustainable development also comprises an ethical imperative: justice in the shared use of the environment; e.g. balancing the environmental quality against resource use is one of its basic elements. Moreover, environmentally sustainable development has to consider following basic principles [13]:

- *consistency* that balances societal and economic use of resources against the carrying capacity of the environment,
- an increase in the *efficiency* of resource use, and
- *sufficiency*, i.e. change of lifestyles as well as resource wasting consumption and production patterns.
- Institutional aspects comprise organisational and procedural aspects including the actors, who promote and materialise an environmentally sustainable development.

4 Research and action fields of environmental urban development

Transferring the general concept of environmentally sustainable development to environmental urban development requires a conceptual framework for relevant

research and action fields [14]. They can be classified by the dimensions they address:
- *Space management* in a two-dimensional or spatial view,
- *Resource management* in a three-dimensional or "functional" view,
- *Spatio-temporal management* in a four-dimensional view, and
- *Process management* in a "five-dimensional" or procedural view.

Consistency, Efficiency and Sufficiency are relevant objectives of space, resource and spatio-temporal management; institutional aspects are relevant for the process management. They all are relevant for both, growing and shrinking urban regions, though with different priorities, that have to be defined by the local communities.

4.1 Space management

In order to reduce environmental pressures and maintain the environmental carrying capacity, an effective steering of land use requires space management. Space management is the data-based activity to monitor and align the patterns of land use and land(scape) functions to the desired goals. Criteria that should be considered in *quantitative space management* include aspects like:
- density of buildings and mixture of uses,
- re-use and recycling of building areas as well as commercial and industrial wastelands, and
- compensation of the land utilization for housing, industrial, commercial, and traffic zones.

In many European regions new settlements like family houses, commercial zones and shopping centres are destroying natural and semi-natural landscapes; a process that should be controlled by legislative orders. In old industrial areas which are now abandoned, another problem predominates: Due to a high density of buildings with high percentages of soil-sealing there is a lack of greenspaces for the inhabitants in their surroundings. Within a city quarter a good balance between open space (especially urban green areas) for recreation and urban density has to be found [15].

A *qualitative space management* aims at the careful and environmentally sound use of surface and soil. Not only has the land use itself to be taken into account, but also its functionality and the drivers of its use intensity.

Several *approaches* to space management in regional and urban planning already exist. Spatial and environmental plans classify areas and place constraints on land use. Regional plans control land use e.g. by defining priority, provisory, and suitability areas. Large cities attempt space management in their surroundings, which includes open spaces in "Regional Parks". However, this list is by far not complete. In the summary, these instruments cover only parts of a space management; research needs still remain. The existing approaches to space management have to be extended at regional and local scales in the following aspects:
- *Co-operative development of guidelines for sustainable land use:* Land use guidelines allow for steering towards sustainable development; they should serve as base for land use decisions. They should meet and make more

explicit the basic principles consistency, efficiency, and sufficiency. Finding them in co-operative processes by the discussion of all relevant societal groups enhances their acceptability.

- *Consideration of environmental, health and nature protection aspects by environmental planning:* a space management towards an environmentally sustainable development requires also an integrative handling of environmental, health and nature protection aspects and their consideration in spatial planning. A process of segregation according to income and ethnical groups can be observed in many cities [16]. The result is that the people with higher income are living in areas with better environmentally quality whereas the poorer people are living in environmentally less favoured areas e.g. in houses along the main roads. Due to this effect on health controlled by the household income, there is the need to consider and define minimum standards for the environmental conditions in urban regions as a social aspect of spatial planning.

- *Open space networks and habitat systems* are useful for both nature protection and human recreation purposes in all cities and urban regions.

- *Use of economic instruments:* an effective control of land use requires supplements to spatial planning and a change in the general conditions of planning. The *general* steering of land use can be managed efficiently by economic instruments, e.g. financial incentives, taxes and contracts with private investors or actors. The spatial plans then serve as framework for the *detailed, spatial development.*

- *Development of a land use register:* To date, the real land use and its intensity often cannot be stated exactly, because an adequate procedure, allowing for a periodical gathering of recent information on land use changes, is missing. Detailed information on the density and distribution of building structures, open spaces and technical infrastructure are a basic prerequisite for a land use management towards environmentally sustainable development. In the complex research area of monitoring land use changes, there was a good progress during the last twenty years so that we can hope to have good monitoring procedures on a high spatial resolution within the near future.

The measures presented above are challenges for spatial and environmental planning, because they partly require new organisational structures and instruments, and a close co-operation of spatial and environmental planning administrations.

4.2 Resource management

Subject to resource management conceptions are not only the resource uses in cities and urban regions, but also the exchange processes of resources between (urban) regions partly on global scale [17].

Main objective of a *quantitative resource management* is the reduction of use, fluxes, and emission of materials, energy and waste (materials, air, water). Beyond that, the potential risks of materials and energy should be taken into account by a *qualitative resource management.*

Aspects of resource management have been realized e.g. by pilot projects, by industrial re-use of resources and recycling products. Also sale and sales promotion of regional products are part of a resource management. But until yet, the perspectives and constraints of a resource management in cities and urban regions have not yet been investigated systematically. Details of an urban-regional resource management are still unclear, but the general need for development can be characterised as follows:

- *Co-operative identification of guidelines for sustainable resource management:* the carrying capacity, the efficiency of resource use and the sufficiency in lifestyles can serve as basic principles for the use of resources by production, housing, and consumption.
- Elaboration of *material and energy flux analyses* [18] that allow for accounting and assessing the resource uses and setting priorities to actions.
- *Development of an equivalent data base*: To date, information on material and energy fluxes in and between urban regions is barely available. In order to construct a resource management system at affordable costs, the most important material and energy fluxes have to be identified and monitored.
- *Involvement of the resource user:* Because the producer and the consumer use resources, a resource management system should integrate both groups, and both should be involved in the development of a resource management system. Here, the gap between the people's knowledge about environmental problems and their behavioural consequences have to be taken into account.

The development and implementation of a resource management system will be difficult, because the expansion of functional networks, the European integration and globalisation processes cause international and global transfers of goods and economical pressure on companies and households. Material and energy fluxes are linked to an extent that it is necessary to identify which products and materials can be subject to an urban-regional resource management in an effective way.

4.3 Spatio-temporal management

The time span of several generations, which is relevant to environmental precautions and long-term stability, and which is a basic part of the sustainable development concept, is not adequately grasped by standard policy-making as well as in business planning and urban and regional planning; they realise mostly short-term up to mid-term time horizons. However: trying to take into consideration the long-term perspective causes considerable epistemological, conceptual and methodological problems because the future development of urban systems is unpredictable and therefore planning activities often fail to anticipate unexpected events, trends and developments. To deal with such problems and with long-term perspectives in complex systems is a domain of future research which supplies a set of methods designed to support the process of thinking about the future, of forecasting and of analysing global change [19]. The analysis of related spatial and temporal structures should take into account the relationships between societal time and spatial use in order to optimise both mutually in all development and planning tasks.

A mapping of the spatio-temporal uses of land and infrastructure can document uses and their intensity dependent on where and when they happen, so that both, "under-use" and "over-use" can be identified. The analysis and documentation of use intensities will deliver the necessary, basic information to steer towards a balance or compensation of use intensities.

Especially in shrinking urban regions we find new, temporarily limited categories of land use (e.g. beach volleyball or sheep grazing on fallow land within the city) [20]. This new land use concepts emerge out of the needs of cities inhabitants together with special opportunities (unused land in shrinking cities). A new approach of spatial-temporal management therefore has to take into account that these new land use concepts often are organized from the inhabitants living nearby in a bottom-up approach.

A *"policy of time"* could help to find long-term perspectives for cities or urban regions that allow for steering the urban development towards an environmentally sustainable development.

4.4 Process management

The shift in importance from formal state-planning to informal project-planning and public-private partnerships requires an adjustment of the organizational structures and instruments of spatial and environmental planning – and especially the introduction of a *management procedure* including the setting of objectives, monitoring, and controlling. In order to develop projects within the framework of environmentally sustainable development, a management approach to planning and supplementing instruments is required (Fig. 1):

- *Strategic orientation of planning:* a planning, that is realised by many actors, is a political and especially a communication process. In order to facilitate a democratic control of negotiations and results, planning processes need a strategic orientation of planning at all political levels. A national strategy for (environmentally) sustainable development can supplement regional and local strategies, containing guidelines, principles, aims, and targets of environmentally sustainable development.
- *Vertical co-operation:* a vertical co-operation and co-ordination between the different political levels - the international, national, Land, regional and local level - is necessary. This vertical co-operation is well known in formal spatial planning as "feedback-principle"; it should be transferred to and used by informal planning, regional development initiatives and agenda initiatives, too.
- *Horizontal co-operation and co-ordination:* formal planning, informal planning and development as well as the activities of regional and local agenda 21-initiatives should be co-ordinated in order to avoid divergences between political and planning activities as well as inefficacy and inefficiency in planning.
- *Evaluation and control:* the „de-formalisation" of planning requires monitoring and assessment of spatial development results with sustainability indicators. This evaluation shall allow for control, whether the economic,

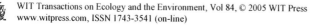

social, environmental and cultural development meets the requirements of environmentally sustainable development.

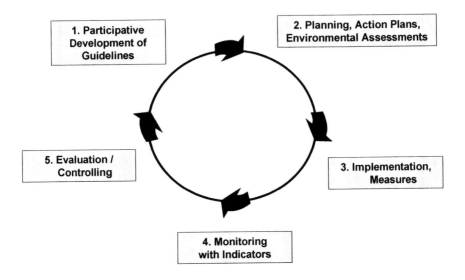

Figure 1: Management cycle as central element of process management.

5 Conclusions

Despite the differences between growing and shrinking cities and urban regions, environmental problems remain severe in many areas of both. The mixture of growth and shrinkage in the same city and urban region does not require completely different approaches, but locally adjusted solutions. Temporarily limited new land use categories in shrinking cities are organized preferably in a bottom-up approach by the inhabitants and therefore are *not planned* in a traditionally sense of the word *planning* Developing space, resource and spatio-temporal management and a new process-oriented and co-operative planning culture requires interdisciplinary and trans-disciplinary work and research. We are at the beginning of this process where the formal instruments have to be complemented by new participatory approaches using strategic as well as economic approaches. A strategic orientation of planning, that encompasses a strategy for sustainability, with aims and target concepts at all political levels can provide guidelines to decisions and help to legitimise the results of negotiations. The application in practice will show if this approach is successful.

References

[1]   United Nations, World Urbanization Prospects – The 1999 Revision. Population Division, Department of Economic and Social Affairs, United Nations Secretariat, 2001.

[2]   Sieverts, T., Zwischenstadt. Bauwelt Fundamente 118. Braunschweig/Wiesbaden, 1996.

[3]   Sieverts, T., Die Stadt in der Zweiten Moderne, eine europäische Perspektive. In: Informationen zur Raumentwicklung nr. 7/8, pp. 455-473, 1998

[4]   Baccini, P. & Oswald, F. (eds.), Netzstadt. Transdisziplinäre Methoden zum Umbau urbaner Systeme. ORL + EAWAG, ETH Zürich. Zürich, 1998.

[5]   Lütke Daldrup, E., Die perforierte Stadt – Eine Versuchsanordnung. In: Keim, K.-D. (ed.): Regenerierung schrumpfender Städte – zur Umbaudebatte in Ostdeutschland. REGIOtransfer 1. Erkner, pp. 193-203, p. 198, 2001.

[6]   Bengston, D.N., Fletcher, J.O., Nelson, K.C., Public Policies for Managing Urban Growth and Protecting Open Space: Policy Instruments and Lessons learned in the United States. In: Landscape and Urban Planning 69, pp. 271 – 286, 2004.

[7]   Atkinson, A., Dávila, J.D., Fernandes, E., Mattingly, M. (eds.), The Challenge of Environmental Management in Urban Areas. Ashgate. Aldershot, p. 5., 1999.

[8]   Herbst, H., The Importance of Wastelands as Urban Wildlife Areas - with Particular Reference to the Cities Leipzig and Birmingham. UFZ-Bericht nr. 2. Leipzig, 2003.

[9]   Baccini, P. & Bader, H.P., Regionaler Stoffhaushalt. Spektrum Akademischer Verlag. Heidelberg, 1996.

[10]   Chambers, N., Simmons, C., Wackernagel, M., Sharing Nature's Interest, Ecological Footprints as an Indicator of Sustainability. Earthscan, London and Sterling, 2001.

[11]   Dávila; J.D. & Atkinson, A., Organisation and Politics in Urban Environmental Management. In: Atkinson et al., The Challenge of Environmental Management in Urban Areas. Ashgate. Aldershot, pp. 193-202, 1999.

[12]   WCED (World Commission on Environment and Development), Our Common Future. Oxford University Press, New York, 1987.

[13]   Weiland, U., Environmentally Sustainable Development of Cities and Urban Regions - Challenges for Spatial and Environmental Planning. In: Bastian, O. und Steinhardt, U. (eds.): Development and Perspectives in Landscape Ecology - Conceptions, Methods, Application. Kluwer Academic Publishers. Dordrecht/Boston/London, pp. 397-189.

[14]   Tjallingii, S.P., Ecopolis: Strategies for Ecologically Sound Urban Development. Backhuys Publishers, Leiden, 1995.

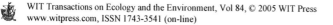

[15] URGE-Team, Making Greener Cities – A Practical Guide, UFZ-Bericht Nr. 8, Stadtökologische Forschungen Nr. 37, UFZ Leipzig-Halle GmbH (Leipzig), 2004.

[16] Tönnies, G., Demographischer Wandel in Großstadtregionen. In: ARL Nachrichten 3, pp. 47 – 48, 2004.

[17] Atkinson, A., Dávila, J.D., Fernandes, E., Mattingly, M. (eds.), The Challenge of Environmental Management in Urban Areas. Ashgate. Aldershot, p. 3., 1999.

[18] Haberl, H., Fischer-Kowalski, M., Krausmann, F., Weisz, H., Winiwarter, V., Progress Towards Sustainability? What the Conceptual Framework of Material and Energy Flow Accounting (MEFA) can offer. In: Land Use Policy 21, pp. 199 – 213, 2004.

[19] Glenn, J.C. & Gordron, T.J., Futures Research Methodology – Version 2.0. American Council for the United Nations University, Washington, DC. The Millennium Project, CD-ROM, 2003.

[20] Bundesamt für Bauwesen und Raumordnung (ed.), Zwischennutzung und neue Freiflächen. Städtische Lebensräume der Zukunft. Berlin, 2004.

Can we plan to protect our environment? Spreading urbanization in the state of Louisiana

I. Maret & H. Blakeman
College of Urban and Public Affairs, University of New Orleans, USA

Abstract

Accused of being the dark side of the American Dream, sprawl illustrates how spreading urbanization can be costly for our environment, our society and our future. In most studies, sprawl is approached broadly and limited to the edge of large and fast-growing urban areas. Current analyses underestimate the extent of the development of new urban forms in previously rural areas relatively far from the urban core, especially in slow-growing urban regions. Sprawl is endemic to small towns as well as large cities, spurred largely by interstate and highway bypasses. This paper suggests that sprawl should be scrutinized as a complicated and diverse land use change. It explicates with GIS and remote sensing approaches the variety and complexity of urban sprawl regions in Louisiana, using population and land use data. This research focuses on the characteristics of new urban forms in the region of New Orleans, Louisiana (LA), looking particularly at St. Tammany Parish. This parish grew at a faster rate in the nineteen-nineties than any other parish in Louisiana. Most of the growth occurred in unplanned, uncoordinated clusters or in unincorporated areas outside of existing cities. This paper examines the consequences of sprawl on the environment, focusing on the link between types of urbanization and the loss of wetlands in St. Tammany Parish, LA, from 1982 to 2000. It then analyzes the diversity of smart growth policies needed to deal with these sprawling situations.
Keywords: sprawl, sustainable planning, wetlands, urban growth, smart growth policies, Geographic Information Systems (GIS).

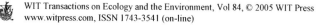

1   Introduction

Sprawl, the major urbanization pattern of the 20th century, not only occurs on the edge of major fast-growing metropolitan areas like Houston and Atlanta, but also in slow-growing urban regions. Hence, this fragmented urban land use landscape is witnessed in the relatively slow-growing urban region of New Orleans, Louisiana. The New Orleans metropolitan area (MSA) is composed of 8 parishes (counties) surrounding Lake Ponchartrain (Figure 1). Table 1 shows that the central parish in the region, Orleans Parish, lost population between 1990 and 2000, while most of the other parishes experienced some growth.

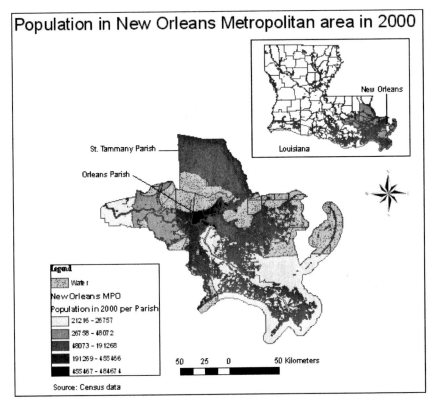

Figure 1:   Population in New Orleans MSA.

Between 1990 and 2000, St. Tammany Parish experienced the fastest growth within New Orleans MSA and in the entire State of Louisiana, as its population grew by 32.4% and another 8.6 % between 2000 and 2003. Most of this growth took place outside of towns. St. Tammany's new constructions are usually composed of piecemeal subdivisions and isolated malls standing outside the geographical jurisdiction, and therefore out of the planning and regulatory influence of local governments.

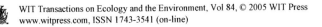

Table 1:   Population trends in New Orleans.

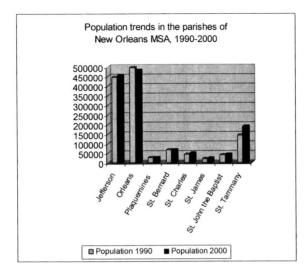

Barras, *et al.* [1] found that at the same time, the State of Louisiana is losing 24 square miles of wetlands each year. Originally considered as wastelands, wetlands have since been proven to be productive habitats for flora and fauna. In Louisiana alone, 50 % of the residents live in coastal parishes, according to the US Census Bureau [2]. Since the majority of Louisiana's wetlands are located in the coastal zone, this coastal urbanization further stresses these sensitive wetland habitats.

Researchers working on sprawl often focus on its definition and its localization.   This work will first analyze, with a GIS approach, the patterns of urban growth in St. Tammany Parish. We will then investigate the relationship between types of urbanization and the degradation and destruction of very valuable natural resources, wetlands. Finally, the analysis will frame a discussion on possible policy responses.

2   Why should we study spreading urbanization and its consequences on wetlands loss?

Unplanned urban spread began to be a major affliction for many cities in the 20th century. Christened "sprawl," this urban growth pattern is accused of being costly not only for local governments, but also for public health and the environment. Malpezzi [3], Ewing *et al.* [4], Gordon and Richardson [5], Galster *et al.* [6], are attempting to capture the nature and extent of the new urban landscape. Characterized by Harvey and Clark [7] as a spreading urban pattern at declining densities, it has the distinction of consuming land for urban purposes at a pace exceeding the rate of population growth.   Ewing states that it uses excessive space in a disorderly manner and at declining densities, with a leapfrogging behavior, jumping into the hinterland, and forcing infrastructures to catch up. Downs [8] cites some of its consequences, among them the fragmentation of open space, the automobile dependence, and the increase of air pollution.

Few researchers are investigating the relationship between sprawl and the loss of wetlands. Ehrenfeld [9] confirms the link between land-based urbanization and the destruction of wetlands, decline in water quality and food chain contamination in the Gulf of St. Vincent, Australia. The federal Clean Water Act (CWA) [10] defined "wetlands" as those areas that are inundated or saturated by surface or ground water at a frequency and duration sufficient to support, and that under normal circumstances do support, a prevalence of vegetation typically adapted for life in saturated soil conditions. Wetlands generally include swamps, marshes, bogs and similar areas. These habitats are vital for protecting the environment and public health. Some of their assets are to filter pollution, purify our drinking water, recharge groundwater aquifers, and absorb floodwaters. This last quality is particularly important in flood-prone areas like South Louisiana. In 1999, the General Accounting Office [11] estimated that approximately 290,000 acres of wetlands are nationally lost per year. National Research Council data [12] shows that since the 1700s, New York has lost more than 60% of its estimated original 2.562 million acres of wetlands. We present in this analysis the relationship between types of urbanization and the loss of wetlands in St. Tammany Parish between 1982 and 2000. Since sprawl thrives on new highway construction, we will also assess the influence of roads on wetland destruction.

3 Sprawl and wetland destruction in St. Tammany Parish

3.1 Localization of wetland loss in St. Tammany Parish

Though the central and northern parts of Louisiana are still somewhat rural, the southeast portion of the state has become increasingly urbanized, especially along the two corridors of Interstate 10 and Interstate 12. Most of Louisiana's large cities are in or near the Coastal Zone, which is influenced by the Gulf of Mexico and contains the majority of Louisiana's wetlands. Lafayette, Baton Rouge, New Orleans, Hammond, Slidell and Mandeville are all in or adjacent to the Coastal Zone. Many of the urban regions of the Coastal Zone are expanding their impervious surface area in gargantuan bites, resulting in an increasing pressure on wetlands in and near urban areas. St. Tammany Parish, in the period 1982 and 2000, most of which is in the Coastal Zone, provides the most dramatic example.

Figure 2 illustrates the urban and habitat changes between 1982 and 2000. Within these 18 years, urbanization has exploded. In the western portion of the parish, the most radical growth took place in the Mandeville/Covington area. The area north of Mandeville and the strip between Highway 190 and Interstate 12 show the most dramatic increases. The City of Mandeville itself experienced a 48% increase in population between 1990 and 2000. As a result, the urban regions of Mandeville and Covington are progressively merging and the area is losing its rural identity. Mandeville also expanded along the coastline of Lake Ponchartrain, building on upland forest, wetland forests and marshes. In the Slidell area, less dramatic patches of growth occurred between Interstate 12 and the Pearl River wetland area. Most of the growth is occurring directly to the east of the city, along Highway 190. This expansion of the built environment continues above Interstate 12, hugging the edge of the Pearl River wetlands to the north. Despite clustering around incorporated areas, it is clear that spreading urbanization did not ignore St. Tammany's outlying extremities. The unincorporated areas between Mandeville, Madisonville, Covington and Abita Springs experienced major increases of their urban landscapes. The remote sensing imagery illustrates the highly fragmented pattern of urban development.

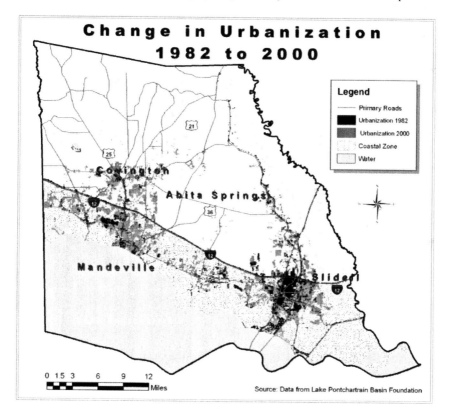

Figure 2:   Urban change in St. Tammany Parish between 1982 and 2000.

3.2 Spatial patterns of wetland loss

According to the Lake Ponchartrain Basin Foundation [13], between 1982 and 2000, 11,000 acres of marsh and nearly 34,000 acres of wetland forests were destroyed. In areas where the wetlands are not being eliminated, urbanization butts up to the edge. While this does not destroy the wetlands, urban pressure can degrade wetlands over time, rendering them uninhabitable for flora and fauna. Figure 3 presents the localization of wetlands converted to urbanization between 1982 and 2000. The comparison between Figure 2 and Figure 3 illustrates the relationship between scattered urbanization and the destruction of marsh and wetland forest.

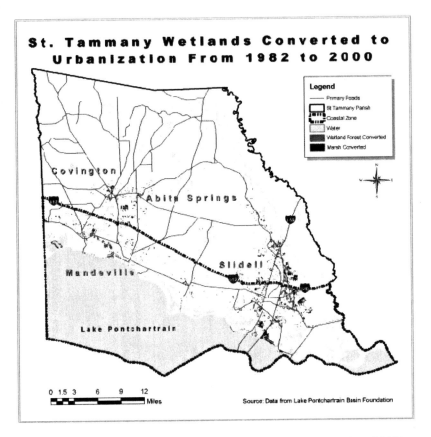

Figure 3:   Wetlands converted to urbanization between 1982 and 2000.

Most of the destruction of wetlands is located in or next to urbanized areas. The conversion pattern is highly patchy, demonstrating the fragmentation of the urbanization. The wetland division also follows the main road corridors, especially in the northern part of Slidell.

4 Does sprawl lead to more wetland loss?

Many researchers offer methods, indexes, and models to quantify sprawl. Mapelzzi and Guo [14] conduct their analysis at a specific time. Hess *et al.* [15], and Galster *et al.* [6] focus their research on the study of the edge of major metropolitan areas. Most studies use census data at the tract or county level to run their investigation, sometimes adding remote sensing data. As sprawl is multifaceted, we did not limit our study at the adjacent proximity of the central city. Harvey and Clark [7] admit that sprawl is a contemporary urban growth pattern, unsustainable over time, best pictured by trends in population density. We used population data from the 1990 and 2000 census, at the block level, to increase accuracy and precision. The census defines "urban" as any contiguous block of greater than 1000 people per square mile or 390 people per square kilometer. We used ArcView spatial analyst to create 200-meter grids for 1990 and 2000, which can be manipulated directly at the map level. We individualized different types of urban processes related to trends in densities. We note that potentially sprawling areas in St. Tammany Parish are areas that encounter low population density in 2000, while having a population density growth between 1990 and 2000 above the parish average: eqn (1).

$$PS_j = [X_j \leq ZLD < Lu_j] \bigcap [IS_j \geq X_{Change\ ij}] \qquad (1)$$

X_i = Mean Population Density in year "j"

ZLD = Zone of Low Density (<390)

Lu_j = Limit Urban (Lu < 390 pop./sq. km) in year "j"

IS_j: Intensity of Sprawl

$X_{Change\ ij}$ = Mean Density Change from year "i" to year "j" (>20)

$\bigcap$ = indicates that both conditions need to be satisfied for places to be considered part of the urban sprawl

Figure 4 shows that potentially sprawling areas (low density and population gain) are not limited to the edge of the central city of New Orleans (in Orleans Parish), but enter deeply into the hinterland, encroaching on natural habitats. The fragmented landscape of the northern part of St. Tammany Parish testifies to an invasion of new urban scenery and lifestyle in previously rural areas.

These trends in density reflect the residential housing construction patterns witnessed in the spreading areas. Many reasons can explain the tendency for development outside of incorporated areas. Among them, we can assert that undeveloped or underdeveloped land is likely more readily available and less expensive outside of cities. Second, developers try to escape municipal land use control. Finally, homebuyers try to fulfill the American dream and prefer to live in a rural atmosphere far from the problems of the inner city. Therefore, they tend to locate outside of city limits on large lots. We see, in Figure 4, a critical increase in potentially sprawling areas in the south of Slidell, near bridge connections to Orleans Parish. It is likely that people live in St. Tammany Parish and commute to Orleans Parish, to work in New Orleans' city center. The potentially sprawling areas are also heavily present between Covington and Mandeville and on the eastern side of Mandeville. They are also closely linked with roads and highways, especially US 190 between Mandeville and Slidell, as well as US 10 between Slidell and Pearl River and to the north. Luis Martinez from the Ponchartrain Institute for Environmental Sciences created a model with ERDAAS Imagine to understand the relationship between wetland loss and highways. We looked at wetland loss from 0.5 miles from a primary road to 2 miles. The results confirm the close connection between habitat change and roads, as most of the wetland loss between 1982 and 2000 occurred within 0.5 miles of a primary highway.

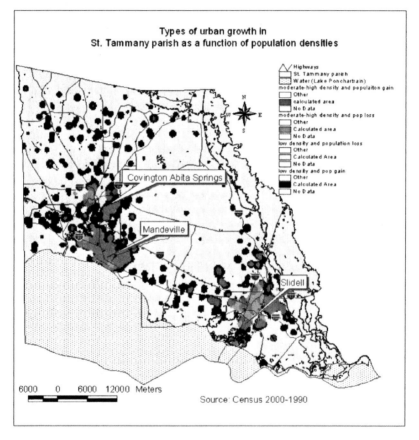

Figure 4: Potentially sprawling areas in St. Tammany Parish.

5 What mediation can be used to protect wetlands while expanding planned urban growth?

5.1 Attempts at the federal level

At the current growth rate, by 2025, urban areas will occupy over 138,000 acres of St. Tammany, or 19% of the parish. Penland *et al.* [16] state that by 2025,

206,000 acres or 28.6% of the parish will be urbanized. If the current trend continues, a large portion of this development will replace wetlands. Despite the recent education about the importance of wetlands, poor development practices continue to encroach on them at an alarming rate. The federal government enacted laws in the 60's and 70's (National Environmental Protection Act, 1969; Clean Water Act, 1972) to maintain environments like wetland habitats. The Clean Water Act protects all waters of the state, including wetlands, from pollution. Section 404 of this act provides a regulatory process for dredging or filling in wetlands. Most farming practices are allowed in wetlands without the penalty of mitigation, as long as the hydrology is not altered. The Swampbuster section of the Farm Bill does give incentives to those farmers that do not clear wetlands, but clearing is allowed. The US Army Corps of Engineers, the governmental agency responsible for permitting wetland removal, allows the filling and draining of wetlands of less than one acre without a major permit. These practices clearly do not control the removal of wetland flora or fauna. The EPA reports that, since 1979, the Corps of Engineers have been petitioned for approximately 150,000 permits to fill wetlands. During this time, only 11 were denied [17].

5.2 Comprehensive planning and smart growth

The new comprehensive plan of St. Tammany Parish [18] shows an awareness of existing inefficiencies in planning coordination. This plan aims for a more comprehensive approach to land development throughout the parish. Elements of the plan include approaches to Critical and Sensitive Habitats, such as wetlands, and Natural Hazards, including flooding. The parish intends this plan to bridge the gap between land use, transportation, housing and protection of critical areas. Another goal of the plan encourages the use of sustainable development, or smart growth principles for future growth. The term "smart growth" is increasingly used to characterize tools to facilitate sustainable development. As an example, the plan promotes Planned Units Developments (PUD's) that protect critical and sensitive habitats by increasing density on the total site. This approach tends to enable urban growth while protecting wetlands and other sensitive habitats. The parish and the municipalities are realizing the challenges associated with sprawling growth and are starting to work together in a more holistic manner. Other smart growth incentives are needed to promote sustainable development. McElfich [19] explains that with wetland ordinances, local governments can require storm water plans or flood plain management to protect wetlands from runoff and non-point pollution. The challenge for St. Tammany Parish is to develop and implement smart tools for growing in a more sustainable, comprehensive and coordinated way.

6 Conclusion

Coastal erosion and unsustainable growth habits are destroying Louisiana's wetlands. With the use of GIS and remote sensing imagery and analysis, we have shown that urban sprawl is turning Louisiana's wetlands into cookie cutter subdivisions. Partition of governance, lack of strong federal policy guidance, and pressure of development have created a fragmented landscape of isolated communities and unlinked pieces of natural habitats. In recent years, planners and environmentalists have recognized that Smart Growth tools can lead to a more sustainable development for current and future communities. Nevertheless, while St. Tammany Parish seems to be headed towards implementing a more orderly and efficient future pattern of urban expansion, pressure from growth is constant. A real awareness and coordination have to exist at all the different levels of governance for sustainable planning policies to have success.

References

[1]   Barras, J.A., Beville, S., *et al*, *Historical and Projected Coastal Louisiana Land Changes: 1978-2050*: USGS Open File Report 03-334, 2003.

[2]   Louisiana 2000 Summary Population and Housing Characteristics; US Census Bureau Web Site. (Coastal parish population total was calculated based on the sum of the populations of the 20 coastal parishes: Ascension, Assumption, Calcasieu, Cameron, Iberia, Jefferson, Lafourche, Livingston, Orleans, Plaquemines, St. Bernard, St. Charles, St. James, St. John the Baptist, St. Martin, St. Mary, St. Tammany, Tangipahoa, Terrebonne, and Vermilion). http://www.census.gov/prod/cen2000/phc-1-20.pdf.

[3]   Malpezzi, S., *Estimates of the Measurements and Determinants of Urban Sprawl in US Metropolitian Areas*. Center for Urban Land Economics Research, University of Wisconsin: Madison, 1999.

[4]   Ewing, P., *et al*, Measuring Sprawl and Its Impacts; Smart Growth America, www.smartgrowthamerica.org/sprawlindex/sprawlindex.html

[5]   Gordon, P., & Richardson, H., Are compact Cities a Desirable Planning Goal? *Journal of the American Planning Association*, Winter, p. 99-105, 1997.

[6]   Galster, G., Hanson, R., *et al*., *Wrestling Sprawl to the Ground: Defining and Measuring an Elusive Concept*, Fannie Mae Foundation: Washington, D.C., 2000.

[7]   Harvey, R.O. & Clark, W.A.V., The Nature of Economics and Sprawl, *Land Economics*, 41 (1), 1965

[8]   Downs, A., New Visions for Metropolitian America. Brooking Institution: Washington, D.C., 1994.

[9]   Ehrenfeld, J.G., Evaluating wetlands within an urban context, Urban Ecosystems, January 2000,vol.4, no.1, p.69-85.

[10]   United States Environmental Protection Agency (USEPA). Clean Water Act Website, Washington, D.C., http://www.epa.gov/region5/water/cwa.htm.

[11]   General Accounting Office.

[12]   National Research Council.

[13]   Lake Ponchartrain Basin Foundation Website. Habitat Change in St. Tammany Parish; New Orleans, www.saveourlake.org.
[14]   Malpezzi, S., & Guo, W.K., Measuring "Sprawl:" Alternative Measures of Urban Form in U.S. Metropolitian Areas. Center for Urban Land Economics Research, University of Wisconsin: Madison, 2001.
[15]   Hess, G.R., Salinda, S.D., *et al.* Just What is Sprawl Anyway?, unpublished paper, North Carolina Forestry Department: Raleigh, www4.ncsu.edu:8083/~grhess/papers/sprawl.pdf.
[16]   Penland, S., D. Maygarden, et al. Environmental Atlas of Lake Pontchartrain, United States Geologic Survey: New Orleans, 2002.
[17]   Understanding the Clean Water Act Website; River Network, Portland, http://www.cleanwateract.org/Pages/c7.htm.
[18]   St. Tammany Parish, *New Directions 2025*, Land Use Plan, 2001.
[19]   McElfich, Jr., J. M. Nature Friendly Ordinances: Local Measures to Conserve Biodiversity, Environmental Law Institute: Washington, D.C., 2004.

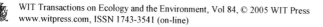

The role of soil organic matter content in soil conservation and carbon sequestration studies: case studies from Lithuania and the UK

C. A. Booth[1], M. A. Fullen[1], B. Jankauskas[2], G. Jankauskiene[2] & A. Slepetiene[3]

[1]EAS-SAS, Research Institute in Advanced Technologies (RIATec), The University of Wolverhampton, Wolverhampton, U.K.
[2]Kaltinenai Research Station of the Lithuanian Institute of Agriculture, Silale District, Lithuania
[3]Chemical Research Laboratory of the Lithuanian Institute of Agriculture, Kedainiai District, Lithuania

Abstract

Soil organic matter (SOM) data are presented from two long-term European experimental research sites: (i) SOM data from a soil conservation site in the U.K. and (ii) SOM data from a carbon sequestration benchmarking site in Lithuania. Detailed SOM information, which also incorporates soil organic carbon (SOC), is vitally important because it plays a fundamental role in both soil conservation and carbon sequestration studies. Land management of pedogenic carbon is a recognized means of improving soil fertility, reducing soil erosion rates, enhancing soil structural stability and promoting carbon sequestration. Therefore, its benefits extend from local to global scales. For instance, the first case study illustrates the environmental benefits of changes in SOM content before (as bare soil) and after (converted to grassland) the adoption of the soil conservation technique of set-aside. The second case study introduces various analytical approaches used to calculate SOM, and demonstrates the potential difficulty of international carbon benchmarking, as part of the global policy to ameliorate climate change.

Keywords: soil erosion, runoff plots, agriculture, grasslands, global warming, climate change, carbon benchmarking, IPCC, Kyoto Protocol.

1   Introduction

Soil organic matter (SOM) content influences many soil properties, including water retention, extractable bases, capacity to supply macro- and micro-nutrients, soil aggregate stability and soil aeration. SOM is increasingly recognized as an indicator of soil quality, that is, a component of biosphere sustainability and stability [1]. Soil organic fraction accounts for 50-90% of the cation exchange capacity (CEC) of mineral surface soils, which allows macronutrient cations (K, Ca, Mg) to be held in forms available to plants. Through CEC, organic matter also provides much of the soil pH buffering capacity [2]. Nitrogen, phosphorus, sulphur, and micronutrients are stored as constituents of SOM, which are slowly released by mineralization, thus aiding plant growth. Humic acids are constituents of SOM and these accelerate soil mineral decomposition, releasing macro- and micro- nutrients as exchangeable cations.

Soil organic carbon (SOC), the major component of SOM, consists of micro-organisms cells, plant and animal residues at various stages of decomposition, stable 'humus' synthesized from residues and nearly inert and highly carbonized compounds, such as charcoal, graphite and coal. Carbon is a major food source for soil fauna. Increasing SOM, especially SOC, changes the biological properties of soils. Therefore, increased SOC generally increases soil fauna and thus improves biodiversity. SOM plays a central role in increasing soil porosity, thus increasing infiltration rates. In turn, this increases the water holding capacity of soil and makes tillage operations easier. The resultant increased water availability for plants decreases both runoff and the pollution of watercourses with agrochemicals.

Impacts of SOM enrichment on soil carbon dynamics are well documented [3, 4]. Conversion of natural vegetation to agricultural land-uses can decrease SOM and, conversely, conversion of cultivated land back to natural vegetation can replenish SOM [5, 6] and return lost soil carbon via increased soil carbon storage [2]. Therefore, increased grass production will increase SOC and SOM and, thus, help ameliorate global-warming by sequestering carbon from atmospheric CO_2 into the soil store [7].

A particular concern in many European areas is the general decline in SOM. According to the European Soil Bureau, based on the limited data available, nearly 75% of the total area analysed in the Mediterranean region of Southern Europe has a low ($\leq 3.4\%$) or very low ($\leq 1.7\%$) SOM content. Typically, agronomists consider soils with $<1.7\%$ organic matter to be in a pre-desertification stage. The problem is widespread. For instance, SOM values for England and Wales show the percentage of soils with $<3.6\%$ organic matter rose from 35% to 42% in the period 1980-1995, which is chiefly due to changing management practices. For the same period, in the Beauce region, south of Paris, SOM decreased by half, which is attributed to the same reasons [8]. Because SOM decline is a crosscutting issue that also affects associated soil parameters, such as fertility, erosion and conservation, plus carbon sequestration estimates, it is extremely difficult to approximate its true environmental and financial cost.

With these concerns and issues in mind, this work presents SOM data from two European long-term experimental research sites: (i) SOM data from a soil conservation site in the U.K. and (ii) SOM data from a carbon sequestration benchmarking site in Lithuania.

2 Strategies for soil conservation

The extent and severity of erosion on European soils has markedly increased over the last fifty years, particularly on arable land. Unfortunately, soil conservation in Europe has not generally received sufficient attention, until recently [9]. Set-aside is a scheme designed to provide farmers with a subsidy to leave land uncultivated and, in doing so, act as a possible soil conservation measure [6, 10]. In the prevailing economic climate, it is feasible that steep to moderate slopes with erodible soils, and other vulnerable parts of fields (i.e. depressions, minor dry valleys and land adjacent to water courses), be put into non-rotational set-aside [11, 12]. This could decrease erosion rates and potentially increase soil organic matter content, with concomitant decreases in soil erodibility.

In the U.K., agri-environment schemes aim to secure environmental benefits above those of Good Farming Practice and cross-compliance. Introduced in 1987, to implement EU Council Regulation 797/85, they were designed to prevent loss of habitat and landscape features associated with intensification at sites targeted by the Environmentally Sensitive Areas (ESA) Scheme. Subsequently, in 1991, the Countryside Steward Scheme (CSS) was established to provide incentives to landowners, farmers and other land managers to take specific measures to conserve, enhance and/or re-create important landscape types. In 1994, the Habitat Scheme (HS) was initiated to create, protect and enhance wildlife habitats by removing land from agricultural production and promoting environmentally sound land-management practices. Shortly after this, in 1995, the Moorland Scheme (MS) was launched with the objective of protecting and improving the upland moorland environment. In 1998, the Arable Stewardship Pilot Scheme (ASPS) was created to assess alternative arable management options for conserving and enhancing farmland biodiversity [13]. More recently, in December 2003, the UK government initiated a new agri-environment initiative, known as the Environmental Stewardship Scheme (ESS), which encourages farmers to deliver simple, yet effective, environmental management of their land (http://www.defra.gov.uk/erdp/reviews/agrienv /default.htm).

3 Strategies for sequestering carbon to the soil store

Global CO_2 concentrations are increasing and it is useful to examine these changes in terms of carbon 'sources', 'sinks' and 'pools'. The current gross increase in atmospheric CO_2 is 6.5 Gt of carbon per year (1 Gegaton or Gt is 10^9 t). This comes mainly from the 'sources' of burning of fossil fuels with a further 1.6 Gt from deforestation. The CO_2 'sink' in terrestrial ecosystems (vegetation and soils) is believed to be ~2.0 Gt C per year, while the oceanic sink absorbs about a further 2.7 Gt C per year. Therefore, the net increase in atmospheric CO_2 is ~3.4 Gt C per year. It is estimated total amounts of carbon in the soil 'pool' is ~1550 Gt organic C and 1700 Gt inorganic C. The latter is mainly in the form of calcium carbonate ($CaCO_3$). Both of these are much greater than the pools in either the atmosphere (750 Gt C) or in all living organisms (550 Gt C). Therefore, if carbon can be taken from the atmosphere, a small increase in the soil organic pool (0.1-0.2% per year) could counteract the current increase in CO_2 content of the atmosphere (~1.5 parts per million by volume per year) [14].

Considerable organic carbon can be sequestered into soils, as carbon is an integral part of soil organic matter (SOM). Soil organic carbon (SOC) constitutes about 55-60%, typically about 58%, of SOM. The potential to sequester atmospheric carbon within the soil store is a growing paradigm in soil science. The consensus is that carbon sequestration is not a panacea to global warming. However, sequestration would form a valuable contribution and allow some extra time while solutions to the problems are sought.

4   Soil carbon modelling

Carbon cycle models provide a valuable tool for understanding and predicting the turnover of soil organic carbon and, in doing so, assist national and international carbon sequestration estimates. To improve soil carbon modelling performance and reliability, and to demonstrate the rate and success of set-aside, it is paramount that all governments and agencies obtain national and regional SOM data to act as a benchmark for future studies. Thus, they should direct their policy to monitor the status of their national soils and to achieve proper soil use and conservation [9]. Models require the input of characteristic soil and climate data, such as soil texture, SOM, rainfall, temperature and evapotranspiration [15]. Therefore, transferable soil data, beyond those of institutional and national boundaries, has international importance for soil carbon model inclusion and quantification of the global carbon budget. Unfortunately, to date, differences between international protocols employed to determine SOM content produce different estimates and interpretations.

Universal or harmonized quantification of SOM concentrations is essential. Data comparability could be achieved by harmonization of analytical protocols. At present, due to methodological differences between regional and national laboratories, problems of SOM data comparison and acceptance exist, particularly where results are presented for international publication or inclusion in soil carbon models. Consequently, there is a need to develop transfer functions between analytical protocols used to determine SOM content.

5   Case studies: soil conservation and carbon sequestration

This work presents results of two case studies (i) SOM data from a long-term soil conservation site in the U.K. and (ii) SOM data from a carbon sequestration benchmarking site in Lithuania.

5.1 Soil conservation: the Hilton Experimental Site, UK

Soil conservation investigations, employing the set-aside approach, are being conducted at the Hilton Experimental Site, Shropshire, U.K. (52.0°033'5.7''N, 2.0°19'18.3''W) (Figure 1). The site covers 0.52 ha with an upper elevation of 67.46 m and slopes to the south and west. The region experiences a temperate climate with a mean annual precipitation at Hilton of 648.3 mm.

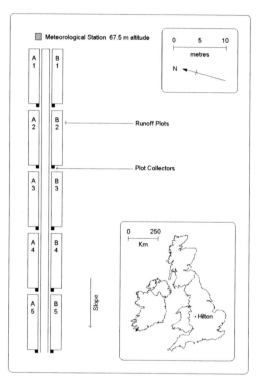

Figure 1:   Plan of the field plots at the Hilton Experimental Site, UK.

An array of ten 25 m^2 (10 x 2.5 m) plots was constructed (1981-82) on the slope beneath the Hilton meteorological station, varying from moderately sloping (7°, 12%) to moderately steeply sloping (15°, 27%). After several years in a bare condition, the array of plots was put into set-aside, being sown with a temporary ley grass mixture on 22/04/1991 [6]. Seeds consisted of a mixture of perennial ryegrass (<u>Lolium perenne</u>) (varieties: Liprior, Condesa, Meltra, Antrim and Sabel), Timothy (<u>Phleum pratense</u>) and Huia White clover (<u>Trifolium repens</u>), spread at a standard application rate of 13 kg ha^{-1} (~80 g per 25 m^2), as advised by the U.K. Ministry of Agriculture, Fisheries and Food (MAFF), now known as the Department of the Environment, Food and Rural Affairs (DEFRA). Subsequent set-aside management followed U.K. Ministry of Agriculture regulations [16]. These included two grass cuts between July and September and the grass cuttings retained on the plots. Fifty topsoil (0-5 cm deep) samples (~60-80 g dry weight each) were removed using a hand-trowel (~10 cm width) from the experimental plots in December 1985, 1988, 1990 and April 1991, 1993, 1995, 1999 and 2001 (n = 400). Five samples were removed from each plot from interrill positions at 2, 4, 6, 8 and 10 m on the south side of plots on each sampling occasion. Soil organic matter contents of the fine-earth fraction (<2 mm) were determined by loss-on-ignition at 375°C for 16 hours [17].

On the 10 bare soil plots, during a monitoring period of more than 5 years (1985-1991), soil organic matter significantly decreased (Table 1). For this period, average total erosion was 47.2 t ha^{-1} y^{-1}. During the ley establishment period (20/05/1991-19/12/1991) erosion rates were moderate, with a mean plot erosion rate equivalent to 0.82 t ha^{-1}. However, vegetation monitoring suggested that once cover was ~30%, runoff and erosion rates notably reduced. Conversion of the 10 plots to set-aside reversed the trend of declining soil organic matter contents, which then significantly increased, especially in the first four years. Mean SOM content increased from 2.04% by weight (1991) to 3.11% (2001), compared with nearby permanent grassland values of ~4.5%. Erosion rates on the set-aside plots with a developed ley cover were very low, the mean rate over 69 plot years was 0.52 kg y^{-1} (S.D. 0.36). This is equivalent to a mean rate of 0.21 t ha^{-1} y^{-1} (S.D. 0.14).

Table 1:   Long-term SOM data (% by weight) for field plots at the Hilton Site.

Plot	Dec. 1985	Dec. 1988	Dec. 1990	April 1991	April 1993	April 1995	April 1999	April 2001	n =
A1	1.90	1.66	1.39	1.49	2.10	2.66	2.39	2.71	40
A2	2.40	2.06	1.74	1.89	2.05	2.91	2.78	2.59	40
A3	2.99	2.62	2.50	2.41	2.80	3.00	3.30	3.18	40
A4	2.81	2.56	2.31	2.43	2.78	2.73	3.22	3.40	40
A5	3.43	3.02	2.93	2.56	3.05	3.34	4.00	3.76	40
B1	2.06	1.78	1.67	1.52	1.78	1.95	2.94	2.63	40
B2	1.89	1.45	1.43	1.45	1.75	2.38	2.88	2.71	40
B3	2.45	2.10	2.23	1.94	2.61	3.08	3.42	3.47	40
B4	2.46	2.31	2.38	2.18	3.26	2.68	3.31	3.03	40
B5	3.05	2.90	2.76	2.55	2.78	3.44	3.39	3.62	40
Mean	2.54	2.24	2.13	2.04	2.50	2.82	3.16	3.11	400
S.D.	0.51	0.52	0.54	0.44	0.57	0.60	0.64	0.68	

Pooled t (1985 v 1991) 5.24, P <0.001, d.f. = 98; (1991 v 2001) -9.23, P <0.001, d.f. = 98

Erosion rates were unresponsive to slope angle, suggesting leys are highly effective, even on steep slopes. Therefore, plot results confirm the logical suggestion that conversion of steep slopes with erodible soils to grass would greatly benefit soil conservation. Furthermore, there is considerable potential for set-aside to be targeted on steep and erodible land [5, 18].

5.2 Soil carbon sequestration: the Kaltinenai Experimental Sites, Lithuania

As a result of geopolitical changes, land use has changed markedly in the Baltic States (Estonia, Latvia and Lithuania). The collapse of the Soviet Union, in 1991, meant the guaranteed market for arable crops produced by the Baltic States was unavailable. This promoted land use change from arable production to grassland. For instance, in Lithuania, land use changed from predominantly arable (59.4%) in 1991 to grass (71.4%) in 2001. Although these changes were originally perceived as negative, in hindsight, there are potential environmental benefits. For instance, the Baltic States are increasingly viewed as a carbon sink. This has global implications because, as already mentioned, atmospheric carbon is increasingly stored in the soil system and thus helps ameliorate global warming. Furthermore, carbon sequestration assists the Baltic States adhere to international agreements, such as the Kyoto Protocol and the Agenda 21 for the Baltic region (the international agreement to improve environmental conditions in and around the Baltic Sea). In the longer term, it is possible that, states responsible for sequestering carbon will receive 'carbon credits'; that is, payments received from the international community to sequester carbon. Therefore, the Baltic experience provides a useful case study for environmental managers and policy makers. Specifically, negative circumstances (i.e. initial agricultural collapse) can be turned into positive developments.

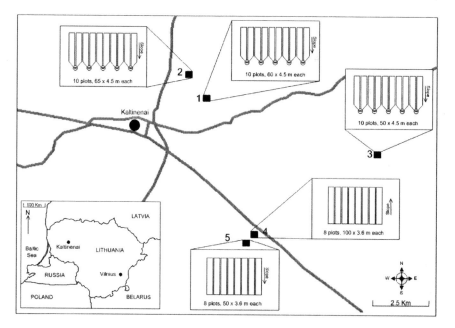

Figure 2:   Plan of the field plots at the Kaltinenai Experimental Sites, Lithuania.

On-going post-Soviet agricultural transformation of Lithuania, from predominantly arable to grass production, provides a timely and unique opportunity to study carbon sequestration at a period of rapid agricultural change. For reasons mentioned earlier, it is imperative to possess background information on the current status of soil organic matter content. In doing so, this 'snapshot' provides a fixed-point against which it is possible to evaluate future long-term changes. Globally, numerous field-sites are 'benchmarked', collectively providing the basis for evaluations of changed soil properties.

In 2002, as part of a joint Anglo-Lithuanian investigation into soil carbon sequestration, samples were removed from 46 experimental soil plots at the Kaltinenai Experimental Sites, in the Zemaiciai Uplands of west-central Lithuania (55°34', 22°29') (Figure 2). These are permanent plots, 16 of which have been operational since 1982 and 30 since 1993 [19]. Soil samples were removed, which included both topsoil (0-20 cm depth) and subsoil (20-40 cm depth), thus providing an archive of 92 soil samples. SOM content for both the topsoil and subsoil horizons was determined by five separate techniques: (i) the traditional Western Europe approach of the loss-on-ignition method [17], (ii) the East European Tyurin titrimetric method [20], (iii) the Tyurin photometric method [21, 22]; (iv) the USDA Walkley-Black method [23] and (v) the Vario-EL III dry combustion approach.

Table 2 shows summary SOM benchmark data. There are noticeable differences between the results of each technique. Therefore, this highlights that when reporting analytical results, care must be taken to specify the precise analytical technique used and stresses the difficulties in comparing international data sets.

Table 2:   Summary soil organic matter data (n = 92 soil samples).

Analytical Technique	Mean	S.D.
Walkley-Black	2.14	0.74
Tyurin photometrical	2.05	0.62
Tyurin titrimetrical	1.84	0.67
Loss-on-ignition	2.93	1.00
Dry combustion	1.94	0.70

Despite the determination of organic matter content being a routine procedure carried out in soil analytical laboratories throughout the U.S. and other Western countries, there is no satisfactory universal method for determining SOM content. It can be determined indirectly by measuring SOC content and multiplying the result by the ratio of organic matter to organic carbon normally found in soil. Direct determination of organic matter usually involves destruction of the organic fraction by oxidation or ignition of the soil at high temperature. Soil weight loss is taken as a measure of organic content. However, the oxidation method has serious limitations, mostly because the oxidation process is incomplete, and the extent of oxidation can vary between soils.

This work highlights universal or harmonized quantification of SOM concentrations is essential and data comparability can be achieved by harmonization of analytical protocols. At present, due to methodological differences between regional and national laboratories, problems of SOM data comparison and acceptance exist, particularly where results are presented for international publication or inclusion in soil carbon models. One way of resolving this issue is for global use of the same technique. Until such times exist, alternatively, there is a need to develop transfer functions between SOM analytical protocols using 'best fit' or regression equations, which transform data sets from one format to another. However, the latter approach is not entirely accurate and data conversion errors exist.

6   Relevance and importance for sustainable planning

These case studies illustrate important planning and policy issues. Researchers are facing multiple environmental problems and are becoming increasingly involved and responsible for global environmental management. However, this requires a holistic approach. In the case of carbon sequestration we must consider soil and climate as dynamically-interacting, mutually-adjusting systems. Thus, we need to consider the effects of our environmental management, both in terms of effects on the 'source' or zone of export (i.e. removing carbon from the atmospheric system) and the 'sink' or zone of import (i.e. importing carbon into the soil system). Likewise, the study also stresses the importance of scale, as the issues are relevant at global, national and local scales.

In trying to comprehend global changes, we face many challenges. These include problems of data comparability, with different countries using slightly different procedures to assess the same soil properties. Therefore, it is important we must move towards harmonizing analytical procedures. Notable steps have already been taken in this direction, with the Kyoto Protocol recommending standardized approaches to the analysis of SOC. However, harmonization in turn poses challenges. How do we compare new international databases with old national databases? Therefore, an important approach is cross-calibration of national datasets, so that important historical data can be incorporated into long-term investigations. However, cross-calibration can produce some errors. In terms of international comparisons, we face problems not only of different analytical procedures, but also different definitions of the parameters. Nevertheless, rather than ignore the complexity of the problems, it is imperative we advance our knowledge and understanding to solve these problems and improve our management of our environment and its resources. As highlighted in the case study of the Baltic States, it was possible to change negative circumstances (i.e. initial post-Soviet agricultural collapse) into positive developments (increased carbon sequestration). Therefore, in the face of these and other major global challenges, we cannot afford to be too pessimistic, as it is possible to turn negative developments to our advantage.

7 Conclusions

SOM influences the biological, chemical and physical properties of soils and its benefits extend from local to global scales. Soil conservation and carbon sequestration are mutually important issues, coupled by the complexity of changes in SOM and the carbon cycle.

Set-aside has been shown to be a highly effective soil conservation measure, which can quickly and significantly increase soil organic content. That said, increased soil organic contents also contribute to soil carbon sequestration. Therefore, in accordance with long-term international strategies (e.g. the Kyoto Protocol, 1997), it is essential that land managers possess a thorough understanding of the long-term response and benefits of converting agricultural soils to grasslands and/or adopting grass ley set-aside for inclusion in future strategies and policy. Much more SOM benchmarking of international soils will make this an achievable goal and improve the harmonization of global SOM databases to enhance international estimates of soil carbon sequestration rates.

Acknowledgements

The help of colleagues, from each institution, with fieldwork is gratefully acknowledged. Some of the presented data formed part of a pilot-project funded by the Leverhulme Trust (F/00630B), to whom all authors gratefully acknowledge their financial assistance.

References

[1] Kogut, B.M. & Frid, A.S., Comparison of humus determination methods in soils. *Pochvovedenie*, **9**, pp. 119-123, 1993. (In Russian).

[2] Lal, R., Kimble, J.M., Follett, R.F. & Stewart B.A., (Eds.) Soil Processes and the Carbon Cycle. CRC Press, Boca Raton, Florida, pp. 609, 1998.

[3] van Kessel, C., Nitschelm, J., Horwath, W.R., Harris, D., Walley, F., Luscher, A. & Hartwig, U., Carbon-13 input and turnover in a pasture soil exposed to long-term elevated atmospheric CO_2, *Global Change Biology*, **6**, pp. 123-135, 2000.

[4] Hagedorn, F., Maurer, S., Egli, P., Bucher, J.B. & Siegwolf, R., Carbon sequestration in forest soils of soil type, atmospheric CO_2 enrichment and N deposition, *European Journal of Soil Science*, **52**, pp. 619-628, 2001.

[5] Fullen, M.A., Soil organic matter and erosion processes on arable loamy sand soils in the West Midlands of England. *Soil Technology*, **4**, pp. 19-31, 1991.

[6] Fullen, M.A., Effects of grass ley set-aside on runoff, erosion and organic matter levels in sandy soils in east Shropshire, U.K. *Soil & Tillage Research*, **46**, pp. 41-49, 1998.

[7] Lal, R., Soil management and restoration for C sequestration to mitigate the accelerated greenhouse effect. *Progress in Environmental Science*, **1**, pp. 307-326, 1999.

[8]   Commission of the European Community, *Towards a thematic strategy for soil protection*. Communication from the Commission to the Council, the European Parliament, the Economic and Social Committee of the Regions. Brussels, 2002.

[9]   Fullen, M.A., Arnalds, A., Booth, C.A., Castillo, V., Kertesz, A., Martin, P., Souchere, V., Sole, A., & Verstraeten, G., Government and agency response to soil erosion risk in Europe, In: Soil Erosion in Europe (Eds) J. Boardman & J. Poesen, John Wiley & Sons publishers, (in press), 2005.

[10]   Chisci, G., Perspectives on soil protection measures in Europe. In: Rickson, R.J. (Ed.), Conserving Soil Resources: European Perspectives. CAB International, Wallingford, England, pp. 339-353, 1994.

[11]   Ministry of Agriculture, Fisheries and Food, *The Soil Code*. MAFF Publications, London, England, pp. 66, 1998.

[12]   Environment Agency, *Best farming practices: profiting from a good environment*. Environment Agency Publications, Bristol, England, pp. 57, 2001.

[13]   Ecoscope Applied Ecologists, *Review of agri-environmental schemes – monitoring information and research and development results*. Final report for the Department of Environment, Food and Rural Affairs, London, 2003.

[14]   Fullen, M.A. & Catt, J.A., *Soil Management – problems and solutions*. Arnold Publishers, London, pp. 269, 2004.

[15]   Smith, P., Powlson, D.S., Glendining, M.J. & Smith, J.U., Potential for carbon sequestration in European soils: preliminary estimates for five scenarios using results from long-term experiments. *Global Change Biology*, **3**, 67-79, 1997.

[16]   Ministry of Agriculture, Fisheries and Food, *Set-Aside*. Advisory Leaflet PB 0299, MAFF Publications, London, England, pp. 23, 1991.

[17]   Ball, D.F., Loss-on-ignition as an estimate of organic matter and organic carbon in non-calcareous soils. *Journal of Soil Science*, **15**, pp. 84-92, 1964.

[18]   Chambers, B.J. & Garwood, T.W.D., Monitoring of water erosion on arable farms in England & Wales. 1990-94. *Soil Use & Management*, **16**, pp. 93-99, 2000.

[19]   Jankauskas, B. & Jankauskiene, G., Erosion-preventive crop rotations for landscape ecological stability in upland regions of Lithuania. *Agriculture, Ecosystems & Environment*, **95**, pp. 129-142, 2003.

[20]   Aleksandrova, L.N. & Naidenova, O.A., *Laboratory Practice in Soil Science*. Kolos, Leningrad, 1976. (In Russian).

[21]   Orlov, D.S. & Grisina, L.A., *Guide in Chemistry of Humus*. MGU, Moscow, 1981. (In Russian).

[22]   Nikitin, B.A., 1999. A method for soil humus determination. *Agricultural Chemistry*, **3**, pp. 156-158, 1999.

[23]   USDA, Primary characterization data. In: *Soil Survey Laboratory Information Manual*. NSSC, SSL, Lincoln, Nebraska, pp. 9-133, 1995.

The 'Sefton Coast Partnership': an overview of its integrated coastal zone management

A. T. Worsley[1], G. Lymbery[2], C. A. Booth[3], P. Wisse[2] & V. J. C. Holden[1]

[1]*Natural, Geographical and Applied Sciences, Edge Hill University, Ormskirk, Lancashire, U.K.*
[2]*Coastal Defence Unit, Ainsdale Discovery Centre Complex, Southport, Merseyside, U.K.*
[3]*Environmental and Analytical Sciences Division, Research Institute in Advanced Technologies (RIATec), The University of Wolverhampton, Wolverhampton, West Midlands, U.K.*

Abstract

The Sefton Coast Partnership (SCP), based in Sefton, Merseyside, UK, is set within the context of and reported as an example of Integrated Coastal Zone Management. It has developed out of a well-established and successful Management Scheme and, since its inception, attempted with varying success to develop a 'working partnership' which has sustainable management at its heart and which is responsible for conservation and the needs of the local community. The history, function and structure of the SCP are described together with the problems that emerged as the partnership developed.
Keywords: ICZM, partnership, sustainable management, Sefton.

1 Introduction

The coastal zone is hugely significant in terms of sustainable management since this is where human activities affect and are inseparable from marine and terrestrial processes and environments both in developed countries and the Third World. Integrated management therefore requires a holistic, geographic approach and, in order to be successful, action at the local and regional level which is supported by the national government. This paper introduces the Sefton Coast Partnership as an example of Integrated Coastal Zone Management (ICZM) in practice. This should not be taken to imply that the Partnership is ideal in every sense but that it illustrates the practical application of ICZM principles in the management of a valuable and dynamic environment. The emergence of the Sefton Coast Partnership in an area with a well-established management tradition highlights how ICZM with 'partnership' at its core may be the best way forward.

2 Location

Sefton is located on the North West coast of England between the estuaries of the Ribble and the Mersey (Figure 1). It is a sedimentary coast approximately 36kms long situated within the eastern Irish Sea, because of this location wave action is limited by the length of fetch, although the location also leads to a significant tidal range of 10 metres. The large conurbations of Liverpool and Manchester lie within easy travelling distance for those wishing to make day-trips.

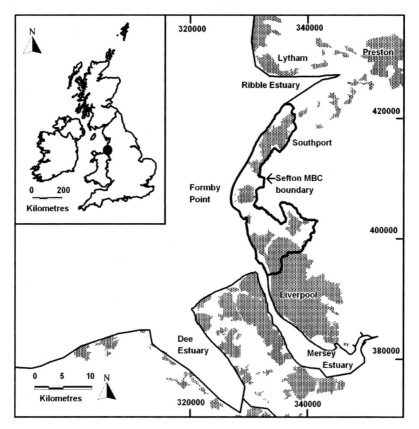

Figure 1:   Location map of the Sefton coast and surrounding areas, NW U.K.

3   Recent history

The recent evolution of the coast cannot be separated from human activities, in the north, around the Ribble estuary, the principal activities to influence the coast are land reclamation (Figure 2) and the dredging of a channel and subsequent maintenance with training walls within the Ribble, for the Port of Preston (now closed). The location of the dredged channel on the north side of the estuary accelerated the development of salt marsh on the south side that has subsequently been exploited through reclamation, mainly for agriculture, but seaward of the town it has been reclaimed for recreation and development; and, to some extent, to maintain the seafront adjacent to the beach (Plate 1a).

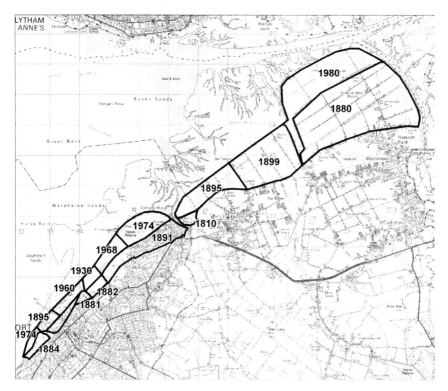

Figure 2:   Location map of the areas of reclamation and their dates, along the north Sefton coast.

To the south, the Port of Liverpool expanded towards the mouth of the estuary and required increased channel depths to cater for larger ships over a longer tidal period. Working with the Port, in the late 1960's, the local Council developed coastal defences in front of Crosby (Plate 1b), reclaiming land for recreation and making beneficial use of the material excavated for expansion of the port.

In the central area, subsequently referred to as Formby Point, sand dunes are the dominant features (Plate 2). These have experienced periods of accretion and erosion with the latest period of erosion commencing circa 1900. Prior to this date landowners had encouraged dune formation using traditional techniques, trees were planted on rear dune areas to control wind blown sand and as a crop to be harvested at a later date. It is perceived that the onset of erosion around 1900 might have been caused by the dredged channel for the Port of Liverpool refracting wave energy on to the Point [1], since this time the Point has been receding at an average rate of 4.5 metres per year, but this diminishes to the north and south until areas of accretion are reached.

(a)   (b)

Plate 1:   Coastal defence features along the Sefton coast (a) Southport sea-wall during its construction and (b) Crosby sea-wall.

(a)   (b)

Plate 2:   Coastal erosion features at Formby Point (a) Erosive face of foreshore dunes and (b) Former pedestrian pathway standing above the present, lowered, beach-level.

4 Context for 'Integrated Coastal Zone Management'

4.1 ICZM: towards working partnerships?

As part of European Commission recommendations, member states are required to undertake a stocktake of the current management of their coastal zones considering the various interests, roles and concerns of all sectors at all levels; the relevant legislation and policy; and to identify inter-regional organisations and co-operation structures [2]. This work has been carried out in two reports, one for Scotland [3] and one for England [4]. The work of coastal partnerships in the north-west of England has also been examined [5].

Typical problems of delivering ICZM through working partnerships that were identified by participants are:
- Inadequate connections between plans
- Lack of strategic overview and direction
- Gap between plan making and plan implementation
- Lack of resources to implement plan
- Unbalanced contributions and commitment from partners
- Lack of power to take actions forward
- Problems with decision making, difficulties in reaching consensus
- Problems engaging stakeholders [3, 4. 5].

None of the reports attempt to define 'partnerships' although all make significant reference to them. A summary of the types of partnerships that they identify would be multi-stakeholder, multi-sectorial, often voluntary, seeking to achieve agreed objectives through some form of joint working, often meeting as steering groups, boards or forums and having documented aims, objectives and action plans.

All three reports agreed that partnerships had a role to play in the delivery of ICZM, considering them important to facilitate the exchange of information, involve all stakeholders, resolve conflict, breakdown sectorial barriers and establish joint objectives. There were also concerns expressed in relation to the need to clarify roles and responsibilities, ensure democratic accountability and the need to undertake monitoring and evaluation of partnerships [6].

The principals of ICZM for reference are [2]:
- Broad perspective
- Long term perspective
- Adaptive management
- Local specificity
- Working with natural processes
- Involvement of all parties concerned
- Support and involvement of relevant administrative bodies
- Use of a combination of instruments

It is worth considering, at this stage, why a partnership is a useful mechanism to deliver these principles, but first it is necessary to clarify what is understood to be a partnership in this context. A useful definition is supplied by the Audit Commission [7], who uses the term when describing otherwise independent bodies who have agreed to co-operate to achieve a common goal and create a separate structure and plan to achieve the goal or goals. They then go on to consider reasons for working in partnership, one of which is to reduce the impact of organisational fragmentation, a particular problem on the coast. A working partnership promotes joint ownership, motivates participants, identifies and consolidates common ground; and provides "a vehicle for effective and positive change" [8], but perhaps most importantly it promotes communication.

The problems listed above and the principals for ICZM make it necessary not only to bring the relevant stakeholders together but to ensure that they communicate, so that conflicting objectives can be identified and reconciled. It also enables opportunities to be identified and better use to be made of resources. This will be illustrated with some examples below.

4.2 Sefton Coast Partnership

The case study is the Sefton Coast Partnership, which was established as the Sefton Coast Management Scheme in 1978 after a wide-ranging consultation exercise. Whilst its principal remit was conservation, this was considered within the context of urban regeneration in the surrounding area. For this reason, issues such as the development of recreation, education and the creation of jobs were considered to be important [9]. Problems giving rise to the need for the Management Scheme relate to the conflict between recreational pressures, the desire for nature conservation (Plate 3), the desire to maintain the sand dune system as a coastal defence and ineffective development control. Further complicated by the (then) structure of local government, which split the geographical area of the scheme between two authorities, a reorganisation led to the area being administered by one authority [10, 11] (Plate 4).

(a)   (b)

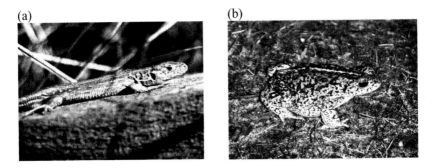

Plate 3:   Examples of important rare species found at the Seftion coast (a) sand lizard *(Lacerta agilis)* and (b) Natterjack toad *(Bufo calmita).*

At its establishment the scheme was under the overall supervision of the Steering Group assisted by an advisory Working Party through which the project officer reported (Figure 3). Only the elected representatives of the local authority had voting rights on the Steering Group, it is noted that the Steering Group is an advisory body and as such has no direct authority over member organisations [9].

It is also stated that the plan developed for the scheme is advisory but seeks to provide commonly agreed goals and a schedule of actions that are agreed to be required in an effort to co-ordinate these actions and to introduce them into partners budgetary planning processes [11].

(a) (b)

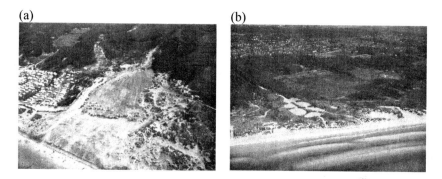

Plate 4: Aerial photographs of the National Trust section of Sefton coast (a) before management, taken 1972 and (b) after management, taken 1997.

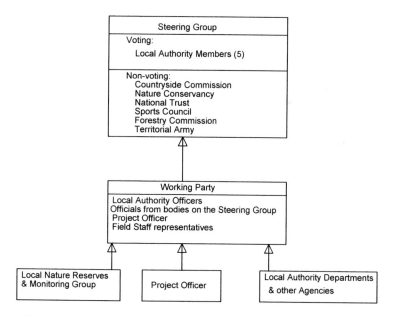

Figure 3: Structure of the Sefton Coast Management Scheme [9].

The partnership was based on guidance from the Countryside Commission (CC) in 'Local Authority Countryside Management Projects' [13]. This identified the need for a co-ordinated approach to address problems that fall into the following two categories:

 WIT Transactions on Ecology and the Environment, Vol 84, © 2005 WIT Press
www.witpress.com, ISSN 1743-3541 (on-line)

- Problems too complex to be dealt with by individual land managers but too small or short term to be of major concern to local authorities.
- Problems that cannot be solved by statutory planning instruments such as development control [13].

The CC focuses on the role of the project officer who, under the general supervision of a steering group and with "substantial delegated financial and administrative responsibilities"(ibid, p3), can work with stakeholders to address issues of conflict and identify and progress opportunities. They emphasise the need for the project, or partnership, to be related to government actions and policy and see the management plan as the mechanism for this. They also see the management plan serving other function such as promoting public acceptance of actions; identifying opportunities and conflicts; defining objectives; setting out methods for resolving conflicts and doing work; identifying a work programme and linking this to longer term goals. Within the management plan of the Partnership a vision was set out (see below) that acts as a brief overarching statement that all partners could agree with.

> Vision Statement of the Sefton Coast Partnership: *"Our vision is for the Sefton Coast to be managed to ensure the conservation of one of the most important coastal areas in Europe for nature while being an asset to a healthy local economy and providing a much needed area for the quiet enjoyment of the countryside. Specifically, we accept the joint responsibility to ensure that the integrity and natural value of the dune system and estuaries is protected in perpetuity as one of the series of European nature areas."* [14]

In the early part of its life the partnership achieved some high profile, high value successes across a range of land ownerships and disciplines; evidence of which can still be seen on the site. It was observed at this time that this work would reduce the need for major physical works with low-key maintenance being the principal physical works carried out by the partnership subsequently [13, 15]. These high profile successes relating to the rejuvenation (over twenty years ago) of a substantially degraded area of sand dunes are still referred to by Partners as one of the major successes of the Partnership.

An important aspect of the work undertaken within the Partnership was bringing the most vulnerable parts of the coast under the control of organisations that shared a common interest in conserving coastal areas [16]. It should be said that corporately the Council has maintained a strong view that an integrated approach to the management of the coast is the optimum method of managing this resource giving evidence to the House of Commons Environment Committee to this effect in 1991 [17].

During the nineties the Partnership continued in much the same format with minor changes such as an increase in the number of Councillors represented on the steering group and a number of new members. All steering group meetings were open to the public [18]. There were no more major physical works carried out although under the Partnership there were a number of successful bids for

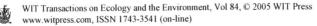

funding for projects developing nature conservation management and examining tourism in the area, amongst other initiatives. However, a number of Partners have related their feelings about the growing frustration that was felt by the non-voting members of the steering group during this time. This manifested itself through more infrequent attendance at the steering group and more emphasis was placed on the sub-groups where practical issues could be addressed.

Following discussion between the principal partners it was decided a reorganisation of the Sefton Coast Management Scheme was needed, and to discuss this a forum was arranged with an independent chair [18]. Following the forum, the Sefton Coast Management Scheme was re-launched as the Sefton Coast Partnership in 2000 [14].

The principal change associated with the move from Management Scheme to Partnership was one of power; the revised organisation all Partners had voting rights and the Councils representation was reduced from eight Councillors to three. The Chair was taken up by one of the voluntary organisations and while the Council was still a Partner it was identified that the partnership should be independent of the Council. The structure of the partnership was still to be determined at this stage but it had been identified that representation needed to be broadened. The existing vision statement was endorsed for the reformed partnership and new Partners to accept.

5 Conclusions

This description of the Partnership and its setting is important for two reasons. Firstly, the Partnership exists in its particular format because of the local characteristics, both temporal and spatial. It came about because of concerns over the physical state of the coast and so has to be considered within the context of societal attitudes and priorities at that point in time. The second reason this description is important is its concentration upon the management aspects of the Partnership; ICZM is by definition about the management process so it must consider what form this management process takes and what the nature of the organisation that delivers it is.

The transformation from Management Scheme to working partnership in the Sefton Coast Partnership is also an important example of how ICZM can be implemented with sustainability at its core. Sustainable management of the coastal zone, particularly on the light of global climate change, requires fluid and responsive strategies together with a mechanism which allows for rapid response to physical environmental change. The Partnership and ICZM in Sefton reflect strongly the local natural environment and its management history and this may be significant to success or failure in the future.

References

[1] Pye, K. & Neal, A., Coastal dune erosion at Formby Point, north Merseyside, England: causes & mechanisms, *Journal of Marine Geology*, **119**, 39-56, 1994.

[2] Official Journal of the European Communities, *Recommendation of the European Parliament and of the Council of 30 May 2002 concerning the implementation of Integrated Coastal Zone Management in Europe*, 2002/413/EC, 2002.

[3] ITAD Ltd & BMT Cordah Ltd, *Assessment of the effectiveness of local coastal management partnerships as a delivery mechanism for ICZM*, Scottish Executive Social Research, Edinburgh, 2002.

[4] Atkins, *ICZM in the UK: A Stocktake*, HMSO, Norwich, 2004.

[5] DETR, *Research into Integrated Coastal Planning in the North West Region*, DETR, London, 2000.

[6] Lymbery, G., *A sustainable environment through partnership – an examination of multiagency, multidisciplinary partnership working & its relevance for environmental management using the Sefton coastal zone as a case study*, Edge Hill University College, Unpublished M.Sc. Thesis, 2004.

[7] The Audit Commission, *A fruitful partnership – effective partnership working*, The Audit Commission, London, 1998.

[8] Harrison, R., Mann, G., Murphy, M., Taylor, A. & Thompson, N., *Partnership Made Painless - A joined-up guide to working together*, Russell House Publishing, Lyme Regis, 2003.

[9] Houston, J.A. & Jones, C.R., The Sefton Coast Management Scheme: Project and Process, *Coastal Management*, **15**, pp. 267-297, 1987.

[10] Evans, S., *Dune Management - A Study of the Sefton Coast, Merseyside*, unpublished research report, Liverpool Polytechnic, 1980.

[11] The Coast Management Scheme Steering Group, *Coast Management Scheme - Plan for coastal management between Hightown and Birkdale*, Sefton Council, Bootle, 1983.

[12] Sefton Council, *Coast Management Plan Review*, Sefton Council, Bootle, 1989.

[13] Countryside Commission, *Local Authority Countryside Management Projects - A guide to their organisation*, Countryside Commission, Cheltenham, 1978.

[14] Sefton Coast Management Scheme, *Annual Report 2000*, Sefton Council, Bootle, 2001.

[15] Sefton Council, *Sefton Coast Management Scheme* (leaflet), Sefton Council, Bootle, 1981.

[16] Sefton Council, *Visit to the Dune Coast at Ainsdale Sands and Formby Point by the Policy and Resources (Land and Development) Sub-Committee*, Bootle, 1980.

[17] Sefton Council, *Memorandum of Evidence to the House of Commons Environment Committee*, Sefton Council, Bootle, 1991.

[18] Sefton Coast Management Scheme, *Annual Report 1999*, Sefton Council, Bootle, 2000.

Collaboration between researchers and practitioners within the context of Integrated Coastal Zone Management: a case study of the north Sefton coast

V. J. C. Holden[1], G. Lymbery[2], C. A. Booth[3], A. T. Worsley[1],
S. Suggitt[1] & P. Wisse[2]
[1]*Natural, Geographical and Applied Sciences,*
Edge Hill University College, Ormskirk, Lancashire, U.K.
[2]*Sefton Coastal Strategy Unit, Ainsdale Discovery Centre Complex,*
Southport, Merseyside, U.K.
[3]*Environmental and Analytical Sciences Division,*
Research Institute in Advanced Technologies (RIATec),
The University of Wolverhampton, Wolverhampton, West Midlands, U.K.

Abstract

This paper reports on a case study of the north Sefton coast where work is currently underway to provide high resolution analysis of contemporary coastal processes, occurring on the salt marsh, with an interrogation of a sizeable archive of data in various forms, also being undertaken to develop a picture of the historical development of the location. The collaboration brings together academic and practitioner sectors and is multidisciplinary in nature. The findings are to be utilized to inform stakeholders with regard to future strategic coastal management planning. This is particularly important in this location due to the influences of sea level change, changing sediment dynamics and anthropogenic factors. The location provides an important site in terms of its requirement for an integrated approach to its management, with the area having a number of demands placed upon it based on the resources that it offers. The collaboration is strengthened by the recognition of the Sefton Coast Partnership to improve understanding of coastal processes operating in the location. The process of the research is divided into the analysis of contemporary sediment samples, artificial marker horizons, historical data and sediment cores, and modelling. The research has the objective of informing long term strategic planning by using a multidisciplinary and holistic approach to coastal management. The benefits of this collaborative approach are outlined.
Keywords: multidisciplinary coastal management, Ribble Estuary, salt marsh.

WIT Transactions on Ecology and the Environment, Vol 84, © 2005 WIT Press
www.witpress.com, ISSN 1743-3541 (on-line)

1 Introduction

The Ribble estuary, in north-west England, is a classic funnel shaped estuary, measuring almost 11km wide at its mouth and being 20km in length [1]. The estuary has been recorded as covering between 70 and 100 km^2 when exposed at low water [1]. The north Sefton coast salt marshes are located on the southern edge of the Ribble Estuary, extending southwards towards the town of Southport, with the southernmost fringes reaching almost to Southport Pier. The marshes are internationally recognized as being of major importance for their provision of habitats, being designated as a Site of Special Scientific Interest (SSSI), a Special Protection Area (SPA) and a RAMSAR site.

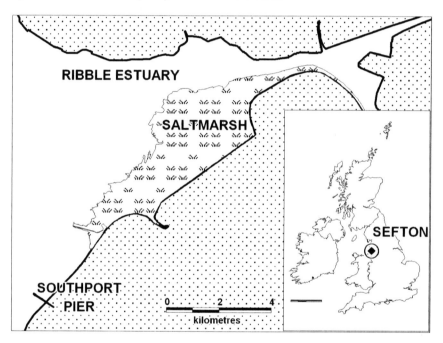

Figure 1:   Plan of the north Sefton coast. Based on the Ordnance Survey map © Crown Copyright produced by Sefton MBC under licence No. LA076317.

The location provides an important site in terms of its requirement for an integrated approach to its management, with the area having a number of demands placed upon it based on the resources that it offers. The understanding of the impacts of human activity in the area are crucial to its management, with tourism and recreation being a key economic factor in the local area, with the recreational beach associated with the town of Southport and bird watching on the marshes being major attractions for visitors and the local population. Human impacts from industry and commerce are also economically and socially important. Land reclaimed from the marshes for agriculture, sand extraction and waste disposal through the construction of the Coast Road are examples of how the location has been changed by human actions. Furthermore, issues such as pollution of both land and water are also anthropogenically-induced factors that are crucial to understand to ensure integrated future strategic management. The understanding of the environmental issues surrounding the area, particularly those involving the management of wildlife and those controlled by legislation and EU Directives such as the Habitats Directive, are crucial to the integration of management strategies. The understanding of all these anthropogenic and environmental factors need to be combined with the physical processes operating in the area, such as changes in the channels in the Estuary, sea-level changes and increasing vegetation.

The development of wetland environments is controlled by the changing balance between tidal regime, wind-wave climate, sediment supply, relative sea level and wetland vegetation [2]. Changes in this balance will result in future movements, further to those already brought about by previous changes in the dynamics. By assessing those changes that have already and are currently occurring and by assigning potential causal rationale to them, it is possible to identify likely future implications of changes in any of the controlling factors. Salt marshes in particular are responsive to changes in relative sea-level due to their nature of being a dynamic soft sediment coastal type [3]. The dynamic nature of the coast will result in the future responses of the coast being complex, particularly where influenced by human impacts [2]. It is anticipated that the long term effects of sea-level rise will cause a slow landward encroachment of the high and low water lines, leading to previously stable coastlines to react with an increased level of erosion, increased siltation, raised groundwater, drainage impedance, saline intrusion and migration of ecological zones [3, 4].

2   The Sefton Coast Partnership

The Sefton Coast Partnership (SCP) was originally established as the Sefton Coast Management Scheme in 1978 after a significant consultation amongst Statutory Bodies and local stakeholders. Its principal remit was nature conservation and coastal defence. The initial problem which gave rise to the need for the Management Scheme was conflict between recreational pressures, the desire to preserve the valuable sand dune habitat, and concerns over coastal defence. The Partnership comprises a range of organizations and bodies representing the interests of landowners, users, and other stakeholders. It comprises a Board, with a Working Party to support the Board and a number of task groups reporting to the Working Party. Whilst it has no statutory powers it seeks to achieve consensus amongst the partners in order to realize the commonly agreed vision of the Partnership.

Even before the formation of the partnership, there had been a long established recognition of the need to improve understanding of coastal processes. Previously, research into understanding was carried out on a more fragmented basis and in relation to specific issues, such as the effects of construction of training walls within the estuaries. Within the Partnership, the recognition has continued, being now more coordinated, and takes a long-term perspective. An illustration of this is that a specific task group has been established to address research, and that on two previous occasions, Sefton Metropolitan Borough Council (SMBC) have sponsored PhD research projects, as well as other more conventional research projects commissioned through consultants.

The specific partners associated with this collaborative piece of research are Edge Hill, who chair the Research Task Group, and the Technical Services Department of SMBC, who take a lead on geomorphology with particular reference to future coastal change. It is worth noting that SMBC are now looking at up to 100 years hence when considering future coastal change, as a requirement of policy development.

3 How the collaboration contributes to Integrated Coastal Zone Management (ICZM)

ICZM is a process for delivering sustainable development, which seeks to be multisectoral and multidisciplinary. This collaboration brings together the academic and practitioner sectors as well as encompassing a range of disciplines, principally engineering, geomorphology and sedimentology. When considering the collaboration against the principles of ICZM it will be shown within the following case study that it is taking a long-term perspective and has local specificity. It is also taking a holistic approach by taking into account a wide variety of influences, and through improved understanding of natural processes it facilities working with them.

4 Case study of the north Sefton coast

4.1 Background

Recent observations from Sefton Metropolitan Borough Council and from concerns expressed by local residents through various media have indicated a change in the sedimentation balance of the outer estuary, with muddy areas developing in a southerly direction towards the town of Southport's central coastal tourism attraction of the pier. This influx of mud is considered a major aesthetic issue by the local community, with potentially serious implications for the local tourism industry. The rapidity of this change coupled with the environmental, social and economic value of the salt marsh also makes it essential that investigations are undertaken into the sedimentology of this section of coastline to establish benchmark information on the processes occurring. The Ribble Estuary Shoreline Management Plan [5] identified sea-level rise and salt marsh spread as two issues within the management of the particular area of coast. The management issues are appreciable from a number of standpoints, such as nature conservation, sea defence, navigation and industrial activity.

This research therefore provides a permanent record and database of the current situation and historical development of the north Sefton coast salt marshes that can be utilised to inform with regard to sea level change. Using this baseline data, other factors such as vegetation characteristics are being investigated to evaluate and model future changes, thereby contributing to the strategic planning of coastal change management. Sefton Coastal Partnership in their 2001 Annual report identified a need to "collate all existing salt marsh data" [6] to enable it to be used in an integrated manner across partnerships.

The data collected during this field work and subsequent laboratory analyses is being used with historic evidence such as aerial photographs and historic maps and charts, to determine the precise nature of coastal changes, the causes of these changes and then used as a predictive tool to anticipate future changes. This process can be sub-divided into the analysis of contemporary sediment samples, artificial marker horizons, historical data and sediment cores, and modelling.

4.2 Contemporary sediment samples

Samples of the top few centimetres of sediment were collected from the study area, representing the contemporary surface sediment. A sub-sample of the bulk sediment was retained from each sample, with a portion of the remaining sample being fractionated into specific grain size fractions, namely sand (2 mm to 63 μm), silt (63 μm to 2 μm) and clay-sized (<2 μm) materials. This was followed by a series of environmental magnetics tests on the bulk and individual size fractions of each original sample.

To allow the future modeling work to assign potential source areas for the contemporary sediment to essentially trace the provenance of the sediment, further sediment samples have been collected from other regional sources. Potential marine-based samples have been collected from the Irish Sea bed, and from a series of locations throughout the Mersey estuary and Liverpool Bay. In addition, intertidal sediment samples have been collected from Formby Point to the south, and the coastline to the north of the Ribble estuary (Fleetwood, Blackpool and Lytham). Samples of potential terrestrial sources of sediment have been collected from a number of rivers that drain into the Ribble Estuary (above their Normal Tidal Limits). By fractionating these 'source' samples in an identical manner to the contemporary 'Southport' samples, and by then carrying out an identical set of magnetics measurements on these samples, it is then perceived that it will be possible to carry out a provenance analysis of the contemporary sediments from the salt marsh surface [7, 8, 9, 10]. From there, it is envisaged that the origin of the contemporary sediments can be identified, allowing high resolution mapping of the sediment dynamics of the coastline.

4.3 Artificial marker horizons

Artificial marker horizons have been established at the study site to determine the level and subsequent rate of vertical accretion of the salt marsh. The measurement of this rate is crucial to understanding the response of the salt marsh to sea level rise, with the balance between the surface elevation of the marsh, through the process of vertical accretion, and a rise in sea-level being critical, [3, 11]. If the rate of accretion is lower than that of local sea-level rise, then the marsh will become submerged and effectively lost to the sea. If the rate of accretion is higher than that of sea-level, then the marsh will develop further; and if the two levels are overall equal, then the system will reach equilibrium, [3]. Artificial marker horizons are based on the principle of having a known surface that is distinguishable from the surrounding sediment. The markers were all established at a known depth, and from that point in time onwards, any sediment being deposited on the marker can be measured.

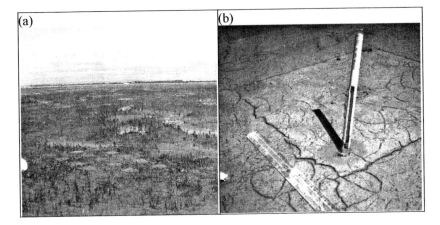

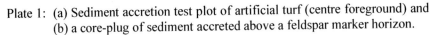

Plate 1: (a) Sediment accretion test plot of artificial turf (centre foreground) and (b) a core-plug of sediment accreted above a feldspar marker horizon.

Marker horizons will establish a spatially orientated baseline of the rates of accretion of contemporary sediments occurring upon the surface of the marsh. The sites under investigation exhibit significantly different characteristics, with varying stages of saltmarsh development. Thirteen sites are being investigated, with six marker horizons established at each site (total number of markers = 78). The materials selected as markers range from the previously proven materials of feldspar and brick dust [12, 13, 14, 15, 16, 17, 18], through to those used for different purposes but in similar environments (artificial turf), to those previously untested in this context (limestone, polypropylene and 'undisturbed'). This research is aiming to establish a basis to enable long-term monitoring of accretion rates, whilst allowing a comparison between the different material types and monitoring techniques.

All the marker horizons are being sampled approximately every two months to provide a cumulative rate of accretion, whilst potentially being able to demonstrate any variations in accretion due to seasonality or tidal conditions. The mineral markers of limestone, feldspar and brick dust are sampled initially by recording percentage cover, until sufficient sediment has accreted on the surface of the marker to allow small scale coring. The polypropylene, artificial turf and undisturbed markers are all being monitored by measuring down to the surface of the marker (or surface of the saltmarsh in the case of the undisturbed marker) using depth probes. In addition to the regular monitoring, the elevation of each of the undisturbed marker pegs was recorded at the time of installation by a survey company contracted by Sefton Metropolitan Borough Council, which is repeated annually. This will give a further high definition comparison with the accretion figures being recorded throughout the year, whilst also giving an indication of the applicability of the undisturbed marker method to conditions on the saltmarsh such as compaction and subsidence of the marker pegs.

4.4 Historical archive data and sediment cores

A significant archive of historical and contemporary data has been made available to this research by Sefton MBC. This data is in the form of aerial photographs; maps, charts and plans; historical photographs; published and unpublished reports; topographic data; survey data; vegetation survey data; and sediment survey data. Some data is already digitized, with other data being in original 'hard copy'.

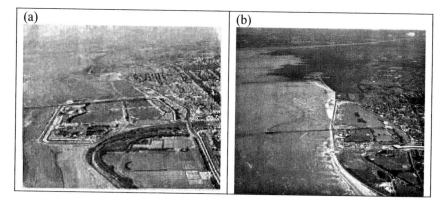

Plate 2: (a) Southport, looking north, pre reclamation, *ca.*1960s; (b) Same view, after reclamation, 1995. Photographs supplied courtesy of Sefton MBC.

The digital data such as aerial photographs and topographic data is being analysed using a Geographical Information System (GIS). The former provide a wealth of information regarding changes in the saltmarsh, such as vegetation changes and changes in the edge of the salt marsh over time. A large number of historic plans and maps, dating from the 18th Century are also available for the research to map changes in channel positions within the Ribble Estuary, which are significant for the sediment dynamics and morphology of the area. In addition, survey data relating to the profile lines being studied in this research are being used to analyse changes in elevation, beach profile, and movements of morphological features such as channels. Data of this type is available dating from 1913. More recently, topographic surveys of the coastline have been conducted using GPS systems to monitor the elevation of the coastline. This data is also available digitally to allow for spatial and temporal analysis in a GIS.

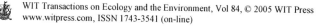

Sefton MBC have also granted unlimited access to their archive of historical photographs relating to the coastline, many of which are invaluable in providing additional evidence for many of the changes identified in the location. The archives also hold a substantial library of reports and both published and unpublished data, which can be accessed for the purposes of this research that would otherwise be unavailable. These include many Government published reports, and documentation relating to the sand extraction licenses in Southport, along with many unpublished reports produced by sub-contractors and consultancies.

To further enhance the historical data, sediment cores will be taken from each marker horizon location (thirteen in total), to establish the historical nature of the sediment deposited along the coastline over time. The data produced from this analysis will be used in conjunction with the archived data being made available by Sefton MBC to create a full picture of the development of the salt marsh with evidenced reasoning as to the current environmental setting.

4.5 Modelling of future change

Modelling of potential future changes will be undertaken based upon the known baseline information obtained throughout the research, incorporating the contribution of various sediment sources, both at the present day and during the Late-Holocene. This will facilitate determination of the relative importance of changing sea level, regional and local wind and wave activity, sediment supply, climate fluctuations and anthropogenic factors on the past, present and future evolution of the coast.

5 Conclusions

The collaborative research therefore links to the principles of ICZM, as it carries through it an underlying objective of informing long-term strategic planning, which reinforces the ability to adapt management strategies accordingly. The multi-disciplinary approach to investigating the development of the coast also links to the principle of adopting a broad holistic approach to coastal management.

When carried out successfully, there are numerous benefits to all parties in working collaboratively. For the academic researcher, there is an obvious benefit in provision of access to data sets that may otherwise be unobtainable (for example commissioned consultancy reports), and also to networks and individuals who may be of benefit both directly to the research and in terms of raising awareness of the work. It can also lead to the development of a means of mentoring and knowledge support additional to that of the academic institution. The multidisciplinary nature of the supervisory and advisory team is particularly beneficial to the progression of the research by offering different specialisms of the team to benefit the methodological development. For the practitioner or industrial sponsor it allows a level of control of the outputs generated by the research, particularly if regular contact is maintained throughout the programme of work. The practitioner will also have a greater ownership of the research, and through the ongoing involvement in the work can develop a better understanding of the issue.

There are also significant benefits to the local area to working in this way, through the collaborative research leading to a greater understanding at all levels which through the Sefton Coast Partnership can be used to inform stakeholders, allowing future sustainable policy development. Through this experience of collaborative working, although many areas of the research have been designed to have local specificity, there are many areas that are generic to both the disciplines and the method of working.   There are therefore considerable implications for the transfer of knowledge from this research to other national and international situations. In terms of methodology, the findings of the different materials for use as artificial marker horizons can be applied to many other UK and northern European coastal settings. Similarly there can be beneficial transfer of this method of working across not only geographical regions but also disciplines.

Acknowledgements

This research forms part of the research development programme funded by Edge Hill University College, to whom VJCH gratefully acknowledges receipt of a bursaried Ph.D. studentship. All authors would like to thank Sefton Metropolitan Borough Council for their financial assistance through project sponsorship and technical support and assistance provided with fieldwork. Assistance and support from the following bodies is also gratefully acknowledged: English Nature, Proudman Oceanographic Laboratory, Mersey Docks and Harbour Company, Centre for Environmental and Fisheries Advisory Service (CEFAS), Ibstock Brick Ltd, and Tarmac North Wales Ltd.

References

[1]   Sefton Metropolitan Borough Council, *Guide to the Sefton Coast Database*. Sefton MBC, Bootle, 1983.
[2]   Viles, H. & Spencer, T., *Coastal Problems*. Edward Arnold Publishers, 1995.
[3]   Haslett, S.K., *Coastal Systems*. Routledge, London, 2000.
[4]   Pethick, J., Coastal management and sea-level rise. *Catena*, **42**, pp. 307-322, 2001.
[5]   Ribble Estuary Shoreline Management Partnership, *Shoreline Management Plan*. Sefton MBC, Bootle, 2002.
[6]   Sefton Coastal Partnership, *Annual Report*. Sefton MBC, Bootle, 2001.
[7]   Yu, L. & Oldfield, F., Quantitative sediment source ascription using magnetic measurements in a reservoir-catchment system near Nijar, S.E. Spain. *Earth Surface Processes & Landforms*, **18**, pp. 441-454, 1993.
[8]   Lees, J.A. & Pethick, J.S., Problems associated with quantitative magnetic sourcing of sediments of the Scarborough to Mablethorpe coast, Northeast

England, UK. *Earth Surface Processes & Landforms*, **20**, pp. 795-806, 1995.

[9]   Lees, J., Evaluating magnetic parameters for use in source identification, classification and modeling of natural and environmental materials. In: Walden, J., Oldfield, F. & Smith, J.P. (Eds) *Environmental Magnetism: a practical guide*. Technical guide, No. 6. Quaternary Research Association, London, pp. 113-138, 1999.

[10] Walden, J., Slattery, M.C. & Burt, T.P., Use of mineral magnetic measurements to fingerprint suspended sediment sources: approaches and techniques for data analysis. *Journal of Hydrology*, **202**, pp. 353-372, 1997.

[11] Reed, D.J., The response of coastal marshes to sea-level rise: Survival or submergence? *Earth Surface Processes & Landforms*, **20**, pp. 39-48, 1995.

[12] Cahoon, D.R. & Turner, R.E., Accretion and canal impacts in a rapidly subsiding wetland II. Feldspar marker horizon technique. *Estuaries*, **12**, pp. 260-268, 1989.

[13] Wood, M.E., Kelley, J.T. & Belknap, D.F., Patterns of sediment accumulation in the tidal marshes of Maine. *Estuaries*, **12**, pp. 237-246, 1989.

[14] Shi, Z., Recent salt marsh accretion and sea level fluctuations in the Dyfi Estuary, central Cardigan Bay, Wales, UK. *Geo-Marine Letters*, **13**, pp. 182-188, 1993.

[15] Cahoon, D.R., Reed, D.J. & Day, J.W., Estimating shallow subsidence in microtidal salt marshes of the southeastern United States: Kaye and Barghoorn revisited. *Marine Geology*, **128**, pp. 1-9, 1995.

[16] Cahoon, D.R., Lynch, J.C. & Powell, A.N., Marsh vertical accretion in a southern California estuary, U.S.A. *Estuarine, Coastal & Shelf Science*, **43**, pp. 19-32, 1996.

[17] Roman, C.T., Peck, J.A., Allen, J.R., King, J.W. & Appleby, P.G., Accretion of a New England (U.S.A.) salt marsh in response to inlet migration, storms, and sea-level rise. *Estuarine, Coastal & Shelf Science*, **45**, pp. 717-727, 1997.

[18] Ford, M.A., Cahoon, D.R. & Lynch, J.C., Restoring marsh elevation in a rapidly subsiding salt marsh by thin-layer deposition of dredged material. *Ecological Engineering*, **12**, pp. 189-205, 1999.

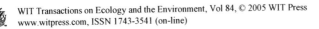

Application of P-S-R framework on the sustainable utilization of shallow artificial lakes management

H.-C. Su[1], L.-C. Chang[2] & S.-Y. Hsieh[3]
[1]*Construction and Disaster Prevention Research Center,
Feng Chia University, Taichung, Taiwan, Republic of China*
[2]*Department of Civil Engineering, National Chiao Tung University,
Hsinchu, Taiwan, Republic of China*
[3]*Institute of Planning and Hydraulic Research, Water Resources Agency,
Ministry of Economic Affairs, Taichung, Taiwan, Republic of China*

Abstract

Water resources management and drainage face a great barrage with the higher and higher density of urban development. However, for development of a modern city, the ecology, landscape, and detention ponds are necessary and welcome features. Furthermore, how to expand the functions of the above ponds as multi-purpose shallow constructed lakes might be helpful. There are conflicts between different purposes practically, such as ecology and detention, ecology and water supply. Then it is necessary to adjust the operation strategies of each consideration purpose to reach a maximum efficiency. This study applies the pressure-state-response (P-S-R) framework which is developed from OECD to analyze the available operation rules for water supply, flood detention, and ecosystem maintenance. Furthermore, a suitable strategy could be compromised between the above purposes, and necessary facilities could be designed. A study case is herein proposed and analyzed throughout P-S-R processes, and then the indicators and considerations are offered at the end.
Keywords: pressure-state-response, shallow constructed lake, water supply, flood detention, ecosystem maintenance.

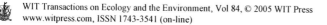

1   Introduction

The problem of limited water resources allocation has increased during the past decades owing to the fast economic development and population increase. Hence artificial lake development is one water resource strategy instead of reservoirs in Taiwan. However, the artificial lakes with large area are also a problem on land, environment impact, water source, construction cost, and so on. Therefore, the detention ponds, ecosystem ponds, and the landscape ponds could be also thought of as other such artificial lakes with small-scale region. However, assessment of flexible operation strategies is important when considering sustainable water use for different purposes.

This study uses the P-S-R (Pressure-State-Response) framework to assist the decision maker for artificial lakes construction and management. More recently, the P-S-R framework has been tested by the national and international organisations (ANKARA 1998). In Taiwan, from 1998, the National Science Council initiated and sponsored an integrated research project to establish sustainable development indicators (SDI). The SDI for Taiwan, which was selected, based on an extended PSR model and the salient features of Taiwan, highlight the linkage between the impact of social and economic pressures on the state of the environment and resources and related institutional responses (Yeh and Lee [11]).

As established above, the lands gain is an important factor for each project about artificial lake construction in Taiwan. More recently, there is a tendency for the artificial lakes of different scales to be designed for multi-purpose utilization. Constructed shallow lakes are dynamic systems that change in response to internal and external inputs and processes How to make a complete consideration between the different purposes is a great challenge to decision-makers. The P-S-R framework used in this study does enable decision-makers to scope complex problems surrounded by uncertainties in a comprehensive, yet understandable way.

For urban development, detention ponds are a necessary facility on flood control and for stormwater storage for a few days in general. Besides, the collect rainfall could be further used for landscape, emergencies, and so on. Therefore, one detention pond at Tainan Science Park, Taiwan is adopted for this case study. Assessment indicators are selected based on the P-S-R framework, to help decision-makers to possess the function including making use of water supply, flood detention, and ecological environment. Moreover, a stable cycle of water flow is projected to preserve the quality and quantity of water sources together with the balance and cycling system of the ecosystem.

2   Sustainable framework the P-S-R model

There are numerous frameworks to assist decision makers on sustainable management. OECD created a conceptual framework, and named at the Pressure-State-Response (P-S-R) in 1994. As a result, it is clearly known that the framework is as follows (ANKARA 1998).

(i)   comprising both human activities and the natural environment
(ii)   landing itself to the presentation of a wide range of environmental phenomena
(iii)   emphasising the causal link between how economies operate and how this impacts the environment

This framework was tested by the national and international organisations. The main categories in the P-S-R framework are (Muskoka Watershed Council 2003):

(i)   Indirect and underlying direct pressure, including human activities that cause environmental change
(ii)   The physical, chemical, and biological condition or state of the natural world, plus human health and welfare.
(iii)   Response or change in policy or behaviour by governments, private sector, households and individuals, including efforts to ameliorate environmental conditions.
(iv)   Effect on ecosystem, human health and human welfare

The framework could be established as in figure 1. Moreover, four relevant questions can be asked (Muskoka Watershed Council [5]):

(i)   What is happening in the environment? (state)
(ii)   Why is it significant? (effects)
(iii)   Why is it happening? (pressure)
(iv)   What are we going to do about it? (social response)

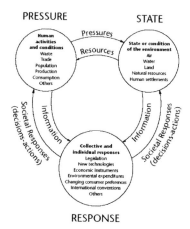

Figure 1:   P-S-R framework demonstration (Pintér et al. [7]).

3   The sustainable development indicators

Within the P-S-R framework, the following types of indicators can be established (OECD):

(i)   Indicators of environmental pressures correspond to the "pressure" box of the PSR framework. They describe pressures from human activities

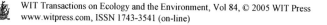

exerted on the environment, including the quality and quantity of natural resources.

(ii) Indicators of environmental conditions correspond to the "state" box of the PSR framework and relate to the quality of the environment and the quality and quantity of natural resources. As such they reflect the ultimate objective of environmental policy making. Indicators of environmental conditions should be designed to give an overview of the situation (the state) of the environment and its development over time, and not the pressures on it.

(iii) Indicators of social responses correspond to the "response" box in the PSR framework. Social response indicators are measurements which show to what degree society is responding to environmental changes and concerns. Societal responses also include actions for the preservation and the conservation of the environment and natural resources.

In general, environmental indicators serve to reduce the complexity of environmental problems and to increase the transparency of the possible trade-offs involved in specific policy choices. The National Council for Sustainable Development (NCSD) at the Executive Yuan in Taiwan has been extremely proactive in promoting efforts towards the development of a set of Taiwan's sustainable development indicators based on P-S-R framework from 1998. This study will firstly consider the developed indicators which have been defined by NCSD.

4 Case study

4.1 Study area

One of the detention ponds at Tainan Science Park Taiwan is examined in this case, and named the shallow artificial lake in this work. The shallow artificial .lake is of area 5 ha., maximum water depth 2m, watershed 100ha. Two reference water depths are proposed, one is 30cm and named the ecosystem maintain water depth, another is 1m and named the landscape maintain water depth. There are no natural water sources around. The primary purpose of the shallow artificial .lake is flood detention for sure; the others are ecological environment and water supply. For the purposes of water supply and flood detention, more water/storage is better which conflicts with the purpose of ecological environment. How to make an acceptable operation policy between the above three purposes is a question to decision-makers.

4.2 Sustainable indicators development

This study is a demonstration for assisting decision-makers to construct an assessment plan using P-S-R framework before artificial lakes building. For individual purpose, the operation goal and environmental impact factors should be firstly understood. Then the possible policies and assessment indicators are further recommended. Moreover, the assessment indicators can be thresholds between the three purposes in operation. Using P-S-R framework, the related statements for individual purpose are as follows.

4.2.1 Purpose of flood detention

The main point is how much flood will be stored for flood detention purpose. Hence the volume of the artificial lake is the most important. The indicators through P-S-R framework could be stated as follows.

1. Task — keeping a maximum storage volume before Stormwater warning
2. Pressure indicator — Rainfall (Stormwater)
3. State indicator — Artificial lake volume following time, hydrological parameters (e.g.: Manning's N), geological parameters (e.g.: roughness, slope, land use), soil erosion, water quality
4. Response indicator (policy) — Investigation of candidate sites of artificial lake, vegetable around the artificial lake, evaluation of flood detention volume, operation rules and facilities of flood inlet (detention) and outlet (drainage)
5. Assessment indicator (threshold) — Effects of Flood detention: $\left(Q_p - Q_{pb} \middle/ Q_p \right) \times 100\%$

   where Q_p is the peak before artificial lake construction, Q_{pb} indicates the peak after artificial lake development

4.2.2 Purpose of water supply

The main point is how much water will be supported for water supply purpose. The indicators through P-S-R framework could be stated as follows

1. Task — Maximum obtainable water supply
2. Pressure indicator — Water sources, rainfall
3. State indicator — Artificial lake volume following time, water quality, moisture content
4. Response indicator (policy) — Stable water source volume, a flexible water supply strategy, standard of water quality, Investigation of candidate sites of artificial lake, investigation of land use within watershed
5. Assessment indicator (threshold) — Effects of water supply, a general approach is amount and duration of water shortage:

   $$\text{Shortage Index (SI)} = \frac{100}{N} \sum_{t=1}^{N} \left(\frac{TS_t}{TD_t} \right) r$$

   where N is the number of analysis days, TS_t indicates annual shortage (annual demand volume minus annual volume supplied), and D_A is annual demand volume. Usually SI=1 is adopted in Taiwan.

4.2.3 Purpose of ecological environment

The main goal is to construct a healthy water environment, and, minimum water is necessary to conserve. This study concentrated on a multipurpose artificial lake design; hence biodiversity could not be used. From numerous researches, nutrient is the most important factor in this kind of interior water body (Hondzo and Stefan [4], Cao [2]). The most sources of nutrients are phosphorus from our reservoirs investigation (Taipei Feitsui Reservoir Administration [8]). The indicators through P-S-R framework could be stated as follows

1.	Task	Keeping a proper water environment and supporting a healthy habitat for ecosystem
2.	Pressure indicator	Environmental impact, including human behaviour, climate disturbance, etc.
3.	State indicator	Habitat types, water quality (nitrogen, phosphorous, etc.), algae, nutrient, Biodiversity,
4.	Response indicator (policy)	Environmental monitoring and maintain plan, nutrient control, distribution and design of geomorphology around artificial lake, investigation of original species, vegetable around the artificial lake
5.	Assessment indicator (threshold)	Nutrient index (could be adopted before the artificial lake contribution): phosphorous concentration
		Biodiversity (after artificial lake development, thru the environmental monitoring plan)

4.2.4 Multi-purpose: flood detention, water supply and ecological environment

From the above statement, some conflicts could be observed obviously. For example: one of pressure indicators to ecological environment purpose is disturbance from human behaviour, however, the water supply and flood storage/drainage are disturbance for ecosystem. For the purposes of water supply and flood detention, the more water supply and storage capacity the better. Nevertheless, the minimum ecosystem water must be conserved all the time. Accordingly, the assessment indicator for each purpose could be a threshold when defining operation rules including the above three purposes.

4.3 Results

This case proposed flexible operation rules through P-S-R framework, and further adopted a system dynamics (SD) package, Vensim, as the analysis tool to examine whether to pass threshold values. A demonstrated artificial lake system is drawn as figure 2. The proposed operation rules considering water supply, flood detention and ecological environment purpose are summarized as follows.

(i) 600 m³/day is the daily public water demand: When water depth is higher than landscape maintain water depth, daily water demand is reduced as 80% of demand. Water supply strategy stops when the water depth is lower than ecosystem maintained water depth.

(ii) Water in the lake will be drained out to channel, till ecosystem maintains water depth, 24 hours before a stormwater warning.

(iii) A wetland is designed upstream of the artificial lake, and absorbability is assumed 50% of phosphorous of inflow.

(iv)   A fundamental lake model in the ecosystem is adopted to simulate the relationship between phytoplankton, phosphorous, light, and so on.

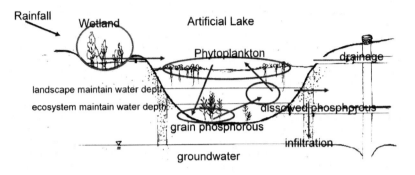

Figure 2:   Artificial Lake System illustration.

Using the SD package, Vensim, to simulate the above proposed operation rules, and one year rainfall records from the Taiwan Central Weather Bureau are adopted as a runoff evaluation. The commutated assessment indicators are:

(i)   Effects of flood detention =22.6%. Numerous experiments made at Taiwan demonstrated that the flood detention effect larger than 18% is acceptable through benefit cost ratio analysis (Water Resources Planning Institute 2004).

(ii)   Water supply: Shortage Index (SI) =1.521. Usually, SI which is larger than and equals to 1 is receivable for water supply purpose.

(iii) Ecological environment: phosphorous concentration during one year is kept lower than 40µg/L.

The above three indicators are satisfied with threshold, hence the above proposed strategies of each purpose are receivable.

5   Conclusions

Residence environment improvement is a tendency for all developed countries; Taiwan also faces the challenge especially for urban regions. The landscape and detention ponds are agreeable to fit ecosystem need and support public water use in the meantime. However, how to define a flexible operation strategy between each purpose is an important issue. The P-S-R framework which is developed by OECD may be satisfactory. Moreover, this study adopted the P-S-R framework and applied it on a proposed case, then some conclusions can be illustrated as follows.

(i)   The strategies of water use/storage capacity and necessary facilities can be much more clear for each purpose (here is public water supply, flood detention and ecosystem maintenance) using P-S-R framework. For example, a minimum ecosystem maintenance water depth is important to keep whenever daily public water supply and flood detention is a top priority.

(ii) Assessment indicators which are thresholds could be easily found throughout the P-S-R framework and easily evaluated. In this case study, shortage index SI, Effects of flood detention and phosphorous concentration are an assessment index for water supply, flood detention and ecological environment separately.

(iii) This study finally utilizes a SD package, Vensim, to link and simulate the assessment indicators under proposed strategies of each purpose. However, the proposed strategies are agreeable when all the three assessment indicators satisfy the threshold; otherwise the strategies must be re-planned.

(iv) Urbanized shallow lakes (ponds) would become more and more important on local microclimate, landscape, water accessible space, emergency water or public water need, and so on. However, lands for constructed shallow lakes are not easy to gain, especially for a country with a high density population such as Taiwan. Artificial lakes are consequently designed for multipurposes as a considerable public construction. The whole system and analyzed scheme could be developed further, e.g., evaportranspiration, a real lake ecosystem model, public water need for a novel community.

Acknowledgements

This study was supported at 2004, by Institute of Planning & Hydraulic Research, Water Resources Agency, Ministry of Economic Affairs, Taiwan, Republic of China.

References

[1] ANKARA, National and International Environment and Sustainable Development Indicators, 1988

[2] Cao, S.-S., *Ecosystem of Lakes and Reservoirs*, 2003. (in Chinese)

[3] Hammond, A., Adriaanse, A., Rodenburg, E., Bryant, D., Woodward, R., Environmental Indicators: A Systematic Approach to Measuring and Reporting ion Environmental Policy Performance in the Context of Sustainable Development, World Resources Institute, Washington, DC., 1995.

[4] Hondzo M., Stefan, H.G., Long-term lake water quality predictors, *Water Research*, 30(12), pp.2835-2852, 1996

[5] Muskoka Watershed Council, Indicators of Watershed Health, 2003.

[6] OECD Environmental Directorate, OECD Key Environmental Indicators, 2004

[7] Pintér, L., Zahedi, K., Cressman, D.R., *Capacity Building for Integrated Environmental Assessment and Reporting: Training Manual,*

International Institute for Sustainable Development, United Nations Environment Programme & Ecologistics International, Ltd., 2000.

[8] Taipei Feitsui Reservoir Administration, *Study on Ecosystem Simulation for Feitsui Reservoir's water quality monitoring*, 2000. (in Chinese)

[9] Water Resources Planning Institute, Water Resources Agency, Ministry of Economic Affairs, *Study on Sustainable Utilization of Multi-purposes Artificial Lakes*, Taichung, Taiwan, 2004. (in Chinese)

[10] WCED, Our Common Future, Oxford University Press, UK, 1987.

[11] Yeh, Jiunn-Rong & Lee, Ling-Ling, Sustainable Development Indicators for Taiwan, *Newsletter of the International Human Dimensions Programme on Global Environmental Change*, 2002.

Asset management for environmental infrastructure

A. R. Perks[1], S. Devnani[1], R. Denham[1] & M. N. Thippeswamy[2]
[1]R.V. Anderson Associates Limited, Ontario, Canada
[2]Bangalore Water Supply and Sewerage Board, Bangalore, India

Abstract

New models for asset management applicable to the needs of secondary cities and towns can help achieve more sustainable public water services, operated on a sound technical and financial basis, and more responsive to customer needs. This paper describes Guidelines for Asset Management prepared by R.V. Anderson Associates Limited (RVA) with the financial assistance of the Canadian International Development Agency (CIDA). The guidelines were intended to promote pragmatic asset management practices in India, based on pioneering work carried out by RVA in Canada, coupled with the firm's planning, design and operations experience in India over the last 10 years. The approach is illustrated through an example Cost of Service determination for the City of Bangalore using readily available operating data and information.
Keywords: water, asset management, cost of service, operations, maintenance, private sector, capacity building, partnership.

1   Introduction

Environmental infrastructure, such as water supply, wastewater treatment and solid waste systems, is the foundation for all urban settlements. However, such infrastructure is very capital intensive, and must be developed over many decades at significant cost and investment. These investments may be implemented with development assistance loans to exacting international design standards. But once commissioned, the management capacity is often not present in the local municipalities that are now responsible for operations and maintenance in India. The result has often been rapid deterioration of physical assets, and a downward spiral of poor service, inadequate revenues, and declining investment. Asset Management practices can help break this cycle.

2   Asset management

Asset Management is essentially a planning process intended to reduce operational costs, increase operating efficiency, and maximize the service reliability of each component and the system as a whole [2, 12]. An Asset Management Plan is the first step towards operating the utility on a sustainable technical and financial basis.

2.1 Implementing asset management

The initial step involves preparing an inventory or "register" of the assets and determining their current condition according to an appropriate rating or scale. Only then can the optimal operational costs and capital investment needed to renew the infrastructure over its entire life cycle be estimated. Initially, the approach may be limited in terms of the level of detail applied, because only aggregate data (technical and financial) is usually available at the outset.

The utility operator can then prepare cost estimates to determine the replacement value of existing assets. The replacement cost method usually provides a suitable basis for evaluation.

A good understanding of the general condition of the entire asset base is necessary to enable assessment of future needs for repairs, rehabilitation and replacement. Often, current condition data is not available, or is incomplete, and surrogate indicators, such as installation date and breakdown records, are needed. The accumulated data can be used to identify the type of investments required during the lifecycle of each group of assets, such as treatment plants, pump stations or distribution networks. The different investment activities required over the life of the assets may include routine O&M, rehabilitation and replacement activities.

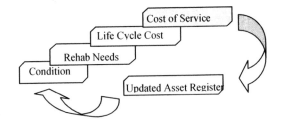

Figure 1:   Asset management.

The next step is to generate a life cycle cost profile for each main component and the system as a whole. The timing of investments can be assigned on the basis of operating information and the estimated remaining life of the asset.

The final step is to estimate the cost of service so that this can be compared with current or projected revenues, and appropriates adjustments made to the cost or revenue base to ensure sustainability. Section 4 demonstrates this approach for the Bangalore water system.

2.2 Cost models

It is important to have a good understanding of capital and operational costs when developing an asset management plan. Water supply capital costs in Asia are typically in the range of US$75-125 per person, including treatment and distribution infrastructure.

Annual operations & maintenance and routine renewal costs would be in the range of 5% per annum. This is consistent with recent North American experience [5, 7, 12], although little published information is available to calibrate this against international conditions.

Rehabilitation of assets with long life spans, such as water systems, is often estimated on a straight-line depreciation basis. Therefore, assets with a 50 year lifespan would be assessed a replacement charge of 2% per annum. According to recent benchmarking studies, most utilities are still investing well below this level at the present time.

Existing debt repayment obviously varies widely depending upon the history of each utility and the economic and political conditions under which it has been operated. However, most well run utilities would endeavour to keep debt charges below the level of 30% of the annual operations and maintenance costs.

The above considerations provide a framework for a simple asset management model for water supply systems. This could be further broken down into purification, distribution, and administration costs (typically in the range of 30%, 30%, and 40% respectively). On this basis a typical investment of $125 per person would break down as follows.

Table 1:   Asset management model for water supply.

Water Supply Capital Asset Value (CAV) per person	$125.00	
Annual O&M cost @ 5% of CAV		$6.25
Treatment and Purification cost @ 30% O&M	$1.88	
Distribution and Storage cost @ 30% of O&M	$1.88	
General and Administrative costs @ 40% of O&M	$2.50	
Renewal of short life assets @ 2% of CAV per annum		$2.50
Debt repayment @ 30% of annual O&M Cost (maximum)		$1.90
Per person annual cost		$10.65

Assuming a water consumption of 100 l/c/d, then these costs would be reflected in a water rate of about $.29 per cu.m. of water consumed. This is similar to many reported water O&M costs throughout Asia and Africa.

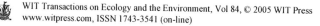

In terms of O&M costs, the data available [1, 3, 4, 6, 8, 9, 11, 13] included several recent benchmarking documents for Asia and Africa, supplemented by RVA project files. These generally reported typical O&M costs of $.15-$.45 per cubic metre of water sold. In order to take the wide variability of the data into account, special attention was given to utilities reporting an operating ratio close to 1.0 as being indicative of those agencies in which O&M costs and revenues would be roughly in balance.

One of the lessons learned from this assessment is that the basic O&M cost for water service seems to be affordable in most instances. However, rehabilitation and replacement costs, as well as debt servicing costs, can drive up water service costs significantly.

3 Best management practices

Some other "Best Practices" should be kept in mind when developing an Asset Management Plan. Specific examples and illustrations have been drawn from typical Canadian and/or international guidelines and case studies [1, 2, 6, 10].

3.1 Level of service

A better understanding of the level of service to be provided can then be applied to building customer awareness, monitoring performance against key indicators, and developing asset management strategies for improved service delivery. Important technical and functional performance indicators may include water quality and quantity, O&M program, capital and operational cost, health and safety, and customer service. It is usually preferable to adopt a few simple, measurable indicators rather than a complex matrix of factors.

3.2 Demand forecasting and management

Because of the level of investment and the lengthy planning-design-construction cycles involved, 20-25 year planning horizons are usually used for environmental infrastructure.

In the past, it was usually sufficient to extrapolate past water consumption trends or use established guidelines, and this may still be appropriate for small systems. However, due to rapidly changing economic factors and increasing emphasis on conservation and demand management, some type of modelling or analysis is now usually required.

A related activity is Demand Management, which seeks to actually modify water use and consumption patterns in order to optimise the performance of existing facilities, reduce or delay the need for new facilities, and generally deliver a more sustainable service.

The main options for implementing Demand Management include customer education, resource substitution, operations improvements, usage regulations, or conservation incentives. Often, a combination of these techniques in a program approach works best. An aggressive demand management program, for example, can reduce revenues faster than costs, creating a financial crisis for the utility.

3.3 Condition assessment

A good understanding of the current condition of a utility's assets and their performance characteristics is important to decisions about maintenance, rehabilitation and replacement needs, and avoiding premature replacement and high lifecycle costs.

Regular condition assessment activities using a variety of tools and techniques are the preferred method of collecting data, assigning priorities and building a database upon which to develop maintenance strategies. This may be used to predict, even in an approximate manner, the effective remaining life of each major component of the system.

3.4 Risk management

Risk management procedures are increasingly being applied to identify and evaluate the types of risks and failures that the agency faces, and to develop a risk management plan that establishes the critical risks, the consequences of failure, and steps to avoid or reduce those risks.

Specific types of risks that may be considered on a corporate or departmental basis might include health and safety, competitiveness in the market, financial, investment, public liability, and life cycle risks related to specific assets.

3.5 Maintenance management

Maintenance management systems are intended to manage those maintenance activities necessary to keep the assets close to their original condition and capacities. The development of new monitoring and control technologies has enabled many utilities to move away from unplanned, corrective maintenance and adopt a planned, programmed approach. The cost savings and performance improvement of a planned, preventative approach can be dramatic, and this represents one of the best management practices in the industry worldwide.

4 Cost of service

This section provides an example of a cost of service assessment prepared as part of an asset management program for the water distribution system of Bangalore, India [1,9].

The intent was to identify the investment needs and costs to rehabilitate or replace portions of the water distribution system over the next 10-20 years, as well as to help identify other considerations that should be employed to minimize the life cycle costs and operational risks. Figure 2 shows the rapid growth experienced by the City.

It is apparent that Bangalore experienced early significant growth in the decades between 1935 and 1955, 1965 and 1975 and most recently between 1985 and 1995. The population growth of this last decade seems to be continuing into the 21st century at unprecedented rates. In fact, the population has doubled from 3 million to 6 million over the 20-year period from 1981 to 2001. While some components of the system are new or have been recently replaced, there are many parts of the water system that are approaching the end of their service life, or have already been abandoned.

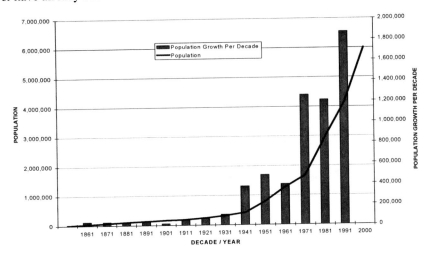

Figure 2: Bangalore population.

Table 2: Replacement costs.

Item	Quantity	Unit	Replacement Cost (million Rs)	%
Water Plants	5	Total	2,640	3
Transmission P S's	3	no.	6,130	6
Distribution P S's	56	no.	500	0.5
Transmission Mains	373	Km's	6,040	6
Internal Transmission Mains	808	Km's	7,850	8
Feeder/Dist'n Mains	24,340	Km's	68,520	67
Overhead Tanks	51	no.	338	0.3
Ground Level Reservoirs	40	no.	7,620	7
Valves	16,774	no.	450	0.4
Connections & Meters	307,900	no.	2,520	2
Bore wells	3,120	no.	465	.5
Stand posts	13,510	no.	80	0.1
			103,153	**100**

4.1 Inventory and replacement value

Bangalore gets its water from the relatively newly constructed Cauvery system. This system is comprised of the Cauvery Water Treatment Plant, Stages I to IV, as well as the smaller Arkavathy system. The Bangalore Water Supply and Sewerage Board (BWSSB) operates 3 sets of booster pumping stations and over 373 kilometres of transmission main to bring the water to Bangalore. Within the City of Bangalore, there are 51 elevated tanks; 40 in-ground reservoirs; and 56 water pumping stations. In addition, the water distribution system is comprised of 808 kilometres of internal transmission lines, 24,340 kilometres of feeder and distribution mains, 16,774 valves and 307,900 water services and meters. Figure 3 summarizes the inventory of the BWSSB water system.

Table 2 shows that the total replacement cost of the water system is approximately Rs 103,153 million. The internal transmission, feeder and distribution mains constitute almost 70 percent of the total replacement cost of the entire water system. Since the current population in Bangalore over 6 million, the replacement cost of the water system is considered to be approximately Rs 17,200 per capita.

4.2 Renewal requirements

Figure 3 illustrates the projected replacement costs for the water system over the next 100 years based on the age, remaining service life and replacement cost for the components. Assumptions regarding the rate of replacement for the electrical and mechanical components of the systems, and the water distribution networks, were discussed with the BWSSB staff prior to calculations.

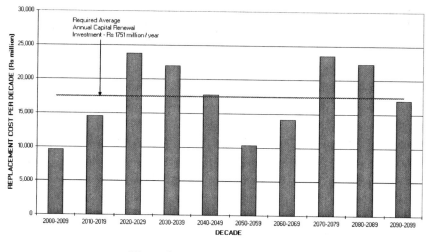

Figure 3:   Replacement cost.

Figure 3 also indicates that at least Rs 17,510 million should be invested in the water system over the next 10 years (approximately Rs 1,751 million per year). It should be noted that the projected costs over the next 20 years are somewhat less than the average requirement, however, expenditures that will be required over the third, fourth and fifth decades of this century are relatively high since significant elements of the system will reach the end their service lives and will require replacement. There however may well be a significant backlog in renewal of the many of the water distribution system components constructed prior to 1950 that have not yet been replaced, and therefore will need to be replaced. This may result in a significant increase in investment required in the first and second decades (2000-2020). This can be ascertained after a detailed condition assessment of these assets is carried out.

The BWSSB therefore needs to extend the service life of the existing water infrastructure by implementing both a pro-active maintenance system and an aggressive rehabilitation program, and establish a "Water Replacement Reserve Fund", in order to establish the funding that will be necessary to undertake this work.

All of this highlights the need to "level out" the spending needs. An aggressive rehabilitation program could successfully extend the useful life of infrastructure components and help to reduce the capital investment needs over the medium and long term.

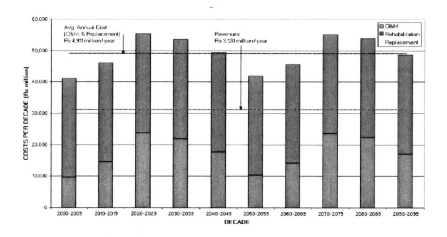

Figure 4: Life cycle costs.

4.3 Life cycle costs

Figure 4 illustrates the life cycle costs for the water system as the sum of the O&M costs, rehabilitation costs (where appropriate) and replacement costs. The average annual cost over the next 100 years is estimated to be Rs 49,110 million per decade, Rs 4,911 million annually, for the water system. It has been assumed that the O & M expenditures for the existing components will remain fixed over this period at the current level of Rs 3,160 million annually with revenues at Rs 3,120 million annually. Total annual costs are expected to decrease initially and then increase dramatically over the period from 2020 to 2050 due to the fact that a large percentage of the existing system will reach the end of its service life during this time. This cycle is repeated again before the end of the century.

4.4 Financial impacts

The information generated identifies the projected shortfall in funding, and establishes that the funding increase required will be in the magnitude of 157%. It can easily be seen that revenues are significantly less than the long-term financial requirement for operations and replacement cost for the water system estimated to be Rs 4,911 million per year.

4.5 Potential impact on water rates

Currently, Bangalore almost recovers its current capital and operating costs, with a slight deficit in most years. The current water revenues (Rs 3,120 million) would have to be increased by 52% (excluding inflation) in order to cover the projected cost for maintenance, rehabilitation and replacement of the water system over the next 100 years (Rs 4,911 million per year on average). The total revenue stream, and all its components, should be reviewed in light of the apparent need for a significant increase in water rates.

4.6 Other findings and recommendations

This preliminary assessment powerfully illustrates the "gap" that can exist between the water revenues and the total annual cost of operations and replacement of the infrastructure. In order to meet the needs of the water users of Bangalore in the future, it will be necessary to deal with this funding gap through implementation of an increase in water rates, a reduction in operational and replacement costs, or a combination of the these strategies. Other technical and managerial suggestions to help "level out" infrastructure spending include; rationalization of water rate structures; a proactive meter replacement program; a maintenance management system; an unaccounted for water reduction program; and a review of current design standards.

5 Summary

The guidelines described in this paper can assist municipalities and public utilities to prepare a program of asset management that will help achieve sustainable costs and revenues for their water system. The tools and techniques presented can be implemented by operations staff relying upon commonly available data and information.

The procedures for preparing an asset management program and a cost of service assessment to help ensure sustainable service delivery were demonstrated for the Bangalore water system. It is expected that many municipal agencies elsewhere in India, and throughout Asia, have similar needs and could benefit from the same approach as discussed herein, requiring about 8-12 weeks of specialist input.

Even using relatively basic data and information for Bangalore, it is apparent that water rates must be increased significantly in order to cover the life cycle costs of the system components and maintain an acceptable level of service. Water rate increases will be a function of the ability of a municipality to implement the programs outlined above. The more successful these programs are in extending the service life of the infrastructure, reducing losses and thereby reducing costs, the less the rates will have to be increased.

References

[1]   R.V. Anderson Associates Limited, "Asset Management for Environmental Infrastructure", prepared for Karnataka Urban Development Corporation and Bangalore Water Board, CIDA, Ottawa, November 2003.

[2]   R.V. Anderson Associates Limited, "Ahead of the Wave: A Guide to Sustainable Asset Management for Canadian Municipalities", prepared for the Federation of Canadian Municipalities, February 2002.

[3]   Asian Development Bank, "Second Water Utilities Data Book – Asian and Pacific Region", Arthur McIntosh, Cesar E. Yniguez, ed., Manila, October 1997.

[4]   Department for International Development, "SPBNet Africa Water Utility Partnership: Report of Performance Indicators", Stephen Ramsey, Peter Mobbs, WRC plc, Wiltshire, December 2001.

[5]   Ontario Water Works Association, "Survey of Municipal Water Rates and Operations Benchmarking in Ontario", 2001.

[6]   Asian Development Bank, "Philippines: Water Supply and Sanitation Sector Profile", Philippines, November 2001.

[7]   Halifax Regional Water Commission, "Accountability, Sixth Annual Report", Halifax Regional Municipality, Halifax, March 2002.

[8]   World Bank, "Returns to Scale in Water Systems in Developing Countries, Some Econometric Evidence", Nicola Tynan, August 2003

[9]   Bangalore Water Supply and Sewerage Board, "Handbook of Statistics 1997-98 & 1998-99", 2000

[10] "International Infrastructure Management Manual – Version 1", Institute of Public Works of Australia, Sydney.

[11] World Bank Institute, "Water Tariffs and Subsidies in South Asia" Paper 3 – Tariff Structures in Six South Asian Cities, December 2002.

[12] Canadian Civil Engineer, "Asset Management: Moving from Concept to Reality", Vol. 19 No. 5, Montreal, December 2002/January 2003.

[13] R.V. Anderson Associates Limited, "International Price of Water", a paper prepared for the World Bank, Washington, D.C., 2004.

The global sustainable development with emphasis on sustainable ecotourism

A. Estelaji[1], H. Mojtabazadeh[2], M. Ranjbar[3] & R. Sarvar[4]
[1]Azad University Varamin Branch
[2]Azad University Tehran markazi Branch
[3]Azad University Hamedan Branch
[4]Azad University Shar-e-Rey Branch

Abstract

The developmental strategies of the world may fall into following categories: Physical strategies; Economic strategies; Socio-Cultural strategies; Regional-spatial strategies. Based on these strategies, various approaches have been followed in different countries. Considering the globalization development process throughout the world, and the urgent need for attention to worldwide development it can be assumed that the universally accepted approach is "Life territory sustainable development". Planning for sustainable ecotourism and tourism is accordingly assumed to serve as a very important factor for realising this objective. The number of world tourists today has risen from 626,000 annually to 1.6 billion. The total income from tourism will reach $445 billion by the year 2020. In planning for global sustainable development many other factors, including a close organic relationship between tourism and socio economic, cultural and ecological with aspects, survival and biological cooperation, as well as basic well-thought relations of human societies with ecological surroundings need to be taken into consideration. Accordingly, sustainability should be a target for development plans at global, regional, urban and rural levels. Also, applied guidelines and approaches need to be developed in this regard. This article, as a result of the authors' research efforts, is thus an attempt to provide, through following procedures, an approach to global sustainable development with emphasis on "sustainable ecotourism and tourism": analysis and explanation of developmental strategies with emphasis on ecotourism and tourism; identification of needs and deficiencies of the world's human society in the process of the world's development; presentation of guidelines, and principles needed to design and develop urban perspective with emphasis on ecotourism and tourism; determination of appropriate policies for a better management of the tourism industry with emphasis on sustainable tourism and ecotourism.
Keywords: ecotourism, sustainable development, environmental economy, global development, management.

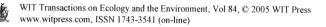
WIT Transactions on Ecology and the Environment, Vol 84, © 2005 WIT Press
www.witpress.com, ISSN 1743-3541 (on-line)

1 Introduction

Ecotourism industry is growing so rapidly at global level that the current era may soon appear as the age of ecotourism. This holds true to the extent that tourism industry has, over the past decade, experienced growth rates as much as 120% and 60% in terms of number of tourists and revenues, respectively. As predicted by the World Tourism Organization, these figures will be three times by 2020. A majority of countries are, thus, trying to achieve sustainable development through improving tourism industry by both reinforcing its strengths (advantages) and alleviating its weaknesses (disadvantages). This article is accordingly an attempt to describe global sustainable development with emphasis on ecotourism industry. To do this, it is imperative to introduce first the important approaches to tourism development planning.

2 Major approaches

The major approaches to tourism development planning may fall into following categories:
- Enhancement – oriented approach
- Economic approach
- Industrial – centered approach
- Physical – spatial approach
- Community – based approach (social - oriented)
- Sustainable development and ecotourism approach

Generally speaking, sustainable development and ecotourism approach is dealt with as the last adopted approach in this regard.

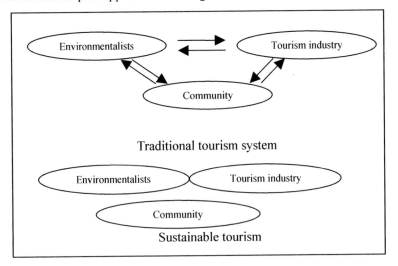

Figure 1:   Participation for tourism sustainable development.

WIT Transactions on Ecology and the Environment, Vol 84, © 2005 WIT Press
www.witpress.com, ISSN 1743-3541 (on-line)

As shown in figure 1, three aspects are highlighted in sustainable tourism. Environmental protection and cultural heritage, as two major aspects involved in this process, are coupled with another aspect, i.e. "Capacity – building" as a key concept. All these aspects need to be finally put into effect within the framework of the latter though integrated local policies and planning. Sustainable development, not only preserves cultural and natural resources, but also may well increase the capacity for generating viable incomes and job opportunities. Thus, as a model for development, the objectives of sustainable tourism are:

a) Improving the host society's quality of life (living standards);
b) Providing visitors with qualitative experience; and
c) Preserving quantity of the environment as a dire need for both the host society and visitors.

Development of sustainable tourism may link tourists and providers of tourism facilities or services with environmentalists and indigenous communities so as to move towards improving the quality of life as a whole.

3 Nature–based tourism and the determinants of resort potentialities

Nature–based tourism has experienced an overwhelmingly rapid growth. National parks, wild life reserves or habitats, natural attractive and spectacular sceneries, or virgin areas are major places visited in this kind of tourism. The most important ecological factors that affect potentialities or capabilities of resorts (recreational areas) are as follows:

- The land structure and physical qualities; including topography, geomorphology, geology and soil;
- Water; including the quality in terms of recreational uses;
- Vegetation coverage; including the economic, tourism and recreational values;
- Wild life; including the economic, tourism and recreational values; and
- Climatology; including seasonal and monthly temperature, and annual precipitation.

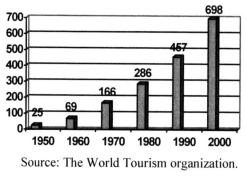

Source: The World Tourism organization.

Figure 2:   Worldwide tourism growth.

As stated by the World Tourism Organization, nature–based tourism has earmarked some 7% of entire economy of tourism industry at international level. Studies of the World Resources Institute also reveal some 4% annual growths for tourism industry; while this figure for nature–based tourism is as much as 30%

4 Ecotourism and the impact on local empowerment

Tourism industry has been flourished in our country, due to the increased demands by high–income groups to visit remotes natural areas for recreational purposes. The disturbing challenge, however, is that unutilized virgin areas are desperately vulnerable and fragile in environmental and cultural terms. Nevertheless, the recognized potentials of tourism are so evident that leave no doubt to emphasize on it for both empowering local communities and preserving the environment. This well indicates that environmental protection and improving the living standards of local communities need to be taken in to consideration as two key concepts when planning for ecotourism. Indeed, ecotourism must mainly aim at providing the appropriate basis so as to meet socio–economic needs of local communities. This kind of ecotourism serves directly towards intrinsic objectives of ecotourism that would allow controls by local communities to preserve environmental resources and benefit from ecotourism activities.

5 Global perspective of ecotourism development and the role in economic development

The burgeoning of tourism affects directly the economic conditions and the growth rates of economic indices. According to a recent report of IMF, GDP growth in the world would be some 3.2% in 2003, which is equal to that of 2002(see table1). A majority of developed economies, including major tourism markets in North America, Western Europe, and Japan, still suffer from low economic growth. However, it is expected that economic indices will improve, however progressively and slowly, during the second half of the year 2003.IMF, also estimates the economic growth to be as high as 4.1% in 2004. It has been anticipated that in America Region, the economic growth rates in 2003 and 2004 would be respectively 2.1% and 3.7%. USA and Canada will experience the highest growth rates. In Latin America, also, countries will enjoy considerable growth rates. Europe will witness a growth rate equal to 2%. This figure for Euro Area will be about 1.1%. Countries in Europe Region, Central and Eastern Europe, and Russian Federation are expected to experience a growth rate between 3.4% to 4% in 2003. Estimates also show that apart from some exception cases, European economic growth will rise to some degree in 2004 to reach an average equal to 2.8%. Asian countries, unlike the Japan's depressed economy, are expected to enjoy an economic growth rate as high as 5% for years 2003 and 2004. This figure, however for China is forecasted to be some 7%.

Table 1: GDP growth rates by fixed prices.

average	Trend (%)		Actual prediction (%)			
(1995-2002)	2004 in relation to 2003	2003 in relation to 2002	2004	2003	2002	
3/5	+	=	4/1	3/2	3/0	world
2/7	+	=	2/9	1/9	1/8	Developed economies
4/9	+	+	5/8	5/0	4/6	Developing economies
3/0	=	=	¼	4/0	4/1	In-transition economies
2/4	+	=	2/8	2/0	1/8	Europe
2/2	++	+	2/3	1/1	0/8	Euro Area
¼	++	+	1/9	0/5	0/2	Germany
2/4	++	=	2/4	1/2	1/2	France
1/7	++	+	2/3	1/1	0/4	Italy
¾	+	=	3/1	2/2	2/0	Spain
2/9	++	+	1/8	0/6	0/3	Netherlands
2/2	++	+	2/2	1/1	0/7	Belgium
2/2	+	+	2/4	1/5	0/9	Austria
2/6	+	+	2/5	2/0	1/6	England
¼	++	+	1/7	0/6	0/1	Swiss
2/7	+	-	2/1	1/6	1/9	Switzerland
2/9	+	+	4/3	3/4	2/9	Central and Eastern Europe
3/0	-	-	3/5	4/0	4/3	Russian Federation
3/3	++	+	3/7	2/1	1/7	America
3/5	++	=	3/6	2/2	2/4	USA
2/2	+	-	3/2	2/8	3/4	Canada
2/0	++	++	4/2	1/5	-0/1	West Area
3/9	+	++	3/5	2/8	1/5	Brazil
-0/5	++	++	3/7	2/3	0/9	Mexico
-0/5	++	++	4/5	3/0	-11/0	Argentina
4/7	++	--	13/4	17/0	-8/9	Venezuela
1/1	+	=	5/1	4/9	4/9	Asia-pacific
3/9	=	+	1/0	0/8	0/3	Japan
4/4	+	-	3/7	3/0	3/8	Australia
4/8	+	-	4/5	4/1	4/6	Asian newly-industrialized countries
4/2	+	--	5/3	5/0	6/1	South Korea
2/9	+	-	3/7	3/2	3/5	Taiwan
4/4	+	+	3/3	3/0	2/3	Hong Kong
6/3	+	+	3/5	3/0	2/2	Singapore
8/1	=	=	6/5	6/3	6/5	Asian developing countries
5/6	=	-	7/5	7/5	8/0	China
½	+	=	5/9	5/1	4/9	India
3/5	+	-	¾	4/0	4/3	Indonesia, Malaysia, Philippines, Thailand
2/7	++	+	5/2	3/9	3/4	Africa
3/1	+	=	4/2	2/8	3/0	South Africa
2/0	=	++	¾	3/6	1/9	Middle East
4/6	-	++	3/1	4/0	2/1	Saudi Arabia
	+	+	3/5	3/0	2/0	Egypt

Source: World Tourism Organization. Adopted form IMF Report
1%< ++
0/2% < + < 1%
-0/2% <=< 0/2%
-1% < - < 0/2%
-->-1%

6   Needs of human society in the process of global development with emphasis on ecotourism

Rapid development of ecotourism in the world, coupled with the crucial role it can play in the economic development of countries, has made it quite imperative for planners of sustainable development to focus on the basic needs of human society throughout the world. However, this should be done with special reference to ecotourism.

7   The principles for designing and developing settlements with emphasis on ecotourism

Regarding the above –mentioned issue, the principles for and the benefits of designing and developing settlements may fall into following categories:

- Making site–surveys and developing settlements according to the natural potential of the environment (establishing balance between natural and man – made environments);
- Preserving and developing farmlands and natural sites;
- Directing populations and activities (particularly industrial ones) in large areas towards sustainable development;
- Coordinating structures with natural environmental models;
- Alleviating consumption of natural resources and generation of pollutants;
- Providing settlements with vital constituents needed for survival;
- Developing and fitting out centers for physical exercises and medical services;
- Enlarging the green space between settlements, and combining land uses and buildings on an appropriate basis;
- Redesigning settlements for making optimized use of climatic parameters; and
- Linking urban development systems with rural areas and the natural surrounding sites (using intact nature of rural areas to make peripheries of urban areas clean and wholesome).

8   Conclusion

As the last approach adopted for development planning, sustainable development needs to be planned on the basis of ecotourism potentials or capacities. The major ecological factors that influence these capacities are stated hereunder:

- Geomorphology structure;
- Water; including the quality for recreational purposes;
- Wildlife; including the economic, tourism and recreational values; and

- Climatology; including seasonal and monthly temperature as well as annual precipitation.

As mentioned before, the widespread capacities of ecotourism or nature-based tourism may well serve not only to empower local communities, but to develop the global economy as well.

Regarding, thus, the need for emphasis on ecotourism in the process of managing and planning for sustainable development at global level, the following recommendations are proposed:

1. Focusing on the needs of the human society with respect to the issues raised in this article;
2. Designing and developing settlements according to the mentioned principles or rules;
3. Taking advantage of flora and fauna, and ecosystems sustainability as a set of zoological and herbal wildlife, for ecotourism (ecotourism and biological diversity);
4. Increasing public knowledge of ecotourism; promoting environmental culture among people; and providing different educational levels with training courses on ecosystems (ecotourism and education);
5. Paying attention to the issues such as protection of natural resources, conservation of soils and ecosystems, or the harmful affects of some activities on natural resources (ecotourism and natural resources);
6. Making precise evaluations of employment–generation process, different services provided, and national revenues (ecotourism and economy);
7. Establishing an appropriate tourism center. This would, naturally, calls for adequate facilities or systems that directly affect the soundness of natural settings or the environment of any specific area. It is, thus, imperative to conduct more precise and more specific assessments at both local and national levels, as far as the impacts of the related activities are concerned;
8. Developing tourism industry dose not necessary call for large economic investment. It should be recognized that ecotourists are not interested in five–star hotels or other luxurious facilities. Rather, they are mostly attracted by limited natural facilities, or the chance for pastime in natural spaces:
9. Providing clear and attractive maps or brochures for ecotourism touring programs serves as a very effective means for introducing or advertising natural potentials of ecotourism;
10. Taking advantage of the concerned governmental units is necessary for controlling purposes where private sector is involved in ecotourism industry;
11. Making optimized use of electronic traveling information systems, including internet, for reservations or other accommodation services would contribute to brisk up tourism industry; and

12. Planning for development or tourism industry must be based on "nature" as the central issue, with the highest priority delivered to "environmental protection".

References

[1]   Castells M.2000 Grass rooting the space of flows in wheeler et al. (Eds) 2000 cities in the Telecommunication Age, the fracturing of Geographies. London and New York. Rout ledge

[2]   Ead. J. (Ed). 1997 living the Global City Clobalization as local process. London and New York. Rout ledge

[3]   Estelaji. A.Reza and Shariat Panahi. M. Vali 2003 Natural touristic attraction in desert and semi desert area. Tehran. Shahr-e-Rey. Azad university

[4]   Estelaji A.reza. Sustainable development 2002. Tehran Ministry of Jihad f. Agriculture. 2002.

[5]   Fennell. D. A. 1999. Ecotourism on introduction. Rout ledge. London

[6]   Frey, H.F. 1999. Designing the City, toward a more sustainable Urban from London. Spon

[7]   Fillon. Fren. L. 1997. The Economics of Global Ecotourism. Paper presented at the fourth world congress and National parks and protected Areas, Venezuela.

[8]   Hetzer. N. D. 1995. Environment Tourism culture. Links.

[9]   Graham. S. and Marvin, S. 2000 urban planning and the Technological future of Cities in wheeler et al. (eds) 2000 Cities in the Telecommunication Age. London and New York. Rout ledge

[10]   Goodwin. H. 1995. Tourism and Environment. Biologist 42(3): 129-133

[11]   Nelson J.G. 1994. The spread of Ecotourism. Some planning implication. Environmental conservation 21(1). 248-255

[12]   Ross, S wall. G 1999 Ecotourism: towards congruence between theory and practice. Tourism management (20)123-132

[13]   Reads. E. 1997. Planning in the future or planning of the future London and New York. Rout ledge

[14]   Scheyvens R.1999 Ecotourism and the Empowerment of Local communities Tourism Management (20). 245-249

[15]   The international Ecotourism society. 2000. Ecotourism statistical fact sheet.

[16]   Tarvati .H. Ayafat. S.A. 1992 sustainable development agenda for the 21st century.

Challenges in the environmental management of post-military land conversion

K. C. Fischer, W. Spyra & K. Winkelmann
Brandenburg University of Technology in Cottbus, Germany

Abstract

In 1994, after nearly 100 years of military use, the last Soviet forces withdrew from the Königsbrücker Heath. Constant artificial disturbance from military activity on this training range in Saxony, Germany, had changed the natural ecosystem from forest into open land. Now, due to the absence of military disturbance, the open lands have begun to reforest. As a result, a host of uncommon open land species face a potential loss of habitat. The Forest for Saxony Foundation (*Stiftung Wald für Sachsen*) owns this land and manages its conversion. The foundation takes on the challenge of disposing the waste from wide-spread ammunition and defusing the conflicts between the landscape's various interest groups including the public, hunters and conservationists. This paper provides a forum to discuss the unique challenges and management tools used in the conversion of the Königsbrücker Heath.
Keywords: conversion, demilitarisation, ecological management, hazardous waste, forest succession, natural preservation, open land management, GIS.

1 Introduction to demilitarisation and conversion

The end of the Cold War signalled and end to the bi-polar weapons race and a start to world-wide disarmament. Both NATO and former Warsaw Pact nations committed to demilitarising many of their bases and properties. Demilitarisation meant dismantling military capabilities. Personnel were decommissioned, radar systems were dismantled, and rockets were taken from storage depots, emptied of their fuels and destroyed. After military potential was removed, military properties entered a stage of conversion. This second stage was essential in order to nullify the possibility of remilitarisation and to establish an alternative peacetime use for the former military property.

WIT Transactions on Ecology and the Environment, Vol 84, © 2005 WIT Press
www.witpress.com, ISSN 1743-3541 (on-line)

Conversion involves transferring the ownership and management responsibilities of military property back into civilian hands. When military property is marketed and sold to a civilian buyer, the new owner takes on full responsibility for the land. Conversion requires an extraordinary amount of time, money, planning and commitment, as well as interdisciplinary cooperation and idea sharing among property owners, scientists, planners, environmentalists and the public.

In what had once been the front lines of the Cold War, the reunified Germany faced the monumental task of demilitarising the properties of the four occupying powers: France, Great Britain, the United States and the Soviet Union. On account of the expanse of land involved and the high level of hazards left after the withdrawal, the impact of the Soviet forces in former East Germany was especially problematic. The Bonn International Center for Conversion [1] reports that in the German Democratic Republic, 450,000 hectares of land were utilized by either the National People's Army or the Soviet Red Army. This made up 4 % of the total land area.

As agreed in Germany's reunification treaty, the Soviet forces were made responsible for the demilitarisation of all occupied properties in eastern Germany. The final Soviet troops withdrew in 1994, leaving the burden of conversion to the newly reunited German government. Since property management was designated as a state matter and not a national concern, the states each determined their own strategy for conversion.

2   Conversion at the Königsbrücker Heath

In 1997, for the ceremonial cost of one Euro, the Free State of Saxony sold the training bases at Königsbrücker Heath and Zeithain to the Forest for Saxony Foundation, or FSF, (German: *Stiftung Wald für Sachsen*). Along with the over 9,500 hectares of land, the state government also endowed the FSF with 25 million German Marks (€ 12.5 million) to invest in conversion and management projects. The FSF accepted the full liability and responsibility for the former military land and committed to dismantling the remaining military infrastructure in order to allow the landscape to return to nature.

The foundation's long-term goal is the proliferation and protection of forests in Saxony. By promoting the growth of healthy and productive forests, the FSF provides a means for combating climate change through the reduction of CO_2 and cares for natural wildlife and ecosystem preservation. With a size of 7,500 hectares, the Königsbrücker Heath is the foundation's largest single territory and also the largest single area of undeveloped land in Saxony. It is an island of wilderness in an area dominated by human-planned agriculture and forestry landscapes. Located in the Upper Lusatia region, the Königsbrücker Heath lies 31 kilometers north of Dresden.

Seven thousand hectares of the former training base had already been declared a nature reserve in 1992. At that time, the land was littered with buried ammunitions and other military waste. In 1998, the FSF [2] reported that over 500 built structures, including barracks, recreation centres and administrative buildings remained around the edges of the training grounds. According to land manager Roland Schiller [3], masses of garbage remained from the more than 20,000 Russians who had lived and worked on the base during Soviet occupation. After nearly a century of use by German and Russian armies, the landscape was nearly void of forest. Routine explosions and burnings on the training range had replaced the native forest ecosystem with a heather and grass landscape. Areas where tanks conducted driving and shooting exercises had become open sand, barren of nearly all vegetation.

Figure 1: An aerial view of the Königsbrücker Heath reveals that nature is reclaiming with trees what once was kept open by military training activities.

According to Mr. Schiller [4], today the Königsbrücker Heath is the sixth largest nature reserve in Germany. Such an undisturbed habitat is unique in heavily developed and densely populated Germany. This landscape provides habitat for golden eagles, wild boars, deer, beavers and several other wild animal species. In addition to a host of common vegetation such as broom, heather, oak and pine, rare plants have also taken root here such as the medicinal arnica (*Arnica Montana*), the flesh eating round-leaved sundew (*Drosera rotundifolia*) and an orchid species, the speckled knabenkraut (*Dactylorhiza maculate*). From the barren and scorched terrain left by years of military exercises, a diversity of ecosystems and habitats has developed. Along the banks of the Pulsnitz and the Otterbach rivers are natural wetlands and pools resulting from beaver dams. In the marshlands surrounding the ponds and natural lakes roost grey harriers and ducks, and the calls of the cuckoo and magpie echo from the trees. The rapid degree of recovery and succession is astounding. From atop the landscape's highest point, the *Königshöhe*, Russian officers used to observe the military training exercises below. Today the deserted sandy ground has been populated by a dense pioneering stand of birch and aspen.

Although forest promotion and nature preservation are the two leading objectives on the Königsbrücker Heath, an essential element of conversion is removing dangers from the property and finalizing a sustainable peacetime usage. The nuclear warheads once stored here and the launching areas directed at western Germany have now been removed. What remains today of a former vital military community are empty buildings and an array of hazardous waste. Weathering and wildlife have helped expose unexploded ordinances, UXOs, buried or overlooked during demilitarisation. Upon assuming management responsibilities in 1997, the FSF's [5] first task was to clear 78 kilometres of roadways of all UXOs. A six metre buffer zone on each side of the roadways assures that emergency personnel, managers and conservationists have safe access to the conversion area. Despite these efforts, the innermost sections of the Königsbrücker Heath are still so heavily contaminated by UXOs that all access is forbidden.

3 Interest group challenges

Negotiating the demands and preferences from the range of interest groups on the Königsbrücker Heath is an additional challenge to the conversion process. The interests of the property owners are often in conflict with one or more of the other groups. Such conflicts cause a rift between a group of workers who must cooperate in order to ensure progress. The following examples introduce the key actors in the conversion of Königsbrücker Heath and explain the issues where conflicts arise.

3.1 The property owners

The Forest for Saxony Foundation is based in Leipzig and has an outpost in the town of Königsbrück. At the outpost, the Königsbrücker Heath property manager is joined by an administrative assistant and a professional hunter. The three perform the task of managing the former training range and working with local citizens to further public understanding about the dangers of the conversion site. Due to the heavy degree of UXO pollution, access to the base is granted only with a permit issued by the FSF. Public hunting is strictly prohibited. Both these restrictions frustrate the local citizens.

Mr. Schiller, the land manager at the Königsbrücker Heath, has lived in a village bordering the training range his entire life. He has childhood memories of swimming in the local lakes with the families of Russian officers. During the demilitarisation process, Mr. Schiller was employed by German officials to monitor and report on the completeness of the operation. No one knows this landscape better than he, and no one understands the complexity of managing a landscape of this size better than the manager himself. The natural beauty of the

Königsbrücker Heath makes it a gem in the eyes of many. Hunters salivate at the abundance of game; the public yearns to hike, ride bicycles and picnic in the green nature; foresters see a potential for forest development; and nature conservationists fight to keep the land wild. Mr. Schiller often stands as mediator between the various interest groups.

3.2 The hunter

The FSF hunter, Hartmut Löwe, has the responsibility of preventing animal overpopulation and protecting the diversity and health of the Königsbrücker Heath forest. Mr. Löwe is a certified master hunter and is responsible for one of the most favourable hunting territories in Germany. Foxes, wild bores, roe deer, red deer and hares live in abundance in this undisturbed terrain. Aside from occasional sanctioned hunting events, Mr. Löwe is the only hunter who roams this territory. His enviable hunting range often places him in a difficult position vis-à-vis the local hunters. "Hunters get crazy if someone has a desirable territory where they can't hunt," says Mr. Löwe [6]. "It becomes an almost erotic obsession, as if one man had the most beautiful wife and the rest spite him for it."

Aside from the hostility he receives from other hunters, Mr. Löwe also faces conflict with the conservationists who keep a watchful eye on him, making sure he does not hunt within the prohibited nature reserve.

3.3 The citizen

Nine villages surround the 7,500 hectares of land managed by the FSF. Expansion of the training grounds under the National Socialists in 1938 required the evacuation of nine additional villages. Prior to its military use, the Königsbrücker Heath was a known hiking and recreation area. Current local residents still know the beauty of the landscape and are eager to obtain access to it. Especially beloved is the *Königshöhe*. Although merely 194 metres high, the *Königshöhe* is the highest point between northern Saxony and Sweden. The view from atop this ridge is pure nature and provides a rare opportunity to retreat from urbanization. There is currently no public access to the *Königshöhe*.

Public access onto the Königsbrücker Heath is a hotly debated issue. In the eyes of the public, the transfer from military to civilian property is not complete without a provision for public access. On the other hand, the dangers associated with UXOs and the disturbance public access could have on the developing ecosystem are reasons to prohibit open access.

In May 1999, a 250 hectare section of the Königbrücker Heath was re-opened to the public. Hundreds of citizens gathered to celebrate the end of 92 years of blocked access. The FSF [7] reported the preparation costs for opening the 250 hectares came to nearly €300,000. The majority of the cost went to tearing down military buildings and finding and disposing UXOs. The pubic celebrated the return of this piece of their homeland and continue to demand more access to the landscape.

3.4 The conservationist

The *Naturbewahrung Westlausitz e.V.* (NBW) is the conservationist society responsible for developing and implementing environmental protection measures in the Königsbrücker Heath. Conservationists routinely deny requests to open areas of the nature reserve for recreation. According to the NBW, the former military terrain should be kept undisturbed and totally protected. The NBW compares their vision for the Königsbrücker Heath with the United States' National Park concept: the land should be allowed to return to nature and remain permanent wilderness. To achieve this, the Königsbrücker Heath must be completely protected from disturbance and development.

Although the FSF agrees that the nature reserve should remain protected, they disagree with the NBW's insistence on complete access prohibition. Instead, they maintain a preference for limited entrance through hiking trails.

4 Environmental management strategies

Over 93% of the Königsbrücker Heath is nature reserve and thus stands under legislation of the German environmental protection laws. Within the reserve, all hunting is prohibited as is the removal of any plant, animal or natural product. Management strategies developed by the FSF must fit within the guidelines of the habitat protection plan as well as meet the other goals of the foundation (i.e. forest propagation, disassembly of military potential and encouragement of public awareness). Such a task requires cooperation from a variety of fields.

4.1 The nature reserve

The 7,000 hectares of nature reserve have been divided into three protection levels. In the largest section, which makes up 80% of the total reserve, the land is to be allowed to develop completely without human interference. This area provides a unique possibility for scientists to research the process of succession in a variety of ecosystems and habitats. Approximately 15% of the reserve has been designated as a managed ecosystem area where measures are taken to control succession and to maintain the current habitat, which is an open landscape. The remaining area forms a border around the nature preserve and serves as a buffer zone from the outside environment. In this area, forest management activities and controlled public access is allowed.

The Beaver Experience Trail is a project developed by the NBW conservationists to encourage public awareness of the flourishing beaver habitat on the Königsbrücker Heath (see Figure 2). The trail is approximately one kilometre long, 400 meters of which are inside the buffer zone of the nature reserve.

This window into the wild is a compromise between the NBW and the FSF to allow public access to the land without the access extending too far into the preservation area. Additional "window" projects are planned for the future.

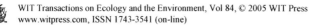

Figure 2: Signs forbid entrance to the former training area while designating the boundaries of the nature preserve (left). Tenacious beavers make a noticeable impact on the landscape at Königsbrücker Heath (right).

4.2 Wildlife management

Wildlife management sometimes means promoting the life of a certain species while taking the life of another. For most of the large animals on the Königsbrücker Heath, humans are the only natural predators. It is therefore necessary for humans to hunt as a means of wildlife management. Like many German establishments, hunting is a highly regulated and heavily bureaucratic undertaking. A professional hunter has a territory for which he or she is responsible. The hunter must kill a quota of animals yearly to maintain optimal health of the species and of the forest ecosystem. Failure to meet this quota results in a fine. The foundation sells the meat from the animals to local butchers and restaurants.

4.3 Open land management

An end to military activity has allowed nature to recover and succession to begin to take its course. The expansion of forest means the shrinking of the open landscape and thus the shrinking of a habitat supporting valued endangered species. Both conservationists and land managers would like to see the Königsbrücker Heath eventually develop into a mosaic of habitats and ecosystems, both forested and open. Immediate action is required, however, to preserve the remaining open landscapes.

Heather (*Calluna vulgaris*) and broom (*Cytisus scoparius*) are the most common vegetation species present in the open landscape. Both species depend on periodic disturbances to remove old growth and allow for rejuvenation. The constant explosions and fires caused by military exercises supported the development of this ecosystem, which is uncommon in Upper Lusatia.

Several methods are available for open land management, but not all are suited for the Königsbrücker Heath. The level of UXO pollution rules out the use of fire, although it is easy and inexpensive. When naturally occurring fires do occur on the Königsbrücker Heath, fire fighting personnel must practice extreme caution to avoid possible explosions.

The safest, but most labour-intensive method of open land management is a combination of manual management with a reliance on natural rejuvenation. In this method, a labour force of knowledgeable workers periodically removes unwanted succession species from a given plot of land. Natural rejuvenation can come from natural weathering or from grazing animals. In natural weathering, extreme winter frosts and periods of dryness cause old plant matter to become brittle and drop off. Grazing animals who feed on the living plant matter provide another method of natural disturbance. These natural methods are the most benign options in regard to natural preservation and are, thus, the NBW conservationists' preferred methods for the Königsbrücker Heath.

Another possible method is the use of domesticated grazing animals such as sheep and goats. Sheep and goats have been used on the Zeithain conversion area to keep land open for over ten years with positive results. Grazing animals would be set onto designated land areas where succession is in the earliest stages. This method is currently being tested on a plot outside the natural preservation area at the Königsbrücker Heath. Using domesticated animals to ensure grazing instead of relying on wild animals enables managers to more precisely direct the open land management onto a chosen area.

4.4 Spatial management tools: GIS and remote sensing

In May 2003, a team of environmental engineers from the Brandenburg University of Technology in Cottbus, Germany, completed and put into operation a Geographical Information System (GIS) for the Königsbrücker Heath. The computer-based spatial analysis tool consists of a digital map with several layers of information that can be viewed individually or together as integrated themes. The GIS covers all aspects of the conversion area's natural and anthropogenic elements. Topographical data, road networks, a vegetation map, hazardous area zoning, and nature preserve boundaries are examples of the some 25 available themes. Regular updates to the system ensure the most up-to-date information can be used for planning. A manager might use this tool, for example, when trying to locate a safe, forested place, outside the nature preserve area, on which to develop a visitor information centre. One could use the GIS to layer the hazardous area zones with the nature preserve boundary and vegetation map, and by studying the overlapping and free areas, locate potential sites.

The Königsbrücker Heath GIS is valuable not only to land managers, but also to other administrative groups. By viewing the locations of fire look-out towers, water ways and emergency transportation routes, fire fighters can effectively and safely combat fires. Conservationists can use the vegetation and topographical data to predict the location of ecosystems and form strategies for maintenance and monitoring.

Another form of spatial analysis used on the Königsbrücker Heath is the use of aerial photos (see Figure 3). Comparing historical images with current photos and vegetation patterns can reveal sites of suspected hazardous waste. The Brandenburg University of Technology in Cottbus is currently developing a GIS theme including the historical land use of the Königsbrücker Heath. Once added to the larger GIS, this theme will provide information from the three phases of military occupation: the German Imperial Army, the Third Reich, and the Soviet Armed Forces. Knowing the historical use of a land area helps to predict the types of ammunition or otherwise hazardous waste that might be found there.

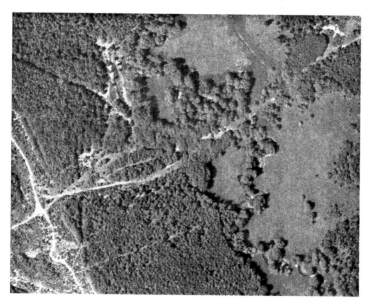

Figure 3:   Aerial photos of the Königsbrücker Heath are used to locate water ways and vegetation patterns. This photo shows a military road (bottom left) and a river wetland (right).

The ability to detect hidden waste greatly reduces the risk of damages to humans or the environment. A total hazardous waste clean-up on the Königsbrücker Heath would cost an estimated € 80 million. The resources for a complete clean-up are not available, so the FSF must prioritise and clear the most dangerous areas first. No records of waste burial locations are available for the past 50 years. Without remote sensing capabilities, finding dumping sites will depend on chance findings such as in 2003, when wallowing wild bores uncovered a dumping site with over 200 tonnes of highly toxic material.

5 Conclusion

Independent of conservationists and land managers, nature continues to re-claim the former training base at the Königsbrücker Heath. This vast terrain is an anomaly in the highly developed and subdivided German cultural landscape. Although the size of the former training range has allowed wilderness to regain its domain, this landscape is still a green island in the midst roadways, industrial parks and villages. The military potential has been taken away, but the lure of forested land in a society eternally hungry for natural resources makes the land on the Königsbrücker Heath tempting to many. Whether this reserve of over 75 square kilometres will remain protected remains a question of political will.

The Forest for Saxony Foundation and its cooperative partners are well on their way to successfully transforming the Königsbrücker Heath. With each demolished building and each destroyed explosive, the process of turning a war preparation zone into a zone of ecological triumph continues. Cooperation between an interdisciplinary group of agencies and experts has made possible the conversion and management of the Königsbrücker Heath. The challenge for the future will be defusing the conflicts among these interest groups to integrate know-how and experience into sustainable solutions.

References

[1]   Bonn International Center for Conversion, www.bicc.de

[2]   Forest for Saxony, Stiftung Wald für Sachsen stellt sich ihrer Verantwortung als Eigentümer in der Königsbrücker Heide, *Wald für Sachsen: Informationsblatt der Stiftung Wald für Sachsen*. Quarterly Newsletter: Issue 3, p. 1, 1998.

[3]   Schiller, R. Personal communication, 19 May 2004, Property Manager, Stiftung Wald für Sachsen, Königsbrück, Germany.

[4]   *ibid*

[5]   Forest for Saxony, Issue 3, p. 1, 1998.

[6]   Löwe, Hartmut. Personal communication, 27 May 2004, Chief Hunter, Stiftung Wald für Sachsen, Königsbrück, Germany.

[7]   Forest for Saxony, Erstes Teilstück des ehemaligen Truppenübungsplaztes Königsbrück an die Bevölkerung übergeben, *Wald für Sachsen: Informationsblatt der Stiftung Wald für Sachsen*. Quarterly Newsletter: Issue 2, p. 1, 1999.

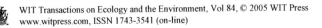

Section 5
Waste management

Multicriteria evaluation of alternative wastewater treatment processes at municipality level

K. P. Anagnostopoulos[1], M. Gratziou[2] & A. P. Vavatsikos[1]
[1]*Department of Production and Management Engineering, Democritus University of Thrace, School of Engineering*
[2]*Department of Civil Engineering, Democritus University of Thrace, School of Engineering*

Abstract

Wastewater treatment has been a highly developed issue during the two last decades in Greece, particular considering the need to comply with the requirements of the European Union directive 91/271. Although all participants in the decision making process generally agree on the necessity of interventions, a systematic opposition frequently emerges when the interventions are concretised and touch upon citizens' reality in their local societies. At the same time, various approaches on centralized or decentralized wastewater management and the available treatment processes form a complex environment for sound decisions from the authorities at municipal and regional level. In this context, a rationalization of the decision-making process is required in order to deal with conflicting objectives. We propose a generic multicriteria approach, based on the Analytic Hierarchy Process (AHP), for the evaluation of alternative scenarios concerning wastewater treatment processes at municipality level. Evaluation scenarios are developed with respect to the number, size, treatment method, and location of plants. Multicriteria process selection is a part of a decision support system where location algorithms and GIS tools are combined in order to define the number of the alternatives and the location of the plants. We also discuss the retained evaluation criteria, land requirements, environmental criteria, construction and operating costs, etc. The application of this approach is illustrated through a case study. A sensitivity analysis is also performed in order to investigate how sensitive the ranking of the alternatives is to changes in the importance of the hierarchy criteria. The results obtained show that this approach is a viable tool and offers good communication with decision-maker.
Keywords: AHP, multicriteria evaluation, wastewater treatment plants, appropriate wastewater treatment.

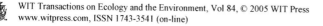

1 Introduction

In order to avoid the serious effects of wastewaters in the environment, current legislation requires an appropriate wastewater treatment, which permits the accomplishment of quality objectives in receiving waters after the effluents discharge [1–5]. This obligation had as a result the rapid increase of wastewater treatment plants (WWTPs) during the last two decades in many countries, including Greece.

In order to comply with the EU legislation, the effort in Greece, up to now, was focused on the construction of treatment plants in the major cities of each prefecture. However, in many cases important environmental problems emerge in non-sewered rural areas with small population equivalent (p.e.) number where no treatment exists [6, 7]. Particular interest present settlements or agglomerations with less than 2000 p.e., that already have or they are about to have sewerage, and those that are not included to the EU legislation but should be taken into account due to sustainability considerations [9].

The planning of full-scale interventions at prefecture level becomes quickly very complex, if we take into account the number of treatment methods, restrictions in their implementation [2, 8], receivers dilution capability, the existent networks and plants, and the cost of constructing conduits to connect an agglomeration with the treatment plants. Moreover, decision making must take into consideration not only quantitative but qualitative criteria as well [6, 8, 9, 10].

In the present paper the Analytic Hierarchy Process (AHP), a well-known multicriteria method, is used in order to evaluate alternative wastewater treatment processes (WWTP) at municipality level with the use of economic, social and environmental criteria. As briefly explained in section 2, this work is part of a GIS based decision support system for the planning of wastewater facilities at prefecture level.

2 Location and allocation of the WWTPs

The proposed multicriteria evaluation is the third of a three steps procedure for the planning of wastewater facilities at prefecture level. In the first step, the agglomerations that demand wastewaters treatment, the receivers for the final discharge of the effluents and space availability are specified by spatial analyses using GIS tools. In this way alternative processes are evaluated according to their performance on serving the same amount of p.e. and to the ability to achieve the same treatment level as it is defined by receivers' sensitiveness [1, 11, 12].

In the second step centralized or decentralized treatment options are considered. Since the cost of the needed conduits is getting outstanding as their length grows, decentralized treatment is preferable. In order to determine the number and the locations of the plants the notion of pole is introduced. A pole is defined as a single agglomeration or as an aggregation of agglomerations and the implementation of a plant for handling with the wastewaters by each pole is considered as a feasible scenario. For a catchment area where N agglomerations are settled, the number of the possible poles varies between 1 (fully centralized treatment) and N (a treatment plant for each agglomeration). For the minimization the cost of conduits, a minisum algorithm is applied for finding the agglomeration from which the distances from all the others to a pole gets minimum. This agglomeration is poles absolutely median, and the plant is located to its neighbourhood.

Finally, since every pole is considered to be a feasible scenario for the implementation of a plant, in any possible case multicriteria analysis is performed for selecting the most preferable treatment process for handling poles wastewaters. The final choice is taken in favour of the scenario with the lowest budget, as it is formed by the cost for the construction of the facilities and the needed conduits.

3   The multicriteria approach to WWTP selection

3.1   The analytic hierarchy process

Developed by T. L. Saaty, the Analytic Hierarchy Process (AHP) is a multicriteria method for dealing with complex decision-making problems in which many competing alternatives (projects, actions, scenarios) exist. The alternatives are ranked using several quantitative and/or qualitative criteria, depending on how they contribute in achieving an overall goal. AHP is based on a hierarchical structuring of the elements that are involved in a decision problem. The hierarchy incorporates the knowledge, the experience and the intuition of the decision-maker for the specific problem.

The evaluation of the hierarchy is based on pairwise comparisons. The decision-maker compares two alternatives A_i and A_j using a criterion and assigns a numerical value to their relative weight. The result of the comparison is expressed in a fundamental scale of values ranging from 1 (A_i, A_j contribute equally to the objective) to 9 (the evidence favoring A_i over A_j is of the highest possible order of affirmation). Given that the n elements of a level are evaluated in pairs using an element of the immediately higher level, an n×n comparison matrix is obtained.

$$
\begin{array}{c|cccc}
K & P_1 & P_2 & \cdots & P_n \\
\hline
P_1 & 1 & a_{12} & \cdots & a_{1n} \\
P_2 & 1/a_{12} & 1 & \cdots & a_{2n} \\
\vdots & \vdots & \vdots & \vdots & \vdots \\
P_n & 1/a_{1n} & 1/a_{2n} & \cdots & 1
\end{array}
$$

Figure 1:   Pairwise comparisons matrix A of actions P_i with respect to criterion K.

The decision-maker's judgments may not be consistent with one another. A comparison matrix is consistent if and only if $a_{ij} \times a_{jk} = a_{ik}$ for all i, j, k. AHP measures the inconsistency of judgments by calculating the consistency index CI of the matrix. The consistency index CI is in turn divided by the average random consistency index RI to obtain the consistency ratio CR.

The RI index is a constant value for an n×n matrix, which has resulted from a computer simulation of n×n matrixes with random values from the 1-9 scale and for which $a_{ij} = 1/a_{ji}$. If CR is less than 5% for a 3×3 matrix, 9% for a 4×4 matrix, and 10% for larger matrices, then the matrix is consistent [13].

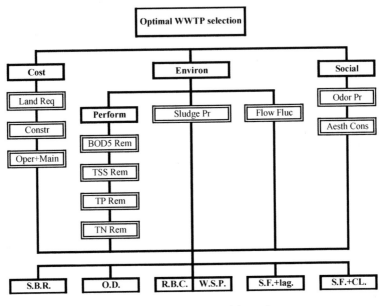

Figure 2:   Problems hierarchy.

3.2 The structure of the hierarchy

In our model, Analytic Hierarchy Process is used for the selection of the most preferable wastewater handling technology in a pole. This is achieved with the use of a four level hierarchy by which Compact sequential batch reactor (SBR), oxidation ditch (OD), rotating biological contactor (RBC), waste stabilization ponds (WSP), horizontal subsurface flow constructed wetlands with lagoon (SF+Lag) and horizontal subsurface flow constructed wetlands with chlorination (SF+CL) are evaluated with the use of three sets of criteria (Figure 2) [8, 9]. Analytically these criteria are:

1. Cost Criteria (Cost). This category consists of the cost for the required land for each alternative (Land Req), the construction cost (Constr) and the operation and maintenance costs (Oper&Main). The model is supported by a database which is supplied with the cost estimations for a range of population equivalent [3, 8, 14, 15].

2. Environmental Criteria (Environ). Alternatives are evaluated according to the quality of the effluents using the percentage removal of biochemical oxygen demand (BOD Rem), solids in suspension (SS Rem), nitrogen (TN Rem)

phosphorous (TP Rem), , with respect to the amount of the produced sludge by each process (Sludge Pr), and finally their response ability to hydraulic flow fluctuations (FlowFluc) [2,6,16].

3. Social Criteria (Social). Treatment plants are described as undesirable facilities and when they are located near to inhabited agglomerations give rise to neighbourhood opposition. In order to take into account these effects social criteria are also included in the hierarchy, odour problems provoked by each one of the alternative processes implementation (OdorProb) and aesthetic considerations (AesthCons) [1,7,16].

Table 1:   Second and third level criteria priorities estimation.

1st Level Criteria	Priorities		2nd Level Criteria	Priorities		3rd Level Criteria	Priorities	
	Local	Global		Local	Global		Local	Global
Cost	0,500	0,500	Land Req	0,112	0,056			0,056
			Constr	0,540	0,270			0,270
			Oper&Main	0,348	0,174			0,174
Environ	0,333	0,333	Perform	0,661	0,220	BOD Rem	0,333	0,073
						TSS Rem	0,333	0,073
						TN Rem	0,167	0,037
						TP Rem	0,167	0,037
			Sludge Pr	0,208	0,069			0,069
			Flow Fluct	0,131	0,044			0,044
Social	0,167	0,167	Odor Prob	0,750	0,125			0,125
			Aesth Cons	0,250	0,042			0,042

4   Model application

The presented model is applied in Evros prefecture and more specifically at the municipality of New Vissa. Two catchment's areas are identified by spatial analyses. In the first one agglomerations of Vissa (3190 p.e.), Kavilli (1650 p.e.) and Sterna (990 p.e.) are settled and in the second Kastanies (1430 p.e.) and Rizia (1870 p.e.). Multicriteria evaluation process is applied in the second case in order to select the best treatment plant for serving a total of 3300 p.e.

According to the AHP methodology, second level criteria are evaluated via pairwise comparisons with respect to the overall goal (selection of the best treatment process), while third level criteria are evaluated for their relative importance to the criterion they belong (Table 1). Finally, the alternatives are compared according to their performance in each one of the third level criteria using common scales for the quantitive parameters, and AHP scale of weights for the qualitive criteria. The priorities from the pairwise comparison matrices are weighted and alternatives are ranked according to their total sum (Table 2). AHP can be successfully used by a certain group of interest or can be applied through a group decision process. In the second case it is possible serious debates to arise during the weights assignment process. For example the regional authorities who fund the facilities constructions consider their cost of higher importance. The opposite is obtained when the municipality authorities assign weights since operations and maintenance costs as well as social criteria are considered as more significant. When a compromise is not reached, priorities derived using the geometric mean of the participants proposed weights.

Table 2:   Local, global, and overall priorities of the hierarchy alternatives.

Alternatives Evaluation Criteria	S.B.R.		O.D.		R.B.C.	
	Local Priorities	Global Priorities	Local Priorities	Global Priorities	Local Priorities	Global Priorities
Land Req	0,364	0,020	0,364	0,020	0,113	0,006
Constr	0,199	0,054	0,112	0,030	0,133	0,036
Oper&Main	0,127	0,022	0,120	0,021	0,150	0,026
BOD Rem	0,173	0,013	0,173	0,013	0,155	0,011
TSS Rem	0,169	0,012	0,169	0,012	0,163	0,012
TN Rem	0,111	0,004	0,111	0,004	0,111	0,004
TP Rem	0,122	0,004	0,122	0,004	0,122	0,004
Sludge Pr	0,051	0,004	0,051	0,004	0,093	0,006
Flow Fluct	0,069	0,003	0,069	0,003	0,118	0,005
Odor Prob	0,254	0,032	0,254	0,032	0,180	0,023
Aesth Cons	0,095	0,004	0,095	0,004	0,095	0,004
Overall Priorities	3rd	0,172	5th	0,147	6th	0,138
Alternatives Evaluation Criteria	W.S.P.		S.F.+Lag.		S.F.+Cl.	
	Local Priorities	Global Priorities	Local Priorities	Global Priorities	Local Priorities	Global Priorities
Land Req	0,034	0,002	0,056	0,003	0,068	0,004
Constr	0,201	0,054	0,203	0,055	0,152	0,041
Oper&Main	0,225	0,039	0,212	0,037	0,167	0,029
BOD Rem	0,173	0,013	0,164	0,012	0,164	0,012
TSS Rem	0,140	0,010	0,180	0,013	0,180	0,013
TN Rem	0,296	0,011	0,185	0,007	0,185	0,007
TP Rem	0,305	0,011	0,165	0,006	0,165	0,006
Sludge Pr	0,238	0,016	0,303	0,021	0,263	0,018
Flow Fluct	0,248	0,011	0,268	0,012	0,228	0,010
Odor Prob	0,062	0,008	0,125	0,016	0,125	0,016
Aesth Cons	0,143	0,006	0,286	0,012	0,286	0,012
Overall Priorities	2nd	0,181	1st	0,193	4th	0,168

Sensitivity analyses enable the decision maker to investigate how sensitive the ranking of the alternatives is to changes in the importance of the criteria. In the appendix, six different options for the final rank of the alternatives are presented considering two major scenarios for the hierarchy's criteria. In the first scenario (first three diagrams) the final ranking of the alternatives is examined according to changes in the importance among the second level criteria (one diagram for each criterion) while all the other priorities are assumed as constant. In the second scenario (last three diagrams) the same procedure is repeated for the cost subcriteria. It is obtained that conventional systems can get more preferable, for the examined amount of p.e., only when an over evaluation of the social criterion is taking place or in areas where the cost of land is extremely high.

5 Conclusions

Multicriteria analysis is a powerful approach to decision making problems, especially to the wastewater treatment plant selection, in which economic, technical and social criteria must be taken into consideration in order to achieve an optimal evaluation of the alternatives. We have proposed a generic approach based on the Analytic Hierarchy Process multicriteria method for selecting wastewater treatment plant at municipality level. This approach has been proved to be a workable and flexible tool that offers good communication between engineers and decision-makers. The model can be used for agglomerations up to 10000 p.e., using each time the appropriate costs estimations. Finally constraints (geological, temperature etc), in appliance of natural systems, obtained using GIS based tools could reduce the number of the candidate solutions, while the presented poles' methodology determines the optimal location for the selected treatment plant.

Appendix

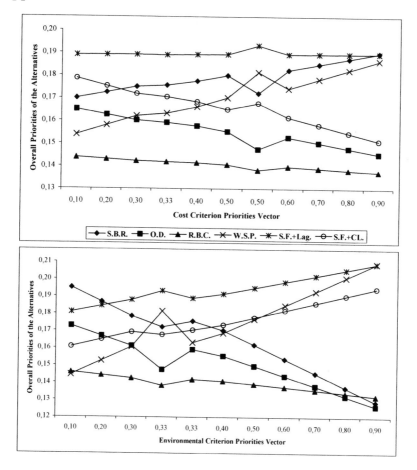

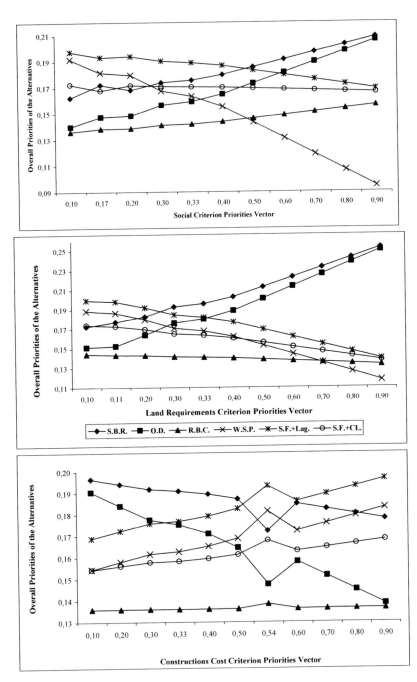

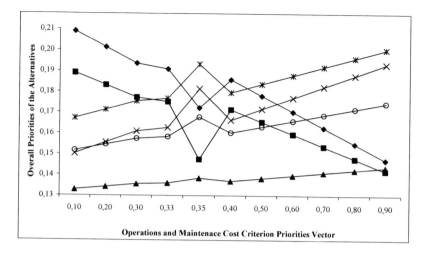

Operations and Maintenace Cost Criterion Priorities Vector

References

[1]   Metcalf-Eddy., *Wastewater engineering-Treatment, Disposal, Reuse*, McGraw-Hill, 4th Edition, N. York, 2003.
[2]   Angelakis A.N., Tchobanoglous G., *Wastewater engineering-Natural treatment systems and effluents retrieve, reuse and disposal*, Crete University Publications, Iraklio, 1995 (in Greek).
[3]   Gratziou M., *Functions for wastewater treatment plants cost evaluation*, Ph.D. thesis, Democritus University of Thrace, Xanthi, 1998 (in Greek).
[4]   Tsagarakis K.P., *The treatment of municipal wastewater in Greece*, Ph.D. thesis, School of Civil Engineering, University of Leeds, Leeds 1999.
[5]   CEC., Council Directive 91/271/EEC concerning urban waste-water treatment, *Official Journal of the European Community*, L135/40, 1991.
[6]   Garcia J., Mujeriego R., and Obis J.M., Wastewater treatment for small communities in Catalonia (Mediterranean Region), *Water Policy*, **3**, 341-350, 2001.
[7]   Hoffmann B., Nielsen S.B., Elle M., Gabriel S., Eilersen A.M., Henze M. and Mikkelsen P.S., Assessing the sustainability of small wastewaters systems-A context-oriented planning approach, *Environmental Impact Assessment Review*, **20**, 347-357, 2000.
[8]   Adenso-Diaz B., Tuya J., and Goitia M., EDSS for the evaluation of alternatives in waste water collecting systems design, *Environmental Modelling and Software*, **20**, 639-649, 2005.
[9]   Abu-Taleb M.F., Application of multicriteria analysis to the design of wastewater treatment in a nationally protected area. *Environ Egg and Policy* (**2**), pp. 37-46, 2000.
[10] Aravosis K., Kungolos A., Legkas K., Makkas A., Patsis K., Methodology development for the evaluation of alternative processes for the treatment of the wastewaters. www.prd.uth.gr/research/DP/2003/uth-prd-dp-2003-19_gr.pdf. 2003 (in Greek).

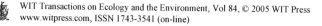

[11] Gratziou M., Alternative choices of wastewater management in Thrace, *Proc. of the International conference on ecological protection of the planet earth bio-environment and bio-culture*, June 2003, Sofia, Bulgaria, pp. 303-308, 2003.

[12] Kotsovinos N. and Gratziou M. *Natural treatment for wastewaters treatment*, Democritus University of Thrace Publications, Xanthi, 2005 (in Greek).

[13] Saaty T.L. *Decision making for leaders*, RWS Publications, 3rd Edition, Pittsburg, 1995.

[14] Tsagarakis K.P., Mara D.D., Angelakis A.N., Application of cost criteria for selection of municipal wastewater treatment systems, *Water, Air and Soil Pollution*, **142**,187-210, 2003.

[15] Gratziou M., Analysis of wastewater treatment plant cost, *Proc. of the 2nd International conference on water resources management in the ERA of transition*, September 2002, Athens, pp. 529-537, 2002.

[16] Balkema A.J., Preisig H.A., Otterpohl R., and Lambert F.J.D., Indicators for the sustainability assessment of wastewater treatment systems, *Urban Water*, **4**, 153-161, 2002.

Environmental diagnosis methodology for municipal waste landfills as a tool for planning and decision-making process

M. Zamorano[1], E. Garrido[1], B. Moreno[1], A. Paolini[2] & A. Ramos[1]
[1]*Escuela Técnica Superior de Ingenieros de Caminos, Canales y Puertos, Department of Civil Engineering, University of Granada, Granada, Spain*
[2]*Civil Engineering, Department of Hydraulics and Sanitary, Centrocidental Lisandro Alvarado University, Barquisimeto, Venezuela*

Abstract

In Europe, a Council Directive passed in 1999 provided for the regulation of waste disposal in landfills. This was a specific piece of legislation aimed at environmental control of new and currently operational installations. As a result it has become necessary to adapt currently operational release points to make them compatible with the new legislation. This new situation has obliged the different environmental organisations to carry out a stocktaking of release points in order to draw up a Conditioning Plan or a Closing Plan in accordance with the Directive. The present study describes a new methodology by which environmental diagnosis of landfill sites may be carried out, involving the formulation of environmental indexes which give information about the potential environmental problems of currently operational landfills. The indexes provide information related to location, design and operation in order to help draw up action plans for the conditioning or closure of the landfill site and to prioritize the order of actions required.
Keywords: municipal solid waste, landfill, environmental impact assessment, landfill sealing, landfill design, landfill recovering.

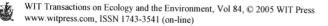

1   Introduction

1.1   Environmental impacts of waste landfilling

The increasing quantities, inappropriate treatment and final disposal of waste can result in negative impacts not only to public health and to the environment but also as a result of the social and environmental effects these activities generate [1, 2]. Damage to the environment due to poor waste management can be avoided by implementing environmentally sensitive waste management techniques, involving minimisation, composting, recycling, reuse and waste-to-energy programmes [3, 4]. However, solid waste disposal in landfills remains the usual method of disposal in the vast majority of cases [5, 6].

Landfills were initiated largely as a result of the need to protect the environment and society from adverse impacts of alternative methods of refuse disposal such as open-air burning, open-pit dumping, and ocean dumping [5]. Although they have eliminated some impacts of old practices, new problems have arisen, primarily due to gas and leachate formation. Besides potential health hazards, these concerns include fires and explosions [5, 7], vegetation damage [8], unpleasant odours [9], landfill settlement [10], ground and surface water pollution [11, 12], air pollution [13] and global warming [14].

1.2   The impact of the European Landfill Directive

The European Union Directive 31/1999 for controlling the landfilling of waste was under discussion for many years prior to its publication. The overall aim of the Directive is to prevent or reduce as far as possible any negative impacts on the environment due to the landfilling of waste. In particular, it is concerned with preventing pollution of surface and groundwater, pollution of soil and air pollution. To meet these objectives, several measures are required aimed at improving the design, operation and management of landfills and also at restricting the types of waste that are allowed to be landfilled.

The Landfill Directive was due to be incorporated into the national law of each EU member state by July 2001. Examples of countries implementing the Directive are Spain [15], the United Kingdom [16] and Finland [17].

Member States are obliged to take measures to ensure that landfills which had already been granted a permit or which were already in operation when the Directive came into force, do not continue to operate unless the requirements are met within a maximum of eight years after the date of the legislation. In consequence, environmental organisations have been obliged to carry out a stocktaking of release points located in their territory in order to draw up a Conditioning Plan or a Closing Plan for each site, depending on the environmental problems found in each case. These plans need to include the specific permission conditions listed in the Directive and to outline any corrective measures which the operators consider necessary to comply with the Directive requirements [18]. In the specific case of Spain, the deadline for the Conditioning Plans was the end of 2002; however, it has been shown that 52% of landfills do not yet have a plan [15].

1.3 Methodologies for evaluating waste landfill environmental impact

The first step in applying the Directive is to inspect the landfill sites and to study their environmental impact. This in turn involves carrying out an environmental diagnosis of the landfill to identify the various problems. A number of authors have worked on different methods for evaluating environmental impact in the design plans for new landfills [19], and methodologies have also been developed to study public opinion with regard to the siting of new landfills [20]. These studies are of limited relevance to our research since we are concerned with landfills which are currently in operation. Nevertheless, on the basis of these methods, further methods have been developed to carry out environmental diagnosis in operational facilities, with the aim of resolving particular problems in certain provinces or groups of municipalities. In most cases, these methods involve stocktaking of local natural phenomena in order to compile lists of impacts in the landfills where monitoring was undertaken, but the sphere of application is limited and it is no possible to take decisions about their control, closing, sealing or recovering [15].

Accordingly, we have developed a new methodology with the objective of providing sufficient data to determine the environmental problems generated by waste landfills and to control their operational state. The methodology has already been applied to a large number of landfills and some changes are being incorporated to correct specific shortcomings and to create software that will facilitate application of the methodology.

2 Methodology description

The methodology is based on the use of environmental indexes designed to provide quantitative assessment of the environmental interaction between the release point and potentially affected environmental elements (surface water, groundwater, atmosphere, soil and health). In addition, assessment is made of the environmental value of each environmental element taken into account, as well as of the operational state of the landfill from the environmental point of view [15, 21].

The methodology may only be applied to municipal solid waste landfills classified as non-hazardous waste landfills by the Directive 31/1999 [18]. Territorial application of the methodology may include countries in the European Union and any other country where similar legislation exists, or indeed where there is no legislation or the legislation is less prescriptive than this Directive [15].

2.1 Environmental Landfill Impact Index (ELI)

The methodology obtains a general index called the *Environmental Landfill Impact Index* [15, 21]. This index characterizes the overall environmental state of the landfill, obtaining values between 0 and 25 with classifications of 'very high', 'high', 'average', 'low' and 'very low' (Table 1). It is expressed by eqn. (1), where ERI$_i$ is the Environmental Risk Index for each environmental element.

$$ELI = \sum_{i=1}^{i=5} ERI_i \qquad (1)$$

Table 1: Classification of different indexes.

Very low	Low	Average	High	Very high
0≤ELI<5	5≤ELI<10	10≤ELI<15	15≤ ELI<20	20≤ELI≤25
0≤ERI$_i$<1	1≤ERI$_i$<2	2≤ERI$_i$<3	3≤ERI$_i$<4	4≤ERI$_i$≤5
1≤eV$_i$<1.8	1.8≤eV$_i$<2.6	2.6≤eV$_i$<3.4	3.4≤eV$_i$<4.2	4.2≤eV$_i$≤5
0≤Pbc$_i$<0.2	0.2≤Pbc$_i$<0.4	0.4≤Pbc$_i$<0.6	0.6≤Pbc$_i$<0.8	0.8≤Pbc$_i$<1
0≤Pbc-s$_i$<0.2	0.2≤Pbc-s$_i$<0.4	0.4≤Pbc-s$_i$<0.6	0.6≤Pbc-s$_i$<0.8	0.8≤Pbc-s$_i$≤1
0≤Pbc-o$_i$<0.2	0.2≤Pbc-o$_i$<0.4	0.4≤Pbc-o$_i$<0.6	0.6≤Pbc-o$_i$<0.8	0.8≤Pbc-o$_i$≤1

2.2 Environmental Risk Index (ERI)

The *Environmental Risk Index* determines the environmental impact potential for each environmental element, reflecting whether or not interaction exists between the release point or landfill and the characteristics of the environment [15, 21]. It is expressed by eqn. (2), where Pbc$_i$ is the Probability of Contamination and eV$_i$ is the Environmental Value, both for each environmental element ($_i$). The index obtains values between 0 and 5 with classifications of 'very high', 'high', 'average', 'low' and 'very low' (Table 1).

$$ERI_i = \sum_{i=1}^{i=5} (Pbc_i \times eV_i) \qquad (2)$$

2.3 Probability of Contamination (Pbc)

The *Probability of Contamination* for each environmental element depends on the scale of operation, as well as waste characteristics and the spread of disposals in the landfill environment [15, 21]. It may obtain values between 0 and 1 and is classified as 'very high', 'high', 'average', 'low' and 'very low' (Table 1).

In order to assess contamination probability, a number of landfill variables are selected for each environmental element. All variables have a theoretical justification of their state, which is closely related to the biochemical and physical processes directly or indirectly affecting the environmental elements. The variables are based on guidelines established in the European Council Directive 1999/31/EC and they are classified in two groups: (i) variables related to operation of the landfill (for example, in the case of contamination probability of groundwater, these variables are: compaction, waste and organic matter types, age of landfill, covering material, waterproofing of release vessel, control of liquid leachate and surface drainage systems); and (ii) variables related to the siting of landfill (for example, in the case of contamination probability of groundwater, these variables are: pluviometry, permeability, release-point localisation in surface runoff, fault, seismic risk, and release-point localisation in flood-water storage volume).

Probability of Contamination for each environmental element is expressed by eqn. (3) where n is the number of variables affecting each environmental element, CRI_j is the Contamination Risk Index for each variable $(_j)$, CRI_{jmin} is the minimum value obtained by the CRI for each variable and CRI_{jmax} is the maximum value obtained by the CRI for each variable.

$$Pbc_i = \frac{\sum_{j=1}^{j=n} CRI_j - \sum_{j=1}^{j=n} CRI_{j_{min}}}{\sum_{j=1}^{j=n} CRI_{j_{max}} - \sum_{j=1}^{j=n} CRI_{j_{min}}} \qquad (3)$$

2.3.1 Contamination Risk Index (CRI_j)

Evaluation of each variable $(_j)$ may be obtained by the *Contamination Risk Index (CRI_j)* for each variable, whose expression is shown in eqn. (4):

$$CRI_j = C_j \times W_j \qquad (4)$$

In this expression, C_j is the classification of the variable and provides information on the situation of the release point or the interaction between disposal processes and environmental characteristics related to the variable [15, 21]. The range of values may be 1, 2, 3, 4 or 5.

W_j is the weighting of each variable. Values may be 1 or 2, depending on the relationship between the variable and the concept of 'structural elements' at the release point; the structural elements considered are: the existence of organic matter, humidity and density of wastes. These three concepts participate in the main biochemical and physical processes produced in the release point and cause production of gas and leachate, affecting all variables and providing greater weighting to the different landfill variables [15, 21]. For example, the variable 'leachate control' affects the environmental elements of surface water, groundwater and atmosphere, obtaining in each case a weighting of 2 since the variable is directly related with the structural element 'humidity' and thus with a higher production of leachate, with the consequent risk of contamination.

W_j also reaches a value of 2 when the variable directly affects the structural elements, although these may not be directly related to the environmental elements. For example, the variable 'Distance from population point' contemplates the distance between the landfill and the nearest population point, including isolated settlements, and this affects the environmental element 'human health'. In this case the variable is directly related with a pollution risk to the health of the inhabitants of the population point.

Justification and classification of the variable 'Distance from population points' is shown in Table 2. Classification is carried out on the basis of criteria established by research into congenital and chromosomal [22] anomalies observed in people living near landfills, as well as Spanish legislation concerning hazardous and unsanitary activities and other studies relating the presence of low or high-density population zones near release points to their environmental impact [23]. The same justification and quantification is applied to all the other variables and environmental elements.

Table 2: Classification and weighting of the variable 'Distance from population points' for the environmental element 'human health'.

Condition	Justification	W_j	C_j
Landfill very close	High-density urban settlement at close distance (under 2 km)		5
Landfill close	Rural area with several developments or urban industrial area at close distance (under 2 km)		4
Landfill at medium distance	Rural area with disperse developments at some distance (between 2 and 3 km)	2	3
Landfill far	Few and disperse constructions at some distance (between 2 and 3 km)		2
Landfill very far	No developments in area (over 3 km)		1

2.3.2 Probability of contamination due to landfill site and probability of contamination due to landfill operation

Taking into account the rate expression for Probability of Contamination for each environmental element, two further indexes are obtained. These provide information about the suitability of the location of the landfill and its operational state, and again apply to each environmental element: *Probability of Contamination due to landfill site ($Pbc\text{-}s_j$)* and *Probability of Contamination due to landfill operation ($Pbc\text{-}o_j$)*. The rate expression used to quantify these indexes is represented by eqn. (4); however, variables included in this expression are restricted to those related to the location of the landfill in the first case, and those related to the operation of the landfill in the second case. The variables may obtain values between 0 and 1 and are classified as 'very high', 'high', 'average', 'low' and 'very low' (Table 1).

2.4 Environmental value (eV)

The concept *Environmental Value* is designed to identify and quantify the environmental assessment of each environmental element in the area of the landfill. The index takes into account the relationship between the landfill environmental and/or social and political characteristics and the emissions in the release point [15, 21]. Values range between 1 and 5 for each environmental element, with classifications of 'very high', 'high', 'average', 'low' and 'very low' (Table 1).

Table 3: Justification and quantification of the characteristic 'use of water' for the environmental element 'surface water'.

A_3	Use of water	1	Not for use by humans
		2	Irrigation/agricultural
		3	Industrial, recreational, street cleaning, garden irrigation
		4	Drinking water, co-existing with other supply sources
		5	Drinking water, exclusive supply source

In the case of surface water, four characteristics are used to quantify Environmental Value: type of surface water flow (A_1), type of surface flow branch line (A_2), use of water (A_3), existence of animal or vegetable species (A_4). The rate expression used to quantify these four characteristics is represented by eqn. (5). Each characteristic may obtain values of 1, 2, 3, 4 or 5 and some may acquire a weighting coefficient value of 2 due to their relative importance; for example, the characteristic 'use of water' has a weighting coefficient of 2 in the case of the environmental element 'surface water'. Table 3 shows justification and quantification in the case of the characteristic 'use of water'. The same justification and quantification is applied to the other characteristics and environmental elements.

$$eV_{surfacewater} = \frac{A_1 + A_2 + 2 \times A_3 + A_4}{6} \tag{5}$$

3 Summary of results

The methodology described makes it possible to carry out an environmental diagnosis of urban waste landfills providing sufficient data to determine the set of environmental problems posed by each landfill. The results obtained, formulated in a series of environmental indexes, may be used in various ways: (i) as a tool for studying the suitability of landfill sites and for monitoring their operation; (ii) for application in the development of projects aimed at conditioning landfills with the objective of continuing their use with reduced environmental impact and in accordance with the new legislation; and (iii) for application in closing, sealing and reinsertion projects in cases where termination of landfill operation is required. The information provided by each index is summarized below.

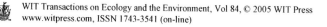

3.1 Environmental Landfill Impact Index (ELI)

This index provides information regarding the overall set of environmental problems posed by the landfill. Applied to different landfills in the same study area, the ELI can be used to draw up lists of priority actions. Landfills with greater ELI values would receive higher priority of action since they pose greater environmental problems.

3.2 Environmental Risk Index (ERI)

Once the overall set of environmental problems posed by the landfill has been determined by means of the ELI, the ERI for each environmental element may be studied. For each landfill, the ERI indicates which environmental element or elements are most affected by the presence of wastes, making it possible to determine the extent of deterioration in each case.

3.3 Environmental Value (eV)

The eV is considered as a relative environmental value, since it aims to identify and quantify the relation between the environmental and socio-political characteristics of the landfill and the landfill emissions, as well as the environmental importance of each element in the surroundings of the landfill. The eV thus provides information concerning the suitability of the landfill location.

3.4 Probability of Contamination (Pbc)

This concept calculates the greater or lesser risk of impact for each environmental element owing to the location and/or operation of the landfill. The difference between the Probability of Contamination and the Environmental Risk Index is that in the first case, risk of environmental impact of the landfill is calculated without taking into account the environmental value of the area in which the landfill is situated. Two landfills with the same contamination probability (for example 0.5) for an environmental element might obtain two different contamination risk indexes (for example 2.5 -average- and 0.5 -very low-) because they have different environmental value for this environmental element (5 and 1 respectively).

By means of the two types of Pbc it is possible to determine how the location and scale of operation of the landfill intervene in the overall set of environmental problems. In turn, this may help to establish the guidelines which need to be followed for their solution.

Finally, individual analysis of the contamination risk indexes obtained for each variable provides information concerning the actions which need to be carried out in the conditioning or closure and plans. For example, it may be necessary to improve control of leachates or biogas, or to construct facilities for the collection of surface runoff, etc.

Acknowledgements

This research is part of an R+D Project funded by the Spanish Ministry of Science and Technology entitled "Design and implementation of methodologies for the environmental diagnosis of urban waste landfills and waste dumps".

References

[1]   Diaz, L.F., Savage, G.M. & Egerth, L.L., Alternatives for the treatment and disposal of healthcare wastes in developing countries. *Waste Management*, in press, 2005.

[2]   Garrod, G. & Willis, K., Estimating lost amenity due to landfill waste disposal. *Resources, Conservation and Recycling*, **22**, pp. 83-95, 1998.

[3]   Read, A.D., Philips, P. & Robinson, G., Landfill as a future waste management option in England: the view of landfill operators. *Resources, Conservation and Recycling*, **20**, pp. 183-205, 1997.

[4]   Burford, C., The UK waste strategy. *IWM Conference Proceedings*, pp. 82-85, 1995.

[5]   El-Fadel, M., Findikakis, A.N. & Leckie, J.O., Environmental impacts of solid waste landfilling. *Journal of Environmental Management*, **50**, pp. 1-25, 1997.

[6]   Mato, R.R.A.M., Environmental implications involving the establishment of sanitary landfills in five municipalities in Tanzania: the case of Tanga municipality. *Resources, Conservation and Recycling*, **25**, pp. 1-16, 1999.

[7]   Raybould, J.G. & Anderson, D.J., Migration of landfill gas and its control – a case history. *Journal of Engineering Geology*, **20**, pp. 75-83, 1987.

[8]   Gilman, E.F., Flower, F.B. & Leone, I.A., Standardized procedures for planting vegetation on completed sanitary landfills. *Waste Management & Research*, **3**, pp. 65-80, 1985.

[9]   Deipser, A. & Stegmann, R., Biological degradation of VCCs and CFCs under simulated anaerobic landfill conditions in laboratory test digesters. *Environmental Science and Pollution Research*, **4 (4)**, pp. 209-216, 1997.

[10]   Edgers, L., Noble, J.J. & Williams, E., A biologic model for long term settlement in landfills. *Proceedings of the Mediterranean Conference on Environmental Geotechnology,* (M.A. Usmen and Y.B. Acat., eds), Cesme, Turkey, pp. 177-184, 1992.

[11]   Chofqi, A., Younsi, A., Lhadi, E.K., Mania, J., Mudry, J. & Veron, A., Environmental impact of an urban landfill on a coastal aquifer (El Jadida, Morocco). *Journal of African Earth Sciences*, **39**, pp. 509-516, 2004.

[12]   Nevenka, M., Bozena, C., Marijan, A., Svjetlana, A. & Zdenkan, T., Assessment of groundwater contamination in the vicinity of a municipal solid waste landfill (Zagreb, Croatia). *Water Science and Technology*, **37(8)**, pp. 37-44, 1998.

[13] Shen, T.T., Nelson, T.P. & Schmidt, C.E., Assessment and control of VOC emissions from waste disposal facilities. *CRC Critical Reviews in Environmental Control*, **20**, pp. 43-76, 1990.

[14] Pearce, F., Methane: the hidden greenhouse gas. *New Scientist*, **6**, pp. 37-41, 1989.

[15] Calvo, F., Moreno, B., Zamorano, M. & Szanto, M., Environmental diagnosis methodology for municipal waste landfills. *Waste Management*, in press, 2005.

[16] Burnley, S., The impact of the European landfill directive on waste management in the United Kingdom. *Resources, Conservation and Recycling*, **32**, pp. 349-358, 2001.

[17] Kettunen, M. & Vuorisalo, T., History and development of Finnish landfill research: impacts of legislative changes and EC policies. *Resources, Conservation and Recycling*, **44**, pp. 51-71, 2005.

[18] Council Directive 1999/31/EC of 26 April 1999 on the landfill of waste. Official Journal of the European Communities. L 182. 16 July 1999. 0001-0019.

[19] Carter, L., Ward, C.H., Ginger, W. & McCarty, P.L., *Methods for assessment of groundwater pollution potential.* John Wiley & Sons. New York, 1997.

[20] Al-Yaqout, A.F., Koushki, P.A., & Hamoda, M.F., Public opinion and siting solid waste landfills in Kuwait. *Resources, Conservation and Recycling*, **35**, pp. 215-227, 2002.

[21] Calvo, F., Moreno, B., Ramos, A. & Zamorano, M., Implementation of a new environmental impact assessment for municipal waste landfill as tool for planning and decision-making process. *Renewable and Suitable Energy Reviews*, in press, 2005.

[22] Vrijheid, M., Dolk, H., Stone, D., Abransky, L., Bianchi, F., Fazarinc, I., Arne, G., Nelen, V., Robert, E., Scott, J.E.S., Stone, D. & Tenconi, R., Chromosomal congenital anomalies and residence near hazardous waste landfill sites. *The Lancet*, 359, pp. 320-322, 2002.

[23] Villalobos, M. *Gestión de residuos sólidos urbanos e impacto ambiental.* Editorial TAL, pp. 285-305, 1991.

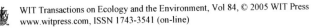

Economic evaluation of small capacity domestic wastewater processing units in provincial or rural areas

M. Gratziou & M. Tsalkatidou
Department of Civil Engineering, School of Engineering,
Democritus University of Thrace, Greece

Abstract

This paper aims at a comparative evaluation of the total cost of urban sewage processing units for several treatment systems, appropriate mainly for small capacity plants. The studied systems were: Oxidation Ditch (O.D.), Trickling Filter (T.F.), Rotating Biological Contactor (R.B.C.), Compact Sequential Batch Reactor (S.B.R.), Waste Stabilization Ponds (S.P.) and Subsurface Constructed Wetland Systems (C.W). For each system, operating and construction costs are calculated as flow rate functions for a 40-year operating period. Cost calculation is based on the analysis of its several components such as energy consumption, chemical consumption, personnel salaries, maintenance expenses, construction materials and their respective quantities, required mechanical equipment and land value. All pecuniary flows, in order to be comparable, are converted into current value. For each case total and partial costs are expressed as functions of the plant capacity. The annual operating and maintenance (O&M) cost, the project cost, as well as the total construction, maintenance and operating cost for 40 years of operation (Present Value) can be expressed as functions of flow rate, of the form $a+bQ-cQ^2$; whereas energy cost can be described by a linear function of flow rate, of the form $a+bQ$, with excellent approximation. The coefficients a, b, c, for the various treatment methods examined and for every cost category are summarized in tables. All treatment methods exhibited, for the several categories of cost per E.P. examined, strong positive scale economies, especially for plant capacities up to 5000 E.P. Wastewater treatment by natural methods is the least expensive choice in every case. The classification of the treatment methods from the least to the most expensive one depends on plant capacity. The classification of the treatment methods based on their cost for different plant capacities is provided.
Keywords: cost evaluation, domestic wastewater, processing units.

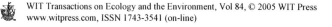
WIT Transactions on Ecology and the Environment, Vol 84, © 2005 WIT Press
www.witpress.com, ISSN 1743-3541 (on-line)

1   Introduction

At times when energy and financial resources are restricted the engineer or the decision maker in general, targeting sustainable development, should decide on technical solutions that comply with the environmental and social constraints, at a minimum energy and financial cost.

The engineer, while aiming at reaching the social and environmental targets, has a variety of technological options available to choose from. The range of these choices however is restricted from the outset due to several factors, with cost being the most important.

This paper provides a comparative evaluation of the total cost of domestic wastewater treatment systems, appropriate for relatively small capacity units. The E.P. (equivalent population) ranges from 100 up to 20,000.

Kotsovinos *et al* [1] reported that for urban sewage processing units within the studied E.P. range, the least expensive from all the variations of the Activated Sludge method is the Oxidation Ditch. Therefore, in this paper we examined and evaluated the following treatment systems: Oxidation Ditch (O.D.), Trickling Filter (T.F.), Rotating Biological Contactor (R.B.C.), Compact Sequential Batch Reactor (S.B.R.), Waste Stabilization Ponds (S.P.) and Subsurface Constructed Wetland Systems (C.W).

All methods include a preliminary treatment stage, sludge dewatering using drying beds and chlorination as disinfection. Dewatering using a band filter press results approximately in a 40% cost increase according to Gratziou and Ikonomou [2]. Only in the case of the waste stabilization ponds, a different disinfection method was chosen. The ponds system consisted of an anaerobic, a facultative and two maturation ponds in series. An imhoff tank is used for primary treatment in the constructed wetlands. As an alternative in the constructed wetlands method, we examined the case of disinfection achieved using a maturation pond (lagoon). It should be noted that in units with capacities up to 5,000 E.P. and in the case of conventional treatment systems, disinfection with UV provides better results, i.e. up to 10% savings [1].

For the cost to be calculated, it is divided into its components, such as energy consumption, chemicals' consumption, personnel salaries, maintenance costs, construction materials and their quantities, mechanical equipment, land cost, amortizations. All pecuniary flows, in order to be comparable, are converted into current value assuming an 8% interest rate for a 40-year timescale. For the calculations, typical costs in Greece are considered. For each case, scale economy and the functions of total cost (present value), project cost and O&M cost, in relation to unit capacity, are estimated along with the annual energy cost functions.

The information provides a first detailed level for general planning and a technique for quick financial evaluation of the treatment systems. The aim of evaluating expenses in pollution control is the minimization of the expenses required for the achievement of a certain water quality target. This procedure should not be mixed with economic optimization terms that refer to maximization of the production yield and minimization of the cost. This procedure is based on the rationale that the lower wastewater treatment system cost still has to meet the legal specifications for water quality instead of actually dictating them. Therefore all designed units can treat with the same efficiency sewage of the same qualitative and quantitative characteristics.

2   Methodology

Cost estimation is based on the identification of its elements which are then cost accounted. The calculation of the several elements quantities was achieved with the development of standardized plans for various flows and a change in flow rate. In the approach of real data expenses, construction details are determined clearly enough for an adequate calculation of the elements required for cost estimation such as material quantities, working man-hours etc.

2.1 Methodology for the calculation of quantities and construction expenses

The most important building expenses for the construction of any treatment unit can be classified as follows:
- Tanks and other concrete or steel constructions.
- Installed equipment.
- Building and housing.
- Channeling with pipes, insulation and support.
- Electrical work, control systems and other installations.

Andreadakis and Chalkia [3] reported that the first four elements can be precisely evaluated and generally account for 85% of the total main expenses. The remaining elements cost can be calculated as a percentage of the total expenses. Building demands depend on the housed equipment and are calculated as quantities (i.e. m^2). The estimated electrical expenses are incorporated as a percentage to the mechanical equipment expenses, the latter involving: the purchasing equipment cost, the installation cost and other secondary expenses. The purchasing cost of the mechanical equipment is a function of size or capacity.

The construction of wastewater treatment plants depends not only on the construction of the processing units, but also on the completion of the supporting plant and piping network, in order for the whole unit to be operational. These construction expenses of the processing units were found to represent 35% to 50% of the total construction cost; piping expenses range between 15%-20% [4].

Other important construction costs are contractors' profit and contingent expenses. Since these costs are calculated based on the total construction cost, net procedure expenses are multiplied by a percentage that defines a value for contractors' profit and contingent expenses. In Greece the enacted contractor's profit percentage amounts to 18% while contingent expenses to 15%. Total construction expenses are calculated as the sum of processing units' expenses, other construction expenses (service networks, surrounding area etc), contractors' profit and contingent expenses.

The calculation of the project cost, besides construction cost, includes non construction expenses related to planning, design and land cost. Non construction expenses are expressed as a percentage of the total construction expenses, e.g. 2% for legal expenses, 15% for the study fee, 3.5% for planning etc [5]. Land cost was assumed as 1,500€ per 1,000m².

2.2 Methodology for the calculation of operating and maintenance cost

The analysis of the operation and maintenance expenses involves:
-Personnel salaries, labor wages for maintenance and operation.
-Necessary operating electrical energy.
-Material required for repairs.
-Chemical substances and other demands.
-Replacement program.
The personnel required for each treatment unit depends on the size of the latter. The total man-hours requirements and therefore the salaries expenses are related to plant size.

The electrical energy consumed for the treatment is the total sum of the energy consumed in each part of the unit.

Replacement cost is applicable on all those construction elements which have a lifespan shorter in duration than the planning period and therefore need to be replaced during the latter. Replacement cost is assumed to be equal to the initial cost of those elements.

2.3 Calculating present value

Total present value is the sum of the present values of all partial costs. For the calculation of present value, land cost was not considered since we assumed that the present salvage land value is equal to its current value. Inflation was also not considered as it was assumed that the general inflation percentage influences rather similarly all the alternative solutions.

3 Results

3.1 Cost functions

Total cost (Present value) and project cost can be estimated as functions of flow rate, in the form of $a + bQ - cQ^2$ or alternatively in the form of $a + bQ$; the annual operating and maintenance cost (O&M) can also be expressed in terms of flow rate, in the form of $a + bQ - cQ^2$, whereas energy cost is described by a linear function of flow rate in the form of $a + bQ$. These functions are all excellent approximations and applicable the majority of treatment systems. The coefficients a,b,c for each studied system and for every cost category are presented in the tables below. Cost is expressed in € and flow rate Q in m³/d, with a flow rate range $15 \leq Q \leq 30,000$ m³/d.

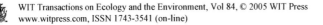

Table 1: Coefficients a,b,c of the Total Cost function, $K_T = a + bQ - cQ^2$.

Processing	Coefficients			R^2
	a	b	c	
Oxidation Ditch	2×10^6	1773.7	0.1633	0.9925
Trickling Filter	2×10^6	1801.9	0.188	0.9945
Rotating Biol. Cont.	1×10^6	2097.5	0.255	0.9915
Compact SBR	714,973	2113.9	-	0.9994
Waste Stab. Ponds	759,259	1490.8	0.174	0.9947
Const. Wetlands-Lag.	511,466	1636.9	-	0.9981
Const. Wetl.-Chlor.	793,000	1704.5	-	0.9965

Table 2: Coefficients a,b,c of the Project Cost function, $K_p = a + bQ - cQ^2$.

Processing	Coefficients			R^2
	a	b	c	
Oxidation Ditch	805,023	1347.9	0.1315	0.9924
Trickling Filter	814,468	1485.9	0.1423	0.9967
Rotating Biol. Cont.	598,940	1621.2	0.1883	0.9941
Compact SBR	101,566	1582.3	-	0.9993
Waste Stab. Ponds	251,190	1202.7	0.1136	0.9976
Const. Wetlands-Lag.	101,566	1582.3	-	0.9993
Const. Wetl.-Chlor.	277,105	1597.8	-	0.9987

Table 3: Coefficients a,b,c of the O&M Cost function, $K_{O\&M} = a + bQ - cQ^2$.

Processing	Coefficients			R^2
	a	b	c	
Oxidation Ditch	48,123	44,105	0.0047	0.9929
Trickling Filter	47,020	30,288	0.0042	0.9866
Rotating Biol. Cont.	42,550	30,080	0.0041	0.9923
Compact SBR	38,964	54,722	0.0038	0.9980
Waste Stab. Ponds	27,167	21,010	0.0036	0.9797
Const. Wetlands-Lag.	30,544	17,089	0.0033	0.9489
Const. Wetl.-Chlor.	38,887	22,591	0.0037	0.9750

3.2 Cost per equivalent population – scale economies

Table 5 presents the total cost per Equivalent Population for 40 years of plant operation for different treatment methods and for plant capacities of 100 E.P., 1,000 E.P., 5,000 E.P., 10,000 E.P. and 20,000 E.P. Positive scale economies are observed; they are very strong for capacities up to 5,000 E.P., especially for conventional systems.

WIT Transactions on Ecology and the Environment, Vol 84, © 2005 WIT Press
www.witpress.com, ISSN 1743-3541 (on-line)

Table 4:   Coefficients a,b of the energy cost function, $K_E = a + bQ$.

Processing	Coefficients			R^2
	a	b	c	
Oxidation Ditch	10,372	12.830		0.9999
Trickling Filter	10,342	1.2646		0.9942
Rotating Biol. Cont.				0.9903
$15 \leq Q \leq 1000$ m^3/d	11,556	1.048	0.0005	0.9993
$1000 < Q \leq 1500$ m^3/d	16,062	0.282	-	0.9999
$1500 < Q \leq 1800$ m^3/d	182.57	1.0783	-	0.9374
$1800 < Q < 30000$ m^3/d	17,631	0.1863	-	
Compact SBR	9,842.1	32.344		0.9999
Waste Stab.Ponds	293.2	0.3209		0.9319
Const.Wetlands-Lag.	293.2	0.3209		0.9319
Const.Wetl.-Chlor.	9733.2	0.3209		0.9319

Table 5:   Total cost per equivalent population.

Processing \ E.P.	Present Value Cost per E.P. (€/E.P)				
	10^2	10^3	5×10^3	10^4	2×10^4
Oxidation Ditch	14,300	1950	598	390	281
Trickling Filter	13,900	1900	582	381	268.5
R. Biol. Cont.	13,900	1820	530	397	270
Compact SBR	6,394	1024	460	387	349.5
Waste Stab.Ponds	6,010	1010	366	255	187
Const.Wetl.-Lag.	4,107	729	351.5	300.5	267
Const.Wetl.-Chlor.	5,905	975.5	434	335.5	290

Similarly, Tables 6 and 7 summarize construction cost per Equivalent Population and the annual operating and maintenance cost per Equivalent Population respectively.

Table 6:   Construction cost per equivalent population.

Processing \ E.P.	Project Cost per E.P. (€/E.P)				
	10^2	10^3	5×10^3	10^4	2×10^4
Oxidation Ditch	7049	1039	361	248	186.5
Trickling Filter	6939	1049	379	267	201
R. Biol. Cont.	6289	891	309	258	187
Compact SBR	2174	403	228	210	202
Waste Stab.Ponds	1742.5	428.5	216.5	168.5	136.5
Const.Wetl.-Lag.	1031	324.5	250	243.5	235
Const.Wetl.-Chlor.	1827	463	302.5	260	245.5

Table 7:   Annual operating and maintenance cost per equivalent population.

Processing \ E.P.	O&M Cost per E.P. (€/E.P)				
	10^2	10^3	$5x10^3$	10^4	$2x10^4$
Oxidation Ditch	419.58	55.90	16.10	10.21	7.03
Trickling Filter	415.04	52.89	13.75	8.19	5.11
R. Biol. Cont.	392.95	48.75	12.31	7.79	4.85
Compact SBR	346.61	48.17	15.81	11.13	8.56
Waste Stab.Ponds	231.42	31.21	8.41	4.97	2.96
Const.Wetl.-Lag.	419.58	55.90	16.10	10.21	7.03
Const.Wetl.-Chlor.	415.04	52.89	13.75	8.19	5.11

4   Cost evaluation - conclusions

Analyzing total cost results, it can be highlighted that an increase in capacity corresponds to a decrease in cost per m^3 of sewage or per E.P. Sewage treatment using natural methods is in every case the least expensive option. Table 8 presents a classification of the wastewater treatment methods (from the cheapest one to the most expensive one) for different plant capacities.

For plant capacities up to 5,000 E.P. the Constructed Wetlands-Lagoon system is the most economic option. If disinfection is achieved by chlorination, total cost rises by 33.7%, construction cost by 43% and the annual O&M cost by 28%. Total cost rises by 28% if a Waste Stabilization Ponds system is chosen. The Compact S.B.R. method increases total cost by around 40%, while construction cost is almost double for capacities up to 2,000 E.P.; for greater capacities no significant differences are observed. The R.B.C. systems total cost is double, while for capacities up to 2,000 E.P. the cost is actually three-times greater. Additionally construction cost triples but the O&M cost is slightly reduced for R.B.C. In the Trickling Filter method, total cost is 2.5 times greater than the Constructed Wetlands- Lagoon system. Oxidation Ditch is the most expensive option for these capacities, its total cost being 2.5 times greater and construction cost triple.

For greater capacities up to 20,000 E.P., Stabilization Ponds are found to be the least expensive option, followed by the Constructed Wetlands-Lagoon systems which increase total cost by 10-20% depending on plant capacity. Construction cost increases from 30% up to 60%, while O&M cost is reduced by 5% in comparison to Stabilization Ponds. When Chlorination is used as disinfection, construction cost rises by 7% and the annual O&M cost by 34%. There is actually a 12% increase in the total cost of the unit. The use of Trickling Filters results in a 45-55% increase of the total cost, a 40-60% increase of the construction cost and a 67% increase of the O&M cost. Oxidation Ditch raises total cost by 50-60%, construction cost by 30-55% and doubles O&M cost. The Rotating Biological Contactor treatment increases total cost by 45-65%, construction cost by 30-60% and O&M by almost 60%. For capacities between 8,000 and 20,000 E.P. the Compact Sequential Batch Reactor treatment is the most expensive option. Total cost is between 50 and 85% higher, construction cost between 20-40% higher and O&M cost is 2.5 times greater.

Table 8: Classification of wastewater treatment methods according to total cost.

E.P.		
$<10^3$	$10^3<<5x10^3$	$5x10^3<<8x10^3$
Const.Wetland.-Lagoon	Const.Wetland.-Lagoon	Stabilization Ponds
Const.Wetland- Chlor.	Stabilization Ponds	Const.Wetland.-Lagoon
Stabilization Ponds	Const.Wetland- Chlor.	Const.Wetland- Chlor.
S.B.R.	S.B.R.	S.B.R.
R.B.C	R.B.C.	Trickling Filter.
Trickling Filter	Trickling Filter	Oxidation Ditch
Oxidation Ditch	Oxidation Ditch	R.B.C.
E.P.		
$8x10^3<<14x10^3$	$14x10^3<<16x10^3$	$16x10^3<<2x10^4$
Stabilization Ponds	Stabilization Ponds	Stabilization Ponds
Const.Wetland.-Lagoon	Const.Wetland.-Lagoon	Const.Wetland.-Lagoon
Const.Wetland- Chlor.	Trickling Filter	Trickling Filter
Trickling Filter	Const.Wetland- Chlor.	R.B.C.
Oxidation Ditch	Oxidation Ditch	Oxidation Ditch.
R.B.C.	R.B.C.	Const.Wetland- Chlor.
S.B.R.	S.B.R.	S.B.R

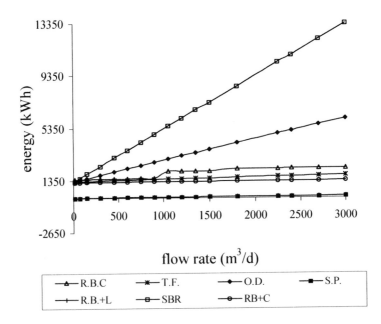

Figure 1: Energy consumption for different wastewater treatment methods.

The classification of the examined treatment methods according to their energy consumption from the least to the most energy demanding is as follows: Waste Stabilization Ponds and Subsurface Constructed Wetlands Systems with Lagoon are the least energy consuming methods, exhibiting almost zero energy demands, followed by Constructed Wetland Systems with Chlorination. Trickling Filters are 5% more energy demanding than Constructed Wetlands with Chlorination, Rotating Biological Contractors require 15% more energy and Oxidation Ditches need 65% more, whereas Compact Sequential Batch Reactors consume 55% more energy compared to Oxidation Ditches (Figure 1).

References

[1] Kotsovinos, N., Gratziou, M. & Tsalkatidou, M., Cost analysis and evaluation of conventional urban sewage processing units. *Proc. of the 3rd International Conference on Ecological Protection of the Planet Earth*, Istanbul, pp.77-78, 2005.

[2] Gratziou, M. & Ikonomou, S., Cost evaluation of urban sewage processing units, *Proc. of the 5th International Conference on Environmental Technology HELECO 2005*, Athens, 2005.B45 pp63-63

[3] Andreadakis, A. & Chalkia, A. Cost accounting of sewage treatment plants through statistical analysis of data in Greece, *Proc. of the 5th National Conference of the Greek Hydrotechnic Union*, Larissa, 1992. (In Greek) pp 243-251

[4] Metcalf and Eddy Inc., *Water Pollution Abatement Technology: Capabilities and Costs*, Public Owned Treatment Works: Springfield, VA, 1995.

[5] Gratziou, M. *Functions for Evaluating Urban Sewage Processing Cost*, PhD thesis, Department of Civil Engineering. Democritus University of Thrace, Xanthi, 1998. (In Greek)

Medical waste management in Greece: the case of Thessaly region

S. Bakopoulou, A. Kungolos & K. Aravossis
*Department of Planning and Regional Development,
University of Thessaly, Volos, Greece*

Abstract

The main objective of this study is the evaluation of medical waste management in Thessaly region, Greece. Nowadays, medical waste treatment and disposal is one of the most important problems in many countries. The reason is simple. Medical waste and specifically infectious medical waste disposal could be extremely dangerous, especially if it is not controlled, according to the basic principles of waste management. Our research was carried out in the 5 hospitals (1 university and 4 general hospitals) that operate in the region of Thessaly and our findings have shown that most of hospitals use the method of steam sterilization in a mobile treatment unit for their waste treatment. More specifically, private companies, which deal with medical waste treatment, visit the hospitals once per week and sterilize the waste in the mobile unit. On the other hand, the university hospital uses the method of incineration for its waste treatment. Regarding the incinerator, it should be noticed that it is a double chamber incinerator. The primary combustion chamber is used for the waste incineration and the secondary combustion chamber is used for the incineration of the fumes. This incinerator operates without the necessary equipment for the air pollution minimization. The medical wastes that are produced in the other medical facilities in the region are disposed without specific care for the environment. It is the outcome of our research that planning about the optimal medical waste management is essential in the effort to achieve an integrated medical waste management according to the principles of sustainable development.
Keywords: medical waste, Thessaly region, waste treatment, waste disposal, incineration, waste sterilization.

1 Introduction

In recent years and particularly during the last two decades, the environmental dimension is considered as an extremely important dimension, which should be taken into account during the procedure of regional planning and development. The *new dogma* is, now, the securing of development sustainability, which is based on the fundamental ecological principles of solidarity between generations, resource renewal etc [1]. Taking in mind this evidence, we understand that waste management and especially medical waste management is by all means significant in an effort to achieve the desirable sustainable development.

Medical waste is generated by healthcare, veterinary and research centres, laboratories and pharmaceutical plants. This group also includes dispersed sources of residues from home treatment (dialyses, administration of insulin, etc). Medical waste is in fact a varied mixture of different kinds of rubbish – from typically municipal ones (food, secondary raw materials, etc), through toxic chemicals (drugs, reagents, etc), to infectious ones (syringes, instruments, post-surgical waste). Numerous studies [2, 3, 4] have shown that an estimated 75 – 90% of waste originating within medical facilities has a municipal character. The remaining 10 – 25% of waste (infectious, pathological, etc) is deemed to require special treatment. The reason is simple. Infectious medical waste is considered to be a special category of waste because of its high potential for contaminating the environment with pathogenic factors and bacteria and thus represents a higher risk to health. For example, contaminated needles and syringes represent a particular threat and may be scavenged from waste areas and dump sites and be reused. World Health Organization has estimated that, in 2000, injections with contaminated syringes caused 21 million hepatitis B virus (HBV) infections (32% of all new infections) and 2 million hepatitis C virus (HCV) infections (40% of all new infections) [5].

Taking into account all this evidence about infectious medical waste dangers, as well as the main philosophy of sustainability, this paper aims at presenting the problems related to medical waste management in Thessaly region, Greece and suggesting optimum solutions in order to minimize environmental and health hazards. It is essential to realize that an integrated management is desirable.

The problem in Greece is significant. Regarding medical waste management, there have not been a lot of studies not only in Thessaly region, but also in Greece. For this reason our search is considered to be important and our findings could be used from the qualified authorities as a base for strategic medical waste management planning, not only in regional level, but also in national level, since such planning does not exist at time.

2 Medical waste management in Greece

The total number of hospital beds in Greece reaches up to 57000, according to data collected in 1999. Taking in mind this number, as well as the fact that the average production quantity of medical solid waste per day in Greece is

2 kg/bed, we understand that about 114 tn of medical waste are produced every day in Greek healthcare centres [6]. The corresponding waste quantity per year is 14000 tn [7]. An estimated 15% of this quantity corresponds to infectious waste, while the remaining 85% corresponds to waste with a municipal character. The distribution of medical waste production to Greek regions is depicted in the following figure.

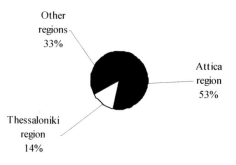

Figure 1: Distribution of production quantity of medical waste per year in Greek regions.

According to specific data collected from a statistic research, which was held in 1998, the 37% of all healthcare centres in Greece uses the method of incineration for its waste treatment [6]. The corresponding incinerators are very old and they operate without the necessary equipment for air pollution minimization. Normally, the toxic emissions and especially dioxin and furan emissions from such incinerators are important because of the high percentage of plastic (i.e. PVC) in medical waste composition [2]. The remaining 63% of Greek healthcare centres disposes its waste without care for the environment and without any prior treatment (Figure 2). This evidence shows that great threats for public health and environment are thus arising.

Figure 2:   Medical waste treatment in Greek healthcare centers (1998).

One incineration unit, which is equipped with all essential instruments for air pollution minimization, as well as an electronic system for on-line controlling of pollutant emissions, was constructed in recent years in Attica prefecture. Unfortunately, a few hospitals carry their waste in this unit because of the high economical cost. Still, the majority of Athens hospitals treats its waste in very old incinerators without the necessary equipment for air pollution minimization or disposes its waste without any prior treatment. It should be mentioned that the corresponding unit treats usually 3 tn of medical waste per day, while its treatment capacity reaches up to 30 tn of waste per day [8].

3   Medical waste management in Thessaly region

The region of Thessaly is situated in the central eastern part of Greece and includes prefectures of Larissa, Magnesia, Trikala and Karditsa (Figure 3). The population of the region in 2001 reached up to 754393 inhabitants within an area of 14037 Km^2 (53.7 inhabitants/km^2).

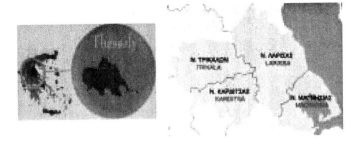

Figure 3:   Location of Thessaly region in Greece.

According to data collected from the National Statistic Office of Greece, 37 healthcare centres operate in Thessaly region at time. These include 4 general hospitals, 1 university hospital (in Larissa city), 1 military hospital (in Larissa city) and 31 private healthcare clinics. 17 primary health-care centres operate in region, too [9].

Our research regarding medical waste management was carried out in 2004 in the 5 hospitals (4 general and 1 university) of the region. Information and data was gathered mainly from personal interviews from qualified authorities in hospitals, as well as from official documents and scientific literature.

3.1 University hospital of Larissa city

The total number of beds in Larissa university hospital is 645. Taking into account this number, as well as the fact that the average production quantity of medical solid waste per day in Greece is 2 kg / bed [6], we understand that about 1290 kg of medical solid waste are produced every day in this hospital. The

193.5 kg correspond to infectious wastes, while the remaining 1096.5 kg correspond to municipal ones.

The hospital has put into practice the segregation at source. More specifically, small bins of different colour are placed in specific rooms inside the hospital in order to enable the personnel to dispose the different waste fractions at suitable places. For example, the red bins (Figure 4) are used for the infectious waste collection, while the black ones are used for the municipal waste collection. Special plastic bins for the collection of syringes and sharps (Figure 5) are not used. This is a very important disadvantage, since sharps and especially syringes represent a great threat for the public health.

Figure 4:   Example of red bins for the collection of infectious waste.

Figure 5:   Special bins for the collection of sharps.

Some other disadvantages that have been noticed in this hospital are related to the improper segregation. During our research, we have found out that the real daily quantity of infectious waste, which is collected in the red bins, is about 900 kg. If we compare this quantity with the value of 193.5 kg (see above), we can clearly understand that the segregation is not applied according to the basic guidelines of medical waste treatment.

After having been collected in the red bins, the infectious waste is lead to the treatment unit. This is a double chamber pyrolytic incinerator, which operates at a temperature of 1100°C. The primary combustion chamber is used for the waste incineration while the secondary one is used for the incineration of the fumes so as the air emissions to be minimized. Normally, waste is introduced into the primary chamber that is heated up to a sufficient temperature in order to distil the waste. Gases leaving the distillation chamber are mixed with a continuous airflow in the afterburning chamber and held at a temperature of 900°C – 1100°C by co-firing of natural gas. Essential equipment for air emission minimization does not exist, as well as a modern on-line gas emission measurement system. This system is required for the continuous monitoring of air emissions, which contain fly ash (particulates) composed of dioxins, furans, heavy metals, and gases such as oxides of nitrogen, sulfur, carbon, and hydrogen halides.

3.2 General hospitals

There are 4 general hospitals in Thessaly region, each in every capital of prefecture. The capacity (number of beds) of the general hospital of Larissa city is 300 beds, as well as the capacity of the general hospital of Volos city. The corresponding capacity of the general hospital of Karditsa city is 240 beds, while general hospital of Trikala city capacity is 221 beds. A quantity of 600 kg of medical wastes and more specifically 90 kg of infectious wastes and 510 kg of municipal ones are being produced every day in the general hospital of Larissa city, as well as in Volos city hospital. On the other hand, in the hospital of Karditsa city about 72 kg of infectious wastes and 408 kg of municipal ones are being produced every day, while in the hospital of Trikala city about 66.3 kg of infectious wastes and 375.7 kg of municipal ones are daily being produced.

All these hospitals use the segregation at source, too. The procedure is the same as in university hospital. There are red and black bins in every hospital for the collection of infectious and municipal waste respectively. The method of treatment that is used in all these hospitals is the method of steam sterilization in a mobile treatment unit. More specifically private companies visit each hospital one or two times per week and sterilize the infectious waste in the mobile unit. Steam sterilization is based on exposure of shredded infectious waste to high-temperature and high-pressure steam. It inactivates most types of microorganisms, if temperature and contact time are sufficient. The sterilization process requires that waste be shredded before treatment. The main disadvantage of this method relates mainly to the fact that the process is inappropriate for the treatment of anatomical waste and animal carcasses, and it does not efficiently treat chemical or pharmaceutical wastes [2]. Regarding the sharps, it should be noticed that there are significant concerns if the sterilization method can inactivate the pathogenic microorganisms because the formulation of the syringes, for example, prevents in many cases the entrance of steam in the interior area of the syringe.

The main problems that have been noticed in these hospitals relate also to the improper segregation. We have found out that the quantity of infectious waste that is being sterilized is greater than the normal quantity, which can be estimated by the values (quantity/bed) that were taken from the Greek scientific literature [6] (see above).

3.3 Other healthcare centres in the region

As mentioned above, our research about the medical waste management in Thessaly region was carried out in the university hospital of Larissa city and in the 4 general hospitals, each in every capital of prefecture. Although, during this research we have found out that most of the other healthcare centres that operate in the region, from primary healthcare centres to the private clinics, do not perform proper management of their waste and dispose them without care for the environment. It is worth mentioning that the doctors in private clinics do not segregate their waste, so the infectious wastes are disposed usually together with the domestic ones.

The main results of our research are depicted in Figure 6 and Table 1.

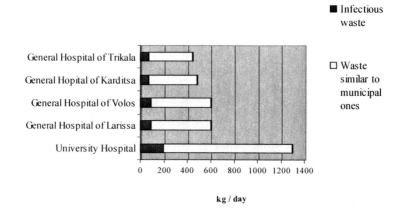

Figure 6:   Waste production quantity per day in the hospitals of Thessaly region.

Table 1:   Infectious medical waste treatment methods in Thessaly region.

Healthcare center	Treatment method
University hospital	Daily incineration in a double chamber incinerator
4 general hospitals	Steam sterilization in a mobile treatment unit 1 time per week
Rest healthcare centres	Disposal without treatment

4 Conclusions and suggestions

In this study, the medical waste management in Greece and more specifically in Thessaly region was examined. Our main conclusion is that the problem of medical waste management in Greece is extremely significant. The reasons relate to insufficient methods of treatment and improper segregation.

Bearing in mind all this evidence, we easily understand that the formulation of objectives and planning for their achievement are important for improving medical waste management at national and regional level. Planning requires the definition of a strategy that will facilitate careful implementation of the necessary measures and the appropriate allocation of resources according to the identified priorities. This is important for the motivation of authorities, health-care workers, and the public, and for defining further actions that may be needed.

First of all, it is important that all the qualified hospital authorities should focus in the proper medical waste segregation and especially in sharps segregation. No matter what final strategy for treatment and disposal of wastes is selected, it is critical that wastes are segregated (preferably at the point of source) prior to treatment and disposal. This most important step must be taken to safeguard the occupational health of hospital workers, as well as public health. Education and training of all hospital personnel is a very important step for the segregation success. It is really important that all the qualified authorities can really understand the contribution of a successful segregation at source to the minimization of infectious waste stream, and thus to the most efficient and least expensive treatment and normally to less health and environmental risks.

On the other hand, establishing clear guidelines, which emphasize at waste reduction, will keep waste management problems in focus. New emphasis needs to be put on waste reduction of hazardous materials. For example, hospital waste management would benefit from a policy of a phase out of mercury-based products and technologies. Digital and electronic technology is available to replace mercury-based diagnostic tools. This would also be a purchasing and investment decision.

Research for detecting the real advantages and disadvantages of the existent treatment methods is essential, as well as research for discovering new more effective treatment methods. It would also be helpful, if the use of PVC plastic in the healthcare tools construction were forbidden in every country. It is widely known that the incineration of such plastic produces dioxins and other pollutants, which pose serious human health risks not only to workers but also to general public through food supplies.

At national level, the corresponding Greek Ministry of Health should develop clear plans and policies for the proper management and disposal of wastes. A national management plan will permit healthcare waste management options to be optimized on a national scale. A national survey of healthcare waste will provide the relevant agency with a data base for identifying actions on a district, regional, and national basis, taking into account conditions, needs, and possibilities at each level. An appropriate, safe, and cost-effective strategy will be concerned principally with treatment, recycling, transport, and disposal options. Education and training of hospital personnel is also significant, in order to assure that these plans will be put into practice and maintained. The establishment of a system of continuous controls in the Greek hospitals for the assurance of the implementation of the above plans is significant as well.

The regional planning of medical waste management represents another crucial point, which should be paid attention to. We mean that the corresponding ministry should decide whether it is better to construct one medical waste treatment unit in each region or every hospital should treat its waste separately. This decision may only be made through a cost-benefit analysis in order to determine which scenario is more effective.

At regional level, every hospital should develop one specific plan for its waste management. The main guidelines of this plan will be similar to the guidelines of the national plan. The commitment of responsibilities by the hospital authorities regarding the infectious waste management is by all means desirable. An effective cost-benefit analysis should also be developed in every hospital in order to determine the most effective treatment method, not only from a cost – benefit aspect, but from an environmental point, too.

The private clinics and the primary health care centres should be forced to implement the segregation at source. Private qualified companies should provide secure collection and transportation of infectious waste from the private clinics or the primary health care centres to one hospital treatment unit. This measure represents a very significant step and it should be considered carefully from the responsible authorities.

In general an integrated system of medical waste management in the whole of Greece and more specifically in the area of Thessaly region has to be achieved through the commitment of responsibility both by doctors, hospital personnel, responsible authorities and the local society. Education of doctors and hospital personnel represents a very significant point in this process. The media should also contribute in the effort for effective medical waste management by informing the local society how important such management could be for the protection of public health and environment.

References

[1] Beriatos E. and Katsakiori Z. "The Greek institutional framework in the field of planning aiming at the protection of the environment" *in the proc. of the 6th International Conference on Protection and Restoration of the Environment*, eds A.G. Kungolos, A.B. Liakopoulos, G.P. Korfiatis, A.D. Koutsospyros, K.L. Katsifarakis and A.D. Demetracopoulos, Skiathos, Greece, Vol. III, pp. 1447-1455, 2002.

[2] World Health Organization - WHO *Safe management of wastes from health-care activities*, edited by A. Próss, E. Giroult and P. Rushbrook, Geneva, 1999.

[3] Basel Action Network - BAN "Eleven Recommendations for Improving Medical Waste Management", Burlington, Vermont, 1999.

[4] Henry J.G. and Heinke G.W. *Environmental Science and Engineering*, Second Edition, Prentice Hall International Editions, New Jersey, 1996.

[5] World Health Organization - WHO "Safe health-care waste management: Policy paper", Geneva, 2004.

[6] Xirogiannopoulou A. *Solid medical waste management*, Laboratory of Heat Transfer and Environmental Engineering, Department of Civil Engineering, Aristotle University of Thessaloniki, Thessaloniki, 2000 (in Greek).

[7] Gekas B., Frantzeskaki N., Katsibela E. *Hazardous waste management technologies*, Tziolas publications, Thessaloniki, 2002 (in Greek).

[8] Kathimerini Newspaper *Medical waste pollution dangers*, Publication of December 4th, Athens, 2003 (in Greek).

[9] National Statistic Office of Greece *Number of healthcare centers and beds in Greek regions, 1999/2000*.

Potential for construction waste minimisation through design

M. Osmani, A. D. F. Price & J. Glass
Department of Civil and Building Engineering,
Loughborough University, UK

Abstract

Recent figures published by the UK Government reveal that construction and demolition waste in the UK is around 90 million tonnes per annum, including an estimated 13 million tonnes of unused material. Furthermore, the introduction of new *legislation*, the emergence of new technologies and practices in both waste disposal and recovery, and the rising tide of public awareness are all conspiring to change the face of waste management. The opportunities and responsibilities to minimise construction waste rest with clients, contractors, suppliers and designers (architects/engineers). The aim of this paper is to investigate the feasibility of construction waste reduction through design. The paper evaluates current government policies and waste practices in the UK construction industry; and identifies problems for the implementation of effective waste minimisation during the architectural design stage of building projects. The objective of the paper is to develop a framework for a doctoral study entitled 'Construction Waste Minimisation by Design' which is investigating the role of architects in reducing construction waste. The paper covers: waste management and minimisation policies; strategies and industry practice construction for waste management and reduction; waste production; and current methods of monitoring; and designing out onsite wastage. The paper concludes that current waste-reduction processes mainly concentrate on the physical minimisation of construction waste and identification of site waste streams, i.e. the when onsite waste has already been produced. It recommends the adoption of a proactive approach to waste minimisation, as legislative and fiscal measures are likely to increase. The content should be of interest to building designers who have a decisive role in helping to reduce waste at all stages.
Keywords: UK, waste management, waste minimisation, legislation, design waste, building design.

WIT Transactions on Ecology and the Environment, Vol 84, © 2005 WIT Press
www.witpress.com, ISSN 1743-3541 (on-line)

1 Introduction

Emerging sustainable building practices offer an opportunity to create environmentally-sound and resource-efficient buildings by using an environmental approach to design. Achieving sustainable *building design* is closely linked to the way the construction industry deals with its waste. A study by the World Resource Institute of material flows in a number of industrialised countries, showed that a half to three quarters of the annual material consumed was returned to the environment as waste within one year (Hutter [1]). Minimisation of construction waste can occur at various levels along the supply chain, the opportunities and responsibilities to minimise construction waste lie with clients, designers, contractors and suppliers. Reducing physical waste could be achieved by redirecting the focus to the design stage of projects so that there will be no onsite waste to manage. The aim of the paper is to examine the potential for construction waste reduction through design. It reviews: *UK* Government waste policies and *legislation*; current terminology; classifications of types and origins of waste; and approaches to address waste reduction by design.

2 Definitions of construction waste

There is no generally accepted definition of construction waste. One common definition of construction waste, as issued by the European Council Directive 91/156/EEC , is "any substance or object which the holder discards or intends or is required to discard" (Directive 91/156/EEC [2], Article 1, Letter a). This definition applies to all waste irrespective of whether or not it is destined for disposal or recovery operations. However, Skoyles and Skoyles [3] defined *construction waste* as a material "which needed to be transported elsewhere from the construction site or used on the site itself other than the intended specific purpose of the project due to damage, excess or non-use or which cannot be used due to non-compliance with the specifications, or which is a by-product of the construction process". Similarly, the adopted definition of *construction waste minimisation* for this research is "the reduction of waste at source, by understanding and changing processes to reduce and prevent waste" (Environmental Agency [4]).

3 Waste management policies

In 1996, the *UK* Government produced a strategy 'Making Waste Work', having for objective the reduction of controlled waste going to landfill by 60 per cent (DETR [5]). Controlled waste is the most hazardous category of waste such as materials and components that exhibit toxicity. It includes waste arising from works of demolition, construction and preparatory work. In its consultation paper on 'Less Waste More Value', the Government considered how goals for *waste minimisation* might be set out and how these long-term ambitions might be translated into medium term targets (DETR [6]). This was followed by the

Government publication of a consultation paper, 'A Way with Waste', which proposed changing public and industrial attitudes to waste, and product design for re-use and re-cycling (including the requirement that manufacturers take back used goods) and better markets for recycled materials (DETR [7]). In response to the demands of the Landfill Directive [8], and other European directives on waste, the *UK* Government launched the Waste Strategy 2000 report (DETR [9]). The Strategy reflects the Government's belief that the amount of commercial and industrial waste sent to landfill sites can be cut by increasing landfill taxes and introducing new regulatory controls that challenge not only the way waste is disposed of but also its production. Waste Strategy 2000 sets out a target to reduce by 2005 the amount of industrial and commercial waste sent to landfill to 85 per cent of land filled in 1998 (DETR [9]). In examining performance against the waste targets set out in the Strategy, a report by the Environmental Audit Committee's highlighted the fact that "no target has been set for waste minimisation. The resources available…have been largely directed at recycling projects rather than waste minimisation efforts" (The Environmental Audit Committee [10], Paragraph 28).

As the Government is committed to *waste minimisation*, the construction industry should anticipate the impact of new and increasingly stringent regulations and by doing so it should adopt a proactive approach towards *waste minimisation*. In addition to environmental and financial benefits, the voluntary initiative should allow it to plan ahead and put in place a coherent and integrated waste reduction strategy.

4   Waste legislation

Most legal frameworks on *waste management* in the *UK* derive from European Union directives. Directive 75/442/EEC, also known as the Waste Framework Directive, provides the overall structure for an effective *waste management* regime within the EU. Over the past decade, the *UK* Government introduced new acts and policies to tighten the control on waste generation and disposal. The key acts that have brought about changes in the *UK* construction waste disposal practices during the last few years are summarised below.

- Waste Minimisation Act 1998 enabled local authorities to make arrangements to minimise the generation of waste in their area by working with local businesses, without placing any obligation on them to carry out such initiatives.
- The Climate Change Levy aim is to encourage the non-domestic sectors (i.e. industry, commerce and the public sector) to improve energy efficiency and reduce emissions of greenhouse gases.
- Aggregates Levy has been set at £1.60 per tonne of aggregates produced. This Levy should force the construction industry to look closely at its sources of raw materials and seriously consider reducing its consumption of virgin raw materials by using recycled materials and waste products.

- The Landfill Tax increased the standard rate of landfill tax from £14 to £15 per tonne. The standard rate of landfill tax will subsequently be increased by £3 per tonne per annum starting in 2005, up to a medium- to long-term rate of £35 per tonne.

The *waste management legislation*, particularly the Landfill Tax should act as disincentive to waste production. However, as yet this does not appear to have seriously reduced the amount of waste production, the Government is likely to introduce other fiscal measures and *legislation* in the future, which will push the construction industry towards a closed loop production system.

5 Types of construction waste

It is estimated that it is as much as 30 per cent of the total weight of building materials delivered to a building site (Fishbein [11]). The disposal of construction waste accounts for more than 50 per cent of overall landfill volumes in the *UK* (Ferguson et al. [12]). In terms of weight, brick masonry and concrete present by far the largest potential for recycling in the building sector (Emmanuel [13]). This has been supported by the findings of comprehensive research conducted across USA, *UK*, China, Brazil, Korea and Hong Kong, which compared the types and volumes of construction waste in these countries (Chen et al. [14]). The types and composition of onsite wastes are highly variable, depending on the construction techniques used. For example, "there will be very little waste concrete and timber forms for disposal if pre-cast concrete elements are adopted" (Poon et al. [15]). However, Guthrie and Mallett [16] split construction and demolition waste into three categories, materials which are: potentially valuable in construction and easily reused/recycled, including concrete, stone masonry, bricks, tiles/pipes, asphalt and soil; not capable of being directly recycled but may be recycled elsewhere, including timber, glass, paper, plastic, oils and metal; and not easily recycled or present particular disposal issues, including chemicals (i.e. paint, solvents), asbestos, plaster, water and aqueous solutions. Coventry et al. [17] went further by identifying seven different types of waste: bricks, blocks and mortar (33%); timber (27%); packaging (18%), dry lining (10%); metals (3%); special waste (1%); and other waste 10%. McGrath [18] used a case study approach to audit types of building materials wasted on three different types of construction projects: social housing; leisure development; and a restaurant. The results demonstrated that the most significant waste stream in all three case studies was inert material comprising soil removed during the construction and the clean up of the site. Packaging, that includes all plastic wrappings, plastic bubble wrap and cardboard, was another major contributor to waste generation.

6 Origins of construction waste

There are a variety of different approaches to the classifications of the main origins of construction waste. For example, Bossink and Brouwers [19] classified sources of construction waste according to the nature and technology of using materials into building products such as concrete, bricks and wood. Whereas Craven et al. [20] grouped construction waste sources into design; materials procurement; materials handling; operations; residual or leftover scraps. A similar approach was taken by Ekanayake and Ofori [21] who categorised construction waste according to design, operational, material handling and procurement sources. The authors revealed that a substantial amount of construction waste is closely related to design errors. They ranked design changes, while construction works are in progress and the lack of information on the drawings, as the most significant contributors to waste generation. They also identified other design related waste causes i.e., complexity of detailing, selection of low quality materials and lack of familiarity of alternative products. They ranked the highest 'operational' waste contributors as damages to subsequent works, errors by tradesmen and improper planning, while inappropriate storage facilities at site and loose forms of material supply to the site were the major waste generation actors due to 'material handling'. 'Procurement' wastage was mainly related to over-ordering of building materials. Waste can also occur during the design stage due to errors in contract clauses or incomplete contract documents (Craven et al. [20]; Bossink and Brouwers [19]). Furthermore, Nguyen et al. [22] classified the sources of construction waste into two phases: pre-construction and construction. During the pre-construction phase, waste occurs during: planning and designing (e.g. lack of coordination with standardisation of materials and extra materials ordering, estimating); and purchasing (e.g. over allowance and materials' variable dimensions; and finally manufacturers and suppliers (e.g. goods are damaged during delivery and loading). They cited a number of sources leading to generation of waste during the construction phase: operational waste due to the nature of the construction process (e.g. time pressure, poor craftsmanship, lack of supervision and poor work ethics); access to site for delivery vehicles, methods of loading and off-loading are all causes of waste related to transportation and delivery; and storage where waste is generated by poor site management failing to provide adequate protection for materials.

According to Baldwin et al. [23] waste is generated during the design process for a number of reasons: 'building complexity', through the emergence of a variety of design specialities and responsibilities within the same project leading to design changes; 'co-ordination' and 'communications' problems due to the multi-disciplinary nature of design projects where the information that passes to contractors is highly variable and open to misinterpretation contributing inevitably to waste generation. Therefore, there is a need to: understand the underlying causes of *design waste*; change processes and practices; and adopt a holistic approach to *building design*.

7   Designing out construction waste

Coventry and Guthrie [24] defined *design waste* as "the waste arising from construction sites both by acts and by omissions on the part of the designer, including opportunities to reduce waste lost by not using reclaimed materials".

Adopting an integrated design philosophy should reduce the amount of raw material used and therefore the amount of wasted resources discarded.

7.1 Addressing waste minimisation through design

The extant of literature reveals various approaches, guidelines and strategies to reduce design-generated waste. These broadly cover four major axes of the design process to include: contract language; design issues and construction techniques; building materials specification; and education.

7.1.1 Contract language
CRiBE [25] highlighted that contract and contractual agreement stages play important roles in reducing waste through incorporating *waste minimisation* activities by means of the use of specifically-oriented contract tender clauses. Dainty and Brooke [26] and GMV [27] suggested using contractual clauses to penalise poor waste performance. Greenwood [28] went further to call for a fully integrated *waste minimisation* system at the contractual stage that "should identify and communicate the responsibilities for *waste minimisation* between all project stakeholders".

7.1.2 Design issues and construction techniques
There is a general consensus in the literature that design variations and changes can lead to considerable amounts of design-generated waste. Coventry et al. [17] pointed out that variations frequently change the type or quantity of the building materials required. Dainty and Brooke [26] identified standardisation of design as a construction method to improve buildability and reduce the quantity of off-cuts. Gibb [29] argued that standardisation and prefabrication of both building layouts and components result in less waste. Design for deconstruction, is seen by several authors to be an efficient way to reduce waste (Greenwood [28]; and Skoyles and Skoyles [3]).

7.1.3 Building material specification
Waste can be reduced in a number of ways by specifying the use of efficient framing techniques, standard size supplies, prefabricated materials and the incorporation of green building materials into the design. Designs that require more material than necessary, through over-specification of the material quantities, facilitate generation of waste (Greenwood [28] and Nguyen et al. [22]). Coventry and Guthrie [24] recognised the role of design to reduce surplus excavation materials, which form one of the most important waste streams of a construction project.

7.1.4 Education
The *building design*er needs to have a voluntary approach towards *waste minimisation* promotion and education, in particular bringing the associated financial benefits to the attention of the client. The flow of information and dissemination of best practice to reduce *design waste* will require investment and publicity in technology and education to reshape societal attitudes to waste

disposal. This will involve partnerships between national government, local authorities, industry, the media and community organisations.

8   Discussion

Waste minimisation can be viewed as a threat requiring ever-increasing expenditure on end-of-pipe technologies to meet ever-increasing *legislation*, or as an opportunity to cut costs and improve performance. The choice should be obvious, but there is a need for a culture change. This requires re-engineering current practice to contribute to a cleaner environment through efficient and cost effective sustainable *waste minimisation* strategies. However, for *waste minimisation* to be effective and self-sustaining, it is important that all stakeholders along the construction supply chain adopt a more proactive approach in dealing with waste, i.e. designing out waste. In recognition of the responsibility of the architectural profession, through its leading role in project management and a key player in the construction industry, architects should move beyond the concept of 'Eco-efficiency' through bolt-on environmental strategies and strive to adopt 'Eco-effective' practices by implementing a holistic approach to design.

9   Conclusion

The current thinking of *waste minimisation* practices is heavily focussed on the physical minimisation of construction waste and identification of site waste streams. Tools, models and techniques have been developed to help handle and better manage onsite waste generation. While these tools facilitate auditing, assessment and benchmarking, a waste source evaluation approach does not offer long-term benefits, as it fails to address the causative issues of waste production.. The impact of *legislation*, particularly the 'Landfill Tax' and 'Aggregate Levy', and its effects on the behaviour and practices of the construction industry has resulted in a number of research studies. The last few years witnessed the publication of *waste minimisation* and recycling guides, which give broad guidance for *building design*ers to adopt sustainable *waste minimisation* approach in their projects. However, the recommendations in these guides do not realistically relate waste to all parameters of the designers' environment, including the complex design and construction process across the supply chain. In addition to this, they do not specifically identify waste-stream components in relation to their occurrence during the design stages. Consequently, the current research in the field addresses various issues related to waste when it has already been produced. The approach of this research is to assess *waste minimisation* potential through source reduction, via a focused effort to eliminate building material waste before it is generated. Therefore, this research, entitled, 'Construction Waste Minimisation by Design', endeavours to track site waste backwards and relate it to the associated design stage where it occurs.

Important questions arise from reviewing the literature: is waste inevitable, or can factors and processes responsible for its creation be changed or modified to

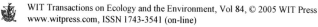

reduce its occurrence? is there a particular stage in the building process at which waste occurs or does it occur in all stages? which stages of the design life cycle lead to waste? how do we address *design waste*? and finally how can *building designer*s adopt *waste minimisation* as an integral part of the design process?

10 Methodology and way forward

The next stage of the research will be a focussed literature review on *design waste* by investigating and assessing existing frameworks and methodologies; best practice; and benchmarking. Building on the initial findings, and as a primary survey, two sets of questionnaires will be designed and administered to the two key players of the construction industry: one will be destined to architects, aiming to ascertain their views on *design waste* practices within their profession and the associated barriers; and the second will be sent to contactors to investigate their current responsibilities and methods of site *waste management* and auditing. This will be followed by field work on live sites to conduct interviews with contractors and site personnel to identify underlying causes of site waste and explore the relationship between waste generation and the design process. A framework will be developed, implemented and validated to map the creation of physical waste across the various design stages. The original contribution of the research will be through the development of a set of recommendations to assist building designers in integrating and sustaining *waste minimisation* strategies in their projects.

References

[1]   Hutter, C., *The Weight of Nations -Material Outflows from Industrial Economies*, World Resources Institute: Washington, 2000.
[2]   Directive   91/156/EEC,   http://europa.eu.int/smartapi/cgi /sga_doc?smartapi!celexplus!prod!DocNumber&lg=en&type_doc=Directi ve&an_doc=1991&nu_doc=156
[3]   Skoyles, E.R. & Skoyles, J.R., *Waste Prevention on Site*. Mitchell: London, 1987.
[4]   Environment Agency, *Waste Minimisation Good Practice Guide – Revised*, Lincoln, 2001.
[5]   DETR, *Making Waste Work: A Strategy for Waste Minimisation in England and Wales*, The Stationery Office: London, 1995.
[6]   DETR, *Less Waste More Value*, The Stationery Office: London, 1998.
[7]   DETR , *A Way with Waste*, The Stationery Office: London, 1999.
[8]   *The Landfill Directive* -99/31/EC, http://europa.eu.int/eurlex/pri/en/oj/dat /1999/l_182/l_18219990716en00010019.pdf
[9]   DETR , *Waste Strategy 2000*, The Stationery Office: London, 2000.
[10]   The Environmental Audit Committee's Fifth Report of Session 2002-03, Waste: An Audit, HC99, 2003.

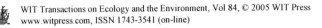

[11] Fishbein, B.K., *Building for the Future: Strategies to Reduce Construction and Demolition Waste in Municipal Projects*, INFORM: New York, 1998.

[12] Ferguson, J., Kermode, N., Nash, C.L., Sketch, W.A.J. & Huxford, R.P., *Managing and Minimizing Construction Waste*: a Practical Guide, Institution of Civil Engineers: London, 1995.

[13] Emmanuel, R., Estimating the environmental suitability of wall materials: preliminary results from Sri Lanka. *Building and Environment*, 39 (10), pp. 1253-1261, 2004.

[14] Chen, Z., Li, H. & Wong, C.T.C., An application of bar-code system for reducing construction wastes. *Automation in Construction*, 11(5), pp. 521-533, 2002.

[15] Poon, C.S., Yu, A.T.W. & Ng, L. H., On-site sorting of construction and demolition waste in Hong Kong. Resources, *Conservation and Recycling*, 32(2), pp. 157-172, 2001.

[16] Guthrie, P. and Mallett, H., *Waste Minimisation and Recycling in Construction*, CIRIA Special Publication 122., CIRIA: London, 1995.

[17] Coventry, S., Shorter, B., & Kingsley, M., *Demonstrating Waste Minimisation Benefits in Construction*, CIRIA C536, CIRIA: London, 2001.

[18] McGrath, C., Waste minimisation in practice. *Resource, Conservation and Recycling*, 32(3-4), pp. 227-238, 2001.

[19] Bossink, B.A.G. & Brouwers, H.J.H., Construction waste: quantification and source evaluation. *Journal of Construction Engineering and Management*, 122(1), pp. 55–60, 1996.

[20] Craven, D.J, Okraglik, H.M. & Eilenberg, I.M., Construction waste and a new design methodology. *Proc. of the First Conference of CIB TG 16 on Sustainable Construction*, ed. C.J. Kibert, Tampa: Florida, pp. 89–98, 1994.

[21] Ekanayake, L.L. & Ofori, G., Construction material waste source evaluation. *Proc. of the 2nd Southern African Conference on Sustainable Development in the Built Environment: Strategies for a Sustainable Built Environment*, Pretoria, 2000.

[22] Nguyen, B., Gupta, H. & Faniran, S., Waste Minimisation Strategies in the Construction Industry- A Geelong Case. *Proc. of Young Waste Professionals Conference*, NSW Waste Board: Sydney, 1999.

[23] Baldwin, A., Keys, A. & Austin, S., Designing to encourage waste minimisation in the construction ndustry, *Proc. of CIBSE National Conference*, Dublin , 2000.

[24] Coventry, S. and Guthrie, P., *Waste Minimisation and Recycling in Construction -Design Manual*, CIRIA SP134, CIRIA: London, 1998.

[25] CriBE, *Waste Minimisation Through Counselling Building Project Teams & Collecting of Building Project Teams and Collecting Waste Arising*. Welsh School of Architecture: Cardiff University, 1999.

[26] Dainty, A.R.J. & Brooke, R.J., Towards improved construction waste minimisation: improved supply chain integration. *Structural Survey*, 22(1), pp. 20-29 , 2004.

[27] GMV-*Greenwich Millennium Village, Reduction, Re-use and Recycling of Construction Waste*: A Project Management Guide. BRE: Watford, 2003.

[28] Greenwood, R., *Construction Waste Minimisation* –Good Practice Guide, CriBE: Cardiff, 2003.

[29] Gibb, A., *Standardisation and Customisation in Construction*: A review of Recent and Current Industry and Research Initiatives on Standardisation and Customisation in Construction. CRIPS: London, 2001.

Vinyl 2010: the European PVC industry's approach to sustainability

M. Griffiths
Vinyl 2010, Brussels, Belgium

Abstract

One of the most promising approaches to bridging corporate and government roles toward sustainability are Voluntary Agreements (VA) made by industry.

Vinyl 2010, involving the entire industry, from raw-material production to post-consumer waste, sets out commitments on production, additives and waste management and operates through projects covering technology, research, organisation and communication.

Vinyl 2010 has established a Monitoring Committee with representatives from the European Parliament, the European Commission and trade unions.

The Vinyl 2010 initiative takes on even further significance in the context of an enlarged EU with 25 or more member states. VAs are an efficient way of transferring best practice.
Keywords: PVC Industry, Voluntary Commitment, waste management, product stewardship, Monitoring Committee.

1 Introduction

Everyone's future depends on sustainable development and each of us has a role to play in making it a reality, personally as consumers and collectively as public authorities, governments and private sector companies.

The PVC industry has accepted this challenge. We have been working very hard for several years and now we have an innovative voluntary approach covering the whole industry chain.

PVC is one of the most widely used plastic materials in the world and plays a vital role in each of the three pillars of sustainable development.

Right from the start, PVC contributes to saving energy and resources, because its production makes optimal use of mineral oil and utilises common salt, a plentiful resource. PVC is durable, strong and lightweight and fulfils the demanding requirements of applications that underpin our modern lifestyle. It also lasts a long time with about 50% of all PVC applications having an in-service life of more than 35 years.

In Europe over 23,000 companies work with PVC, employing approximately 530,000 people and generating a turnover of more than €74 billion.

Sustainable development is not just about the economy. It is about quality of life. PVC enhances the way we live thanks, for example, to reliable and sterile medical and food packaging, sheathing against shocks for electrical cables, and by many hi-tech and leisure applications.

2   The role of a responsible industry

Private enterprise creates value for society. Sustainable development is about bringing value in the long term to everyone in terms of quality of life, social advancement and environmental protection. Government's role, including European Union institutions, is to shape and sustain a framework that will help and encourage society, and thus private enterprise, advance toward sustainability.

One of the most promising approaches to bridge corporate and government roles are Voluntary Agreements (VA) by industry. However, industry and government are bound by a common challenge: VAs must be credible and the implementation transparent. At the same time implementation controls must not hinder and disincentive the emergence of VAs.

2.1 Vinyl 2010: a concrete example of an integrated management system

Based on demanding managerial and scientific criteria, the Voluntary Commitment [1] of the European PVC industry is a 10-year plan with fixed targets and deadlines to improve production processes and products, invest in technology, minimise emissions and waste and boost collection and recycling.

Vinyl 2010 is the legal entity set up to provide the organisational and financial infrastructure to manage and monitor the actions undertaken as part of the Voluntary Commitment. It groups European vinyl resin manufacturers, plastic converters and producers of stabilisers and plasticisers. The four members are: the European Council of Vinyl Manufacturers (ECVM), the European Plastics Converters (EuPC), the European Council for Plasticisers and Intermediates (ECPI) and the European Stabilisers Producers Associations (ESPA).

2.2 Vinyl 2010 commitments and results

2.2.1 Manufacturing
- Cut raw material and energy consumption where economically and ecologically warranted.
- Review progress on an annual basis.

PVC Resin Producers:
- Minimise environmental impact through compliance with the ECVM Industry Charters [2, 3].

Plasticiser Producers:
- Conduct research to help policy-makers make informed decisions;
- Add to the already comprehensive available scientific data about plasticisers;
- Ensure that plasticisers are used safely, in line with the final conclusions of the EU risk assessments;
- Conduct material lifecycle analysis to identify additional possible improvements to the product and its use; compile a database on various PVC plasticisers.

Stabiliser Producers:
- Phase out cadmium stabilisers in the European Union by 2001 (done). Continue to work with the European Commission on targeted risk assessments.
- Work together with the rest of the lead industry and the independent consultants appointed with the approval of the Dutch authorities to compile the necessary data for a full EU risk assessment on lead.
- Continue to research and develop alternative stabilisers to the widely used and highly effective lead-based systems as part of a commitment to replace lead stabilisers by 2015;
- Produce yearly statistics on stabiliser consumption by converters.

2.2.2 Waste management
- Actively support an integrated waste management approach. Use raw materials as efficiently as possible and utilise the most sustainable end-of-life options.
- Work with stakeholders to research, develop and implement the necessary recycling technologies to achieve targets. Total PVC post-consumer waste recycling is expected to reach 200,000 tonnes per year in Europe in 2010.
- Commitments on waste management (recycling to ultimate disposal) operating today through more than 20 projects covering technology, research, organisation (recycling schemes) and communication (best practice).
- Target of 25% recycling of collectable, available PVC post-consumer waste from pipes, windows profiles and roofing membranes reached in 2003, the target of 50% is expected in 2005.
- Projects funding of €4.2 million in 2004 and considerably greater allocation of resources in terms of time and effort; total expenditure of about €16 million over the last 4 years.

2.3 Research innovation and best practice for an integrated approach to waste management

The European PVC industry is working to develop an integrated waste management approach and environmentally responsible solutions for managing its products at the end of their useful life. It aims to maximise the efficient use of raw materials and to develop the best end-of-life treatment option per waste stream:

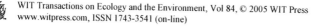

- Window profiles, pipes and fittings and roofing membranes: commitment to recycle at least 25% by 2003 and 50% by 2005 of the collectable, available PVC waste.
- Flooring: commitment to recycle at least 25% by 2006 and 50% by 2008 of the collectable, available PVC waste.
- Coated Fabrics: project started in 2002 with a study to look into contributing to the recycling targets of Vinyl 2010 with the collection of data and planned test projects in Germany and France.

Several approaches are followed to reach these targets: mechanical recycling, feedstock recycling, energy recovery and disposal. The PVC industry is currently working to establish effective integrated waste management solutions for both short and long life PVC products.

2.3.1 Mechanical recycling

At the end of their life, PVC products can be recycled and reused for production of the same or similar applications. However, mechanical recycling makes ecological and economic sense only where sufficient quantities of homogeneous, separated and sorted waste are available. Products such as pipes, roof coverings and window profiles are currently being recycled in this way. Mechanical recycling of mixed plastic waste is also possible to a limited extent. Main project supported by Vinyl 2010 are:

- *Vinyloop*: the Vinyloop® process is a mechanical recycling process in which a selective solvent dissolves the PVC resin matrix, releasing the additives and the secondary materials, resulting in a regenerated PVC compound.
- *Light Concrete*: the purpose of this feasibility study is to evaluate whether PVC waste from building demolition can be recycled as an aggregate for making light concrete – and thus re-used in buildings.

2.3.2 Feedstock recycling

Feedstock recycling is particularly well suited to mixed plastics waste. A number of feedstock recycling technologies are currently under development. All are based on the principle of breaking down PVC into its chemical components, which can then be recovered for re-use within a range of industrial processes to manufacture new products. In the case of a PVC rich feedstock, hydrochloric acid is one of the main components recovered via this method. This can be re-used as a raw material in the PVC production process. Main project:

- *DOW/BSL Project*: feedstock recycling plant capable of treating high chlorine-containing waste. Initial trials demonstrated that the technology is robust and suitable to treat large quantities of most kinds of PVC waste.
- *Stigsnaes RGS-90 Project*: hydrolysis plant, for conversion into a two-step process for the recycling of PVC waste products.
- *Redop Process*: the Redop – derived from 'Reduction of iron ore in blast furnace plants by plastics from waste' – process targets the mixed-plastics segment of municipal solid waste.

2.3.3 EuPR recycling study and Recovinyl initiative

In 2002, EuPR conducted a study on PVC mechanical recyclers in the EU. The aim of this study was to better understand who these independent third party recyclers are, what their business is, how they recycle post-consumer PVC waste and whether they are ready to invest in additional capacities.

The main problem with post-consumer waste is to ensure a steady supply of secondary raw material to these recyclers in order to justify their investments.

In an effort to help ensure steady supply, recyclers and other interested parties have agreed to set up a consortium called Recovinyl SA to facilitate the collection, dispatching and recycling of post-consumer PVC waste across Europe. It involves all stakeholders from consumers, Industries and municipalities to waste management companies and recyclers. Its aim is to ensure a steady supply of PVC waste for recycling and consequently support the Vinyl 2010 sectoral targets.

Recovinyl is designing, testing and implementing a collection system offering financial incentives to collectors that sort and bring PVC waste to accredited recyclers. This system should ensure the collection of 40,000 tonnes of PVC post-consumer waste by 2010. Recovinyl is working in synergy with the sectoral associations of Vinyl 2010 to expand the collection schemes and make them self-supporting.

In 2005, Recovinyl plans to concentrate its activities in the Benelux, France, the UK and Germany with the setting-up of a network of collection points composed of affiliated collectors and accredited recyclers. The activity will mainly consist of negotiating with local governments, developing contacts, identifying recipients for collection, setting a database, developing guidelines and organising trainings for collection centres.

2.3.4 Energy recovery

Incineration with energy recovery ensures that the calorific value of oil used in PVC production is recovered, potentially after many years of efficient service. Incorporating PVC waste in controlled municipal incinerators reduces the need for additional fuel. A number of independent studies have demonstrated that adding PVC to an incinerator waste stream in which chlorine is naturally present does not increase the generation of potentially harmful emissions. The PVC industry is currently involved in the development of appropriate techniques for handling solid waste residues arising from the pollution control processes employed when incinerating municipal waste containing PVC.

2.3.5 Life cycle analysis review of PVC

The LCA-methodology allows applying sound bookkeeping methods to establish a balance of pros and cons, including aspects of materials consumption, environmental aspects and end-of-life considerations.

The life cycle analysis (LCA) review does not form part of the industry's Voluntary Commitment but was mentioned in the European Parliament resolution on the Commission's "Green Paper on environmental issues of PVC" (2001) as regrettably missing.

The European Commission in 2002 therefore commissioned a consortium led by PE Europe (Stuttgart), an independent consultant, to conduct a review of existing LCA studies on PVC for many applications including flooring, toys, window profiles, coatings and medical devices. ECVM, ESPA and ECPI collaborated actively to the LCA review by providing existing LCA studies and comments. The last version of the report was signed off in 2004.

The review investigated more than 100 life cycle documents and reviewed in depth 30 LCA studies. The conclusions of the review are well balanced. It confirms that PVC is a material like any other, depending on the application and on its use, and that there is no reason to treat PVC differently from any other material.

These results also appear to be consistent with the findings of a draft report issued in December 2004 by the US Green Building Council's PVC Task Group. This two-year study concludes that the environmental and health impacts of PVC used in building applications are comparable to those of competing materials.

3   Conclusions

The Voluntary Commitment of the PVC industry is an effective approach towards sustainability, emphasising:

- *Cradle to grave approach* - It is (to our knowledge) the only Voluntary Commitment involving the entire upstream and downstream chain – from raw-material production to post-consumer waste in a single industry.
- *SME's contribution* - With its 23,000 companies, Vinyl 2010 is a model for Corporate Governance aimed at Sustainable Development and Durable Consumption because it looks at the entire life cycle of a product and because it actively includes the Small and Medium Sized Enterprises.
- *Transparency* - It actively involves stakeholders and policy makers, with an independent Monitoring Committee to follow the implementation of the Voluntary Commitment that currently includes representatives from the European Parliament, the European Commission and trade unions. Vinyl 2010 hopes to enlarge representation and welcomes participation by environmental and consumer NGOs. Furthermore Vinyl 2010 publishes a yearly Progress Report [4] verified by DNV Consulting and audited by KPMG for the financial figures and the tonnages of product recycled.
- *EU enlargement* - The Vinyl 2010 initiative takes on even further significance in the context of an enlarged EU. Rigid regulatory approaches are unlikely to be effective, as they will not answer market diversities, local financial constraints or the consumer's behaviour. VCs, by contrast, are an efficient way of transferring best practice to the East bypassing complex legislative process.
- *Social Responsibility* - The issue of Corporate Social Responsibility is becoming more and more relevant in contemporary society. We believe Voluntary Commitments from industry are part of the need for Corporate Social Responsibility to make effective progress on sustainable development.

References

[1]   Vinyl 2010, The Voluntary Commitment of the PVC Industry, 2001, www.vinyl2010.org.

[2]   ECVM, Industry Charter for the Production of VCM and SPVC, 1995, www.ecvm.org.
[3]   ECVM, Industry Charter for the Production of EPVC, 1999, www.ecvm.org.
[4]   Vinyl 2010, Progress Report 2005, www.vinyl2010.org.

Wood production utilizing raw sewage in Ojinaga, Chihuahua, México

M. Tena Vega[1], J. Mexal[2], G. Barragan[1], H. O. Rubio[1]
& M. Sosa C.[3]
[1]Campo Experimental La Campana-Madera del Instituto Nacional de Investigaciones Forestales Agricolas y Pecuarias, Mexico
[2]New Mexico State University, Las Cruces NM, U.S.A.
[3]Facultad de Zootecnia de la Universidad Autonoma de Chihuahua

Abstract

The objective was to evaluate a commercial forest plantation using raw sewage in Ojinaga, México. A total of seven materials were used: three genetic lines of *Eucalyptus camaldulensis*, three of *Populus deltoides* and one of *Robina pseudoacacia*. Each genetic line was considered as a treatment and six repetitions were used. Forty nine plants were established in each treatment and the evaluation was performed on the 25 most centrally located plants. A total area of 1.5 ha was used for the experiment. Completely randomized designs were used. Plant height, diameter and plant survival were determined 33 months after planting. The genus *Eucalyptus* presented the best performance reaching a plant height of 7.78 m, a diameter of 7.8 cm and a 96.2% survival. *Populus* showed a plant height of 6.24 m, a diameter of 5.4 cm; but poor survival with 55.1%. Although *Robinia* genus had a good plant survival (86.9%) it was the worst in plant height (5.04 m) and diameter (3.5 m). Wood production from irrigation with raw sewage may be a feasible alternative to using water and fertilizer in the state of Chihuahua.
Keywords: forest, plantation, raw sewage, Eucalyptus, Populus, Robina.

1 Introduction

The forestry sector in México is going through a severe crisis. On one side, the demand of goods and services of forest resources has increased in a constant way; on the other side, the offer has diminished in a great proportion. The main factor that has patronized the increase in the demand is the demographic growth; wish has been of more than 3% yearly, with a population of more than a 100 million people. On the contrary, the offer has diminished drastically, due to the large deforested areas and the presence of plagues and diseases on forested areas. Other of the factors is the lower capacity of response of the forest to unpredicted phenomena like drought that has specially affected northern México, where the States of Durango and Chihuahua, provide a considerable offer of forest derived products. This contrasts between offer and demand, have conduced to a well marked deficit in the supplying of raw material for the forest industry, especially of cellulose and paper. For this reason, it is observed the necessity of promoting projects that let reduce the distance between the offer and demand.

The forest commercial plantations have acquired importance due to the growing demand of cellulose material in the world [1]; which covers approximately 0.6% of the world commercial forested surface. These plantations participate with near 30% of the total production of wood for industrial purposes, 70% of which are consumed by the cellulose and paper industry. It is estimated that the world industry consumes 500 million cubic meters of wood annually. The 20% (100 million cubic meters) of this volume are obtained of fast growing plantations [2].

México counts with 56.8 million hectares of wooded surface of forests and jungles. In the 70's, 8 million cubic meters were extracted annually. In the last years the observed trend is a decrease in the production, so much that in 1995 the national production was of 6,302,417 cubic meters and for October of 1996, they were only 5,368,421 cubic meters extracted [3]. Even with the descent of production of wood in the country forests, the social pressure is bigger over it with the increase of demand of products derived from forest vegetation [4].

An alternative that has been implemented with success in other countries of the world, is establishing commercial plantations. These plantations grow wood products in an intensive way, beside the employment and an economic spill between other advantages [5]. A problem with this type of production, due to the behavior of the specie for arid and semiarid zones of México is the scarce water, for what it is required the use of water that is not used for other goods and services. In this study sewage water was used, which in the moment of establishing the project were not used. The objective of this study was to asses under irrigation conditions, the adaptation of fast growing species of the genus *Populus*, *Eucalyptus* and *Robinia*. It is expected that the results here presented be useful as a base line for establishing commercial plantations in the nearby areas of Ojinaga, Chihuahua and other similar regions of the Country. Other aspect is the contribution to eliminate the water and soil pollution and improve the environmental conditions.

2 Materials and methods

The plantation was established on the Rio Bravo riverside, 3 kilometers east from Ojinaga City in Chihuahua, in a private land named "La Juliana", which latitude and longitude are 29° 34' North and 104° 24' West. The altitude is 841 meters over sea level. According to the climate classification of C.W. Thornwaite, the region's climate is (Ebro) very dry, temperate with deficient rain in all the year seasons and extreme, with an average precipitation of 288 mm, and a mean annual temperature of 21.5 °C and extreme temperatures of from - 12°C to 48°C. Most of the year, winds come from Northeast (NE), with an average speed of 29.6 km/h. The probability of occurrence of hail for the region is very small, since in the last 10 years of observation, there was a maximum of two times per year, which can occur in the months of April, May and June [6].

The soil conditions in the experimental plots are very variable. It can be observed from heavy clay soils to sandy soils with gravel [7]. It was used a total of seven materials; from which, three were *Eucalyptus camaldulensis* lines, three of *Populus deltoids* and one of *Robinia pseudoacacia*. Each material was considered as a treatment, and there were used six repetitions. This gave a total of 42 experimental units with 49 plants for each treatment, assessing the 25 central plants.

For effects of this work and for making the analysis of the response variables (survival, height and diameter) the information was analyzed under a completely random design with seven treatments and six repetitions. The treatments were distributed in the field under a completely random design. To test the difference between means, it was made an analysis of variance (ANOVA) for each one of the variables, using a significance level of 0.01 and when the null hypothesis was rejected it was used the Tukey test for the mean comparison [8, 9].

The response variables evaluated after 33 months of establishment were; Height, diameter and survival. The height was measured with a suunto clinometer, from the base in the soil until the tip of the tree. The diameter was measured at 1.3 meters using a diameter tape. The survival variable was evaluated considering two possible results, "living plant" or "dead plant". In some cases no plant was found, so it was considered dead. The species used in the treatments were: 1) *Eucalyptus* camaldulensis 4019; 2) Eucalyptus camaldulensis 4016; 3) Eucalyptus *camaldulensis* SC5; 4) *Populus deltoides* 197; 5) *Populus deltoides* 029; 6) *Populus deltoides* 367 and 7*) Robinia pseudoacacia*.

The cultural labors previous to the establishment of the study were the soil plough and furrow for establishing the plantation, same that were made with an equipped agricultural tractor. There were formed the experimental plots of 0.02 hectares each, planting 49 trees (7 x 7), using a useful area of 25 central plants (5 x 5) with a spacing of 2 x 2 meters between furrows and plants, which gives a density of plantation of 2,500 plants per hectare. The total area of the experiment was 1.5 hectares. The plantation was made on the days 17, 18 and 19 of April 1997. Previously there were marked the definitive sites for each species, and the treatments plants were placed according to the experiment design. The plantation was made under the system of common stump, with a 15 centimeters diameter by 20 centimeters deep, making this with manual shovels. The plant was collocated into the stump, previously tearing the bag, covering it and having especial care to compact the soil to eliminate the air. After this process the establishing irrigation was made.

3   Results and discussion

In table 1, it can be observed that at 33 months of establishment of the plantation, the genus *Eucalyptus* was the one that presented the best development in height (7.78 meters) as in diameter (7.8), as well as in survival with a 96.2%; in second place, in growth it was for the genus *Populus* that presented a height of 6.24 meters and a diameter of 5.4 centimeters. On the other side *Populus* had the less survival rates with barely 55.1%, surpassed by the genus *Robinia* that obtained a survival rate of 86.9%, but had the lower height development (5.94 meters) and in diameter. (3.5 centimeters).

There were found highly significant differences in the plants height, were the treatment 6 outstands with a mean of 8.95 meters. The Table 1 shows the results of the test of means comparison. These results are similar to those reported by Hassey et al., [10] whom established essays of species and clones of fast growth to obtain fire wood in Yuba Country Foot – Hills in California, U.S.A. The objective was to know the behavior of the species in a six year study were *Eucalyptus camaldulensis* obtained a height of 9.72 meters.

Table 1:   Means comparison of eight in three species of trees.

TREATMENT	MEANS*
6. Populus deltoides 367	8.95 a
1. Eucalyptus camaldulensis 4019	9.39 ab
2. Eucalyptus camaldulensis 4016	8.05 ab
3. Eucalyptus camaldulensis SC5	6.89 abc
5. Populus deltoides 029	6.33 bc
7. Robinia pseudoacacia	5.03 cd
4. Populus deltoides 197	3.43 d

*Means with the same letter are equal statistically.

The result of the ANOVA for the diameter variable, indicates that existed a highly significant difference between the treatments, were the treatment 1 outstands (*Eucalyptus* 4019), with an average diameter of 8.48 cm followed by treatment 4 (*Populus* 367) with 7.91 cm. These results are superior to the ones found in the species and clones essays established by Hasey et al., (1988) were *Eucalyptus camaldulensis* obtained a diameter of 8.8 cm at 43 months of establishment. The lowest values were presented in the treatments 4 (*Populus* 197) and 7 (*Robinia pseudoacacia*) with average diameters of 3.15 cm and 3.50 cm, respectively. After, it was conducted a means comparison to this variable according to the Tukey procedure, to know the existent degree of difference between the treatments, indicating that treatment 1 and 6 (Table 2), are the ones that show the highest values and similar between them. The treatments 2 and 3 behaved similarly between them, followed by treatments 5, 7 and 4 were the last two show the lowest behavior and analog between them.

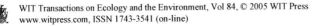

Table 2:   Means comparison of diameter in different species.

TREATMENT	MEANS*
1. Eucalyptus camaldulensis 4019	8.48 a
6. Populus deltoides 367	7.91 a
2. Eucalyptus camaldulensis 4016	7.58 ab
3. Eucalyptus camaldulensis SC5	7.51 ab
5. Populus deltoides 029	5.26 bc
7. Robinia pseudoacacia	3.50 c
4. Populus deltoides 197	3.15 c

*Means with the same letter are equal.

With respect to survival variable, the ANOVA detected a highly significant difference between the treatments, were the treatments 3 (*Eucalyptus camaldulensis* SC5), 2 (*Eucalyptus camaldulensis* 4016) and 1 (*Eucalyptus camaldulensis* 4019) outstand, with an excellent survival rate of 99, 96 and 93% each, followed by the treatments 7 (*Robinia pseudoacacia*) and 6 (*Populus deltoides* 367), were the first with an 86% and the second with 85%, show a very good survival rates at 33 months of its establishment. The treatment 5 with a 67% (*Populus deltoides* 029) and the 4 with 17% (*Populus deltoides* 197) are the lowest values, been able to consider the first as acceptable, and the second as a treatment of very low survival. The existing difference between treatments, according to Tukey, indicates that in treatments 3, 2 and 1, there was not any difference between them, followed by treatments 7, and 6 that are similar between them; treatments 5 and 4 behaved completely different from the others.

Table 3:   Mean comparison of survival of different species.

TREATMENT	MEANS*
3. Eucalyptus camaldulensis SC5	99.3 a
2. Eucalyptus camaldulensis 4016	96.0 a
1. Eucalyptus camaldulensis 4019	93.0 a
7. Robinia pseudoacacia	86.6 ab
6. Populus deltoides 367	85.3 ab
5. Populus deltoides 029	62.6 b
4. Populus deltoides 197	17.3 c

*Means with the same letter are equal.

The survival shown by *Eucalyptus camaldulensis* at 33 months of establishment, has a similar trend to that reported by [11] in an essay with several eucalyptus species with the objective of observing their behavior and after that take them to an intensive management for paper pulp production in Napa Country California, U.S.A. were *Eucalyptus camaldulensis* obtained a survival rate of 88% at 75 months of establishment.

It is important to make clear that in this work the treatments were analyzed under a completely random design as mentioned before, observing that treatment 4, in its repetitions 2 and 3, obtained a 0% survival rate, for what the statistic program analyzed it with values of zero, showing this treatment low values in the height and diameter variables. In a practical point of view and considering the mean of all the living trees of the *Populus deltoides* specie, it shows higher mean values for this variables (5.15 for height and 4.7 centimeters for diameter), going over *Robinia pseudoacacia*. This is mentioned looking for the reader to take care about this case according to its point of view about the results of this work.

4   Conclusions

According to the results obtained at 33 months of establishing the plantation it can be concluded that:

1. The essayed species adapted favorably to the agro climatic of the region.
2. The tested species are considered good candidates as fiber producers using sewage water for irrigation.
3. The genus *Populus* and *Eucalyptus*, in general, showed an excellent development, allowing one to expect a harvest 6 or 7 years after establishment.
4. It is required to test faster growing species, especially *Robinia*, because this is the one that shows a lower development than *Populus* and *Eucalyptus.*
5. There is a chance of establishing 200 hectares of plantations with sewage water irrigation.

References

[1]   Martínez, B.A. 1996. El cultivo de las plantaciones forestales comerciales. Memoria de la Primera Reunión Científica Forestal. México, D.F.
[2]   Sosa, C.V. 1995. Política Nacional de Fomento a las Plantaciones Forestales Industriales, Simposio sobre Reforestación Comercial. Pub. Esp. No. 65. INIFAP, México, D.F. 11-69.
[3]   SEMARNAP, 1997. Reunión e Informe de avance del Programa Estatal de Reforestación en el estado de Chihuahua (Inédito). Subsecretaria del Medio Ambiente, Recursos Naturales y de Pesca. Delegación Estatal Chihuahua.
[4]   Alarcón, B.M., Iglesias, G.L., and Armendáriz, O.R. 1996. La producción planta de pino en vivero, bajo diversos tratamientos, para reforestaciones comerciales. Memoria del Simposio sobre Reforestación Comercial. Pub. Esp. No. 65. P. 65.
[5]   Eguiluz, P.T., Saldívar, C.D., and Torres, P.J. 1992. Estudio Técnico financiero para el establecimiento de plantaciones forestales comerciales bajo riego en el Valle de Mexicali. Genética forestal, Chapingo México.
[6]   Tarango, S., Berzoza, M., and Nuñez, S.R. 1986. Diagnóstico para el plan de Investigación en el Campo Experimental de Ojinaga, Chihuahua.
[7]   Núñez, S.R. 1998. Informe Anual de Investigación. INIFAP-CEDEL. Chihuahua, México.

[8]   Rubio, H.O. and Jiménez, J. 1996. Procedimientos estadísticos para la comparación de medias en la experimentación científica. Folleto Técnico Marzo-29 p.

[9]   Rubio, H.O. 2003. Estadística Experimental. Práctica, Útil y Sencilla. Chihuahua, México.

[10]   Hasey, K.J., Standford, B.R., Connor, J.M., and Sachs, M. R. 1998. Low elevation foothill fuelwood plantation. California Agriculture, Vol. 42, No. 6. University of California; 21-22.

[11]   Donaldson, R.D., Lebranc, W., and Standford, B.R., 1988. Seven year performance of Eucalyptus species in Napa Country, California. California Agriculture, Vol. 42 No. 7. University of California; 19-20.

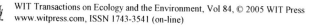

Alleviation of environmental health impacts through an ecosystem approach – a case study on solid waste management in Dhaka City

I. M. Faisal[1] & S. Parveen[2]
[1]SouthAsia Enterprise Development Facility, Bangladesh
[2]State University of Bangladesh, Bangladesh

Abstract

This study examines environmental health and safety problems associated with urban solid waste management and provides a set of interventions options using the ecosystem approach. In particular, it investigates the health problems faced by child waste-pickers of Dhaka City, who collect recyclable and reusable items from garbage bins and landfill sites. The study tracks down these problems with the help of an impact-pathway based analysis. It then develops a set of intervention options through extensive multi-stakeholder consultations and interviews. The recommendations formed thereby have been presented in an impact-intervention matrix. The intervention matrix addresses each part of the impact-pathway from source to health impacts, and explores a range of policy tools to devise 'integrative' and 'sustainable' interventions. Based on urgency, ease of implementation and resource requirements, the paper also indicates tentative time-frames these interventions.
Keywords: solid waste, health impact, intervention matrix, ecosystem approach.

1 Introduction

Dhaka City, the capital of Bangladesh with a population of about 10 million, is growing at a rate of 3.72% per year. Nearly 70% of this population lives in the jurisdiction of the Dhaka City Corporation (DCC) that covers an area of 360 sq. km. On average, 4,000-4,500 tons of solid waste is generated everyday in the City, with a per capita contribution of about 0.5 kg per day (Islam [1]).

The waste stream fraction of Dhaka city is 46.8% domestic, 21.8% street sweeping, 19.2% commercial, 12.9% industrial and 0.5% clinical (MMI [2]).

Analysis of physical composition of mixed waste shows that the primary component is food waste (70.12%), and about 80% of the municipal solid waste is of organic origin and biodegradable. Of the remaining 20%, about 10% is paper, plastic, rubber and leather; the remaining part is contributed by metals, glass, ceramic, cloth and so on.

The DCC collects and disposes approximately 50% of the solid waste, most of which is taken to Matuail – a 70-acre 'open dump' being used as the primary landfill site for Dhaka since 1994. Around 16% of the solid waste is recycled, mostly by the informal sector (households, hawkers, waste pickers) and a significant 50% is discarded into streets, drains, ditches, canals and open spaces (ADB [3]; DCC [4]). The cycle of generation, disposal and recycling of solid waste in Dhaka City is shown in fig. 1.

At present, there is no separate collection or disposal system in Dhaka for clinical waste. Everyday, an estimated 200 tons of clinical waste and another 5000 tons of industrial waste are generated within the city, all of which are disposed in the same garbage bins used for household waste and eventually disposed in the landfill sites. As a result, the residents of Dhaka are being exposed to the additional health risks from contaminated, toxic, or hazardous clinical and industrial wastes on daily basis.

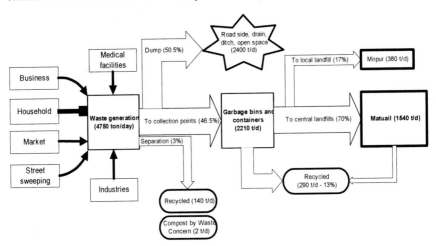

Figure 1:   Waste generation, disposal and recycling in Dhaka (adopted from Memon [5]).

Such inadequate and unsafe solid waste management practices have immediate and inescapable consequences: filthy streets littered with garbage, scavengers scouring garbage bins, and human waste pickers handling waste without any precaution. In addition, indiscriminate solid waste dumping clogs up drains and fills up water bodies leading to drainage congestion and water logging. Mosquitoes breed in these stagnant waters, and spread deadly diseases such as malaria and dengue. Thus, the absence of a comprehensive solid waste management system poses major environmental health risks to the residents of major urban centres in Bangladesh.

In this backdrop, this paper presents an in-depth assessment of the environmental health risks faced by the child waste-pickers of Dhaka based on a comparative epidemiological study. It then presents a set of intervention options identified through extensive consultative sessions and summarized in the form of an impact-intervention matrix.

2 Methodology

The study is primarily based on information collected through field survey, interview of key informants, and multi-stakeholder roundtable sessions. The health impacts have been assessed through a comparative epidemiological study, where two groups, each comprised of 75 children, were randomly selected, interviewed and given medical examination. The exposed group (waste pickers) worked at the central landfill at Matuail; the control group (non-waste pickers) came from a different neighbourhood with similar socio-economic background. The type and extent of health and safety concerns faced by the child waste-pickers have been identified and estimated using point and prevalence rates. The extent of additional health risk faced by the waste-pickers vis-à-vis the control group has been examined by employing descriptive statistics and   multiple regression technique to statistically capture the influence of risk and confounding factors.

Options to alleviate the health impacts have been explored as per the 'ecosystem approach.' First, the impacts have been linked to the corresponding stressors and sources, and the results have been summarized in an 'impact-pathway' table. Possible intervention options to minimize these impacts have been identified through in-depth analysis of system components and extensive stakeholder interview and consultation. Two seminar-cum-roundtable sessions were arranged to explore both 'hard' (material flow and technology) and 'soft' (social, economic, legal, institutional) options. Summary of these sessions have been presented in the 'Impact-Intervention Matrix' that reflects the collective assessment and recommendations of over 100 representatives from all stakeholder groups.

3 Environmental health impacts

The present mode of solid waste management by the DCC poses a number of environmental health risks. First, the city does not have separate waste disposal systems for clinical and industrial wastes. Everyday, some 500 hospitals, clinics and pathological laboratories generate 200 tons of waste, about 15% to 20% of which are extremely hazardous that include infectious waste, pathological waste, sharps, and a small amount of pharmaceutical and chemical wastes (Rahman et al. [6]). Moreover, several thousand industries located within the city (including the 'hot-spots' at Hazaribagh and Tejgaon) generate hazardous solid wastes that contain corrosives, toxic chemicals and heavy metals. Both clinical and industrial wastes are dumped in municipal landfill sites or in open fields and ditches exposing the city residents to unknown health hazards.

Second, about half of the solid waste generated in the city – some 2,250 tons a day- is not collected at all, which may include some medical and industrial wastes. Often, wastes are not collected on time and seen rolling on the streets attracting scavengers and unwanted biota.

Third, the most serious health risks are faced by the human scavengers: around 6000 to 8000 of them work in the streets and at landfill sites as waste pickers. A preliminary survey indicates that nearly 50% of them are children under the age of 15, and about half of them are girls. Due to their marginal and impoverished social status, these child-workers are compelled to work in the most unhygienic conditions without having access to most basic amenities such as drinking water and sanitation at workplace.

The cumulative health impacts of all these threats on the city population are unknown – no study has so far been conducted to scientifically link these risks with health impacts. However, a number of recent studies have examined the occupation health hazards faced by the waste pickers of Dhaka, who worked in the streets or at the Matuail landfill site [7, 8, 9]. Shamsad [8], and Parveen and Faisal [9] have identified stressors and sources corresponding to the health and safety impacts (table 1). The waste pickers face a whole range of health risks: from minor on-site problems such as insect bite to major health concerns such as bronchitis, hepatitis, and physical injury.

It was found that in most cases, no medication is used or doctor consulted. The waste pickers resort to over-the-counter medicine or take a day-off only if the ailments become grave and debilitating.

Table 1:   Impact path-way of common health problems.

Health problem	Stressor	Source
Allergy, skin disease	All types of waste	All waste sources
Headache, dizziness, nausea	Pungent smell	Exposed organic waste
Cuts and bruises, tetanus, gangrene, physical injury	Sharp / pointed objects, heavy machineries	Hospitals and health centres, households, landfill machineries
Asthma, bronchitis, eye irritation / infection	Dust, fume, smoke	Burning of plastic, tire, incineration, wind
Pain, inflammation, infection	Insect bites	Bare foot/hand
Worms, diarrhoea, dysentery, cholera	Drinking water, dirty hand or utensils	Lack of sanitation; poor personal hygiene
Malaria, dengue, meningitis	Mosquito bite	Pool of stagnant water, garbage pile, landfill
TB, bronchitis, hepatitis, AIDS etc.	Contaminates / clinical waste	Hospitals and health centres
Sore, infection, metabolic disorders, cancer	Acid, alkali, toxic chemicals, radioactive materials	Industrial or clinical waste

Parveen and Faisal [9] have further extended these findings by conducting a comparative epidemiological study of the health impacts using 'exposed' and 'control' groups. By comparing point and period prevalence rates of different health problems faced by these groups, they show that the child waste-pickers of Dhaka suffer significantly more compared to the 'non-waste picking' control group (fig. 2). It is evident from fig. 2 that at the time of the survey, child waste-pickers suffered from 30% more skin problems, 40% more eye, respiratory and general health problems, 47% more aches and pains, and 20% more gastro-intestinal ailments. The difference is even greater if period prevalence rates for skin and eye related problems are compared. The most significant difference is noted for fever – 62% more waste pickers suffered from some kind of fever during a six-month period prior to this survey compared to the control group.

By employing the multiple regression technique, Parveen and Faisal [9] also show that there are statistically significant association between the point and period morbidity indices (cumulative frequency of all health problems as reported by the respondents) and the risk factor – waste picking. This confirms the generally held view that a significant part of the health problems affecting the waste pickers are due to their hazardous occupation, and the rest of the impacts are outcomes of other socio-economic and environmental factors.

Table 2 shows the statistical associations between the point morbidity index and the confounding and risk factors: age, gender, monthly family expenditure, family size, and group of the respondent. The regression coefficients and t-statistics support a number of important conclusions: (i) the exposed group is much more vulnerable to health problems than the control group; (ii) younger children tend to suffer more from health problems compared to older ones; (iii) girls suffer from more health problems compared to boys; (iv) morbidity is positively correlated to family size (crowding); and, (v) morbidity is negatively correlated to family expenditure (better nutritional and health care). The overall goodness of fit of the linear multiple regression model is satisfactory as indicated by $R^2=0.69$ and $F=64.42$ for a combined sample size of 150. Another linear model suggested similar relationship between the period morbidity index and the above mentioned set of dependent variables.

Table 2: Statistical association between point morbidity index and risk / confounding factors.

Model variables	Coefficients		t	Sig.
	B	Std. Error		
(Constant)	6.274	1.665	3.768	.014
Age	-.334	.107	-3.116	.002
Gender	1.675	.564	2.970	.003
Family expenditure	.000	.000	-1.841	.068
Family size	.559	.218	2.562	.011
Group	8.681	.620	14.002	.000

Note: Dependent Variable: Point morbidity index. $R^2=0.691$, $F=64.424$, $N=150$.

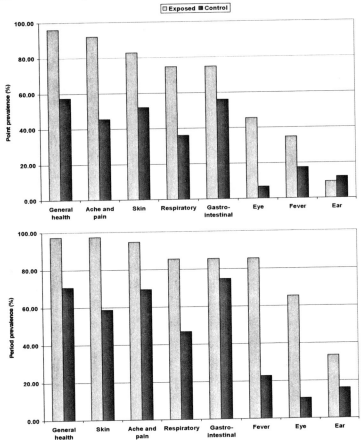

Figure 2: Point and period prevalence rates for the exposed and control groups.

4 Alleviation of impacts

4.1 Ecosystem approach

The ecosystem approach to human health requires an understanding of the complex interplay between the society and the environment shared by a group of people [10, 11]. It begins with an analysis of the system, which is comprised of 'system description' and formation of the 'issues framework.' Thus, at the analysis level, both 'hard' and 'soft' system components and interactions between these components are taken into account. Once results from system analysis are available, the process goes through two additional phases: synthesis and implementation. Ecosystem approach requires full stakeholder consultation at all stages. Further, it is essential to have a monitoring and feedback component in the last leg of the process. This is to ensure that the entire process remains 'alive' and 'adaptive' to changes in system components and interactions. This entire process has been schematically shown in fig. 3.

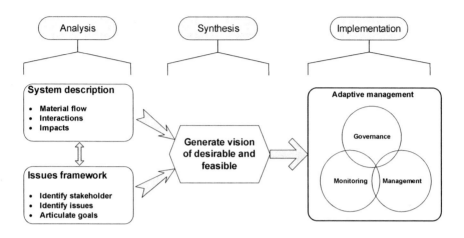

Figure 3:   Schematic representation of the ecosystem approach (adapted from Kay et al. [12] and NESH [13]).

This approach has been employed in this study to identify and quantify the health impacts (analysis) and to generate a set of intervention options through extensive consultation with the stakeholders (synthesis). Note that implementation of the intervention options would require a general consensus at the policy level as well as commitment of a significant amount of time and resources on part of the stakeholders. As such, the 'implementation' part is beyond the scope of this study; perhaps a follow-up study may attempt to elaborate on this part.

4.2 Intervention options

A simplistic and drastic approach to solving most of the health problems created would be to remove all waste pickers from streets and landfill sites. However, this is neither possible nor desirable due to social and economic reasons. In fact, it would be immoral to displace the waste pickers, who are providing a valuable service to the society through waste recycling, without providing them with an alternative livelihood. The presence of waste pickers and the informal recycling sector in the city are indications of a lack of 'holistic' solid waste management plan. Thus, the possible intervention options should not be centred around the garbage bins or landfill sites; rather a broad or ecosystem approach is needed to ensure that the issues are dealt with in an integrated and sustainable manner.

With this purpose in mind, a number of key informants were interviewed and two seminar-cum-roundtable sessions were arranged in January 2005 to have extensive multi-stakeholder consultations. All major stakeholders including representatives from Dhaka City Corporation (DCC), private waste management organizations, NGOs, the City Development Authority (RAJUK), relevant ministries, donor agencies, universities, urban planners and the civil society participated in these events. On both occasions, keynote papers were presented by experts, followed by roundtable sessions. This approach has allowed identification and synthesis of a series of intervention options pertaining to the entire cycle of waste generation to disposal. The key interventions options along with the suggested time-frame for implementation have been summarized in table 3 in the form of an impact-intervention matrix.

It is evident from the impact-intervention matrix that a whole range of technical, socio-economic, environmental, regulatory and institutional interventions would be needed to provide a sustainable solution to the problem of urban solid waste management. Note that the interventions presented in the matrix are not comprehensive enough to fully address all the issues. Rather, these options have come out as the most important and essential ones during the roundtable sessions and one-to-one interview with key informants and experts.

The interventions suggested in the matrix collectively incorporate the ecosystem approach, which is both integrated and sustainable. For example, both 'hard' and 'soft' options have been provided for each segment of the impact-path way, thereby ensuring an integrated approach. At the same time, a range of policy tools have been utilized to ensure that the resulting system evolves as socially, economically and environmentally sustainable over time. Regarding priority and order of implementation, the interventions have been grouped into short term (one to two years), medium term (three to five years) and long term (more than five years) as per the consensus reached during the roundtable sessions.

5   Concluding remarks

This study has identified the most important set of intervention options for integrated and sustainable management of urban solid waste as per ecosystem approach. These interventions, when implemented, would alleviate the environmental health and safety risks presently faced by the residents of Dhaka City, and the waste pickers in particular. Although additional study would be needed to prepare a detailed 'blue print' for implementation, certain measures, particularly the short term ones, may be introduced immediately without incurring much cost or difficulty. Some such measures have already been introduced, e.g., community-based waste collection, awareness campaigns by NGOs and limited health services for the waste pickers. Some other options, on the other hand, are likely to be very challenging, e.g., introducing at-source separation of waste, full-cost based waste service fee, and formalization of the recycling sector. Successful adoption of these measures would require major 'social engineering' efforts to sensitize all stakeholder groups and induce a cultural shift in the way solid waste has been dealt with in Bangladesh for decades.

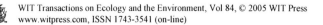

Table 3: Impact-intervention matrix.

	Interventions →	Institutional	Technical	Socioeconomic	Environmental	Regulatory
Source	Household Market and business Industry Medical facilities Street sweeping	Community-based waste collection (S)	Separation of organic and inorganic waste (L)	Market-based collection fee proportional to waste volume (M)	Composting from organic waste; reduce, reuse, recycling (M)	New anti-littering law with steep penalty (M)
Stressors	Hazardous chemicals Pathogens Sharp objects Odor	Separate system for clinical and industrial waste (L)	Incinerator, autoclave, dispenser (M)	Awareness campaign (S)	Separate site for hazardous waste (M)	Enforcement of pollution laws (L)
Media	Land (solid waste) Air (odor and dust) Water (leachate)	Timely collection and disposal of waste (S)	Sanitary landfill (M-L)	Awareness campaign (S)	Removal of street-side bins; setting up collection depots (L)	Law banning 'open dump', landfill in major cities (M)
Vector & reservoir	Insects, flies Mice Birds Cats and dogs Waste pickers	Timely collection and disposal of waste (S)	Sanitary landfill (M-L)	Alternative livelihood for waste pickers (M-L)	Removal of street-side bins; setting up collection depots (L)	Law banning 'open dump', landfill in major cities (M)
Receptors	Waste pickers Family members Neighbors Reusable materials traders	Formalize the recycling sector (M-L)	Sanitary landfill (M-L)	Alternative livelihood for waste pickers, incentive for recycling (M-L)	Water supply, sanitary latrine (S)	Regulatory support for the recycling industry
Health impacts	Diseases Cuts and bruises Discomfort Accident	Community health center and free treatment (S)	Sandal, mask, cap, picking rod (S)	Awareness campaign on personal safety & hygiene (S)	Water supply, sanitary latrine (S)	Pro-poor health policy (M)

Note: S = short term (1-2 years); M = medium term (3-5 years); L = long term (more than 5 years).

References

[1] Islam, A. Z. M. S., Solid Waste Management in Dhaka City, unpublished paper, Dhaka City Corporation, 2003. http://www.iges.or.jp/kitakyushu /Successful%20Practices/SP%20 (Analyzed)/Solid%20Waste/3%20Dhaka%20(Paper.pdf

[2] MMI (Mott Macdonald International), Solid Waste Management Draft Technical Manual, in association with Cuplin Planning Limited, Engineering and Planning Consultants Limited, Dhaka, 1991.

[3] ADB (Asian Development Bank), Dhaka City Management Reform Pilot Project: Final Report, BCAS: Dhaka, pp.61, 1998.

[4] DCC (Dhaka City Corporation), Solid Waste Management of Dhaka City, Dhaka City Corporation, pp. 9. 1999.

[5] Memon, M. A., Solid Waste Management in Dhaka, Bangladesh: Innovation in Community Driven Composting, 2002. http://www.iges.or.jp/kitakyushu/Meetings/Thematic%20Seminar/Solid% 20Waste/Supplementary/2%20Solid%20Waste%20Management%20in%2 0Dhaka.pdf.

[6] Rahman, M. H., Ahmed, S. N., & Ullah, M. S., A study on hospital waste management in Dhaka City, Proc. Of the 25th WECD Conference, Integrated Development for Water Supply and Sanitation, Addis Ababa, 1999.

[7] Khanam, K. A., Socio-Demographic Characteristics and Morbidity Pattern of Waste Pickers of Dhaka City. National Institute of Preventive and Social Medicine (NIPSOM), Dhaka, 2000.

[8] Shamshad, R., Occupational Health Hazard of the Scavenger Children in Matuail Landfill Site, Unpublished Thesis, Department of Environmental Studies, North South University, Dhaka, 2003.

[9] Parveen, S. & Faisal, I. M., Occupational Health Impacts on the Child Waste-pickers of Dhaka City, paper presented at Environmental Health Risk 2005, Bologna, Italy, September 14-16, 2005.

[10] Feola, G., & Bazzani, R., Challenges and Strategies for Implementing the Ecosystem Approach to Human Health in Developing Countries: Reflections from Regional Consultations, IDRC, Ottawa, 2001.

[11] Forget, G., & Lebel, J., An Ecosystem Approach to Human Health, International Journal of Occupational and Environmental Health, supplement to 2(7), pp. S3-S38, 2001.

[12] Kay. J., Regier, H., Boyle, M. & Francis, G., An Ecosystem approach for Sustainability: Addressing the Challenge of Complexity, Futures, 31(7), pp. 721-742, 1999.

[13] NESH (Network for Ecosystem Sustainability and Health), NESH's Adaptive Ecosystem Approach to Environmental Stewardship, 2005. http://www.ecologistics.com/nesh/aea.html

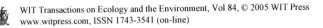

The PVC industry's contribution to sustainability in the building and construction sector

M. Piana
Centro di Informazione sul PVC, Milan, Italy

Abstract

In the building and construction sector, in addition to technical specifications and price, specific environmental and ecological requirements are frequently written into public and private tenders.

An informed choice of materials, as well as technical and architectural solutions, can contribute to energy saving and to minimising environmental impact, whilst increasing a building's comfort. Furthermore, the sustainability of different materials is also becoming a criterion of evaluation for certifications and for international eco-efficiency standards.

The European PVC industry, through its organisation Vinyl 2010 (which involves the entire upstream and downstream chain – from raw-material production to post-consumer waste), is working hard to guarantee the eco-compatibility of PVC products and applications (the B&C sector absorbs about 60% of PVC production).

Efforts in this area include an integrated approach to waste management (from collection and recycling schemes to ultimate disposal) with several projects covering technology, research and organisation. It also covers the promotion of best practice in technical solutions of PVC applications: for example, 'intelligent' windows with excellent insulation can save up to the equivalent of 16 kg of CO_2 per year; membranes and flooring that result in less energy for heating and cooling houses; light concrete with increased thermal insulation properties; or projects like the 3LH (3 litre house).

Keywords: PVC sustainability, recycling, sustainable building, energy saving.

WIT Transactions on Ecology and the Environment, Vol 84, © 2005 WIT Press
www.witpress.com, ISSN 1743-3541 (on-line)

1 Introduction

Human activity needs energy and any use of primary energy sources has an environmental impact, whether significant or not.

Energy consumption has grown in parallel with human history, and evolves in conjunction with the variation of the energy source employed and life styles [1]. Below is a view of estimated yearly energy consumption per human being throughout history:

10,000 years ago	100 K Tep (1 tep = 11,600 KWh)
5.000 years ago	350 "
XIV century	850 "
XX century	2000 "

Limiting energy use means to limit consumption and the benefit we get from it. On the other hand, to reconcile economic development with respect for the environment is a moral duty - this is the great challenge for a sustainable future.

2 The responsible consumption of the energetic resources: the role of the building sector

Buildings have a significant role to play in energy consumption worldwide and the resulting emissions of pollutants (energy consumption of the final utilisation in residential buildings is shown in fig.1). At the same time, there are wide margins for improving energy efficiency and therefore environmental impact – for example residential buildings are responsible for 21% of CO_2 emissions and tertiary buildings for 10.5%.

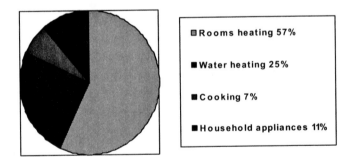

Figure 1: Energy consumption of the final utilisation in residential buildings (source ENEA).

Energy consumption is growing worldwide. Yet, only in the most industrialised countries thanks to the gradual shift to less pollutant fuels (i.e. gas instead of oil), and to better thermal insulation of buildings, is the increase in emissions less than the absolute consumption of primary energy.

The EU Green Paper identified a reduction in energy consumption as the first step towards a more efficient management of buildings [2].

Recent estimates show a potential saving of 22% by 2010. The achievement of this objective would reduce energy consumption by 55 millions Tep, equivalent to a decrease of 100 millions tonnes of CO_2 (20% of the Kyoto target for the EU).

The most striking thing about this is that this level of savings could be achieved with increased use of simple technologies. These are already on the market and cost efficient, for example technology to improve the thermal performances of buildings.

This is especially important in terms of the use of renewable energy sources. In a traditionally constructed building, renewable sources (i.e. sun energy) do not feature because of inefficient insulation and the inability thereof to guarantee the entire energy needs. Yet, the contribution of renewable sources can be relevant in a building where energy consumption is very limited, but it only makes sense if there is an excellent thermal insulation.

2.1 The European directive on energy performance in B&C

The main issue we must address is how to stimulate the adoption of measures to save energy in the framework of European general strategy guidelines [3]. It is important to act fast as inefficient buildings represent a heavy burden that will weigh on the shoulders of future generations.

The European Commission issued the Directive 2002/91/CE on energy performance in the building and construction sector. The aim of the directive is to create a framework to allow member states to coordinate the regulation of the sector. The main elements of the proposal are:

1. The creation of a common integrated method of calculating the energy performance of buildings. The calculation tools must take into account all the factors that contribute to the energy balance of a building, such as: sun contribution, ventilation and heating energy, heat recovery, orientation, thermal insulation etc.
2. Application of minimal standards on energy performances in new buildings and renovations.
3. Energy certification of new and existing buildings based on a common method of calculation. These certifications can represent an incentive for buyers/tenants, as a result of possible savings on management costs.
4. Inspection and specific evaluation of heating and cooling plants.

2.2 Savings through the improvement of the building "system"

On average new buildings (in the EU) lose about half as much heat compared with buildings built before 1945. The total energy consumed in new buildings is 60% of the energy consumed in old buildings. Renewing standards of thermal insulation, and improving the efficiency of plants installed in existing buildings, can contribute to achieving energy saving and cost efficiencies.

A European initiative to improve the energy performances of buildings (which results in the application of regulations on thermal insulation similar to the ones already existing in some member states across the Union), has the potential to bring significant energy savings to the EU as a whole.

 WIT Transactions on Ecology and the Environment, Vol 84, © 2005 WIT Press
www.witpress.com, ISSN 1743-3541 (on-line)

2.3 Some experiences in Europe

2.3.1 The German pragmatism

The German government has set itself the target for the coming years of 25% reduction of CO_2 emissions compared to the levels of 1990, equivalent to 35 million tonnes per year. The unusual nature of the German experience lies in the simplicity of the approach with its strongly conservative strategies to minimise energy consumption. It prefers well established and proven solutions to spectacular architectures.

One approach, known as *Niedrigenergiehaus* (NEH), has an annual consumption limit of about 70 kWh/m^2 (specific yearly consumption), with a saving of 30% compared to new buildings in compliance with the 1995 standards, and of 50% compared to previous standards. It naturally gives rise to the so called *Passivhaus* concept. This concept deals with the thermal resistance of the envelope that must be reinforced with an adequate insulation thickness; the use of high efficiency windows; and the elimination of thermal bridges.

A similar reduced energy requirement, equivalent to about 150 litres of gas oil for heating a 100 m^2 house during the entire winter, is equivalent to a more than 75% reduction in consumption compared to a *Niedrigenergiehaus*, and 85/90% reduction in comparison to a building in Italy built according to the law 10/91 (where the typical consumption is between 100 and 150 kWh/m^2 year), this comparison is reported in table 1.

In Germany PVC window profiles cover about 55% of the market, and are the most used, in line with the NEH standards.

Table 1:   Estimated energy balance by different standards.

	Traditional building	Law 10/91 (Italy)	Standard Passivhaus
Dispersion for transmission	5,513 kWh	2,260 kWh	625 kWh
Dispersion for ventilation	916 kWh	618 kWh	82 kWh

2.3.2 France and the HQE process

In France, the most well known concept of sustainability in building and construction, called environmental high quality (*Haute Qualitè Environmental, HQE)*, consists of 14 targets (*cibles*). These summarise the main aspects of sustainable development and are grouped into four themes (construction, management, comfort and healthiness).

In order to significantly reduce the energy needs of the B&C sector, the French Government issued in 2000 a new *Reglementation Thermique* (RT 2000), which imposes more restrictive consumption limits compared to the previous 1988 regulation. The aim is to obtain an energy saving of at least 20% for new buildings, and, by 2010, to decrease present energy consumption in existing buildings by 22% with interventions of retrofit.

2.3.3 The Dutch approach

In The Netherlands, after the first experiences of ecological building that took place at Rotterdam at the end of the 80s, and the inclusion of recommendations on the choice of materials for new buildings into the Building Code of Amsterdam, the Government is strongly committed to sustainable buildings. It therefore launched in 1995 the *Sustainable Building Plan: Investing for the future*, supported by fiscal incentives for five years. Even if the declared objective of reaching the target of 80% of new houses built according to the criteria of eco compatibility was not fully achieved, it did succeed in spreading this concept widely into Dutch practices.

2.3.4 The Swiss concept of Minergie

The Swiss Government set the target of 10% reduction in CO_2 emissions by 2010, to be achieved through incentives towards more efficient construction techniques. The result of this approach is the Minergie standard, table 2.

Table 2:   Standard Minergie: limit values.

	Yearly specific consumption	Average U for envelop	Average U for windows
Current legislation	85 kWh/m^2 (305 MJ/M^2)	0.3 W/m^{2}K	1.6 W/m^{2}K
Standard Minergie	45 kWh/m^2 (160 MJ/M^2)	0.2 W/m^{2}K	1.3 W/m^{2}K
Standard Passivhaus	15 kWh/m^2 (53 MJ/M^2)	0.1 W/m^{2}K	0.8 W/m^{2}K

The aim of Minergie is to promote the use of construction strategies and techniques that make the reduction of energy dependence of non renewable sources possible in a cost-efficient way. Furthermore, the standard sets other objectives such as healthiness of internal air, thermal comfort (winter and summer), noise protection, and urges the use of renewable energy. Experience to date from new constructions shows that the additional costs compared to a traditional building are about 2/3 %, easily recoverable in few years thanks to the savings from reduced heating costs. The Minergie concept has now spread widely in Switzerland, and in fact, many banks grant loans and financing at more favourable conditions for those buildings that have this mark. By applying this criterion on a large scale, it has the potential to halve CO_2 emissions, equivalent to an annual reduction of 10 million tonnes.

3   The characteristics of tomorrow's construction techniques

Considering the above, it is possible to define the necessary characteristics of future construction techniques:

1. ***project suitability***: the designer must be able to incorporate specialised and different materials in order to meet project requirements - in particular an

opportune variation of thickness and of functional schemes to meet the desired levels of energy consumption.

2. *lightness*: this is fundamental to reduce resources during construction phases, for the management and dismantling of the building, and to guarantee a more effective management of the yard.

3. *evolution:* a building is not an immutable and fixed object, but an organism that over time is subject to obsolescence, and to variation of its hosted functions. Construction techniques must be naturally aligned to maintenance, to the substitution of parts, to volumetric variations, image makeovers (through the change of the external aspect) and to change of function (flexibility).

4. *reversibility:* at the end of the useful life, when a building cannot be 'reused' for other functions, a selective demolition must be possible in order to reuse or recycle certain components.

3.1 The choice of materials

The materials used in the B&C sector are numerous; they use different sources of raw materials; are manufactured with diverse processes; and are used with imprecise modalities.

This is the reason why it's not easy to tackle the theme of environmental compatibility in the B&C sector.

Unfortunately, magic methods in terms of the choice of materials and eco-compatible systems are not known, and not available at the moment. There are systems that exist to try and analyse the life cycle of products in the most scientific and holistic way possible. These have created a method that allows comparisons, even if not exhaustive. Obtaining usable comparisons, however, will depend on the consistency of the methodology.

The comparison can be based on the quantity of raw materials used, rather than on the energy consumed, or CO_2 emissions. The choice of materials will take into account:

- environmental compatibility
- quality of materials
- product performances such as for example:

thermal transmittance	$\rightarrow$	pollution/resources
acoustic insulation	$\rightarrow$	welfare
recyclability	$\rightarrow$	environment
hygiene	$\rightarrow$	safety

The Life Cycle Analysis - LCA is one of the most common methods for the evaluation of the environmental impact of a product. The Society of Environmental Toxicology and Chemistry (SETAC) has defined guidelines for the definition of LACs, which have then been integrated into the ISO 14040 standard.

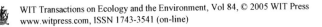

4 Energy saving in buildings: the contribution of PVC

In 2002, the European Commission commissioned a consortium led by PE Europe (Stuttgart), an independent consultancy, to review existing LCA studies on PVC for several applications, including flooring, toys, window profiles, coatings and medical devices. The review investigated more than 100 life cycle documents and reviewed 30 LCA studies in depth. It has confirmed that PVC is a material like any other, with both stronger and weaker points depending on the application and on its use, and that there is no reason to treat PVC differently from any other material.

Furthermore, PVC applications such as windows profiles, insulating membranes and flooring, make a positive contribution to energy savings, as low cost and eco-efficient solutions.

4.1 The example of PVC windows profiles

By making the right informed choice of fastening, this offers a low cost solution with a very high energy efficiency. Fastenings include windows, doors, shutters, etc. that can be realised in wood, tin, PVC, mixed materials or steel.

An evaluation of the use of thermal insulations is an integral part of energy saving, which corresponds to the ability of windows to avoid the passage of heat from the internal environment to the outside in winter and vice versa during summer.

Table 3:   Thermal transmittance in windows' profiles.

Kind of glass	Air space nominal thickness	Profile material	Window transmittance U (W/m^{2}K)	Average transmittance day/night window with screen U (W/m^{2}K)	
				Shutters	Others
Single-glazed	-	Wood, PVC	5.0	3.7	4.7
		Metal	5.8	4.2	4.8
Double-glazed	6	Wood, PVC	3.3	2.6	2.9
		Metal	4.0	3.1	3.4
	8	Wood, PVC	3.1	2.5	2.8
		Metal	3.9	3.0	3.3
	10	Wood, PVC	2.4	2.7	
		Metal	3.8	2.9	3.2
	12	Wood, PVC	2.9	2.4	2.6
		Metal	3.7	2.9	3.2
Double window	> 30	Wood, PVC	2.6	2.1	2.3
		Metal	3.0	2.5	2.7

PVC windows fitted with cave structured profiles (that have a very low thermal conductibility value, about 1,000 times inferior to Al), achieves excellent values of thermal insulation, as shown in table 3.

Research conducted by the Centro di Informazione sul PVC [4] demonstrates that modern PVC window profiles, thanks to optimal performance in terms of insulation, can contribute to a 20% reduction of heating costs in an average flat. This corresponds to an equivalent saving of 200 litres of gas oil per year. As a solution this leads to both economic and environmental benefits, equivalent to the reduction of pollutant emissions in the atmosphere equivalent to 16kg of CO_2.

For these reasons, the use of PVC window profiles has been included, for example, in the materials that satisfy the Passivhaus criteria.

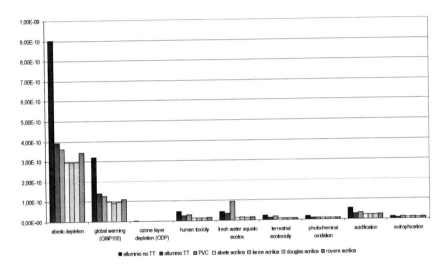

Figure 2:   Politecnico of Milan: LCA results.

A recent study on the LCA of wood, PVC and tin windows profiles, realised by the Politecnico of Milan, showed that PVC and wood profiles have a good environmental impact, fig. 2.

4.2 The 3-litre-house

The BASF 3-litre-house project in Ludwigshafen has set a record in conserving energy. The tenants did not even need the equivalent of three litres of heating oil per square meter of floor area per year to heat the house. What this shows, is that an older building that has been refurbished taking energy consumption into account, conserves more energy than a new low-energy house. In addition, it is much more efficient than an unrenovated older building, which uses 20 litres of oil per square metre per year.

Besides focusing on good insulation, designers also pay a lot of attention to avoid "thermal bridges," where heat leaves the house through building elements. Modern energy-saving buildings, like the 3-liter-house, are constructed in accordance with the philosophy of the airtight building envelope. The utmost care is therefore taken to ensure that no air whatsoever flows outside, causing unchecked heat losses at windows, doors, edges and joints. A ventilation system provides fresh air, by drawing the stale air from the kitchen and bath to a heat exchanger. This then converts up to 85% of the heat into fresh air, which, after being filtered and adjusted to a pleasant temperature, can flow into the living room and bedrooms.

4.3 PVC recycling in B&C sector

Collection and recycling of B&C PVC products is managed by the European PVC industry within the framework of Vinyl 2010 and its Voluntary Commitment. Based on demanding management and scientific criteria, the Voluntary Commitment is a 10-year plan with fixed targets and deadlines to improve products and production processes, to invest in technology, to minimise emissions and waste and to boost collection and recycling.

Window profiles, pipes and fittings and roofing membranes: commitment to recycle at least 25% by 2003 and 50% by 2005 of collectable, available PVC waste. Flooring: commitment to recycle at least 25% by 2006 and 50% by 2008 of the collectable, available PVC waste.

Vinyl 2010 supports studies and research on possible eco-compatible PVC applications such as light concrete. Light concrete is found in certain applications for building where low weight and the highest thermal and sound insulation characteristics are required, such as with floors or walls. This application is a solution in the recycling of non-pure PVC waste from demolitions.

5 Conclusions

The application of innovation, science and technology to reconcile economic development with respect for the environment - this is the big challenge for a sustainable future which is being played out in all the field of human activity.

In the building and construction sector, the contribution design makes to energy savings is very important. Energy certification for buildings as proposed by recent European and Italian regulations, may certainly offer tools and methods to make the attainment of this aim a reality.

The choice of PVC applications (windows, insulating membranes, flooring, etc.) is a way to achieve superior energy efficiency in a relatively simple way throughout the entire life cycle.

References

[1] Piana, M., *Realtà e false credenze* - Proceedings of the Conference "Costruire ECO" - Centro di Informazione sul PVC, Milan, 2004.
[2] Piana, M., *Prestazioni energetiche dei serramenti secondo le direttive comunitarie* - Proceedings of the SAIE DUE Conference, Bologna, 2004

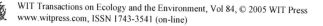

[3] Corrado, V., *Le regole della certificazione energetica degli edifici -* Proceedings of the SAIE DUE Conference, Bologna, 2004.
[4] Piana, M., *Pieni e vuoti: tecnologie dei serramenti in PVC,* Centro di Informazione sul PVC, Milan, 2004.

Dynamic modelling software for the analysis of different waste valorization scenarios in the cement production process: a new step on sustainability

J. Arias[1], C. Gutierrez-Cañas[1], M. Larrion[1] & C. Urcelay[2]
[1]*Department of Chemical and Environmental Engineering,
University of the Basque Country, Spain*
[2]*Cementos Lemona S.A., Spain*

Abstract

Larger widespread public concern about sustainability as an answer to the huge pressure put on the medium by the accelerated degree of development is bringing about the emergence of analytical tools with the purpose of assessing environmental damage relating to industrial products or activities in general.

According to this project's vocation a new experimental tool, based on generic LCA (Life Cycle Assessment) software aided by a process simulator, is developed to carry out the assessments of several scenarios of waste valorization in the cement process.

Starting from a preset base case of zero alternative material usage, the program recalculates environmental impacts of the evolved process taking into account deviations in pollutant emission levels and benefits of waste recovery versus new resource consumption.

The results of these analyses will help with decision-making issues concerning the selection and dosage of most adequate waste according to comparison between data obtained from the different scenarios proposed, assuring in this way the minimisation of environmental impact in the recovery/valorization of these alternative materials.

Keywords: decision support, LCA, cement, process simulation, waste management, software, dynamic tool.

WIT Transactions on Ecology and the Environment, Vol 84, © 2005 WIT Press
www.witpress.com, ISSN 1743-3541 (on-line)

1   Introduction

1.1 The path towards sustainability

Deeply rooted in mankind's mind has always been the persistent desire to excel itself. The truth is that although while under control it is an incredibly valuable mechanism to overcome new challenges and take the most out of limited resources and opportunities, when this pure ambition turns wild it is easy to lose global perspective and start running the risk of compromising future chances due to disproportionate forcing of the present ones.

This tangible threat, nowadays more than ever a harsh reality of the present, has made us think about the necessity of an ideal towards which we should walk together; a path in which future needs are not endangered by the fulfillment of current necessities: the path towards sustainability.

It is clear that many pitfalls await us in this struggle for sustainability's sake, but at the same time we can count on a wide range of tools to aid us in the task of taking the right decisions to advance a new step towards our goal: In this sketched context can be located the software we have developed for the cement production process.

At this point, the next questions we have to answer are: firstly, what has cement production process to do with sustainability? -Soon we will have a look at its main environmental threats and opportunities, primarily waste valorization-

And then, in which way can this tool contribute to achieve the desired objective? We will explain how the software tool can offer decision-making support by comparing environmental impacts in different scenarios of waste usage-.

1.2 The cement production process. Threats and opportunities

Simply put, cement-manufacturing process consists in three basic stages:
1. Raw materials acquiring
2. Raw mix grinding and burning: Clinker manufacture
3. Clinker and additives grinding: Cement production

As a result, cement (the most demanded industrial product worldwide) is obtained, but on the way, a toll, in the form of environmental impact must be paid as in every other human activity.

Exactly, on one hand the main environmental issues associated with cement production are raw materials depletion, emissions to air (note we have not mentioned neither wastewater nor solid waste -as cement process is an almost no-waste process-) and above all the amazingly intensive energy consumption EIPPCB [1].

However, on the other hand, certain peculiarities found in the cement manufacture (very high flame temperatures and long periods of contact between combustion gases and materials —more than 2000°C and 5-6 s- in an alkaline environment) makes it possible to dispose efficiently of incinerable waste taking advantage of its material and energy content as well, hence surpassing in some cases other alternatives for waste disposal CEMBUREAU [2]

Therefore, according to the European directives, which establish the priority order as far as waste destination is concerned (1. Minimize 2. Reuse 3. Recycle 4.Valorization 5. Final Disposal), the cement kiln offers solutions for the three last options.

This way, using these alternative materials and fuels in cement plants, not only can be enhanced the cost-effectiveness of process but also does enable the environmentally compatible management of a wide range of waste VDZ [3]

1.3 The role of the software tool

In spite of this unique potential, we must be aware of the fact that not every single alternative material can be valorized and its composition is often limited by the high quality standards imposed on the product. It is also important that new elements introduced do not have a pernicious effect on emissions and, generally speaking, on the environmental performance of the process, as, under some circumstances, the benefits we achieve, for example, saving in new resources consumption might be hindered by an increase of the amount of certain pollutant released into the atmosphere.

And here is when our tool goes into action. Thanks to its predictive nature, and starting from a preset base case of zero alternative materials usage, the program is able to recalculate environmental impacts of the evolved process comparing its performance with the base case.

Therefore, after carefully watching the results, decisions can be made concerning the convenience of valorizing a specific waste type, allowing as well ulterior comparison with other possibilities of disposal (such as incineration).

2 Describing the software tool

2.1 Global perspective

Having come this far, it is about time we take a deeper look into the software itself:

  *How does it accomplish its task?

  *How is it structured?

  *and... What kind of data does it exactly need?

As can be seen in the simplified diagram represented in figure 1 the tool comprises two main modules:

- The clinker burning process model (labeled BURNMOD) , developed in Aspen Plus 12.1, which taking into account the materials and fuels used in the process as well as the operation parameters preset by user, calculates the output (basically, the product –clinker- and airborne emissions)

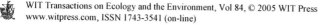

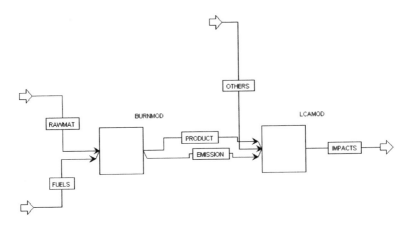

Figure 1:   The two main modules and the links established between them.

- The Life Cycle Assessment model (labeled LCAMOD), developed in SimaPro 6.0, which, based on LCA methodology and fed by the output of the previous model and other considerations (such as electricity consumption, resources depletion, etc.), presents the impacts generated by the process.

So, considering it as a whole, the software is able to predict environmental impacts from *any* scenario of waste usage proposed by the user (hence the *dynamic* attribute), establishing comparisons among them or between a specific case and its corresponding base case.

2.2 The clinker burning process model

On the course of thinking about the functionality of the software soon it was clear the obvious necessity of being able to anticipate changes in emission levels and clinker composition brought about by the introduction of alternative materials and fuels in the cement manufacture.

Comprising more than thirty blocks and up to one hundred streams, the BURNMOD was created to carry out this task. It can be easily depicted with the aid of figure 2, where we can observe the main parts, inlets and outlets it includes.

2.3 The life cycle assessment model

At the very end, the purpose of the tool is to predict impacts from a given set of raw materials and fuels (*scenario*); the LCAMOD carries out this final job by transforming data calculated in the previous model into impacts and considering any other information available concerning the process life cycle.

This life cycle assessment approach provides us with a holistic view of the environmental performance of the process, making it possible to analyze the global effect of waste management in the cement process without displacing ecological burdens temporally or locally Larrion [4].

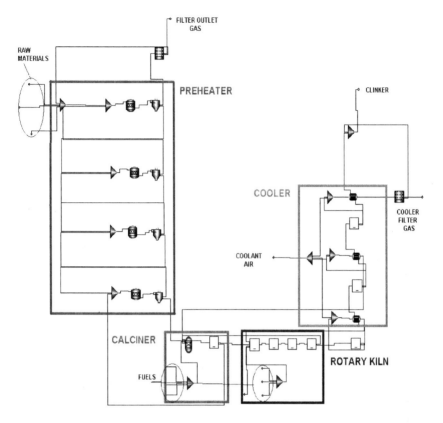

Figure 2:   BURNMOD. Parts, inlets and outlets.

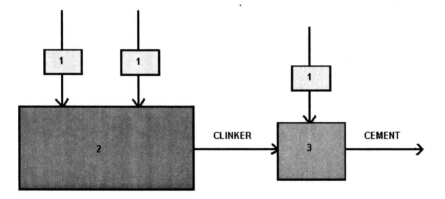

Figure 3:   LCAMOD. Main blocks and relations among them.

The diagram represented above (figure 3) shows in an unsophisticated way the three different kinds of "blocks" the model is arranged into:

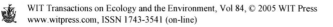

- In these <u>yellow blocks, #1</u>, is stored the inventory associated with the winning and feeding of each of the materials that somehow take part in the process (raw materials, fuels, additives, etc.). There is one of these for every different material fed into the system
- The <u>green block, #2</u> contains input and output inventory of the kiln; consequently is strongly linked to BURNMOD as it provides a significant part of this information. However it goes far beyond this because data concerning electricity consumption, ancillary resources, etc. are added.
- The <u>blue block, #3</u>, adds the environmental burdens related to clinker manufacture to those of cement grinding (including additives consumption –considered in the #1 blocks connected to block #3-)

3 Results. Practical example

3.1 The base case

After this description of the tool, now is the suitable moment to set up a practical example and see it in action.

In table 1 a simplified summary of the input describing the hypothetic base case of a certain cement plant is indicated. With these data available and having preset the parameters, it is feasible to run the model and obtain an overall view of the process.

Table 1: Base case input summary.

Input	Unit	Value
Raw mix flow	Kg/h	165000
Raw mix composition	$\%CaCO_3$	79
	$\%SiO_2$	13
	$\%Al_2O_3$	3
	$\%Fe_2O_3$	2
	$\%H_2O$	3
Fuel flow	Kg/h	11800
Fuel composition	$\%C$	86
	$\%S$	3
	$\%H_2O$	2
Additives flow	Kg/h	4320
Additives composition	$\%CaSO_4$	90
Electricity	MJ/h Raw mill	9492
	MJ/h Coke mill	1814
	MJ/h Cement mill	17692
	MJ/h Others	18540

By means of this analysis we can, for example, gather information regarding the impact categories where the process is predicted to have a more notorious effect (see figure 4; normalized results are shown; note these impact categories vary depending on the impact assessment method selected –in this example Eco-indicator 99 PRè Consultants [5] has been chosen-; it is best to perform several different assessments in order to ascertain conclusions drawn are reliable).

Also discerning the contribution of each part of the process is possible by having a look at the colour pattern of any particular bar.

In spite of the fact that global charts like the previously shown are quite easy to understand, at this point we might be wondering, just as an example: what are the foremost substances that contribute to raise the climate change category?, or what is the exact amount of carbon dioxide released along the whole life-cycle?

In these cases, when necessary, further level of detail can be acquired, just inspecting the data calculated (figure 5)

3.2 The alternative case

Until now, we have presented some of the program capabilities to carry out assessments and display them in a detailed or graphic fashion; however, its true potential is revealed when comparing several scenarios, thus serving as a backup for decision-making.

Let us suppose the same manufacture plant mentioned before, urged by local government, is considering substitution of half its primary fuel – coke – for alternatives such as worn car tyres and meat and bone meal (table 2)

Table 2:   Key values for the alternative case.

Percent of fuel energy input substitution	52 %
Percent substituted by tyres	28 %
Percent substituted by meat and bone meal	24 %

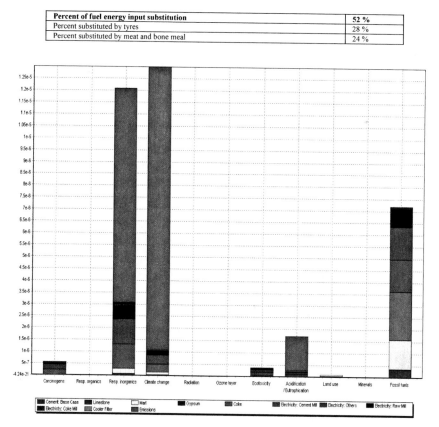

Figure 4:   Environmental impacts predicted for the base case.

No	Substance	Compartment	Unit	Total
	Total of all compartments		DALY	1,99E-7
	Total of airborne emission		DALY	1,99E-7
1	Carbon dioxide	Air	DALY	1,98E-7
2	Methane	Air	DALY	8,64E-10
3	Carbon monoxide	Air	DALY	3,54E-10
4	Dinitrogen monoxide	Air	DALY	5,25E-11
5	Ethane, 1,2-dichloro-1,1,2,2-tetrafluoro-, CFC-114	Air	DALY	1,24E-12
6	Methane, tetrafluoro-, FC-14	Air	DALY	2,92E-13
7	Propane	Air	DALY	1,18E-13
8	Butane	Air	DALY	1,14E-13
9	Ethane, hexafluoro-, HFC-116	Air	DALY	4,64E-14
10	Methane, dichlorofluoro-, HCFC-21	Air	DALY	1,23E-14
11	Methane, chlorotrifluoro-, CFC-13	Air	DALY	9E-15
12	Methane, dichlorodifluoro-, CFC-12	Air	DALY	6,43E-15
13	Methane, trichlorofluoro-, CFC-11	Air	DALY	4,7E-15
14	Methane, chlorodifluoro-, HCFC-22	Air	DALY	1,43E-15
15	Methane, dichloro-, HCC-30	Air	DALY	5,66E-18
16	Chloroform	Air	DALY	3,88E-18
17	Methane, tetrachloro-, CFC-10	Air	DALY	-1,1E-14
18	Methane, bromotrifluoro-, Halon 1301	Air	DALY	-1,04E-11
	Nitrogen	Air	kg	1,59
	Carbon dioxide	Air	g	944
	Oxygen	Air	g	227
	Water	Air	g	57,2
	Nitrogen oxides	Air	g	1,36
	Carbon monoxide	Air	g	1,1
	Sulfur dioxide	Air	mg	557

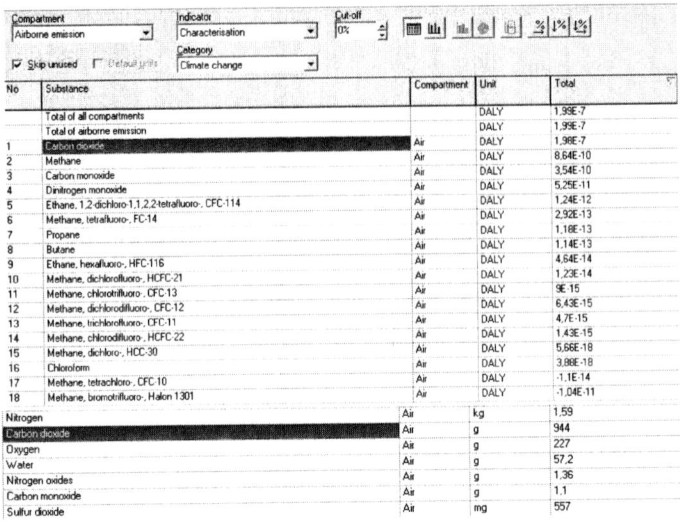

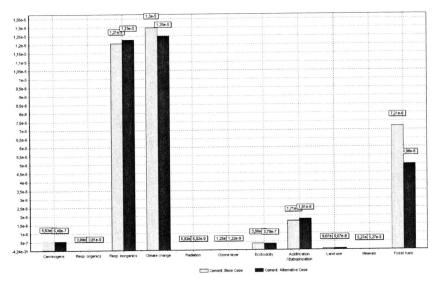

Figure 5: A deeper look into the data calculated.

Figure 6: Comparison between the two cases.

How would these changes alter the environmental performance of the modified process?

Which specific impact categories would be predictably favoured and which would not?

To answer this intriguing questions a new run is made after which the "compare" function is used to generate a straightforward picture of deviations in environmental impacts of the evolved process (figure 6).

4 Discussion and conclusions

The model has been executed; the results have been displayed and finally the moment of decisions has arrived. In this last section we will show how the tool can point out guidelines to support them:

Returning to the case previously presented (figure 6), it is quite remarkable the difference between the two bars in 'fossil fuels' category (note that what really matters here are not the absolute values but the difference itself, which allows to establish comparisons): logically, the introduction of waste as a fuel for the cement process helps with saving fossil resources.

Also, according to the model predictions, there is a slight decrement in 'climate change' impact (due to a reduction in global carbon dioxide releases by 4%). However, the tool warns of a possible small increment in 'acidification' and 'respiratory inorganics'.

If these two lastly commented factors are not critical, the inclusion of alternative fuels in this plant that has served us as an example, seems not only to have few contraindications but also to improve the overall process' environmental performance

In addition to this, we must not forget that, after all, it is waste what we are valorizing in the process, so another question that might just come up -at least under the government's point of view- is whether the cement kiln is the best way of disposing this waste (when comparing with other options such as incineration or dumping).

As we have observed in figure 5, the tool is able to provide detailed enough information to support this kind of decisions as well. In case credentials are required, the cement plant manager could submit a report based on these data to the local authorities showing the emission levels predicted in the new scenario for asked pollutants.

Afterwards, it would be government's task to gather data regarding the other alternatives, compare them, and objectively select 'the best option'.

A few last words

Frankly, 'the best option' is not always that easy to be discerned because other economic or social factors -not considered in this tool- take part as well, and by any means must be ignored.

In spite of this fact, we are sure that this software tool will help with clarifying waste management criteria for cement production process, as far as environmental issues are concerned, by anticipating impacts under a life-cycle perspective prior to implementation.

To sum up, it is clear that alternative materials and fuels valorization is a quite demanding practice and requires strict analysis, monitoring and constant information. However, superior cost-effectiveness and advances made towards a more sustainable process are without any doubt worthwhile rewards.

In that sense, in the context of an increasing desire for ensuring our present needs without compromising future chances, we can count on this dynamic modelling software to take cement production towards a new step on sustainability.

References

[1] EIPPCB, BREF for the Cement and Lime Manufacturing Industries, 2001
[2] CEMBUREAU, Environmental Benefits of Using Alternative Fuels in Cement Production, 1999
[3] VDZ, Environmental Data of the German Cement Industry, 2002
[4] Larrion M., Revisión Estratégica del Proceso de Producción del Cemento Pórtland (ACV), PROMA 2001 Environmental Engineering Congress
[5] PRè consultants, http://www.pre.nl/eco-indicator99/default.htm

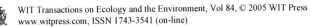

Waste statistics surveys

M. Zitnik
Department for Environment and Energy Statistics,
Statistical Office of the Republic of Slovenia

Abstract

In the European Union the modern environmental protection policy and related legislation focus on preventing negative impacts on the environment that are the result of activities conducted by people. These nevertheless strive to do this also by abandoning the use of harmful substances, activities and procedures, the effects of which can cause permanent damage to the environment.

The fundamental principle of environmental protection is thus prevention.

For enforcing this principle, basic information must be provided on the basis of which certain measures can be adopted. The data on the amount of waste generated and on waste management are also very important for proper policy-making. For the data to be relevant and correct, it is, of course, necessary to implement accurate data collection, processing and analysis, which is provided by statistical surveys in these fields. However, these surveys need to be harmonised with the legislation governing the field of waste in individual countries as well as in the European Union.

The paper attempts to show individual waste streams, statistical collection of these data, their processing and requirements that we have to take into consideration in our work (Waste Statistic Regulation).

Keywords: waste, statistical survey, handling of waste, list of waste, waste statistics regulation, NACE classification.

1 Introduction

Waste is any material or object, which the owner or possessor cannot or does not want to use, does not need, is disturbing or damaging to him and he discharges it, intends or has to discharge it.

Waste is also any material or object which is to be collected, processed, disposed or transported as prescribed due to environmental protection or other public benefit [2].

Despite intensive efforts to reduce the amount of waste, it keeps increasing every year, and is consequently harming the environment. Harmful impacts on the environment, which are related to waste, are mainly the pollution of subterranean and surface waters, the pollution of soil, our health is endangered by poisonous gas emissions, dust particles, scents and the greenhouse effects which all result from methane emissions from waste landfill sites.

Accurate records on the existing waste amounts and waste management are of vital importance for the prevention of dangerous waste-related influences, proper environmental policy, and for proper decisions in this area. Data on the existing waste amounts and waste management are obtained with the help of waste statistics surveys.

Bringing the waste data collection in line with the standards, laid down by the European Union, is one of important steps to be taken by every EU Member State. The statistics on waste data collection in an individual country is of key importance for satisfactory control in the area of waste politics and its future course.

2 Lifecycle of industrial and municipal waste

2.1 Industrial waste

From its origin to its final recovering or disposal procedure waste goes through a number of different stages or travels a number of different paths.

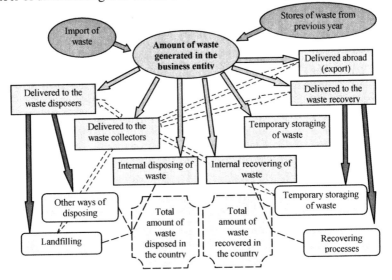

Figure 1:   Cycle of industrial waste.

Industrial waste is the result of production and service activities in individual business entities. Business entities can then decide whether to reuse that waste in the production process or to dispose it on their own. That is the case of internal waste management, which includes the internal waste recovering and/or disposing process. However, business entities can leave that waste to other business entities for future waste recovery or disposal. In that case waste goes from waste collectors to waste recyclers or disposers, or directly to waste recyclers or disposers who finally recycle or dispose waste.

2.2 Municipal and similar waste

The cycle of municipal waste is slightly different. Municipal waste is mostly produced in households, which landfill it into waste containers for mixed municipal waste, separately into waste containers designated for separate collected fractions (e.g. paper, glass, packaging), or deliver it to the waste collection centres. The collection of municipal waste is then conducted by public waste services, which transport the mixed municipal waste to public waste landfill sites, and separately collect waste to processors or waste removers.

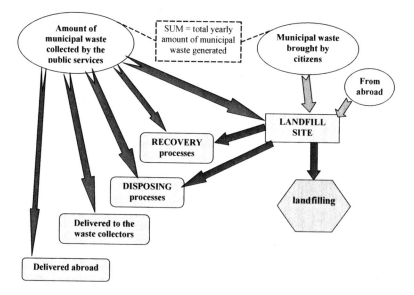

Figure 2:   Cycle of municipal waste.

3   Requirements and needs for a statistical data entry

Regarding the waste cycles, the collection of data on waste can be conducted in a number of ways. Statistical data collection for industrial waste is conducted via three different sources.

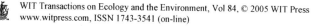

The first source of the statistical data in the EU is the business entity, where waste is generated. Here the following can be controlled: the amount of waste generated, the types of waste, the amount of internally recovered or disposed waste, the amount of temporarily stored waste and the amount of waste, handed over to another business entity with the intention of recovering and/or disposing this waste. The act [2] regulates that waste is to be temporarily stored up to a year after it has been produced, before the final recovery or disposal procedure. The business entity also communicates the accurate data on the amount of waste, transported abroad or exported.

This method of data collection is very accurate, as the data are received from the source; however, it demands a lot of effort and is expensive due to a large number of business entities. It is difficult to include all business entities, coming from a certain country and being potential waste producers, into the survey. It is therefore wiser to implement sample survey, and later recalculate the results to the total population.

The second source of statistical data are waste collectors. Waste collectors are those business entities that have a waste collecting licence, issued by the competent ministries. Waste producers hand waste over to waste collectors who then transport it to recyclers or disposers. Data received from waste collectors are seen as a control bridge between waste producers and waste recyclers and/or disposers. Very important data, received from data collectors, is the amount of waste, imported into a country with the intention of managing that waste in that country, and the amount of waste, received from business entities with the intention of exporting it out of the country.

The third source of statistical data on waste is waste recyclers and/or disposers, who have to obtain a waste collecting licence, issued by the competent ministries. Only those types of waste are to be recycled or disposed, and only according to those procedures, for which a licence has been issued. Waste recyclers and/or disposers communicate the data on the amount of waste and on recycling and/or disposing methods of the individual types of waste.

To ensure comparable results, waste statistics is to be prepared according to the set classification system, in an appropriate form, and within specified time limits after the reference year has ended. These conditions are laid down in the Waste Statistics Regulation [1], according to which the MS statistical offices are required to communicate data to the Statistical Office of the European Communities - Eurostat.

3.1 Waste Statistics Regulation [1]

The Waste Statistic Regulation (WSR) was adopted in November 2002. All EU Member States will have to meet the Regulation requirements and from June 2006 onwards communicate the required data for the year 2004.

In line with the Directive, waste statistics will cover the areas of waste development, recovery and disposal, waste export and import. When preparing the statistics, the countries must apply the statistics waste nomenclature (EWC-Stat).

The collection of data, which must meet the quality and accuracy conditions, can in some countries be conducted with the help of statistical surveys, administrative and other sources, statistical evaluations on the basis of samples or assessments of assessors in the area of waste, or with the combination of the above-mentioned possibilities.

In order to reduce the administrative burden on small business entities, the statistical survey do not include business entities with less than 10 employees, except for those, which significantly contribute to waste production with their activity. WSR also defines that waste statistics must encompass all areas of activity from A to Q according to the NACE Rev 1 Classification, which means that all service activities are included as well, as shown in Table 1. The data communicated must also include waste produced in households and waste resulting from recovery and/or waste disposal procedures. Data on waste must be deployed according to the EWC-Stat list. The unit for all types of waste is 1000 tonnes, whereas the quantity of dry material is additionally indicated for the waste group 'sludge'.

Table 1:   Activities according to NACE classification.

1	A	Agriculture, hunting and forestry
2	B	Fishing
3	C	Mining and quarrying
4	DA	Manufacture of food products, beverages and tobacco
5	DB+DC	Manufacture of textiles and textile products + Manufacture of leather and leather products
6	DD	Manufacture of wood and wood products
7	DE	Manufacture of pulp, paper and paper products; publishing and printing
8	DF	Manufacture of coke, refined petroleum products and nuclear fuel
9	DG+DH	Manufacture of chemicals, chemical products, man-made fibres + manufacture of rubber and plastic products
10	DI	Manufacture of other non-metallic mineral products
11	DJ	Manufacture of basic metals and fabricated metal products
12	DK+DL+DM	Manufacture of machinery and equipment + Manufacture of electrical and optical equipment + Manufacture of transport equipment
13	DN without 37	Manufacturing n.e.c.
14	E	Electricity, gas, steam and hot water supply
15	F	Construction
16	G-Q except 90 and 51.57	Services activities: Wholesale and retail trade; Repair of motor vehicles, motor cycles and personal and household goods + Hotels and Restaurants + Transports, storage and communications + Financial intermediation + Real estate, renting and business activities + Public administration, defence and compulsory social security + Education + Health and Social Work + Other community, social and personal activities
17	37	Recycling
18	51.57	Wholesale of waste and scrap
19	90	Sewage and refuse disposal, sanitation and similar activities
20		Waste generated by households

Statistics must be prepared for all recovery and disposal facilities. The waste statistics excludes the facilities if their activity in waste management is limited to recycling of waste on the site, where the waste was generated.

Statistics on recovering and disposal procedures has to be prepared for a number of working facilities and to focus on their performance and total quantity of waste, processed according to the procedures of incineration, operations which may lead to recovery and disposal (other than incineration).

In recovering and disposal it has to be marked, according to which procedure of recovery (R) or disposal (D) the waste was managed. The recovering procedures are divided into 13 different groups (from R1 to R13) and the disposal procedures into 15 groups (from D1 to D15).

3.2 The waste statistics questionnaire

In case of statistical data collection through a statistical survey adequate questionnaires and methodological materials must be prepared. The questionnaire structure and appearance are not set out by the Regulation, thus each country makes its own questionnaire for data collection.

These questionnaires, completed by the reporting units, help obtain the relevant data. These questionnaires may contain individual questions on reporting units, their activity and the types of waste they generate. At the same time they also contain tables that include numerical data on quantities and types of generated waste and waste management.

Questionnaires on waste are very extensive and it is difficult to complete them in most EU Member States, therefore methodology materials containing precise instructions for their completion are enclosed.

3.3 Valid lists of waste

Individual countries can conduct a statistical survey on waste with the help of different lists of waste. Lists to be used in line with the current legislation in force in the EU are EWC-Stat[1] and List of Waste (LoW) [2]. Nevertheless, individual countries can establish their national classification lists of waste, according to which data are collected. However, these lists must be harmonised and translatable into required formats. The required data on waste, classified according to EWC-Stat will have to be transmitted to Eurostat by the Statistical Offices. Therefore a conversion table from LoW can already be found in the Regulation [1].

3.3.1 EWC-Stat
The above-mentioned WSR lays down the EWC-Stat Classification List, which is prepared in relation to the material basis of waste and encompasses 30 types of different waste. Waste is further classified into hazardous and non-hazardous waste. Data on the quantity resulting is needed for each group of waste.

Table 2:   EWC-Stat list.

	Code	Description	Type	
1	01.1	Spent solvents	-	Hazardous
2	01.2	Acid, alkaline or saline wastes	Non-hazardous	Hazardous
3	01.3	Used oils	-	Hazardous
4	02	Spent chemical catalysts Chemical preparation wastes	Non-hazardous	Hazardous
5	03.1	Chemical deposits and residues	Non-hazardous	Hazardous
6	03.2	Industrial effluent sludges	Non-hazardous	Hazardous
7	05	Health care and biological wastes	Non-hazardous	Hazardous
8	06	Metallic wastes	Non-hazardous	Hazardous
9	07.1	Glass wastes	Non-hazardous	Hazardous
10	07.2	Paper and cardboard wastes	Non-hazardous	-
11	07.3	Rubber wastes	Non-hazardous	-
12	07.4	Plastic wastes	Non-hazardous	-
13	07.5	Wood wastes	Non-hazardous	Hazardous
14	07.6	Textile wastes	Non-hazardous	
15	07.7	Waste containing PCB	-	Hazardous
16	08	Discarded equipment	Non-hazardous	Hazardous
17	08.1	Discarded vehicles	Non-hazardous	Hazardous
18	08.41	Batteries and accumulators wastes	Non-hazardous	Hazardous
19	09	Animal and vegetal wastes	Non-hazardous	-
20	09.11	Animal waste of food preparation and products	Non-hazardous	-
21	09.3	Animal faeces, urine and manure	Non-hazardous	-
22	10.1	Household and similar wastes	Non-hazardous	-
23	10.2	Mixed and undifferentiated materials	Non-hazardous	Hazardous
24	10.3	Sorting residues	Non-hazardous	Hazardous
25	11	Common sludges	Non-hazardous	-
26	11.3	Dredging spoils	Non-hazardous	-
27	12.1+ 12.2+ 12.3+ 12.5	Mineral wastes (excl combustion wastes, contaminated soils and polluted dredging spoils)	Non-hazardous	Hazardous
28	12.4	Combustion wastes	Non-hazardous	Hazardous
29	12.6	Contaminated soils and polluted dredging spoils	-	Hazardous
30	13	Solidified, stabilised or vitrified wastes	Non-hazardous	Hazardous

3.3.2 List of Waste (LoW)

The classification list of waste, which is in compliance with the Regulation of the European Commission [2] and is valid from the year 2001, classifies waste according to its origin and regardless of its material basis. It is divided into 20 thematic groups of waste, which are further divided into waste subgroups, and the subgroups are further broken down into individual types of waste. Each waste, indicated in the Classification List, has a six-digit code. In addition to this code, the hazardous waste also carries the following mark: *.

Classification list of waste thus encompasses 839 types of waste, 405 types of which are hazardous waste.

Individual groups of waste are:

Group 01	Wastes resulting from exploration, mining, quarrying, and physical and chemical treatment of minerals
Group 02	Wastes from agriculture, horticulture, aquaculture, forestry, hunting and fishing, food preparation and processing
Group 03	Wastes from wood processing and the production of panels and furniture, pulp, paper and cardboard
Group 04	Wastes from the leather, fur and textile industries
Group 05	Wastes from petroleum refining, natural gas purification and pyrolytic treatment of coal
Group 06	Wastes from inorganic chemical processes
Group 07	Wastes from organic chemical processes
Group 08	Wastes from the manufacture, formulation, supply and use (mfsu) of coatings (paints, varnishes and vitreous enamels), adhesives, sealants and printing inks
Group 09	Wastes from the photographic industry
Group 10	Wastes from thermal processes
Group 11	Wastes from chemical surface treatment and coating of metals and other materials; non-ferrous hydro-metallurgy
Group 12	Wastes from shaping and physical and mechanical surface treatment of metals and plastics
Group 13	Oil wastes and wastes of liquid fuels (except edible oils, and those in chapters 05, 12 and 19)
Group 14	Waste organic solvents, refrigerants and propellants (except 07 and 08)
Group 15	Waste packaging; absorbents, wiping cloths, filter materials and protective clothing not otherwise specified
Group 16	Wastes not otherwise specified in the list
Group 17	Construction and demolition wastes (including excavated soil from contaminated sites)
Group 18	Wastes from human or animal health care and/or related research (except kitchen and restaurant wastes not arising from immediate health care)
Group 19	Wastes from waste management facilities, off-site waste water treatment plants and the preparation of water intended for human consumption and water for industrial use
Group 20	Municipal wastes (household waste and similar commercial, industrial and institutional wastes) including separately collected fractions

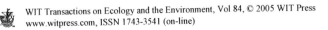

4 Workflow of the statistical survey

The statistical survey is conducted according to the pre-defined procedures:

- preparation of methodology for the survey implementation;
- preparation of methodology materials in accordance with the set methodology;
- preparation of questionnaire for data collection;
- selection of target group (reporting units);
- preparation of directory of reporting units according to the requirements, set out in the Regulation [1];
- sending of the questionnaires and methodology materials to reporting units;
- collection of completed questionnaires;
- preparation of a programme for data entry and control;
- visual and computer control of acquired data;
- contacting reporting units and correcting mistakes;
- processing of final data;
- preparation of publication tables;
- analysis of results, acquired by the survey;
- publication of results in internal, national and international publications.

5 Conclusion

The basic principle of the environmental protection is preventing negative impacts of man on the environment. For the implementation of this principle, statistical information must be provided, on the basis of which final decisions are adopted at the local or on state level. Information on environmental problems of the economic development is necessary for the policy-making of balanced development. On the next level the information is transformed into environmental accounts. Environmental accounts are indicators that point out, how much different layers of the society contribute to national and international environmental aims.

Quality data acquired with the help of statistical surveys are needed to establish adequate and accurate indicators of environment. The cooperation between reporting units and data collection offices is of vital importance for the quality data collection and precise analyses. The bigger the cooperation, the more qualitative and accurate is the environmental indicators, which lead to better political solutions.

The state of the environment we live in greatly depends upon human beings, and with timely action and/or correct solutions only can we keep it clean and useful for generations to come.

References

[1] The Waste Statistic Regulation: Regulation (EC) No 2150/2002 of the European Parliament and of the Council of 25 November 2002 on waste statistics (Text with EEA relevance), Official Journal L 332, 09/12/2002 P. 0001 - 0036
[2] Rules on waste management, Official Journal of the Republic of Slovenia No. 20/01 and 13/03

Development of fuel briquettes from oil palm wastes

M. S. Aris[1], S. Hassan[1], O. Mamat[1] & K. Sabil[2]
[1]Department of Mechanical Engineering,
Universiti Teknologi Petronas, Malaysia
[2]Department of Chemical Engineering,
Universiti Teknologi Petronas, Malaysia

Abstract

Current utilization of oil palm waste is used in mill boilers to produce steam, and electricity through a back pressure turbine. The reuse of waste material reduces operation costs, negative environmental effects and dependency on conventional fuels. This paper focuses on the development of briquettes from oil palm waste to enhance its utilization as fuel. Several aspects of improvement to the physical properties as well as energy content were taken into account in this study. A total of eight tests were conducted for different ratios of shell, fiber and binder mixtures as well as varying the type of binder material used. Varying briquette pressing pressures were also considered in these tests. Results show good physical properties in terms of durability, impact and compressive strength for a 36:54:10 ratio by mass of fiber, shell and waste paper briquette with 5.7% ash and 5.24% moisture content. The gross calorific value of 22.4 MJ/kg indicates good energy content of the briquette. The briquette pressing pressure of 159 MPa was used after discovering that it had an outright positive effect on almost all physical and energy components for all combinations tested. The results obtained from this study shows a 36% increase in energy content from a similar study conducted on oil palm briquettes using other binder material. There was also a substantial increase in physical properties for the above ratio and binder material as compared to studies conducted by others
Keywords: fuel briquettes, oil palm waste, briquette mixture ratio.

 WIT Transactions on Ecology and the Environment, Vol 84, © 2005 WIT Press
www.witpress.com, ISSN 1743-3541 (on-line)

1   Introduction

Malaysia is the world largest producer and exporter of palm oil. In terms of the world oil and fat exports, the country contributes 51% and 62% respectively [1]. For three consecutive years since 2001, the production of crude palm oil (CPO) in Malaysia had increased from 11.80 to 13.35 million tones. In these three years as well, the total export value of palm oil products constituting of CPO, palm kernel oil, palm kernel cake, oleo chemicals and finished products had increased from RM 14.22 billion to RM 26.15 billion. The increasing trend in production and exports were mainly due the expansion of the oil palm planted area, well distribution of rainfall and constant sunshine throughout of the year. The total area under oil palm cultivation in 2001 was approximately 3.5 million hectares, while in 2003, it increased to 3.79 million hectares.

In oil palm crops, fresh fruit bunches (FFB), CPO and palm kernel oil constitute only 10% of the total FFB. The remaining 90% are waste material and identified as fibre, shell, empty fruit bunches (EFB) and palm oil mill effluent (POME).

Studies indicate the potential for energy recovery from oil palm waste due to its significant carbon content. The low ash and sulfur contents are also desirable qualities to have in a fuel.

1.1   Waste from the palm oil process

The waste generated in a typical palm oil mill is significant. With the current number of operating palm oil mills standing at 370 throughout the country, the amount of waste produced is estimated to be 16.5×10^6 ty^{-1} [2]. This figure is substantially higher when compared to the 6.425×10^6 ty^{-1} estimated municipal solid waste (MSW) produced in the country [3]. Although a portion of the oil palm waste is reused to fire up the mill boilers, the remaining amount is left as heaps of waste close to the mill. Open burning is sometimes used to rid of the access waste. Attempts to reuse the waste as fertilizers in the oil palm plantation prove to be only a temporary solution due to the limited quantity used. Furthermore, the economic feasibility of reusing the waste as fertilizers is questionable due to its application limitations and low demand. External usage of oil palm waste can be explored with the use of current technology. However this involves cost and the need for a constant volume of supply for it to be commercially viable.

One of the best options available to handle oil palm waste is to take it through the biomass densification route i.e. Briquetting or Pelleting. The end product expected from this process is a higher density fuel having reasonable mechanical and combustion properties. This will allow for improved storage and handling as well as energy content per kg of briquette produced. The development of fuel briquettes therefore, is a method of improving the energy recovery potential from oil palm waste. The utilization of oil palm waste as fuel is further supported by the increasing production of biomass energy from its current contribution of 14% of the world's energy needs [4]. Also, owing to the fact that biomass waste is "carbon neutral", the reuse of oil palm waste for energy recovery would address environmental concerns over burning fuel by increasing the use of renewable energy in our energy supply.

1.2 Palm briquettes

Briquetting involves the compaction of biomass at very high pressures. Ground oil palm particles and binder material are compressed in a die to produce briquettes. These products have significantly smaller volume than the original biomass and thus have a higher volumetric energy density (VED) making them a more compact source of energy, easier to transport and store than natural biomass.

The briquettes not only can be used as the mill boiler fuel, it could also be transported for use elsewhere without significant storage and handling issues to resolve.

The comparison from previous studies on the mechanical and combustion properties of current oil palm briquettes against some selected waste materials (rice husk, coconut fiber, peanut shell and sawdust) show reasonable values to prompt further investigation. A higher heating value (HHV) of 16 MJ/kg as compared to 16.5 and 17 MJ/kg for peanut and coconut fiber respectively was indicative of its good combustion properties. It had a moderate shear strength (100bar die pressure) of 35 N as compared to coconut fiber – 70 N and sawdust – 95 N.

Apart from having reasonable combustion and mechanical properties, other factors justifying the development work of oil palm fuel briquettes include the current access waste scenario at palm oil mills, environmental issues relating to the burning of fossil fuels, energy savings and the storage and handling of waste fuel.

2 Methodology

The focus and objectives of this development work was the improvement of the oil palm briquettes' mechanical and combustion properties. This was achieved through conducting tests, to identify the best combination of fiber, shell and binder weight ratios. The constraint imposed for this study is that all the components forming the briquettes had to be made from 100% waste material, including the binder.

The process involved in the development studies include identifying appropriate waste materials, binders, briquette preparation at different mixture ratios, testing for combustion and mechanical properties and analysing results.

The waste material selected was oil palm waste after considering the factors mentioned earlier. The binder material selected for testing was waste paper. Starch was also used at some point for comparison purposes. The combination of tests to determine the mechanical and combustion properties were based on the amount of fiber, shell and binder material used. The samples were prepared according to the following ratio. For presentation purposes, the samples are referred to using the percentage of shell and fiber over the total weight of shell and fiber instead of the total weight of the sample (with binder).

Table 1:   Sample identification.

Sample No.	Shell, % of total sample weight	Fiber, % of total sample weight	Binder, Fixed at 5% of total sample weight	Binder type	Shell, % of shell and fiber weight	Fiber, % of shell and fiber weight	Load (kN)	Pressure (MPa)
1	54	36	10	Paper	60	40	200	159
2	45	45	10	Paper	50	50	200	159
3	36	54	10	Paper	40	60	200	159
4	54	36	10	Starch	60	40	200	159
5	45	45	10	Starch	50	50	200	159
6	36	54	10	Starch	40	60	200	159
7	54	36	10	Paper	60	40	150	119.35
8	54	36	10	Paper	60	40	100	79.57
9	54	36	10	Paper	60	40	50	39.78
10	54	36	-	-	60	40	200	159
11	-	100	-	-	-	100	200	159
12	100	-	-	-	100	-	200	159

The maximum load applied during the test was limited to the pressing equipment capacity. The amount applied however was comparable to previous work [5, 6] conducted for oil palm and other waste material combinations. Only nominal values of the results associated with the samples tested are presented in this paper.

2.1 Experimental setup

The type of experiments conducted was selected based on previous work by other researches [2, 4, 5, 6]. This was to ensure the results obtained had a basis for comparison. Strict standard procedures outlined in the ASTM guidelines were maintained throughout the experiment to guarantee repeatability and quality of the data obtained.

Sample preparation was an important task in which would determine the outcome of the study. A total of 12 sample types were studied and for each sample type, 3 briquettes were prepared for testing. The sample preparation procedure consisted of pretreatment, grinding and sieving, preparation and mixing of binder material and pressing.

There were a total of eight tests for the mechanical and combustion properties conducted in this study. The mechanical tests involved Crack (drop test), Stability (relax density), Durability (% remaining mass) and immerse test (water resistance). The combustion property tests were Proximate/Ultimate Analysis (ASTM D3172-97-1999, D3173-96-1999, D3175-89a-1999), Burning Rate (TGA) and Calorific Value (Bomb Calorimeter).

3 Results and discussions

The results reported some interesting findings in relation to the mechanical and combustion properties of the oil palm briquettes. The test results and discussions are presented in the following order:

1.   Combustion Properties – Ultimate and Proximate Analysis, Ignitability, and Calorific Value
2.   Mechanical Properties – Crack, Stability, Durability, Immersion and Compressive Analysis.

3.1 Combustion properties

3.1.1 Ultimate and proximate analysis
Results from the ultimate and proximate analysis conducted using the appropriate standards are shown in the following tables.

Table 2:   Proximate analysis.

No	Sample	Moisture (%)	Volatile Matter (%)	Fixed Carbon (%)	Ash (%)
1	60:40 Paper	5.24	68.04	21.00	5.71
2	50:50 Paper	10.29	67.25	20.40	6.06
3	40:60 Paper	6.51	67.03	18.79	6.33
4	60:40 Starch	6.68	69.43	21.12	5.76
5	50:50 Starch	7.41	68.40	19.31	5.87
6	40:60 Starch	7.27	67.28	16.55	6.90
7	60:40 (150kN)	7.35	68.56	21.49	5.60
8	60:40 (100kN)	6.06	68.33	20.15	5.45
9	60:40 (50kN)	N/A			
10	60:40	5.17	65.95	23.53	5.35
11	Fiber	8.02	67.02	16.63	8.33
12	Shell	N/A			

Table 3:   Ultimate analysis.

No	Sample	Carbon %	Hydrogen %	Nitrogen %	Sulfur %
1	40:60 (p)	42	7.055	0.827	0.349
2	40:60 (s)	41.99	5.743	5.427	0.109
3	50:50 (p)	42.075	5.868	0.582	0.117
4	50:50 (s)	43.435	5.635	0.521	0.149
5	60:40 (p)	45.7	6.229	0.806	0.113
6	60:40 (s)	40.995	5.306	6.987	0.089
7	60:40:00	42.335	4.682	2.694	0.1
8	60:40 (150kN)	40.065	4.912	0.476	0.071
9	60:40 (100kN)	45.025	5.092	0.901	0.111
10	60:40 (50kN)	43.78	5.647	1.146	0.038
11	Fiber	N/A			
12	Shell	N/A			

The above analysis was used to determine the elemental content of the briquettes at the respective mixture ratios and pressing pressures. The content would have a direct effect on the energy content and emissions (burning stage) of the briquette as well as secondary effects on the mechanical strength.

It can be seen that the shell rich briquette (60: 40) contains higher amounts of carbon as compared to the other mixtures both at low and high pressing pressures. This mixture also had lower sulfur content throughout the pressure range and also when starch was used as a binder. The findings were further confirmed thorough the proximate analysis results for fixed carbon.

In terms of ash and moisture content, the shell rich briquette recorded low values. The moisture amount indicates higher energy content of the briquette while the low ash reduces residues and operational difficulties. Volatile matter however was higher for the shell rich briquette at 100kN while having close values for the other mixture ratios and pressing pressures. Volatiles are also considered to contribute to good burning characteristics.

3.1.2 Ignition test
The ignitability of a briquette is important as it determines the time taken for the fuel to light up. Based on the results obtained, it can be seen that the shell rich briquettes was 55% faster to ignite as compared to the fiber rich sample, in which indicates good ignition quality. The shorter ignition time for shell rich samples could be attributed to its higher fuel density as compared to the fiber rich sample. This finding was also found to be true for other waste fuel briquettes as reported by Bhattacharya et al [8].

3.1.3 Calorific value
The calorific value of a fuel is often used as a main measure of fuel quality. The tests conducted in this study had found significant improvements in the calorific

value of the fuel briquettes as compared to other studies [2, 3, 5, 6]. Among the samples tested, the fiber rich briquette proved to have possessed higher calorific value compared to the shell rich sample. The use of starch binder with the shell rich sample however proved the opposite. The excellent results from the use of starch binders however only worked for the shell rich sample. When used for other mixture ratios, the calorific value seems to decrease. The following figure shows the calorific values of the samples tested and also in comparison with different waste materials done by others.

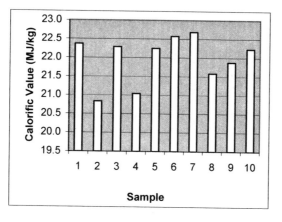

Figure 1:   Calorific value of samples.

It is also worth mentioning that higher calorific had resulted for briquettes pressed at higher pressures. This reason behind this observation is due to the increase in density of the fuel briquettes.

3.2 Mechanical properties

3.2.1 Crack analysis
As part of the briquette strength assessment, a crack analysis was performed via a drop test. At 0.83 m, a radial crack propagation of 26 mm suggest that the 50:50 shell-fiber-paper mixture was the most intact. When compared with the starch binder, results show a drastic improvement for the fiber rich sample. On the whole the starch bounded samples displayed slightly better results for all the mixture ratios. This was expected due to the glutinous nature of starch as compared to paper. Similar results were also observed from an earlier research work conducted by Hussain et al [2].

3.2.2 Stability analysis
An important mechanical property of fuel briquettes made from waste material is its stability or expansion length. Readings of briquette diameter recorded within a 1 week period as suggested by Chin and Siddiqui [10] saw no expansion. Readings taken after week 3 however recorded a maximum 4.6% increase among samples tested. This value is very much lower when compared to briquettes

made from other materials which reached as high as 150%, as reported by Wamunkonya and Jenkins [4].

The fiber rich samples with paper binders recorded the least expansion after the 3 week period. The reason could be related to the length of the fibers and paper which acted to hold the briquettes together for a longer time.

An obvious finding related to the briquette pressing pressures was that the expansion length had decreased as a result of increased pressure. Also observed was the larger expansion for samples without binders as compared to those with binders, justifying the need to include it in the sample mixtures.

3.2.3 Durability analysis
Results obtained show higher durability for samples using paper binder as opposed to starch, between 98.8% and 99.5%. The durability was also higher for fiber rich samples and those made at higher pressure. There are similarities between the durability and stability analysis in that the fiber rich samples seem to have a stronger hold over the briquettes, hence resisting expansion and shattering.

3.2.4 Immersion test
The immersion or water resistance test was popular amongst researches as it was performed by Hussain et al [2] and Yaman et al [6] for oil palm and other waste material. The results from this study show comparable values to olive refuse and paper mill waste [6] but rather substandard when compared to the work done on oil palm briquettes as reported by Hussain et al [2].

For the samples tested in this study, the fiber rich, high pressure and starch bounded briquettes seem to have displayed better water resistance results at 36 seconds. Faster immersion time was recorded for the 50:50 and 60:40 samples. Both binders showed similar trends with starch recording higher immersion time of between 31 to 36 seconds. The presence of starch in the sample seems to have had an effect on the water resistance of the briquettes. The earlier comparison with the work done by Hussain et al [2] was valid as they had used a high starch mixture in their briquette sample.

As for the immersion test for briquettes pressed at different pressures, as expected, higher pressures produced briquettes which were more resistant to immersion. The immersion time ranged from 23 to 27 seconds for pressures between 100 and 200 kN (60:40 sample) respectively.

3.2.5 Compression test
All the samples placed under a compression force of 5 kN managed to withstand the load, suggesting high briquette compressive strength. Due to equipment limitation, the tests had to be terminated at the current test value. However, earlier work done on oil palm briquettes [2], indicate much lower briquette compressive strengths. This was probably due to the much higher briquette height used. The height chosen for the current study was only 5 mm and had proven to withstand high compressive loads especially from buckling failure.

4 Conclusions

From the experiments carried out, it was generally found that the shell rich briquette (60:40) with waste paper binder recorded good combustion properties. Although the mechanical properties (immersion, crack and durability) were better for the fiber rich samples, the difference in results were not far off. This was an indication that the shell rich briquette possessed suitable fuel briquette qualities and should be further studied for dimension optimization. This study also suggests the use of waste paper as the binder material based on the good test results obtained. The usage of 100% waste material should also be a factor supporting the use of waste paper in fuel briquettes.

There is high commercial potential for the development of fuel briquettes from oil palm waste and future studies should take it a step further. Other potential waste materials should also be explored and to find the optimum component mixture for the briquettes. As mentioned earlier, cost factors should also be included in future studies for commercial evaluations to be made possible.

References

[1]   Malaysian Palm Oil Board, www.mpob.gov.my
[2]   Hussain, Z., Z, Zainal, Z, Abdullah. Briquetting of Palm Fiber and Shell from the Processing of Palm Nuts to Palm Oil. Biomass and Bioenergy, pp. 505-509, 2002.
[3]   Sivapalan, K., Muhd Noor, M.Y., Sopian, K., Samsuddin, A.H., Energy Potential from Municipal Solid Waste in Malaysia. Renewable Energy, pp. 559-567, 2003.
[4]   Wamunkonya, L., Jenkins, B., Durability and Relaxation of Sawdust and Wheat Straw Briquettes as Possible Fuel for Kenya. Biomass and Bioenergy, pp. 175-179, 1995.
[5]   Demirbas, A., Physical Properties of Briquettes from Waste Paper and Wheat Straw Mixtures, Energy Conversion and Management, pp. 437-445, 1999.
[6]   Yaman, S., Sahan, M., Haykiri-Acma, H., Sesen, K., Kucukbayrak, S., Production of Fuel Briquettes from Olive Oil Refuse and Paper Mill Waste. Fuel Processing Technology, pp. 23-31, 2000.
[7]   Demirbas, A., Combustion Characteristics of Different Biomass Fuels. Progress in Energy and Combustion Science, pp. 219-230, 2004.
[8]   Bhattacharya, S.C., Shetcha, R.M., Biotechnology and Economic. RFFIC Asian Institute of Technology, Bangkok, 1990
[9]   Turns, S.R., An Introduction to Combustion, Concepts and Applications, MCGraw Hill, Inc, Singapore, pp. 1-67, 1996
[10] Chin, O.C., Siddiqui', K.M., Characteristics of Some Biomass Briquettes Prepared Under Modest Die Pressures. Biomass and Bioenergy, pp. 223-228, 2000

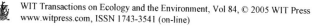

Section 6
Resources management

Potential assessment of the use of green energy to meet the electricity demand in a land aquafarm

C.-M. Lai[1] & T.-H. Lin[2]
[1]Department of Construction Technology, Leader University, Taiwan
[2]Department of Mechanical Engineering,
National Cheng-Kung University, Taiwan

Abstract

Due to the widespread aquaculture at coastal areas in Taiwan and high wind power potential at the sites, it is worth carrying out the potential assessments of green energy used for aquaculture in Taiwan. This study aimed at the practical installation of a small-scale wind power system. First, the weather data acquired from the newly installed weather station, the Weibull Probability Distribution and power curve provided by the generator manufacturer were used to analyze the wind power potential. After the design and planning had been completed, the small-scale wind power system was installed, being sponsored by the supporting industry. A detailed account of the installation procedure and solutions to the encountered problems were presented in the text.
Keywords: renewable energy, wind power, aquaculture.

1 Introduction

The geographical location of Taiwan is such that it has the opportunity to generate much wind power, mainly on the west coast and on nearby islands such as the Pescadores (Peng-hu). There, the annual average wind speed exceeds 5–6m/sec, yielding a wind power density of over $250W/m^2$ at 10 m height, which value favors the development of wind power. Based on an assessment of domestic wind energy and the government plan entitled, "Challenge of 2008: Project for National Development", the Energy Resource Committee of Taiwan decided in June 2000 to promote wind power over the long term. A total capacity of 1500MW is expected to be reached by the year 2020, including an

WIT Transactions on Ecology and the Environment, Vol 84, © 2005 WIT Press
www.witpress.com, ISSN 1743-3541 (on-line)

onshore capacity of 1000MW and an offshore capacity of 500MW. Fig.1 shows the primary target of wind power developed in Taiwan. Due to the widespread aquaculture at coastal area in Taiwan and high wind power potential in their sites, it is worthy to carry out the technical potential assessments of small-scale wind power system used for aquaculture in Taiwan. This study aimed at the assessment of the practical installation and operation performance.

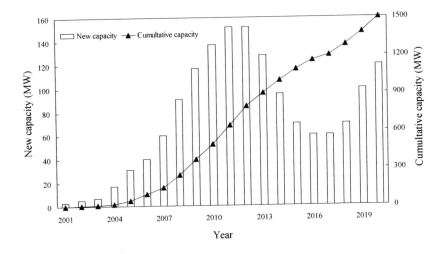

Figure 1:   Primary target of wind power development in Taiwan.

2   A brief introduction to the wind power system

The application logic of large-scale wind power systems differs completely from that of small scale power systems. Large-scale wind power systems are established to increase domestic power capacity, by connection to the electricity network. Small-scale wind power emphasizes "self-reliance". The generated power is provided to regional industries, which thus reduce their dependency on power from utilities. In Taiwan, the main benefit is to reduce the peak power load. Small-scale wind power can be subcategorized into three types - micro, mid-range and mini one, as depicted in Table 1 [1]. The components of a small-scale wind power system and their special features are described in Reference [2]. The uncertainties in the quality of wind (related to a lack of wind or a wind speed that is too low to start up the turbines) and the periods of demand for energy are such that a small-scale power system must use sub-devices to reduce the risk of power leakage. These sub-devices include battery systems, diesel generators, solar power systems or power generated from utilities, among others.

A simple small-scale wind power system includes a main body (turbines and generator), a charging controller, a battery system, current inverters or a utility connection system, among others, as shown in Fig. 2. The application modes of such components can be varied. For instance, the input to the connection

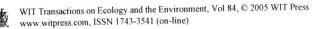

box/charging controller not only receives power generated from wind, but also can be connected to a photovoltaic system, an emergency system or a diesel generator.

Table 1:   Classification of small-scale wind power system [1].

category	Power output (KW)	Radius of the turbine (m)	Max. rotation speed (rpm)	Generator	Applications
micro	1	1.5	700	PM	Electric fences, yachts
mid-range	5	2.5	400	PM or induction	Remote houses
mini	20-50	5	200	PM or induction	Remote community

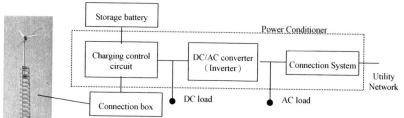

Figure 2:   Illustrative diagram of the small-scale wind power system.

3 Local wind resource assessment

3.1 Analytical method for predicting long-term wind energy availability

The Weibull Probability Distribution (h(v)) is a mathematical expression which has been found to provide a good approximation to the measured wind speed distribution [2].

$$h(v) = \left(\frac{k}{c}\right)\left(\frac{v}{c}\right)^{(k-1)} e^{-\left(\frac{v}{c}\right)^k} \qquad (1)$$

where,

$h(v)$ =probability associated with wind speed v in a certain period. Unit: %

v =wind speed Unit: m/s

k =shape parameter Unit : dimensionless

c =scale parameter Unit : m/s

K and c are important parameters, and can be determined from the average wind speed V and the standard deviation σ.

$$C=V/0.89 \tag{2}$$
$$V=c\,\gamma\,(1+k) \tag{3}$$
$$\sigma^2=c^2\,(\,\gamma\,(1+2/k)-\gamma\,(1+1/k))\quad(\gamma : \text{Gamma Function}) \tag{4}$$

when the height of the wind-power devices (H_2) differs from the height at which the wind-speed is measured (H_1), a formula proposed by G. Hellman, can be used to predict the wind speeds at height H_2

$$V_2 = V_1\left(\frac{h_2}{h_1}\right)^\alpha \tag{5}$$

where α is the friction coefficient of the surface. The site of this research was on a plane, and therefore, α is fixed at 0.15 in this study [2].

3.2 Wind speed measurement

The guidelines for properly planning and designing wind-power systems depend on accurately estimating wind energy potential. The power system in this investigation was located in a suburb close to the ocean. Its background environment differs greatly from those of the central weather bureau ground stations, since both Tainan station and Yung-Kang station that in cities. Weather information from the Tainan Salt Factory from 1983 to 1995, and detailed weather information recorded to help in the planning of the Cheng-Si Li Coastal Recreation Area by the Tainan City Government, was obtained. However, the data from such reports cover only up to 1995. Given the changes in the landscape, the actual wind-speed recently at the site must be understood. A weather measurement station at a height of 4m was activated next to the aquafarm (DAVIS Instruments) to measure factors such as the wind-speed, the direction of the wind, the temperature and the humidity and rainfall. The sampling interval was fixed at 10 minutes.

4 Planning, designing and establishing a small-scale wind power system

4.1 Planning and designing

The wind power system adopted herein had a small capacity. All components of the system are easily available on the open market for small-scale power systems. The designed and established electrical supply system therefore met the requirements for generating low-voltage electricity.

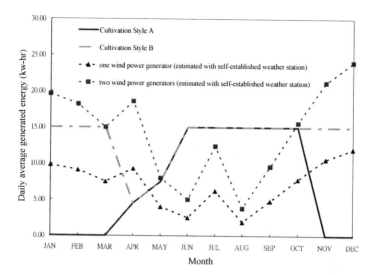

Figure 3:   Electricity demand and estimated energy output of wind power.

(1) Demand for power

The type of aquatic product, the amount of oxygen required, the scale of the aquafarm, the water circulation devices and the equipment in the farmhouse all affect the demand for power and the mode of operation.   A milkfish aquafarming generally uses one of two cultivating styles, as illustrated in Fig. 3.

   (a) Style A: Cultivation period of six months.
      Every March, young fish are released into the aquafarm; October is the harvesting month. Gas irrigators, as shown in Fig.4, are operated for promoting oxygen exposure from dusk to dawn of the following day. In the initial stage of the cultivation, only one gas irrigator is required for an aquafarm with an area of about 1000 m^2 and the operating time is short. However, as the young fish grow, the second gas irrigator is used and the operation time is gradually increased. This is the most often used approach to cultivating milkfish in aquafarms in Taiwan.

Figure 4:   Gas irrigators can be easily found at an aquafarm in Taiwan.

(b) Style B: Year cultivation (also called "through the winter cultivation")
The young fish are allowed to grow until after the harvesting month of October; they are harvested only in the following year to meet the demand of the market.

(2) The adoption of the small-scale wind-power system
The monthly and annual energy generation data with a 1.05 safety margin can be estimated from the monthly distributive data derived from the weather statistics and the power curve of the GaleForce Passat 1.4kW wind power generator, as shown in Fig. 3. The ratio of theoretical energy generation to actual energy generation can be estimated for each generator. Hence, the number of generators and the type of generators that should be used to replace to satisfy the demand for energy can be determined. Table 2 presents the load coverage for the two cultivation styles.

Table 2:   Estimation of the electricity generation.

Measured weather data	Jan.	Feb.	Mar.	April	May	Jun.	July	Aug.	Sep.	Oct.	Nov.	Dec.
Monthly average wind speed (m/s)	4	3.7	3.2	3.7	2.2	1.8	2.78	1.68	2.44	3.59	3.67	4.12
Standard deviation of wind speed	1.81	1.59	1.69	1.3	1.2	0.98	1.35	0.96	1.35	1.31	1.27	1.37
k (shape parameter)	2.37	2.46	2.03	3.11	1.65	1.94	2.19	1.84	1.9	4.02	3.17	3.04
c (scale parameter)	4.51	4.14	3.66	4.14	2.42	2.03	3.14	1.89	2.75	2.99	4.1	4.59
Electricity information (GaleForce Passat@1.4KW)												
Daily average power output (W)	430	399	329	408	175	110	272	83	211	342	465	526
Daily average energy output (kWh)	9.8	9.1	7.5	9.3	4.0	2.5	6.2	1.9	4.8	7.8	10.6	12
monthly energy output (kWh)	304	255	140	279	124	75	192	59	144	242	318	372
Relationship between energy output and demand (one wind power generator @1.4KW) unit：%												
Load coverage ratio of Style A	100%	100%	100%	100%	53%	17%	41%	13%	32%	52%	100%	100%
Load coverage ratio of Style B	65%	61%	50%	100%	53%	17%	41%	13%	32%	52%	71%	80%
Relationship between energy output and demand (two wind power generators @1.4KW) unit：%												
Load coverage ratio of Style A	100%	100%	100%	100%	100%	33%	83%	25%	64%	100%	100%	100%
Load coverage ratio of Style B	100%	100%	100%	100%	100%	33%	83%	25%	64%	100%	100%	100%

Note: Safety Margin was set to be 5%.
    ▨ : energy output that can not meet the demand (estimated).

The results reveal that under the common cultivation style (Cultivation Style A), one small-scale power generator can supply sufficient energy only in the early stage of the growth of the young fish, for around 1.5 months.   The generated electricity is insufficient after mid-April. Two wind power generators also cannot provide enough power in May. At the peak hours, even two sets of generators cannot meet the demand for energy for Style A Cultivation. The low wind speed in the summer and autumn at the research site is responsible for the lack of energy generated even when the number of devices is increased. One set of wind power generators could not provide sufficient energy to meet the demand in the one-year cultivation mode (Style B Cultivation). However, the strong northeastern wind in winter at the research site enables the generated energy to meet the need for electricity from October to the following March. The same problem arises in summer and autumn when the power output is too low. Therefore, the other climatic feature, high exposure to sun, is considered. The high potential for wind-power and the solar energy at the research site, given that they appear to generate power in a complimentary manner makes worthwhile the study of the potential for using a small-scale wind and supplementary photovoltaic power system.

Figure 5:   The wind power tower was installed on an RC foundation.

Figure 6:   The turbines were built on the ground and integrated into the frame.

Figure 7:   This study used a power crane to suspend the entire tower frame.

4.2 Establishment

The correctness of the installation strongly influences the safety and efficiency of a small-scale wind power system. The steps in the installation must be followed to prevent accidents.

5   Conclusion

This work analyzed the wind power potential, using a Weibull Probability Distribution based on weather data acquired from the Central Weather Bureau and a newly installed weather observation station. The wind power system used in this work had a small capacity and the components of the system are commonly available on the market. The design and construction of the power system were suitable for lower-voltage use. After the design and planning had been completed, small-scale wind power systems were installed, being sponsored by the supporting industry. Accurate and detailed account of the installation procedure and the solutions to the encountered problems were presented.

Acknowledgement

The authors would like to thank the National Science Council of the Republic of China for financially supporting this research under Contract No. NSC 90-2623-7-426-001.

References

[1]   Claudsen PD, Wood DH. Research and Development Issues for Small Wind Turbines. Renewable Energy 1999; 16: 922-927.
[2]   Mukund RP. Wind and Solar Power System. CRC Press 1999.

Sustainable management of human water consumption: a preliminary case study in North-eastern Portugal

N. Haie[1], J. E. R. Queirós[2] & L. F. Fernandes[3]
[1]Civil Engineering Department, University of Minho, Campus of Azurem, Guimaraes, Portugal
[2]Townhall Assembly of the Municipality of Bragança, Portugal
[3]CETAV, Universidade de Trás-os-Montes e Alto Douro (UTAD), Portugal

Abstract

Portugal is experiencing a drought. Since April, 2005, about 80% of the country, including our study area, has had a severe to extreme drought. Hence, there are a lot of difficulties with regards to the current water needs for human consumption, agriculture, ecosystem, etc. This is a scenario that can repeat itself more often in the future because of the effects of climate change. Proper water management is one of the key issues that can make sustainability practical.

We studied and utilized a multi-dimensional model in order to capture the dynamics of water use in Portugal. To begin with, we used a municipality in the North-eastern part of the country called Bragança. Although it is more humid than the southern municipalities, nonetheless, it has had severe water problems this year. We used four different dimensions to understand the sustainability of the water supply system of the municipality. These are: price, quantity of the water used, quality of the water used, and the mode of life. Their values were in binomial form: price (free / pay, as some part of the system operated free of charge), quantity of water (low / high, a threshold was defined to separate the two levels), quality of water (satisfactory / unsatisfactory, as related to the legal norms), and mode of life (rural / urban, a crude first step characterization of this social parameter). The results show that the worst scenario reflects the following situation (free, high, unsatisfactory, rural). And the best is (pay, low, satisfactory, urban). This preliminary study has made the authorities of the municipality more aware of the problems of the system and a number of them are being solved. However, to make the model more useful towards a sustainable management, its further refinement is underway, to be also applied to other regions.
Keywords: human water consumption, North-east Portugal, multi-dimensional model, quantity and quality of water, water price, mode of life.

WIT Transactions on Ecology and the Environment, Vol 84, © 2005 WIT Press
www.witpress.com, ISSN 1743-3541 (on-line)

1   Introduction

Water—long thought of as being a never ending resource—has become one of the major problems of this new century. Either it is too much and causes floods that devastate whatever is on their way or not much of it is available and causes countless human sufferings and deaths. Particularly of great importance is the amount of water necessary in each region for human consumption. Worldwide some 6,000 children die every day from diseases associated with unsafe water and poor sanitation [1]. On the other hand the phenomenon of climate change is affecting more and more the normal water availability of the regions.

The first Earth Day was celebrated in 1970, some 35 short years ago. In the meantime, environment takes great proportions and now sustainability is the greatest challenge before the human race. " …, it was hardly a secret—or even a point in dispute—that progress in implementing sustainable development has been extremely disappointing since the 1992 Earth Summit, with poverty deepening and environmental degradation worsening." [2].

Portugal is experiencing a drought. In April, 2005, about 80% of the country, including our study area, has a severe to extreme drought [3]. Hence, there are a lot of difficulties in regards to the current water needs for human consumption, agriculture, ecosystem, etc. This is a scenario that can repeat itself more often in the future because of the effects of climate change. Water is one of the key factors, if not the key factor, in great parts of Portugal.

In this study, we are trying to understand in a better way the inter-relationships between various players in order to make water management more sustainable for the future.

2   A preliminary model

The European Water Framework Directive [4] is a legal instrument in many countries of the European Union. Its articles refer to the necessity of dealing with the price, quantity of the water used and its quality. But water, as essential as it is in all aspects of life particularly for human consumption, is also related to the mode of life of the inhabitants of a region. Hence, these four dimensions formed our preliminary model for assessing the sustainability of water consumption systems in Portugal.

Data and reliable measurements is one of our major problems. Consequently early on we decided to use qualitative data, at least as a first trial, in order to characterize the water systems. A binary approach seemed sufficient to conclude some of our first results. So the dimensions got the following values:

- Price (P): the impact of price on sustainability is very important and indeed an important factor in any management scheme [5]. But besides doing a full range economic analysis and the fact that part of our systems are free, we decided to make a division on those who pay (whatever the amount) and those who use the system for free. Hence the values for this parameter are: free (f) or pay (p).

- Quantity of water used (Q): This is the quantity of water consumed at the level of analysis (parish or municipality). It is of great importance particularly for a country with drought scenarios as Portugal. In order to use a two-valued parameter, a threshold was defined as to be the average value of the water consumed for all the system. A minimum per household or some other values could have been used. In any rate, this threshold water consumption gives the values for this parameter as low (l) or high (h).
- Quality of water used (L): No doubt one of the important dimensions of any water model for human consumption is its quality. Quality is determined according to the national norms in vigour. But norms are of different categories, one being more tolerable than the other, for example a toxic substance. The determination of whether a substance has violated its norms or not, sometimes is very costly and out of reach of some systems. According to these legal specifications, the value of the quality of water used can be satisfactory (s) or unsatisfactory (u).
- Mode of life (M): Different people in different countries have different habits and their water use changes. Such changes can be linked to a number of socio-economic indicators for a full range of types of living. Because Portugal is the 2nd most rural country in the European Union [6], for the time being, two values were used for this descriptor: rural (r) or urban (u).

Figure 1:   Localizing the District of Bragança.

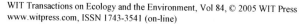

3 Application

3.1 The study area

Bragança is the name of a North-east Portuguese District (Figure 1), a Municipality and a city. The Municipality consist of 49 parishes, 3 of them being urban and 46 rural [7]. The average area of a parish is 24 km^2 with a population density that ranges between about 3 and 1560 habitants/km^2. The average temperature is about 12.2 °C and an average rainfall of about 740 mm. The first canal structure for water distribution dates back to the 1st century A.D. Today the water supply system is divided between the City Hall of Bragança (a central system) and each individual parish. There exist 108 of these independent smaller water supply systems. Also there are those who use wells to get to groundwater for their use.

3.2 Results

The following figures depict some of the results produced for the current case. Figures 2 and 3 give the prices and the mode of life in relation to the population. As can be seen, almost half of the population live in either urban or rural, with the former living in only about 5% of the area of the municipality. It is also typical of all the districts of the country that most of its parishes are of the rural type. Although most of the municipality pays for the water services, but 35% of the population is still using free water. This indeed is one of the problems and socially very difficult to solve.

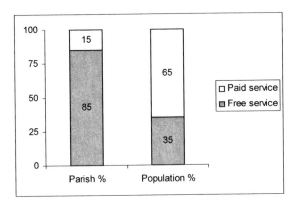

Figure 2:   Prices of the water used.

The relations of the quantity of water used are illustrated in Figures 4 and 5. The urban population uses some 5 m^3 per habitant per month of water. On the contrary of the rural area that triples that amount. The weighted average of these two values gives 9 m^3 which has served for comparison purposes.

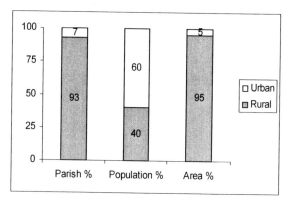

Figure 3:   Mode of life in the Municipality.

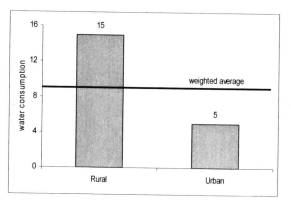

Figure 4:   Quantity of water used (m³/habitant/month) for different modes of life.

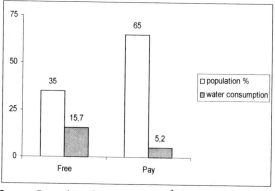

Figure 5:   Quantity of water used (m³/habitant/month) vs. price.

Figures 6 and 7 portray the quality of the water used in the Municipality of Bragança. During last few years, on the average, about 10% of the analyses were found outside of the allowable limits (Legally Unsatisfactory Results). However some of these LURs, are alarming and needed immediate care.

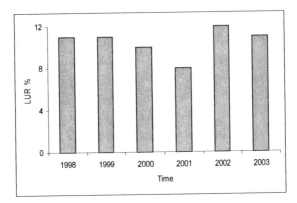

Figure 6: Legally unsatisfactory results (violation of the allowable limits) for the Municipality of Bragança.

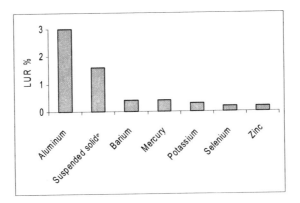

Figure 7: LUR (Legally unsatisfactory results, violation of the maximum allowable limits) for a few parameters for the Municipality of Bragança.

Residual Chlorine is one of the major problems of the municipality. Almost 75% of analyses showed results outside the Lower and Upper Allowable Limits: LAL of 100 and UAL of 500 mg/L (Figure 8). Its solution is not easy because there are 108 independent water supply systems and the local capacities for handling such situations is very limited, particularly in the rural areas.

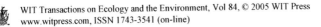

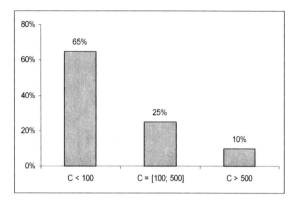

Figure 8: Average concentration of residual chlorine (C, mg/L) for the year 2002 for the Municipality.

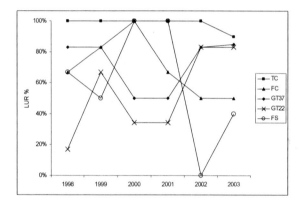

Figure 9: LUR in the parish of Gimonde, a rural area with the worst quality results.

Figures 9 and 10 show LUR for selected parishes. Gimonde, a rural area showed the worst results. Rossas, having the highest population density, showed results that are alarming. How does a water system grow to be sustainable, such as becoming more resistant to these abnormalities?

Table 1 shows the relationships between the 4 dimensions discussed in this paper. It also shows these relations for an ideal water supply system. To better understand the table, make questions based on the first column. For example: In an urban area (Mu), should we use high quantity of water (Qh)? Table shows that for the municipality in study, the answer is not defined because some use high quantity and others low. However in an ideal system, the answer should be "No" (N). Of course there should be care in how Qh has been defined.

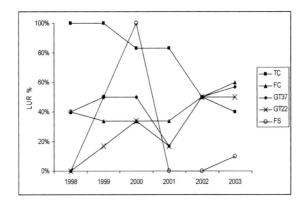

Figure 10: LUR in the parish of Santa Comba de Rossas, a rural area with the highest population density

Table 1: Relationships of the 4 dimensions used in characterising the water supply systems of the Municipality of Bragança vs. an ideal system.

	Pf	Pp	Ls	Lu	Ql	Qh
Ls	-/N	Y/Y				
Lu	Y/N	-/N				
Ql	-/N	Y/Y	Y/Y	-/N		
Qh	Y/N	Y/Y	-/-	Y/N		
Mr	Y/Y	Y/Y	Y/Y	Y/N	-/Y	Y/N
Mu	-/N	Y/Y	Y/Y	-/N	Y/Y	-/N

However to analyse Table 1, it should be noted that it portrays a bi-dimensional function and consequently some apparent contradictions. In reality the policies for sustainable development of the systems should be defined in response to multiple factors. Anyhow, for the Municipality of Bragança, the Table found some problems that needed solutions.

4 Conclusions

Sustainable planning is the greatest issue of our time. Conceptually very easy and appealing but trying to put it in practice and manage systems have proved and will continue to prove very difficult. The fundamental reason for such an apparent discrepancy is the extreme complexity inherent in a sustainable system, hence holistic and unified approaches are very necessary.

Water touches almost everything in our civilization. It is a complex phenomena coupled with another multifaceted issue – climate change. Consequently water resources management is one of the key problems in the world of sustainable development. It is obvious that not only quantity and quality of the water used for human consumption are of paramount importance, but the prices and the economy of the services as well as the mode of life of the individuals play important roles. Particularly in drought situations, like Portugal, groundwater becomes a strategic resource and its sustainable use equally strategic [8].

Our case study with the Municipality of Bragança, showed that a rather cursory analysis of the parameters of the water supply system can indicate severe problems, that the local population, politicians and institutions were not aware. It is important to analyse the systems in multiple dimensions through proper indicator development. It was found that the free water accessible by a sizable portion of the municipality is unsustainable and although the values for the year 2003 shown above are not final, the trend indicates an unsustainable system. Residual Chlorine is indeed one of the major problems and the authorities now are determined to deal with it.

References

[1] International Year of Freshwater 2003, accessed on 10 of May of 2005, http://www.un.org/events/water

[2] Johannesburg Summit 2002, accessed on 11 of May 2005, http://www.johannesburgsummit.org

[3] National Institute of Water, "Seca em Portugal Continental: Relatório Quinzenal, 15 de Abril de 2005", (in Portuguese), 2005

[4] Water Framework Directive (WFD), "Directive 2000/60/EC of the European Parliament and of the Council of 23 October 2000 establishing a framework for Community action in the field of water policy". Official Journal of the European Communities 22.12.2000, L 327 pp. 1-72.

[5] Ferreira da Silva, Júlio, Naim Haie and J. Pereira Vieira, "Custos instantâneos de "Produção" de Água Potável - Enfoque nos sistemas com origens afectadas pela intrusão salina", (in Portuguese), IV SILUSBA - Simpósio de Hidráulica e Recursos Hídricos dos Países de Língua Oficial Portuguesa, Coimbra, 24-26 Maio 1999.

[6] United Nations Population Fund (UNFPA), "The State of World Population 2004", www.unfpa.org

[7] Queirós, Joaquim, "Qualidade da Água para Consumo Humano no Concelho de Bragança – Estado Actual e Perspectivas Futuras", (in Portuguese), Master these, 2004.

[8] Haie, N., "Groundwater Resources per Inhabitant Indicator", Groundwater Resources Sustainability Indicators, UNESCO, Paris, 7-9 April 2004

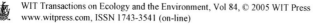

Updating the institutional debate in sustainable water management and planning

K. F. Wong
Department of Geography and Environmental Science,
University of Bradford, U.K.

Abstract

While acknowledging the contributions of the neo-institutional thinking in sustainable water management, this paper challenges the inadequate understanding of institutions in shaping human action in water consumption and financing. Strong belief in the efficiency of new formal institutional arrangements by active process of institutional design and crafting in pursuit of optimal resource management fails to consider the social impact on, and the cultural influence of, the public's perception of sustainable use of water. This paper also shows that over-reliance on legal regulations can create disincentives. Downplaying the socially-embedded institutions undermines the effectiveness of bureaucratic institutions. The case study of England and Wales casts doubt on the universal application of the design principles for disregarding social and cultural contexts.
Keywords: sustainable water management, institutions, privatisation, decentralisation, community participation, England and Wales.

1   Introduction

Current calls for new institutional reforms in water management by the World Bank [1], OECD and the European Union marks a significant concept difference from the previous ones. Underpinned by a new set of institutional thinking, the Sustainable Water Management Framework departs from the dualism between state ownership and full privatisation, and moves towards the partnerships amongst privatised water companies, public regulators and the community. Institutional strengthening by decentralisation, stakeholder participation and effective enforcement, as the Framework suggests, can simultaneously achieve water efficiency, social equity and ecological sustainability.

The new strategic water management is under the influence of neo-institutionalism. The neo-institutional theory asserts that the failure of achieving sustainable use of water lies in inadequate incentives and weak regulatory arrangements. Institutional intervention, by purposefully crafting desirable forms of rules, regulations and coordination with water agencies, is an attempt to provide a long-term solution with low enforcement costs.

The Framework has made significant contributions since it takes a holistic approach to water resources. It re-focuses on demand-side management (Griffiths [2]). There are, however, concerns about the universal application of the institutional design and crafting, without adequately addressing the contextual and cultural specificity (Mehta *et al* [3]).

The objective of this paper, therefore, is to explore the neo-institutional approach to water management and examine the effectiveness of the new institutional arrangements. It also aims to seek a better understanding of the role of institutions in water governance, and to uncover the latent tensions within the Framework. England and Wales are chosen as a case study in this paper because they have experienced a dramatic change in water institutional structures.

2 Sustainable water management framework

The sustainable water management framework is summarised in Figure 1. The World Bank, the European Union and the International Water Association are the key players in promoting the new institutional reforms. The five elements in the Framework are: privatisation, decentralisation, stakeholder participation, effective enforcement and monitoring, and appropriate application of technology.

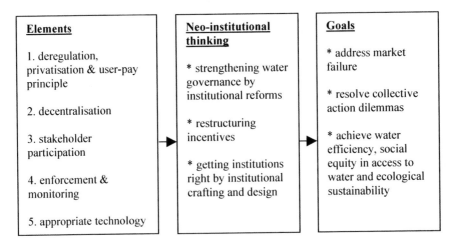

Elements	Neo-institutional thinking	Goals
1. deregulation, privatisation & user-pay principle	* strengthening water governance by institutional reforms	* address market failure
2. decentralisation	* restructuring incentives	* resolve collective action dilemmas
3. stakeholder participation		* achieve water efficiency, social equity in access to water and ecological sustainability
4. enforcement & monitoring	* getting institutions right by institutional crafting and design	
5. appropriate technology		

Figure 1: Sustainable water management framework. (Author's original diagram, ideas inspired by World Bank, OECD, EU.)

It is claimed that implementing privatisation by selling the previously state-owned water enterprises to private investors brings competition, and therefore better services. The principle of full recovery of costs of water services is considered to provide adequate incentives for efficient use of water. A decentralised approach to water regulation transfers the major responsibility to the market and the municipalities. Stakeholder participation represents a bottom-up approach. By information sharing and increasing transparency, different stakeholders feel the ownership of, and share the responsibility for, water management (Petresin [4]). Effective monitoring and enforcement mechanisms lay down clear rules about what water-using behaviour is desirable. Sanctions are applied to 'bad apples' who fail to comply with the regulations.

2.1 Neo-institutional thinking

Neo-institutionalism is distinct from old institutionalism in two aspects: firstly, it takes a broader view of institutions. Institutions do not simply mean regulations or organisations, but 'rules of the game'. It focuses not merely on the constraining nature of institutions, but also the enabling side in shaping human action (Ostrom [5]). Secondly, it does not conceive the state and private companies as necessarily mutually exclusive in water governance. It promotes the idea that they can work together closely as strategic partners. The public (to be precise, community) is also encouraged to take part in decision-making processes to feel responsibility for sustainable water management.

The failure to achieve better water management, the neo-institutionalists claim, lies in inadequate incentives, weak governance and inefficient regulatory and legal arrangements. The market alone is unable to achieve both water efficiency and social equity at the same time because of the complex nature of water. The solutions, they propose, are to restructure water-related institutions in order to get the incentives right, to redefine water as economic goods, and to change the role and perception of the public and private sectors in the water industry. Success in attaining social equity in access to water, economic efficiency and ecological sustainability lies in having 'right' institutional arrangements. The right organisational structures help to identify rights and responsibility of different stakeholders. High level of public participation generates social capital and sense of ownership that facilitates water planning. Effective enforcement and monitoring is intended to deter free-riding behaviour, so as to align individuals' private interests with collective outcomes. These new institutional arrangements are regarded as a low-cost mechanism since they secure a self-enforcing form of governance (Mansuri and Rao [6]).

There are three forms of institutions: judiciary, bureaucratic and socially-embedded. Judiciary institutions comprise the law and regulations which determine the water ownership and structure of authority. Clear sets of rights and responsibilities are laid down, so that both water and sewage providers and water users know what is expected of them. Sanctions, such as threatening to cut water supply, are used to deter free-riding behaviour and to ensure water efficiency. Bureaucratic institutions are water-use organisations and committees which make decisions about rules, access and distribution. In contrast, socially-embedded institutions are social values and norms which govern and shape our water-using behaviour. These three forms of institutions, however, are not mutually exclusive. The neo-institutional approach marks a shift from the traditionally predominant supply-oriented modes of planning to the demand-side. Distinct from neo-liberalism, the Framework promotes the 'private-public' synergy and takes a more positive view on the role of the state and community.

3   Case study: England and Wales

England and Wales have witnessed a dramatic historical transformation in water management over the past thirty years. The water industry was nationalised before 1979. The privatisation scheme under the Conservative regime in the early 1980s, however, was influenced by a strong belief that market competition was the best way to promote water efficiency and to safeguard the interests of customers. Economic regulations, therefore, were kept at a minimum level at an interim stage of deregulation. The responsibility for environmental regulation was assumed to be transferred to the shareholders in the privatised companies (Summerton [7]).

However, pressure on the government to envisage adequate regulatory protection of consumers against the interests of service providers was mounting. In 1989, the government introduced a dual system: privatised companies were responsible for providing clean water and sewage treatment while the environmental and drinking water regulation was the responsibility of separate public bodies. All these changes mark the influence of both domestic and international pressure. The changing socio-economic-political circumstances in England and Wales suggest economic arguments alone are unable to promote strategies for water institutional reforms. They require social legitimacy and political capacity. The Water Framework Directive by the European Union came into force in 2000. The paradigm shift about the understanding of the nature of water as both economic and public goods also plays a role in encouraging stronger regulation and legislation in water governance.

3.1   Regulatory structure

The regulatory framework functioning in England and Wales is summarised in Table 1. Ten water and sewage companies and 16 water companies are responsible for distributing and managing potable water supply and waste-water treatment. They are also required to design, implement and maintain the water infrastructure. Different public bodies oversee the water sector in different aspects. The Drinking Water Inspectorate (DWI) evaluates the quality of drinking water. The Office of Water Services (OFWAT) is an economic regulator which monitors the water price levels. The Environment Agency (EA) is responsible for monitoring the water environment.

Experiences in England and Wales appear to suggest that successful water management lies in strategic partnership amongst private service providers, the government and different regulators (Kinnersley [8]). The clear and simple institutional and regulatory arrangements provide adequate incentives for efficient governance. This managerial structure also tries to show that privatised water companies, under strong profit-seeking pressure, are not necessarily incompatible with long-term benefits for consumers and the environment. Whether these claims are valid in reality will be discussed in the subsequent section.

Table 1:   The division of labour in water provision and regulation.

Authority	Duties
Water companies	* provide potable water to consumers and operate and maintain infrastructure facilities
Drinking Water Inspectorate (DWI)	* evaluates the quality of drinking water
Office of Water Services (OFWAT)	* monitors water price levels
Environment Agency (EA)	* supervises waste treatment and prevents air and water pollution

4   Limitations of the neo-institutional approach

How likely are these new institutional arrangements, established with a strong focus on privatisation, regulation, decentralisation and community participation, to provide the answer to sustainable water management in England and Wales? Conceptually, the institutional perspective to strategic water management takes a 'pick and choose' approach in institutional designs. New and efficient institutions are carefully moulded, while the old and inefficient ones are abandoned or forced to transform. It also shows an instrumental view on institutions. Rules are purposefully crafted to produce desirable forms of collective action (Ostrom [5]).

The problem of this approach is that it considers institutional building as a 'unilinear model of institutional evolutionism' (Cleaver [9]) which assumes that new institutional reforms necessarily move towards higher efficiency. Another limitation is that the planned institutional interventions are designed to minimise uncertainty (Mehta *et al* [3]). Petresin [4] also argues that this approach fails to recognise the complexity of the social and natural worlds and the unpredictable outcomes of human action.

4.1 Institutions create disincentives

OECD suggests the development and application of a strong legal framework to ensure the sustainable use of water. This is based on an assumption that regulations, stressing obligation and coercion, give the right signals for individual water users to align their private interests with collective outcomes.

Regulations also guide water service providers to provide an appropriate level of service with an acceptable performance at an acceptable cost to customers. Under a right institutional framework, institutional scholars believe that the conflicts between environmentalism and entrepreneurialism are reconcilable.

Evidence, however, shows a rather different picture - regulations hinder, rather than enhance, the adoption and implementation of sustainable practices. Foxon *et al* [10] point out that: 'the imposition of institutional systems and regulatory targets will encourage the adoption of less sustainable technologies or solutions by the water industry'. In other words, the heavy reliance on laws and regulations in the water industry merely encourage seeking 'quick wins' rather than long-term, strategic and more innovative sustainable initiatives. Due to the profit-driven nature, private water companies do not have a strong incentive to do more than meet current environmental regulations. Berndtsson and Hyvönen [11] also find out that it is the laws and regulations which obstruct the implementation of sustainable alternatives to water-based sanitation system. In their words, 'conventional water-based sanitation systems are fully legal, and even mandated by the legal system' (p526). In addition, standard regulations have difficulty in meeting inter-regional variations.

4.2 Playing down the role of socially-embedded institutions

As discussed before, there are three forms of institutions: regulatory, bureaucratic and socially-embedded. In the sustainable water management framework, however, more emphasis is on the first two forms, but less on the third. Institutionalists tend to believe that formal institutions, such as laws, regulations and water organisations, are effective in ensuring effective use of water. It is also believed that 'inefficient' socially-embedded institutions are challenged and gradually be replaced by 'robust' formal institutions. The neglect of informal institutions, however, has negative impact on water sustainability. The dualism of formal and informal institutions also fails to see the interactive nature of institutional building.

Informal or socially-embedded institutions are defined as social values, norms, habits and routines guiding our everyday lives, including water consumption and perception of alternative water innovations. These institutions are the products of social and political practices. They are powerful in influencing our water-using behaviour because water-related norms and practices 'think on our behalf' (Douglas [12]), and they can both facilitate and constrain individuals in switching to more sustainable innovations. For example, to explain the failure of the riparian buffer zones in England, Ducros and Watson [13] interviewed the affected farmers about their goals, motives and values. Recognising the role of socially-embedded institutions explains why the technically sound policies can result in limited impact. Decisions made by customers are not always confined by formal institutions. The water metering system, for example, is expected to be an effective demand management measure since it is intended to increase customers' sensitivity to water consumption and the costs. Evidence, however, shows that households in the North of England deliberately consumed more water during the drought in 1995 in order to protest against the mismanagement of the Yorkshire Water company (Haughton [14]).

4.3 Over-simplification of agency

Providing adequate incentives is the central idea in the sustainable water management framework. This takes an economistic view of human behaviour, arguing that individuals take actions by constantly making the appropriate calculation of cost and benefit. This resonates with the rational choice theory, assuming that human beings are necessarily selfish and calculating, and thus they tend to cheat and abuse water. In order to avoid water wastage, heavy reliance on regulations and monitoring, such as metering, are in favour. Sanctions are considered as necessary to punish non-compliance. In the principle of water charging, Figueres *et al* [15] make this assumption explicit: 'paying for water makes people more responsible for their demand, as they *often ask for more than they really need*' (p202, my emphasis). The case of BedZED (a new housing development in the London Borough of Sutton), however, demonstrates that, even without coercion, tenants are willing to cooperate and rarely put sanitary towels, nappies or condoms down the toilets or drains (Shirley-Smith [16]). This example suggests that individuals can act altruistically and   cooperatively for sustainable development.

Agency here is defined as individual's capacity to act. The tendency to reinforce the role of water users as 'customers' or 'consumers' is problematic since this has simplified the complexity of agency. Assigning clear rights and responsibilities to customers is considered as an act of empowerment which gives them a strong sense of ownership. Encouraging customer-orientation to develop financially viable water and sanitation services regards customers as rational individuals who make water-related decisions based on economic rationality. The cost-benefit analysis attempts to establish links between the kind of service that benefits the stakeholders and what they are willing to contribute in cash. The customer-orientation, however, does not necessarily guarantee higher transparency or a louder voice to water-users in the process of decision-making. The regional privatisation of the water market in England means that water companies have a monopoly of water distribution and sewage disposal within their franchise areas. Customers cannot vote with their feet by switching to another water utilities, no matter how dissatisfied they feel about the quality of water service. In addition, the main concern of water companies is to maintain financial returns and satisfy investors and shareholders. The needs of their customers are not really a very high priority. Empowering customers to ensure higher water efficiency and sustainability, therefore, remains a myth because customers lack the real power to challenge the status quo.

4.4 Paradoxes within the sustainable management model

There are latent tensions within the strategic water framework which needs to be addressed properly. The three levels of dilemmas are: the 'efficiency-equity' paradox, the conflicting interests between water customers and shareholders, and the tension between the demand- and supply-side management. Petresin [4] proclaims that: 'water must be managed and conserved in a fair and efficient manner' (p6). This highlights that an equitable access to water is a social right. However, at the policy level, achieving water efficiency without undermining social equity needs a fine balance. Increasing water prices, for example, helps to improve efficiency, but it has negative impact on the livelihoods of the poor. Encouraging the public to participate in decision-making is also an attempt to resolve the 'efficiency-equity' paradox by instilling the sense of right of, and responsibility for, water conservation. Community participation, however, is not necessarily good for the poor since active participation demands extra time, resources and energy from the poor. Participation may be used merely as a means to improve project efficiency and to get funding from the government, rather than as an end itself to increase community ownership and commitment.

Some writers may take the view that the tension between shareholders and customers is not necessarily problematic. The obligation of the water companies to generate revenues for shareholders forces them to improve water efficiency which will then lower water prices and improve environment in the long run. In reality, however, water companies face tremendous commercial risks in business continuity. The pressure to meet the rising expectation of shareholders means that the larger the price cap, the greater the returns they can provide for shareholders. The profit-seeking image of water companies, portrayed by the media, also undermines trust between the public and the companies. When the services fall short of customers' expectations, it will easily trigger off the blame-game. During the drought in North England in 1995, for instance, the water companies accused the public of being 'culturally ignorant about the value of water' (Haughton [14]).

The sustainable water management framework plays down the dimension of power. In England, improving drinking water quality and efficiency of water use still depends heavily on development in science and technology. It is not to deny the contribution of technical know-how towards sustainability, but the traditional 'predict and provide approach', devising engineering solutions to satisfying human needs, remains strong. The blue-print ideas about project planning and implementation still dominate the intervention and institutional reforms. This atmosphere creates an unfavourable condition for community participation since local knowledge is not highly valued. The demand-side management would then easily be hijacked by the supply-oriented.

5 Conclusions

This paper has examined the currently influential neo-institutional approach to sustainable water management. The central idea of this approach is to build strategic partnership amongst private water companies, the government, public regulators and the community to achieve efficient water governance and financing. Policies such as decentralisation, community participation, effective monitoring and use of sanction, are all intended to restructure the incentive mechanisms, to craft the right forms of institutions, and to build a clear structure of authority that water companies and users can follow.

This paper does not deny the contributions that the neo-institutional thinkers have made in re-focusing the significance of institutions in shaping human action. Defining water as both economic and public goods helps to recognise that the market alone cannot achieve water efficiency, social equity in access to water and ecological sustainability. My research, however, has exposed the wide gap between the neo-institutional theory and current water realities in the case study of England and Wales. The discrepancy can be explained by the instrumental view on, and inadequate understanding of, institutions. Strong belief in the efficiency of new formal institutional arrangements by the active process of institutional design and crafting in pursuit of optimal resource management fails to consider the social impact on, and the cultural influence of, the public's perception of sustainable use of water. This paper has also showed that over-reliance on legal regulations can 'unwittingly' create disincentives. Downplaying the socially-embedded institutions undermines the effectiveness of bureaucratic institutions. My other paper [17] also uses the case study of England and Wales to illustrate that implementing sustainable water management is contextually specific, and that the universal application of the design principles is problematic.

In addressing the shortcomings, it is suggested that institutional interventions in future should consider both the micro and macro process of institutional strengthening. Institutional building cannot be separated from people's belief and livelihoods. Micro contexts matter since they provide the conditions that shape water access and consumption on the one hand and willingness and capability to pay on the other. By far, little research has been done on how individuals respond to new water regulations. Qualitative studies then should complement quantitative research to investigate the effectiveness and desirability of sustainable water management. Furthermore, the narrow focus of the sustainable water management framework on water aspects only fails to pay sufficient attention on a wider environmental concern. Only by integrating strategic water programmes into land and economic planning can the holistic approach of water management be genuinely achieved.

Acknowledgement

This paper is part of the WaND Project (Water Cycle Management for New Developments), funded by EPSRC. The writer takes full responsibility for the opinions and views expressed therein.

References

[1]   World Bank, World Development Report: Sustainable development in a dynamic world – transforming institutions, growth and quality of life. Washington, D.C., 2003.

[2] Griffiths, M., The European Water Framework Directive: an approach to integrated river basin management, Publication: European Water Association, 2002.

[3] Mehta, L., Leach, M., Newell, P., Scoones, I., Sivaramakrishnan, K. & Way, S.A., Exploring understandings of institutions and uncertainty: new directions in natural resource management, IDS discussion paper 372, Institute of Development Studies: University of Sussex (UK), 1999.

[4] Petresin, E., Slovenian water management and EU – challenge and opportunity. European Water Association, 2003.

[5] Ostrom, E., Crafting institutions for self-governing irrigation systems. ICS Press: San Francisco, 1992.

[6] Mansuri, G. & Rao, V, (eds). Evaluating community driven development: a review of the evidence. Development Research Group, The World Bank: Washington. D.C. (1st draft), 2003.

[7] Summerton, N., The British way in water. Water Policy, 1, pp.45-65, 1998.

[8] Kinnersley, D., Privatised water services in England and Wales: a mixed verdict after nearly a decade. Water Policy, 1, pp.67-71. 1998.

[9] Cleaver, F., Reinventing institutions: Bricolage and the social embeddedness of natural resource management. The European Journal of Development Research, 14(2), pp.11-30, 2002.

[10] Foxon, J., McIlkenny., G., Gilmour, D., Oltean-Dumbrava, C., Souter, N., Ashley, R., Butler, D., Pearson, P., Jowitt, P. & Moir, J., Sustainability criteria for decision support in the UK water industry. Journal of Environmental Planning and Management, 45 (2), pp.285 301, 2002.

[11] Berndtsson, J. & Hyvonen, I., Are there sustainable alternatives to water-bases sanitation system? Practical illustrations and policy issues. Water Policy, 4, pp.515-530, 2002.

[12] Douglas, M., How institutions think. Routledge: London, 1987.

[13] Ducros, C & Watson, N., Integrated land and water management in the United Kingdom: narrowing the implementation gap. Journal of Environmental Planning and Management, 45 (3), pp.304 -423, 2002.

[14] Haughton, G., Private profits – public drought: the creation of a crisis in water management for West Yorkshire. Transactions of the Institute of British Geographers, 23 (4), pp.419 -433, 1998.

[15] Figueres, C., Tortajada, C. & Rockstrom, J., (eds). Rethinking water management: innovative approach to contemporary issues. Earthscan: London, 2003.

[16] Shirley-Smith, C., Setting up water management for BedZED. Conference 'Planning for water: a major challenge for the government's new sustainable communities. London, 21 Oct, 2004.

[17] Wong, K. F., Sustainable water management in England – What can we learn from the developing world?. Engineering Sustainability Journal (forthcoming).

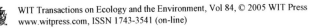

Beyond weights and discounting: decision analysis tools for integrated planning

L. Holz, G. Kuczera & J. Kalma
University of Newcastle, Australia

Abstract

An evaluation of management options can be supported with formal decision analysis tools which attempt to integrate objective and subjective information. There seems, however, to be little exploration of decision analysis tools beyond weights and discounting for the formalisation of value judgements. This paper argues that we need to look beyond weights and discounting for tools which may better reflect value judgements about: intergenerational equity and; balancing economic, social and environmental outcomes. The paper presents some alternative tools for articulating value judgements in integrated assessment.
Keywords: decision analysis, sustainability, weights, discounting.

1   Introduction

Option evaluation, in light of sustainability concerns, often requires stakeholders to weigh up a number of conflicting outcomes. Numerical weights are often assigned to each outcome to formalise this value judgement. If, for example, stakeholders consider ecosystem value to be twice as important as agricultural value, they may assign weights of 0.66 and 0.33 respectively. These weights can be used in various ways to aggregate the estimated agricultural and ecosystem performance data to simplify option evaluation. Option evaluation is further complicated by the need to consider the temporal dimension. The stakeholders, for example, may have to consider the forecasted ecological and agricultural outcomes of a project over a 30-year period. The economics literature supports the use of discount rates to simplify this evaluation problem. A discount rate allows the aggregation of data over the 30 years, albeit with less importance attached to both positive and negative impacts occurring further into the future.

A discount rate thus represents a value judgement with potential intergenerational equity implications.

Weights and discounting allow for integrated evaluation in that different types of data may be aggregated. These tools can be used to formalise value judgements about triple bottom line and intergenerational equity considerations. Weights and discounting are not the only means for formalising value judgements about these issues though. Section 2 briefly argues that we need to look beyond weights and discounting to find evaluation tools which are more effective at facilitating articulation of such value judgements. Section 3 examines methods other than applying weights, which can be used to explore and articulate preferences when multiple outcomes need to be considered. Section 4 outlines some alternative approaches for dealing with the temporal dimension.

2 Limitations of weights and discounting

Many authors argue that time preference is irrelevant when it comes to multigenerational evaluation. This is because "whole societies are quasi-immortal...and cannot be described as 'impatient'" [1] therefore positive time preferences do not apply. The focus shifts from 'what I want as a utility-maximizer' to 'what we ought to do as a society' [2]. Also, positive time preference may be a result of risk averseness [3] in which case discount rates represent an inflexible framework to handle such values [4]. Fearnside [1] argues that the moral implications of discounting are not obvious to the wider public. He advocates that weights have clearer moral implications. Intergenerational weights effectively assign voting power to each generation.

Multiple criterion decision-making (MCDM) tools, like weighting methods, can support decision making when there are different outcomes to consider. Many, [5,6,7], have recognised the need for MCDM tools to facilitate communication and a learning environment in order to aid the decision making process. There is some suggestion however, that MCDM tools may in fact discourage dialogue. There is concern, for example, that the assignment of weights may heighten conflict [8], especially if the discussion is abstract rather than context sensitive [9]. The assignment of weights to decision criteria may be a quick way to identify the core ideologies but it does not capture what is and is not negotiable for that stakeholder. Hajkowicz et al. [10] also lists concerns such as the complexity and time required for some weighting methods while Söderbaum [11] says that the "ideological orientations are often treated in a way... that is far from the vocabulary and conceptual framework of actors in public debate".

If discounting and weighting methods are to be used to aggregate subjective and objective data in option evaluation, then the resulting tradeoffs need to be examined for congruence with stakeholder preferences. Sumaila and Walters [12] argue that conventional discounting often does not correlate with human preferences due to altruistic behaviour. The congruence of aggregate evaluations with stakeholder preference is particularly a concern where questions of value are not sensitive to the decision context. A prime example of this is that many techniques for obtaining weights do not take into account the range of scores on each criterion. Imagine, for example, that a rural stakeholder stated that agricultural value was more important than ecosystem value in a land management project. If however, the set of options under consideration all perform quite well agriculturally, then the stakeholder may attach a higher weight to ecosystem performance.

In sum, there are concerns about whether weighting methods and discount values are appropriate for communicating value judgements. Their ability to facilitate articulation of value judgements and the resulting 'accuracy' of aggregated evaluation outcomes are two key issues. Padilla [13] argues that to adequately address intergenerational equity we need to move beyond making modifications to weights and discount rates. Section 3 illustrates two styles of exploration of value judgements in MCDM that move beyond assigning weights to criteria. Section 4 examines a number of alternative methods to incorporate intergenerational equity concerns into decision analysis, including Padilla's evaluation process.

3 Balancing economic, social and environmental outcomes

There are arguably three primary approaches used to explore MCDM preferences, as outlined in Figure 1. The first approach is to determine the relative importance of the criteria by which strategies are to be evaluated. Typically this involves the assignment of some weight to each criterion. These weights may then be used in additive value functions or in outranking methods to produce a partial or complete ranking of strategies.

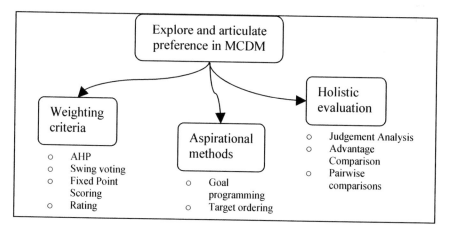

Figure 1: As illustrated, weighting criteria is not the only means to explore and articulate preferences in MCDM. The aspirational methods refer to criteria outcomes rather than the criteria themselves; in holistic evaluations strategies are evaluated based on their overall performance in a more intuitive manner.

The second approach to exploring value judgements is through reference to aspirational levels. Here the user specifies some outcome which is deemed satisfactory or desirable. The option which comes closest to this outcome is identified as the preferred decision. This approach is used in goal programming methods. This approach could be enhanced with the use of an interactive and iterative approach where (i) the user has an opportunity to gradually alter their aspirational levels in response to available strategies or (ii) where the search for strategies is guided by aspirational levels. An online overview of goal programming resources can be found through the University of Portsmouth [14].

Finally, the third approach to exploring value judgements is through holistic comparison of strategies. Here, users may be presented with a small number of options at a time and asked to weigh up the costs and benefits of each, usually through the use of some visualisation tool. The statement of preference may be used to remove unattractive solutions and direct the search for the preferred option, or it may be used to derive weights for the decision criteria. The former approach is utilised by Ximing et al. [15] and Soderberg and Kain [16] and in Multiple Objective Linear Programming techniques. The latter approach is used in multiple regression analysis techniques such as Judgement Analysis [17].

In order to better identify what performance outcomes are most important to stakeholders, an aspirational method called 'Target Ordering' was developed by the authors of the present paper. This method was also created to improve the context sensitivity of user value statements and ensure greater user control of tradeoffs between criteria while retaining simplicity. Table 3 illustrates, in the context of a water supply case study, how value judgements are articulated with this approach. This aspirational method can give a complete ranking of strategies.

Initial feedback from a workshop involving the water planning community indicates that the aspirational and holistic evaluation techniques more effectively enable articulation and communication of value judgements than weighting techniques.

Table 1:   Articulating preferences in water resource management with the Target Ordering method.

Imagine for a moment that you are in charge of supplying water to a large metropolitan centre. Now imagine that your predecessor was very ineffective and that you are faced with a high risk of running out of water (1% chance), frequent water restrictions (30% of time) and poor environmental performance (1210kWh/month and 15% of natural river flows). The decision criteria and associated targets are illustrated below. You decide that reducing risk from 1% chance of running out to 0.5% chance of running out is absolutely essential and that you would like to reduce risk to 0.3% chance before thinking about anything else. You would then like to reduce the frequency of restrictions to 15% after which you would start to think about making some environmental improvements. Your next decision is whether to improve river flow to 35%, reduce energy consumption to 1200kWh/month, reduce frequency of restrictions to 10% or reduce risk to 0.15% chance of running out.

The 'must-have' targets are used as hard constraints. Any strategy which does not achieve a 'must-have' target performance level is given an overall score of zero. The 'should' and 'could-have' prioritisation of targets is used to develop a preference value score for each strategy. The targets which are more important (i.e. to be achieved first) are assigned a higher weight. For example, the intermediate step from 0.5% to 0.3% <u>risk</u> (rank 3) has a higher weight than the intermediate step from 30% to 20% <u>frequency</u> of water restrictions (rank 4). The overall score for strategy s is then a combination of the weight assigned to each intermediate step and the normalised score for strategy s on each intermediate step:

$$score(s) = \sum_{n=Nmust}^{Ntargets} weight(n) * normscore(n,s) \qquad (1)$$

where Nmust = number of must-have targets, Ntargets = total number of targets, weight(n) is the weight assigned to the target with rank n and normscore(n,s) is strategy s' normalised score for target interval with rank n. The normalised score ranges from 0 to 1 and can be thought of as a percent achievement of the current target interval. For example, if a strategy achieves 0.4% risk, then normscore(3,s) is equal to 0.5 since only half of the interval (0.5%,0.3%) is achieved.

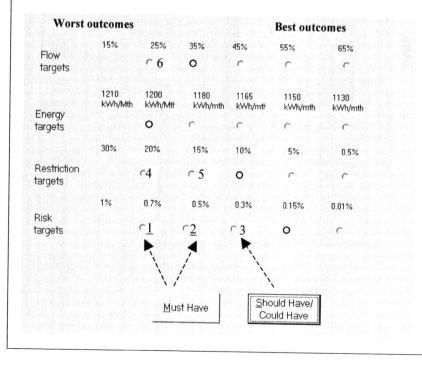

4 Balancing present and future outcomes

4.1 Evaluation of trends

Perhaps the simplest way to analyse temporal flows of costs and benefits is through graphical tools highlighting trends. Figure 2, for example, illustrates the projected regional water demand from a variety of management strategies over a 100-year period. From this, it is possible to qualitatively assess intergenerational equity. Visualisation tools may be useful if holistic evaluation methods are used. In the case of a large number of strategies or criteria, or where equity considerations must be quantified, visualisation tools will not suffice.

It may be possible to quantify trends. Sustainable Seattle [18], for example, categorises indicators based on declining, improving or neutral trends. This information may either be utilised holistically or, if preferences or constraints on the rate of change can be obtained, a ranking of strategies may be achieved quantitatively. When the predicted trends are complex, it may not be useful to represent the trend through a simple statistic. For example, several strategies in Figure 2 exhibit non-linear and multi-directional trends.

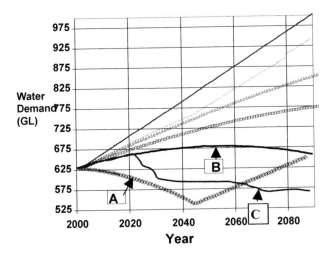

Figure 2: Hypothetical time series of predicted regional mains water demand under different demand control strategies.

4.2 Max-min rule

Within economic literature a frequently quoted interpretation of justice comes from Rawls [19] notion of 'pure procedural justice'. A common interpretation is that the option which minimises the worst possible outcome should be chosen [20, 4]. This is referred to as the max-min rule as the aim is to maximise the minimum possible welfare. This rule is often criticised for its sensitivity to

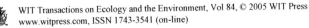

starting conditions: "For a society starting with poverty this means that it will endure poverty over all succeeding generations" [4]. The max-min rule suffers from further constraints though.

The max-min rule assumes complete egalitarianism and/ or completely risk adverse behaviour. The 'veil of ignorance' principle can be interpreted as decision making under uncertainty. Here, some degree of risk/ inequality may be preferred, if the resulting potential gains are worthwhile. Secondly, issues such as long-term trends, uncertainty of information and duration of poor and good performance are of relevance to intergenerational equity. In Figure 2 for example, if minimising water demand was the only objective, strategy A would be chosen under the max-min rule. Strategy C however has better long term prospects than strategy A. Strategy C has a short period of increasing water consumption initially, but sustains a reduction in consumption over the medium and longer terms. The max-min rule narrowly focuses on the welfare of the worst off (in this case the population in 2020), potentially to the detriment of intergenerational efficiency and better long-term trends.

4.3 Measures of fairness

Matheson et al. [21] defines three measures of fairness which may be employed to measure intergenerational equity. The first considers a fair outcome in relation to the relative stakeholder contributions, or what is deserved. The second measure considers fairness as an equal distribution of impacts. The third measure considers the needs of each group. Deviations from proportionality, equality and satisfaction of needs are aggregated separately but they may be weighted and averaged into an overall intertemporal fairness measure. This is certainly a more sophisticated approach to intergenerational equity however it is reliant on specifications of need and warranted proportion. It is possible also, that the aggregation of deviations across all generations may disguise an unfair distribution of burden.

4.4 Measures of reliability, resilience and vulnerability

Loucks [22] quantifies sustainability through measures of reliability, resilience and vulnerability of various economic, environmental, ecological and social criteria. These measures require specification of satisfactory and unsatisfactory performance levels. Reliability measures the probability that a strategy will fail to achieve satisfactory performance over some time period. Resilience measures the speed of recovery made from an unsatisfactory performance. Finally, vulnerability aggregates both the severity and duration of failure. This approach does not consider the temporal distribution of failures, therefore may be not be sufficient as an intergenerational equity measure. One generation may, for example, suffer most of the failures, which may be inequitable. This would not be revealed through measures of reliability, resilience or vulnerability of time series data.

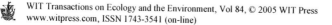

4.5 Procedurally rational analysis

Padilla [13] offers a procedure for considering intergeneration equity in the evaluation process. A critical question is whether the strategy compromises sustainability. This seems to be interpreted by Padilla as the interdisciplinary task of determining if future capacity is jeopardised. If a strategy does not jeopardise future capacity then temporal preferences should be articulated through intergenerational weights. A critical part of Padilla's evaluation process is what should be done if future capacity is jeopardised. Where it is not feasible to avoid or compensation for harm the project should not be implemented.

4.6 Target ordering approach

Rather than apply weights to each generation, the Target Ordering approach starts by specifying the "must", "should" and "could-have" outcomes for each generation. Rather than ask "does it compromise sustainability" the Target Ordering approach, as illustrated in Figure 3, asks "does it fail must-have requirements for any generation"? If there is no option which achieves all must-have requirements for each generation then deviations from must-have targets are analysed. This is somewhat akin to the fairness measure of; 'deviations from satisfying needs', as outlined in section 4.3. If it is perceived that future generations have different needs, then different 'must have' targets can be specified for that generation. Similarly, if it is felt that different outcomes should be achieved sometime in the future, then different 'should have' outcomes can be specified. This flexibility provides a tool to specify a planned path out of poverty or other poor performance levels.

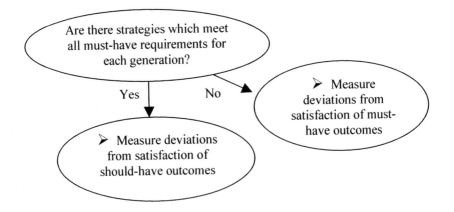

Figure 3:   Target ordering analysis and intergenerational equity.

An aggregate score is derived for each option by adding the degree of deviation from "must" or "should-have" outcomes in each generation. It is possible, with the aggregation of each generation's deviation score, that an unfair distribution of burden is disguised. Therefore other measures may be useful such as the max-min analysis of the deviation scores. A max-min analysis in this context does not need to suffer from sensitivity to initial conditions. This is because different "must" and "should-have" targets can be set for each generation. Hence if poor conditions prevail now, then the targets can be relaxed for the short term. The other concerns with max-min analysis, as outlined in section 4.2 would still hold. The decision makers would need to weigh up the aggregate and max-min analysis. They need to consider how important it is that each generation achieves an equal proportion of their wants and needs (max-min); and how important it is that there is efficient achievement of wants and needs across generations (aggregate). The max-min and aggregate measures could be combined into a single measure. This could be achieved, for example, through assigning some weight to each measure or through a Target Ordering analysis.

5 Conclusion

While weights and discount rates may predominate, there is a need to find more effective means to formalise value judgements in planning. This paper has given a brief overview of why we need to look beyond weights and discount rates and outlined several methods for doing so. Each method, including the new Target Ordering method introduced by the authors, has its own strengths and limitations and many of these have been examined. It is hoped that this brief overview will inspire planners to engage with a broader set of decision analysis tools which may allow more effective articulation of value judgements in sustainability planning.

References

[1] Fearnside, P.M., Time preference in global warming calculations: a proposal for a unified index. Ecological Economics, 41, pp.21–31, 2002.

[2] Sagoff, M. Aggregation and deliberation in valuing environmental public goods: A look beyond contingent pricing. Ecological Economics, 24, pp.213–230, 1998.

[3] Roelofsma, P.H.M.P., Modelling intertemporal choices: An anomaly approach. Acta Psychologica, 93, pp.5-22, 1996.

[4] Nijkamp, P. & van den Bergh, J.C.J.M., Operationalizing sustainable development: dynamic ecological economic models. Ecological Economics, 4, pp.11-33, 1991

[5] Belton, V. & Stewart, T.J., Multiple Criteria Decision Analysis: An Integrated Approach, Kluwer Academic Publishers, 2002.

[6] Pereira, A.G. & Quintana, S.C., From Technocratic to Participatory Decision Support Systems: Responding to the New Governance Initiatives. Journal of Geographic Information and Decision Analysis, 6(2), pp.95-107, 2002.

[7]   Stahl, C.H., Cimorelli, A.J. & and Chow, A.H., A New Approach to Environmental Decision Analysis: Multi-criteria Integrated Resource Assessment (MIRA). Bulletin of Science, Technology & Society, 22(6), pp.443-459, 2002.

[8]   MIKA, Notes from MIKA-workshop: Methodologies for integration of knowledge areas, Swedish national research programme (Urban Water), 2002.

[9]   Mintzberg, H., The rise and fall of strategic planning, Pearson Education, London, 2000

[10]   Hajkowicz, S., Young, M., Wheeler, S., MacDonald, D.H., & Young, D., Supporting Decisions: Understanding Natural Resource Management Assessment Techniques. A report to the Land and Water Resources Research and Development Corporation, CSIRO Land and Water, Australia, 2000.

[11]   Söderbaum, P., Decision Processes and Decision-making in relation to Sustainable Development and Democracy – Where do we stand?. ESEE Frontiers 2 Conference European Applications in Ecological Economics, Tenerife, Canary Islands, 2003

[12]   Sumaila, U.R., & Walters, C., Intergenerational discounting: a new intuitive approach. Ecological Economics, 52, pp.135– 142, 2005.

[13]   Padilla, E., Intergenerational equity and sustainability. Ecological Economics, 41, pp.69–83, 2002.

[14]   University of Portsmouth, Goal Programming Resources, www.tech.port.ac.uk/research/mmg/GPResources.html

[15]   Ximing, C., Lasdon, L. & Michelsen, A. M., Group Decision Making in Water Resources Planning Using Multiple Objective Analysis. Journal of Water Resources Planning and Management, 130(1), pp.4-14, 2004.

[16]   Soderberg, H. & Kain, J.H., Integrating Knowledge or Aggregating Data-Multi-Criteria Approaches for sustainable water and waste systems. DMinUCE London, 2002.

[17]   Stewart, T.R, Judgement analysis: procedures. Human Judgement. The SJT View, ed. B. Brehmer & C.R.B Joyce., Amsterdam, Elsevier Science Publishers B.V., 1988.

[18]   www.sustainableseattle.org/

[19]   Rawls, J. A theory of justice, Oxford University Press, 1999.

[20]   Woodward, R.T., Sustainability as Intergenerational fairness: efficiency, uncertainty, and numerical methods. American J. Agri. Econ., 82, pp.581-593, 2000.

[21]   Matheson, S., Lence, B. & Fürst, J. Distributive fairness considerations in sustainable project selection. Hydrological sciences, 42(2), pp.531-548 1997.

[22]   Loucks, D.P., Quantifying trends in system sustainability. Hydrological Sciences, 42(4), pp.513-530, 1997.

Means to ends: success attributes of regional NRM

J. A. Williams[1], R. J. S. Beeton[1] & G. T. McDonald[2]
[1]School of Natural and Rural Systems Management,
University of Queensland, Australia
[2]CSIRO Sustainable Ecosystems, Australia

Abstract

Whilst the investment in natural resource management in Australia both in financial and regulatory terms is at its highest point, Australia's natural systems are in decline. This trend in degradation of the resource base is seen worldwide with studies indicating that humanity's collective demands on natural resources first surpassed the earth's regenerative capacity around 1980. The complexity of natural resource management, which is socially an evolving 'discipline of disciplines', creates challenges for society. With the continual degradation of the natural resource base, the past and present approaches to natural resource management in Australia could be assumed to be failing. NRM is recognized in the 21st century as having an assumed importance as a development strategy, because of the claims that it can contribute towards sustainable livelihoods, thus NRM has two facets: the natural resource base and the institutional arrangements to maintain these. Australia is presently going through a transformation with the evolution of a regional NRM systems approach. The paper reports a hypothesized model of a sustainable regional NRM system for Australia that will be tested by a subsequent study.
Keywords: sustainable, regionalism, trans-disciplinary, success attributes, regional NRM system, literature model, means, ends, organisations and their governance, people and their attitudes, decentralised democracy.

1 Introduction

Natural Resource Management (NRM) in Australia has the explicit objective of achieving sustainable utilisation of major resources, such as land, water, air, minerals, forests, fisheries and wild flora and fauna [3]. Together, these resources provide the ecosystem services that underpin human life [4]. Lawrence *et al* [5] found that NRM has until relatively recently had its main focus on soils, hydrology, agronomy, biology, ecology and a host of other 'natural' dimensions. Rasmussen and Meinzen-Dick [6] portray concepts of sustainable NRM as a technical-ecological matter on the one hand, or an economic issue on the other. This dichotomy is too simplistic and if either approach were sufficient natural resource degradation problems would be easily resolved.

In practice NRM is an evolving field with varying paradigms. New paradigms for NRM have been proposed by academics, planning theorists and practitioners [7]. Farrington and Baumann [8] claim that NRM is recognised as having an assumed importance as a development strategy because of the claims that it can contribute towards sustainable livelihoods. In this context NRM has two facets: the natural resource base and the institutional arrangements to maintain these and the wide acceptance that social, ecological and economic factors are inextricably linked; to address one is to necessarily intervene in another.

1.1 Trans-disciplinary nature of NRM

The World Bank [4] recognises the trans-disciplinary nature of NRM. This study focuses on the integration of planning/geography, political science, sociology, economics, psychology, ecology and agri-environmental systems to explore and identify the complexities and success attributes of NRM, fig.1 [9].

1.2 Sustainable regional NRM defined

A sustainable regional NRM system's ability to achieve its objectives requires essential components, characteristics and relationships. Superficially the NRM literature suggests [3] that NRM is being driven towards a regional approach in Australia, however many more factors are influencing this approach. Privatisation trends, growing fiscal constraints at state levels, globalisation, neo-liberalism, reorganization of the roles of the state and the market, reorganization of society around a different vision of development and democratic decentralization of natural resources are proposed as the main drivers for a regional approach [10]. Natural resources and the environment are identified as one of the six key global drivers and trends for the globe over the next twelve years [11].

If sustainable regional NRM is a response to these drivers, how best can sustainable regional NRM be defined? For the purposes of this paper Regional NRM is defined as the institutional intermediary between the economy and the formal institutions of the state to deliver ecologically sustainable development, hence sustainable regional NRM has a responsibility to the sustainable management of natural resources and the building of civil society. This could be proposed as a new democratic form, with the role of the state being to make self-regulation possible and effective and the role of civil society being to democratise the state and the market to deliver sustainable NRM.

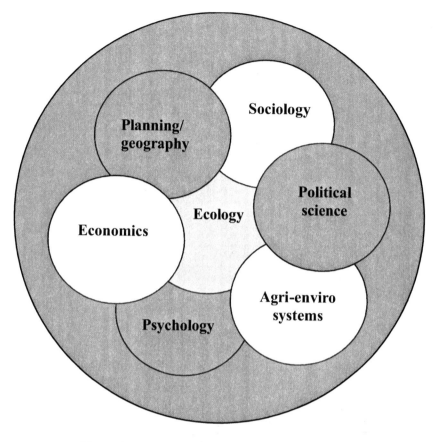

Figure 1:   Trans-disciplinary nature of NRM [9].

2   Overview of regional NRM approaches in Australia

In Australia since European settlement new and old disciplines have been integrated and melded with the emerging NRM approaches, fig. 2[10]. The history of NRM in Australia presents itself in a dissected form, with the literature tending to divide NRM in time and history into a number of approaches. The process has been accretive with agricultural aspects of soil conservation [12,13]; conservation and environment movements [14]; resource degradation [15,16]; ecological thought and action [17]; environmental history and policy [18,19], the social sciences and the many versions of landcare and catchment management approach [12,13,20,21,22] all joining an ever widening field of study and action.

Often each discipline failed to acknowledge other players' aspirations and attempts at NRM. Much of the literature focuses on the natural resource management occurring since European settlement in the late 1700's. This epistemological and ontological chaos highlights the need for greater understanding of what NRM is and how it is evolving. In particular this chaos highlights the failure to recognise that Australia was in essence an aboriginal farm with empirically derived management systems prior to European settlement [23].

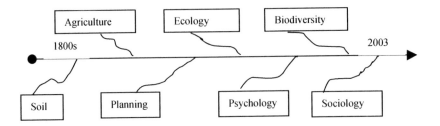

Figure 2:   Integration of new disciplines over time.

In the late 1980's the Australian Landcare movement emerged and was coupled with a catchment management approach and public participation with significant government and community investment through programmatic approaches such as the National Soil Conservation Program (NSCP), the National Landcare Program (NLP) and the Natural Heritage Trust Phase 1 (NHT1). This period is often posited as the most significant approach to natural resource management in Australia since European settlement [24]. Also since 1980 there has been an increase of National and State NRM legislation in response to community, national and international expectations.

From the early 1990's till 2002 there was significant investment in evaluation of the effectiveness and efficiency of these various NRM programmatic approaches with sixty-five completed evaluations of NHT1 alone [25]. There is a divergence of views about the effectiveness and efficiency of the NRM experiment. While there are demonstrated outcomes in awareness raising of NRM issues the continued degradation of the natural resource base in Australia would indicate that the objectives were not achieved. The Australian National Audit Office (ANAO) in 2001 asserts ' *the ANAO notes that there has still been little progress in relation to finalising the design of an overall performance information framework. Consequently there has been limited capacity to measure the results in concrete terms – that is, terms of what impact the NHT has had overall and what progress has been made towards the program goals such as conservation, repair and sustainable use of Australia's natural environment*' [26]. McDonald and Morrison [27] also identify that severe problems of fragmented policies and uncoordinated implementation undermine NRM in Australia. Results from the various reviews of NRM approaches such as the NHT1 and the NLP have generated a plethora of national discussion papers, reports and proposed models [1,3,28,29,30,31,32,33,34,35,36].

This process contributed to the development of a new approach towards NRM in the form of the Australian Government's 2001 investment regimes namely the National Action Plan for Salinity and Water Quality (NAP) and the

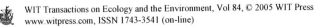

Natural Heritage Trust Phase 2 (NHT2). This change required a new delivery mechanism over six years from 2002 to 2008 where investments are delivered at national, regional and local levels. Regional investments are the principal delivery mechanism and require investment to be made on the basis of an accredited, integrated NRM Plan developed by the regions. This approach has led to the formation of 56 Regional NRM bodies across Australia.

3 What are the success attributes of a regional NRM system?

The success attributes of each of the disciplines in Figure 1 were initially identified randomly to create starting points. As these were investigated the cross-disciplinary complexities became obvious and to further progress the discussion, an ordered system was required to analyse the attributes of NRM and progress model development. This required consideration of key elements of the nature of the system and the grouping of cross-disciplinary factors. Ascher [37] suggests that identifying the key elements creates a means to better cope with complexity and the effects of organisational interests. The key elements were sequenced for progression in the development of a sustainable regional NRM model. This sequence was based on the hypothesis that people and their attitudes drive sustainable NRM outcomes. The key elements hypothesised as facilitating an analysis of sustainable NRM are:

1. People and their attitudes;
2. Organisations and their governance;
3. The third way: regionalism the new panacea;
4. Building societies capacity for sustainable NRM: means to ends.

3.1 Learning from international and national experiences

To better inform these key elements a literature review was undertaken. Common themes identified in the international experiences indicated that major factors in the success of a regional NRM system [10] were

- the stakeholders and their communities,
- organisations and their governance,
- power relations,
- conflicts of interest,
- negotiation processes between actors,
- participatory processes,
- collective action,
- relationships, devolution and
- stakeholder selection.

Adger et al [38] indicates that NRM decisions made by individuals, civil society and the state often involves questions of economic efficiency, environmental effectiveness, equity and political legitimacy with a multi-disciplinary approach required to understand NRM decisions that seek to identify legitimate and context-sensitive institutional solutions that produce equitable, effective, efficient and enduring NRM outcomes.

Common themes emerging from the literature review of NRM experiences in Australia [10] identified necessary success attributes as:

- clarification of property rights and duty of care;
- clarifications of roles and responsibilities,
- change management methods for groups and individuals,
- credible and legitimate institutions, information sharing,
- performance criteria indicators and targets,
- participative approach, adequate investments,
- incentives and concessions for public good conservation and
- coordination and integration.

Australia demonstrates much in common with the international experience: people and their interactions, power relations and legitimate organisations are key issues if a sustainable regional NRM approach is to succeed. Sustainable NRM is to do with people and their organisations and the attitudes they adopt which profoundly affect their behaviour. This confirms Doran's [39] characterisation of NRM as a 'people problem' requiring intervention strategies that have emphasis on communication and persuasion to reconcile conflicting interests and to facilitate cooperation.

3.2 People and their attitudes

The literature review of people and their attitudes highlighted the need to define and scope what constitutes a society or 'community of interest' in a sustainable regional NRM context the possible intervention method to be identified. Historical and cultural factors need to be considered and scoping of how that community of interest 'undertakes their business' needs to be understood prior to intervention. Successfully intervention requires:

- the identification of the players of sustainable NRM;
- the agents required to bring about positive change;
- the personality traits required of those agents;
- scoping of the contextual environment (rules) the players and agents are working in and
- scoping of the relations of power that exist.

It is crucial to have all the players of NRM included in the conflict resolution process. The success attributes for people and attitudes demonstrates that for efficient, effective and enduring sustainable NRM requires: an understanding of the players in the conflict; an understanding of the agents and their motivations, interactions and psychological contracts; the relations of power that exist; the contextual environment of the conflict; an adaptive management approach and long time frames [10].

3.3 Organisations and their governance

Barzilai [40] describes organisations as structured social systems consisting of groups of individuals working together to meet agreed objectives. Governance, which generally refers to the 'rules of the game' of organisations, was used to better understand the contextual environment that the players and agents of a sustainable NRM are imbedded in. For the purposes of this discussion the organisational players in sustainable NRM have been identified as three distinct groups: government, the corporate sector and civil society or the not-for-profit sector. Within each of these organisational players are a variety of interest groups and agents, however the common thread to each of these players is that their own particular governance actually frames their existence, evolution and progress. Importantly analysis of each player's governance provides a clear picture of roles and responsibilities. The analysis of the different levels of governance that exists in society provides more insight into what types of institutions are required to enable sustainable NRM.

The review of organisations and their governance demonstrates that there are key criteria to determine good governance of any organisation. An effective, efficient and enduring approach to sustainable NRM organisations requires the following attributes of good governance [10]:

- participation;
- transparency;
- responsiveness;
- consensus orientation;
- equity; effectiveness and efficiency;
- legitimate institutions;
- accountability; strategic vision;
- an adaptive management approach and
- independent evaluation and auditing

3.4 Regionalism

Giddens [41] characterises regionalism as the renewal of social democracy. This approach has arisen as a response to the reform driven by globalisation and its effects on the world socially and economically. This third way approach is often referred to as 'new regionalism' as it represents an alternative to two failed models of regional development: top down, state led and directed approaches on the one hand and free market dominated approaches on the other. Regionalism would focus on governance rather than government with a focus on partnerships between government, the private sector and not for profit organisations [42]. Regionalism in this discussion refers to sub-national areas known as regions that may be defined in different ways depending on the spatial scope and objectives of the intervention policy [43].

Regions are regarded as significant in that it is the level where social organisation, institutional interaction and coordination can be more adaptive. The main benefits identified of a regional approach are the opportunity for meshing processes of community participation with the broader scales of government. In Australia regionalism is seen as a strategic approach to facilitate sustainable NRM at a local level. The literature to date identifies that effective, efficient and enduring sustainable NRM requires the following attributes:

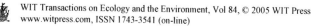

- successful decentralisation strategies,
- all forms of decentralisation to be present and
- clear unambiguous objectives of the intervention strategy to facilitate regionalism.

Monitoring and evaluation of intervention strategies that include before and after evaluations and the anticipated performance in the absence of the intervention are key requirements to enable measurement of the success of the intervention strategy whilst including a flexible and adaptive management approach [10].

3.5 'Means' and 'ends' in a sustainable NRM system

There are many references [1,3,26,27,28,30,31,32,34] to the need to build the capacity of governmental, corporate and civil society sectors to enable sustainable regional NRM however there is a divergence of assumptions of what are the 'means' and what are the 'ends'. Assumptions about people and their attitudes, organisations and their governance and regional decentralisation can produce a variety of regimes where tools themselves are often confused with 'ends'. 'Means' refers to the methods, processes and instruments that are required to achieve an outcome (ends) and for sustainable regional NRM 'means' come in many forms including management systems and tools. Australia's past attempts at sustainable NRM show that awareness and activity does not necessarily equate to outcomes. McDonald [44] warns of the concerns that the present evolving regional NRM arrangements in Australia appear to be focussed again on outputs rather than outcomes.

4 The hypothesised model

This dilemma demonstrates the need for determining the difference between 'means' and 'ends' in a sustainable regional NRM system and assists in the identification of essential foundation attributes required as the first stage of progress in the building of an appropriate system. We propose a model to progress a sustainable regional NRM system approach. This model presents a process that is based on foundation attributes, agent based interactions and 'means' to affect the 'ends' of regional sustainable NRM being resilient sustainable ecosystems, sustainable communities, decentralised democracy, changing social behaviours and changing landscape scenarios. Figure 3 provides a first rendition of the model.

Subsequent testing of the model is presently underway in Australia to evaluate the current regional NRM system approaches using the massive national experiment where a diversity of approaches is evident. This study is using both qualitative and quantitative data to determine whether the current regional NRM systems in Australia are effective, efficient and enduring and if not why not. It is anticipated that this subsequent study will test and improve our hypothesised model.

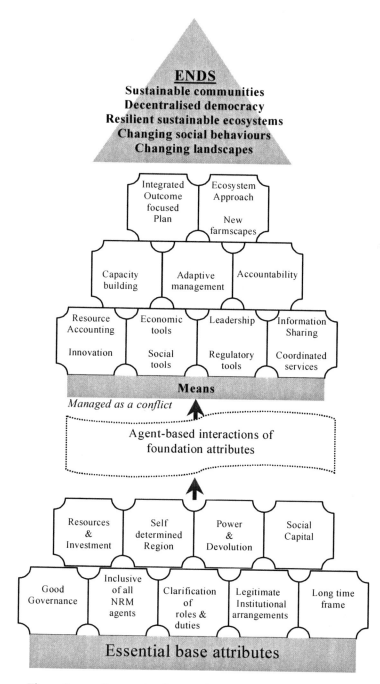

Figure 3: Success attributes of a regional NRM system.

5 Conclusion

For a sustainable regional NRM system to achieve its objectives requires essential components, characteristics and relationships. The many success attributes identified and their disciplinary sources demonstrate the potential systems complexity in sustainable NRM approaches. Recent initiatives to improve resource management indicate vulnerability to inappropriate interest-driven actions, which can result in patterns of perverse outcomes. Common criticisms of the Australian NRM approaches to date are the short programmatic nature of investments and the lack of long term, legitimate arrangements for a collaborative regional approach. The development and testing of this model is anticipated to assist the progression of sustainable regional NRM in Australia.

References

[1]   Prime Minister's Science, Engineering and Innovation Council (PMSEIC), *Sustaining our Natural Systems and Biodiversity* Australia, 2002.

[2]   Brown, R.L; *Rescuing a Planet under stress and a civilization in trouble* WW Norton & Company New York, 2003.

[3]   National Natural Resource Management Task Force *Managing Natural Resources in Rural Australia for a sustainable future* Canberra, 1999.

[4]   World Bank *Natural Resources Management* *http://lnweb18.worldbank.org/essd/essd.nsf/GlobalView/NRM.pdf/$File/N RM.pdf*

[5]   Lawrence, G *A;* Higgins, V & Lockie, S; *Environment, society and Natural Resource Management* Edward Elgar Cheltenham, 2001.

[6]   Rasmussen, L.N & Meinzen-Dick, R; Local Organizations for Natural Resource Management lessons from theoretical and empirical literature *IFPRI Environment & Production Technology Discussion Paper 11*, 1995

[7]   Lachapelle, P.R; McCool, S.F & Patterson, M.E Barriers to effective Natural Resource Planning in a 'messy' world **16(6)** pp 473-490, 2003.

[8]   Farrington, J & Baumann, P; *Panchayati Raj and Natural Resource Management: How to decentralise management over natural resources* www. panchayats.org/dnrm_introsalr.htm 2000.

[9]   Adapted from: Avery, S.K; *Resource Management Decision Support: The CCSP Plan* Climate Change Science Program Workshop Colorado, 2002

[10] Williams, J Unpublished Dissertation Brisbane, 2005.

[11] Centre for Future Studies, www.futurestudies.co.uk

[12] Campbell, A; *Landcare communities shaping the land and the future* Allen & Unwin Sydney, 1994.

[13] Cary, J.W & Webb, T; Landcare in Australia: community participation and land management. *Journal of Soil and Water Conservation* **56(4)**, pp.274-278

[14] Hutton, D & Connors, L; *A history of the Australian environment movement* Cambridge University Press Cambridge, 1999.

[15] Bolton, G; *Spoils and Spoilers Australians make their environment 1788-1980* Allen & Unwin Sydney, 1988.

[16] Heathcote, R.L & Mabutt, J.A; *Land, water and people geographical essays in Australian Resource Management* Allen & Unwin Sydney, 1988,

[17] Mulligan, M & Hill, S; *Ecological Pioneers* Cambridge University Press Cambridge, 2001.

[18] Dovers, S; (ed) *Environmental History and Policy: still settling Australia* Oxford University Press Melbourne, 2000.

[19] Dunlap, T.R; *Nature and the English Diaspora* Cambridge University Press Cambridge, 1999.

[20] Australian Landcare Council *The Future of Landcare discussion paper* Canberra, 2001

[21] Blake, J; Landcare, where has it come from and where to now *National Landcare Conference Proceedings* Darwin, 2003

[22] Kirner, J; Radio Interview Australian Broadcaster www.abc.net.au/rn/science/earth/stories/s112638.htm

[23] Flannery, T; *Beautiful Lies* Black Inc. Melbourne, 2003.

[24] Lloyd, B; Landcare: a community based approach to sustainable development *Proceedings IFA Annual Conference Sydney,* 2001.

[25] Australian Government Department of Agriculture, Fisheries & Forestry *Natural Heritage Trust Phase 1 Final evaluation scope and terms of reference* Canberra, 2003.

[26] Australian National Audit Office *Performance Information for Commonwealth Financial Assistance under the Natural Heritage Trust* Commonwealth of Australia Canberra, 2001.

[27] McDonald, G & Morrison, T; Integrating natural resource management systems for better environmental outcomes *Paper for the Australian Water Summit* Sydney, 2003.

[28] Prime Minister's Science, Engineering and Innovation Council (PMSEIC) *Moving Forward in Natural Resource Management Report* Australia, 1999

[29] Business Leaders Roundtable *Repairing the Country: leveraging private investment* Allen Consulting Group Sydney, 2001.

[30] National Farmers Federation/Australian Conservation Foundation *National Investments in Rural Landscapes* The Virtual Consulting Group & Griffin nrm Pty Ltd, 2000.

[31] Australian State of the Environment Committee *State of the Environment* CSIRO Publishing Collingwood, 2001.

[32] Wentworth Group *Blueprint for a living continent* WWF Australia, 2002.

[33] Industry Commission *A full repairing lease* Inquiry into Ecologically sustainable land management Commonwealth of Australia Canberra, 1998.

[34] Standing Committee on Environment & Heritage *Public Good conservation: our challenge for the 21st Century* Parliamentary paper 231/2001 Canberra, 2001.

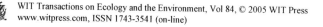

[35]   National Land & Water Audit www.nlwra.gov.au
[36]   NRM National Steering Committee *A discussion paper for developing a National Policy Canberra,* 2000.
[37]   Ascher, W; Coping with Complexity and organizational interests in Natural Resource Management *Ecosystems* **4(8)** pp.742-757, 2001.
[38]   Adger, N; Brown, K; Fairbrass, J; Jordan, A; Paavola, J; Rosend, S; Seyfang, G; *Governance for sustainability* www.uea.ac.uk/env /cserge/pub/wp/edm/edm_2002_04.htm
[39]   Doran, J; Intervening to achieve co-operative ecosystem management *Journal of Artificial societies and Social Stimulation* **4(2),** 2001.
[40]   Barzilai, K; *Organizational theory* Case Western Reserve University Cleveland, 2003.
[41]   Giddens, A; *The third way; the renewal of social democracy* Polity Press Cambridge, 1998.
[42]   Rainnie, A; New Regionalism in Australia: limits and possibilities *Proceedings Social Inclusion and New Regionalism Workshop* Brisbane, 2002.
[43]   Bureau of Transport and Regional Economics *Government Interventions in pursuit of regional development: Learning from experience* Working Paper 55 Canberra, 2003.
[44]   McDonald, G; Regional NRM: what is in place and why *Proceedings EIANZ Seminar* Brisbane, 2003.

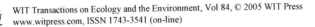

Aspromonte National Park: a study of the energy flows as a support tool for the sustainable management of protected areas

M. R. Giuffrè[1], V. Grippaldi[2] & R. F. Nicoletti[3]
[1]DASTEC, Department of Art, Science and Techniques of Building,
Faculty of Architecture of Reggio Calabria, Italy

Abstract

The Aspromonte National Park, which is set entirely in the province of Reggio Calabria, is a protected area of 70,000 hectares. It has been the subject of a preliminary study aimed at detecting and investigating the most important issues in the field of energy, with the purpose of supporting a sustainable energy plan. This paper presents a summary of the main results obtained from the analysis of the energy flows, which are spread over the territory of the protected area itself and parts of the small towns whose territory belongs only partially in the area of the Aspromonte Park. The analysis has been carried out in three different steps: collecting the required territorial data, analysing the consumption of energy, and evaluating the potential of the renewable resources already existent in the aforementioned territory of the Park. Through the creation of suitable maps, it has been possible to discern the areas having the highest potentiality with regards to the use of renewable sources of energy. The representation of the results is thus a useful tool which can be used in the process of planning and management of the area itself and which is also, along with other cultural, social and environmental information, the first step towards the definition of a Sustainable Energy Plan for the area of the Aspromonte National Park.
Keywords: sustainability, renewable energies, protected areas.

1 Introduction

The issues and problems related to energy are indeed central ones among the politic and development strategies of the EU members; in fact, EU in the recent program "Intelligent Energy for Europe" has underlined, among the main goals, the increase of 1% a year of the energy efficiency and the increase of use of energy from renewable sources, within 2010, as of 22.1%.

The objectives proposed by the Energy and Transport General Department are actually a challenge to achieve in the next few years.

The aim of this paper is to supply the starting tools for an oriented information system, which is of paramount importance to support the policies of sustainable development; in particular, with regards to protected areas, this implies the necessity to analyse the energy flows and the level of efficiency of the networks of distribution of energy.

An analysis of the sources of energy in a wide and complex territory, as the National Aspromonte Park one, cannot set aside the analysis of the existing relations among anthropic system, socio-economic and environmental system.

In this particular case, the process of management of anthropic systems is pretty inadequate to make the many variables involved work as best as possible; hence, all the initiatives, aimed at enhancing the knowledge about the activities in the area of the Park and the adjacent ones, are of paramount importance.

The issue of environmental impacts and sustainability of development is a very important part of this frame, which also increases the overall complexity of the analysed problems.

A study about the Aspromonte National Park aimed at defining the tools for a Socio-Economic Plan for the Park is described in this paper, which reports the results of the analysis of the consumption of power and the main aspects from which this study originates.

In fact, the aim of the study is describing the results of the analysis of the energy flows in the whole territorial system of the Park, and the methodology which has been used to detect the typical aspects of the use of energy in the territory of the Park itself.

The identification of the typical schemes of the consumption of energy in the territory of the Park provides the preliminary data whose further analysis and detection allow to define the apt and suitable scenarios for a rational and sustainable Development Planning.

2 The territory involved in the study

The territory which has been analysed is included in the boundaries of the Aspromonte Park consist of 70.000 hectares and 36 municipalities. The part of territory involved in the study is exactly equivalent to the area included in the boundaries of the Park and the one that comprehends the territory of the Municipalities, given that the overall balance of the energy flows mainly depends onto anthropic activities carried on in the municipality areas. The analysed area is, with regards to its orography, pretty complex, in fact some parts of it are actually coastal ones whilst other ones are about 1500 metres high. In Figure 1 the boundaries of both the Park and the municipalities involved in the study are shown.

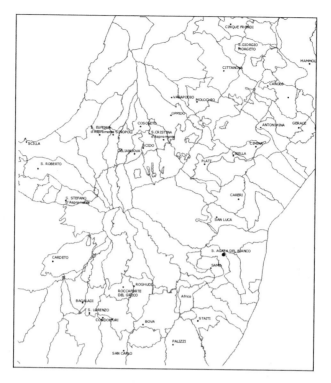

Figure 1:   The territory involved in the study.

3   The demand of power supply

A preliminary analysis has shown that electric energy is the main source of energy being used in the territory of the Park, hence the decision to deepen the detection of the demand of energy with regards to this particular type of power.

It is noticeable that carrying on the analysis of the demand of power supply to the territorial scale, allows to obtain interesting results especially with regards to the fact that the tools used to detect the consumption of energy also allow to create thematic maps that contain information regarding both spatial and time parameters.

In the following description, the structure of the available data is reported and it is possible to notice that there is a lack of in depth details referred to the time and space distribution of the data regarding the consumption of energy.

3.1 The data provided by ENEL

The data used for the analysis have been supplied by the Italian electric company (ENEL) and in particular, by the branch of it that distributes the energy. The database consists in a series of 1930 records reporting the municipality, the category of activity and the consumption of energy per year referred to 2001.

With regards to the structure of the Informative System from which the data have been obtained, it is important to underline that:

- the current method used by ENEL for evaluating the consumption of energy and the related database is mainly based onto the survey of the consumptions for each individual user (in particular, the energy meters reading) with annual reading and integrations with statistical studies;
- the position of the meter readings is not geo-referred hence it is not possible to analyse the consumptions of energy with disaggregated methodologies;

Besides, it has to be underlined that the network of distribution of energy is structured in five levels of aggregation, in particular: Municipality, Area, Street, Line, Socket. In particular, the municipality represents the whole area of the town; the Area is obtained sectioning the municipality area in few units; the Street represent the aggregations of about one thousand users and it corresponds to a group of streets of the town area or, for instance, a quarter; the Line represents a functional electric branch composed by some hundred users; the Socket is the power meter of a user. It has been esteemed that the optimal level of aggregation of the data should be referred to the monthly or seasonal consumptions either of the Street or the Line; nonetheless, in spite of the fact that the data are all included in the Informative System, the data regarding the Street and the Line are not actually available for the analysis. Besides, the data regarding the Sockets are not releasable by the Electric Company due to the necessity to protect the privacy of the users. Actually, the above mentioned Information System has been setup mainly for general procedures of administrative management, and then the requested data for a detailed analysis are not easily available.

3.2 The annual consumption of energy

In order to analyse the different anthropic activities, the existing about one hundred product categories have been aggregated in eighteen groups, as shown in Table 1.

As shown in the table, the annual overall consumption of energy in the analysed area is about 283 GWh/year.

The distribution of consumption of energy per activity and per area is shown in Figure 2, which represents the consumption of energy with regards to aggregated categories.

In order to point out the size of annual consumption with regards to each group and each municipality, suitable charts that show the distribution in frequency of the consumption have been created.

In particular, these charts are aimed at evaluating, with regards to the territory of the Aspromonte Park, the demand of energy per category; besides, they allow us to identify the percentages of the consumption of energy with regards to geographical distribution.

The frequency of consumption related to housing category, shown in Figure 3, demonstrates that in most of the cases the annual consumptions is about 2GWh/year.

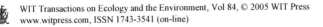

Table 1:   The annual consumption of power for aggregated categories.

Code number	CATEGORY	Consumption (MWh)
2000	Houses	144688
2001	Industry	3386
2002	Building industry	6200
2003	Commerce	18578
2004	Tourism	14789
2005	Food industry	15037
2006	Health services	4577
2007	Civil service	3219
2008	Transports	1743
2009	Enterprise	4111
2010	Education	1776
2011	Industry (with regards to energy)	670
2012	Manufacturing activities	136
2013	Communications	3710
2014	Irrigation	978
2015	Services to infrastructural networks	27254
2016	Services to waterworks	28113
2017	Other	4527

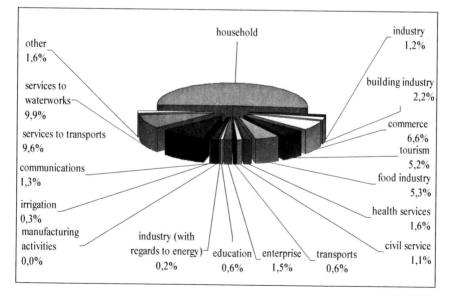

Figure 2:   Categories and related consumption of energy.

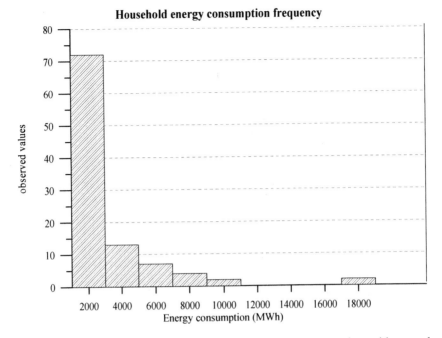

Figure 3: Distribution in frequency of the energy consumption with regards to houses.

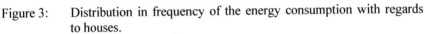

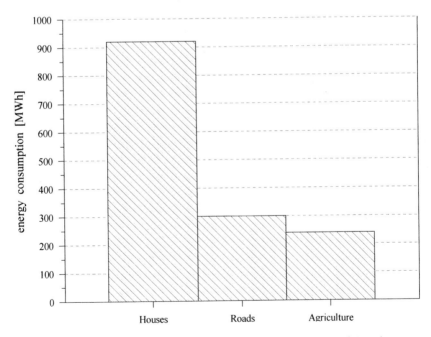

Figure 4: The main consumptions for the municipality of Cosoleto.

WIT Transactions on Ecology and the Environment, Vol 84, © 2005 WIT Press
www.witpress.com, ISSN 1743-3541 (on-line)

This result provides important information in order to identify possible interventions aimed at producing energy to be used in a given category.

A further analysis can be made by elaborating histogram charts, as the one shown in Figure 4, about the municipality of Cosoleto, and which reports the category in the x-coordinate and the consumption in the y-coordinate. The chart allows us to display the consumptions in terms of absolute value with regards to each category that, when aggregated, forms the category of housing. This approach allows us to point out the maximum, minimum and mean consumptions with regards to each category; this information allows not only to evaluate the level of socio economic development of each municipality involved in the study, but also, to underline the differences existing between the municipalities.

The information attainable from the described graphs can be further analysed with regards to the consumptions of energy related to the single municipality. This approach allows us to analyse this issue more in-depth, going from the evaluation of the i-th category to the evaluation of the individual characteristics of each municipality. The analysis per single municipality is therefore aimed at identifying the relative and absolute contributions of each of the aggregated categories; besides, it represents the necessary database that allows us to draw possible scenarios of future development.

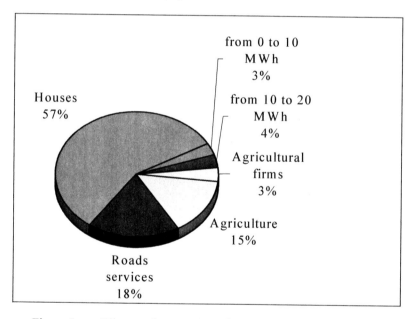

Figure 5:   The prevalent consumptions for the town of Cosoleto.

Instead, in Figure 5 it is represented the distribution of consumptions in terms of relative percentages; in particular, the chart shows the results with regards to the town of Cosoleto.

3.3 The thematic maps

With reference to the structure of the database supplied by ENEL, it is noticeable that it's quite difficult to create a thematic map of the consumptions, with regards to aggregated category, having a spatial resolution larger than the municipality level; nonetheless, it is possible to use, with regards to some of the categories, further variables.

For example, with regards to the category of houses, the variable to be used is represented by the number of buildings not set in the urban areas: in fact, if further informations lack, the ratio between number of inhabitants scattered over the territory and those living in the urban areas allows to esteem the requirement of energy of a given territory.

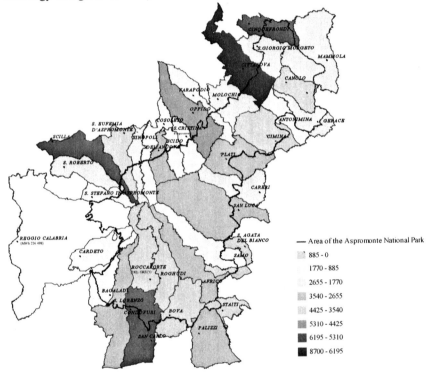

Figure 6: Thematic map of the consumption for the housing category.

A thematic map presenting the consumption of energy related to the housing category without reference to its distribution over the territory is shown in Figure 6.

4 Conclusions

The results obtained from the study allow to draw some important conclusions regarding methodological aspects; in particular, with regards to the implementation of a SIT aimed at the development of the protected area referred to the use of the energy and especially, of the energy obtained by renewable sources.

In fact, the presented results show that the information attainable from the proposed charts are actually preliminary ones, hence, the necessity of a more in-depth study appears evident; at present though, the existing system of organization and management of data cannot supply such results, in the short period.

Analysing the results obtained from the analysis, it is noticeable that, even though there are great differences between the municipalities involved in the study, the main categories are those regarding the housing, the services to waterworks and transports.

This first stage of information regarding the amount of annual consumptions, the considered categories and the relative percentages of each municipalities, defines the distribution of the existing level of economic development of the territory and can be used as a starting tool for the definition of apt scenarios of both intervention and development in the field of energy.

References

[1]   ENEA Rapporto Energia e ambiente 2001, L'analisi.. Rome 2001.
[2]   Il Parco Nazionale dell'Aspromonte. Università degli Studi di Reggio Calabria. Domenico Corso. Reggio Calabria 1999 - Jason editrice.
[3]   Piano del Parco. Ente Parco nazionale del Gran Sasso e Monti della Laga. Ente Parco Nazionale del Gran Sasso e Monti della Laga 1999.
[4]   Primo Rapporto sullo Stato dell'Ambiente in Calabria. Regione Calabria. Dicembre 2000. Regione Calabria 2000.

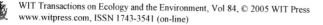

Urumiyeh, a unique lake exposed to danger: challenges and sustainable approaches

R. Sarvar, H. Mojtaba Zadeh, A. Estelaji & M. Ranjbar
Islamic Azad University, Shahr-e-Rey section

Abstract

Urumiyeh is the name of a lake located in the north-west of Iran, commonly known by various names such as Chichest, meaning white and shining, a name given many ages before it was recorded in the writings of historians. Miyeh means 'Ma' (water), and the initial syllable of the word (i.e. Ur) means land and fire. However, due to the fact that Zoroaster belonged to this land, the word Urumiyeh seems relevant to both interpretations.

Besides the primeval and sacred nature of this lake, it is regarded as one of the most significant, vast, and highest lakes in the plateau of Iran. Moreover, it enjoys many unique and exclusive natural features as well as having many beautiful environmental areas. It has already been recognized by UNESCO as being among 59 global storage spots in the world and is formally identified in their records.

However, several factors are having a detrimental effect on the lake and its environment, giving rise to the steady elimination of the lake's outstanding features. Therefore, it requires prompt and serious attention, both at national and international levels to address the problems. The main aim of our research in this article is to identify the key problem areas and to propose remedial action.

Keywords: sustainable development, sustainable planning, national park, environmental impact assessment, protected areas.

1   Introduction

Urumiyeh Lake usually covers 4000 to 6000 square km of the region. Its length is between 120 to 160 km from north to south and its width changes from 15 to 60 km. The height of the lake is 1265 meters and the depth is between 4 and 50 meters. The water of the lake is provided by a pond of 3500 square km and is excessively salty (there are 111 to 155 kg salt in each square meter). Therefore, no fish can live there except a species of crustacean called Artemia.

The lake is recognized as the second most salty lake in the world, with a reputation for its beauty, its varied scenery and its animals, and enjoying unique specific features capable of maintaining a sustainable tourism industry. However, the following factors have given rise to the steady elimination of the lake's outstanding features:

- Regression and decrease of water due to the hydrological imbalance of the basin
- Increase of salt in the lake and threat of crustacean's lives.
- Rapid growth of the region's population and daily-increase of sewage entering the lake through the rivers.
- Gradual increase of contamination-generating industries in the surroundings.
- Application of certain incompatible projects done without prior study pertaining to "the evaluation of environmental effects."
- Weakening of the ability to sustain animals and thousands of migratory birds
- Decline of the level of environmental values in the surrounding protected areas
- Increase of soil erosion and waste water in the basin

The main aim of this article which is the result of many years scrutiny of the writers, centers around:

1) Recognition of attraction sites and identification of specific environmental values.
2) Study and introduction of factors threatening the survival of creatures in this unique living-place.
3) Deducing appropriate approaches and implementing sustainable planning.

The methodology of research is based on the studies and actual visits to the area, as well as using library resources.

2   The condition of the case study area

Uromiyeh Lake (about 5000 square kilometers) located in the north-west of Iran, with 1265 meter altitude, is one of the most important and invaluable water ecosystems of Iran and the Middle East. It is the biggest lake in Iran. Due to its natural and ecological characteristics it was considered as the national park, Ramsar site, in 1975, and as a protected area in 1977 by UNESCO.

Uromiyeh Lake is in the center of an enclosed drain, and all ground and underground water sources drain into it. Its intense saltiness is the result of high evaporation and continuous sediments of its salt, Fig 1.

Figure 1:   The location of the lake.

3   Ecological and non-ecological features of the Uromiyeh Lake

3.1 Non-ecological features

1- The most important parts of the nearby area of the lake, which is about 51876 square kilometers include: mountain areas 38%, hills 21%, plateaus and high lands 11.2% and the lake itself which is about 130×40 km with an average depth of 5.4m (about 13 m in the north) and a volume of 31 million cubic meters.

2 - Due to its altitudes and height, its weather is very cold in winter and moderate in summer.

3 - From geology perspective, this area is the result of the vicinity of The Alborz and Zagros heights that influenced the tectonic aspects of the area as faults, fractures, volcanic activities, and other tectonic phenomena.

4 - The water of the Uromiyeh Lake is supplied by 21 rivers (14 permanent and 7 seasonal rivers). The average annual volume of flowing water is about 5316 million cubic meters.

5 - All the ground water of this area, excluding Ajichai flows in salty places, has a desirable quality.

6 - The average level of the lake water has been 1276 above sea level (from 1965-2000) but after this period the development of water sources has led to its reduction to 2.66 m.

3.2 Ecological features

1 - There are about 1500 plant species in the Uromiyeh lake area (about 15% of the total plant communities in Iran). The biggest plant variations are in mountain areas and the least ones in salt areas.

2 - The lake contains a large amount of green and edible algae that provide the basis of the food-chain.

3 - In the ecological area of the lake there are 27 different mammals, 212 birds, 41 reptiles, 7 amphibians, and 26 fish species, Fig 2.

4 - The lake is a suitable place for large groups of water birds (especially ducks and waders). It also provides the opportunity for the greatest colony of flamingos in Iran (more than 20,000 pairs). In this area, 11 species of birds, exposed to the threat of world extinction, have been recorded.

5 - Since two types of mammals, Iranian yellow deer (Dama mesopotamica) and Armenian Ram (ymelini ovis orientalist), which are exposed to destruction, have been transported to the Islands of the lake National park, the rate of their population has increased .

6 - The most important invertebrate type of the lake is Artima Urmiana, one of the domestic shrimp of salt water.

Due to the lack of fish in the lake, this type is very important to provide food for birds (especially flamingos). Since the lake water has become too salty, the shrimps cannot grow and therefore its population will decline.

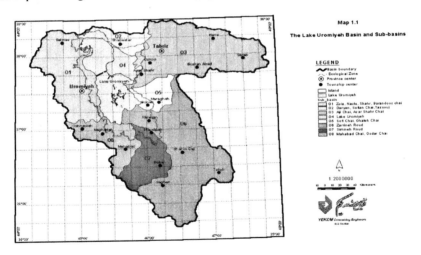

Figure 2:   The boundary of the ecological area.

4   The bio-environmental values of the Uromyieh Lake

* This ecosystem is a unique example of enclosed water area (in Iran and Middle East) that all ground and underground water sources flow into a salty lake.

- It is considered as a major biosphere source by UNESCO.
- There are many invaluable international ponds around it e.g. Qare Qeshlaq, Noorooz lou dam, Mimaneh, shoor gol and yadgarlou.
- The great variation of wild-life (including 11 species which are exposed to world threat).
- It provides the opportunity to refine the contaminants.
- The function of surrounded ponds in providing underground water, preventing the flow of salt water to the place of birds.
- Providing beautiful waterscape, great climate, various islands, natural sludge, with treatment effects, opportunity for sailing, possibilities for wild animals and tourism industry.(table1)

5 Bio – environmental critical points

The critical points of the ecological area of the Uromiyeh lake include 17 stations, each with particular features (especially ponds), and the lake itself. The important features of the lake are as follows. See Fig 3.

1- Consisting of dry lands, such as: Kaboodan, Arezoo. Ashk, Spir, and Doqoozlar Islands (IBA[4] DR[3] NP[2] RS[1])

2 - Garde Qare Qeshlaq (Marsh, Morass, Mire quagmire)

3 - Qit and Meymand pass (defile, bottleneck, Gorge) (IBA an NHA[5])

4 - Norooz lu dam

5 - Islamic peninsula (NHA)

6 - Shoor Gol (RS and IBA)

7 - Yad Gar lou (RS and IBA)

8 - Darge sangi (Threshold) (Rs and IBA)

9 - Gapi/Baba Ali Gapi/lake (RS and IBA)

10 - Qare Gol Pond (NIBA[6])

11 - Aq ziarat (IBA)

12 - Cani Barazan (NIBA)

13 - Sheitan Abad (NIBA)

14 - Islam Abad/Jahood Abad (NIBA)

15 - Gapi Qazan and Garoos (NIBA)

16 - Jamal Abad (NIBA)

17 - Changiz Goli (NIBA)

Explanation: 1- Ramsar site, 2- National park, 3- Biosphere storage (Bio-sphere), 4- The important area of birds, 5- The no hunting place, 6- The major international area of birds.

There are other places around the lake which are not recognized, but they are very important for these ecosystems, and they have to be managed. They are as follows:

1- Zarineh Rood delta

2- Simineh Rood delta

3- Mahabad River delta

4- Nazloo Chai delta

5- BARAndooz Chai delta

6- Shahr Chai delta
7- Soofi Chai delta
8- Mardooq Chai delta
9- Soofian Chai delta
10- Aqaj Chai delta
11- Roze Chai delta
12- Godar Chai delta

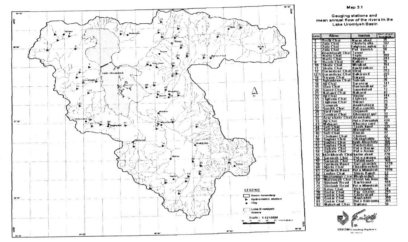

Figure 3: Gauging stations and mean annual flow of the rivers in the Lake basin.

6 The threats and influences of human activities on the Uromiyeh lake ecosystem

1- The human population in this area has increased from 2.6 in 1355 to 4.3 million in 1996 which in turn resulted in new problems.

The increasing average rate of population was about 2.6% in the past two decades, (4.14% in urban areas and 0.55% in rural areas). The migration from rural to urban areas (especially men) has been increasing in recent years.

2- Although people have lived in this area for thousands of years, the agricultural and industrial activities, the fundamental projects, and projects to develop water sources have been improved only in recent decades. These measures have had remarkable effects on the ecological situation of the Uromiyeh lake and the critical areas. The decline of the function of this ecosystem as well as the changes of pond areas, especially in the critical places of the south of the lake, is the new problem.

3- Although there were variations in the lake level, there were great changes for Ramsar Sites in the south of the lake. Due to developing of the agriculture, establishing the drains and deviational dams, as well as the recent drought,

Yadegar lou pond, Darge sangi, the Gapi lake of Baba Ali are all under threat of being destroyed.

4- The lands can be used as follows: grass lands 63 %, dry farming lands 17.3 %, wet farming lands and orchards 11.8 %, and the forests, salt lands, while ponds, dams, swamps and the plains are 7.9%. In 70% of these lands there has been erosion at an intense rate.

The great slope, the form of erosive geology weak plant covering in sustainable farming are the causes of erosion (in the area). The great sediment rate in the lake threatens the ecological stability.

5- The major project on the fundamental development is calantary highway that passes the Uromiyeh lake and the national park (Ramsar site). This highway has influenced the integration, hydrodynamic features, quality, quantity and the salt rate of the lake.

6- The developmental projects of ground and underground water sources provide about 4690 million cubic meter of the lake water that has a great effect on the quality and quantity of the water sources that flow into the lake, which in turn affect the lake's ecosystem.

7- It is predicted to use 1.3 milliard cubic meters up to the year 2021. If it is done there will be serious problems, Fig 4.

- As the lake level reduces, the lake salt rate will increase.
- According to a long term statistics this rate will be changed – from 235 grams in each liter (in 1980-1993) to about 272- 275 grams. In this salt rate, Artima, the base of the food chain in the lake, cannot survive, so the flamingos and other birds have to leave the area (as happened in the recent drought).

8- People use the different products of the lake and the near by ponds as: Artima / bamboo, salt, and water birds. They are in the following situation:

- Due to intense salt rate in the lake, the Artima population is reduced.
- Since salt water flows in the fresh water area, picking of the bamboo is stopped.
- Because of the lake contamination, salt extraction has been reduced.

9- In addition to the aforementioned cases, it has other advantages.
Mud treatment, fishing, fish breeding areas in the nearby ponds and rivers, tourism industry, and amusement programs.

10- The activities of management protecting are just allocated to the protected areas, and they do not have any positive effect on the environment.

11-According to studies, people use the Uromiyeh lake differently and can be classified to environmental values, productions, and services. Sustainable development of these activities and stability of ecosystem have been threatened by human activities, therefore, the new process represents two great influences of human activities on the lake:

- the population density near the lake which causes increasing pressure on the natural sources and environment.
- the emergence of new cities and their development, the development of industrial plants and service industries are the basic factors destroying the environment.

 WIT Transactions on Ecology and the Environment, Vol 84, © 2005 WIT Press
www.witpress.com, ISSN 1743-3541 (on-line)

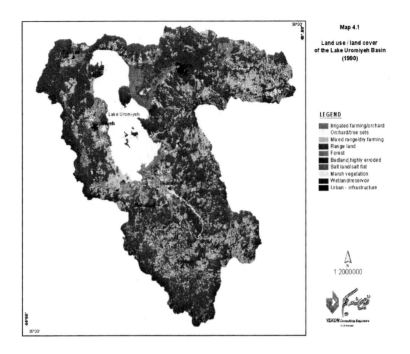

Figure 4:   Land use in the Uromiyeh Basin.

7   The present process in sustainable development

The local people's needs have been provided by the lake for thousands of years. These values have potentialities of development and sustainable use.

Unfortunately, it has been observed that the development process is not continuous and sustainable and the lake ecosystem is declining. The reduction and decline of the ecological situation in the lake have had a negative effect on the social-economic values and possibilities of the lake, particularly in the past decade. The major changes are:

- Reduction of size, volume, and water level of the lake which resulted in changing the lake waterscape and also the moderate climate of the area.
- Due to the destruction of the life zone and increasing the lake's saltiness, high changes in life have occurred. The ecological-cycle of Artima declined, the breeding of flamingos stopped, and the bird population reduced.
- Because of the new ecological of Artima, its fishing is being stopped.
- The traditional salt taking is being reduced and it may have a contaminating effect on salt quality. Developing the regional industries depend on using modern technology to remove these contaminants.
- The nearby bamboo, tamarisk, and grass-sward areas are completely destroyed, which in turn has demolished the grass lands for regional animals and reduced the bamboo industry.
- The number of water birds, as well as their hunting area is also reduced.

- Since the underground water sources of the down areas have been used and the water source projects developed, the lake level and the water volume of nearby fresh ponds has decreased.
- The projects of the development of water sources in the high areas around the rivers resulted in flowing salt water to the rivers near the lake.
- The rate of contaminants in hygienic sledges has been increased, which has a negative effect on the tourism industry.

Increasing the use of flowing water to the lake and the recent droughts represent the in unsustainable development of the area. Therefore the reduction of the fresh water sources flow into the lake is a serious danger for the lake ecosystem and all related parameters (Fig 5).

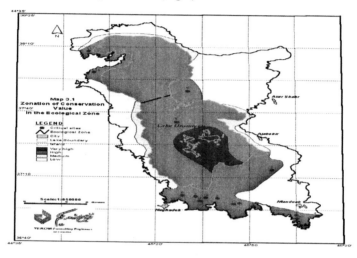

Figure 5:   Conservation zones of value in the ecological zone.

8   Guided and practical suggestion

1. Controlling the population rate.
2. Providing strategic programs to use land water and soil sources.
3. Promoting the knowledge of related groups and private companies (N.G.O).
4. Considering and applying the assessed principles of the bio – environmental effects of related great projects.
5. Changing the water way and direction of minor zab to zarine road area.
6. Protecting the international ponds.
7. Preparing programs to revive the Ramsar site (the Gapi Lake, shoorGol, yadgarlou, sangi Dorageh).
8. Doing exact hydrological studies about all aquiferous and watershed areas.
9. Managing the effective methods to optimal use of water sources.
10. Studying and applying cultivative systems appropriate to the water sources.
11. Studying the effects of artima fishing on the flamingos' life.

12. Prohibiting and stopping human activities in heron and other bird communities.
13. Providing and controlling the no hunting zone.
14. Cooperating of all international and national organizations to protect this critical and important area from the destruction.

Table 1: The summary of multiple values assessment of The Uromiyeh Lake.

Ecosystem values	Explanation	Significance	Major users	Population users (person)	Economic values ($1000)
Moderating the climate	Moderating the hot weather, Increase of rain	Area	The inhabitants, farmers and food sellers	414 millions	9
Life diversity	The special life zone of uromiyeh Artima, flamingos, herons, water birds, winter birds, plant diversity	Local, national, international	Rural people, tourists, people live on the way of the flight of the migratory birds, viewers, the Uromiyeh Lake, researchers, and students	730/000, million people, 25000	9
Views and sights	Lake, topography, islands, national park and biosphere storage	Local, national, international	Rural people, tourists	Millions of people	9
Pond establishing	—	—	—	—	—
Artima fishing	300- 400 thousand tones of preserved artima, 20-40 thousand tones of fishable Artima	Local, national	Fishery , environment organization and the related organs	75	75000
Grass and livestock grazing land	Pickable Astragalus – Fistalia	Local	Rural people and farmers	1.5 Million	9
Water birds' hunting	Being declined	Local	Lake near by farmers	160	2.15
Bamboo picking up	No existence	Local	Rural people	9	9
Salt taking	3.2 million storage	Local	Rural people, workers, industrial areas of salt taking	500	1000
Hygienic and treatment mud	Traditional drug	Local	Local tourist	730/000	9
Fishing	—	Local	Rural people	9	9
Services	—	Local		—	—

Supplying ground water sources	Fresh water ponds, supplying ground water sources	Local	Rural people, farmers, industrial workers (artisan)	All people	9
Preventing from the advancing of salt water		Local	Rural people, farmers, industrial workers	9	9
	Fresh water ponds supply underground water sources and preventing from flowing and advancing of salt water to the Uromiyeh Lake				
Tourism	Water scope and view, entertainment place	Local, national	Tourism industry	—	—
Training and research	Scientific and research potentialities	Local, national	School students and university students	730 / 000	3 .5
Commercial significance as food for shrimp	—			27000	9

References

English
[1]   About Lake gori gol, website:http/ramsar.org
[2]   About Lake kobi, website:http/ramsar.org
[3]   About Lake uromiyeh, website:http/ramsar.org
[4]   About Shur gol, yadegarlu and dorgeh sangi Lakes, website:http/ramsar.org
[5]   About the ramsar convention (ramsar speak), website:http/ramsar.org
[6]   doe,undp.text of convention on biological diversity (undp/cro) undp/gef/nbsap secretariat,may 2000.
[7]   Guidelines on Management planning for Ramsar sites and other wetlands, website:http/ramsar.org
[8]   Information on Ramsar wetland Lake obi, website: http:/ramsar.org/Lake IUCN Red list categories, www.http/iucn.org/themes/Ramsar
[9]   National Committee of Sustainable Development National Action Plan for Environmental Protection, Department of the Environmental Protection, Department of the Environment, Ramsar Advisory Missions: Report No.31,1999
[10]   The Criteria for Identifying Wetlands of International Importance, Email:wiap@wiap.nonionet.agro.net
[11]   YEKOM Consulting Engineers. Workshop Report: the First Workshop on Applying the Ecosystem Approach to the Management to Lake Uromiyeh(2_4 July 2001), Yekom Consulting Engineers,2001.

[12] Ziaie, Z.A Review of the Lake Uromiyeh Ecosystem /the First Workshop to Appling the Ecosystem Approach to the Management to Lake Uromiyeh (2-4 July 2001), Yekom

[13] Consulting Engineers, 2001.

[14] Odisho Unestablished information plants in W. Azarbijan, Research Center of Forest and Ranhelands in W. Azarbaijan.

[15] Rose, P.M.& Scott, D.A.,1997,Waterfowl population Estimates, Second Edition wetlands International Publication No.44, Wetlands International, Wagenin gen, The Netherlands.106pp

Persian

[16] Advisor Engineers of Power Ministry, 1994. The studies of The Second step of Shahid Kalantary Highway Near The Uromiyeh Lake. Vol.2.Hydrological studies of The Uromiyeh Lake. The Last Report.

[17] Advisor Engineers of Power Ministry, 1994.The studies of The Second step of Shahid Kalantary Highway Near The Uromiyeh Lake. Vol.1.Hydrological studies of The Uromiyeh Lake. The Last Report.

[18] Asri.1999.The Plant Covering of Salt Swamp Of The Uromiyeh Lake.

[19] Education Ministry. 1996. Geography of West-Azarbaijan Province. Iran Publishing Co.

[20] Education Ministry Geography of Kurdestan Province. Iran Publishing Co.

[21] Gamab Advisor Engineers Company, 1998. The Iran's Water Comprehensive Plan, The Uromiyeh Water Area.

[22] Iran Advisor Engineers.1997. The Comprehensive Studies of Agricultural Development of Aras and Uromiyeh Water Areas, Water Complicated Process. Vol.38.ch. Ground waters.

[23] Iran Oil Company. Iran Geology organization. 1978 Iran Map. West_North. No.1

[24] KarAmooz.G.1996.The Study of Salt Reduction of the Uromiyeh Lake. Power Ministry Water Research Center.

[25] Shahraby.1986. organization map geology Uromiyeh NO.3

[26] The Budget and Program Organization.1999 The Third Plan Law of the Cultural, Social and Economical Development of the Islamic Republic of Iran.

[27] The Environmental Protecting Organization, 2001. The Approved Collection of The High Council of Environmental Protection.

[28] The First Advisor Engineers. 2002. The Uromiyeh Lake Environmental Management Project.

[29] The Report on the Study of the Management Capacity of the Uromiyeh Lake.1997.

[30] The Secretary of the Leyal, Assembly, and Information Affairs of Agriculture.1996. The Collection of Agricultural Rules (A long-term plan of west- Azarbaijan Development). Agriculture Ministry.

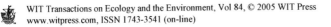

Carrying capacity assessment of Slovene Istria for tourism

I. Jurincic
Turistica, College of Tourism Portoroz,
University of Primorska, Slovenia

Abstract

The method of carrying capacity assessment has been found to be a useful tool for saturation prevention as well as for implementing sustainable tourism development strategies in Slovene Istria. It has been found that sustainable tourism development allows for variations in tourism development intensity in the region. The aim of sustainable tourism development is a long-term optimal use of tourism resources without negative impacts on the natural, social and economic environments.

The major constraints that will have to be considered if tourism development is to be sustainable are: waste water collection and treatment, lack of car parks, road and rail transport, sea water quality, potable water resources, solid waste disposal and management, and last but not least the dissatisfaction of the local community and tourists with tourism. The development of more accommodation facilities would not be reasonable without investments in general infrastructure facilities. Measures for increasing carrying capacity have also been suggested.

Keywords: carrying capacity, sustainable tourism, indicators, tourist destination, regional planning, geographical information systems.

1 Introduction

Today the development of tourism demands careful planning. The environmental impact of tourism is harmful and has frequently been uncoordinated with other users of the land. Moreover, the fragility of the environment has been seldom taken into consideration. Tourism development has been often led by individual investors who put profitability in the first place. To make the situation worse, this has been repeatedly done with complete disregard for tourism development vision in a destination or region. Development potentials of the area have not been fully considered when planning economic development. Such tourism development can damage the reputation of a destination. Its long term damage can be felt in decreasing demand and uncompetitive prices of services as well as in increased pressure on natural and other resources. It can lead to devaluation of resources and dissatisfaction or even opposition by local community. In this way ample accumulation becomes impossible, consequently the present tourism offer cannot be complimented and it is not possible to introduce a new offer. As a result, the long term development of a destination is jeopardized. Cases of this kind can be frequently met all over the world, unfortunately and inevitably also including Slovenia.

In order to avoid such serious consequences, all tourism development potentials have to be periodically assessed on a level of the country, region and local community. To be able to do that we have to devise tourism strategy in due time in cooperation with the tourism industry, municipality, state and local inhabitants. The strategy has to be adjusted to changing circumstances in the area and economy. Only by doing so, a long term sustainable tourism development can be ensured in the region and country [1].

Prompt and integrated physical planning, which places the intervention planned in the strategy into the environment, is a key factor of sustainable tourism development. It has to involve the representatives of the tourism and other industries in the region, different experts, local inhabitants, state and local government. They have to communicate and negotiate in the process of drawing up legal documents and take into consideration the results of carrying capacity analysis for different activities.

Although the carrying capacity analysis (CCA) method has been used successfully throughout the world, it has not been established in Slovenia yet. Therefore I intend to illustrate its applicability in the process of implementing the principles of sustainable tourism in Slovenia.

2 Hypothesis

We intend to test the following hypothesis:
The carrying capacity analysis (CCA) method is a suitable tool for the prevention of saturation in a tourist destination as well as for the implementation of sustainable tourism development in a region.

The tourism industry which ignores the carrying capacity of the region in a long term jeopardizes its development or even existence and makes a negative impact on the overall development of the region. The hypothesis is going to be empirically tested in the case of Slovene Istria.

3 Method

World Tourism Organization (WTO) and United Nations Environment Program (UNEP) recommend that apart from wholesome physical planning in the region and efficient tourist destination management we should make carrying capacity analysis for individual tourist destinations and areas [2, 3].

By making CCA for tourism we calculate the maximum number of visitors to a region or a tourist destination that can come at the same time without causing irreparable ecological and socio-cultural damage to the environment. The carrying capacity method recommended by UNEP has been slightly modified. The changes and supplements are considered to be necessary to make more adequate CCA possible in Slovenia and some other developed regions being compared. The analysis has been made by using computer assisted Geographical Information System (GIS) Idrisi [4]. The carrying capacity indicators for tourism specific to Slovene Istria that we consider most important have been determined on the basis of similar experiences abroad described in literature [5].

Firstly, the present capacity of individual carrying capacity indicators is going to be defined. Later on we are going to determine if appropriate measures can increase their capacity in the future. It is going to be done by comparing the current indicator capacity with the maximum carrying capacity limit for the chosen tourism development scenario by the year 2020. Both the planned and possible improvements in different development programs and strategies suggested by local inhabitants and tourists will be taken into consideration.

On the basis of assessed carrying capacity of individual indicators and taking into consideration the indicators that are at the lowest level in spite of the planned improvements, we are going to determine the carrying capacity of the region expressed the maximum number of tourists allowed to stay in the region at the same time. In the conclusion we are going to propose some measures that could be taken in order to monitor and increase the calculated regional carrying capacity for tourism and that will enable the implementation of the selected tourism development scenario by the year 2020.

After the sustainable tourism development scenario had been chosen we started the process of carrying capacity assessment of Slovene Istria. Relevant carrying capacity indicators for tourism have been determined and later divided up into three groups:

1. physical - ecological: beaches (sq m of beaches), sea water quality, potable water quality, solid waste collection and treatment, air quality and parks and green areas (quantity, condition),
2. infrastructural: accommodation capacity, potable water quantity, sewage disposal, road traffic, car parks, railway transport, sea transport, marinas and moorings and air traffic.
3. sociological - psychological: local inhabitant satisfaction with tourism and overall tourist satisfaction.

We did not follow the procedure found in literature and regrouped the indicators. The physical, ecological and infrastructural parameters or indicators were due to their importance in Slovene Istria divided into two groups: physical - ecological and infrastructural, comprising general and tourism infrastructure.

Inhabitant and tourist opinion polls suggest that they are highly sensitive to the condition of the environment and infrastructure. The next two groups of indicators, socio-demographic and psycho-political were joined into one group called socio-psychological indicators.

Physical, ecological and infrastructural indicators are crucial in the process of defining the overall carrying capacity of Slovene Istria. Numerous examples of CCA for tourism in the world so far confirm that these factors are deciding with destinations in developed countries, Slovene Istria being one of them. In underdeveloped and developing countries it has been found out that socio-demographic and psycho-political carrying capacity indicators are more deciding.

The present carrying capacity of each indicator has been evaluated by using the following categories: not exceeded, unsustainable and exceeded. If it has been established that the indicator carrying capacity has not been exceeded, we used the category "not exceeded". It has also been defined whether it is possible to increase the capacity, and if it is, we listed the measures that may be used to increase the carrying capacity. For instance, the carrying capacity of accommodation capacity is "not exceeded", the annual average shows the 35% occupancy rate in the year 2003.

If it has been established that the carrying capacity on an indicator has already been exceeded, we used the category "exceeded". For instance, sewage disposal system as it still does not include all settlements in the region and cleaning devices do not allow for all phases of cleaning.

The category "unsustainable" has been used to describe indicators with a carrying capacity that has not been exceeded, but is nearing the carrying capacity limit or in the long term threatens the fragility of the environment in every sense of the word. For this reason we call attention to the measures that need to be taken as soon as possible to sustain their use in the long term. Such an example is sea water quality. If the complete sewage system for all settlements is not built in due time with all suitable cleaning devices, the water might become unsuitable for swimming.

4   Carrying capacity assessment

By analyzing 17 key indicators of carrying capacity in the region in order to develop sustainable tourism it has been established that: 5 indicators (29%) exceed the capacity limit, with 8 indicators (47%) the carrying capacity is unsustainable and 4 indicators (24%) do not exceed the capacity limit.

Carrying capacity has been exceeded in the following indicators: sewage disposal, car parks, road traffic, marinas and moorings and air traffic. It has been established that disposal of sewage is the weakest indicator. The current capacity of this indicator allows for no more than 18,000 tourists. In spite of the planned sewage system upgrade, the peak season capacity will not meet the requirements of the present maximum number of tourists, especially if we take into consideration both, registered and unregistered tourists. The project of sewage system building allows for the unexpected and expected increase of inhabitants and increased demands of the industry. The planned reserves would be sufficient for 29,200 tourists.

The next carrying capacity indicator is the lack of parking lots. In peak season we are currently short of 6,175 parking lots. By the year 2020 the number is expected to rise to 7,750 taking into account a mere 30% increase in the number of registered tourists. In high season demand exceeds the supply of car parking facilities everywhere and the problem presents a huge obstacle to accessibility. Multi-storey car parks have to be built in urban areas and car parks in the vicinity of junctions and public transport stations by the year 2020. However, the problem has to be solved together with the improvement of public transport. Such solution would be environmentally sound and it would result in the decrease of car parks needed in urban and tourist centers.

The third indicator is road traffic. It has to be stressed that the impact of road traffic on overall carrying capacity evaluation in a region is considerable. It has a negative impact on several indicators, such as car parks, air quality, the satisfaction of local inhabitants and overall satisfaction of tourists. Congestions become critical in high season, on holidays and at weekends. Apart from building highways we have to improve bus transport by introducing smaller coaches throughout the year and start passenger transport by the sea between our coast and towns of the northern Adriatic. The proposed introduction of tram or intercity rail connecting our coast with Italy and Croatia is a good but expensive idea. We must not forget cycling, an alternative means of transport mainly within and between urban areas.

The analysis has shown that infrastructure includes the most important limiting indicators preventing the sustainable development of tourism in the region. Marina carrying capacity in high season has been exceeded and the number of moorings throughout the year is inadequate. It leads to the fact that one day trippers in marinas moor their vessels in prohibited areas and pollute the sea.

The carrying capacity of antiquated airport in inadequate and it makes landing possible just for small, obsolete and noisy aircraft. Upgrading the airport would allow for modern quieter planes which would be most important due to its vicinity to an extremely fragile area around salt pans in Secovlje. Therefore we support modernization in concordance with impact assessment and propose limiting the volume of traffic by imposing high ecological taxes.

The sustainable development of tourism calls for measures which would improve the carrying capacity of presently inadequate infrastructure. Apart from this it is necessary to implement measures for increasing the capacity of indicators demonstrating unsustainable carrying capacity: beaches, sea water quality, solid waste disposal, parks and green areas, potable water quantity, railway transport, satisfaction of inhabitants with the effects of tourism and overall satisfaction of tourists.

First we have to ensure the adequate quantity of potable water and the substitute for the quantity lost because of possible disruptions in supply from Croatia. We also have to increase the capacity of water supply to provide uninterrupted supply in case of drought in peak season. The execution of the building plan for the accumulation in Padez would provide the quantities of potable water needed for the 30% increase in tourist arrivals by the year 2020.

The present way of solid waste collecting and disposing is unsustainable. A regional system has to be established, the plan was outlined in the Regional Development Program of South Primorska by the year 2007.

On the beaches the maximum standard of 10 sq m per swimmer has already been exceeded, on the other hand the minimum standard of 6 sq m per swimmer is likely to allow for the 30% increase in accommodation capacity projected by the year 2020. Most popular beaches tend to be overcrowded in high season. Natural beaches tend to be disorderly, but as they are also less crowded it would be possible to spread the tourist load to such areas. In this case it would be urgent to build ample facilities and introduce minimal measures for the protection of swimmers as well as the environment. The capacity of beaches can be increased by building swimming pools, at least one third of them should be indoors to be operational all the year round. Although one of the possible measures could be also to extend the coastline by building artificial lagoons, it has to be thoroughly investigated and the impact on the environment must be considered.

The quality of sea water is still within the criteria for swimming waters. However, in some places it occasionally does not meet the criteria or is nearing the limits of acceptable. In order to improve the quality of sea water it is urgent to improve the treatment of rain fall and the existing sewage system with cleaning devices.

The present railway transport is not efficiently used. The planned building of the second track will enable the use of faster trains and open the door to Slovene Istria for tourists from faraway countries. The areas covered by parks or other green areas have to be increased and not the other way round. In case they have to be built up due to the infrastructure it has to be done after a careful consideration and they have to be replaced afterwards. The region should distinguish itself as a cultural landscape where public and private green areas prevail and are used for outdoor recreation.

The negative attitude of local inhabitants towards tourism is caused by inadequate infrastructure in high season which has a considerable impact on the quality of life. In general mass tourism makes negative impact on the environment. The upgrading of infrastructure will undoubtedly improve the attitude of local inhabitants who should be also invited to take an active part in planning the tourism development. Local inhabitants should also get involved in tourism offer and be encouraged to start their own enterprise.

Tourists coming to Portoroz find accommodation in the resort satisfactory, which cannot be said for the rest of the offer in the destination. They miss variety in the events and entertainment offered, they think beaches should be in a better condition and that there should be more car parks available. They feel they should be better informed about the tourism offer. They are disturbed by noise in Portoroz. Service providers should cooperate when conceiving and carrying out projects. To put it in a nutshell, the management of a tourist destination should be more efficient. In 2003 the survey conducted in the high season in several coastal towns led to the same conclusion. This should be taken into account when planning the sustainable development of tourism in the whole region. We should try to maximize guest satisfaction in the areas where tourism is well developed and avoid dissatisfaction of tourists in the areas where tourism is still to be developed.

The implementation of measures meant to maintain the present capacity has to continue. In addition, we have to start carrying out measures meant to improve the exploitation of capacities of the following indicators, with which the carrying capacity is not exceeded: potable water quality, air quality, accommodation capacity and transport by sea.

The proper quality of potable water is ensured by the cleaning device in Cepki and the implementation of security measures in the protected areas around the source of the river Rizana in the municipality of Koper. In some other areas water sources still need to be protected by taking precautionary measures.

Estimate of air quality is based on insufficient data since the monitoring of air quality has not been established yet. It should be done in the foreseen future to make it possible to take the measures for the prevention of excessive pollution in the region.

When it comes to accommodation capacities, we should first use the present capacities more efficiently and only after we have done so start thinking about the building of new ones. More emphasis should be put on the inefficient transport by sea which has to be developed by building suitable passenger terminals in transport centers in the vicinity of urban areas. We should particularly boost the development of ship transport between towns and tourist resorts in the northern part of the Adriatic sea.

The analysis of carrying capacity has shown that the region can presently accept the maximum of 18,000 tourists. The carrying capacity is limited by the indicator disposal of sewage, which has the lowest capacity. By building the sewage system and the cleaning devices planned to be finished by the year 2008 the carrying capacity of the region will increase to 29,200 tourists. However, this will not meet the needs of the maximum number of tourists in peak season, which amounts to a total of 33,750. According to this limitation the maximum number of tourists coming in the peak season should be decreased, especially if we want to deal with the sewage by the rules. This is the conservative scenario regarding the number of tourists, but it would improve the quality of swimming water and sustainable development.

5 Measures for carrying capacity implementation and monitoring

The assessment of carrying capacity of the region should be regarded as a tool to be used by tourist destination managers in order to plan and carry out the sustainable development of tourism in the region. It functions as guidance in making long term decisions as well as decisions taken on a daily basis. The process of carrying capacity analysis and its implementation play a very important role in education and make those who are involved in the process of tourism planning aware of the importance of sustainable development in the region.

Nevertheless, we have to be aware of the fact that the estimated carrying capacity is not fixed and does not determine the maximum number of tourists once and for ever. When the circumstances used to define it change and when we resort to appropriate strategic planning, we can increase the capacity and similarly it can be decreased by acting recklessly or by resorting to inappropriate tourism development. For this reason it is necessary to plan measures for the carrying capacity increase.

The most urgent measures for the increase in carrying capacity are as follows: the complementation of the existing sewage system, the improvement of public transport with special emphasis on transport by the sea, the construction of multi-storey car parks together with the prompt reaction to the lack of parking lots in critical areas, the provision of a supplemented quantity of potable water and encouragement of economical water and energy consumption, increase in the use of renewable sources of energy, selective collection of solid waste and recycling throughout the region, better care for public and private green areas, recycling water for irrigation systems, more diversity and better quality of tourism offer in the region.

In order to extend tourism offer over the whole year and to increase the occupancy of tourism capacities we should: build heated and indoor swimming pools, build various sports, recreational and entertainment facilities and start different activities, rebuild and promote old towns and villages and other cultural heritage, organize various cultural, entertainment, sports and recreational events throughout the year, create opportunities for shopping tourism, promote congress tourism, offer interesting excursions to towns, countryside and nearby tourist destinations, also by sea (Postojna cave, Lipica, Skocjan caves, Karst, Venice, Croatian Istria, etc) throughout the year, include protected areas into tourism offer, constantly improve tourism offer according to market trends (ecotourism, adventure tourism, active tourism...), create ecological brand for the whole region as a tourist destination.

The most urgent measures for the development of tourism in the countryside that would lead to good use of available resources in the whole region and complement littoral tourism offer are as follows: building accommodation facilities in the countryside, particularly by renovating the existing buildings that present local architecture, building the network of walking, cycling, riding and theme trails, reviving cultural heritage and inclusion of natural attractions, events and produce sales, offering various local specialties and wines, boosting the development of entrepreneurship in the countryside and educating local inhabitants and developing cross-regional cooperation in the countryside and within the whole region (Karst, Croatia, Italy).

Steps that have to be made in order to extend the season throughout the year and to develop tourism in the countryside are intertwined and produce a synergistic effect. By extending the season and expanding tourism over the whole region we would make a better use of a very expensive infrastructure which is currently fully exploited just in peak season. In this way we would also achieve its profitability. In this way we would also relieve the strain put on indicators by exceeding the carrying capacity limit and avoid the need to invest in infrastructure. Simultaneously tourism income would be increased and tourism offer would be easier improved and complimented.

By offering various events and excursions we complement tourism offer and achieve satisfaction of tourist, extend their stay and in this way also the season. Spreading the tourist load over the whole region would reduce the number of tourists on beaches and on some roads, solve the problem of parking, sewage and as a result increase the carrying capacity of the region.

6 Conclusions

However, first we have to deal with the indicators where the carrying capacity limit is already exceeded or is unsustainable. At the same time we have to be aware of the fact that the investments are long-term and most local communities are not able to cope with them on their own. Government, EU structural funds and other investors (strategic partners, EBRD, World Bank) will be needed for the implementation of plans. Further investment in tourism infrastructure is recommended as it makes possible the quality improvement, the extension of the tourism season and better use of present accommodation capacities.

Only in this way we can develop sustainable tourism in accordance with physical, ecological, infrastructural, sociological and psychological capacity of the region.

A good use of GIS can facilitate the close monitoring of carrying capacity and such a system is much needed in every tourist destination. Apart from this, there should be also such a common information system for all service providers that would include a common reservation system, marketing and promotion of a destination. Needless to say, only such organization and equipment, together with well-qualified staff, would ensure that regional tourist offices manage a tourist destination efficiently and competently. To sum up, it is necessary to change the carrying capacity by improving the tourism destination management.

References

[1] Jurincic, I., Sustainable development of tourism on Slovene Littoral, and carrying capacity assessment. *Public enterprise* **16**, pp. 345-357, 1998.
[2] UNEP/MAP/PAP, *Guidelines for carrying capacity assessment for tourism the Mediterranean coastal area.* Split, 1996.
[3] World Tourism Organisation, *What tourism managers need to know – A practical guide to the development and use of indicators of sustainable tourism.* Madrid,1995.
[4] Eastman, J.R., *Idrisi 32: Guide to GIS and Image Processing.* Clark University: Worcester, 1999.
[5] Coccossis, H., Mexa, A. & Collovini, A., *Defining, measuring and evaluating carrying capacity in European tourism destinations.* University of Aegean: Athens, 2002.

The role of industries in air pollution and guidelines: a case study of the city of Tabriz

H. Mojtabazadeh
Azad University, Tehran Centre Branch

Abstract

The emergence of the renaissance and invention of the steam engine was the beginning of the industrial revolution era, which resulted in the introduction of a large number of industrial complexes as a basis for new investments and the development of the societies.

In the light of this issue, some countries (the present developed countries), which were regarded as the pioneers of industrial revolution, were able to continue their way so as to become industrialized, especially in the last three decades of the 19th century, and it was due to the advantages they had, like specialized manpower and wealth. This also caused a gap between prevention societies and underdeveloped countries. From that time on, some of the underdeveloped countries, which were in search of finding a way to compensate for the lag, hastily decided to become industrialized while disregarding the hazardous aspects of this phenomenon on their environment (ecological problems).

Our country Iran, as well as other countries, in its second developing program decided to consider industrialization in its long term program, therefore the city of Tabriz with a population of over 2 million was selected as the core of the industrialization in this project. In this study the researcher noticed that because of some problems like inaccurate planning and inappropriate location finding for the industrial complexes in Tabriz, it has had a negative impact on air pollution.

Right now the city of Tabriz is suffering from some sort of air pollution like other big cities. This article attempts to name some of the key components that have to be considered before implementation of any industrial project.
1. Location finding for any manufacturing site in accordance with geographical conditions.
2. Classification of the industries according to the amount of pollution they may have.
3. Study of the impacts of environmental pollution that is caused by industries.
4. Presentation of applied guidelines for minimizing the environmental problems.
Keywords: industry, pollution, environment, sustainable development.

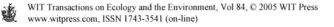
WIT Transactions on Ecology and the Environment, Vol 84, © 2005 WIT Press
www.witpress.com, ISSN 1743-3541 (on-line)

1   Introduction

Nowadays, cities are considered to be the most populated places. Villagers and farmers gradually leaving their habitats and prefering life in the big cities. As a result, cities becoming more and more populated.Yet people have their own needs, they need to find a job, they ask for a better way of life and a raise in their income.

Right in the beginning of the century industrialization and expansion of the factories became the main concern of the developing countries.

The city of Tabriz in Iran, that could hold a large population in it turned to become as one of the industrial poles in the country. Within the years 1967-1975 the city of Tabriz was the subject of new changes and developments. But in the process of industrialization and installation of the manufacturing sites and factories, some decision makers and executive managers did not try to take the geographical and topographical conditions of the city into their considerations, therefore, the city of Tabriz became more and more polluted and the peoples, social health and hygiene were endangered.

The consequences of all these wrong measures were the imposition of large amount of expenses on people.

In this article the researcher is not only trying to manipulate the present problem but is also in search of finding a solution to the problem that can be implemented in Tabriz and in the other similar places in the other parts of the world.

2   Industrial location finding regarding the geographical conditions of the place

Tabriz is the center of east Azerbaijan province and is located in the North west of Iran, within the 46.17 degrees east longitudinal and 35.05 degrees north latitudinal position.

In other words, the city of Tabriz is on the outskirts of Sahand mountain and east west of a place which is called Tabriz plain. The natural land of Tabriz looks like a big ditch which is surrounded by mountains on three sides. It is only in the west that the city opens up into plain lands of brackish type that is the result of the functions of the conical section of a river. The city's elevation from the sea level is between 11350-12550 meters with a general slope of the land towards the west.

At present most of the big industries and pollutants are located in the south west of Tabriz. In spring southwest wind is blowing high and in the fall and winter it seems to be considerably high. Because of the inversion phenomenon, the situation in Tabriz gets much worse in winter.

Fumes, smoke coming out of thermal power plants and Tabriz refinery exhausts are taken directly towards the city. One can vividly see the moving pollutant materials that are coming towards the central part of the city. The natural slope of the land from east to west and the specific topographical position

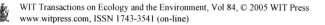

causes the height of the inversion layer to be lower in the east with regard to the west.

For this reason, inversion layer in the east drops down earlier than from the west and this will cause a faster exchange of atmosphere in the east.

Since these big industrial contaminating sources, with their 75.55% contamination materials are among the most important sources of Pollution, their dreadful impacts on environmental social, economic and health aspects of human beings are of great concern. Therefore, all the attempts should be in the direction of finding appropriate locations with more emphasis on having an understanding of the geography of peoples social and behavioral way of life as well as trying to eradicate the echo logical and environmental problems.

3 Classification of the major industries according to the amount of contamination they make in the place of study

Generally speaking there are three categories of industries that cause air pollution.

1. Industries that cause air pollution in their process of production: such as chemical and petrochemical industries.
2. Industries that the fuel of which causes pollution: such as thermal power plants.
3. Industries that both in the process of production and utilization of different types of fuels pollute the air such as Foundries, Moulding industries and Oil refineries.

The city of Tabriz suffers from five different types of pollutants:

1. Tabriz oil refinery
2. Tabriz thermal power plant
3. Tabriz brick burning furnaces across the road
4. Kaja abad brick burning furnaces
5. Asphalt making units

4 Industries and their impact on contaminating the environment

There are different factors and sources of air pollution that have been observed in the place of study with their amount of pollution.

Table 1.

Air contamination sources	Percentage
All means of transportations	0.49%
Factories, houses and businesses	0.77%
Major industrial sources	98.74%
Total	100%

Source: Mojtabazadeh Hossein, Tabriz industrial development, University of Tabriz 1999.

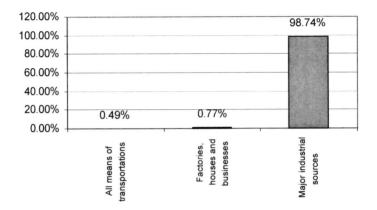

Figure 1:   Percentage of the air pollutants in the city of Tabriz.

From the point of view of the amount of air contamination Tabriz Thermal power plant is the second after Tabriz refinery. The amount of the fuel that is used for the production of an average of 700 Megawatts power per hour by the two steam units of the power plant is about 179.9 cubic meters per hour or 4,317,600 liters per day or 4102 tons of mazut per day.

Regarding the minimum percentage weight of sulfur (2.5%) and conditions governing the power plant, the type and the amount of contamination materials are shown in the following table.

5   Type and the amount of contaminating materials of Tabriz thermal power plant

Asphalt factories in Tabriz and its suburbs are among the other sources of contamination. There are about 17 asphalt unit factories that 7 of them can be found in Laleh Dareh Cie in southwest of Tabriz and the rest are located in the suburbs.

Table 2.

Air contamination material	Amount tonnages per day	Remarks
Carbon Mono Oxide	22%	Sulfur oxides May exceed to 246.1 ton per day in the case of any increase in the percentage of sulfur weight
Organic gases	1.99	
Nitrogen Oxide (No2)	54	
Sulfur Oxide (So2)	205.1	
Particles	5.2	
Total	266.3	

Source: Hossein Mojtabazadeh industrial development of the city of Tabriz, Tabriz University 1999.

Contamination sources in asphalt factories in Tabriz are: circulatory driers, lifters, screeners, mixers, storing pits, preservation of sands in open areas. Among the different contaminating sources, circulatory driers are the biggest sources of dust and dirt spreading.

Heavy traffic that is caused by different means of transportations and the consumption of different fuel products by houses, companies and small industries in Tabriz suburbs are other sources of air pollution. Urban developments, winds flowing from the west and inversion phenomenon are other intensifying factors.

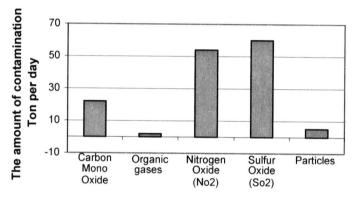

Figure 2:   Type and the amount of contaminating materials from Tabriz thermal power plant.

6   Conclusions, implications and suggestions for the limitation of Tabriz ecological problems

The results of the above study show that because of the geopolitical conditions of the city of Tabriz and regarding the population of the city at that time, the executive measures for that implementation of the industrialization pattern in Tabriz have been taken for the fulfillment of benefits of people not only in Tabriz but also in the area, and is quite justifiable. But what remains unsolved, is the issue of disregarding the political and economic criterions in the project and not observing the geographical, topographical conditions of Tabriz like: the direction of the blowing of the wind and the amount of the rainfall, and all this has disturbed not only the ecology of the area but also deteriorated the economic condition of the people.

A comparison of the past and the present situation in Tabriz will clarify the results of this scientific study. According to a report from the bureau of statistics of Iran in 1965, every 2 minutes 5 of the people of Azerbaijan (particularly from Tabriz) entered the capital city of Tehran. And in the process of implementation of these industries and up to 1982 the situation reversed, and people not only left Tabriz but also many people from the other cities moved to Tabriz.

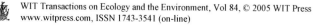 WIT Transactions on Ecology and the Environment, Vol 84, © 2005 WIT Press
www.witpress.com, ISSN 1743-3541 (on-line)

But later on, since 1984, with the expansion of the air pollution, people decided to leave their hometowns and emigrated to the other places which has caused the drain of the brains and the capitals from the city has imposed large amount of hygiene and cure expenses on the people. This problem right now is regarded as one of the main concerns of the local executive managers.

The implications of this study with some suggestions will not only stop the inauspicious phenomenon of air pollution but also prevent emigration in accordance with technological growth. It is only in this case that we can enjoy our environment.

7 Suggestions

1. Establishment of a green belt between the populated areas and those of polluting industries.
2. Avoiding the establishment of the new pollutant industries.
3. Replacement of the pollutant industries with the new ones.
4. Filtration of the polluting industries in accordance with the international standards.
5. Replacement of the fossilized fuels and means of producing energy.
6. Drain aging the sewage to the barren and unpopulated lands.
7. Establishment of hygiene training centers that can help the workers and the local residences.
8. Equipping the local means of transportations with CNG type of burning.
9. Establishment of new towns regarding the climatic conditions and advantages of the place.
10. Appropriate location finding for the industries regarding the geopolitical conditions of the place.

References

[1]   7-Bahram Soltani, K: collection of theories of urbanization methods and Environment, Tehran, Environment protection organization, 1365 (1986)
[2]   Clark Michael. S. Horizons in physical Geography Macmillan Edac London 1987
[3]   Dioxides C.A the Human settlement that wended 1914 McGraw Hill Nel
[4]   Eshkevari, S.H: principles and theories of area planning, university of Tabriz, 1378 (1998)
[5]   Executive manager of the Sahand new town, Tabriz city Detached Developmental location finding, Tabriz 1365 (1986)
[6]   Hosseinzadeh Dalir,K: Tabriz the Great, An urbanic Area for programming and planning, Tabriz university, 1378 (1998)
[7]   Keith smith Environmental hazard Routledge London 1992
[8]   Konya Allan Design primer for Hot climate the Architectural Press Ltd lor 1980 p 12-13
[9]   Petr akos George urban concert ration and Agglomerate a tion Econ urbann studies No 1992

[10] Raoofi, M: The Role of small industries in East Azerbaijan province industrial development, Tabriz university, 1366 (1987)
[11] Reis M a Leonard. The urban press Free press 1964
[12] Shokohi, H: Urban Geography, Tabriz university, 1379 (1999)
[13] The main office of the Environmental protection organization of the province, A survey and a study on the air contaminating source of Tabriz, Tabriz 1367 (1988)
[14] Zahedi, M: Coupenic, method of finding Azerbaijan Meteorological condition, Tabriz university, 1378 (1998)
[15] Zamorredian, M.J principles and theories of Civil Engineering, university of Mashad, 1367 (1988)

The Solar D House

M. Garrison
School of Architecture, The University of Texas at Austin, U.S.A.

Abstract

The Solar Decathlon provided a national forum for competition among fourteen university student teams, each of which designed, built, and operated a totally solar-powered home with a home office and their transportation needs using a solar-charged vehicle. The competition took place on the National Mall in Washington D.C., where each house was constructed and operated from September 18 to October 10, 2002. The competition consisted of ten contests focusing on energy production, energy-efficiency, design, thermal comfort, refrigeration, lighting, communication and transportation.

1 Introduction

Professor Michael Garrison of the School of Architecture directed the University of Texas at Austin (UT) Solar Decathlon team along with Pliny Fisk, co-director of the non-profit Center for Maximum Potential Building Systems in Austin, Texas. The graduate student team developed a design that features an open building system using a reusable kit of parts that sits lightly on the land and forms the superstructure around a mobile utility environment. Our investigations suggest that progressive technologies offer solutions to the serious emerging challenges of energy efficiency and sustainable development and thereby become a strong design shaping force. These progressive technologies: photovoltaic (PV) power, passive solar heating, daylighting, natural ventilation, and solar hot water heating were integrated with concepts of affordability and energy conservation to help promote an ideology of sustainable architecture.

2 Design

Given the fact that the competition brief implied a portable and temporary structure that could be erected in a few days without the use of heavy cranes, the

UT Solar Decathlon House is built for change. Gone are nails and glues, cast in place concrete footings and structural welds. In their place are screws, pre-cast foundation pads and structural bolts. The major difference between these scenarios is in the connections between parts; the UT House can come apart and adapt without the destruction of materials.

The UT Solar Decathlon House separates the layers of utilities, structure and infill walls. The entanglement of utilities normally hidden behind gypsum board walls is replaced with utility runs that are in the structural columns and beams and can be accessed easily without disruption to the walls. Likewise the disentanglement of utilities from walls enables controls and utility lines of all types to evolve with technology enhancement.

Figure 1:   Airstream functions as a mobile utility environment.

3   Mobile utility environment

Our team modified a standard Airstream trailer to meet the plumbing (kitchen, bathroom and laundry) needs of the competition. The team "gutted" the Airstream down to the frame and several layers of Icynene insulation were installed so that a better buffer against the exterior climate was established. The interior was finished with bamboo flooring and recycled aluminum wall and ceiling panels. New interior cabinetry was added to house the Airstream's energy and water efficient appliances including a specially made energy-efficient Sunfrost-D.C. refrigerator, an Equator dishwasher that uses only 4.75 gallons (18 liters) per cycle, an Equator combination washer- dryer that uses only 8.27 gallons (31.3 liters) per cycle, a CookTek induction cook top, a General Electric flash-bake oven and a Sun Oven solar cooker for the outside grill. An integral bamboo table and bench were constructed to serve as the dining room and energy efficient lighting was added that consumes less than .5 watts per square foot (joule/sec per .092 square meters). The UT Solar Decathlon Airstream receives all of its power through a series of BP Solar and ASE photovoltaic (PV) arrays. The creative integration of an Airstream trailer into our scheme has the added benefit of isolating all the heat and humidity producing equipment from the rest of the house enabling the rest of the house to have lower internal gains.

4   Environmental controls

In order to make the solar decathlon project work effectively with the sun as its sole power source we employed energy conservation techniques including using, caulking, R-30 wall and Roof Structural Insulated Panels, and double-pane Low-E, Argon filled windows and doors. Secondly, we integrated into the Design energy efficient environmental controls strategies divided into five systems:

* Natural and solar induced ventilation
* Passive solar gain and/or shading
* Daylighting
* Solar hot water heating and Hydro-Air Mechanical Heating and Cooling
* Photovoltaic power

The first three systems are passive, meaning that no electricity or mechanical parts are involved. The last two are active, since they involve the pumping of water and electrical generation via of PV cells.

4.1 Ventilation

In order to reduce the dependency on active cooling, natural ventilation was designed as the primary means of cooling for much of the year. Since the building relies solely on solar power to supply all its needs, designing for ventilation allows the active cooling loads to be reduced. Back up cooling loads are provided by small Hydro-Air hydronic fan coil units coupled with an ice-battery (thermal storage) unit.

The project goal was to channel prevailing breezes into the building, increase their velocity so as to maximize the perceived cooling effect, and to ensure that all of the inhabited volume of the spaces had effective air movement.

The solar decathlon house is based on the principles of a historical dog run house scheme that emphasizes natural ventilation cooling and was designed to be a demonstration of natural ventilation and other "green building " techniques for an energy-efficient and comfortable home.

The house is a rectilinear configuration, with the dog run corridor bisecting the plan running from south to north. The living spaces are arranged on both sides of this corridor, with door openings onto the corridor and window openings out of the sides and north wall of the house. The plan is staggered to provide opportunities for creating pleasant outdoor rooms that take advantage of the breezes. When a summer breeze sweeps through the central corridor, it creates a

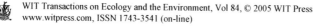

low-pressure zone along its path. Simultaneously, the breezes striking the front and sidewalls of the house, finding only small windows to penetrate, create high-pressure zones. The combination of these two pressure conditions, in turn forces an accelerated airflow through the openings in the front and sidewalls of the house. The window openings can be controlled to modulate the velocity and channel the direction of the airflow.

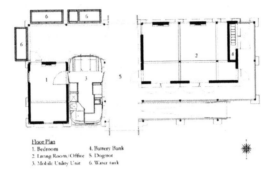

Floor Plan
1. Bedroom   4. Battery Bank
2. Living Room/Office 5. Dogtrot
3. Mobile Utility Unit 6. Water tank

Figure 2:   UT Solar Decathlon House Plan, based on a dog run (5) scheme to maximize natural ventilation.

Because summer breezes in Washington D.C. are most active in the morning and late afternoon the dog run porch is used during these periods for immediate cooling ventilation and for "loading" the house with morning coolness that is retained in walls, floors and furniture. Conversely, the evening breezes are used to "flush" the house of heat that accumulates during the afternoon.

The volume of air that flows through a structure is governed by the size of the window openings. The velocity of air movement through the structure is maximized, creating the greatest cooling, when the area of outlets is greater than the area of inlet openings. The careful sizing and placement of air inlets and outlets greatly enhanced the cooling effect of cross ventilation. The window outlet air for the solar decathlon house is two times the inlet area. CFD simulations determined than an 8 mile per hour (1.6 kilometers per hour) breeze could achieve up to 50 air changes per hour moving at a speed of 566 (fpm) feet per minute (172.5 meters per minute). Air moving at 566 fpm will increase the upper temperature range of the house interior bioclimatic comfort zone.

Once the window schemes were worked out, the team built a physical 3/4 inch (1.9 centimeters) scale model and tested it at the University of Texas Pickle Research Center wind tunnel facility. The wind tunnel test confirmed that a 2 to 1 north south ratio of windows worked if the north openings were spread out. High north wall vents were effective, the dog run was the breeziest part of the house and openings in the east and west walls are essential when the breeze is along an E-W axis.

During the heat of the day a ventilated air space with a PV roof over a radiant barrier shields the ceiling from intense solar radiation. Continuous soffit vents at the eves of the roof overhang vent the attic. The air is exhausted at the peak of the roof using a continuous metal ridge vent. The reflective roof, a radiant roof barrier, a ventilated air buffer and R-30 Structural Insulated Roof Panels keep the mean radiant temperature of the ceiling cooler. The broad roof overhangs; a radiant wall barrier, light exterior colors, and R- 30 Structural Insulated Wall Panels also keep the mean radiant temperature of the walls cooler. The cooler mean radiant surface temperatures and the use of ceiling fans extend the upper limit of comfort zone and minimize the need for additional active, or mechanical cooling.

4.2 Passive solar heating

Although the Solar Decathlon competition ran from late September to early October 2002 in Washington D.C., which had generally mild weather at that time, the project was designed for high performance during cold winter months and hot summer periods in Austin, Texas where it makes its home. The goal was to use direct gain to trap solar radiation during the winter days and to have a highly insulative thermal envelope that prevents this heat from escaping during the night in order to reduce the reliance on active mechanical heating. Based on Visual DOE-3 simulations passive solar heating was found to be adequate in maintaining comfortable conditions in winter inside the house. An optimum balance point between maximizing heat gain and minimizing afternoon overheating was achieved with a south-facing glazing ratio of 1.2 square feet of glazing per square foot of conditioned floor area. This glazing ratio is calculated to provide up to 72% of the solar heating fraction while minimizing the diurnal temperature swing. A back-up heating system that uses hot water supplied to small fan-coil units is designed to provide the make-up heating required for cool morning periods in Washington D.C. and in Austin, Texas.

Figure 3:   Passive solar heating through south facing windows.

4.3 Daylighting

To reduce the need for artificial lighting and therefore reduce the demand for solar power, natural daylight was the primary source of lighting. Daylighting reduces the need for excessive amounts of electrical lighting required to illuminate the space. However, too much daylighting may produce glare and an unacceptable amount of heat gain.

Figure 4:   Daylighting of the solar decathlon interior.

Good daylighting is achieved in the dogtrot design by providing bilateral lighting, (light from two sides). A deep roof overhang along the south elevation controls glare.

Using the rectilinear daylight simulator at The University of Texas at Austin, we were able to test the light intensity in various locations within our 3/4" = 1' scale model. Light sensors were affixed at a height of 30" (scaled) above the floor. Using the daylight fraction method, we were able to convert values into footcandles specifically for a typical overcast Washington D.C. sky. We found that it was not difficult to achieve the minimum intensity (15 footcandles) of uniform light at the work plane throughout the building during the middle of the day. Furthermore, with the narrow plan (13.5' deep), the daylighting was relatively balanced.

4.4 Solar water heating

The solar decathlon project employs an evacuated solar water system manufactured by Thermo Technologies to reduce the need for electric solar water heating. The direct pump system uses an electric circulating pump to move heat from the 30-tube manifold evacuated tube solar collector to a 90-gallon water storage tank.

A differential controller turns the circulating pump on or off as required. There are two sensors, one at the outlet of the collectors, and the other at the bottom of the tank. They signal the controller to turn the pump on when the collector outlet is 20°F warmer than the bottom of the tank. It shuts off when the temperature differential is reduced to 5°F. The philosophy behind this design is that the cost of heating your collectors with hot water from you tank is low cost freeze protection if only required occasionally. These systems are commonly used in the Sunbelt, and only where freezing is a rare occasion. The annual total BTU's collected per square meter (10 tubes) equals 3,602,086 for Washington D.C., and the annual total BTU's collected per square meter for Austin, Texas equals 4,625,681. Beyond domestic hot water use the hot water in the tank was used in conjunction with a Hydro-Air hydronic fan-coil unit to provide back up heating during extreme conditions.

Figure 5:   Evacuated tube solar hot water collectors.

4.5 Photovoltaic (PV) power system

To meet the power needs of the solar decathlon's modern home-office, a stand-alone solar photovoltaic power system forms an integral part of the design. A stand-alone system has to have a battery bank that services a certain number of dark days, which in our case was designed for 3 dark days. This does not imply that the battery bank will discharge entirely if there are three moderately cloudy days. PV modules continue to produce power from natural ambient light during cloudy days, although at greatly reduced efficiency, and so the batteries received some charge during cloudy periods during the competition and power in the batteries was not a real problem even during several days of cloudy weather.

The 3.6 kW PV collector array, which covers a portion of the roof area above both the bedroom and living room sections of the house, supplies power that is routed through Schottky diodes, lighting arrestors and charge controllers to a battery bank. The PV arrays were mounted at an incline angle of 20 degrees to the horizontal and face due south.

Figure 6:   Solar PV system-25 BP solar PV panels and 6 ASE PV panels on the solar decathlon house in Austin, Texas.

4.5.1 Load analysis

All the electric loads in the home are supplied from the battery bank. This ensures that each load receives a steady power supply irrespective of weather conditions and time of day. Power from the batteries flows through a Trace SW5548OG Inverter that coverts the DC input into a sine wave AC output to service all the loads in the house except the refrigerator. The power then flows to an AC panel-board that consists of breakers for each circuit and one main circuit breaker (MCB). The office, Airstream, solar car, and the bedroom are each on separate circuits.

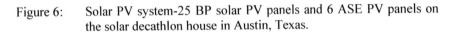

Table 1:   PV output.

MONTH	Sun hrs/day	Total Power (Wh)
		25 BP+6 ASE
Jan.	2.81	10326.75
Feb.	3.85	14148.75
Mar.	4.69	17235.75
Apri.	5.61	20616.75
May	5.58	20506.50
Jun.	5.78	21241.50
July	5.75	21131.25
Aug.	5.53	20322.75
Sept.	4.8	17640.00
Oct.	4.29	15765.75
Nov.	3.69	13560.75
Dec.	2.79	10253.25
Yearly		**202749.75**

Retail costs quoted by PV panel suppliers were in the range of $10,000 a kW, thus a 3.6 KW system would retail for $36, 00 and a 7.68 would be $76,800 dollars. We believed that it was important to demonstrate that a solar PV system be affordable so we used a more economical 3.6 KW systems. During the competition we found the 3.6 kW systems adequate for our needs if we managed the load and did not utilize every appliance and charge the electric car at the same time. Our load analysis revealed that we needed a capacity of 1,107 Ah (accounting for 3 dark days) to power the system. We installed 20-Trojan L-16 6V batters to meet our storage needs.

Table 2 shows that the energy needs of the house average 10.33 kWh a day, theoretically creating surplus energy that could be used to charge the electric vehicle.

Table 2:   Total power requirements.

Inverter Powered Appliance	Whrs/day
17" Computer Monitor	300.0
Computer/Web Server	1320.0
19" Television	480.0
Inkjet Printer	17.5
Washer-Dryer	35.7
Dishwasher	1450.0
Cook top	1800.0
Differential Controller	800.0
Slow Pump	850.0
Lighting	1176.0
Ceiling Fans	150.0
Microwave	450.0
Bio Radiant Hydronic System	1500.0
Total	10329

4.5.2 Transportation analysis

The electric car provided to each team for the "Getting Around" competition is a Ford Th!nk Neighbor. The competition organizers recommend that each team charge their car with excess energy generated by their PV system and then analyze how much mileage they will get out of their car. For each full 8-hour charging, the car has a range of 30 miles. The chart below depicts how many miles can be driven per month depending on potential excess power.

Figure 7:   Ford Electric Think Car adjacent to the UTSOA solar decathlon.

Table 3:   Electric vehicle power consumption.

Month	Total Power	Excess Power	
	Wh/month	Wh/month	miles/month
January	309802.5	-67.50	
February	424462.5	114592.50	249
March	517072.5	207202.50	450
April	618502.5	308632.50	671
May	615195.0	305325.00	664
June	637245.0	327375.00	712
July	633937.5	324067.50	705
August	609682.5	299812.50	652
September	529200.0	219330.00	477
October	472972.5	163102.50	355
November	406822.5	96952.50	211
December	307597.5	-2272.50	
Total	602492.5	2364052.5	

5   Conclusion

During the competition the 3.6 kW PV powered solar house provided enough excess power to run the solar electric car 100 miles per week. This distance was adequate to provide for all the grocery shopping and the transportation needs of the home and home office. Although the winning school's 7.68 kW competition entry was able to run their solar electric car 250 miles per week, the UT solar decathlon house easily met the daily supply of energy for its occupants to survive and prosper in today's society and did so at a more affordable PV array size of only 3.6 kW.

References

[1] Hartkopf, V., V. Loftness, P. Drake, F. Dubin, P. Mill, and G. Ziga. <u>Designing the Office of the Future: The Japanese Approach to Tomorrow's Workplace</u>. New York: John Wiley & Sons, 1993

[2] Allard, F., <u>Natural Ventilation In Buildings,</u> London: James & James, 1997.

[3] Sick, F., and T. Erge, <u>Photovoltaics In Buildings,</u> London: James & James, 1998.

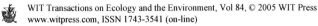

A computational model based planning approach for integrated resource management with a case study

S. Mingshan, P. Shuihong, Z. Xiusheng & H. Jiankun
Contemporary Management Research Center/Energy Environment Economy Institute, Tsinghua University, Beijing, People's Republic of China

Abstract

Regional sustainable development issues, such as sustainable city development and environmental rehabilitation, are complicated management issues. The integrated resource management approach and its related technologies can be applied to these issues. Computational model based planning is required in the institutional design, such as establishment of a tradable water rights system, when an integrated management approach is applied.

Computational model based planning is applied to environmental rehabilitation in Tarim valley for integrated resource management. Tarim valley is situated in the south of Xinjiang Autonomous Region in China. A tradable water rights system could be one of the institutional reform schemes for water resource management. But simulation results show that it is necessary to integrate a tradable grass quota system into the institutional design.

To analyze the economic impact of tradable water rights and a tradable grass quota system, a joint multi-product water rights and grass quota trade model with transaction cost is developed. The model integrates ecological improvement and agricultural activities into a system. The variational inequality approach is applied to transform the game-theory models into computational models. The results of model simulation show that a joint tradable water rights and grass quota system will encourage participates to conserve the water and grass resources at the same time. The study also shows that a computational model based planning approach could provide both qualitative and quantitative results for sustainable region planning.

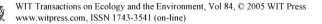
WIT Transactions on Ecology and the Environment, Vol 84, © 2005 WIT Press
www.witpress.com, ISSN 1743-3541 (on-line)

1 Introduction

Regional sustainable development issues, such as sustainable city development and environmental rehabilitation, are complicated management issues.

According to Jackson and Keys [1] management issues can be depicted in 2 dimensions: complex and divergence. As for the dimension of complexity the problem contexts can be spread along a continuum, ranging from simple to complex. As for the dimension of divergence the issue can be unitary, pluralist or conflictual. Therefore, complicated systems can be complicated unitary systems, or complicated pluralist systems or complicated conflictual systems, or a mix of them.

As the problem becomes more complicated the breakthrough was to abandon the method of trying to include in a model all the myriad of interacting variables that appear on the surface of the problem context. The theoretic research on complexity and chaos after 1960's has contributed to the development of methodology for complicated management systems [2].

Along the dimension of divergence the breakthrough came when the aim of producing one single objective model of a problem situation was abandoned. The trick was to make subjectivity central in the methodological process and to work with a variety of models of the world.

There are 2 groups of works to deal with complicated management issues: the rapid approach, and the game theoretic approach. The rapid approach applied human experience and integrated it into the research. The rapid approach includes "Soft OR" [3], the Wuli-Shili-Renli approach [4], the Rapid Rural Appraisal [5], Participant Observation, and others [6]. Game theory is moving ahead very rapidly now and the breadth and depth of its application to economics, political science, management science and other areas is spectacular. Game theory can provide the basic models for some of the components of systems.

Our experience has indicated that many of the challenged problems we encounter are integrated complicated management issues and we can not divide the issues into some separated issues. Therefore, based on the case of natural resource management, we have built the integrated resource management framework [7], and developed the approach [8] and relevant technologies for complicated management issues [9].

A complicated management issue can be modeled as an integrated management system. An integrated management system is a system comprised of inputs, transformations and outputs. Their inputs can be human resources, natural resources, or man-made resources, or a combination of them. The output can be transformed human resources, transformed natural resources, or man made products, or a combination of them.

The integrated management approach is a system approach to guide the management practices for natural resources, human resources, and man-made resources under the situation of fierce competition and high uncertainty. Integrated management includes vertical integration and horizontal integration.

The relevant technologies for an integrated management approach include flow analysis, characteristics analysis and transformation analysis [9]. The flow analysis includes material flow analysis, energy flow analysis, information flow analysis, and value flow analysis. The characteristics analysis included externality analysis, sustainability analysis, and effectiveness analysis. The transformation analysis includes planning, incentive scheme design and information mechanism design. In this paper we explain these technologies. To overcome the challenge of uncertainty in the analysis a participatory research approach (PRA) is also applied.

2 Background of case study

The Tarim River is 2,179 kilometers long. It is the longest inland river in China. It runs west to east along the northern edge of the Taklimakan Desert, the biggest moving desert in China, and flows into Taitema Lake. The main stream of Tarim is divided into the upper reaches of 495 kilometers, the middle reaches of 398 kilometers, and the lower reaches of 428 kilometers. The glaciers and accumulated snow of the mountains nourishes the Tarim River, which flows through the Basin and nurtures the oases embedded along the edges of the Basin [10].

The Tarim River is mainly fed by six tributaries: the Konqi, Weigan, Kaxgar, Yarkant, Hotan, and Aksu Rivers. Today, the Tarim is mainly replenished by the Aksu and Hotan, and in the flood period, by the Yarkant. The main stream retains a volume of about 398 million cubic meters on average [10].

The river plays an important role in the economic and social development of the Xinjiang Uygur Autonomous Region. It has for a long time been irrigating towns and oases in the river valley area. There were many famous towns in the valley when the "silk road" passed through.

Tarim valley is a major production base of quality cotton, pears and apricots in China. The total cotton production in this valley is about 10% of the total production in the country. The natural gas well in the valley is the starting point of the West East Natural Pipeline Program in China. The Tarim Valley is home to 7.7 million people. There are 38 counties among 6 regions, with a total area of 920,600 km^2. Household income in the valley is low compared to other areas of China. The net per capita annual income of a rural household is just 1428 RMB Yuan in 1998 [11].

The water resources in the valley are relatively low compared to the China average and the world average, as shown in figure 1.

In recent years, the ecological environment of the Tarim valley has been deteriorating, especially in the lower reaches of the river. Excessive land reclamation, over-grazing and unreasonable use of water in the upper reaches have led to deterioration of the local environment. As a result of irrational exploitation of areas along the river, Taitema Lake dried up in 1972. As the river is on the fringe of the local desert, desertification is also expanding. Ecological degradation is indicated by long-standing droughts, destruction of grasslands and desertification involving severe sand mobilization. The deteriorated eco-system has restricted Xinjiang's social and economic development, and also posed a threat to the environment of other regions of northwest China.

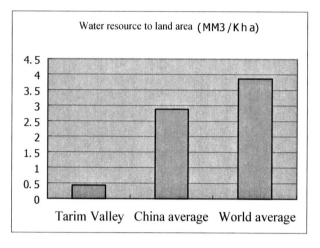

Figure 1:   Water resource in Tarim Valley.

To protect the environment and ecology of this valley, more efforts should be made to control the water usage in the upper reaches, to bring under control the middle reaches and to protect the green belt in the lower part.

There are different options to achieve the objective but the costs of them are quite different. International experiences show that an institutional barrier is one of the barriers for water resource conservation [12]. For example, many cases have showed that a tradable water rights system could be one of the cost effectiveness options.

Therefore, the issues in the Tarim valley are integrated issues with ecological degradation, economic underdevelopment and poverty, which are interlinked with each other. A computational model based planning approach which takes into account different natural resources and economic capacity constraints is necessary for policy analysis and institutional design in the valley.

3   An integrated tradable water rights system and grass quota trade model

3.1 Requirement of integrated models

To analyze the economic impact of tradable water rights system a multi-product water rights trade model is developed [13]. It is a game-theoretic model which simulates the market equilibrium of tradable water rights. In the model there are I participates, $i=1,2,3,..,i,...I$. The economic activities are catalogued into D types, $d=1,2,3,..,d,...D$. The decision variable is production output, and production inputs, such as land, labor, water, water rights. Transaction cost is considered in the model. The utility function of the participant is measured by net benefit from the production and the transaction of water rights. The constraints are land constraint, labor constraint, water constraint, and water rights constraint. It is assumed that the product market is an oligarchy monopoly and the market of water rights is complete competition.

The model simulation shows that establishment of a tradable water rights system will encourage participants to conserve water resources but it cannot encourage participants to allocate more water to grass or wood production. On the other hand, to analyze the economic impact of a tradable grass quota system a grass quota trade model is developed [13].

The model simulation shows that establishment of a tradable grass quota system will encourage participants to conserve their grass resources but it did not encourage households to conserve water resources. The results imply that from the perspective of environmental rehabilitation it is necessary to integrate the grass resources into a water resource management planning approach. The discussion on a field visit also showed that it is important to integrate the water rights system with the grass quota system.

3.2 Integrated tradable water rights system and grass quota trade model

An integrated multi-product water rights and grass quota trade model is developed [13].

In the model there are I participates. The economic activities are catalogued into D types. The decision variable is production output, q_{id}, and production inputs, such as land, labor, water, water rights, grass quota rights. Transaction cost is considered in the model. The objective function and its related constraint are displayed as formula (1) where u_i represents the utility function of participate I which is measured by net benefit from the production and the transaction of water rights and grass quota, A_{id}^m represents land used for production, L_{id}^s represents labour input, $l_{g_i}^k$ represents grass quota, w_{id}^j represents water consumption, and l_i^j represents water quota. $b_{q_i}^k$, o_i^k, $g_{0_i}^k$, $b_{g_i}^k$, b_{id}^m, $b_{I_i}^s$, a_{id}, $\varsigma_{g_i}^k$, e_{id}, and $\varsigma_{g_i}^k$ are parameters.

$$
\begin{cases}
Max(u_i) \\[4pt]
st. \sum_{k=1}^{K} b_{q_i}^k q_{i1} + \sum_{k=1}^{K} \dfrac{2l_{g_i}^k}{o_i^k} + \sum_{k=1}^{K} 2g_0^k \le \sum_{m=1}^{M} b_{g_i}^m A_{i1}^m \\[8pt]
q_{id} \le \sum_{m=1}^{M} b_{id}^m A_{id}^m, d \ne 1 \\[8pt]
q_{id} \le \sum_{s=1}^{S} b_{L_{id}}^s L_{id}^s \\[8pt]
q_{id} \le a_{id} \sum_{j=1}^{J} \varsigma_{id}^j w_{id}^j \\[8pt]
\sum_{d=1}^{D} h_{id}^j w_{id}^j \le l_i^j \\[8pt]
\sum_{d=1}^{D} e_{id} q_{id} \le \sum_{k=1}^{K} \varsigma_{g_i}^k l_{g_i}^k
\end{cases}
\quad (1)
$$

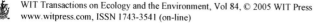

The net benefit can be calculated with sale income minus production cost including water rights cost, grass quota cost, and transaction cost. When market structure for product q_{id} is oligarchy monopoly sale income of product output depends on market price which is affected by the output of participants.

Assuming the market structure for water rights and grass quota is complete competition, the market clearing formula for water rights and grass quota is described by formula (2):

$$\left[\sum_{i=1}^{I} (l_i^{j0} - l_i^{j}) \right] \begin{cases} = 0, & if \ p^{j*} > 0 \\ \geq 0, & if \ p^{j*} = 0 \end{cases} \tag{2}$$

where p^j represents the price for water rights, p_g^j represents the price for grass quota.

4 Simulation of the models and discussion

4.1 Simulation and results

The variational inequality approach can be applied to transform the model into computational models [14]. The modified projection algorithm is applied and it is coded in Matlab.

In the modeling process for the Tarim case participants are the 5 regions: Kezhou, Kashi, Hetian, Akesu, Bazhou. The simulation results show that the cotton production in Kashi and Akesu will decrease by 43% and 19% while the cotton production in Kezhou, Hetian and Bazhou will increase by 160%, 67% and 60% respectively. It also showed that the total cotton production in the valley will decrease by 10%. The simulation shows that mutton production in the valley will increase twofold. This shows that after the establishment of a water rights system and grass quota system participants prefer to plant grass and raise goats rather than cotton production. The simulation shows that the total water consumption for the production activities will decrease by about 40%. This means that sufficient water can be applied for purely ecologically purposes.

4.2 Discussion and recommendation

The results of model simulation show that a joint tradable water rights and grass quota system will encourage participants to conserve the water and grass resources at the same time. Therefore, it is relevant to develop the tradable water rights and grass quota system as an integrated system.

The modeling practice also shows that a computational modeling process could provide both qualitative and quantitative results for sustainable region planning.

References

[1]   Jackson, M. C. and Keys, P., Towards A System of System Methodologies. Journal of the Operational Research Society 35, pp 473-486, 1984.

[2]   Streufert, S. and Swezey, R.W., Complexity, Managers and Organizations. Orlando: Academic Press, 1986.

[3]   Jackson, M., Beyond the Fads: Systems Thinking for Managers. Systems Research, Vol.12 (No.1): pp.25-442, 1995.

[4]   Gao, F. and Gu J., To See Wuli-Shili-Renli Systems Approach from A New View. In J Gu: Systems Science and Systems Engineering. Beijing: Scientific and Technical Document Publishing House, pp157-161, 1998.

[5]   Molnar, A., Community Forestry: Rapid Appraisal. Rome: Community Forestry Note 3 of Food and Agriculture Organization of the United Nation, 1989.

[6]   Ison, R. L. and Ampt, P. R., Rapid Rural Appraisal: A Participatory Problem Formulation Method Relevant to Australian Agriculture. Agricultural Systems, Vol.38 (No.4): pp363-386, 1992.

[7]   Su, M., He, J., Zhou, L. and Gu, S., Integrated Resource Management-- Case Study on Sustainable Wood Energy System, in: Gu J., eds. Systems Sciences and Engineering, Beijing: Scientific and Technical Documents Publishing House, pp157-161, 1998.

[8]   He, J., Su, M. and Wu, H., Integrated Management Approach-System Thinking For Complicated Systems With Alxa Environmental Rehabilitation Case Study, in: Allen, J. K. and Wilby J., eds. Proceeding of 46th Conference of The International Society for the Systems Sciences. Shanghai: ISSS, 2002.

[9]   Su, M., Deng, J., He, J. and Li, G., Integrated Management Technology-System Approach For Complicated Systems With Alxa Environmental Rehabilitation Case Study, in: Allen, J. K. and Wilby J., eds. Proceeding of 46th Conference of The International Society for the Systems Sciences. Shanghai: ISSS, 2002.

[10]   Liu, Y., Jiao, G. and Dai, J., Field Visit Report for Tarim Valley Middle and Down Reach. China Statistics Press: Beijing, 2000.

[11]   Xinjiang Statistics Bureau, Xinjiang Statistics Yearbook 2000. China Statistics Press, 1999.

[12]   Brehm, M.K. and Castro, J.Q., The Market of Water Rights in Chile: Major Issues. Washington D.C.: World Bank Technical Paper, No.285, 1995.

[13]   Su, M. Study on Computational Models and Applications for Marketable Water Right and Grass and Wood Quota Systems in Arid Area. Dissertation Submitted to Tsinghua University for the Degree of Doctor of Management Science. Beijing, 2003.

[14]   Nagurney, A., Network Economics: A Variational Inequality Approach, Kluwer Academic Publishers, 1999.

The areal distribution of applied water above and below soil surface under center pivot sprinkler irrigation system

H. M. Al-Ghobari
*Agricultural Engineering Department, College of Agriculture,
King Saud University, Saudi Arabia*

Abstract

In this study an evaluation of the areal distribution of applied water above and below the soil surface for six center pivot systems was conducted under field conditions, to quantify the subsurface distribution of soil water content and water application on the ground surface. The measured application depth of water and water distribution patterns with the distance from the pivot were presented. Field experimental results showed evidence of the importance of redistribution of the applied surface water. The values of the subsurface uniformity coefficients were higher by approximately 12% than the surface values. It was found that the water within the soil is more uniformly distributed than that applied above the soil surface. An experimental relationship between the uniformity coefficients above and below the soil surface was derived under center pivot sprinkler irrigation systems.
Keywords: water distribution, water uniformity coefficients, center pivot, sprinkle irrigation, nonweighted coefficient of uniformity, water application, areal distribution.

1 Introduction

With population growth in the world, the demand of water is increasing. Hence, the necessity for conservation of water resources increases, particularly in countries of limited water supply, where the agricultural irrigation has traditionally been the major water use sector in these areas, usually in the range of 80 to 90%. The sprinkler irrigation system is widely and universally spread. This is because it has flexibility and water application can be controlled efficiently with it. Center pivot systems are used more than any other irrigation system in the Kingdom of Saudi Arabia due to its high automation level in the wide desert areas. It accounts for more than 80% of the irrigated area and there are more than 20,000 center pivots in the country (Abo-Ghobar and Mohammad, [1]). As the necessity for conservation of water resources increases, the water application uniformity is becoming increasingly important. This increases the need for better-designed and managed sprinkler irrigation systems. Water application uniformity is an important measure of performance used in the design and evaluation of sprinkler irrigation systems. The performance of an irrigation system is described by its uniformity and efficiency. Uniformity refers to the evenness at which water is applied or infiltrated throughout the field and depends on system design and maintenance. Efficiency refers to the amount of water needed for crop production compared with the amount applied to the field and depends on system uniformity and management. It has been demonstrated that the uniformity of irrigation water application has an effect on crop yield (Solomon [14]; Letey [11] and Mantovani et al. [12]).

Numerous investigations and works have been made on the surface distribution of water from sprinklers (Christiansen [4]; Heermann and Hein [9] and Merriam and Keller [13]) and stated the procedures of sprinkler distribution testing above soil surface, e.g. Merriam and Keller [13] and ASAE [3]. A necessary step before calculating an applied water distribution parameter is the accurate measurement of applied water from sprinklers using catch cans or collectors (Fischer and Wallender [6]). Procedures to determine the distribution of water from different sprinkler systems are given in ASAE Standard 5436 [3].

1.1 Uniformity coefficient

Traditionally, center pivot irrigation systems are evaluated by placing a transact of catch cans, uniformly spaced and radially outwards from the pivot point along the lateral. As the machine travels across the transact. The water is caught in the cans, and then the system performance is evaluated from the measured water caught in the cans. Nonuniformity in the center pivot system is assumed to occur more along the lateral than in the direction of travel (Hanson and Wallender [7]). The uniformity of water application could be influenced by many factors. These factors include improper sprinkler nozzling and spacing, wear of sprinklers and pipes, variation in pressure distribution along the lateral, and wind speed and direction during irrigation. Also, the evaluation entailed measuring pressures, system and nozzles flow rates and travel speed of the end tower.

Numerous coefficients of uniformity (CUs) have been developed over the past few decades. These coefficients have been generally accepted as criterion of sprinkler irrigation design. In general, all CUs can be divided into two categories: nonweighted and areal-weighted. Nonweighted CUs are calculated directly from the observations (actual or simulated catch-can data), and each observation is assumed to represent the same land area. The nonweighted coefficient of uniformity (CU) developed by Christiansen [4] is written as:

$$CU = 100\left(1 - \frac{\sum |x_i - \bar{x}|}{n\,\bar{x}}\right) \tag{1}$$

where:

CU = Christiansen's coefficient of uniformity
x_i = the depth in equally spaced catch cans on grid
$\bar{x}$ = the mean depth of water caught in the cans, and
n = number of collectors measured

The above definition required that each catch can represents the depth applied to equal areas could be used to assess the center pivot uniformity along the travel path. But, this is not true for data collected under center pivot irrigation systems where the catch cans are equally spaced along a radial line from the pivot point to the outer end. Heerman and Hein [9] defined the weighted coefficient of uniformity (CU) for center pivot system as:

$$CU = 100\left[1.0 - \frac{\sum_\eta S_s \left|D_s - \dfrac{\sum_\eta D_s S_s}{\sum_\eta S_s}\right|}{\sum_\eta D_s S_s}\right] \tag{2}$$

where:

CU = Heermann and Hein uniformity coefficient
D_s = Total depth of application at a distance S from the pivot point
S = Distance from the pivot point to the collector
s = subscript denoting a point at a distance S
η = number of catch containers

1.2 Distributions above and below soil surface:

Most sprinkler irrigation systems are evaluated by determining the uniformity of water as it is applied to the surface of the soil. The irrigation water interception by the plant, however, influences the distribution of water content within the soil. In reality much attention is given to the evaluation of sprinkler irrigation systems above soil surface and ignoring water distribution uniformity below soil surface due to a lack of knowledge. The concern of the designer is mostly associated with achieving uniformity of the spray in the air above the soil surface rather than obtaining a uniform wetting of the root zone or uniformity of water uptake by crop. However, the yield response of the crop is affected by the water within

 WIT Transactions on Ecology and the Environment, Vol 84, © 2005 WIT Press
www.witpress.com, ISSN 1743-3541 (on-line)

its root zone and therefore, the distribution of water within the soil is more important than its distribution on the soil surface. Thus, the surface uniformity coefficient may not be an appropriate reflector of the actual water distribution below the soil surface. Davis [5] and Li and Kawano [10] raised the importance of the water distribution inside the soil profile and stated that the evaluation of water distribution above the soil surface is not a good indicator of crop yield. Hart [8] showed examples of uniformity coefficient of 60% of water distribution from conventional sprinkler system at the soil surface becoming 76% and 86% after redistribution in the soil for 1 and 2 days, respectively. Alazba, et al. [2] investigated the uniformity of above and below soil surface under one center pivot system with different nozzle heights. They concluded that there was difference between the Cu values of above and below soil surface. However, The effect of redistribution within the soil, is of course, much dependent upon the spatial distance between above-average and below-average applications (Thooyamani and Norum [15]). Thus, the uniformity of application under the sprinkler irrigation system may be improved considerably if the redistribution within the soil profile is taken into consideration.

The above discussion concerning the prediction of uniformity below the soil surface strongly suggests that the current approach to sprinkler system design has limitations. There is a need to establish a more appropriate design method which takes account of how the water applied was redistributed after irrigation in the root zone, and finding a relationship between uniformity of the water above the soil surface and uniformity below the soil surface. The aim of this work is to evaluate the above and below soil surface uniformity of water application of six center pivot sprinkler irrigation systems operating under field conditions, and to find out a relationship between the above and below soil surface uniformity coefficients.

2 Materials and methods

Six low-pressure center pivot sprinkler irrigation systems were used in this study. Each system is 412 m long with uniform nozzle spacing of 2.54 m. There were a total of 154 different sized nozzles. These nozzles provide increasing discharges with radial distance from the pivot point. System description is given in table 1. The spray nozzles from the pivot point up to number 91 were equipped with pressure regulators to keep the pressures within the recommended operating range of small nozzles. The pivot lateral is a steel pipe with two diameters (table 1), and the drop tubes made of PVC with diameter of 19.05 mm and 3 m long.

The evaluation tests were carried out under normal field conditions in the early morning to minimize the effect of evaporation. Wind speeds ranged from 2 to 7 m/s, the air temperature ranged from 14 to 19°c, and the relative humidity ranged from 13 to 28%. Two rows of catch cans were used for each system to measure the uniformity of water distribution in radial direction. The catch can spacing was 8 m with first can at 11.6 m from the pivot point. The speeds of the systems at time setting of 100% during the tests ranged from 6.36 to 6.88 m/min.

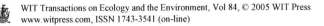WIT Transactions on Ecology and the Environment, Vol 84, © 2005 WIT Press
www.witpress.com, ISSN 1743-3541 (on-line)

The height of spray nozzle was 1.1 m above the top of the catch cans. There was no end-gun sprinkler at the lateral end in any system and the systems were operated nearly on level grounds.

Table 1:   Specifications of center pivot systems used in the study.

Manufacturer: Linsay Zimmatic	Pivot height: 4.3 m
Pipe diameter: Span 1-6=168.22 mm	Tower height: 3.8 m
Span 7-8=141.22 mm	Span length: 52 m
Nozzle type: Senninger (360/cv-m)	Nozzle spacing: 2.54 m
Regulator model: PMR - 15 LF	System age: 10 years

The evaluation indexes of each center pivot above and below soil surface were determined. The weighted coefficient of uniformity (Cu) was used to determine the water distribution in radial direction above the soil surface for each system. For the subsurface water uniformity assessment, the soil water contents (θ) were used and determined gravimetrically at three soil depths (20, 40 and 60 cm). The initial moisture content was determined before the beginning of water application. Soil water content (θ) for each depth was measured after 12, 24 and 36 hours after water application ceased. The soil texture was loamy sand (85% sand, 7% silt and 8% clay).

The uniformity of water redistribution below the soil surface was determined by rewriting the nonweighted coefficient of uniformity developed by Christiansen [4] in the following form:

$$\bar{\theta} = \left(\sum_{i=1}^{N} \theta_i \right) / N$$

$$CU_s = 100 \left(1 - \frac{\sum \left| \theta_i - \bar{\theta} \right|}{N \bar{\theta}} \right)$$

(3)

where:

CU_s = Christiansen's coefficient of uniformity of soil water content
θ_i = the measured soil water content

$\bar{\theta}$ = the mean soil water contents, and
N = number of measured points

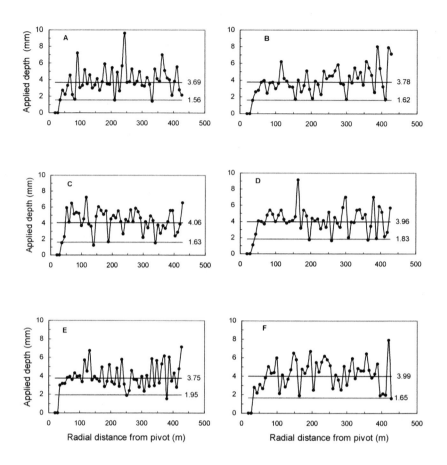

Figure 1: Water distribution patterns in radial direction with the average depths and the average low quarter depths of application from six center pivot systems before maintenance.

3   Results and discussion

The water distribution patterns of the tested center pivot systems above soil surface are shown in Fig. 1. The patterns present the average depth of water caught in each can along the lateral of the pivot. It can be seen from the figures that there was a variation in depth of water applied along the lateral from one system to another, and it can be said that the water was distributed non-uniformly in some systems than the others along the lateral. Also, the values of the average depths and the average low quarter depths of application for each system were determined and shown in figure 1. The weighted uniformity coefficients (Cu) were determined for each system above the soil surface. The values of Cu were 71.9%, 69.2%, 74.7%, 70.7%, 71.4% and 69.9% for systems

A, B, C, D, E and F respectively. The systems were distributing water below the generally accepted level of uniformity (80%). This non-uniformity is attributed to the field operation factors, such as improper nozzling, leakage, and pressure variation along the lateral.

A substantial amount of work has been done to measure and evaluate the uniformity of center pivot systems below the soil surface. The average values of CUs below the soil surface at three different depths and different time of measurements were calculated, and the values were 85.42%, 78.85%, 87.15%, 82.11%, 84.44% and 81.2% respectively for the six systems. It can be noticed that the values of CUs below the soil surface were higher (83.2% an average) than those of Cu above soil surface (71.3% an average). This can be explained by the hydraulic gradients existing within the unevenly wetted soil which causing water movement laterally and vertically within the soil profile, resulting the water within the soil to be more uniformly distributed than the indicated by the surface-measured distribution (Cu). These findings are in agreement with the results of Hart [8] and Li and Kawano [10].

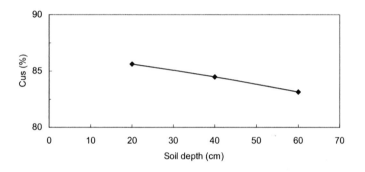

Figure 2: The subsurface uniformity coefficients of water (CUs) as function of soil depth after irrigation from six center pivot systems.

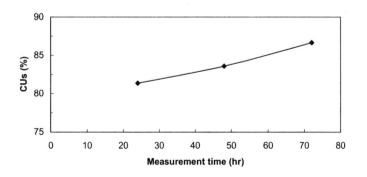

Figure 3: The subsurface uniformity coefficients of water (CUs) as function of time after irrigation from six center pivot systems.

Also, it was found that the values of CUs below soil surface were decreased slightly with the increase of soil depth (Fig. 2) due to the soil water diffusivity, but increase with the time of measurements (Fig. 3) due to the achievement of equilibrium. In general, the water within the soil at any depth and time of measurement was more uniformly distributed than the surfaced-measured distribution of water, and the CUs values were generally above the acceptable uniformity level of design (80%).

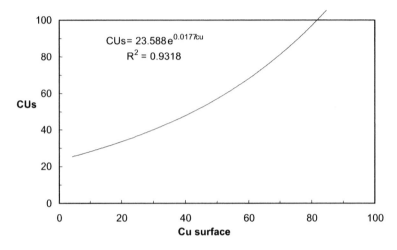

Figure 4:   The relationship between the surface and subsurface uniformity coefficients for center pivot irrigation systems.

Many researchers have studied the function to represent the distribution of water application above soil surface from sprinkler systems. However, the function to represent the distribution of water at different depths of soil profile after infiltration under center pivot systems has not been reported. However, given the difficulties inherent in the above-mentioned work and the above discussion concerning the prediction of redistribution water strongly suggests that an alternative approach to the subsurface evaluation of center pivot performance is to relate the subsurface evaluation indexes to the surface evaluation indexes. Such relationship describing the sprinkler system performance in relation to the prediction of water redistribution is likely to be useful index to the farmer and system designer. The results depicted in Fig. 4 is revealed the type of the relationship between the surface and subsurface uniformity coefficients (Cu and CUs) which was found to be an exponential type with correlation coefficient ®=0.9318, which has the following form:

$$CU_s = 23.588e^{0.0177\,Cu} \qquad (4)$$

This equation can estimate the water distribution uniformity coefficient under soil surface expected from center pivot system instead of the tedious work, which requires the field measurements of soil water contents. The value of Cu should be substituted in the equation as true value not percentage.

4 Conclusion

It can be concluded that all the six center pivot systems were distributing water above soil surface below the generally accepted level of uniformity. But, the water within the soil was more uniformly distributed than the surface-measured distribution of water. The redistribution of water within the soil profile is a function of many irrigation and soil variables, such as depth of water applied, uniformity above soil surface, initial soil water content and soil water diffusivity.

A system designed using the current design criteria for sprinkler irrigation uniformity, such as Cu $\geq$ 75%, or Cu $\geq$ 80% may not be the most economical if the system is mainly aimed at producing desirable uniform soil water distribution. This conclusion may not necessarily apply for arid regions where the irrigation depth for an irrigation event is larger than in humid regions. Therefore, the level of design of the acceptable uniformity of application under the sprinkler irrigation systems should be re-examined with taking into consideration the redistribution of water within the soil profile.

The results revealed that there is an exponential relationship between the surface (Cu) and the subsurface (CU_s) uniformity coefficients. The derived equation may provide a useful guide to potential performance of sprinkler systems in respect to redistribution of water under soil surface, which will lead to the saving of precious resource in areas of limited water supply. Also, the study is expected to draw the attention of sprinkler irrigation system designers and users to consider the previous concept of the evaluation of sprinkler systems above soil surface.

References

[1]   Al-Ghobari, H. M. and Mohammed, F. S. "Survey study about the crust problem in center pivot irrigation pipes in the Kingdom of Saudi Arabia." Agr. Res. Center, KSU, 54, (1995).

[2]   Alazba, A. A.; Al-Ghobari, H.M. and Alotay, A.A. Field Evaluation of Below Soil Surface Uniformity for Center Pivot. ASAE paper No. 992052, 1999.

[3]   ASAE Standards S436 "Test procedure for determining the uniformity of water distribution for center pivot, corner pivot, and moving lateral irrigation machines equipped with spray or sprinkler nozzles." ASAE, Joseph, MI 49085, PP 754-755, . (1994).

[4]   Christiansen, J. E. Irrigation by Sprinkling. California Agricultural Experiment Station, Bulletin 670, 1942.

[5]   Davis, J. R. "Efficiency factors in sprinkler system design". Sprinkler Irreg. Assn. Open Tech. Conf. Proc. Pp 13-50, 1963.

[6]   Fischer, G.R. and Wallender, W.W. Collector Size and Test Duration effects on Sprinkler Water Distribution Measurement. Trans. of the ASAE, vol. 31(2): 538-542, 1988.

[7]   Hanson, B.R. and Wallender, W.W. BI-directional Uniformity of Water Applied by Continuous-Move Machines. Trans. Of the ASAE, vol. 29(4):1047-1053, 1986.

[8]   Hart, W. E. "Subsurface distribution of non uniformity applied surface waters." Trans. Of the ASAE, Vol. 15 (4): 656-661, 666, 1972.

[9]   Heermann, D.F. and Hein, P.R. Performance Characteristics of Self-Propelled Center Pivot Sprinkler Irrigation Systems. Trans. of the ASAE, vol. 11(1):11-15, 1968.

[10]   Li., J. and Kawano, H. The areal distribution of soil moisture under sprinkler irrigation. Agricultural water management, 32:29-36, 1996.

[11]   Letey, J. Irrigation Uniformity as Related to Optimum Crop Production-Additional Research is needed. Irrigation Science, 6(4): 253-263, 1985.

[12]   Mantovani, E. C.; Villobos, F. J.; Orgaz, F. and Fereres, E. Modeling the effects of sprinkler irrigation uniformity on crop yield. Agricultural water management, 27:243-257, 1995.

[13]   Merriam, J.L. and Keller, J. Farm irrigation system evaluation: A guide for management. Utah State University. Logan, Utah, 1978.

[14]   Solomon, K.H. Yield Related Interpretation of Irrigation Uniformity and Efficiency Measures. Irrigation Science, 5(3):161-172, 1984.

[15]   Thooyamani, K. P. and Norum, D.I. Performance of low-pressure center-pivot sprinkler irrigation systems in Saskatchewan. Canadian Agricultural Engineering, 29(2): 143-148, 1987.

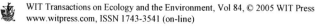

Towards integrated water resources management in Armenia

M. Vardanyan[1], T. Lennaerts[2], A. Schultz[2], L. Harutyunyan[2]
& V. Tonoyan[2]
[1]*Office of Economic Restructuring and Energy, USAID, Armenia*
[2]*USAID Program for Institutional and Regulatory Strengthening of
Water Management in Armenia, PA Consulting Group, Armenia*

Abstract

The Republic of Armenia has made good progress in the transition from a
centrally planned to a market economy. The many state organizations that were
previously involved in providing water management services in the drinking
water, hydropower and irrigation sectors have been consolidated into
autonomous and accountable private, public or cooperative organizations,
supported by an improving legal framework and an emerging regulatory
capacity. This process has already led to improvements in operational
performance. To activate overall water resources management, the Water
Resources Management Agency (WRMA) and its five River Basin Management
Organizations (BMOs) were recently established under the Ministry of Nature
Protection (MNP), which has a broad natural resources mandate. In this paper, it
is argued that the current single biggest challenge of the MNP is to revitalize
water resources monitoring, water use permitting and enforcement, which will be
essential for future basin planning and management. This will require that the
MNP streamline cooperation among its various monitoring and enforcement
agencies and the WRMA/BMOs. At the same time, financial mechanisms need
to be designed to finance these basic water resources management needs, so that
they are sustainable. These priority measures are now being developed in the
first National Water Program (NWP).
*Keywords: Armenia, water resources management, water management agencies,
legal and institutional reform, national water program.*

1 Introduction

1.1 Setting

Armenia is a small, landlocked country in the Southern Caucasus with an area of nearly 30,000 km² and a population of about 3 million. Turkey lies to the west, Georgia to the north, Iran to the south, and Azerbaijan to the east (Figure 1). The borders with Turkey and Azerbaijan are currently closed. A third of the population lives in the capital Yerevan. The country is filled with mountain ranges and plateaus with valleys in between. About 75% of the country is situated at more than 1,500 meters (m) above sea level. The climate is continental with cold winters and warm and dry summers. Average annual precipitation varies from 1,000 mm in the high mountains to 300 mm in the wide and fertile Ararat Valley, which forms the southwestern border with Turkey.

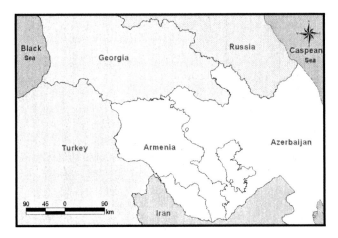

Figure 1:   Southern Caucasus region.

1.2 Socio-economic development

Since 1994, Armenia has been among the most advanced reformist countries in the former Soviet Union. Currently the GDP has almost reached its 1990 level. During the last several years, GDP growth was well above 10% annually. Per capita income in 2003 is estimated at US$ 950 (Atlas method). Factors that contributed to economic growth include: reforms in the electricity sector, growth in exports in a few sectors (diamonds, metals, electricity, processed food), transfers from the Diaspora that fuelled investments and housing construction, and a major program of international assistance.

However, the high levels of economic growth have not yet made up for jobs lost to downsizing or closure of traditional, Soviet era enterprises. Over one-third of the country's workers are unemployed. Armenia's public expenditure budget will remain tight in the medium term. In 2004 the state budget amounted to only US$ 0.8 billion. The country's economic future depends on the government's ability to improve the environment for private sector development, particularly in the industrial sector to sustain the current high economic growth rates, and create jobs to reduce poverty and expand exports.

Water resources play an important role in the economic development of Armenia. Hydropower accounts for 20% of total electricity production. Irrigation accounts for about 80% of total agricultural production, which in turn accounts for almost 25% of GDP.

1.3 Water resources

Most of the rivers in Armenia are small and rapid running. They are grouped in 14 main river basins. The renewable surface water resources amount to 7.2 BCM/year. Armenia possesses considerable renewable groundwater resources, which play an important role in the overall water balance. Groundwater is the source for about 96% of the water used for drinking purposes. Deep groundwater originating within Armenia accounts for almost 1 BCM/year. This constitutes a strategic water reserve for the country. Important deep and artesian groundwater resources are found in the Ararat Valley.

If all water resources are considered, Armenia has more than 3,000 cubic meters per capita per year (m3/c/year). Although Armenia is certainly not "water-stressed", there are spatial imbalances of Armenia's water resource base. There is also significant annual and seasonal variability in runoff of the rivers. About 55% of run-off occurs in the spring months when rainfall and snowmelt is highest. This severe variability causes occasional flooding in spring and local drought conditions in summer. To address seasonal variations of river runoff, the country has built 79 dams with a total reservoir capacity of 1.1 BCM. Most of these dams are used for irrigation.

Armenia's only multi-year water storage is Lake Sevan. The lake, which is situated at an elevation of almost 1,900 m above sea level, covers an area of about 1,200 km² and has a volume of approximately 33 BCM. Through its regulated surface outflow into the Hrazdan River, the lake's waters provide a significant amount of hydropower and irrigation to croplands in the Ararat Valley. Mainly due to excessive water utilization, the original level of Lake Sevan decreased substantially, increasing the threat of eutrophication and largely depleting the lake's storage capacity as a strategic water reserve for multi-purpose use.

1.4 Water uses

Historical trends of water withdrawals for the main intake uses are presented in Figure 2. The figure shows a steady decline in the total water withdrawals for these uses since independence. Between 1989 and 2004, water withdrawal experienced a sharp decline from 3.9 BCM to 1.7 BCM. Industry and irrigation water experienced the most pronounced decline, 63% and 57% respectively.

Irrigation accounted, and still accounts, for approximately 70% of the total surface and groundwater withdrawal in Armenia. The average water intake per ha per year amounts to 8,000 m3. About 40% of the irrigation area depends mostly on high-lift pumping, with pumping lifts of 100 to 500 m. The actually irrigated area amounted to more that 300,000 ha in 1985 and has declined to about 135,000 ha at present. Major factors that have contributed to this decline are the widespread deterioration of the irrigation conveyance systems, high costs of pumping, the disintegration of the former large collective farms into many small private farms (1 to 2 ha), and drainage problems, particularly in the Ararat Valley where groundwater tables are shallow.

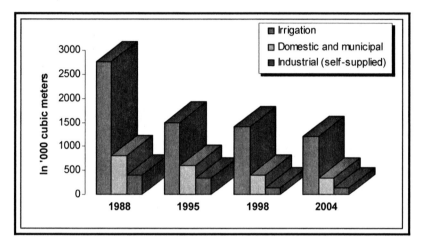

Figure 2:   Historical trends of water withdrawal.

Domestic and industrial water use has also declined since independence, as a result of a decline in economic activity and, more recently, metering and other management measures. Many sewerage systems are old and don't function adequately because of their age and the lack of maintenance. Therefore, most wastewaters are discharged untreated into rivers.

1.5 Water quality

Pollution of Armenia's rivers was extensive during the Soviet period. The current extent of pollution of Armenia's surface waters is not known with certainty because monitoring programs have been hampered by low operational budgets. IWACO et al. [2] conclude on the basis of available data and the implementation of a crash water-quality monitoring program that the water quality conditions of the rivers have improved substantially as a result of the closure of a large part of the traditional industrial enterprises and the decline in irrigated agriculture. The chemical parameters in the surface water were within acceptable limits, except for a few locations downstream of the main cities. However, the exceedances were not considered significant. These findings, if confirmed, will have important implications for water management in Armenia, including the prioritisation of investments.

2 Review of water resources management

2.1 Legal framework

With the assistance of USAID, Armenia adopted in 2002 a new, comprehensive National Water Code [3]. The Water Code shows the way forward for water resources management, in line with international best practice. The Water Code declares Armenian water resources as state property, its use and disposal controlled through economic instruments, employing water use permits to be issued and enforced on the basis of monitoring information, contained in a computerized National Water Cadastre. Important innovations in the Water Code strengthen the basin-oriented principles of water resources management and the importance of public awareness and participation. This has resulted already in the consolidation of Armenia's 14 main river basins into five primary basins at which planning and management functions will be directed (Figure 3).

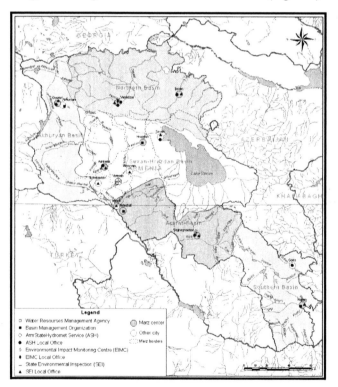

Figure 3:   Principal river basins for planning and management.

A National Water Program (NWP) will provide the strategy and time-phased action program for achieving the different aspects of the Code. The Water Code has, and the NWP will benefit from, the comprehensive knowledge base that has been developed since 1995 with the help of international organizations, including the Lake Sevan Action Program [5], National Environmental Action Plan [4],

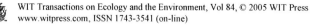

Integrated Water Resources Management (IWRM) Study [1], Sustainable Water Resources Management in Armenia (2000-2004), and Water Management in the South Caucasus (2000-2004).

Nevertheless, this legal framework is new and fresh, endeavours to be quite comprehensive, and will undoubtedly face many challenges as its implementation moves forward. Of overriding importance is the concern that the NWP be financially sustainable. Another major concern has to do with the coherence and consistency among the many existing legal documents. This has led to some confusion in the institutional arrangements.

2.2 Institutional setting

The new Water Code established the Water Resources Management Agency (WRMA) and its five Basin Management Organizations (BMOs), which must become the principal authorities for integrated water resources planning and management. The WRMA is placed under the Ministry of Nature Protection (MNP), which has a broad natural resources mandate, including environmental protection. The MNP also has responsibilities for several other essential water resources management tasks, including the formulation of policies and regulations, water resources monitoring, and the assurance of compliance with regulations and water use permit conditions.

The State Committee for Water Systems (SCWS) and the Public Sector Regulatory Commission (PSRC) were established to manage and regulate the natural monopolies in the provision of operational services in irrigation, hydropower, and municipal water supply and wastewater collection, treatment and disposal. Finally, the Water Code also established the National Water Council (NWC), which is the highest advisory body in the area of matters related to water use and protection. Under the NWC, a Dispute Resolution Commission is organized for resolving disputes related to water use permits.

As a result, Armenia has separated responsibilities for the following three important water management functions: the overall management of water resources, the management of sectoral water services, and environmental protection. It also has separated the management, regulatory and operational functions in the provision of sectoral water services.

Most of the newly established institutions require substantial institutional strengthening and capacity building to enable them to implement the tasks assigned to them in the legal framework. Among other considerations, the NWC can be strengthened to serve as a focal point with the political mandate to synthesize the differing positions and conflicting interests of all water agencies. Another issue is the existing gaps, overlaps and inconsistencies in authorities, responsibilities and tasks among the new and older institutions. A third issue is the lack of coordination and cooperation, including data and information exchange, among the various institutions, in particular at the basin level.

2.3 Overall water resources management

Progress lags in overall water resources management, which involves water resources monitoring, national water planning and coordination, integrated river basin planning and management, water use permits, and compliance assurance and enforcement of regulations and permit conditions, which are all responsibilities of agencies under the MNP. The fulfilment of these activities has been suffering from lack of adequate budgets.

Water resources monitoring is fragmented, and to some degree duplicated among several agencies. To a large degree, the monitoring is conducted according to methods and procedures from Soviet times, albeit at a much lower level of activity. Also the existing National Water Cadastre is incomplete and fragmented. As a result, the availability and the quality of the collected data have declined to the point that the data are considered unfit for planning and management.

The water use permits govern water withdrawals from and pollution discharges into surface waters (rivers, lakes) and groundwater [6]. Currently water use permits are issued by the WRMA, supported by the BMOs. Since the adoption of the new Water Code in 2002, about 500 water use permits have been issued by the WRMA. These include new permits and the renewal of existing permits. The experiences so far suggest that the implementation and enforcement of the water use permitting system has been constrained by deficiencies in permitting regulations and guidelines, insufficient cooperation among agencies of the MNP in the processes of issuance of permits and the assurance of compliance with permit conditions, and capabilities of agencies and their staff.

The inspection of water users to ensure compliance with regulations and permit conditions is fragmented between the WRMA/BMOs and the State Environmental Inspectorate (SEI), also under the MNP. The SEI has weakened considerably during the last several years. The methods, procedures and standards used have little changed since Soviet times [6]. Moreover, there seems to be virtually no cooperation or even information exchange between the SEI and the surface water quality monitoring organizations. Few fines and penalties are being applied or paid for non-compliance, and virtually no legal action has been taken against those who have not paid their fines. Thus, an accurate estimate of current water use cannot be made. Moreover, there is little knowledge as to which organizations or persons are in compliance with permit conditions.

2.4 Sectoral water management

Good restructuring progress has been made in sectoral water management, supported by a legal framework that has separated the management, regulatory and operational functions in the provision of water services in the irrigation, hydropower, and municipal water supply and wastewater collection, treatment, and disposal. The many state organizations that were previously involved in these services have been largely restructured and consolidated into autonomous and accountable private, public or cooperative organizations.

The low level of activities in overall water resources management seems not to have negatively affected progress in the sectoral water services. Nevertheless, the improvement of their operational performance, particularly in irrigation and municipal water services, has been modest until now, mainly due to inadequate funding mechanisms for making the required investments. However, this issue is now being addressed with the assistance of various institutional lenders, donors and the private sector.

One of the pressing issues in the irrigation sector is the sustainability of a substantial part of the remaining irrigation and drainage (I&D) systems, in particular the schemes that depend on high-lift pumping for their water supply. Some of these schemes may be converted to gravity supply. Most pumped schemes, however, will continue to represent a heavy and likely unsustainable financial burden on the Government and the users. The operation and maintenance costs amount to more than US$100/1,000m3 (US$500/ha) for high-lift pumped schemes. These costs are higher than the incremental income of the farmers from irrigation, which may range from US$200/ha to US$400/ha. A further severe reduction of the currently irrigated area of 135,000 ha is likely, particularly if the Government would decide to stop subsidizing irrigation.

2.5 Transboundary water management

The new Water Code recognizes the importance of transboundary cooperation and empowers the Commission on Transboundary Water Resources to address transboundary issues with similar organizations in neighbouring countries. A number of bilateral treaties bind Armenia with respect to the development and use of international waters. A basic requirement for the implementation of these treaties is that proper monitoring and information exchange programs on water flows and water quality are in place [7]. This basic requirement is not yet met, despite the various donor-supported transboundary projects, which mostly have been supporting workshops and legal, policy and planning activities. As a result, hard facts on water quantity and water quality issues between the countries are scarce.

3 Priorities for the National Water Program

3.1 Needs and limitations

The National Water Code requires the preparation of the first National Water Program (NWP), which will provide the foundation for all water management activities in the country. The Code also calls for annual updating of the NWP, with approval of the National Assembly. The preparation of a NWP is a substantial undertaking, requiring the efforts of many different experts, providing data, information and analysis in a variety of fields. The preparation of a NWP is heavily dependent upon availability of reliable data and information. At the moment, recent and reliable data on current water availability, water quality and water usage do not exist. In addition, there are limitations on capability and expertise, within government agencies, to perform some of the needed studies and analyses required for the NWP.

Fortunately, Armenia doesn't face serious overall water management problems in terms of water shortages, water quality or sectoral competition for water (see above). The previous sections indicate that Armenia is blessed with sufficient water resources to serve its current and foreseeable needs. Renewable surface water and groundwater supplies average over 8 BCM/y, whereas total usage reduced from about 4 BCM/y in the late 80s to about 1.7 BCM/y at present. Moreover, the reduction in water use was accompanied by a remarkable improvement in water quality due to the decline in industrial and agricultural output. Thus, there seems no pressing need in the short term for a more holistic integrated approach to water resources management, including the preparation of IWRM plans for the aforementioned five river basins as part of the NWP.

The current lack of "stress" in the water sector provides an opportunity for establishing the right framework for managing the water resources in Armenia for all future needs, including environmental considerations. In this connection, key priorities are the revitalization of the basic water resources management tasks of water resources monitoring, water use permitting, and the assurance of compliance with regulations and permit conditions. With the re-vitalization of these essential tasks, the basic data will become available to enable any meaningful IWRM planning in, say, five years from now, when there will be a real demand for basin planning and management if the economy of Armenia keeps growing at its current high rate. The revitalization of these basic tasks has technical, institutional and financial requirements, which also need to be addressed in the NWP.

The NWP will guide water resources management in Armenia, up until the time when the WRMA and BMOs will be in a strengthened position, and capable of carrying out all their responsibilities under the Water Code in cooperation with the monitoring organizations, enforcement organizations, and the sectoral water supply services. Subsequently, the WRMA and the BMOs, working in concert, will play a key role in the periodic updating of the NWP, including, IWRM planning at the basin level when there is a need for such plans.

3.2 Priorities for the National Water Program

Taking into account the above described issues, needs and limitations, the following priorities will be addressed in Armenia's first NWP.

- Re-design and revitalization of monitoring programs of water resources;
- Strengthening of water use permitting for water withdrawals and pollution discharges;
- Improvement of compliance assurance and enforcement of regulations and water use permit conditions;
- Development of the National Water Cadastre Information System;
- Assessment of the future of irrigation in Armenia;
- Development of planning and analytical capacity;
- Development of cooperative basin management measures;
- Development of financing mechanisms for water resources management;
- Institutional needs assessment for the streamlining of agencies involved in the water sector;

- Harmonization and consolidation of laws and other legal instruments;
- Implementation of the Lake Sevan Action Plan;
- Establishment of water quality management program;
- Protection of environmentally sensitive zones;
- Assessment of drainage requirements in areas reverted to marshes in the Ararat Valley.

References

[1]   World Bank, 2001. Towards Integrated Water Resources Management. Technical Paper. Armenia.
[2]   IWACO et al, 2001. Integrated Water Resources Management Planning. Stage II Final Technical Report. Integrated Water Resources Management Plan Armenian. Funded by World Bank. Armenia.
[3]   Government of Armenia, 2002. Water Code of the Republic of Armenia. Official Bulletin of the Republic of Armenia.
[4]   World Bank, 1998. National Environnemental Action Plan. Main Report and various working group reports. Armenia.
[5]   World Bank, 1999. Lake Sevan Action Plan. Armenia.
[6]   ARD, 2004. Water Use Permitting Guidelines and Water Resources Fees Strategy, Ministry of Nature Protection. Sustainable Water Resources Management Project in Armenia, Funded by USAID. Armenia.
[7]   DAI, 2003. Water Management in the South Caucasus. Final Report. Funded by USAID. Armenia.

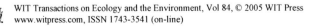

Author Index

Energy and the Environment

Editors: **C.A. BREBBIA**, *Wessex Institute of Technology, UK and* **I. SAKELLARIS**, *Aristotle University, Thessaloniki, Greece*

Considerable developments are now under way in many technical aspects of energy efficiency from general equipment and appliances to building design.

Featuring papers presented at the First International Conference on Sustainable Energy, Planning and Technology in Relationship to the Environment (Energy and the Environment), this book covers a whole range of technological and policy issues.

The following sections are included: Energy and Environment; Energy Resources Management; Energy Markets and Policy; Renewable Energy Resources; Alternative Energy Sources; Energy Efficiency in Buildings; Industrial Energy Issues; Transportation Energy Reduction and Losses; Energy Computer Modelling; and Data Management.

Series: The Sustainable World, Vol 7
ISBN: 1-85312-970-4   2003   384pp
£126.00/US$199.00/€189.00

Beauty and Science

E. TIEZZI, *University of Siena, Italy*

In this book, the distinguished author argues that the aim of science should not be to dominate nature but to live in harmony with it. If we do not make reference to our "common biological origin" (Jean-Paul Sartre) or find the umbilical cord that binds us to nature, his conviction is that we risk destroying the life cycles of our planet. He demonstrates that the role of form, colour, flavour, sound, scent – and beauty – was fundamental for biological evolution, and is still fundamental today for a scientific view of complexity. This is especially so with nature threatened by the linear, mechanistic, arrogant and crude approach of science at the service of a society that "knows the price of everything and the value of nothing".

In order to avert catastrophe, Tiezzi asserts, science cannot be based only on reason but must combine reason, passion, intuition, emotion, logic and "global feeling": science cannot be cold.

Series: The Sustainable World, Vol 10
ISBN: 1-85312-740-X   2004   132pp
£39.00/US$62.00/€58.50

Sustainable Planning and Development

Editors: **E. BERIATOS**, *University of Thessaly, Greece,* **C.A. BREBBIA**, *Wessex Institute of Technology, UK, and* **H. COCCOSSIS** *and* **A. KUNGOLOS**, *University of Thessaly, Greece*

This book features contributions from the first international conference on this subject. Almost 100 papers cover topics including: Environmental Management; Environmental Legislation and Policy; Environmental Impact Assessment; Ecosystem Analysis, Protection and Remediation; Social Issues; and Rural and Urban Planning.

Series: The Sustainable World, Vol 6
ISBN: 1-85312-985-2   2003   1,048pp
£299.00/US$478.00/€448.50

Disposal of Hazardous Waste in Underground Mines

Editors: **V. POPOV**, Wessex Institute of Technology, UK and **R. PUSCH**, Geodevelopment AB, Lund, Sweden

This book contains the results of a three-year research programme by a joint team of experts from four different EU countries. The main focus of this research was on investigating the possibility of using abandoned underground mines for the disposal of hazardous chemical waste with negligible pollution of the environment.

The contributors address many aspects that are common to underground disposal of nuclear waste, such as: the properties and behaviour of waste-isolating clay materials and practical ways of preparing and applying them, development of tools/software to assess the stability, performance and transport of contaminants inside and outside the repository, and risks associated with different repository concepts considering the long-term safety of the biosphere. Information is also included on the selection of site location, design and construction of repositories, predicting degrees of contamination of groundwater in the surroundings, estimation of isolating capacity of reference repositories, and many other relevant issues.

Invaluable to researchers and engineers working in the field of hazardous (chemical) waste disposal, this title will also significantly aid experts dealing with nuclear waste.

Series: The Sustainable World, Vol 11
ISBN: 1-85312-750-7 2006 apx 300pp apx £89.00/US$142.00/€133.50

The End of Time

E. TIEZZI, University of Siena, Italy

"...a compelling fusion of the historical, philosophical and scientific aspects of the struggle towards a new, ecological culture."
ECOFARM & GARDEN

A best seller in Italy, this influential title has now been revised and translated into English for the first time. Tiezzi emphasises the need to reconcile the wants and pace of a modern generation with the hard reality that evolutionary history had already pre-determined a pace of her own. Presenting scenarios of 'hard' and 'soft' sustainability for the future, he poses the critical question: Will the scientific and cultural instruments we have be enough to combat the pressures of unsustainable human behaviour?

Series: The Sustainable World, Vol 1
ISBN: 1-85312-931-3 2002 216pp £49.00/US$75.00/€73.50

WIT eLibrary

Home of the Transactions of the Wessex Institute, the WIT electronic-library provides the international scientific community with immediate and permanent access to individual papers presented at WIT conferences. Visitors to the WIT eLibrary can freely browse and search abstracts of all papers in the collection before progressing to download their full text.

Visit the WIT eLibrary at
http://www.witpress.com